Palestinian and Arab-Jewish Cultures

Language, Literature, and Identity

Reuven Snir

EDINBURGH
University Press

Edinburgh University Press is one of the leading university presses in the UK. We publish academic books and journals in our selected subject areas across the humanities and social sciences, combining cutting-edge scholarship with high editorial and production values to produce academic works of lasting importance. For more information visit our website: edinburghuniversitypress.com

Edinburgh University Press Ltd
13 Infirmary Street
Edinburgh EH1 1LT

First published in hardback by Edinburgh University Press 2023

Typeset in 10.5/13 pt Adobe Text
by Cheshire Typesetting Ltd, Cuddington, Cheshire

A CIP record for this book is available from the British Library

ISBN 978 1 3995 0321 1 (hardback)
ISBN 978 1 3995 0322 8 (paperback)
ISBN 978 1 3995 0323 5 (webready PDF)
ISBN 978 1 3995 0324 2 (epub)

This book was published with the support of the Israel Science Foundation.

Contents

	Preface	vii
	Acknowledgments	x
	Technical Notes	xii
	Notes on Transliteration	xiv
	Introduction	**1**
PART I OCCUPATION, DOMINATION, AND COMMITMENT		**27**
1.	**Performance: In the Service of the Nation**	**35**
	Introduction	35
	First Attempts	38
	Uprooting	44
	Professionalization	50
	Conclusion	67
2.	**Commitment: Verse Drama and Resistance**	**73**
	Introduction	73
	Political Theater	78
	"Ladder of Hunger"	83
	Apocalypticism	88
	Conclusion	91
3.	**Chronicle: The Ongoing *Nakba***	**94**
	Introduction	94
	"I Am the Last Arabs' Sigh"	97
	"Oh, Father, I Am Joseph"	106
	"Will Homer Be Born after Us?"	116
	Conclusion	130

4. Bilingualism: Palestinians in Hebrew **143**
Introduction 143
Reterritorialization 152
"I Melt out of Love" 156
"Hebrew, Arabic, and Death" 162
Conclusion 170

PART II HYBRIDIZATION, EXCLUSION, AND DEMISE **185**

5. Pluralism: Arabs of Mosaic Faith **193**
Introduction 193
Historical Background 194
"A Carbon Copy of *Ibn al-Balad*" 206
"We Are Arabs before We Are Jews" 213
Conclusion 231

6. Spring: "We Were Like Those Who Dream" **241**
Introduction 241
"In the World of Light" 245
"Till Spring Comes" 250
The Shift to Hebrew 261
Conclusion 283

7. Demise: The Last of the Mohicans **291**
Introduction 291
Existentialist Sensibility 293
Mystical and Metaphysical Motifs 300
"Iraq's Days" 303
Conclusion 308

8. Identity: Inessential Solidarities **325**
Introduction 325
Narrativization of the Self 331
Interpellation and Exclusion 336
Globalization 344
Conclusion 349

Epilogue: "Trailed Travellers": Between Fiction, Meta-Fiction, and History **352**

References 376
Index 425

Preface

The aim of the present book is to summarize my studies on Palestinian and Arab-Jewish cultures[1] in both their historical and contemporary manifestations, and to introduce fresh and updated insights based on additional recent investigations. The scholarship on both fields during recent decades seems to have been conducted both in isolation and independently, mainly developed by academics with different areas of expertise. In this vein, I argue that, due to political, ideological, social, and cultural considerations, scholars who insist on exploring them jointly—and who argue that they are very intimately connected—will in fact develop insights that shed light on phenomena that, at first glance, seem to belong only to one scholarly field. However, I argue that in-depth investigations into Palestinian and Arab-Jewish cultures may reveal the advantages of considering that both fields have indeed interacted with one another from both synchronic and diachronic perspectives, with diversifying mutual interplay, since the 1920s. The various chapters of this book refer to this interplay, which is especially important to consider in light of the relevant identities that play a role in the texts and activities being examined here.

In 1988, I published my first contribution to the field of Arab-Jewish culture: "Cultural Changes as Reflected in Literature: The Beginning of the Arabic Short Story by Jewish Authors in Iraq"[2]—it was a Hebrew article on the role that Jewish authors played in the emergence of the Arabic short story in Iraq during the 1920s. That article was incidental to the main focus of my scholarly interests at the time, which centered on modern Arabic

[1] I use the term "culture" here mainly to refer to "all those practices, like the arts of description, communication, and representation, that have relative autonomy from the economic, social, and political realms and that often exist in aesthetic forms, one of whose principal aims is pleasure" (Said 1994, p. xii). As for the term "identity" and parallel terms, see the discussion below.

[2] Snir 1988, pp. 108–29.

literature in general, mainly modern Arabic poetry and neo-Ṣūfī poetics. Gradually, my interest in specifically Jewish literary writings in Arabic grew, and during the last thirty years my publications in Hebrew, English, German, and Arabic have covered various aspects of Arab-Jewish culture and identity. In my early investigations in this field, notions regarding identity and belonging were marginal compared with literary poetic ones. In my first comprehensive work on Arab-Jewish culture, published in Hebrew in 2005, notions of identity played a more significant role, as hinted at by the book's title, *Arabness, Jewishness, Zionism: A Clash of Identities in the Literature of Iraqi Jews*.[3] My main objective in my early publications on the topic was to expose the large corpus of literary texts that Jews wrote in Arabic in the late nineteenth and twentieth centuries, and to analyze them in their appropriate cultural and social contexts, namely, before and after the emigration of Jews from the Arab world to Israel. That is, I set aside theoretical contexts regarding issues of identity, because I was more interested in cultural and literary activities and less in the subjectivities of the people concerned. Later, I would expand my theoretical investigations into the realm of identity in order to understand the internal dynamics in Jewish Arabic literary writings and the interactions between culture and identity. This expansion can be seen mainly in the two books I published on the topic.[4]

One year after the publication of my first study of Arab-Jewish culture, I published my first contribution in the field of Palestinian culture: "A Wound Out of his Wounds: Palestinian Arabic Literature in Israel."[5] This was a Hebrew article dealing with the unity of all branches of Palestinian culture despite the *Nakba* (Catastrophe, Disaster)—the destruction of Palestinian society and homeland in 1948, and the permanent displacement of more than 700,000 Palestinian Arabs—about half of prewar Palestine's Arab population. The destruction of Palestinian society and the Palestinian homeland following the *Nakba* has by no means been an isolated event or series of events, but an ongoing process of uprooting, permanent persecution, and displacement against which background the process of Palestinian nation-building has been accelerating in various fields of Palestinian culture, as will be illustrated below. Also, the Palestinian search for roots has concentrated as well on the revival of various cultural activities less as a subject of historical and literary study and more as a vital and dynamic force in society and as a symbol of the determination of the Palestinian people's efforts to gain their right to self-determination as a nation with a distinctive culture and peculiar

[3] Snir 2005a.
[4] Snir 2015b; Snir 2019a.
[5] Snir 1989, pp. 244–68.

history. One cannot refer to any Palestinian cultural activities, whether in Israel, the West Bank and Gaza Strip, or in other places, without experiencing them against the background of the *Nakba*—it is always there as a kind of background without which anything in the life of the Palestinians may exist, demanding imagery dialogues with other activities in an interplay of reality, culture, meta-culture, and meta-myth.

The interplay between the scholarly fields of Arab-Jewish culture and Palestinian culture reached its climax following the gradual escalation of the Arab–Jewish conflict—the establishment of the State of Israel (1948), which has been the embodiment of the Palestinian *Nakba*, and the subsequent immigration of most Arab Jews to the new Jewish state and the joint "achievement" of this political–ideological conflict, "the pearl in the crown": the implicit unspoken agreement between the two national movements, Zionism and Arab nationalism, to perform a total cleansing of Arab-Jewish culture. As I published many studies on both topics, books and scholarly articles, essays and literary translations, my insights and arguments have not been stable, but have developed and evolved so as to better understand these two unique cultures and the interplay between them. Reviewing the studies I published during the last four decades, I have updated several of them, written new ones, united their method of presentation, and incorporated them all into one overarching framework with two main axes in the belief that such a framework would make it easier for readers to understand my arguments. The present book is a complementary volume to my *Modern Arabic Literature: A Theoretical Framework* (2017), but, unlike the latter's macro-conception, which at times could be subject to the charge of ignoring the nuances and details of isolated topics, the emphasis here in general is on the texts themselves and on specific literary activities—in other words, I will concentrate on the micro-systems that make up the entire system of Arabic literature.

Acknowledgments

I wish to thank the editors and publishers of the following journals for permission to reuse material that has appeared in their pages (in alphabetical order): *Acta Orientalia*, *Arabic Language & Literature*, *Arquivo Maaravi: Revista Digital de Estudos Judaicos da UFMG*, *Asian and African Studies*, *Australian Journal of Jewish Studies*, *Contemporary Theatre Review*, *Der Islam*, *Die Welt des Islams*, *Folia Orientalia*, *HaMizrah HeHadash*, *Hebrew Studies*, *Hispanic Issues*, *Jama'a: Interdisciplinary Journal of Middle East Studies*, *Jewish Social Studies*, *Journal of Modern Jewish Studies*, *Journal of Oriental and African Studies*, *Journal of Theatre and Drama*, *Jusūr*, *al-Karmil: Studies in Arabic Language and Literature*, *Mamlūk Studies Review*, *Mediterranean Review*, *Middle Eastern Studies*, *Miscelánea de Estudios Árabes y Hebraicos*, *Orientalia Suecana*, *Quest: Issues in Contemporary Jewish History*, *Shofar: An Interdisciplinary Journal of Jewish Studies*, and *Virginia Woolf Miscellany*. My thanks go out as well to the following publishers of the books from which material has been reused in the present study (also in alphabetical order): Ben-Zvi Institute for the Study of Jewish Communities in the East, Brill, Dār al-Sāqī, Edinburgh University Press, Harrassowitz Verlag, Harvard University Press, Reichert Verlag, Routledge, and York Press.

This book is the result of research projects that I have been conducting for the last three decades. The projects have been supported by grants and fellowships that I obtained from the Israel Science Foundation (ISF) (1992–1995), the Memorial Foundation for Jewish Culture (1993 and 1998), the Oxford Centre for Hebrew and Jewish Studies (2000 and 2008), the Seminar für Sprachen und Kulturen des Vorderen Orients and Hochschule für Jüdische Studien at Heidelberg University (2002 and 2017–2018), the Wissenschaftskolleg zu Berlin—Institute for Advanced Study (2004–2005), the Seminar für Semitistik und Arabistik at the Free University of Berlin (2004–2005), the Radcliffe Institute for Advanced Study at Harvard University (2009–2010), the Simon Dubnow Institute for Jewish History and Culture at Leipzig University (2015), the Department of Languages and Literatures at the University of Gothenburg (2017–2018), the Herbert D. Katz Center for Advanced Judaic Studies at the University of Pennsylvania (2019), and IMéRA—Institut d'études avancées at Aix-Marseille University (2020).

Finally, as in several of my previous volumes, a special word of thanks and appreciation is due to the editor, Michael Helfield, for his excellent work on the manuscript and for his significant contribution to the final shaping of this book.

Technical Notes

1. Translations are mine unless otherwise indicated.
2. Quotations (generally, but not solely, in poetry) in the original appear wherever the Arabic text is important for the understanding of the arguments presented. The aim is by no means to provide a poetically parallel text in English, especially with regard to verses in the *qaṣīda* form—an elaborately structured ode maintaining the same meter and a single end rhyme that runs through the entire piece, in which each verse is divided into two paired hemistichs, the first being the *ṣadr* and the second being the *ʿajuz*. The generally independent nature of the meaning of each verse usually allows them all to stand alone, and thus these verses have been translated as separate verses, with each hemistich being translated on a separate line.
3. The epigraph appearing at the opening of the book and the epigraphs appearing at the start of its two parts appear in the original and in translation. The epigraphs appearing at the start of its chapters appear in English only; if they are translations, the original Arabic text will appear within the main text of the chapter.
4. Titles of Arabic books and articles are transliterated into English. Titles of Hebrew books and articles are translated into English and identified as such at the end of the translated title. The transliterated Arabic titles are accompanied by their translation immediately afterward in the body of the text but not in the References list. For the system of transliteration from Arabic, see Notes on Transliteration, below.
5. In the titles of one chapter and several subsections, I have incorporated parts of verses that I believe are relevant to the chapter content. For example, in Chapter 3, Section 3, I incorporated the words "Oh, Father, I Am Joseph" from a poem by Mahmud Darwīsh. I have generally done this when I am discussing literary texts and offering my own close reading

of them. Of course, I am well aware that other scholars or laypersons may offer different readings of the texts in question.

6. The definite article ال appears as *al-* throughout the entire book before solar and lunar letters. At the beginning of a surname in the References list, it is not taken into consideration with regard to alphabetical order.
7. Works with one author/editor or two authors/editors will appear with the name or names fully cited. For works with more than two authors/editors, "et al." will be used.
8. In case of a subsequent edition of a book, the year of the first edition is mentioned only when it is significant for the arguments made in previous research—for example, when referring to studies related to the emergence of new modes of literary genres: al-Malā'ika, Nāzik. 1983 [1962]. *Qaḍāyā al-Shi'r al-Mu'āṣir*. Beirut: Dār al-'Ilm li-l-Malāyīn.
9. When referring to sources on the Internet that are being continuously updated, I mention the last time I accessed the relevant website. Readers are encouraged to access the relevant websites in order to familiarize themselves with the most recent information.

Notes on Transliteration

أ؛ ؤ؛ ئ	’i; ’u; ’a	ط	ṭ
ب	b	ظ	ẓ
ت	t	ع	ʿ
ث	th	غ	gh
ج	j	ف	f
ح	ḥ	ق	q
خ	kh	ك	k
د	d	ل	l
ذ	dh	م	m
ر	r	هـ	h
ز	z	و	w
س	s	و (long)	ū
ش	sh	ي	y
ص	ṣ	ي (long)	ī
ض	ḍ	◌ِ; ◌َ; ◌ُ (short)	i; a; u

1. The definite article *al-* is used before solar and lunar letters. The *waṣla* over silent *alif* is systematically ignored.
2. ’(أ) is not indicated when it is at the beginning of a word. ا or آ or ى are transcribed as *ā*.
3. ة at the end of words and names is not transliterated (i.e., *ḥikāya* for حكاية). When it occurs in the first word of an *iḍāfa* (construction), it is transcribed as *t*.
4. A *shadda* (ّ) is represented by doubling the relevant letter.
5. Final *nisba* is transcribed as *ī* (masculine, i.e., *ʿArabī* for عربيّ) and *iyya* (feminine, i.e., *ʿArabiyya* for عربيّة).
6. Arabic words or letters transcribed into Latin characters are generally given in *italics*, except for personal names and names of places and publishers.

7. Anglicized spellings of commonly used names and locations have been retained, and foreign names in transliterated passages generally appear in their English form. In English quotations, transliterated Arabic words appear as is, even if they differ from our preferred system.

لقد صار قلبي قابلا كلّ صـورة فمرعى لغزلان ودير لرهبان
وبيت لأوثـــان وكعبة طائـــف وألواح توراة ومصحف قرآن
أدين بدين الحبّ أنّى توجّـــهت ركائبه فالحـبّ ديني وإيمـاني
– محيي الدّين بن العربيّ

My heart is capable of every form,
A pasture for gazelles, and a cloister for monks,
A place for idols, and the pilgrim's *Ka'ba*,
The Tables of the Torah, and the Koran.
Love is the faith I hold wherever turn
Its camels, love is my belief and faith.
– Muḥyī al-Dīn ibn 'Arabī

Introduction

The present book emerged following my investigations into various branches of Palestinian culture and my studies of specific manifestations of Arab-Jewish identity and culture, as well as in light of the recent theoretical contributions on identity by major cultural theorists and sociologists. Among them, I have been mainly guided by insights introduced by the Jamaican-born cultural theorist Stuart Hall (1932–2014), who argues that "the question, and the theorization, of identity is a matter of considerable political significance, and is only to be advanced when both the necessity and the 'impossibility' of identities, and the suturing of the psychic and the discursive in their constitution, are fully and unambiguously acknowledged."[1] *The Black Atlantic: Modernity and Double Consciousness* by the British historian Paul Gilroy (b. 1956) also inspired me: "Striving to be both European and black requires some specific forms of double consciousness," says Gilroy, but "saying this, I do not mean to suggest taking on either or both unfinished identities necessarily exhausts subjective resources of any particular individual."[2] The writings of poststructuralist professor of rhetoric Diane Davis (b. 1963) have played a role in the development of my arguments on the notions of inessential solidarities, particularly her question: "Is there a way to activate a sense of solidarity among singularities—a way to say 'we'—that doesn't automatically exclude, that doesn't just ask for trouble by simultaneously feeding this craving for communion, for Gemeinschaft (in the name of which any number of 'we's have committed the most horrific atrocities in recorded history)?"[3] Likewise, the insights of the Italian philosopher Giorgio Agamben (b. 1942) have been very helpful for my investigations and studies, mainly his *The Coming Community*, which starts out by stating that "the coming being is whatever being," and

1 Hall 1996, p. 16.
2 Gilroy 1993, p. 1.
3 Davis 1999, p. 639.

ends with the following: "Whatever singularity, which wants to appropriate belonging itself, its own being-in-language, and thus rejects all identity and every condition of belonging, is the principal enemy of the state. Wherever these singularities peacefully demonstrate their being in common there will be a Tiananmen, and, sooner or later, the tanks will appear."[4]

Most helpful for the present book was the notion of "interpellation" suggested by the French Marxist philosopher Louis Pierre Althusser (1918–1990), more especially since no writer, the author of the present study included, can divorce himself from the complexity of his own subjectivity. In the last section of his essay "Ideology and Ideological State Apparatuses (Notes towards an Investigation),"[5] Althusser coined the term "interpellation," theorizing the constitutive process by which individuals acknowledge and respond to ideologies, thereby recognizing themselves as subjects. Stating that (a) "there is no practice except by and in an ideology"; and (b) "there is no ideology except by the subject and for subjects," Althusser comes to his central thesis that "ideology interpellates individuals as subjects." There is no ideology except for concrete subjects, and this destination for ideology is only made possible by the "*category of the subject* and its functioning." With the rise of bourgeois ideology, the category of the subject is the constitutive category of all ideology, whatever its determination, region, or class, and whatever its historical date:

> I say: the category of the subject is constitutive of all ideology, but at the same time and immediately I add that *the category of the subject is only constitutive of all ideology insofar as all ideology has the function (which defines it) of "constituting" concrete individuals as subjects*. In the interaction of this double constitution exists the functioning of all ideology, ideology being nothing but its functioning in the material forms of existence of that functioning. In order to grasp what follows, it is essential to realize that both he who is writing these lines and the reader who reads them are themselves subjects, and therefore ideological subjects (a tautological proposition), i.e. that the author and the reader of these lines both live "spontaneously" or "naturally" in ideology in the sense in which I have said that "man is an ideological animal by nature."[6]

Althusser defines ideological recognition as the act of "interpellation," of identification of a subject and that subject's recognition of him/herself as the one addressed ("hailing")—this recognition "guarantee[s] for us that we

[4] Agamben 2003 [1993], pp. 1, 87. Our use of the term "singularity" here differs from the same term that refers to technological singularity. It is a theoretical moment in time when artificial intelligence will have progressed to the point of radically changing civilization, and perhaps human nature; see Kurzweil 2005.

[5] Althusser 1971, pp. 121–73.

[6] Althusser 1971, p. 160 (emphasis in the original).

are indeed concrete, individual, distinguishable and (natural) irreplaceable subjects."[7] In the context of social science, to be interpellated is to identify with a particular idea or identity. It is the process by which you recognize yourself as belonging to a particular identity. To illustrate how interpellation functions in the context of ideology, Althusser used the example of a policeman who shouts "Hey, you there!" At least one individual will turn around (most likely the right one) to "answer" that call. At this moment, when one realizes that the call is for oneself, one becomes a subject relative to an ideology, and in that case the ideology of law and crime. This is the way in which ideology generally functions, says Althusser, as we are all always caught up in the process in which we voluntarily acknowledge the validity or relevance of some ideology in which we live for ourselves and thus subject ourselves to it. In other words, ideology functions as a mediator between systems of power and individuals; it allows for hegemonic power to reproduce itself by obscuring traditional forms of repression and incorporating individuals into the power structure.

The process of identification thus creates identity, and we recognize ourselves when we are hailed—you identify me, and I become that me that you have identified. I know that it is me who is being called as I unconsciously accept the subject position and it is as if I had always already been there. The apparent freedom with which we recognize and accept that position only serves to cement us further into it. Interpellation can be thought of as being "recruitment," since it invites a person to be in a subject position; it is, however, rarely as specific as being addressed by name, but it is, rather, being addressed as a member of an audience or any collective. When we recognize that we are being spoken to, we not only engage more deeply with the hailing, we also accept the social role being offered to us: young, white, female, gay, athletic, liberal, etc. and, in the context of our present study, Arab, Palestinian, Israeli-Arab, Mizrahi, Arab-Jew, Levantine, Oriental, Sephardi, Black, etc. One can immediately see the connection between interpellation and rhetoric; I will elaborate on this below.

For the purpose of my investigations into the identities of Palestinians and Arabized Jews,[8] I have broadened the scope of interpellation to encompass all human interactions. This process, in Althusser's analysis, occurs chiefly through Ideological State Apparatuses (ISAs)—public/private education, media, religion, the family, etc.—and, when necessary, Repressive State Apparatuses (RSAs)—the police, the army, etc. But since we are always

[7] Althusser 1971, pp. 161–2.

[8] I will use here the term "Arabized Jews" following Brann 2000, pp. 435–54. On the question of terminology, see Behar 2009, pp. 747–71; Levy 2017, pp. 79–103.

already in ideology, we generate systems of ideologies ourselves because we are always already implicated as subjects of and subjects (re)producing interpellation. As "good" subjects, we are always already interpellating others as "subjects" in the "work" of achieving our own recognition. "Man is an ideological animal by nature," says Althusser, and therefore it is not only the school where we learn, the university where we study or teach, or the policeman who interpellates us into a subject position, nor is it only the politician, the preacher, the news editor, the novelist, the film director, or any other adherent of any ideology or "ideology." Interpellation also occurs even if there is no evident agent with clear intention, as, for example, in poetic folk narrative,[9] the mere stare of a poor and helpless child,[10] or memories of a lover.[11] All of them interpellate us, knowingly or unknowingly, into the subject position of belonging in a specific group or relating to a certain identity.

The process of interpellation and hailing always involves both an identity ascribed to someone as a subject and a subject position of the person being interpellated.[12] But, although something is expected and anticipated to be the result of that process, there is no guarantee that the hailing will produce the same effect it initially intended. As a student of literature, I have found Althusser's notion of interpellation illuminative in the study of subjectivities of fictional characters which are the invention of the author's subjectivity, whoever the author happens to be. The fictional characters inflict "real" subjectivities on readers, each reader affected in his very own way. Take, for example, an interpellation that closely resembles Althusser's illustration—the hailing of a policeman and the answer of the interpellated person, and the latter's realization that the call was for him or her, which results in their

[9] Maḥmūd Darwīsh (1941–2008) related how he had been interpellated as an Arab-Palestinian subject by "the poets of celebrations and *zajal* poetic dialogues." In his poem "Qaṣīdat al-Arḍ" ("The Earth Poem") (Darwīsh 1988, pp. 618–31), he recalls the memory of a *zajal* singer whose poems were the first inspiration for his poetry (see also *Mashārif* [Jerusalem and Haifa] 3 [October 1995], pp. 78–9).

[10] See the short story "Naẓra" ("A Stare") by Yūsuf Idrīs (1927–1991) (Idrīs n.d. [1954], pp. 11–12; English translation: Allen 1978, pp. 3–4). The stare in the story is of a fictional character—a poor female child—but one cannot ignore the staring of the narrator and that of the implied author, which represents the stare of the author in specific time and space, and, of course, that of the interpellated reader, whoever the reader may be.

[11] See, for example, the memories of the speaker in Orhan Pamuk's *The Museum of Innocence* (Pamuk 2009). It goes without saying that any reader of the novel, as a human being, cannot escape his or her own experiences—he/she is being interpellated by those very memories into a certain subject position.

[12] Unless it is specifically indicated, identity in the present study refers to a subject's belonging to or being a member of a certain group, whether chosen or ascribed to him or her by other subjects.

becoming a subject relative to the ideology of law and crime. In the first chapter of Fyodor Dostoevsky's *Crime and Punishment*, Raskolnikov, after leaving the room he had rented and walking out into the street, suddenly hears a voice: "Hey, you, German hatter!" It was a drunken man pointing at him and yelling. The young man stops and convulsively clutches his Zimmerman hat—and fear seized him because "some stupid thing like that, some trivial detail can ruin the whole scheme!"[13] The fact that Raskolnikov was interpellated not by a policeman but by a drunkard has nothing to do with the effect of the hailing on his own subjectivity in the context of his future crime and punishment. Readers of Dostoevsky's book are interpellated each in his own way, as well.

The notion of interpellation can be of a more sophisticated nature, as in the "reading" of fiction as we see, for example, in *Nightwood* (1936), a novel by Djuna Barnes (1892–1982).[14] Ann Kennedy shows how Barnes anachronistically extends Althusser's investigation beyond the traditional institutions of the state, examining how our most idealized notions, our safest havens (such as the "private" spaces of love and the maternal that feminist analysis has politicized) are the very means through which subjects experience the contradictory and ambivalent effects of ideology. Deeply embedded in the narrative subject's desire for an identity that will carry forward the continuity of history, our idealized notions are present throughout the novel as systems of nostalgia, transcendence, and wholeness (re)hailing subjects back into an imaginary history of linearity, simplicity, and fulfillment. The suggestive implications of Althusser's analysis appear most explicitly in "Bow Down," the first section of *Nightwood* (pp. 1–28), a novel about love, language, and identity. The author challenges understandings of gender, singularity, and sexuality, suggesting that these categories are unstable, ever-shifting entities. It raises the problem of definition or classification, of whether or not a stable definition of identity can exist while placing us as readers into the experience of being other than what we assume we are.[15]

Since the second half of the previous century, the concept of "identity" has become a prism through which many dimensions of contemporary life are spotted, grasped, and examined. Robert Jay Lifton (b. 1926) published his preliminary versions on what he called "the protean self," which he named after Proteus, the ancient Greek sea god of many forms. On this many-sided self in constant motion, Lifton proffered the following comments:

13 Dostoevsky 1993, p. 5.
14 Barnes 1961.
15 Kennedy 1997, pp. 94–112.

> We are becoming fluid and many-sided. Without quite realizing it, we have been evolving a sense of self appropriate to the restlessness and flux of our time. This mode differs radically from that of the past, and enables us to engage in the continuous exploration and personal experiment ... The protean self emerges from confusion, from the widespread feeling that we are losing our psychological moorings. We feel ourselves buffeted about by unmanageable historical forces and social uncertainties ... We change ideas and partners frequently, and do the same with jobs and places of residence ... Whether dealing with world problems or child rearing, our behavior tends to be ad hoc, more or less decided upon as we go along. We are beset by a contradiction: schooled in the virtues of constancy and stability—whether as individuals, groups, or nations—our world and our lives seem inconstant and utterly unpredictable. We readily come to view ourselves as unsteady, neurotic, or worse.[16]

Later, in the preface of a book published in 1993, Lifton would reveal that in the 1960s, when he first wrote on the concept of proteanism, he had been accused of "contributing to the downfall of Western civilization." He insisted that "the protean self can help people renew their relationships to cultures, Western and non-Western, that are now under duress."[17]

More than twenty years after the contributions of Althusser and Lifton to the understanding of subjectivities, Stuart Hall could point to the veritable discursive explosion around the concept of identity and the fact that it had been subjected to searching criticism; he wonders how this could be explained and where we stood as a result. He says that the deconstruction of the concept of identity was conducted within a variety of disciplinary areas, all of them, in one way or another, critical of the notion of an integral, originary, and unified identity:

> The critique of the self-sustaining subject at the centre of post-Cartesian western metaphysics has been comprehensively advanced in philosophy. The question of subjectivity and its unconscious processes of formation has been developed within the discourse of a psychoanalytically influenced feminism and cultural criticism. The endlessly performative self has been advanced in celebratory variants of postmodernism. Within the antiessentialist critique of ethnic, racial and national conceptions of cultural identity and the "politics of location" some adventurous theoretical conceptions have been sketched in their most grounded forms. What, then, is the need for a further debate about "identity"? Who needs it?[18]

In 2009, the Polish sociologist and philosopher Zygmunt Bauman (1925–2017) wrote that the "discursive explosion" around the concept of

[16] Lifton 1993, p. 1.
[17] Lifton, 1993, p. ix.
[18] Hall 1996, p. 1.

identity "has triggered an avalanche";[19] voices surfaced claiming that after many years at the top of the intellectual parade "identity" had run out of steam;[20] and questions such as "should we say goodbye to identity?"[21] were no longer rare. However, he says, listening to other voices, it is no doubt too soon to wish identities "goodbye." Going a step further is the more definitive idea that identities as mere fictions seem to be less helpful than when the priorities were to resist coercive normative identity formations.[22] In any case, throughout the last decades discussions around the idea of identity have been channeled into two major positions or models: the primordialist and the non-primordialist. The first assumes that there is an essential content to any identity which is defined by common origin or common structure of experience; in the words of Lebanese writer Amin Maalouf (Amīn Maʿlūf) (b. 1949): "It presupposes that 'deep down inside' everyone there is just affiliation that really matters, a kind of 'fundamental truth' about each individual, an 'essence' determined once and for all at birth, never to change thereafter."[23] Although discredited among cultural theorists and sociologists, this view for obvious reasons is popular among politicians, particularly as regards ethnic identity. The second major position, which encompasses all other non-primordialist views regarding identity, including the instrumentalist and the constructivist, argues that identities are constructed through an interplay of cultural reproduction, everyday reinforcements, as well as institutional arrangements.[24]

The non-primordialist position emphasizes the impossibility of fully separate distinct identities. Any identity depends upon its difference from some other identity—"identity is a structured representation which only achieves its positive through the narrow eye of the negative," writes Hall; "it has to go through the eye of the needle of the other before it can construct itself."[25] More than two decades earlier, the English playwright and novelist Michael Frayn (b. 1933) had theorized in a similar vein to Hall, when he seemingly suggested that the protagonist Robinson Crusoe was a human archetype. He tells us that just as philosophers thought the thick stew of human discourse, with all its inaccuracies and assumptions, could in theory be refined down to pure white crystals—"atomic propositions embodying atomic fragments of experience"—so we feel that human society is a construction from

19 Bauman 2009, p. 1.
20 See Du Gay 2009, p. 1.
21 Frosh and Baraitser 2009, pp. 158–69.
22 Frosh and Baraitser 2009, p. 168.
23 Maalouf 2000, p. 4.
24 See Arthur 2011, pp. 4–7 (Introduction).
25 Hall 1991, p. 21.

a series of "atomic individuals," each of them sovereign and entire unto himself:

> We feel that we are Crusoes who have been set down in sight of one another, so that the difficulties of communication and co-operation have been *added* to those of our isolation. As if we are what we are and *then* we enter into relations with the people around us. But man is the child of man. He comes from the belly of another human creature, seeded there by a third. *He can become conscious of his thoughts and feelings only by articulating them in a language developed by communication with his fellows.* Even in his inmost nature he is defined by interaction with other beings around him. What characteristic do we have that can be expressed without relation to others? ... Crusoe on his island would have been neither brave nor resourceful, neither determined nor ingenious, if he had not come from the society of men; if there were not other men across the sea; if there were not a man to tell the story and men to hear it ... No one would—no one *could* talk to himself without having talked to someone else first.[26]

Whereas someone's single identity cannot be explored or challenged without a simultaneous investigation of another or other identities, this is rarely the case in practice. Most investigations in cultural studies deal with the construction of subaltern or marginalized or dominated identities, and rarely are the two ever studied together, as mutually constitutive, as the theory would seem to dictate. It would seem that most of us have gradually become convinced that identity is always a temporary and unstable effect of relations that define identities by marking differences—which implies that the multiplicity of identities and differences and the emphasis on connections or articulations between the fragments or differences are inevitable.[27] Never unified, identities seem to us increasingly fragmented and fractured. Never singular, they seem as well to "multiply constructed across different, often intersecting and antagonistic, discourses, practices and positions." In addition, they are subject to "a radical historicization and are constantly in the process of change and transformation." Actually, identities arise from the narrativization of the self, but the necessarily fictional nature of this narrativization in no way undermines its discursive, material, or political effectivity—"even if the belongingness, the 'suturing into the story' through which identities arise is, partly, in the imaginary (as well as the symbolic) and therefore, always, partly constructed in fantasy, or at least within a fantasmatic field." Identities refer to the meeting point, that very point of *suture*, between, on

26 Frayn 1974, # 67 (my emphasis). Cf. "[L]anguage itself [is] perhaps the most ancient of apparatuses—one in which thousands and thousands of years ago a primate inadvertently let himself be captured, probably without realizing the consequences that he was about to face" (Agamben 2009, p. 14).

27 Grossberg 1996, pp. 89–90.

the one hand, the discourses and practices that attempt to interpellate, speak to us, or hail us into place as the social subjects of particular discourses, and, on the other hand, the processes that produce subjectivities, that construct us as subjects that can be "spoken." All identities are only "points of temporary attachment to the subject position which discursive practices construct for us."[28]

And because we are always in the process of being exposed to new interpellating machines and processes, reacting always consciously *and* unconsciously to them from within our own complicated and unique singular subjectivities, there is no escape from elusiveness and fluidity. Bauman described contemporary society as a place in which everything is elusive and where the disorientation and insecurity caused by living in such a place cannot be solved by parading past certainties and established systems.[29] In other words, identities deal with the past only on the exterior level, simply because they cannot be other than both present- and future-oriented projects. They are about questions of using resources of history, language, and culture "in the process of becoming rather than being: not 'who we are' or 'where we came from,' so much as what we might become, how we have been represented and how that bears on how we might represent ourselves."[30]

Postmodernity and globalization have undoubtedly problematized and invigorated the notion of identity even more so. In traditional premodern[31] societies, as implied in the primordialist model above, in general one's identity was considered to be something fixed, solid, and stable. One was born and died a member of one's clan, of a fixed kinship system, and of one's tribe or group with one's life trajectory fixed in advance. Identity was not problematic and, at most, not subject to any reflection or discussion. Individuals did not undergo identity crises, or radically modify their identity, at least not in the contemporary sense. With modernity, however, as Douglas Kellner (b. 1943) says,[32] identity becomes more mobile, multiple, personal, self-reflexive, and subject to change and innovation. It also becomes social and other-related—the other being a constituent of identity in modernity—but its form is also relatively limited, fixed, and substantial, even though the boundaries of possible identities are continually expanding. There still remains in modernity a structure of interaction with socially defined and

28 The quotations in the last sentences are from Hall 1996, pp. 5–6.

29 Bauman 2004. See also Bauman 2007.

30 Hall 1996, p. 4.

31 I use here the term "modern" not in the temporal sense, but as consisting of three dimensions, namely, a preference for secular rationality; the adoption of religious tolerance with tendencies toward relativism; and individualism.

32 Kellner 1991, pp. 141–77.

available roles, norms, customs, and expectations, among which one must choose, appropriate, and reproduce in order to gain identity in a complex process of mutual recognition. Identity in modernity becomes increasingly problematic; furthermore, the issue of identity itself becomes a problem, as we puzzle over how to constitute, perceive, interpret, and present our self to ourselves and others.[33]

Postmodern thought has by and large rejected the essentialist and rationalist notion of identity building on the constructivist notion, which it in turn problematizes the issue. Kellner refers to the notion of multiple, freely chosen, and easily disposed postmodern identities for multiple circumstances and occasions:

> It appears that postmodern identity tends more to be constructed from *images of leisure and consumption* and tends to be more unstable and subject to change. Both modern and postmodern identity contain a level of reflexivity, an awareness that identity is chosen and constructed. In contemporary society, however, it may be more "natural" to change identities, to switch with the *changing winds of fashion*. While this produces an erosion of individuality and increased social conformity, there are some positive potentials of this postmodern portrayal of identity as an *artificial construct*. For such a notion of identity suggests that one can always change one's life, that identity can always be reconstructed, that one is free to change and produce oneself as one chooses.[34]

In other words, identity does not disappear in contemporary society but has been reconstructed and redefined; it becomes a "freely chosen game, *a theatrical presentation of the self*, in which one is able to present oneself unconcerned about shifts, transformations and dramatic changes."[35] Rather than identity disappearing, it is "merely subject to new determinations and new forces while offering as well new possibilities, styles, models, and forms." The overwhelming variety of subject positioning in an affluent image culture creates "highly unstable identities while constantly providing new openings to restructure one's identity."[36]

Referring to Kellner's suggestions, Bauman says that while the modern problem of identity was how to construct an identity and keep it solid and stable, the postmodern challenge is how to avoid fixation and keep the options open: the catchword of modernity was *creation* while the catchword of postmodernity is *recycling*.[37] Bauman proposes that in the same way

[33] Kellner 1991, pp. 141–3.
[34] Kellner 1991, pp. 153–4 (my emphasis).
[35] Kellner 1991, p. 158 (my emphasis).
[36] Kellner 1991, p. 174.
[37] Bauman 1996, p. 18. Cf. Bauman 1998, pp. 77–102.

as the pilgrim was the most fitting metaphor for modern life, the foremost strategy of life as pilgrimage and of life as identity-building, the stroller, the vagabond, the tourist, and the player jointly offer the metaphor for postmodern strategy, which is motivated by a horror of being bound and fixed.[38] The stroller may imagine him/herself to be a director, though all strollers are the objects of direction; the vagabond is pushed from behind by hopes frustrated and pulled forward by hopes untested; the tourist is a conscious and systematic seeker of new and different experiences; the player's world is one of risks, intuition, and precaution-taking. All four intertwining and interpenetrating postmodern life strategies have in common the tendency to render human relations fragmentary: they are all up against "strings attached" and long-lasting consequences, and "*militate against the construction of lasting networks of mutual duties and obligations.*" They all promote a distance between the individual and the other and cast the other primarily as an "object of aesthetic, not moral, evaluation; as a *matter of taste, not responsibility*."[39]

These ideas are now current and shared by many people, certainly by scholars, writers, and poets. In 1994, a poster put up on the streets of Berlin read: "Your Christ is a Jew. Your car is Japanese. Your pizza is Italian. Your democracy—Greek. Your coffee—Brazilian. Your holiday—Turkish. Your numbers—Arabic. Your letters—Latin. Only your neighbor is a foreigner."[40] Or the following anecdote: in an attempt to discredit one of the Zapatista leaders in southern Mexico, Subcomandante Marcos (Rafael Sebastián Guillén Vicente, b. 1957), government officials tried to put forth the idea that Marcos was gay—in a region where *machismo* still runs strong, it was hoped this would tarnish the leader's credibility. He responded by writing:

> Yes, Marcos is gay. Marcos is gay in San Francisco, Black in South Africa, an Asian in Europe, a Chicano in San Ysidro, an anarchist in Spain, a Palestinian in Israel, a Mayan Indian in the streets of San Cristobal, a Jew in Germany, a Gypsy in Poland, a Mohawk in Quebec, a pacifist in Bosnia, a single woman on the Metro at 10 pm, a peasant without land, a gang member in the slums, an unemployed worker, an unhappy student and, of course, a Zapatista in the mountains. Marcos is all the exploited, marginalised, oppressed minorities resisting and saying "Enough." He is every minority who is now beginning to speak and every majority that must shut up and listen. He is every untolerated

[38] Cf. the fluid identity of the chameleon-like hero in the genre of the *maqāma*: "He is not fixable to just one identity nor to just one place. He is a god-like man, a *theios anēr*, of no identity at all or of all identities at once" (Hämeen-Anttila 2008, p. 34).

[39] Bauman 1996, p. 33 (my emphasis).

[40] According to Bauman 2004, p. 27.

> group searching for a way to speak. Everything that makes power and the good consciences of those in power uncomfortable—this is Marcos.[41]

Then there is the Bulgarian poet Kapka Kassabova (b. 1973); in her poem titled "I Want To Be a Tourist" from her collection *Geography for the Lost*, the speaker tells of an experience that includes more than one or two of the postmodern strategies:

> I imagine my life as a city
> somewhere in the third world, or the second.
> And I want to be a tourist
> in the city of my life.
>
> I want to stroll in shorts and baseball hat,
> with laminated maps and dangling cameras.
> I want to find things for the first time.
> Look, they were put there just for me!
>
> I want a room with musty curtains,
> I want a view of rubbish dumps and urchins,
> I want food poisoning, the dust of traffic
> in the mouth, the thrill of others' misery.
>
> Let me be a tourist in the city of my life.
> Give me overpriced coffee in the square,
> let me visit briefly the mausoleum of the past
> and photograph its mummy.
>
> Give me the open sewers, the stunted dreams,
> the jubilation of ruins, the lepers, the dogs,
> Give me signs in a funny language that I never
> have to learn. Then take my money and let me go.[42]

Kellner's constructed identity from images of leisure and consumption, Bauman's four postmodern strategies, and Kassabova's desire to be a tourist in the city of her life lead us to the notion of globalization, which is one of the major sources for the fresh points of view from which scholars have recently been exploring the concept of identity. There is, for example, the Italian social theorist Alberto Melucci (1943–2001):

> We are migrant animals in the labyrinths of the metropolis; in reality or in the imagination, we participate in an infinity of worlds. And each of these worlds has a culture, a language, and a set of roles and rules that we must adapt to

[41] First published in the *Monthly Review: An Independent Socialist Magazine* 46.4 (September 1994) (according to http://cuadernolatinoamericano.blogspot.co.il/2007/07/subcomandante-marcos-gay.html). Cf. Auron 2012, pp. 34–5.

[42] Kassabova 2007, p. 3.

> whenever we migrate from one to another. Thus we are subjected to mounting pressures to change, to transfer, to translate what we were just a moment ago into new codes and new forms of relation. We transform ourselves into sensitive terminals, transmitting and receiving a quantity of information which far exceeds that of any previous culture. Our means of communication, our work environment, our interpersonal relationships, even our leisure, generate information addressed to individuals who must receive, analyse and store in the memory, and almost always respond with further information.[43]

Since these words were published, all the phenomena and processes that Melucci mentioned have been intensified in a way that any journey into "labyrinths of the metropolis," where "migrant animals" wander, has become so complicated with so many refuges (with at the same time a multitude of dead ends) that traditional notions of identity seem to have lost their conceptual strength. For example, in the postscript of his book *10 Moral Paradoxes* (2007), the Israeli philosopher Saul Smilansky (b. 1962) writes about the future that awaits us:

> Genetic engineering, nanotechnology, and the integration of the biological and the mechanical will enhance human cognitive, physical and emotional capacities. If people can be modified (or modify themselves) radically and repeatedly, questions about identity, choice, value, agency, and responsibility will be transformed in extreme ways ... While our moral world has so far been populated by human beings and, at the margin, other animals, new super (or "trans")-human, sub-human, and dubiously-human (e.g. robotic) beings will people our future societies, requiring thoroughly new ways of thinking about topics such as respect for persons, the sanctity of the body, violence, gender, and equality. Technologies of surveillance, control, manipulation, communication, and knowledge (e.g. as to when people are lying) should redraw the role of personal conscience and self-control versus social forces, and bring up acute questions about the need to safeguard identity, privacy, and autonomy ... New chemical and virtual-reality capacities for the safe and continuous inducement of pleasure will transform human experience.[44]

On the subject of the ethics of identity, Kwame Anthony Appiah (b. 1954) talks about the ethical claims that identities make in the world we human beings have created:

> [W]e make our life *as* men and *as* women, *as* gay and *as* straight people, *as* Ghanaian and *as* Americans, *as* blacks and *as* whites. Immediately, conundrums start to assemble. Do identities represent a curb on autonomy, or do they provide its contours? What claims, if any, can identity groups as such justly

43 Melucci 1997, p. 61.
44 Smilansky 2007, pp. 134–5.

> make upon the state? These are concerns that have gained a certain measure of salience in recent political philosophy ... they are anything but newfangled. What's modern is that we conceptualize identity in particular ways. What's age-old is that when we are asked—and ask ourselves—*who* we are, we are being asked *what* we are as well.[45]

The Internet, as one of the factors and manifestations of globalization, has been embraced so far by 65.6 percent of the world's population.[46] As with any other technological invention, the Internet makes our lives easier—human beings, even those of us who speak out against technology and science (in favor of spirituality and a natural life), tend to adopt and adapt new inventions immediately after they become available. One major aspect of the Internet that relates to identity is this: communication through the Internet, more than through any other means, encourages us to refrain from adherence to one identity, and rather to toy with other identities. This is not to mention the creation of fake identities. The point here is the way the Internet provides us with the ability not to commit ourselves to a single identity. In Plato's *Republic*, Socrates and Adeimantus discuss the origin of the state and the nature of justice and injustice as they appear in the ideal state. Socrates states that the true creator of the state is necessity; it is necessity that is the "mother of our invention," or with another translation "our own need will make it."[47] It may be that the Internet came into existence due to humankind's needs, but its true creator was necessity. In our fluid world, "identities are for wearing and showing, not for storing and keeping." It is because we are endlessly forced to twist and mold our identities, and are not allowed to cling to one identity even if we want to, "that electronic instruments to do just that come in handy and tend to be embraced by millions."[48]

Speaking of globalization, one cannot now ignore what could be called the new cosmopolitan turn of the start of the twenty-first century. Only three years before the turn of the century, Ilios Yannakakis declared "the death of cosmopolitanism." His essay with that same title was published in a book dealing with Alexandria as a "cosmopolitan community." He wrote that "interpretations and definitions of cosmopolitanism run up against each other and are self-defeating," and that "cosmopolitanism filled only an instant of history." Cosmopolitan people were "those who had the world for their culture and mankind as their nation." Referring specifically to

[45] Appiah 2005, p. xiv.

[46] On Internet usage statistics, see at: http://www.internetworldstats.com/stats.htm, last accessed September 5, 2021.

[47] *Republic*, Book II, 369c. See Plato 2000, p. 40; Plato 2006, p. 51

[48] Bauman 2004, pp. 89–90.

Alexandrian cosmopolitanism, he mentioned its urban nature and European cultural roots. The "cosmopolitan spirit" in Alexandria blossomed when economic growth "made it possible for the wealthy merchants to begin a certain social activity within their respective communities." The steady increase of community schools widened the social base of new elites fascinated by modernity; the "increased familiarity with others amongst a relatively young population encouraged an interest in the outside world and emancipated the mentality." French had acquired a dominant position in the eastern Mediterranean, and at this time was thought to be the *lingua franca*. From the end of the 1880s, thousands of immigrants had flowed into Alexandria, filling up the city, and "it was external cultural inputs, especially European, that propped up the community identity." However, soon "cosmopolitanism became diluted by the adopted national culture," since "cosmopolitanism and a strong national sentiment are incompatible." Yannakakis concludes his essay by saying: "Cosmopolitanism was the product of a limited period and singular history—that of the crumbling Ottoman Empire. It lived to the age of a sturdy human being, before disappearing forever."[49]

When Yannakakis' lament for cosmopolitanism was published, some aspects of Alexandrian cosmopolitanism were again emerging in their entirety, and were much more intense. The Internet generation is now considerably much more global than "those who had the world for their culture and mankind as their nation." Instead of French as a *lingua franca*, we have English (or "Globish")[50] in our global village, and migration has been never as intense as in the last decades. In addition, the national cultures that caused the dilution of cosmopolitanism have, in many instances, been replaced by globalized culture. Are we on the verge of a cosmopolitan turnabout?—and, if the answer is positive, why do we not celebrate, as Yannakakis celebrates the nostalgic Alexandrian spirit? And, what is the nature of the cosmopolitan situation compared with the globalized one?

Speaking of cosmopolitanism in the Middle East, one should be very cautious because of the fluidity of the concept and the frequent tendency to use it as anti-nationalist and anti-traditionalist teleology and to grieve for the Ottoman prenationalist paradise lost. Although a contested concept,

49 Yannakakis 1997, pp. 190–4. Cf. Levi 2012, pp. 33–7. For another view, see Hanley 2013, pp. 92–104 ("The conventional image of cosmopolitan Alexandria fails to describe its historical reality because it requires the conjuring of a faceless, voiceless non-cosmopolitan mainstream of poor Muslim Arab Egyptians who, by definition, cannot be cosmopolitan. They exist, submerged as a sort of human ballast in order to elevate the cosmopolitan pinnacle. They are the context that creates cosmopolitan Alexandria, from which they are excluded by definition" (p. 100). On expressions of cosmopolitanism in Levantine literature, see Baladi 2018, pp. 45–56.

50 McCrum 2010.

cosmopolitanism has come to indicate detachment from "parochialisms emanating from extreme allegiances to nation, race, and ethnos."[51] Will Hanley shows how cosmopolitanism in Middle Eastern studies is characterized by a fantasy that clings to scholarly and popular accounts of the Middle East and how it focuses on elites and the invocation of a tag rather than on the pursuit of an idea; the general tone is that of grieving nostalgia. Evidence of social diversity in the modern Middle East can be found in literature, memoir, and film rather than in historiography, since historians have not provided the means to measure cosmopolitanism or to evaluate the claims and respond to the needs of non-specialists interested in diversity. The Middle East's past, Hanley says, is a victim of its moribund present. Prenational Middle Eastern modernity did not exist so as to condemn late twentieth-century nation-states. At this point, the cosmopolitan decline teleology must be overturned, since truly cosmopolitan phenomena are of grave importance to the globalized Middle East, and can be recognized as such only when the concept is rid of its romanticism.[52]

Taking into consideration Hanley's arguments on the necessity to avoid using prenational Middle Eastern modernity as a means of condemning late twentieth-century nation-states, what now makes it possible to talk about some kind of cosmopolitan turn is our belief in the necessity to avoid treating identities as fixed and absolute. Subjectivities are always unfinished and unfinishable, and their characteristics shift widely between multiple perspectives—no single analytic framework can fully account for the inner lives of people and their intersubjective relations. Although the present study cannot pretend to refer in its arguments to non-elitist segments of society, we are not using cosmopolitanism here as a refuge from the nation-state paradigm, as a label or tag devoid of meaningful content, or for the sake of nostalgia. The notion of cosmopolitanism serves here as another dimension of the fragmentation of the notion of identity and as a tool to escape the binary analytical methods in the humanities and social sciences.

In an article published in 2006,[53] the German sociologist Ulrich Beck (1944–2015) and the Israeli sociologist Natan Sznaider (b. 1954) argue that from the beginning of the twenty-first century we have been witnessing a global transformation of modernity that calls for a rethinking and a recon-

[51] Anderson 1998, p. 267. Cf. Starr 2008, pp. 10–11.

[52] Hanley 2008, pp. 1346–67. In his article, Hanley provides a critical discussion of most of the scholarly contributions on cosmopolitanism in Middle East studies, and in particular on Sami Zubaida's descriptions. These he sees as displaying elitism and grieving nostalgia: "Although the plebian majority is necessary to the existence of the cosmopolitan elite, its preponderance is an occasion for grief and nostalgia for a lost age" (p. 1350).

[53] Beck and Sznaider 2006, pp. 1–23.

ceptualization of the humanities and the social sciences by asking for a cosmopolitan turn. There is no uniform interpretation of cosmopolitanism; the boundaries separating it from competitive terms such as globalization, transnationalism, universalism, and glocalization are not distinct; and internally it is traversed by all kinds of fault lines.[54] Yet, according to Beck and Sznaider, all other concepts presuppose basic dualisms, such as domestic/foreign, national/international, local/global, us/them, all of which in reality have become ambiguous. In fact, all these dualities have dissolved and merged together in new forms that require new conceptual analysis. The underlying idea is that the light of the great cultural problems has moved on from a nation-state definition of society and politics—"the modern construct of the nation state is under constant pressure from the forces of globalisation"[55]—to a cosmopolitan outlook. This means that, in doing research or theorizing, we can no longer take it for granted that society is equated with national society; the unit of analysis should no longer be the national society, or the nation-state, or the combination of both. The principle of cosmopolitanism can be found in specific forms on every level and can be practiced in every field of social and political action: in international organizations, in binational families, in neighborhoods, in global cities, in transnationalized military organizations, in the management of multinational corporations, in production networks, in human rights organizations, among ecology activists, and in the paradoxical global opposition to globalization.[56]

The recent changes and developments in our attitude to the notion of identity are a natural outcome of intense globalization, wide migration, growing social and political uncertainty and insecurity, the development of communication, and the turnabout in cosmopolitanism in the above sense; all this and, in addition the heritage of postmodernism, poststructuralism, psychoanalysis, and postfeminism. Such changes and developments, however, could not have happened without what has been described as the market triumphalism in our era that witnessed "the expansion of markets

54 When Tony Judt uses the term "globalization," referring to "the last great era of internationalization" in the "imperial decades preceding World War I," he probably means the era of cosmopolitanism as we intend in the present study. In any event, Judt argues that "the story of globalization combines an evaluative mantra ('growth is good'), with the presumption of inevitability: globalization is with us to stay, a natural process rather than human choice." In his view, however, "we should by now have learned that politics remains national" (Judt 2010, pp. 190–7).

55 Zajda 2009, p. 8.

56 On moral cosmopolitanism, see Appiah 2006. According to Appiah, cosmopolitanism is a dynamic concept based on the idea that we have responsibilities to others that are beyond those based on kinship or citizenship, and that just because other people have different customs and beliefs from ours they will likely still have meaning and value.

and market-oriented reasoning into spheres of life traditionally governed by nonmarket norms."[57] We are all "*in* and *on* the market," Bauman says, "simultaneously customers and commodities. No wonder that the use/consumption of human relations and so, by proxy, also our identities ... catches up, and fast, with the pattern of car use/consumption, imitating the cycle that starts from purchase and ends with waste disposal."[58] Bill McKibben (b. 1960) describes how we surrendered a fixed identity—a community, an extended family, deep and comforting roots—for, "quite literally, the chance to 'make something of ourselves.' Now we create our own identities." And this "making something of yourself" is, more than anything else, an economic task. We are interested in longer lives, fuller tables, and warmer houses, and the community is no longer necessary to provide these things. We change our religions, spouses, places of residence, and professions with ease; "our affluence isolates us ever more. We are not just individuals; we are hyper-individualists such as the world has never known."[59]

These changes and developments in the notion of identity could not have happened without what may be termed the "classlessness" of the bourgeoisie: "If we had once again to conceive of the fortunes of humanity in terms of class," Giorgio Agamben says, "then today we would have to say that there are no longer social classes, but just a single planetary petty bourgeoisie, in which all the old social classes are dissolved: The petty bourgeoisie has inherited the world and is the form in which humanity has survived nihilism."[60] If the petty bourgeois is willing to stop looking for "a proper identity in the already improper and senseless form of individuality," and if one accepts his "proper being-thus" not as belonging to an identity but as a "singularity without identity," then and only then might there be a chance that the bourgeois will enter into community without presuppositions and without subjects:

> The fact is that the senselessness of their existence runs up against a final absurdity, against which all advertising runs aground: death itself. In death the petty bourgeois confront the ultimate expropriation, the ultimate frustration of individuality: life in all its nakedness, the pure incommunicable, where their shame

[57] Sandel 2009, p. 265. Sandel's hero is Robert F. Kennedy (1925–1968), who tried to confront what he called "the poverty of satisfaction," as in the following quotation: "But even if we act to erase material poverty, there is another great task. It is to confront the poverty of satisfaction—a lack of purpose and dignity—that inflicts us all. Too much and too long, we seem to have surrendered community excellence and community values in the mere accumulation of material things" (March 18, 1968).

[58] Bauman 2004, p. 91.

[59] McKibben 2007, p. 96.

[60] Agamben 2003 [1993], p. 63.

> can finally rest in peace ... This means that the planetary petty bourgeoisie is probably the form in which humanity is moving toward its own destruction. But this also means that the petty bourgeoisie represents an opportunity unheard of in the history of humanity that it must at all costs not let slip away. Because if instead of continuing to search for a proper identity in the already improper and senseless form of individuality, humans were to succeed in belonging to this impropriety as such, in making of the proper being-thus not an identity and an individual property but a singularity without identity, a common and absolutely exposed singularity—if humans could ... be only the thus, their singular exteriority and their face, then they would for the first time enter into a community without presuppositions and without subjects, into a communication without the incommunicable. Selecting in the new planetary humanity those characteristics that allow for its survival, removing the thin diaphragm that separates bad mediatized advertising from the perfect exteriority that communicates only itself ... this is the political task of our generation.[61]

"Global capitalism," René ten Bos (b. 1959) explains, "is indifferent to whether products are being sold to Moslems, Christians, Buddhists, Hindus, or atheists. It is also indifferent to national or political identities. It only takes an interest in anonymous and acquisitive citizens."[62] Tim Parks says the same but referring to literature: "The idea that we are absolutely free of any community permits us to engage with all people everywhere. This is why so much international literature is about freedom and favors rebellions against institutions."[63]

Also, the changes and developments in the notion of identity could not have happened without what I might call, following what Guy Debord (1931–1994) prophetically discerned more than fifty years ago, the "complete triumph in our life of the spectacle," the politics we live in, and the decline of being into having, and having into merely appearing. The start of the emergence of the spectacle as a major social power had already been seen in the late nineteenth century. In *The Age of Empire*, Eric Hobsbawm (1917–2012) refers to the identity crisis through which bourgeois society passed from the 1870s to 1914, and shows how the traditional kingdom of high culture was undermined by a formidable enemy: "the arts appealing to the common people and (with the partial exception of literature) revolutionized by the combination of technology and the discovery of the mass market."[64] All three mottos for the chapter from which this quotation is taken are relevant to our argument, but the one Hobsbawm quotes in brief

61 Agamben 2003 [1993], p. 65.
62 See ten Bos 2005, p. 22.
63 *NYRblog*, August 30, 2012.
64 Hobsbawm 1987, pp. 219–20.

from the writings of the Italian playwright and founder of Futurism Filippo Tommaso Marinetti (1876–1944) is most illuminating. Here is the full relevant quotation from a new translation of Marinetti's critical writings:

> The past is necessarily inferior to the future. And that's how we want it to be. How could we possibly see any virtue at all in our most dangerous enemy, the past, that gloomy mentor and abominable tutor? This is why we renounce the obsessive splendors of the centuries that are gone forever and why we cooperate with triumphant machines, which keep the earth enclosed in their net of speed. We connive with the Machine to destroy the poetry of far-off times, of faraway places and of solitude in the wild, the poignant nostalgia of parting, and in their place we set the tragic lyricism of speed in all places, at all times.[65]

When Debord wrote his book, what had been merely a vision of cooperation with "triumphant machines," in this case the machine of the spectacle, had already become a reality. In 221 theses divided into nine chapters, Debord traces the development of modern society in which "all that once was directly lived has become mere representation."[66] Debord argues that the spectacle is the inverted image of society in which relations between commodities have supplanted relations between people and in which passive identification with the spectacle supplants genuine activity. "The spectacle is not a collection of images," he writes, "rather, it is a social relationship between people that is mediated by images."[67] Debord's twelfth thesis reads:

> The spectacle manifests itself as an enormous positivity, out of reach and beyond dispute. All it says is: "*Everything that appears is good; whatever is good will appear.*" The attitude that it demands in principle is the same passive acceptance that it has already secured by means of its seeming incontrovertibility, and indeed by its monopolization of the realm of appearances.[68]

Agamben has taken that insight one step forward, wondering what could be reaped from Debord's heritage in the era of the complete triumph of the spectacle:

> It is clear that the spectacle is language, the very communicativity or linguistic being of humans. This means that a fuller Marxian analysis should deal with the fact that capitalism (or any other name one wants to give the process that today dominated world history) was directed not only toward the expropriation of productive activity, but also and principally toward the alienation of language itself, of the very linguistic and communicative nature of humans, of that *logos*

65 Marinetti 2006, p. 44.
66 Debord 1995 [1967], p. 12. Another translation: Debord 2000 [1967], p. 7.
67 Debord 1995 [1967], p. 12. Another translation: Debord 2000 [1967], p. 7.
68 Debord 1995 [1967], p. 15. Another translation: Debord 2000 [1967], pp. 9–10 (my emphasis).

> which one of Heraclitus's fragments identified as the Common. The extreme form of this expropriation of the Common is the spectacle, that is, the politics we live in. But this also means that in the spectacle of our own linguistic nature comes back to us inverted. This is why (precisely because what is being expropriated is the very possibility of common good) the violence of the spectacle is so destructive; but for the same reason the spectacle remains something like a positive possibility that can be used against it.[69]

Against this theoretical background, one should keep in mind the heritage of the twentieth century, with its fetishization and relentless celebration of difference, or, in other words, the celebration of separate identities. In fact, raising our heads from the books and articles that theorize the notion of identity into the real world, one can hardly deny that reality has been lagging far behind theory. "Since cultural diversity is, increasingly, the fate of the modern world, and ethnic absolutism a regressive feature of late-modernity," says Stuart Hall, "the greatest danger now arises from forms of national and cultural identity—new and old—which attempt to secure *their* identity by adopting closed versions of culture or community and by refusal to engage ... with the difficult problems that arise from trying to live with difference."[70]

Therefore, my analysis and the method by which I will present my arguments herewith are not devoid of some kind of what could be described as "orientational meliorism."[71] This life, as the American pragmatist John Dewey (1859–1952) argued, is neither perfectly good nor bad; it can be improved only through human effort. Certain orientations that a subject can take, Scott R. Stroud tells us, "may be better than others in terms of their adaptive value to the environment (including social environments) and their value in terms of the quality of a subject's experience, and second, individuals can work to improve their experience by changing their orientations toward the world, self, and others."[72] Here is the place to introduce the notion of practical identity, which Christine Korsgaard (b. 1952) characterizes as a normative self-conception, as "a description under which you value yourself, a description under which you find your life to be worth living and

69 Agamben 2003 [1993], p. 80. For more on the alienation of language in Agamben's thought, see Agamben 1999.

70 Hall 1993, p. 361.

71 See Stroud 2007, pp. 185–215. Stroud asserts that the American pragmatist John Dewey presents a useful notion regarding moral development and growth with a focus on attentiveness to one's situation, but also notes that he leaves out extended analysis of how one is to foster such an orientation. He argues that Deweyan moral theory can be supplemented by the methods that Zen Buddhism prescribes to bring attentiveness back to one's experience of activity.

72 Stroud 2007, p. 187.

your action to be worth undertaking."[73] That is to say, our practical identity is both discovered and constructed, generated from the inside and by no means imposed externally. Many aspects of our practical identity are not matters of choice but arise from the constraints that define our situation and the non-voluntary aspects of our identity, such as bodily and intellectual capacities, our sexual and cultural tendencies as well as family relationships. However, due to the reflective nature of our human self-consciousness, as agents we have the capacity

> to call into question whether certain aspects of our identities, and the beliefs, desires, and motives to which they give rise, constitute *reasons* for us ... we can construct a self-conception that then comes to have normative authority for us ... Practical identity is, therefore, both a precondition for and a product of agency.[74]

Global developments have been marking a positive process for the future of society, any society, and people should be encouraged to abandon ideas which advocate oneness. "It's possible, of course," Diane Davis says, "to continue teaching without considering which ways of being-with-one-another our pedagogies promote," to point a finger at another country or at certain organizations within our own countries and to feel righteous, over and above it all:

> [T]he "reason" on which we base our innocence, that thinking-style that masquerades as thinking itself, that sends us scrambling to categorize, to separate the Self from Other, the Same from the not-Same, the poison from the cure ... reason is in deep. It can no longer be counted on to save us from the disaster because it's *implicated* in too many disasters. Don't miss the significance of this: The Nazi Nightmare may not have been the result of "mis-takes" in thinking—it may rather have been the result of a thinking that was too logical, logical to the extreme. After all, the "project of making [One] sense" seems to have been hanging out at the scene of every massive crime against "humanity" recorded in our long and indecent histories—it presided over the holy wars, the Salem witch trials, and the Nazi massacres; it justified the storm of the Desert Storm and the ethnic cleansing in Bosnia; in fact it has been at the bottom of every hate crime buttressed by presumed distinctions in race, sex, class, religion, sexual orientation, etc.[75]

[73] Korsgaard 1996, p. 101. Cf. Atkins 2008, pp. 1, 64–7, 106–10; Davenport 2012, pp. 7–30, 38–57, 63–73, 80–7, 93–118, 123–4, 150–7.

[74] Mackenzie and Atkins 2008, p. 11.

[75] Davis 2000, p. 14. See also Amin Maalouf's words about "mortal identities" or "identities that kill" (Maalouf 2000, p. 26).

We must not forget that Davis published the book from which I have just quoted in the year 2000. Had she published it now, she would have had to add to the records of the "indecent histories" some good new examples.

In order to put on display the complexity of the concept of identity, I will conclude the present theoretical introduction with some sections about identity that the British historian Tony Judt (1948–2010) wrote several months before his death. Judt considers "identity" to be "a dangerous word" because in academic life the word has comparably mischievous uses. Students today can select from a swathe of identity studies: "gender studies," "women's studies," "Asian-Pacific-American studies," and dozens of others. The shortcoming of all these "para-academic programs" is not that they concentrate on a given ethnic or geographical minority, but that they encourage members of the minority to study themselves—thereby simultaneously negating the goals of a liberal education and reinforcing the sectarian and ghetto mentalities they purport to undermine:

> Blacks study blacks, gays study gays, and so forth. As so often, academic taste follows fashion. These programs are byproducts of communitarian solipsism: today we are all hyphenated—Irish-Americans, Native Americans, African-Americans, and the like. Most people no longer speak the language of their forebears or know much about their country of origin, especially if their family started out in Europe. But in the wake of a generation of boastful victimhood, they wear what little they do know as a proud badge of identity: you are what your grandparents suffered. In this competition, Jews stand out. Many American Jews are sadly ignorant of their religion, culture, traditional languages, or history. But they do know about Auschwitz, and that suffices.

Talking about himself, Judt writes that, as an English-born student teaching in the United States, as a Jew somewhat uncomfortable with much of what passes for "Jewishness" in contemporary America, and as a social democrat, he is frequently at odds with his self-prescribed radical colleagues that he supposes he should seek comfort from in the familiar "rootless cosmopolitanism." But that seems to him too imprecise, too deliberately universal in its ambitions:

> Far from being rootless, I am all too well rooted in a variety of contrasting heritages. In any event, all such labels make me uneasy. We know enough of ideological and political movements to be wary of exclusive solidarity in all its forms. One should keep one's distance not only from the obviously unappealing "-isms"—fascism, jingoism, chauvinism—but also from the more seductive variety: communism, to be sure, but nationalism and Zionism too. And then there is national pride: more than two centuries after Samuel Johnson first made the point, patriotism—as anyone who passed the last decade in America can testify—is still the last refuge of the scoundrel. I prefer the edge: the place

> where countries, communities, allegiances, affinities, and roots bump uncomfortably up against one another—where cosmopolitanism is not so much an identity as the normal condition of life. Such places once abounded. Well into the twentieth century there were many cities comprising multiple communities and languages—often mutually antagonistic, occasionally clashing, but somehow coexisting. Sarajevo was one, Alexandria another. Tangiers, Salonica, Odessa, Beirut, and Istanbul all qualified—as did smaller towns like Chernovitz and Uzhhorod. By the standards of American conformism, New York resembles aspects of these lost cosmopolitan cities: that is why I live here.

He concludes with the following:

> Being "Danish" or "Italian," "American" or "European" won't just be an identity; it will be a rebuff and a reproof to those whom it excludes. The state, far from disappearing, may be about to come into its own: the privileges of citizenship, the protections of card-holding residency rights, will be wielded as political trumps. Intolerant demagogues in established democracies will demand "tests"—of knowledge, of language, of attitude—to determine whether desperate newcomers are deserving of British or Dutch or French "identity." They are already doing so. In this brave new century we shall miss the tolerant, the marginals: the edge people. My people.[76]

The present book has two main axes; the first of them is *commitment*. Here, I concentrate on the contribution of Palestinian culture, especially literature and theater, to Palestinian nation-building since 1948. Becoming an essential part of the vocabulary of Arab intellectuals and writers, commitment (*iltizām*) has been employed to indicate the necessity for writers or artists to convey a message rather than merely create an imaginative work for its own sake. The case studies, discussed in the chapters of Part I, relate to Palestinian cultural activities, whether in Israel, the Occupied Territories, or the Palestinian diaspora. All of them are discussed against the backdrop of the 1948 *Nakba,* in which more than 700,000 Palestinian Arabs—about half of prewar Palestine's Arab population—fled or were expelled from their homes. The second axis is *hybridization*. The blending of elements from different cultures is one of the major phenomena in Arabic literature, certainly against the backdrop of its relationship with Islam and its cultural heritage during the last one-and-half millennia. Here, we will focus on the role the Jews have played in Arabic literature in light of their contribution to this literature since the pre-Islamic period, and on the gradual demise of Arab-Jewish identity and culture in recent decades. It goes without saying that similar studies should be conducted about the role that other non-Muslim Arabs have played in Arabic literature, such as the Christian Arabs. This

[76] *New York Review of Books*, February 23, 2010.

book is structured in line with the aforementioned two axes: it consists of two parts, each of which has four chapters, each chapter including an introduction, three sections, and a conclusion. The following is a short description of the parts and chapters of the book.

Part I, "Occupation, Domination, and Commitment," refers to topics related to Palestinian culture in light of the *Nakba* and the ongoing dispossession of the Palestinian people. *Chapter 1*, "Performance: In the Service of the Nation," refers to the emergence of Palestinian drama and theater against the background of the *Nakba* and in light of Palestinian nation-building. The discussion deals with early dramatic and theatrical productions during the first half of the twentieth century, the uprooting of Palestinians after the 1948 War of Independence, the repression of Palestinian cultural activities during the 1950s, the new start and the growth of professional theater after 1967, especially the al-Ḥakawātī Theater, and the nature of contemporary theatrical activities. *Chapter 2*, "Commitment: Verse Drama and Resistance," discusses the various cultures that were integrated into the emerging Palestinian theatrical movement after the 1967 War and during the second dispossession of the Palestinian people. This discussion will be illustrated through a pioneering work, a verse drama by the Israeli-Palestinian poet and dramatist Samīḥ al-Qāsim, titled *Qarāqash* (1969), that was inspired by several different cultures, including Israeli-Hebrew culture. It was also inspired by such famous Western dramatists as Erwin Piscator and Bertolt Brecht. *Chapter 3*, "Chronicle: The Ongoing *Nakba*," deals with the poetry of Maḥmūd Darwīsh, the national Palestinian poet, especially his attempt to provide a chronicle of the ongoing Palestinian *Nakba* in the mid-1980s against the backdrop of the Israeli invasion of Lebanon and the lead-up to the outbreak of the first *Intifāḍa* in the West Bank and Gaza Strip in December 1987. The discussion concentrates on the collection *Ward Aqall* (*Fewer Roses*) (1986), which is unique in its poetic structure and lyrical coherence. *Chapter 4*, "Bilingualism: Palestinians in Hebrew," shows how Palestinian authors became bilingual, changed their cultural loyalties, started to write in another language, and sometimes even abandoned their mother tongue only to pay a heavy price for so doing, certainly when Hebrew culture refused to accept them as equals. The chapter concentrates on the works of the Druze Na'īm 'Arāyidī and the Christian Anton Shammās, referring as well to the Hebrew canonical center's cognitive dissonance toward Palestinian writers in Hebrew.

Part II, "Hybridization, Exclusion, and Demise," is about the involvement of Jews in Arabic literature, which came to a sad end mainly due to the political and ideological conflict in the Middle East. *Chapter 5*, "Pluralism: Arabs of Mosaic Faith," surveys the literary writing of Jews in Arabic throughout the history of Arabic literature, even before the rise of Islam, and concludes with the demise of this literary writing today. Judeo-Muslim symbiosis began at the very birth of Islam, a process in which the Jews played an important role; the Qur'ān provides a solid testimony to this. The chapter refers as well to the immigration to Israel of most of the Jews from the Arab world, as well as to the clash of narratives and the shift to writing in Hebrew. *Chapter 6*, "Spring: 'We Were Like Those Who Dream,'" discusses the literary Arabic activities of the immigrating Arab-Jewish writers in Israel, especially during the 1950s. Among the writers, it was possible to discern two streams parallel to the dominant trends of the local Palestinian literature: those who were supported by the Israeli governmental establishment, on the one hand, and the Communist writers, on the other. These were the years when hopes were still high that the new Israeli society would accept the Arabic language as a legitimate language of local literary creation. *Chapter 7*, "Demise: The Last of the Mohicans," concentrates on the activities of the last Jews writing in Arabic as illustrated in the writing of the Iraqi-Jewish author Isḥāq Bār-Moshe, who started his literary career in Israel after his emigration from Baghdad. Bār-Moshe was one of the few emigrant Arab-Jewish authors who insisted on remaining true to their cultural origins by writing in Arabic even in the late twentieth century, though they realized that they were working in a void and hardly finding any readership inside or outside Israel. *Chapter 8*, "Identity: Inessential Solidarities," is theoretically oriented and discusses the issue of Arab-Jewish identity and the changes in this concept among Arabized Jews. Due to some processes that Arabized Jews had experienced and because of some global developments, they gradually developed a negative sensitivity toward the notion of a stable identity, asserting instead their particular singularities and searching for alternative forms of identification, mostly various kinds of inessential solidarity and belonging

The *Epilogue*, "'Trailed Travellers': Between Fiction, Meta-Fiction, and History," refers to the two core issues around which the present book revolves, the *Nakba* as an ongoing process of uprooting, permanent persecution, and displacement of the Palestinians, on the one hand, and the contemporary demise of Arab-Jewish identity and culture, on the other hand. The aim is to look at both processes, but mainly the second one that suffers from a lack of scholarly attention, sometimes even denial out of populist considerations, through the examination of the relationship between fiction, meta-fiction, and history.

Part I

Occupation, Domination, and Commitment

والهويَّةُ؟ قُلْتُ،
فقال: دفاعٌ عن الذّات ...
إنَّ الهويّة بنتُ الولادة لكنَّها
في النّهاية إبداعُ صاحبها، لا
وراثة ماضٍ. أنا المتعدِّدَ. في
داخلي خارجيٍ المتجدِّدُ. لكنَّني
أنتمي لسؤال الضّحيَّة.
– محمود درويش

And what about identity? I asked,
It is a self-defense ... he said.
Identity is born but
At the end, it is a creation by its owner, not
Inheritance of the past. I am the multiple ... Inside
Me you can find my self-renewing exteriority. But
I belong to the victim's question.
– Maḥmūd Darwīsh

There is general agreement among contemporary social historians that, as a direct corollary of modernity, nationalism appeared on the historical scene only fairly recently. Accepted, too, is the notion that it has its basis in invention, construction, and what noted historian Eric Hobsbawm (1917–2012) has termed "social engineering," which is often deliberate and always innovative, if only because historical novelty implies innovation. Nations as a natural, God-given way of classifying human beings, as an inherent political destiny, are only a myth—the reality is that nationalism sometimes takes pre-existing cultures and turns them into nations, sometimes invents them, and often obliterates pre-existing cultures. The history of the modern Middle East provides ample evidence of how effective this reality can be, as the nation-states that arose there after the First World War clearly serve as evidence of how politics, language, and literature all contributed to the fostering of nationalistic sentiment. Nationalism embraces not only the political but all phases of life—men and women have come to work and produce and live not only for themselves but for the nation; even their truths and their gods have become national. This holds *a fortiori* for the nation-states in the Middle East, where during the last decades of the twentieth century critics and scholars have spoken of the separate Arabic literatures of Egypt, Syria, Iraq, and Lebanon. But by now it is obvious that one should also study the role that literature—or even the creation of literature—has played and still plays in the social engineering that has gone into the making of the nation-state.

Israeli and Palestinian nationalism or nations must be novel, whatever the historic continuities of Jews or Middle Eastern Muslims, since the very concept of territorial states of the currently standard type in their region was barely thought of during the nineteenth century, and hardly became a serious prospect before the end of the First World War. Standard national languages, to be learned in schools and written, let alone spoken, by more than a smallish elite, are largely constructs of varying, but often brief, ages. Thus, along with the search for the gradual legitimization of the Arab nation-state came the invention, for each of them, of a particularist "national" past, which was then disseminated through cultural campaigns in various fields and through the inevitable shifts in educational and cultural policies in the service of indoctrination. As state control of cultural organs and electronic media always comes into play here, caution is required when one encounters nationalistic themes in modern literature with regard to the conclusions one may draw from them. An outstanding case in point is Iraq, where writers and artists were encouraged, in certain periods, to derive their inspiration from the civilizations and cultures that flourished in Mesopotamia-Iraq from remote antiquity to the modern age.[1] But it is very interesting to study the relationship between nationalism and literature in the Palestinian case, where the process of building a nation-state has still not been completed, even though the relevant social engineering has been in full swing for many years, in fact, even since before the creation of Israel. This process has certainly been highly fostered because of the State of Israel's establishment. It cannot be isolated from the larger context of the search for roots, or "the invention of tradition," a phenomenon widespread since the First World War throughout all of the nation-states in the Arab world and one that is very common in recent years among the Palestinians as a part of their efforts to strengthen their national identity and promote their hopes of establishing their independent state. The process of vernacular mobilization first discovers an ethnic past that is serviceable for present needs and then creates a unified and distinctive consciousness and sense of ethnic community and of a politicized common culture. In the Palestinian case, this means accentuating a separate cultural personality and distinguishing it from the wide, inclusive Arab identity. For example, this process included intense cultural activities as a response to the need to recognize and preserve the Palestinian national identity in the face of what is described as the annihilation of Palestinian culture. The Palestinian search for roots has concentrated as well on the revival of folklore less as a subject of historical and literary study and more as a vital and dynamic force in society and a symbol of the determination of the Palestinian people to gain their right to self-determination as a nation with a distinctive culture and peculiar history. In the four chapters in the present part, I will discuss various topics related to Palestinian nation-building and the connections of these topics with literature.

In *Chapter 1*, "Performance: In the Service of the Nation," I will discuss the emergence of Palestinian drama and theater in particular and its connection with Palestinian nation-building. Although Palestine has become fertile ground for cultural activities since the 1920s, especially in the field of poetry, the development of theater was very slow. Palestine, on the margins of the Egyptian cultural center, was never a center for any modern cultural movement in the Arab world during the nineteenth and the first half of the twentieth century. The cultural activities in Palestine prior to the First World War lacked any political strand in the form of a Palestinian consciousness. In this sense, it was not exceptional, since no particular Arabic literature written at the time can be identified as national in the modern political sense. Up to that point, Palestinian literature bore marks of cultural consciousness of a very special nature, but did not reflect the subsequent political

[1] See Snir 2017, pp. 162–3.

consciousness. The first Palestinian theatrical attempts started before 1948, but after the uprooting of the Palestinians following the *Nakba*, there was a significant decline in the activities in the 1950s. The new start followed the 1967 War, which brought about the growth of the professional theater, especially with the establishment of the al-Ḥakawātī troupe in Jerusalem, and the emergence of many other theatrical activities which were incorporated among the Palestinian search for roots. It included as well the use of folklore as a symbol of the determination of the Palestinian people to gain their right to self-determination as a nation with a distinctive culture and peculiar history. As mentioned above, the process of vernacular mobilization first discovers an ethnic past that is serviceable for present needs and then creates a unified and distinctive consciousness and sense of ethnic community and of a politicized common culture.

Chapter 2, "Commitment: Verse Drama and Resistance," will discuss the mixture of various cultures integrated into the emerging Palestinian theatrical movement through a play by Samīḥ al-Qāsim titled *Qaraqāsh* (1969) that became a junction of different sources of inspiration, such as that of the German director Erwin Piscator (1893–1966) who, together with Bertolt Brecht, believed that conveying social and political messages was the prime aim of the theater in a dynamic modern society, and that of Israeli-Hebrew theater side by side with the inspiration of both Russian and Arabic theater. The dramatic text becomes an arena of diversified cultural imprints due to the fact that the Palestinian theatrical movement provides a rare glimpse into the unique historical circumstances that have accompanied the process of Palestinian nation-building. *Qaraqāsh*, among the first Palestinian plays written with an awareness of the Western sense of the genre, is considered by critics to be one of the first printed plays of which Palestinian literature can boast. The dramatist intended it originally to be a contribution to the establishment of a Palestinian theater with a high artistic and intellectual mission, and to impart a political message of great poignancy to the world. Indeed, in the setting of the reunification of the two segments of the Palestinian people after the 1967 War, *Qaraqāsh* denoted the beginning of the professional stage in the modern Palestinian theatrical movement. It was first performed in the West Bank in 1970 by the amateur troupe 'Ā'ilat al-Masraḥ (The Family of the Theater) from Ramallah; however, the military authorities intervened to ban subsequent staging of the play. The 'Ā'ilat al-Masraḥ troupe later formed the nucleus of the Balālīn Theater troupe that was established in 1971, which was the basis for the al-Ḥakawātī Theater and then for the al-Masraḥ al-Waṭanī al-Filasṭīnī (Palestinian National Theater). Moreover, through *Qaraqāsh* one can follow some of the pivotal thematic and poetic aspects of the Palestinian theatrical movement, its literary and ideological background, and the universal as well as particular Arab sources of inspiration.

Chapter 3, "Chronicle: The Ongoing *Nakba,*" deals with a chronicle of the Palestinian people in the mid-1980s against the backdrop of the Israeli invasion of Lebanon in 1982 and the years prior to the outbreak of the first *Intifāḍa* in the West Bank and Gaza Strip in December 1987. In fact, it is a chronicle undertaken by a single poet, the Palestinian Maḥmūd Darwīsh (1941–2008), one of the most popular Arab poets in modern times, especially against the backdrop of the marginalization of poetry within the already marginalized role of literature in the age of mass media and the Internet. The second half of the twentieth century witnessed a shift in the field of poetry, whereas the declarative traditional tone of neoclassical poetry was generally abandoned and poetry had been consigned to being an intimate activity of the lonely reader far removed from the style of the poet as the representative of the tribe. Yet, although the relationship between the poet and the reader has undergone an essential change; poetry in some cases still functions as a register of the experiences of human beings, recording their miseries, feelings, hopes, and trials, if in new ways. Although poets tend to avoid speaking in the name of collective communities, poetry as a means of expressing the agonies and miseries of a collective is still being written. One example is the poetry used by the Palestinians to chronicle their *Nakba* (the catastrophe of 1948) and its unending agonies. The discussion in the chapter will concentrate on the collection *Ward Aqall* (*Fewer Roses*) (1986), which the present writer considers to be one of the peaks of modern Arabic poetry. The *Nakba* is always there as a kind of background without which this poetry cannot exist, but its main concern is a dialogue with other texts and the interplay not only between reality, poetry, and myth but that between poetry, meta-poetry, and meta-myth.

Chapter 4, "Bilingualism: Palestinians in Hebrew," investigates the writing in Hebrew by Palestinians through two models of the attitude to the culture of the majority. Literary bilingualism is not uncommon in societies where a minority culture evolves alongside or within a majority culture, but in Israel this minority culture has been since 1948 under constant threat from the majority culture—Arabic is not only the mother tongue of the Palestinians, it is the very embodiment of the minority's struggle to defend and preserve its religious and cultural heritage. This explains why the phenomenon of Palestinians writing in Hebrew generally has remained limited to Arab writers belonging to the Druze and Christian minorities and took on some significance only in the 1980s, when Anton Shammās (b. 1950), who is a Christian, and Na'īm 'Arāyidī (1948–2015), who was Druze, began to make a name for themselves in Hebrew. Only a small number of Palestinian authors and poets have followed them and now write in Hebrew in addition to Arabic—in rare cases, Palestinian writers write only in Hebrew. Typical of the literary activities of Palestinians who write in Hebrew is their membership in two different, even "hostile," literary systems: the Arabic into which they were born and in which they usually created their first works; and the Hebrew into which they were thrown more or less against their will, even if later they can be seen to embrace it in an act of conscious aesthetic preference. Most of them possess a natural skill and ability of expression in Hebrew, and have mastered the modernist techniques and literary style that enable them to write fluently in the language and sometimes write about the same experience in both Hebrew and Arabic. The discussion will refer as well to the Hebrew canonical center's cognitive dissonance in its attitude toward these two writers and their fellow authors.

Chapter 1

Performance: In the Service of the Nation[1]

A new age for the living dead ... a
foggy murky world where one comes and
goes, speaks and writes, buys and sells, plants
and ploughs, works and meets, faithfully but
uselessly beating the air and striking the wind.
– Maḥjūb, Maḥjūb

1. INTRODUCTION

Until the 1980s, most scholars emphasized that Arabs did not know theater before the nineteenth century. Only during the last three decades have some scholars suggested that there had already existed some sort of a secular and live theater in the premodern Arab world. All scholars, however, agree that the modern Arab theater in its first steps was inspired by the Western theatrical tradition. At the same time, one cannot deny the impact of the ancient heritage on the shaping of the art of Arab theater. The controversy in essence has turned to revolve around the extant or the dominant role of the medieval heritage as vis-à-vis that of the foreign factors and the process through which such interplay took place. Born only in the twentieth century with sufficient testimonies for its various stages of development, Palestinian theater provides a rare glimpse into this process. Unlike other cases presented in my publications, where the same patterns were born independently in both Western and Arabic cultures,[2] the emergence of Palestinian theater is an evident case of interference. Furthermore, this theater would not have appeared in its present form without that peculiar wedding of Western and traditional factors. The inspiration that Arab theater, including Palestinian theater, drew from Western theater was mainly due to the vacuum in this field in Arab culture. As I have previously indicated, interference normally occurs when a target culture lacks a sufficient repertoire to absorb newly needed functions, and tends to be stronger when a body of culture is either

1 This chapter uses material that first appeared in Snir 1995a, pp. 29–73; Snir 1998b, pp. 57–71.
2 See, for example, the topos of "world upside down" (Snir 1994a, pp. 51–75).

in a state of emergence, or in a state of vacuum, or at a turning point in its history.[3] Thus, whenever in need of innovation and unable to use its own repertoire to that end, a literature tends to make use of whatever repertoire is within reach. Though availability may arise as a result of physical contacts, it is nevertheless ultimately determined by the cultural promptness ("openness," "readiness") of the target culture to consider a potential source as "available."[4]

Palestine, on the margins of the Egyptian cultural center, was not a center for any modern cultural movement in the Arab world during the nineteenth and the twentieth centuries. The cultural activities in Palestine prior to the First World War lacked any political strand in the form of Palestinian consciousness, which has since become an integral element of Palestinian literature.[5] In this sense, Palestinian literature is not exceptional, since no particular Arabic literature written before the First World War can be identified as national in the modern political sense. Up to that point, Palestinian literature bore marks of cultural consciousness of a very special nature, but did not reflect the subsequent political consciousness. Nevertheless, Palestinian literary historians and cultural critics have recently taken pains to show that Palestine in the second half of the nineteenth century and the beginning of the twentieth was the center for a distinctive cultural revival.[6] The information they provide is significant but cannot be isolated from the larger context of the eager search for roots, or "the invention of tradition."[7] This phenomenon has been widespread since the First World War throughout all the nation-states in the Arab world, and has been very common in recent years among the Palestinians as a part of their efforts to strengthen their national identity and promote their hopes of establishing their independent state.[8] "The process of vernacular mobilization," states Anthony D. Smith (1939–2016), "must first discover an ethnic past that is serviceable for present needs and then create a unified and distinctive consciousness and sense of ethnic community and of politicized common culture."[9] In the Palestinian case, this

[3] Cf. al-ʻAẓm 1992, p. 159:

> لا ينجح الغزو الثّقافيّ في التّأثير الفاعل والعميق على المجتمع المغزوّ إلّا بمقدار الخواء الثّقافيّ الّذي يقع عليه الغزو. فحيثما توجد ثقافة حيّة نامية متحرّكة تتعامل مع مشكلات عصرها الكبرى وتحدّياته المصيريّة بنجاح معقول وتتفاعل مع قضاياها الوطنيّة والفكريّة والعلميّة والتقنيّة والفنيّة بصورة خلّاقة ينكمش تأثير الغزو الثّقافيّ ويميل فعله إلى التّلاشي تلقائيّا والعكس بالعكس.

[4] Sebeok 1986, I, p. 462.

[5] Peled 1982, p. 141.

[6] See, for example, the comments of Imīl Ḥabībī (1921–1996) and Ḥabīb Būlus (1948–2012) in Urian 1996, pp. 323–45.

[7] Hobsbawm and Ranger 1992 [1983], pp. 1–14.

[8] Snir 1990, pp. 244–5.

[9] Smith 1991, pp. 132–3.

means accentuating a separate cultural personality and distinguishing it from the wide, inclusive Arab identity. In the West Bank, for example, the cultural revival in the early 1970s included the foundation of the quarterly *Majallat al-Turāth wa-l-Mujtama'* (*Journal of Heritage and Society*) by Jam'iyyat In'āsh al-Usra (Association for the Revival of the Family) in al-Bireh.[10] The publication of this journal since 1973, as a major Palestinian intellectual stated, has been a concrete expression of the "pressing need to recognize and preserve the Palestinian national identity in the face of the cultural and national annihilation as attempted by the Zionist Israel."[11] The Palestinian search for roots has not been limited to literature: for example, Palestinian newspapers have started special folklore sections with invited contributions from readers. The folklore here is less a subject of historical and literary study and more a vital and dynamic force in society and a symbol of the determination of the Palestinian people to gain their right to self-determination as a nation with a distinctive culture and peculiar history.

Although Palestine had already become a fertile ground for cultural activities in the 1920s, especially in the fields of poetry and journalism, the development of theater was very slow, particularly in view of the circumstances of the growth and emergence of modern Arabic theater and dramatic literature. Pioneering Arab ventures into modern drama occurred in Egypt in the mid-nineteenth century, although the very first attempt was Syrian: after visiting Europe, the Syrian Christian merchant Mārūn al-Naqqāsh (1817–1855), being impressed particularly by Italian opera, in 1848 wrote and produced at his own house in Beirut a play titled *Riwāyat al-Bakhīl* (*The Story of the Miser*) which drew heavily on *L'Avare* by the French playwright Molière (1622–1673), though it was not a direct translation and involved a great deal of singing.[12] After Mārūn al-Naqqāsh's death, his nephew Salīm al-Naqqāsh (1850–1884) moved the theatrical troupe to Alexandria. Since the second half of the nineteenth century, the influx of Syrian Christian men of letters into Egypt, where they pioneered free journalism and various cultural activities, had been a contributory factor to the lead taken by that country in the Arab renaissance in the nineteenth century. This was due in part to the stimulation provided by Napoleon Bonaparte's expedition at the turn of the century and in part to the drive for modernization embarked upon by the dynasty of Muḥammad 'Alī (1769–1849). From the nineteenth century, Egypt became the center of

[10] On the contribution of the quarterly, first published in April 1974, see al-Sawāḥirī 1980, p. 132.

[11] Ashrawi 1976, p. 9.

[12] Landau 1958, pp. 57–8.

the theatrical movement in the Arab world and has since produced the first notables in the modern Arab theater, such as the Egyptian Ya'qūb Ṣannū' (Jacob Sanua) (1839–1912) and the Syrian Abū Khalīl Aḥmad al-Qabbānī (1836–1902), who was the first Muslim to rise to prominence in this field. Both these men produced their plays in Egypt. The following is an attempt to trace the development of Palestinian theater, in the shadow of the Arab–Israeli Conflict, on the margins of the Egyptian cultural center and against the background of Western impact.

2. FIRST ATTEMPTS

Palestine was removed from the main cultural activities in the Arab world throughout the nineteenth century and the beginning of the twentieth century. Literary historians and cultural critics have attributed this vacuum to the severe economic conditions in Palestine, the widespread illiteracy in the region, the absence of educational institutions, and general cultural backwardness.[13] No Palestinian literature, or any other particular local Arabic literature, bearing distinctive marks of national identity can be found in the nineteenth century. Some poets were writing poems praising the beauty of places, such as Nazareth or Haifa, but without any reference to political circumstances.[14] Only after the revolution of 1908 and the promulgation of the Ottoman constitution of that year did Palestinian national consciousness begin to emerge, but Palestinian literature was still trailing behind the pioneering literatures of Egypt and Lebanon. The general cultural atmosphere in Palestine till the 1920s was characterized, as indicated by the literary historian Kāmil al-Sawāfirī (1917–1992), by "all-encompassing darkness of ignorance, a plain scientific backwardness and widespread illiteracy among its children."[15] After the First World War, the cultural atmosphere began to change: Palestine started witnessing a cultural revival, encouraged both by a political revival, particularly in light of the Zionist activities, and an economic revival, which was due to the British Mandate over Palestine. This revival was encouraged as well by the process of urbanism that major cities of Palestine underwent at the time. For example, Haifa during the Mandate period attracted thousands of Palestinian rural migrants, who constituted a significant portion of its Arab population and contributed to its economic development, participated in political and cultural activities, and formed a connecting link between the city and their villages of origin.[16]

[13] Al-Sawāfirī 1979, pp. 17–31.
[14] Peled 1982, p. 146.
[15] Al-Sawāfirī 1979, p. 31.
[16] Ben Ze'ev 2020, pp. 1–18.

This atmosphere of revival was stimulated by the opening of schools and educational institutions, public libraries, cultural clubs and societies, publishing houses, newspapers and periodicals, and literary organs, and by the growth of intellectual trends. From 1919 to 1921, no fewer than fifteen new Palestinian newspapers appeared.[17] This revival, concentrated especially in the areas of Jerusalem and Haifa, encouraged the development of literary salons by established families, where young poets, writers, and dramatists were invited to read their works.

In addition, a revival of folk and religious culture occurred, which combined such theatrical elements as the *ḥakawātī* (the "storyteller"),[18] who used to tell tales from folk literature, mainly from *Alf Layla wa-Layla* (*A Thousand and One Nights*); *shā'ir al-rabāba* (the singer of the *rebab*, a stringed instrument with one to three strings); and the itinerant storyteller with a "box of wonders" or a "magic box" (*ṣundūq al-dunyā* or *ṣundūq al-'ajab*).[19] Then there are the religious festivals, such as the traditional birthday (*mawlid*) of the Prophet or the birthdays of saints (*mawālid*), the night-time shows during the fast of Ramadan, and the theatrical elements that can be found in other places in the Islamic world[20] in popular peasant

17 Sulaymān 1988, p. 15.

18 On the *ḥakawātī*, the *shā'ir*, and storytellers in the Islamic world, see Lane 1954 [1908], pp. 397–431; And 1963–1964, pp. 28–31; 'Arsān 1983, pp. 353–9; Slyomovics 1987; al-Ṭālib 1987, pp. 106–13; Khūrshīd 1991, pp. 166–7; Slyomovics 1994, pp. 390–419; Berkey 2001; Hanna 2003, pp. 66–8. See also the first section of chapter 8 in Ibn al-Nadīm's *al-Fihrist* titled "Fī Akhbār al-Musāmirīn wa-l-Mukharrifīn wa-Asmā' al-Kutub fī al-Asmār wa-l-Khurāfāt" ("With Accounts of Those Who Converse in the Evening and the Tellers of Fables with the Names of the Books which [They Composed] about Evening Stories and Fables") (Ibn al-Nadīm 1970, II, pp. 712–24; Ibn al-Nadīm 1985, pp. 605–13). On the role of the religious storytellers (*quṣṣāṣ*) in the first decades of the Islamic era, see Tottoli 2002, pp. 86–96, and the references on p. 92, n. 2. For a comparative study of modern and classical storytelling in Arabic literature, see Mustafa 1997.

19 The itinerant storyteller carries the box on his back, puts it down on a trestle at street corners, invites children to part with a small coin to peer through a row of holes at a succession of crude pictures on a roll that he unwinds as he speaks of the deeds of some folk hero (Cachia 1990, p. 135, n. 4; on *ṣundūq al-dunyā*, see also Ḥusayn 1993, pp. 125–6). Modern Palestinian playwrights used *ṣundūq al-dunyā* to allude to the traditional Palestinian theatrical heritage (e.g., Mu'īn Bsīsū's [1927–1984] *Thawrat al-Zanj* [Bsīsū 1988, pp. 119–20, 163–5, 183–5] and Imīl Ḥabībī's *Luqa' ibn Luqa'* [Ḥabībī 1980, pp. 9–14]. The folkloristic dimensions in the play are also emphasized in a report on the staging of the play in 1981 in Damascus by Firqat al-Mukhtabar al-Masraḥī al-Sūrī [*Filasṭīn al-Thawra*, May 22, 1981; according to *al-Jadīd*, June/July 1981, pp. 13–16]). See also the role of the *ḥakawātī* in *Mughāmarat Ra's al-Mamlūk Jābir* by Sa'd Allāh Wannūs (1941–1997) (Wannūs 1989. Cf. al-Ṭālib 1987, pp. 322–31). According to Margaret MacDonald (MacDonald 1999, p. 325), until the 1950s this peep-show phenomenon could ordinarily be seen in Egypt, but after the spread of television and videos it began to gradually disappear.

20 Cf. And 1963–1964, pp. 53–61.

cultures, such as the *dabka* dances,[21] in which a group of dancers, with linked arms, stamp out the rhythm and sing, and the *zajal*, that is, the popular Arabic poetry in strophic form, all of which were performed on special occasions, such as weddings and feasts and even at funeral rituals. However, these folk and popular activities never developed into theater in the Western sense and only with the rise of a professional Palestinian theater during the 1970s did they become associated with theater in the Western sense.

An important forerunner of the first attempts at theatrical activities in Palestine were the performances of the *khayāl al-ẓill* ("shadow plays")—a type of puppet theater in which flat articulated figures are manipulated between a strong light and a translucent screen, so that the audience sees only their shadows. Most of the performances of this type of theater were given during the month of Ramadan, when local troupes were competing with performers from the neighboring Arabic-speaking countries. The Arabs of the Old City of Jerusalem in particular, both young and old, were known to be especially fond of *Karagöz*.[22] In the month of Ramadan 1944, for instance, these shadow plays in Jerusalem were directed by a Syrian performer. They were presented twice nightly, the first show being intended for children and the second for adults, with a background at times historical and at others satirical.[23]

One of the major stimulations for the Palestinian cultural revival, including the theater, was the foundation of Maḥaṭṭat al-Quds or Idhāʿat Filasṭīn (Jerusalem Station or Palestine Broadcasting Station), which began broadcasting on March 29, 1936. The Arabic section of this station, headed by the poet Ibrāhīm Ṭūqān (1905–1941), encouraged men of letters, poets, playwrights, and actors to broadcast their works.[24] The play *Shamshūn wa-Dalīla* (*Samson and Delilah*) by Naṣrī al-Jawzī (1908–1996) was the first to be

[21] These dances, in which a group of dancers link arms and stamp out the rhythm and sing, still figure prominently in various Palestinian cultural activities. On the popular dances, especially the *dabka*, see al-Barghūthī 1979, pp. 72–82. On the songs accompanying the *dabka*, that is, *Dalʿūnā*, see al-Barghūthī 1979, pp. 137–58; Khūrī 1999, pp. 159–60.

[22] *Karagöz*, a word apparently derived from *Qarāqūsh*, Saladin's official, was originally the chief character of the Turkish shadow play, and his figure gave the title to these plays. The Turkish *Karagöz* was copied in other Arabic-speaking countries and was introduced into their own shadow theaters, just as non-Arab countries were similarly influenced by *Karagöz* while under Turkish domination (Landau 1958, pp. 24–5. See also Guo 2020, p. 283 [*karagöz*]).

[23] Landau 1958, p. 38; Snir 2017, pp. 218–19, and the references in n. 179. See also the virtual Matḥaf al-Dumā al-ʿArabiyya (Arab Puppetry Museum), available at: http://museum.arabpuppettheatre.org, last accessed January 27, 2022. See also Tarzi 2022.

[24] Al-Sawāfīrī 1979, pp. 66–72; Ṭūqān 1985, pp. 118–28.

broadcast from the station.[25] This was also the period in which the geographical position of Palestine on the margins of the culturally prestigious Egyptian center helped to encourage the development of local theatrical activities and to stimulate other cultural activities. Egyptian literature, poetry and prose, newspapers and periodicals, visits of dramatic and dancing troupes, and the pioneering Egyptian cinema were all important catalysts for the local revival of Palestinian culture. For the Palestinian intelligentsia, as for any other intelligentsias in other Arab countries, Egypt was the recognized heart of culture for the Arab world.[26] Palestinian intellectuals not only read Egyptian newspapers and periodicals but also contributed to them. Palestinian writers published their works in Egyptian publishing houses, such as the Palestinian writer Isḥāq Mūsā al-Ḥusaynī (1904–1990), whose famous and controversial novel *Mudhkkirāt Dajāja* (*Memoirs of a Hen*) (1943)[27] was published in Cairo and asked the leading Egyptian writer Ṭāhā Ḥusayn (1889–1973) to write the introduction. Some of the first Palestinian dramatists used to publish their works in Egyptian magazines like *al-Hilāl* and *al-Muqtaṭaf*, before publishing them in the local arena.[28] The impact of Egyptian culture upon the growing Palestinian culture in those years was intense: local audiences flocked to watch the performances of the Egyptian troupes that visited Palestine[29] and later became the nucleus for Palestinian audiences, which "demanded" local and original performances. Consequently, groups of amateurs, especially students, began producing and performing plays and dramatic texts. The Palestinian writer and dramatist Imīl Ḥabībī (Emile Habibi) (1921–1996) notes that when he was a school student he acted the role of the thief in a play based on *The Hunchback of Notre Dame* by French poet, novelist, and playwright Victor-Marie Hugo (1802–1885).[30] Yet almost all the dramatic activities were limited to amateurs and took place within clubs and schools without developing into professional troupes. The dramatic texts were based mainly on translations and adaptations of famous Western plays

25 See *Bama* 52 (December 1947), p. 43.
26 See Snir 2017, pp. 150–1.
27 See Snir 1989, p. 134.
28 Landau 1958, p. 103.
29 Among the Egyptian troupes that visited Palestine was that of the renowned actor and director Georges Abyaḍ (1880–1959), who introduced European classical dramas before and after the First World War (Landau 1958, p. 78).
30 That dramatic adaptation of the novel (Hugo 1956 [1831]; Hugo 1937) was presumably based on one of the films that were produced in the beginning of the century. The novel has been translated into Arabic as *Aḥdab Notre Dame* (Hugo 1989). In his short story "Wa-Akhīran Nawwara al-Lawz" ("Finally, the Almond Blossomed"), written after the 1967 War (Ḥabībī 1985, pp. 13–22), Ḥabībī returns to the character of Pierre Gringoire from Hugo's novel. On that story, see Seekamp 1988, pp. 258–60.

in addition to texts based upon Arabic literary texts from non-canonical folk literature. Very few original texts were used, but if so they were generally didactic plays staged for social and religious purposes. Frequent insertion of well-known verses from ancient Arabic poetry into these plays indicates their didactic nature. Due to social and religious considerations only, few females participated in these theatrical activities and female characters were generally converted into male ones.

With the growth and development of the urban middle classes, some serious attempts were made to initiate professional theatrical activities. One of the first professional troupes was Firqat al-Jawzī (The al-Jawzī Troupe) established by the aforementioned Naṣrī al-Jawzī in the mid-1930s. Naṣrī came from a noted Gaza and Jerusalem family, which was known for its cultural and theatrical activities. His troupe was the first to broadcast dramatic texts from the radio station, which both encouraged and directly and indirectly accelerated theatrical activities.[31] Imīl Ḥabībī, who was working at the beginning of the 1940s in the Arabic section of the Palestine Broadcasting Station, notes that actors recited the dramatic texts in a live broadcast.[32] Naṣrī, who continued his intense theatrical activities until 1947, wrote several original plays, including *al-Shumū' al-Muḥtariqa* (*The Burning Candles*), a four-act social moral drama about the suffering of children caused by their father's unhealthy lust.[33] In his ceaseless quest for novel ways to develop the newly emerging local theater, he was also the first Palestinian dramatist to write for children. Among his contributions in this field was the play *Dhakā' al-Qāḍī* (*The Wisdom of the Judge*), describing a famous trial before the Caliph Hārūn al-Rashīd (763–809 CE). In one of his essays prior to 1948, titled "How Can We Encourage the Palestinian Theater?", he mentioned more than thirty troupes active in Jerusalem alone and bearing symbolic names like al-Nahḍa (The Awakening), al-Taqaddum (The Progression), and Iḥyā' al-Funūn (The Revival of the Arts).[34] These troupes, most of them amateur, generally preferred to stage productions based on translations and adaptations of English and French plays. Although the local audiences showed some interest in these plays, rarely was any play performed more than once.

Naṣrī's brother Jamīl al-Jawzī (1915–2005) also contributed to the growing Palestinian theatrical movement; in 1937, he established a theatrical troupe within the Young Men's Christian Association (YMCA) in Jerusalem, making use of translated texts, some of which were from his own original

31 Al-'Awdāt 1992, pp. 93–4.
32 Urian 1996, pp. 323–45.
33 See *Bama* 50 (January 1947), p. 110.
34 *Al-Hadaf*, April 21, 1946, p. 11. Cf. Landau 1958, p. 103.

material. J. M. Landau (1924–2020), who watched one of the plays staged at the YMCA in 1946, testified to the amateurish nature of the production; he also mentioned the attitude of the spectators, who could "not distinguish between sitting in a café or in a theater."[35] The brothers al-Jawzī resolutely pursued their interest in the theater, but since 1948 they have resided in Jordan, and concentrated not on practical theatrical activities but mainly on the historical aspects of Arabic (and especially Palestinian) theater.[36]

Another figure of the pre-1948 Palestinian theatrical movement was Jamīl al-Baḥrī (1895–1930), whose interest in theater accompanied his activities in journalism; he also owned the journal *al-Zahra*, based in Haifa, in which he used to publish his dramatic works. Among these was *Qātil Akhīhi* (*His Brother's Murderer*), a play in three acts that was staged in several theaters in Palestine and Syria. In his translated plays, he used to omit the female roles for lack of actresses, as well as to insert verses from Arabic poetry according to his didactic and educational inclinations.[37]

Palestinian theatrical and dramatic activities prior to 1948, like Palestinian literature in general, were very limited. First attempts were marked by European impact, whether in translation of texts or adaptations. As many of the plays were intended to be staged in schools or by groups of students, their didactic nature was dominant. Moreover, Palestinian theater before 1948 was not generally involved in the national struggle. Prose in general,[38] let alone the theater, was barely concerned with politics and mainly concentrated on didactic aims and entertainment. Direct involvement in the struggle was at that time typical only of poetry, which remained the dominant genre in Arab culture until the mid-twentieth century (*al-Shi'r Dīwān al-'Arab!*). Palestinian poetry served as a weapon in the political struggle, and following the 1917 Balfour Declaration was overwhelmingly concerned with the anti-Zionist and anti-British campaign. It expressed the innermost desires and fears of the Palestinian community and its emotions regarding external threats and the prospects of the foundation of a Jewish national home in Palestine. Although, like many other Arab poets, Palestinian poets before 1948 also wrote dramatic texts, especially verse drama, only a few of these plays were staged successfully. Among those writing for theater before 1948 were Burhān al-Dīn al-'Abbūshī (1911–1995), Muḥyī al-Dīn al-Ḥajj 'Īsā al-Ṣafadī (1897–1974), and Mu'ayyad Ibrāhīm al-'Īrānī (1913–1987). The

35 *Bama* 50 (January 1947), pp. 107–9.

36 Naṣrī al-Jawzī wrote a book on the history of Palestinian theater from 1918 to 1948 (al-Jawzī 1990), and Jamīl al-Jawzī has been active in the press; see, for example, his essay in the Jordanian newspaper *al-Dustūr*, January 29, 1986. See also al-'Awdāt 1992, pp. 91–2.

37 Landau 1958, p. 103; Sayegh 1990, p. 159.

38 On exceptions, see Peled 1982, pp. 157–62.

constraints of the dramatic genre in that period, however, did not allow its development as a weapon in the political struggle.

3. UPROOTING

Following the 1948 War, the greater part of the Palestinian urban intelligentsia, the traditional and social leadership, and most of the property owners abandoned the territories of the State of Israel. Those who remained were generally from the poorer and the uneducated village populations. Most of the cultural activities, including the newly developing theater, were uprooted.[39] Many of the exponents of the young Palestinian theater left the country, giving an impetus to the development of the newly emerging theater in Jordan.[40] Cultural activities among the Palestinians in Israel as well as in the West Bank and Gaza Strip were very limited during that period. The immense shock in the wake of the defeat, the fact that the Palestinian majority in Palestine had become a minority in Israel, the political limitations, and the difficult economic and social circumstances under which the Palestinians were living, whether in Israel or in the West Bank and Gaza Strip, prevented Palestinian writers, poets, and dramatists from working freely. Since theatrical activities require more than merely writing texts and publishing them, the political and socioeconomic circumstances had greater effect than in other cultural fields, and thus ruled out any real progress in the first years following 1948. All that remained from the promising Palestinian theater of the 1940s were a very few amateur troupes, which were mainly based within clubs and schools.

Nevertheless, Palestinian culture, which had emerged and started crystallizing before 1948, did not totally disappear, though it crumbled into two segments—outside Israel and within it. Those Palestinians who were uprooted from their homes following the 1948 War and had become refugees suffered the greater shock and were preoccupied with their daily struggle for existence in the refugee camps, whether in the West Bank or in the Gaza Strip. Despite the educational system established by the United Nations Relief and Works Agency (UNRWA),[41] significant cultural activities, certainly in the field of theater, were almost totally absent. Due to political and economic reasons, the fate of the permanent citizens of the West Bank and the Gaza Strip until the 1960s was mostly similar. Hashemite rule over the West Bank and Egyptian rule over the Gaza Strip was overtly and directly

[39] Snir 1990, pp. 247–8.
[40] Landau 1958, pp. 97, 103.
[41] Al-Sawāfirī 1979, pp. 79–80.

involved in suppressing the publication of any worthwhile literature, especially that of political or social significance. Direct censorship plus control over educational and social institutions, clubs, and all cultural activities, along with relentless political persecution, succeeded in maintaining what one Palestinian critic described as "a standard of ignorance and superficiality of alarming dimensions."[42] Only the regimes' mouthpieces or writers of trashy third-rate literature succeeded in getting their works published, while an underground movement remained scarce and did not reach a significant audience.

Within Israel, the 1950s did witness certain cultural activities, especially due to the efforts made by the Israeli governmental establishment to encourage "positive" cultural activities in the aim of "manufacturing 'quiet Arabs' in Israel."[43] The vacuum created by the disappearance of the urban cultural elite was partially filled by Jewish writers and poets who had immigrated to Israel from Iraq.[44] Some Iraqi Jews with acting experience produced Arabic plays, the first of which, staged in October 1956, was the famous verse drama *Majnūn Laylā* (*The Madman of Laylā*) by the Egyptian poet Aḥmad Shawqī (1868–1932). Jews who had emigrated from Egypt, with a certain amount of real theatrical experience, also contributed to the revived local Arabic-speaking theater, and their first production concentrated on the life of Oriental immigrants in Israel.[45]

Since theatrical activities before 1948 were initiated and consumed by the urban elite classes, the crumbling of these classes in society following the war was almost a death blow to the young Palestinian theatrical movement. Nevertheless, shortly after the war cultural activities among the Palestinians within Israel were showing signs of revival in two opposite directions: one sponsored by the Israeli governmental establishment and the other sponsored by the Communist Party. Several literary organs stood at the disposal of those who were close to the governmental establishment, such as the newspaper *al-Yawm* (*The Day*) (established in 1948 and closed in 1968), the weekly *Ḥaqīqat al-Amr* (*The Fact of the Matter*) (established in 1937 and closed in 1959), and the monthly *al-Mujtamaʿ* (*Society*) (established in 1954 and closed in 1959).

The Histadrūt (The General Workers' Union) played a major role in the Arab sector during these years, organizing and launching "positive" local Arab cultural and literary activities. Needless to say, these activities did not

42 Ashrawi 1976, p. 3.

43 Jamal 2012, pp. 245–64. On the literary activities among the Palestinians in Israel during the 1950, see also Hoffman 2009, pp. 203–54.

44 On the cultural activities of Iraqi Jews in Israel, see Snir 1991, pp. 153–73.

45 Landau 1958, p. 103.

include any criticism of government policy, and avoided dealing with controversial problems. The "positive" cultural and literary activities were initiated and cultivated by means of prizes and literary competitions, as well as through the Arab Book Fund acting under its aegis. This fund, for example, published the book *Fī Mahrajān al-Adab* (*In the Festival of Literature*)[46] containing Arabic-language literary and dramatic works, which had earned prizes in the 1958 Histadrūt competition. The book, whose introduction illustrates the effort to produce "positive" literature,[47] includes two short plays, both using the Palestinian dialect in the dialogues. The first, titled *Taṭawwur al-Qarya al-ʿArabiyya fī Isrāʾīl Khilāla ʿAshr Sinīn* (*The Development of the Arab Village in Israel in Ten Years*),[48] was written by a female Palestinian playwright from Nazareth who preferred not to reveal her name. This play, as reflected by its title, is a good example of the aforementioned "positive" literature. It is the story of a couple, Abū ʿAlī and Umm ʿAlī, who had been living before 1948 in one of the villages in Palestine. They had left their village following the "war of liberation," as the 1948 War is described in the play. After ten years, they returned to Israel to visit their previous birthplace on a symbolic day, May 15, 1958 (on May 14, 1948, the State of Israel was declared). The two Palestinians, amazed by all the development that had occurred during their absence in their original village, promise at the end of the play to inform their relatives outside Israel about the miracles and the wonderful projects in the Israeli Arab villages. The play, portraying the development brought to the "primitive" Arab villages by the Israeli authorities, seems to be pure propaganda without any redeeming literary value and illustrates the nature of the cultural activities sponsored by the governmental establishment. The second play included in the book is *Fatāt al-Yawm* (*Today's Young Women*),[49] written by Ḥabīb Ibrāhīm Karkabī (1929–2015), who was from Shfaram. The play, whose events take place in Nazareth in April 1958, deals with the improvement in the status of women in Arab society in Israel since 1948, and its evident message was to serve the aims of the Israeli governmental establishment's propaganda exactly like the first play. Karkabī has continued to be active in the field of Arabic-speaking theater in Israel, and during the 1970s published several other plays.[50]

Palestinian scholars have generally overlooked the "positive" cultural activities sponsored by the Israeli establishment—the fourth volume of *Encyclopaedia Palaestina*, dedicated to studies about various aspects of

46 Aggassi 1959.
47 Aggassi 1959, pp. 1–3.
48 Aggassi 1959, pp. 119–29.
49 Aggassi 1959, pp. 130–42.
50 Moreh and Abbāsī 1987, p. 196.

civilization, including theater—generally ignores the period 1948–1967, dealing only with the cultural activities before 1948 and after 1967.[51] Not all the cultural activities in Israel during this period, however, were sponsored and directed by the establishment; there were also the leftist writers of the opposition. These writers were active within the framework of the Communist Party, whose intellectuals had not abandoned Israel following the 1948 War, unlike most of the Palestinian elite. The leftist writers faced many difficulties and obstacles, and the establishment employed various means to disrupt their cultural and literary activities. Furthermore, the establishment's implicit ban on Communist writers, Jewish or Arab, inspired those writers close to the establishment to refuse to collaborate with them. Such a polarity was naturally reflected in the literature and readership of both trends, with each having its own writers and audience. The journals of the two camps were fiercely competitive, but the Communist journals stood out, particularly *al-Ittiḥād* (*The Union*), established in 1944, and *al-Jadīd* (*The New*), established in 1953, for their quality and wide circulation.[52] These journals provided avenues of expression for promising new poets and writers—hence, the predominance of Communist literary figures as pioneers in the modern Palestinian literary tradition. Along with the Dār al-Ittiḥād publishing house in Haifa, several other progressive publishers contributed to the increasing output of Palestinian literary figures opposed to the establishment. The lack of freedom and the censorship imposed on leftist writers did not prevent their works from gaining high popularity among the masses within Israel and later, particularly from the mid-1960s, even outside it. The Israeli governmental attempts at suppressing this kind of literature failed entirely and produced contrary results. The charge of endangering the "security of the state," exploited frequently against outspoken Palestinian writers, only enhanced the popularity of those writers and showed them in a heroic light.

The leftist writers did not hesitate to raise their voices in protest and to deal with subjects considered taboo by the establishment-sponsored press. The latter was thus perceived by local Palestinians as the trumpet of the ruling party, and even as anti-Arab. In contrast, a preoccupation with political and social issues was dominant in Communist writing. In order to evade censorship, symbolism was sometimes used, which gradually detracted from the effect of Palestinian literature as a political weapon. The Communist

51 Sayegh 1990. Cf. ʿAlyān 1992.

52 Among the other journals published by the Israeli Communist Party at the time were *al-Darb* (*The Road*) (established in 1951) and *al-Ghad* (*The Morrow*) (established in 1954). On these journals and others, see Moreh 1974, pp. 91–110.

literary writing generally conveyed a worldview whose universality rejected the narrow confines of nationalism and preached equality of rights for all peoples and justice and equality in all human societies.

The two opposing literary trends were in fact sharing a striking, black-versus-white, dichotomy; but while for those close to the establishment, this dichotomy contrasted the dark past to the joyous present, for the Communist writers it was social and universal—between a dark present filled with oppression and a utopian future ruled by justice. The writers of both groups, each from their own viewpoint, preached coexistence, peace, and brotherhood, and believed in their realization. Writers in the 1950s, like Imīl Ḥabībī, frequently emphasized the obligation of Arabic literature in Israel to "carry the banner of Jewish-Arab brotherhood." They were stressing Jewish-Arab cooperation not only in times past but also for the present and future, as well as praising the contribution of Arab-Jewish writers in this field.[53]

The first Palestinian printed play in Arabic to be published in Israel after 1948 was *Ẓalām wa-Nūr* (*Darkness and Light*) (1954) written by Mīshīl Ḥaddād (1919–1997) and Jamāl Qaʿwār (1930–2013). The play, betraying a didactic trend, describes the struggle of a student in a secondary school in Israel wanting to study at the university, despite his father's blindness and poverty. The didactic aim of the play, as indicated in the introduction,[54] directs the plot toward culminating in the student's success despite all the difficulties facing him. Another pioneering play published in Israel in the 1950s was the two-act *Sirr Sharazād* (*The Secret of Sharazād*) (1958), by Najwā Qaʿwār Faraḥ (1923–2015), based on the character of Shahrazad from *A Thousand and One Nights*. The playwright, distinguished by her penetrating studies of human emotions, was one of the first Palestinian female writers in Israel. She also published several volumes of short stories and a collection of poetry in prose,[55] in addition to another play titled *Malik al-Majd* (*The King of Glory*) (1962), which was inspired by the life of Jesus.

The actual Arabic theatrical activities in Israel in the 1950s were limited to troupes of amateurs, particularly in schools. Only in the 1960s did these activities start developing rapidly, first in playwriting and later on in the field of staging. One of the prominent dramatists was Salīm Khūrī (1934–1991), who published several plays.[56] His first play, *Āmina* (title and name of the heroine) (1960), was based on historical events and it preaches, through its eponymous heroine, love and brotherhood among people. His second play

[53] Snir 1991, p. 168.
[54] Ḥaddād and Qaʿwār 1954, pp. 5–6.
[55] See Moreh 1967, p. 169; Moreh and Abbāsī 1987, pp. 174–5.
[56] Moreh 1974, pp. 47–50; Moreh and Abbāsī 1987, pp. 76–9.

was *Warīth al-Jazzār* (*The Heir of the Butcher*) (1960), and one of his most interesting recent plays, *Ba'd al-Aswār* (*After the Walls*) (1983), shows the clear impact of Bertolt Brecht (1898–1956).[57] Salīm Khūrī was also prominent in being one of the forerunners in establishing a Palestinian children's theater.

Till the 1960s, Arabic-speaking theatrical activities for children were limited mainly to amateur troupes in schools. For lack of space, I shall not deal here with the development of Palestinian children's theater, except to mention that in the recent decades this field has been developed extensively as part of the development of Palestinian children's literature.[58] Plays for children have been presented since the 1980s by professional troupes in various frameworks.[59] In addition, the Arabic section of Israeli television has played some role in encouraging Arabic-speaking theatrical activities for children. One of the successes of this section was the series *Sāmī wa-Sūsū* (*Sāmī and Sūsū*), in which the leading roles were played by George Ibrāhīm (b. 1945) and Labība al-Darīnī.

The theatrical activities in the Arab sector in Israel were concentrated in Haifa and Nazareth, both of which were dominant centers of the Palestinian intelligentsia and culture. The establishment of the Beit Hageffen Arab-Jewish Center in Haifa and the Frank Sinatra Center in Nazareth in the early 1960s indicated some change in the attitude of the establishment toward the culture of the minority. Rather than encouraging "positive" culture, a genuine attempt was made to stir up local cultural activities. With regard to theater, the Jewish actor Arieh Elias (1921–2015) was sent to Nazareth where he established a local troupe with the assistance of Palestinian theater people. This troupe staged several plays for al-Masraḥ al-Ḥadīth (The Modern Theater) (established in 1965), prominent among which was the famous aforementioned verse drama *Majnūn Laylā* (*The Madman of Laylā*) by Aḥmad Shawqī.

Theatrical activities among the Palestinians outside Israel were very limited in both playwriting and staging. Nevertheless, some theatrical activities were held in the West Bank, and especially in the framework of the summer festivals in Ramallah and al-Bīra. The director Ṭāriq Maṣārwa established a local troupe, which staged some plays. Several important dramatic texts were written in the 1960s by Palestinian playwrights outside Israel,

57 Cf. Ṭāhā 1990, pp. 113–24. On Brecht's influence on the Palestinian theater, see Snir 1996, pp. 101–20.

58 Sayegh 1990, pp. 239–51.

59 See, for example, the report of the Palestinian dramatist 'Afif Shalyūṭ (b. 1962) about the participation of Arab troupes in the Third Haifa Festival for Children's Theater held in April 1993 (*Mawāqif*, March/April 1993, pp. 113–19).

prominent among whom was Ghassān Kanafānī (1936–1972). Among the plays he wrote before 1967 was *al-Bāb* (*The Door*) (1964), which tells the story of a young man torn between his ideas and the possibilities of acting upon them.[60] The foundation of the Palestine Liberation Organization (PLO) in 1964 prompted cultural activities aimed at strengthening Palestinian consciousness, including the foundation in Damascus of Jam'iyyat al-Masraḥ al-Filasṭīnī (Association of Palestinian Theater) with three prominent aims: stimulating national awareness; presenting experiences of the revolution on the stage; and reviving the Palestinian heritage.[61]

4. PROFESSIONALIZATION

The period after the 1967 War marks paradoxically, despite the defeat of the Arabs, not only the political and social reconciliation of the two segments of Palestinians—those in Israel and those in the West Bank and Gaza Strip—but also the dawn of the era of optimism and rebellion and cultural revival. Palestinian theater developed in this period extensively, and drama in the Western sense, written and staged by professional theater people, came into being. This is also the period marking the end of the involvement of the Israeli establishment in the local Arab cultural arena. The reunification of the Palestinians and the removal of the borders between Israel and the Occupied Territories strengthened the Palestinian identity of the Israeli Palestinians, making the writing of "positive" literature almost impossible. The Palestinian intelligentsia within Israel was beginning to search for a means of consolidating their cultural relations with their brothers in the Occupied Territories. This phenomenon was also accompanied by a change of view in the Arab general public's opinion toward Palestinian literature in Israel. Following the initial shocked response of the Arab writers to the heavy defeat in 1967, they gradually became aware of activities of cultural resistance exercised by the Israeli-Palestinian writers, and especially poets. From being considered in the 1950s almost as traitors by the Arab world because of their readiness to accept Israeli citizenship, after the 1967 War they became heroes. The new political and cultural circumstances brought a worldwide reputation and fame to Palestinian literature written in Israel; it became the central topic of discussion in literary circles and has been widely studied in various Arab countries; local Palestinian poetry began to be broadcast on various Arab radio stations, translated into European and Asian languages, and incorporated into poetry anthologies. Later, novels, short stories, and plays also

60 Sayegh 1990, p. 222.
61 Sayegh 1990, p. 223.

became popular[62] to such an extent that Maḥmūd Darwīsh (1941–2008) felt obliged in 1969 to voice his dissatisfaction with the injustice that critics in the Arab world had done to Palestinian literature by avoiding any objective criticism of it.[63] These critics, in their readiness to accept unconditionally anything that was Palestinian as a positive contribution to the spirit of the nation, prompted a leading Palestinian critic to declare in 1976 that "Palestinian literature is not a spoiled child or mentally deficient person for whom all sorts of excuses and rationalization are to be made. It is responsible enough to demand honesty and responsibility from its readers and critics."[64]

In contrast to its effect on poetry and prose, the 1967 War did not open immediate new horizons for Palestinian theater in Israel. The nature of this art and the lack of financial resources necessary for staging plays in addition to an insufficient familiarity with the dramatic genre were among the major reasons for its delay in development. Nevertheless, some important plays were published following the war, even if most of them were not staged immediately. Outstanding among them is a verse drama titled *Qaraqāsh* (1970) by Samīḥ al-Qāsim (1939–2014), who was one of the most prominent contemporary Palestinian poets—in his poetry "the individual blending with the national and the universal. Through the merging of these three circles, al-Qāsim introduced his modified version of modernism, formulating a holistic, dynamic vision."[65] This play is considered to be one of the first printed plays about which Palestinian literature can boast.[66] Theatrical activities in the late 1960s and at the beginning of the 1970s generally concentrated on the field of writing new original dramatic texts. This phenomenon cannot be isolated from the growth of Palestinian literature in Israel after the 1967 War, but unlike poetry and prose the dramatic text cannot be fully realized without staging. In this regard, there were many difficulties, such as the lack of directors and professional actors—particularly female—and the mainly insufficient budgets. Plays staged in the first years after the war were mainly by amateur troupes functioning without funding and mostly in the centers of the Israeli-Palestinian intelligentsia in Nazareth and Haifa. Although the repertoire of these troupes was based on the repertoire of other Arab theaters, in addition to adaptations of Western plays, more and more original dramatic texts were being staged. Among the prominent theater devotees in

62 Snir 1990, pp. 253–7.

63 See his essay "Anqidhūnā min Hādhā al-Ḥubb al-Qāsī" ("Save Us from This Cruel Love") (Darwīsh 1969, pp. 2–4; Darwīsh 1969a, pp. 113–16; Darwīsh 1969b, pp. 5–6).

64 Ashrawi 1976, p. 58.

65 Ṭāhā 2021, pp. 91–105. The quotation is from p. 96.

66 Ashrawi 1976, p. 55. On *Qaraqāsh*, see Snir 1993d, pp. 129–47; Snir 1995e, pp. 63–103; Snir 1996, pp. 101–20. See also below, Chapter 2.

those years, we can mention Anṭwān Ṣāliḥ (1939–1997) and Victor Qamar (1942–2009), who had also been active in the Arabic section of Israeli television since its inception.

After the 1967 War, the involvement of the Israeli establishment in the local Palestinian cultural arena decreased following the failure of a similar involvement during the 1948–1967 period. Nevertheless, the relevant sections in the Ministry of Education and Culture and the Histadrūt continued to employ Arabic-speaking Jews in order to start new cultural activities. In 1967, the Ministry of Education and Culture inaugurated the al-Nāhiḍ (The Rising) Theater in Haifa, which started as an amateur troupe and later became a professional theater. Its productions, which continued until 1977, concentrated on the events of 1948, particularly the refugee problem, the settlement of Jews in Palestinian lands, and minority rights in Israel, in addition to various aspects of the Arab–Israeli Conflict. The al-Nāhiḍ Theater, which also contributed to the development of the children's theatrical movement, faced many difficulties, like other Palestinian dramatic troupes at the time, and in particular suffered from a lack of funds. Budgetary restrictions were also behind the closure of al-Masraḥ al-Ḥadīth in Nazareth in the mid-1970s. One of the successful theatrical troupes in Israel at that time was Masraḥ al-Ghirbāl. Established in Shfaram in 1977, it organized the First Arabic Theater Festival in Israel in September 1982. Following the festival, Rābiṭat al-Masraḥ al-ʿArabī (The Arabic Theater League) was established on January 8, 1983 in al-Makr.[67]

The revival of Palestinian culture was not limited to the Palestinians in Israel but also included the Occupied Territories, constituting another aspect of the reunification of the two segments of the Palestinian people. Nevertheless, although 1967 was the actual date in which Israeli Palestinians met their fellow Palestinians who until then had been under Hashemite Jordanian or Egyptian rule, the process of discovery and recognition remained rather slow and tentative until the 1970s. The completion of this process coincided with the October 1973 War, which formed a turning point in the uplifting of Palestinian morale. This was also the period in which the cultural activities of the two Palestinian segments were interwoven—a process stimulated by a new self-confidence—after years of defeat. This self-confidence

[67] In July 1983, the League published a one-issue magazine titled *al-Masraḥ* (*The Theater*), which included details about the activities during the festival and was aimed at fostering Arabic-language theatrical activity. An attempt was made in that publication as well as in the activities of the festival not to emphasize the Palestinian national nature of the theatrical movement, hence calling it an Arabic "theatrical movement." This would appear to have been for fear of the authorities' reaction and due to the close links of some of the participants with the governmental establishment.

later emerged, in the words of Ḥanān Mīkhā'īl 'Ashrāwī (b. 1946)—the most prominent Palestinian literary critic of that period—as a:

> distinctly Palestinian energy which was able to withstand the political setbacks of the Arab world and hold its own as a viable force with which the oppressed faced their oppressors and asserted their presence, their rejection of the status quo, and their awareness of their own national identity and consciousness.[68]

This Palestinian unity was climactically expressed on March 30, 1976, that is, *Yawm al-Arḍ* (The Day of the Land), when the Palestinians both in Israel and the Occupied Territories declared a total strike and faced Israeli soldiers with rocks and burning tires. The tragic events that the Palestinians lived through in the 1970s—the September massacres of 1971 in Jordan and the Lebanese Civil War since the mid-1970s—contributed to their cohesion and solidarity. They were convinced that their survival depended primarily on their steadfastness in their own land, and not on external forces. This awareness played an important role not only in the political but also in the social and cultural history of the Palestinians. Moreover, since the 1970s one can speak again about Palestinian culture as a whole, as it was before 1948, rather than the literature within or outside Israel. Both Palestinian segments were becoming closer and more interdependent, despite the various distinctions. This unity was expressed in common cultural interests and in the beginning specifically helped the intellectuals in the West Bank and Gaza Strip to become acquainted with newspapers, journals, and books from throughout the Arab world. Moreover, since there were no copyright laws between Israel and the Arab countries, works by Arab and Palestinian writers, poets, and playwrights were printed and smuggled on both sides, and pirated editions put out by private publishers were the norm. Thus, the progressive political, intellectual, and cultural trends occurring in the Arab world also reached the Palestinians in the Occupied Territories.[69]

Despite this reunification, a great difference remained in the attitude of the authorities toward the Palestinians in Israel and those in the Occupied Territories. While most of the restrictions on the Israeli Palestinians were removed, the Palestinians in the Occupied Territories continued to face the same kind of censorship that had followed the British Mandate emergency laws of 1945.[70] These laws, enforced also on the Arabic newspapers and magazines in East Jerusalem, were very arbitrary in the 1970s and made

68 Ashrawi 1976, p. 2.

69 On how Palestinian intellectuals forged transnational connections through written texts and engaged with contemporaneous decolonization movements throughout the Arab world, challenging both Israeli policies and their own cultural isolation, see Nassar 2017.

70 Sulaymān 1988, pp. 212–218.

frequent use of the argument that this or that publication was a threat to "the security of the state." In that period, for example, the word "Palestine" was considered threatening enough to be censored, even in West Bank children's textbooks.[71] Nevertheless, these years witnessed a revival of Palestinian cultural activities in the West Bank, and especially in East Jerusalem, which became the undisputed capital of Palestinian culture. A prominent role was played by the Palestinian press in East Jerusalem, and specifically *al-Fajr* (*The Dawn*), *al-Sha'b* (*The People*), and *al-Quds* (*Jerusalem*).[72] Recognizing the need to create further channels for literary expression, these newspapers produced literary sections, which have gained immense popularity. The Israeli-Palestinian Communist newspaper *al-Ittiḥād* was banned during that period from being sold in the West Bank in light of the old Jordanian laws, according to which the Communist Party was outlawed and possession of any Communist material was illegal. Nevertheless, *al-Ittiḥād* and the Communist literary journal *al-Jadīd* played an important role in the development of the Palestinian national consciousness. *Al-Jadīd* remained the main literary Palestinian magazine until March 1976,[73] with the publication of the magazine *al-Bayādir* (*The Pastures*), which soon established itself as the leading organ of intellectual and literary Palestinian life. In it, as in *al-Jadīd*, one can read the works of the major recognized and the most promising new literary figures, and at the same time follow the development of contemporary literary trends.[74] Nevertheless, the Palestinian intellectual arena in the Occupied Territories and East Jerusalem has continued to suffer from a scarcity of journals and magazines due to the difficulties in obtaining licenses and financial support. Hence, one of the stimulating factors of the cultural movement in the Occupied Territories was the establishment of several publishing houses, prominent among which was Ṣalāḥ al-Dīn, which was established in 1974 in East Jerusalem and which soon became the major publisher of West Bank intellectual, literary, and political circles. However, the Palestinian cultural revival in the Occupied Territories was not limited in that period to the printed page alone, and various channels of expression were devised to supplement the gaps and circumvent obstacles to freedom of thought and expression. Poetry-reading sessions, panel discussions, seminars, and study sessions have become familiar phenomena on a very wide scale, especially in

[71] Ashrawi 1976, p. 5.

[72] Shinar 1987, pp. 41, 48–52.

[73] On the role *al-Jadīd* played in the development of a Palestinian public sphere, see Nassar 2010, pp. 333–51.

[74] To evade their lack of freedom, writers frequently used pseudonyms to hide their identities (Ashrawi 1976, p. 11).

the West Bank. Literary events, such as the traditional *Sūq ʻUqāẓ*[75] at Birzeit University, have gained increasingly large audiences.

Several indirect attempts were made in Israel during this period to counter the emergence of nationalist and progressive newspapers, journals, and publishing houses. Thus, for example, the authorities sponsored publishing houses that would serve Israeli policy as well as those intellectuals who did not come out openly against it. The most prominent of these publishers were Dār al-Nashr al-ʻArabī and Dār al-Sharq (the latter developed into Dār al-Mashriq in Shfaram), both of which were directly connected with and sponsored by the Histadrūt and the authorities. The prominent organs sponsored by the establishment in that period were the newspaper *al-Anbāʼ* (*The News*), established in 1968 and closed in 1985, and the literary journal *al-Sharq* (*The East*), established in 1970 and still being published.

The aforementioned cultural background was fertile ground for the emergence of one of the most noticeable literary-cultural phenomena of the 1970s—that is, the professional Palestinian theater, which was mainly in the Jerusalem–Ramallah area. The first attempt took place late in 1970 when an amateur troupe called ʻĀʼilat al-Masraḥ (The Family of the Theater) was established in Ramallah and started rehearsals on Samīḥ al-Qāsim's aforementioned verse drama *Qaraqāsh*, until the military authorities banned the staging of the play. The ʻĀʼilat al-Masraḥ troupe formed the nucleus of the al-Balālīn Theater troupe established in 1971 by François Abū Sālim (Abu Salem) (1951–2011). Son of the Hungarian-born French poet Lorand Gaspar (1925–2019) and the French painter and sculptor Francine Gaspar, he was born in Provins but raised in East Jerusalem, where his father took over the management of the Saint-Joseph Hospital from 1954 to 1970. He continued his secondary studies with the Jesuits in Beirut between 1964 and 1968, before being hired as an actor at the Théâtre du Soleil in Paris. This is the time when he made a decision that would change his life:

> J'ai 18 ans, j'annonce à mon père sur la plage de Rawad à Tunis que j'ai l'intention de m'installer en Palestine, à Jérusalem (côté arabe ... à l'Est ...)—où lui-même a travaillé pendant 17 ans et où j'ai grandi—pour y faire du théâtre et soutenir les Palestiniens dans leur combat. Comme l'aurait sans doute fait tout père aimant, il tente de m'en dissuader, au moins momentanément, le temps de faire des études, dit-il, d'acquérir une formation, même en théâtre, mais je suis déterminé et incapable pour l'heure, de prendre le moindre recul. En désespoir de cause, mon père me prodigue quelques recommandations, dont une qui me marque et que je relève comme un défi: "Tu risques de ne jamais te faire

[75] After a famous fair held in ancient times in Mecca at which poetic competitions were held.

accepter. Tu as beau bien connaître la culture et la langue arabes, tu n'es pas de sang arabe!"[76]

He decided to adopt Palestinian identity and integrate himself into Palestinian culture and society, doing everything to hide his Western origins (French and Hungarian), at least in his public life, adopting the surname Abū Sālim instead of Gaspar:

> Ainsi donc, je m'inventai peu à peu une histoire et une identité que je jugeai "acceptable" en Palestine et plus généralement dans le Monde Arabe. J'étais né à Bethléem au lieu de Provins, j'étais de mère française—pour expliquer mon teint "désespérément" pâle—et de père palestinien (ou, variante: palestinien d'origine arménienne, histoire que cela ressemble un peu à la réalité d'une racine arménienne chez une grand-mère de mon père), et je me suis appelé François Abou Salem au lieu de François Gaspar.[77]

Abū Sālim's reconstruction of his new "Palestinian" identity sheds light on the postmodern notion of identity that suggests that one can always change one's life, that identity can always be reconstructed, that one is free to change and produce oneself as one chooses. In other words, identity becomes a freely chosen game, a *theatrical presentation of the self*, in which one is able to present oneself unconcerned about shifts, transformations, or dramatic changes.[78] With his new adopted identity, Abū Sālim returned to Jerusalem in September 1970 and soon became the major figure of the modern theatrical Palestinian movement.[79] He says of that period:

> When I returned from Paris I wanted to create a Palestinian theater, although friends told me it was not the right time. I knew that I could influence through theatrical-political protest more than through joining some militant organization. I did not go for military training to South Lebanon, because I felt that creating the theater would be more effective in keeping our society intellectually awake, during the long nation-building process. It has not been easy to establish a modern theater. They do not always understand the need for a full company, when one storyteller can enact the entire plot.[80]

76 From an unpublished essay written by François Abū Sālim titled "Exclusion—Insertion en Palestine." I thank Katharina Lack, who received the essay in person from Abū Sālim in 2006 (henceforth, Abū Sālim 2006).

77 Abū Sālim 2006. On Abū Sālim, see also Jawad 2013, pp. 1–3, 245–6; Varghese 2020, pp. 27–33, 59–60.

78 Kellner 1991, pp. 153–4, 158 (my emphasis). For more on this notion of identity, see below, Chapter 8.

79 On the emergence of the Palestinian theatrical movement throughout the 1970s, including the process of theater-making itself and the professionalization of the movement, see Nakhle-Cerruti 2020, pp. 611–29.

80 Shinar 1987, p. 134.

One of the major figures in the troupe was the East Jerusalem poet-singer Muṣṭafā al-Kurd (b. 1945), and it included as well Sāmiḥ al-ʻAbbūshī (b. 1943), Hānī Abū Shanab (b. 1951), Nādiyā Mīkhā'īl (b. 1944), and Imīl ʻAshrāwī (b. 1951). The troupe looked for ways to develop a Palestinian theater based upon the idea of addressing the audience in the vernacular (*al-ʻāmmiyya*) and the ability to perform its productions in the towns and villages as well as in cafés (i.e., *masrḥ al-maqhā* ["café-theater"]).[81] On January 22, 1972, the troupe performed the play *Qiṭʻat Ḥayāt* (*A Slice of Life*), which met with great success and attracted[82] audiences from all over the Occupied Territories and from Israel. One of the reasons for its success was the fact that it did not hesitate to criticize the social backwardness of Palestinian society, including the status of women. The troupe also produced some of the masterpieces in Palestinian theater in the 1970s, such as *al-ʻAtma* (*The Darkness*) and *Nashrat Aḥwāl al-Jaww* (*The Weather Forecast*). The same troupe also produced folkloristic shows with dances and songs as well as musicals, such as *al-Kanz* (*The Treasure*) and the dramatized poem *Yūnus al-Aʻraj* (*Yūnus the Lame*) originally written by the Turkish poet Nazim Hikmet (1902–1963). One of the experimental projects of al-Balālīn was titled *Jarīdat al-Masraḥ* (*The Theater's Newspaper*)—a short (about five minutes) theatrical presentation given in the vicinity of schools or in the streets. This was in addition to other activities such as the foundation of the Balālīn Friends Group, lectures on the art of theater, popular plays, and musicals. The professional nature of the troupe was expressed in its leading role in the week-long First Palestinian Theater Festival, which took place in August 1973 in the basement of Ramallah's City Hall, an event in which students and other amateur groups presented their works. The festival was organized by the troupe and included sixteen productions.[83] In addition to these activities, a temporary splinter group from al-Balālīn, Bilā-Līn (Without Mercy), put on the play *Muṣāraʻa Ḥurra* (*Free Wrestling*) to great acclaim. The al-Balālīn theatrical activities were discontinued in 1976 with the deportation of Muṣṭafā al-Kurd, one of its founders and major activists.

Several other amateur theater troupes were formed in the 1970s, such as al-Kashkūl (The Beggar's Bag), which won acclaim for some of its experimental plays, and another troupe, Firqat al-Masraḥ al-Filasṭīnī (The Palestinian Theater Troupe), which won acclaim for its play *al-Ṭāʻūn* (*The Plague*). In 1973, al-Dabābīs (The Pins) was established and met with success for its productions *al-Ḥaqq ʻalā al-Ḥaqq* (*Blame the Blame*) and *Dā'irat al-Khawf*

[81] Sayegh 1990, p. 217.
[82] On *al-ʻAtma*, see Snir 2005d, pp. 5–29.
[83] Shinar 1987, p. 134; Sayegh 1990, pp. 221–2.

al-Ḍabābiyya (*The Foggy Fear Circle*), the latter alluding to Brecht's *The Caucasian Chalk Circle*. Following the staging of *al-Ḥashara* (*The Insect*), the majority of the troupe members were arrested by the authorities.[84] In 1975, another new troupe was established, and it gave itself the name Ṣundūq al-ʻAjab (The Magic Box), alluding to the box of wonders that wandering Palestinian storytellers used in the folk tradition. This troupe won great acclaim with the production of *Lammā Injanenā* (*When We Went Insane*), but was forced to stop the staging following the arrest of its leading actor, Muṣṭafā al-Kurd. Other troupes that were active in the 1970s were al-Frāfīr (The Birds), al-Masraḥ al-Jāmiʻī (The Academic Theater), and al-Warsha al-Fanniyya (The Artistic Workshop). In August 1974, a theater committee was established within the newly founded Association for Work and the Development of the Arts. The intensive theatrical activities of that period also brought about the development of theater criticism with the emergence of some prominent critics.[85]

Almost all the plays presented in that period were written by members of the troupes themselves, and most of these troupes preserved their independence. Financial troubles, lack of qualified actors, and attempts by the authorities to disrupt them caused serious difficulties, which prompted some of the troupes to stop their activities. The attitude of the military authorities to the theatrical movement in East Jerusalem and the Occupied Territories was very arbitrary. The military censor took responsibility for censorship of plays published or staged in the Occupied Territories, while for plays published and staged in East Jerusalem the responsibility was entrusted into the hands of the Council for the Criticism of Films and Plays. However, the Palestinians argued that the attitude of this committee was basically no different from that of the military censor. Out of twenty-seven dramatic works examined by the committee between 1977 and 1984, only seventeen texts were approved, and even these were partially censored.[86] In addition, the authorities banned the staging of plays in the Occupied Territories by troupes from East Jerusalem.

Nevertheless, and despite all the difficulties, a new national Palestinian theater was emerging in the 1970s, stimulated by major writers and poets who began to direct some of their attention to this genre. Palestinian theatrical activities, especially in the Ramallah–Jerusalem area, brought about several attempts to establish a solid national Palestinian theater. One of the

[84] Sayegh 1990, p. 219; ʻAlyān 1992, p. 84.
[85] Sayegh 1990, p. 222.
[86] ʻAlyān 1992, p. 86. Cf. Shiḥāda 1985, pp. 249–52; Shiḥāda 1989, pp. 180–1; Sayegh 1990, p. 218.

first, albeit unsuccessful, attempts made by groups and individuals was to unite under the name of the aforementioned al-Balālīn troupe, but the major event in the development of the national Palestinian theatrical movement was the establishment of the al-Ḥakawātī Theater in East Jerusalem in 1977. The foundation of al-Ḥakawātī, which was to become a synonym for the national Palestinian theater, and its subsequent various activities were the brightest expressions of the cultural unity of all segments of the Palestinian people, namely, those inside Israel and those in the Occupied Territories.

The establishment of the al-Ḥakawātī Theater, a joint project of dramatists, directors, and actors from Israel and East Jerusalem, marked a prominent phase in the professionalization of Palestinian theater. The troupe was founded and developed by François Abū Sālim and a group of theater people, prominent among whom were ʿAdnān Ṭarābsha (b. 1958), Ibrāhīm Khalālyila, Da'ūd Kuttāb (b. 1955), Muḥammad Maḥāmīd, Rāḍī Shiḥāda (b. 1952), Idwār al-Muʿallim (b. 1958), Īmān ʿAwn (b. 1963), ʿĀmir Khalīl (b. 1964), and the actress and costume designer Jackie Lubeck (b. 1952), Abū Sālim's Brooklyn-born Jewish wife. Additional actors, set designers, lighting professionals, and musicians were recruited according to need. The previously mentioned Muṣṭafā al-Kurd, permitted by the military authorities to return in 1982, also joined the troupe. The aim of the founders was to establish a theatrical framework that would contribute to the strengthening of Palestinian culture and to provide an artistic framework that would intensify the political awareness of the Palestinians and become a vehicle for expressing social and political messages. These messages included resistance against the occupation and at the same time protest against negative phenomena in Palestinian society itself. Undertaking the mission to express in dramatic terms the national aspirations of a society under occupation, it could not rely, as had former troupes, on a classical repertoire, though in shaping its own stories and style the troupe drew inspiration from folkloric and traditional sources. The fact that target audiences included intellectuals and professional critics as well as villagers, workers, and merchants and that the troupe was operating under the military government's regulations led it to develop a language of subtle symbols and metaphors, which served as an artistic code between the theater and its audience, using plot, rhetoric, creative-interactive processes, and institutional structures as channels for its nation-building messages.[87]

The theater's name alludes to the traditional *ḥakawātī*—the itinerant storyteller, who used to appear in places such as cafés and public squares, and present his stories based mainly upon ancient folktales and legends. He

[87] Shinar 1987, p. 134.

would accompany his tales with gestures and different voices and would encourage his listeners to react and become involved. This cultural institution of the storyteller disappeared in the mid-twentieth century following the increasing impact of electronic mass media and the development of modern theater and cinema. The relation to the *ḥakawātī* was preserved in some of the activities of the al-Ḥakawātī Theater and its traditional techniques, and even in the specific arrangement of the seating so as to resemble the atmosphere of a public café. The adoption of the storyteller's techniques by the troupe was an act undertaken to indicate the ancient roots of Arabic theater, in what was perceived as a new genre that the Arabs, including the Palestinians, had only recently come to know.[88] These techniques motivated some of the original experiments and improvisations by the troupe in its first years. For lack of suitable available dramatic texts, and due to a desire to experiment, the act of playwriting and devising characters and dialogues became a collective undertaking by the actors themselves and was based largely upon improvisation. Western theatrical concepts too were incorporated into the activities of al-Ḥakawātī. Brecht, as well as the French stage director Ariane Mnouchkine (b. 1939), and the Théâtre du Soleil and le Grand Magic Circus Théâtre of the Argentinian-French theater director and actor Jérôme Savary (1942–2013), the commedia dell'arte, and American slapstick: they all exerted their impact. The rhetoric of al-Ḥakawātī was delivered in Chaplinesque tones, a Brechtian, alienated, "poster theater" style, and a blend of traditional and contemporary symbols. This rhetoric was adopted in order to reach a wide audience, and the plots were full of traditional and mythical characters whose language and behavior bordered on the vulgar. Brash humor served to depict Palestinian and Israeli characters alike. Thus, Israeli civilians, army personnel, and the military authorities were presented in terms as grotesque as those used to present the Palestinian characters.

The first play produced by the al-Ḥakawātī troupe, *Bismi al-Ab wa-l-Umm wa-l-Ibn* (*In the Name of the Father, the Mother and the Son*), was staged during the 1978–1979 season. The play, in circus style, depicted the violent invasion of modernization and occupation into Palestinian life, and illustrates how the stress on the father causes him to put a lot of stress on his wife, who in turn puts stress on her child. The play clearly illustrates one aspect that had become predominant after the 1967 War in Palestinian literature in general, namely, the criticism of Palestinian society and leadership.

[88] On the relation of the Palestinian theater to the ancient storyteller, which was "the corner stone for the beginnings of the local theatre," see Shiḥāda 1989, pp. 173–4; Snir 2017, pp. 218–19, and the references in the notes.

The figures, making their first appearance on the stage inside cages, are the husband Aṭrash (in Arabic: a deaf male), his wife Kharsā’ (in Arabic: a mute female), and their son Muṭī‘ (in Arabic: an obedient male). While the training of the female by the male is announced as a “special trick,” a clever, intelligent, and modern unknown creature, which may symbolize Israel or modernization,[89] sneaks his way in and imposes himself on the tamer’s pets. The stranger stays on while the tamer tries unsuccessfully to get rid of him:

> OK stranger, time’s up! Get lost! Excuse me folks but this is definitely not part of the act. That stranger is taking over! Hey, wait a minute! Where is Aṭrash? Muṭī‘, get back in your cage! Kharsā’, cook dinner! ... The female is on the loose! The offspring is on the loose! I’m losing control!!! ... My act! My creatures! My work! My act![90]

One of the Palestinian critics stated that in this play there is no difference between the “social backwardness and the military occupation ... this society is falling between the hammer of the occupation and the anvil of poverty, economic, social and intellectual backwardness.”[91]

Several plays were staged by al-Ḥakawātī before an Israeli-Jewish audience, causing a great deal of professional and political interest. Among them *Maḥjūb, Maḥjūb,* staged in the 1980–1981 season, gave more than 120 performances. The play, in which the troupe attempted to activate the audience by inciting it against the reactionary character in the play, portrays the Palestinians as a community robbed of their vitality and their creativity:

> A new age for the living dead ... a foggy murky world where one comes and goes, speaks and writes, buys and sells, plants and ploughs, works and meets, faithfully but uselessly beating the air and striking the wind.[92]

This is the dehumanized world into which the antihero Maḥjūb steps, soon to understand that such a bare existence holds no more joy than a peaceful death. He gives up and chooses to die but quickly awakens when his companions unfold his life before him. The core of the play comprises the three long nights of his wake during which his life is narrated, interpreted, and performed. The sequence of mishaps typical of his life begins when, in the excitement of his birth, his father drops Maḥjūb on his head. He leaves school after being reprimanded for asking too many questions. In a series of tragicomic episodes, Maḥjūb is made aware that he does not know who he really is. Before the 1967 War, he refuses to stand up for the Jordanian

89 Shinar 1987, p. 135.
90 Al-Ḥakawātī, *Information Brochure*, 1985 (according to Shinar 1987, p. 135).
91 ‘Abd Allāh 1979, p. 16.
92 Quotations from the English translation distributed to the audience (Shinar 1987, p. 135).

national anthem. He shouts for joy at the radio news bulletin that boasts Arab victory in the war, but droops in despair when he learns the bitter truth. He outwits an Israeli soldier who stops him at a checkpoint, and he is subject to interrogation after the colors of the Palestinian flag are recognized among other colors of his clothing. Maḥjūb is shown as a prospective member of the Israeli Histadrūt workers' union and as a participant in the Jerusalem municipal elections, who upon being caught voting by a TV reporter states: "I didn't vote. I am simply a worker in the building—I sweep the floors." Maḥjūb is also presented as an immigrant who tries unsuccessfully to live in the United States, as a prisoner, and as an advisor to the late Egyptian President Anwar al-Sādāt (1918–1981).

Reflecting all dimensions of Palestinian life, Maḥjūb directs caustic and bitter criticism at the sterile confusion of his brethren's existence, and wonders at the contradictions in the occupiers' lives: on the one hand, they display military power, social organization, and technological skill, but, on the other hand, they are obsessed with a ridiculous security ritual. Thus, whenever Maḥjūb goes out to dispose of his garbage bag, a voice is heard asking "*Shel mi ze? Shel mi ze?*" (i.e., a Hebrew phrase meaning "Whose is this?" often heard upon discovery of a suspicious object). The impact of the American filmmaker Woody Allen's (b. 1935) works on various episodes of the play is clear, as well as the inspiration from Imīl Ḥabībī's *al-Waqā'i' al-Gharība fī Ikhtifā' Sa'īd Abī al-Naḥs al-Mutashā'il* (*The Peculiar Events Surrounding the Disappearance of Sa'īd, the Ill-Fated Pessoptimist*),[93] in which the Palestinian tragedy is presented through the story of Sa'īd, whose image represents ironically the absurdity of the life of the Palestinian people from the perspective of those who remained after 1948.

Another important play staged by the troupe was *Jalīlī, Yā 'Alī* (*'Alī, the Galilean*), which presented the adventures of a Palestinian villager in Tel Aviv, the very heart of the occupiers' country. A circus-like burlesque style is used to portray a series of episodes in the life of 'Alī, who is a refugee and stranger in his own country. He is the

> tragic son, the naïve little boy, the thief in the night, the hot-shot cowboy, the imaginary lover, the silent worker, the steadfast militant, the black and white ... as he moves from the village of his ancestors to the city of his colonizers.[94]

The question of 'Alī's Palestinian identity is thoroughly explored upon his arrival in Tel Aviv: being recognized by the "sheriff," he is ordered to leave before sundown. An Israeli friend he meets in the local saloon advises him to

[93] Ḥabībī 1974; Habiby 1982.

[94] Quotations from the English translation distributed to the audience (Shinar 1987, p. 136).

adopt an Israeli name, Eli, and thus to evade the "sheriff," to court a beautiful Israeli woman, to work, fight, and play "safely."[95] At the end, a couple of Hebrew-speaking thugs enter the stage, shouting that their act will be presented instead—it is called "'Alī, the Terrorist."[96]

One of the plays staged by the troupe and regarded later as a self-fulfilling prophecy was *Alf Layla wa-Layla min Layālī Rāmī al-Ḥijāra* (*A Thousand and One Nights of the Nights of a Stone Thrower*). First presented before the outbreak of the *Intifāḍa*, it portrays a confrontation between a Palestinian youth and the military governor, Gidi, who steals the magic lamp from 'Alā' al-Dīn. The narrator indicates:

> In the tiniest flash of a second, a military governor, a modern man, having stolen the lamp of 'Alā' al-Dīn, swept us away to his control tower, his headquarters, his palace ... I present to you this tale of the magician governor, how he moved us aside and upon his tattered decor, installed himself. I recall it to you in my own Arab spirit and all that has been conserved by my Palestinian memory.[97]

A series of confrontations portrays the Palestinians enduring and triumphing over a thousand and one nights of oppression and humiliation. The military governor loses awkwardly:

> Already a man by the age of ten, the stone thrower child's game with the stones became a gesture of a free man. He saw that nothing remained but the stones themselves to defend his home from the gluttony of the governor, who was gobbling away at the trees, the stars and the sun.[98]

The struggle is presented as a fight between a Palestinian David and an Israeli Goliath: the Palestinian boy armed with stones is confronting the military governor's well-equipped warriors. This struggle, frequently reflected in Palestinian literature since 1967, develops into a Middle Eastern "star war" with flying carpets fighting rockets and laser beams. The satirical confrontation between the occupier Goliath and the occupied David is associated with the struggle between the traditional and the modern. "If they show us this play," says the Israeli-Jewish critic Amos Kenan (1927–2009), "it means that instead of throwing stones at us, they want to talk to us."[99] Nevertheless,

95 The act of changing an Arabic name by a Palestinian into Hebrew in order to live and work safely among Jews is very common among Palestinians and has been frequently illustrated in Hebrew literature, even recently in Eshkol Nevo's (b. 1971) novel *Hare'yon Ha-Aḥaron* (*The Last Interview*) (see Nevo 2018, pp. 126–36).
96 Cf. Snir 2005c, pp. 141–5.
97 Quotations from the English translation distributed to the audience (Shinar 1987, p. 136).
98 Quotations from the English translation distributed to the audience (Shinar 1987, p. 136).
99 Urian 1996, p. 343.

the staging of the play brought about the arrest of the leader of the troupe, François Abū Sālim.[100]

In November 1983, the al-Ḥakawātī troupe leased the al-Nuzha cinema in East Jerusalem for ten years and converted it into the first Palestinian theater in the West Bank. Supported in 1984 by a $416,000 Ford Foundation grant[101] and donations from Palestinian individuals and organizations in the West Bank and abroad, the troupe managed to renovate the building and set it up as their base. The theater was formally opened on May 9, 1984. The main 400-seat hall, a small 150-seat hall, and additional facilities have enabled the troupe to pursue its objectives and to provide facilities for other professional and amateur drama, music, and dance groups. Plays are performed in the new theater by West Bank troupes, such as the al-Jawwāl troupe, the Bayt ʿAnān's ʿĀ'idūn Theater, the al-Sanābil troupe, and some troupes of children's theater. Haifa's Municipal Theater also staged Samuel Beckett's (1906–1989) *Waiting for Godot* in Arabic and Hebrew there. Films have also been screened, including *Les Enfants du Paradis* (*The Children of Paradise*) (1945) directed by Marcel Carné (1906–1996); the Israeli film *Beyond the Walls* directed by Uri Barbash (b. 1946); and *Hanna K.* (1983) by the Greek-French film director Costa Gavras (b. 1933). Musical programs were presented, featuring performances of folk songs, contemporary poems, sing-alongs of popular songs, and nationalist concerts, such as Muṣṭafā al-Kurd's.[102] The activities have included art exhibitions and cultural and political debates.[103]

The first play to be staged in al-Ḥakawātī's own theater in May 1985 was *Ḥikāyat al-ʿAyn wa-l-Sinn* (*The Story of the Eye and the Tooth*). It was directed by François Abū Sālim, and among the actors were Rāḍī Shiḥāda (b. 1952), Hiyām ʿAbbās (b. 1960), and Jackie Lubeck (b. 1952). The play was a landmark in the development of Palestinian theater as a nation-building communications medium.[104] Unlike the previous plays, it is more sophisticated,

100 ʿAlyān 1992, p. 85.

101 In its battle to win the Cold War, the Ford Foundation was the first international agency to fund theater in the "developing world"—the foundation had, by then, established an advanced "cultural development" model for soft-power activities in emerging countries. In a critical evaluation of the impact of international development and conflict-resolution funding on theater in the Occupied Palestinian Territories, Rashna Darius Nicholson shows that financial aid, while ensuring the material conditions for the growth of the Palestinian performing arts, promoted a structural dependency that emptied the language of anticolonial resistance of emancipatory potential, generating a soft, phantom sovereignty for the audience of the international community (Nicholson 2021, pp. 4–22).

102 On these activities of al-Kurd, see *al-Qindīl*, October 1988, pp. 36–7.

103 Shinar 1987, pp. 132, 139.

104 Shinar 1987, p. 132.

employing more abstract terms, a generalized form, surrealist symbols, and a wider use of non-verbal techniques. Music, movement, costumes, puppets, lighting, and sets are put to work, enhancing a theatrical language almost entirely absent from the earlier shows, which relied basically on the spoken word. In the first scene, when tradition is the topic, the musical score is composed of Palestinian country tunes featuring motifs popular in the West Bank villages. The second scene, in which modernity is emphasized, is illustrated with contemporary international rock music, while the musical finale toward the end of the show features a majestic choir performance of the "Kyrie Eleison" (Greek: "Lord, Have Mercy") of Mozart's *Requiem* as a symbol of total destruction and hopelessness. Combinations of visual elements are used abundantly to convey the play's grim message: colorful laundry hanging overhead during the play later turns into grimy rags; shiny paper used to represent the village square and well becomes paler and paler during the *dabka* dance, in which the elders' bodies disintegrate into inanimate objects. Pessimism reaches its peak when, as a result of the "eye and the tooth" war, the families, dressed in typical clothes resembling uniforms, start wandering around the pile of bodies at an ever-slowing pace; the sacks on their backs become heavier and heavier burdens.

The play concentrates on the larger issues of tradition, modernity, identity, war, and peace through a composite process rather than through specific adventures of individual characters. Tradition is blatantly challenged, when the two pairs of twins born by the well refuse to comply with the commitment assumed by their parents when they signed the traditional wedding contract upon the babies' birth. The revolt triggers a long bloody feud between the families, which becomes the central axis of the plot. A *ṣulḥa* reconciliation ceremony between the feuding sides is imposed on the families in a later scene by the neighbors, in which a traditional *dabka* dance is performed by the elders, who did not succeed in forcing their offspring to behave according to tradition. They dance until they disintegrate into an inanimate pile of puppets, which stay put on stage. The past in which the elders determined the younger generation's ways is dead, but it physically obstructs progress, making all action on stage move around the dead bodies. The atmosphere of appeasement is disturbed again in the second part of the play, when a new character, symbolizing Zionism and Israel, makes his entrance. The two sides in the conflict are no longer fathers and sons, but Palestinian and Israelis. The longer their endless war becomes, the greater the losses suffered by both sides, and the weaker they become. The conclusion is far from optimistic: the final words, "how happy are the parents of the bride and the groom on the day of their children's wedding?" refer to Tanza, a Palestinian, and Sarah, an Israeli woman, who fall in love and marry under the shadow of bombs and death. Thus, notwithstanding the common fate of the two sides, no solution is offered to restore mutual respect and normal life. Walking around in blood up to their ankles, the protagonists cannot bring a message of hope for the present or future.

The outbreak of the *Intifāḍa* created a new reality for al-Ḥakawātī, and the troupe went into shock: the artistic framework seemed to be slight in the face of the demonstrations of the masses, the stone-throwers, the dozens of Palestinians killed and wounded, and the thousands in prison. Though no restrictions were placed on the troupe itself, it was not permitted to present its work on the main stage of the *Intifāḍa* (i.e., the West Bank and Gaza Strip). The troupe began to act in a vacuum, unable to reach its audience, although various productions were staged[105] and attempts were made to adjust to the new circumstances.[106] This was why several of its founders and earliest members began to search for other new theatrical frameworks. The original group crumbled, and its leader, Abū Sālim, left for Europe, but not before al-Ḥakawātī had succeeded during its few years of intensive activities in arousing Palestinian awareness and contributing to the forming of a political Palestinian consciousness. Moreover, the theater contributed to the rising of a new generation of actors, of whom several can currently be found seeking their own theatrical paths. The great success of al-Ḥakawātī was despite, and perhaps because of, the constant attempts by the Israeli authorities to disrupt its activities. In order to foil these attempts, the troupe was sometimes aided by Jewish-Israeli theater people who protested against the prevention of freedom of speech.[107] The success of the troupe outside the Palestinian arena was not limited to the Israeli-Jewish domain alone, and the troupe also won great acclaim abroad. Since the early 1980s, it has conducted annual tours in Israel, the West Bank, and abroad, including participation in festivals in England, France, West Germany, Italy, Switzerland, Belgium, Holland, Poland, Scandinavia, Spain, and Tunisia. One of the successful productions abroad was the aforementioned *Ḥikāyat al-ʿAyn wa-l-Sinn* (*The Story of the Eye and the Tooth*), staged at the beginning of 1986 in London. In the late 1980s, al-Ḥakawātī held a long tour of performances in Japan, Europe, and the United States, achieving great success according

[105] According to statistics published by the Association of Palestinian Writers, fifty-two theatrical productions were staged by Palestinians from the Occupied Territories during the first three years of the *Intifāḍa* (*Filasṭīn al-Thawra*, January 20, 1991, p. 30).

[106] For example, staging the plays in daytime in order to bypass the frequent curfews imposed by the authorities (ʿAlyān 1992, p. 87).

[107] See, for example, *Haaretz*, September 11, 1988, p. B6; *Haaretz*, Supplement, September 15, 1989, pp. 9–11; *Haaretz*, September 21, 1989, p. 10; *Haaretz*, February 24, 1992, p. B3.

to the Palestinian press.[108] In 1989, the name of the theater building was changed to al-Markaz al-Thaqāfī al-ʻArabī (the Arabic Cultural Center).

In recent years Al-Ḥakawātī has become, under its new name al-Masraḥ al-Waṭanī al-Filasṭīnī (the Palestinian National Theater), the central framework of the Palestinian theatrical movement. Its own original productions have decreased, and it has increasingly become a framework for various productions of Palestinian theatrical activities and festivals, including puppet and children's theater. In recent years, a new phenomenon has appeared in Palestinian cultural life: festivals of national Palestinian theater, prompted and sponsored initially by al-Ḥakawātī, are convened throughout the Palestinian centers in Israel and the Occupied Territories, encouraging the development of this art and opening new paths and horizons. During several long periods since its establishment, al-Ḥakawātī suffered from a lack of financial resources and during the recent two decades, due to the financial crisis, the activities of the theater have been very limited. In September 2021, al-Ḥakawātī's artistic director at the time, the aforementioned ʻĀmir Khalīl, even called the Palestinian Prime Minister Muḥammad Ishtayya (Shatayye) (b. 1959) to save the Palestinian National Theater from closure.[109] So far, it seems that the Palestinian Authority has taken the necessary steps to find a solution that will guarantee the continuation of this significant Palestinian cultural institution. Khalīl admits that what is happening on the ground in the Occupied Territories is more powerful than any theater or play. Nevertheless, he believes theater does have an important role to play in helping Palestinians cope with the situation they are in and in encouraging a strong, aware, and educated population: "Theatre in the West Bank is more difficult to make, however. They live under occupation and have a Ministry of Culture which doesn't understand theatre, art or culture."[110]

5. CONCLUSION

Palestinian theater, like Palestinian literature in general, has flourished as a direct reaction against the suppression of freedom, particularly since the 1967 War. Its professionalization took a line parallel to the escalation of resistance and has lived up to historical challenges, defying the hardships imposed by censorship, geographical isolation, and lack of education.

[108] For the report about the performances in Japan, see *al-Yawm al-Sābiʻ*, April 10, 1989, p. 32; in Europe, see *al-Yawm al-Sābiʻ*, May 15, 1989, p. 32; and in the United States, see *al-Yawm al-Sābiʻ*, August 7, 1989, p. 32.

[109] Amer Khalil, September 14, 2021, available at: https://www.facebook.com/amer.khalil.56/posts/10158485875021229, last accessed September 18, 2021.

[110] Avaes 2014, p. 27.

Political constraints played a role in leading this theater to develop a style of collective work. Plays are created, especially in the theater in East Jerusalem, through a process of improvisation on agreed topics; they do not rely on written texts. Some troupes claim that their plays were written solely for the benefit of the censorship authorities, "who nevertheless fail from time to time, to grasp the real meaning of the messages."[111] Thus, much variation develops during long months of rehearsal and interaction with the audience, until the plays are finally shaped. Palestinian theater has tried to fulfill the multiple tasks and roles imposed upon it by historical and sociopolitical conditions. Its main purpose has been to reflect the political aspirations of the Palestinian people. Therein lie both its strength and its weakness: it is a political instrument called upon to raise the level of national consciousness, to incite resistance and revolution, to record the trials and experiences of the nation as a whole, and to prepare for and project a better future. It also has the duty of being the social critic, conducting an exacting self-examination and exposure of the ills and problems of a traditional society trying to meet the challenges of progress and development. Finally, it is a part of the dynamic cultural Palestinian movement with the projected vision of self-help and education directed to and rooted in the masses of the Palestinian people. However, sometimes lacking abstract and material security under occupation, it has also lacked the assurance of objective criticism, for most people look to it for its didactic quality.[112]

Palestinian theater developed under the impact of the Arabic heritage, ancient folklore, and contemporary Arabic literature, but it was also inspired by Western theater. A major inspiration for this theater is still exerted by Brecht, especially with regard to the essence, contents, and techniques of the epic theater, which appeals less to the spectator's feelings than to his reason. One cannot overlook too the impact of the Hebrew theater, in view of the fact that many prominent Palestinian actors were graduates of Israeli-Hebrew theater schools. Furthermore, due to the nature of this cultural activity that obliges direct contact with the people, the relation between the Palestinian dramatic movement in Israel and Hebrew dramatic activities is stronger than in any other cultural domain. Palestinian theater has been adopted in its full Western image and practice, but the dramatic impulse in Palestinian peasant culture is still very popular. The two traditions currently exist side by side and are even interwoven: various plays have combined elements from the peasant culture, and some theater troupes perform in the villages and attract large audiences. Essentially, however, the theater is a city

[111] Shinar 1987, p. 138.
[112] Cf. Ashrawi 1976, p. 58.

activity (mainly in East Jerusalem, Haifa, Nazareth, and Ramallah), and its audience is the middle class, the educated, and the politically aware working class. Nevertheless, the Palestinian theme and the revolutionary orientation of most plays have taken Palestinian drama away from the bourgeoisie and the elite and have made it available to a larger segment of society. Like other cultural and literary activities and productions, drama has become a serious means of political education, as reflected in the activities of al-Ḥakawātī. This theater has functioned as a channel presenting some of the most basic dilemmas of Palestinian nation-building. The troupe has raised questions of identity without concealing its affinity with Palestinian, rather than pan-Arab or pan-Islamic, characteristics; it has given expression to the tradition–modernity dilemma, stating its preference for modernity, without however discarding tradition as a source of inspiration and reliance.

During the last few decades, Palestinian theater has developed in several innovative directions, both inside Israel and in the Occupied Territories. For example, Masraḥ al-Maydān in Haifa was founded in 1994 by the leftist Israeli Minister of Education Shulamit Aloni (1927–2014) during Israeli Prime Minister Yitzḥak Rabin's (1922–1995) government. At the beginning, it was named "The Arab-Israeli Theater," but after a few years it was renamed. The theater serves as the artistic community of Palestinian Arabs in Israel, and its productions run throughout the country. The initial budget with the opening of the theater was provided by the Israeli Ministry of Culture and the Municipality of Haifa, but over the years the share of budget from the Ministry of Culture has decreased and the share of the municipality has increased. During the last few years, the theater has faced severe criticism from right-wing Minister of Culture Miri Regev (b. 1965), and it has gotten to the point that the theater is now in danger of closing.[113]

In the Occupied Territories, I can mention Masraḥ al-Ḥurriyya (the Freedom Theater), a Palestinian community-based theater and cultural center that was established in 2006 in the Jenin Refugee Camp. The theater aims to generate cultural resistance through the fields of popular culture and art as a catalyst for social change in the Occupied Territories. The theater's goal is to develop a vibrant and creative artistic community that empowers children and young adults to express themselves freely and equally through art while emphasizing professionalism and innovation. The theater draws its inspiration from a project of care and learning, which uses theater and art

[113] On Masraḥ al-Maydān, see Marom 2005; and the theater's official website at: https://en.wikipedia.org/wiki/Al-Midan_Theater, last accessed August 5, 2019. The theater stopped its activities in 2019, mainly for political reasons, despite protests by Palestinian intellectuals and politicians, see at: https://haipo.co.il/item/316544, November 1, 2021, last accessed November 7, 2021.

to address the fear, depression, and trauma experienced by children in the Jenin Refugee Camp. Set up during the first *Intifāḍa*, the project was run by Arna Mer-Khamīs (1929–1995), an Israeli-Jewish political and human rights activist who devoted her life to campaigning for freedom and human rights, together with women in the refugee camp. Her work was documented in the internationally awarded documentary film *Arna's Children*, which gives some background to the Freedom Theater. The film was directed by Juliano Mer-Khamīs (1958–2011), Arna's son, who in 2006 co-founded the Freedom Theater and was its general director. Juliano's father was the Israeli-Palestinian intellectual Ṣalība Khamīs (1922–1994), who was one of the leaders of the Israeli Communist Party.[114]

On April 4, 2011, Juliano Mer-Khamīs, whose Israeli, Hebrew, Arab, Palestinian, and Arabic identities were struggling inside him, was assassinated. Six months later, on October 1, 2011, François Abū Sālim, with his unique mixture of Hungarian, French, Arabic, and Palestinian identities, committed suicide. There was no connection between the death of two of the most significant figures in the emergence of the Palestinian professional theater, but one can hardly ignore the personal identity crisis that each of them had suffered in his desire to adopt Palestinian identity while struggling to contribute to the emerging local theatrical movement. Both of them encountered a sense of mistrust on the part of the local elites, who tended to view them as semi-foreigners, as *Le Monde* wrote about Abū Sālim after his suicide: "Mais il s'est toujours heurté à un sentiment de méíance de la part des élites locales, qui avaient tendance à le regarder comme un semi-étranger."[115] Almost forty years before his suicide, in attempt to describe the national and existential dilemma of the Palestinian human being under occupation, Abū Sālim inserted the following monologue in his aforementioned play *'Atma* (*The Darkness*):

> خلّيهم يتعلّموا، الموت نهاية متاعب كلّ واحد، أقصر طريقة للموت هي الانتحار، بفرجيكم، بفرجيكم، شبّاك مفتوح، طابق رابع، عمليّة انتحار نظيفة، ثاني يوم اسمك بالجرايد، ليش هي هالعيشة اللي كلّ دقيقة بينطسّ الواحد فيها على مناخيره، في البيت بيظلموك، في الشّارع بيظلموك، في المدرسة بيظلموك، بدّي افرجيهم خلّيهم يتعلّموا، أنا مش ضعيف، بقدر أسوّي إشي كبير، بقدر أنتحر، بخلّي البلد كلّها تهتزّ، طريق الشّهرة شبّاك مفتوح في الطّابق الرّابع.

114 On Masraḥ al-Ḥurriyya, see Wallin 2017; Johansson and Wallin 2018; and the theater's official website at: http://www.thefreedomtheatre.org, last accessed August 5, 2019. See also Handal 2015, pp. 33–5. See also Qabaha 2022, pp. 74–87, whose analysis is based on the documentary film *Arna's Children* that "suspects the possibility of theatre to contain colonial reality and its impact, particularly on children who have been born into it, and it argues instead that performance reinforces this reality and endangers the safety and existence of those involved in it" (the quotation is from pp. 78–9).

115 *Le Monde*, October 11, 2011.

> Let them learn, death is the end of everyone's troubles, the shortest way to die is suicide, I will show you, I will show you, an open window, a fourth floor, a clean suicide operation, the second day, your name in the newspapers, why is this life in which every minute a man becomes sick and tired, at home they oppress you, on the street they oppress you, in the school they oppress you, I want to show them, let them learn, I am not weak, as much as I can do something big, I can commit suicide, I will make the whole country shake, the path to fame is an open window on the fourth floor.

Nevertheless, Palestinian theater is still developing, presenting new concepts, and engaging in fresh interactions with the reality of occupation. For example, in her doctoral dissertation, Najla Nakhle-Cerruti studied the development of spatiality in theatrical texts and its interactions with the real space in which they unfold based on a corpus of six plays produced between 2006 and 2016 by Palestinians.[116] Because of the strong constraints imposed on the Palestinians with regard to their mobility, the practice of the territory represents first of all an experience of identity that marks the conditions of creation and the dramaturgical choices. The theater offers the Palestinian human being a space to tell people about this experience, and it is the testimony that occupies the stage, in various forms of scenic autobiography. Such a testimony becomes a literary object, where the monologized self-narrative allows the Palestinians to express the exile in which they live in its double nature: it is at the same time geographic and psychological. In these scenic tales, the characters end up being confused with the space they describe; literary figures specific to this relationship to space are then developed. Thus, the image of confinement manifests the links between the text and the reality experienced and described. This poetics of space also contributes to the questioning of the myth of Palestine that occupies the texts of this decade, and thus provides a privileged angle to analyze the identity dynamics of the Palestinians in their continuing 1948 *Nakba* and ongoing contemporary tragedies. Referring also to the poetics of space, Maurya Wickstrom argues that theater in the Palestinian case is a place in which a profound practice and exploration of new politics might occur and, in fact, is occurring:

> This means that theatre itself becomes a different kind of space than it has habitually been. This theatre is a space made in the interstices of impossible, brutal situations. It is made as a seizure and remaking of space in places in the world where comprehensive claims on space have been made, and are enforced, through the most unjust and forceful methods. It is made in a place where the divide, suddenly, is not, where the divide no longer appears. It appears

[116] See Nakhle-Cerruti 2019.

> unpredictably, on the stages of theatres where it was not expected. Or it is made in the rubble of destruction and obstructs the aims of neoliberal development.[117]

Concluding this chapter, I will quote from the findings of Elin Nicholson in her doctoral dissertation on theatrical practices of resistance to spaciocide in Palestine:

> Contemporary Palestinian theatre exists in multiple spaces throughout the West Bank and East Jerusalem, including the main urban sites, refugee camps, and the rural hinterland. Both professional and amateur theatre productions are regularly performed and watched throughout Palestine by adults and children alike. Palestinian theatre practices are not monolithic, for they are situated in their immediate locale and respond to the geopolitical environment in which they are located. As a result, theatre forms part of the wider nonviolent resistance movement in Palestine, which has existed since the onset of Zionism, and continues to the present day through a myriad of activities, including cultural activities. As a mode of resistance, Palestinian theatre has numerous objectives, primarily including actively struggling against the continuing expansion of Israeli military and settlement enterprises through empowering both performers and audience members by creating awareness of their situation and envisaging possible solutions, and presenting their version of their everyday experiences to an international audience to garner support. There is an overwhelming aspiration for theatre practitioners to create inspirational, high-quality productions for local and global audiences, which reflect the aspirations and desires of Palestinians in relation to ending the occupation as well as individual goals. Offering "a unique lens into the process of identity formation not least because it incorporates a broad array of the population as agents in the process,"[118] theatrical performance is perceived by those involved as a declaration of both life and culture as an antithesis and antidote to the daily sufferings experienced under the conditions of "bare life."[119]

[117] Wickstrom 2012, p. 188.
[118] Gitre 2015, p. 521.
[119] Nicholson 2014, p. 231.

Chapter 2

Commitment: Verse Drama and Resistance[1]

In every time
In every place
He comes in the form of a human being
Accompanied by death
While the voice is sounding:
He has lived in every time
He has lived in every place
Qaraqāsh,
Qaraqāsh,
Qaraqāsh!!
– Samīḥ al-Qāsim

1. INTRODUCTION

In the previous chapter, I chronicled the emergence of Palestinian drama and theater against the background of the *Nakba* and in light of Palestinian nation-building. The discussion referred to the first dramatic and theatrical attempts during the first half of the twentieth century, the uprooting and the decline after the 1948 War, the repression of Palestinian cultural activities during the 1950s, and the new start and the growth of professional theater after 1967, especially the al-Ḥakawātī Theater, and contemporary theatrical activities. As an extension of the previous chapter, the present chapter illustrates how one dramatic text becomes an arena of diversified cultural imprints. Palestinian theater provides such a rare glance at Palestinian culture because of the unique historical circumstances that have accompanied the process of Palestinian nation-building. This chapter deals with the diversity of cultural dimensions revealed in the Palestinian theatrical voice

[1] This chapter uses material that first appeared in Snir 1993d, pp. 129–47; Snir 1995e, pp. 63–103; Snir 1996, pp. 101–20.

through an examination of the play *Qaraqāsh* (1969) by the Palestinian poet and playwright Samīḥ al-Qāsim (1939–2014).[2] *Qaraqāsh*, among the first Palestinian plays written with an awareness of the Western sense of the genre, is considered by Palestinian critics to be one of the first printed plays of which Palestinian literature can boast.[3] The dramatist intended it originally to be a contribution to the establishment of a Palestinian theater with a high artistic and intellectual mission, and "to impart a political message of great poignancy to the world."[4] Indeed, in the setting of the reunification of the two segments of the Palestinian people after the 1967 War, *Qaraqāsh* denoted the beginning of the professional stage in the modern Palestinian theatrical movement. It was first performed in the West Bank in 1970 by the amateur troupe 'Ā'ilat al-Masraḥ (the Family of the Theater) from Ramallah; however, the military authorities intervened to ban subsequent staging of the play. The 'Ā'ilat al-Masraḥ troupe later formed the nucleus of the Balālīn Theater troupe established in 1971, which was the basis for the al-Ḥakawātī Theater and then for al-Masraḥ al-Waṭanī al-Filasṭīnī (the Palestinian National Theater).[5] Moreover, through *Qaraqāsh* one can follow some of the pivotal thematic and poetic aspects of the Palestinian theatrical movement, its literary and ideological background, and the universal, as well as particular Arab sources of inspiration.

The specific personal and general political and cultural contexts of the late 1960s are essential for an understanding of the play. Paradoxically, the period after the 1967 War, despite the defeat of the Arabs, marks not only the political and literary reconciliation of the two segments of Palestinians—those in Israel and those in the West Bank and Gaza Strip—but also the dawn of the era of optimism and rebellion and the revival of Palestinian culture. Palestinian theater developed in this period extensively, and drama in the Western sense, written and staged by professional Palestinian theater people, came into being. This is also the time signifying the end of the involvement of the Israeli governmental establishment in the cultural arena of the Arab sector in Israel, contrary to the previous period.[6] The reunification of the Palestinians and the removal of the borders between Israel and the Occupied Territories strengthened the Palestinian identity of the Israeli Palestinians, making the writing of "positive" literature impossible.

[2] Moreh and 'Abbāsī 1987, pp. 181–4.

[3] For example, see Ashrawi 1976, p. 55.

[4] Jayyusi 1992, p. 254. The Egyptian scholar 'Alī al-Rā'ī (1920–1999) described the play as "the first political oppereta denouncing fascism and tyranny in our modern literature" (al-Rā'ī 1979, p. 237).

[5] Snir 1995b, pp. 43–9; Snir 2005c, pp. 105–30.

[6] Snir 1995b, pp. 34–7.

Moreover, the Palestinian intelligentsia within Israel were beginning to search for a means of strengthening their national identity and consolidating cultural relations with their brothers in the Occupied Territories. This phenomenon was also accompanied by a change of view in Arab public opinion generally, and particularly among the poets, writers, and critics, toward Israeli-Palestinian literature. Following the initial shocked response of the Arab writers to the heavy defeat in 1967, they gradually became aware of activities of cultural resistance exercised by the Israeli-Palestinian writers, especially the poets. From being considered in the 1950s almost as traitors by the Arab world because of their readiness to accept Israeli citizenship, they became heroes after the 1967 War. The Syrian poet Nizār Qabbānī (1923–1998) described the "defeated [Arab] poets" (*al-shu'arā' al-mahzūmūn*) as eunuchs in the courts of rulers. Addressing the Palestinian resistance poets, in his poem "For the Poets of the Occupied Land,"[7] he announced after the 1967 War the death of traditional Arabic poetry:

شعراء الأرض المحتلّهْ
يا من أوراق دفاتركمْ
بالدّمع مغمّسة، والطّينْ
يا من نبرات حناجركمْ
تشبه حشرجة المشنوقينْ
يا من ألوان محابركمْ
تبدوا كرقاب المذبوحينْ
نتعلّم منكم منذ سنينْ
نحن الشّعراء المهزومينْ
نحن الغرباء عن التّاريخْ
وعن أحزان المحزونينْ
نتعلّم منكمْ
كيف الحرف يكون له شكل السّكّينْ.

[...]

نتعلّم كيف يكون الشّعر
فلدينا قد مات الشّعر
ومات الشّعراء
الشّعر لدينا درويش
يتربّع في حلقات الذّكر
والشّاعر يعمل حُوذِيًّا لأمير القصر
الشّاعر مخصيّ الشّفتين بهذا العصر
يمسح للحاكم معطفه

[7] *Al-Ādāb*, April 1968, p. 4. The poem appeared in many collections, such as Qabbānī 1974, pp. 37–41.

ويصبّ له أقداح الخمر
الشّاعر مخصيّ الكلمات
وما أشقى خصيان الفكر

[...]

محمود درويش. سلاما
توفيق الزيّاد. سلاما
يا فدوى طوقان. سلاما
يا من تبرون على الأضلاع الأقلاما
نتعلّم منكم
كيف نفجّر في الكلمات الألغاما
شعراء الأرض المحتلّة
ما زال دراويش الكلمة
في الشّرق يَكُشّونَ حماما
يحسون كؤوس الشاي الأخضر
يجبَرون الأحلاما
لو أنّ الشّعراء لدينا
يقفون أمام قصائدكم
لبدوا
أقزاما، أقزاما

O poets of the Occupied Land,
O you whose notebooks' pages
Are soaked with tears and mud
O you whose intonations of your voice
Resemble the death-rattle of hanged men
O you whose inkwells' colors
Resemble the necks of the slaughtered
We have learned from you for years,
We, the defeated poets,
We, the strangers to history,
And to the sorrows of the sorrowful
We learn from you
How a letter can take the shape of a knife.
...
We learn from you how poetry should be,
Among us poetry has died,
Also the poets have died,
Poetry among us is like a dervish
Reeling in dervish circles,
The poet works as coachman for the castle's commander,
The poet's lips are castrated in this age
He brushes the ruler's coat

Pouring wine into his glasses
The poet's words are castrated
How wretched are the eunuchs of thought!
...
Maḥmūd al-Darwīsh, greetings!
Tawfiq al-Zayyād, greetings!
O Fadwā Ṭūqān, greetings!
O You who sharpen your pencils on your own ribs,
We learn from you
How to explode mines in words.
O poets of the Occupied Land,
The dervishes of the word are still
Chasing away pigeons in the East
Drinking green tea, ruminating dreams
If only our poets
Were standing in front of your poems
They would seem dwarfs, only dwarfs.

The new political and cultural circumstances disclosed the literary activities of Israeli-Palestinian literature, especially poetry, to Arab public opinion and brought worldwide reputation and fame to some of the poets. Palestinian literature written in Israel became a significant topic of discussion in literary circles and has been widely studied in various Arab countries. Palestinian poetry written in Israel began to be broadcast on various Arab radio stations, translated into European and Asian languages, and incorporated into poetry anthologies. Later, novels, short stories, and plays also became popular in the Arab countries,[8] to such an extent that Maḥmūd Darwīsh (1941–2008), the most prominent contemporary Palestinian poet, felt obliged in 1969 to voice his dissatisfaction with the injustice critics in the Arab world had done to Palestinian literature by avoiding any objective criticism of it.[9] These critics, in their readiness to accept unconditionally anything that was Palestinian as a positive contribution to the spirit of the nation, prompted a Palestinian critic to declare in 1976 that "Palestinian literature is not a spoiled child or mentally deficient person for whom all sorts of excuses and rationalization are to be made. It is responsible enough to demand honesty and responsibility from its readers and critics."[10]

The new cultural atmosphere was fertile ground for the emergence of the most noticeable literary-cultural phenomenon of the 1970s, namely, the professional Palestinian theater, which was mainly in the Jerusalem–Ramallah

[8] Snir 1990, pp. 253–7.
[9] Darwīsh 1969, pp. 2–4. Cf. Snir 2005c, pp. 86–7.
[10] Ashrawi 1976, p. 58.

area. Some important plays were published following the war, although most of them were not staged immediately. Outstanding among them is the aforementioned verse drama *Qaraqāsh* by Samīḥ al-Qāsim, especially against the background of the playwright's own experiences in the few years preceding the writing of the play following the 1967 War: his imprisonment at the beginning of the war, the censorship of his literary works,[11] and his feeling that "on the fifth of June I was reborn."[12]

2. POLITICAL THEATER

There is an unmistakable impact on the play of one of the main issues that occupied the general Arabic literary system in the late 1960s, namely, the issue of *iltizām* (commitment), inspired by the term "littérature engagée" coined by Jean-Paul Sartre in the mid-twentieth century. Sartre excluded poetry from his category, but later critics have generally argued for its inclusion. This term, considered since the 1950s to be an essential part of the vocabulary of Arab intellectuals and writers, was employed to indicate the necessity for a writer to convey a message rather than merely create an imaginative work for its own sake. Although its significance became diffuse and generally denoted a certain measure of nationalism, one of its dominant meanings was the adoption of a Marxist stand.[13] The genre of verse drama chosen by the dramatist was also very popular with committed Arab playwrights in the 1960s, particularly for political criticism. For example, one of the prominent plays of this kind in the 1960s was the verse drama *Ma'sāt al-Ḥallāj* (*The Tragedy of al-Ḥallāj*) (1964) by the Egyptian poet and playwright Ṣalāḥ 'Abd al-Ṣabūr (1931–1981).[14]

Qaraqāsh's eponymous title indicates one of the significant sources of inspiration of contemporary Palestinian, as well as Arabic, theater and literature in general. It alludes to the historical figure of Qarāqūsh, a eunuch

[11] See al-Qāsim 1969a, pp. 30–2.
[12] See al-Qāsim 1969, p. 26.
[13] On *iltizām*, see Slyomovics 1998, pp. 169–98; Snir 2002; Di-Capua 2012, pp. 1061–91; Pannewick and Khalil 2015; Dimeo 2016; Athamneh 2017; Thompson 2017 pp. 207–50; Di-Capua 2018; Creswell 2019, pp. 38–43.
[14] 'Abd al-Ṣabūr 1965 [1964] (English translation: 'Abd al-Ṣabūr 1972). See Snir 1992a, pp. 7–54; Snir 1993, pp. 74–88; Snir 1994d, pp. 245–56. On commitment in Arabic literature, see Snir 2002; Seigneurie 2003; Qutbuddin 2005; Ghazoul 2006, pp. 1–10; Pannewick and Khalil 2015; Snir 2017, p. 51. According to Qussay Al-Attabi, despite the forceful circulation of *iltizām*, the indeterminacy that continued to plague the term contributed to *iltizām*'s popularity—the dissemination of the term was characterized by an intriguing paradox: while *iltizām* failed as a term of literary criticism, it succeeded in fueling robust literary and critical output (al-Attabi 2021, pp. 124–46).

whose full name was Bahā' al-Dīn ibn 'Abd Allāh al-Asadī (d. 1201). Qarāqūsh obtained his liberty and was appointed an amir and then chamberlain. In this capacity, he served the family of the late caliph and is said to have administered his office with great severity, such as preventing the family of the caliph from increasing by separating men from women. Apart from his strictness and cruelty, a series of absurd verdicts are attributed to him in a work titled *Kitāb al-Fashūsh fī Ḥukm Qarāqūsh* (*The Book on the Stupidity of the Judgments of Qarāqūsh*).[15] These verdicts and judgments have nothing to do with statecraft but are court verdicts; they are typical and familiar anecdotes that are equally prevalent among other nations. This was the historical background to a popular and folkloric figure named "Qarāqūsh" (also called "Sultan" in one of the manuscripts), who became notorious as a byword for cruelty and stupidity.[16]

Al-Qāsim was not the first to exploit this historical figure in the theater: in 1933, the Egyptian comedian Najīb al-Rīḥānī (1891–1949) staged the operetta *Ḥukm Qarāqūsh* with music by Zakariyyā Aḥmad (1890–1961). The operetta is about Bunduq Abū Ghazāla, who is fed up with injustice in society and expresses his wish to be the ruler just for seven days in order to save people from their misery. He is even ready to be executed afterward. Qarāqūsh hears him and allows him to rule for seven days so that he can kill him afterward. And indeed, Bunduq Abū Ghazāla assumes his responsibilities as a ruler and hands down his verdicts in a comic manner. Actually, Bunduq reminds us of another figure in al-Rīḥānī's dramatic works, namely, Kishkish Bek, the name al-Rīḥānī gives to a fictitious Egyptian elder or *'Umda*, always interpreted on the stage by the comedian himself.[17] Like Kishkish Bek, Bunduq too passes through various misadventures and his small talk reflects the common-sense attitude of the simple man to all matters concerning social conditions and morals. Through this operetta, like most of his comedies, al-Rīḥānī frankly satirizes various traditional institutions in Egypt.[18]

Al-Qāsim's allusion to the figure of Qarāqūsh in the late 1960s belonged to the then-popular method adopted by Arab poets and playwrights in order to express political and social views. This is, in fact, the strategy of *qinā'*

[15] Ibn Mamātī n.d., pp. 8–28; Sa'd 1990, pp. 70–165. On the motives behind the attributing of such stories to Qarāqūsh, see al-Hilālī 1977, pp. 132–4.

[16] Sobernheim 1978, pp. 613–14; al-Ziriklī 1984, V, p. 193. See also Kishtainy 1985, pp. 54–5; Ibn al-Rāfidayn 1990, pp. 47–50; DeYoung 1992, p. 197; Ḥamza 2000, pp. 341–410.

[17] Landau 1958, pp. 87–8; Allen 1987, p. 259. See also the film *Ḥawādith Kishkish Bek* (*Kishkish's Episodes*) produced in 1934 according to a story by Najīb al-Rīḥānī; for details about the film, see Qāsim 2002, pp. 22–3.

[18] See al-Rā'ī 1993, pp. 335–7.

("mask")—the presentation of ideas and feelings through ancient figures generally from the Arab and Islamic heritage. Al-Qāsim apparently adopted this strategy under the impact of famous Arab poets and playwrights, particularly the Iraqi poet 'Abd al-Wahhāb al-Bayyātī (1926–1999), and the Egyptian poets and playwrights 'Abd al-Raḥmān al-Sharqāwī (1921–1987) and the aforementioned Ṣalāḥ 'Abd al-Ṣabūr. It enabled the playwright to avoid censorship and at the same time to impart universal meaning to his play.[19] Emphasizing this meaning, al-Qāsim defines at the beginning of his work the place and time:

الزّمان: كلّ زمان
المكانْ: كلّ مكان

The Time: every time
The Place: every place.[20]

In every time and place, there exists a tyrant like Qaraqāsh, and in every time and place people rebel against any despotic and arbitrary rule. In order to emphasize this aspect, three groups—ancient Greeks, ancient Egyptians, and modern Europeans—move across the stage in dumb show in the opening scene, all shackled with chains, suffering various tortures and lashed by whips. The last group, the modern Europeans, crosses the stage accompanied by the voice and picture of Adolf Hitler. The scene clearly demonstrates how despotism has had various faces in the course of history but that its logic is one, and a clear analogy is drawn between tyrants in the past history of humankind and the most notorious of them in modern times, Hitler. Preaching the philosophy of aggression as a way out of economic difficulties, Qaraqāsh regards human beings as cannon fodder and lubrication for the war machine. The allusions to the Nazi characteristics of Israeli behavior are clear and unambiguous, and such allusions are widespread in contemporary Palestinian literature and theater. These allusions are emphasized through the analogy between yesterday's victims (the Jews who suffered the despotism of the ancient Greeks, the ancient Egyptians, and the Nazis) and today's victims (the Palestinians, who are suffering the despotism of the Israeli Jews). The relevant message of the play is also expressed in the overture by the chorus:

في كلّ زمانْ
في كلّ مكانْ
يأتي في صورة إنسانْ

[19] See al-Naqqāsh 1991, p. 115.
[20] Al-Qāsim 1970, p. 7.

يأتي فيجيء الموتْ
ويظلّ يدوّي الصّوت:
في كلّ زمان عاش
في كلّ مكان عاش
قرقاش
قرقاش
قرقاش!!

In every time
In every place
He comes in the form of a human being
Accompanied by death
While the voice is sounding:
He has lived in every time
He has lived in every place
Qaraqāsh,
Qaraqāsh,
Qaraqāsh!![21]

The universal human dimensions of the play and its relevancy to all, including the spectators, are also expressed by the note in the printed text:

> The spectators may interrupt the dialogues and express their opinions whenever they want.[22]

This note betrays the inspiration from the German director Erwin Piscator (1893–1966) who, together with Bertolt Brecht (1898–1956), believed that conveying social and political messages was the prime aim of the theater in a dynamic modern society.[23] In his "political theater," and especially in his experimental productions of the 1920s in Berlin, Piscator encouraged the audience to take an active part in events on stage. The impact of Piscator, and especially of Brecht, is evident throughout *Qaraqāsh*, which employs some of their principal theories. The poetry of al-Qāsim is in general heavily inspired by Brecht's poetry, drama, and political ideologies,[24] and he even translated some of Brecht's poems into Arabic.[25] Like Brecht's *The Caucasian Chalk Circle* (1944–1945),[26] *Qaraqāsh* could be described as a fairytale for grown-ups. Outdoor scenes and images of nature abound in

21 Al-Qāsim 1970, p. 9.
22 Al-Qāsim 1970, p. 8.
23 Taylor 1984, pp. 217–18.
24 Al-Qāsim 1969, p. 28; al-Naqqāsh 1991, p. 116.
25 For example, see al-Qāsim 1969, pp. 10–13.
26 Brecht 1962 [1944–1950]. Arabic translation: Brecht n.d.; Brecht 1962 (English translation: Brecht 1969).

both plays, which deal with extremes of good and evil, omitting anything in between.[27] The impact of Brecht is seen in al-Qāsim's leaning toward the balladeer: his villainous rulers, his merciless soldiers, his greedy and rebellious peasants, and his eccentric judge are characters who might have stepped out of a fairytale or ballad, but he also brings much of the human experience into focus as he modulates between stylized action and poetic narration.

Al-Qāsim attempts in *Qaraqāsh* to present the type of epic theater advocated by Brecht, Piscator, and other German theater people of the 1920s. According to Brecht, who also stressed the political significance of the genre and its complete exclusion of empathy, the essential point of epic theater is that it appeals less to the spectator's feelings than to their reason.[28] Al-Qāsim also exploits one of Brecht's principal theories of drama—the *Verfremdungseffekt*, known as the "V-Effect" (Alienation Effect often abbreviated to "A-effect"), namely, the retention of a degree of critical detachment and distance from the play and performance instead of complete absorption by the actor in his role.[29] The dramatist exploits various techniques to keep the audience consciously aware that it is a theatrical performance they are witnessing, and to limit their emotional identification and assimilation with specific characters and situations. The instructions given by the dramatist and the directional approach encouraged by him are that the actor is not required to attempt just to be the character, to present it entirely from the inside, and to endeavor to lose himself in it, but, while understanding its psychological workings, to present it in such a way as to imply an attitude toward the character. The actor's function is accompanied by "extreme simplification in staging ... settings are stripped down, and placards indicate the scene or give information to remove suspense. Machinery and lights are exposed to prevent illusion; stagehands work in full view and instrumentalists playing the music for the songs that punctuate [the] plays are visible to the audience."[30] It is interesting to note that a similar sort of "V-Effect" is known from the ancient theatrical tradition of the Arabs in which the actors were dressed to look like the persons they represented, but did not allow their identity as actors to be effaced by the characters.[31]

[27] Hayman 1984, p. 80.
[28] Taylor 1984, p. 97.
[29] Taylor 1984, p. 12.
[30] Innes 1999, p. 151.
[31] Moreh 1992, pp. 129, 147, n. 43.

3. "LADDER OF HUNGER"

The play is divided into four acts, or pictures (*lawḥāt*), as they are called by the dramatist. Each act opens with the marching onto the stage of two masked men—one laughing and the other crying—carrying a placard with a slogan, different in each act (in the third act, there are two slogans). The first act opens with the slogan

الطّاغوت يصعد إلى العرش على سلّم الجوع

The false god (*al-ṭāghūt*) ascends to the throne on the ladder of hunger.[32]

Through the story of the ascension of Qaraqāsh to the throne, it illustrates how hardships and difficulties can be fertile ground for the rise of totalitarianism. As a result of the drought, the people suffer famine, the granaries are empty, the flocks of sheep are dying, and the wells have dried up. One can hardly forget the first scene of Sophocles' *Oedipus the King* when the priest describes to Oedipus what happens in the city:

For our city, as you yourself can see,
is badly shaken—she cannot raise her head
above the depths of so much surging death.
Disease infects fruit blossoms in our land,
disease infects our herds of grazing cattle,
makes women in labour lose their children.[33]

Against this intertextual background, Qaraqāsh is considered as a savior, and the stage directions describe his appearance on the stage as an ironic mixture of *al-faraj ba'da al-shidda* (relief after misery) known from the medieval *Adab* literature and the *deus ex machina* known from the Greek tradition:

Outside the stage a heavy footfall is heard. A strong wind blows accompanied by smoke and dust. Qaraqāsh enters the stage with strong and confident steps.[34]

However, the spectators have no doubt regarding the ironic description of Qaraqāsh as a false savior, which is also emphasized by the stage directions:

When Qaraqāsh sees his citizens in their silent gloomy condition, he stands with his hand to his waist, touching his sword and looking around at them with superiority and malicious joy.[35]

32 Al-Qāsim 1970, p. 13.
33 *Oedipus the King*, ll. 26–30 (trans. Ian Johnston = Sophocles 2007).
34 Al-Qāsim 1970, p. 16.
35 Al-Qāsim 1970, p. 16.

In this setting, a conflict arises between Qaraqāsh and one of the farmers, who represents the conscience of the playwright and the voice of universal justice. Qaraqāsh suggests solving the misery by calling for an attack on the neighbors and seizing their resources, while the farmer, called by the playwright a "revolutionary farmer" (*fallāḥ thā'ir*), insists that the crisis can and must be solved only by hard and strenuous work on the land. The farmers on the stage, incited by Qaraqāsh, face a dilemma between accepting the logic of an easy demagogic military solution presented by Qaraqāsh or the pacifistic preaching of the revolutionary farmer. However, the suppression of the farmers is poetically expected and anticipated, and the first act ends with the victory of Qaraqāsh and the killing of the revolutionary farmer by his fellow farmers in fulfillment of the slogan at the opening of the act.

Describing the horrors of a country ruled by a despot, the second act opens with the slogan:

قرقاش يحصد حنطة الآخرين ويشرب آبارهم

Qaraqāsh reaps the others' wheat and drinks their wells.[36]

The soldiers, returning from the battlefield at the end of a military expedition by Qaraqāsh, carry the enemy's loot but at the same time many of them are severely wounded. Furthermore, the bodies of the dead soldiers have been left on the battlefield at the personal command of the despot. One of the soldiers wins three medals after his death, but his mother refuses to accept them. She is angered because of the decision not to permit his body to be brought back, and in consequence she is accused of treason. This episode, along with others in the play, alludes to Sophocles' *Antigone*, in which Creon gave orders that the Argive dead were not to be buried, including Antigone's brother Polynices.

The third act opens with two slogans:

حتّى تصبح حاكما بأمرك يجدر بك أن تحرم الشّعب من تراثه
فكرة تذويب الفروق بين الطّبقات وبال على أصحابها

In order to become dictator, you must strip the people of their heritage.
The idea of the removal of the differences between the classes in society is destructive for its originators.[37]

Describing the ways in which Qaraqāsh succeeds in exercising his influence throughout the country, this act portrays his encounter, during a hunting expedition, with a group of joyful farmers reaping the grains in a field. Annoyed to find them singing and dancing, Qaraqāsh is afraid that the noise

[36] Al-Qāsim 1970, p. 31.
[37] Al-Qāsim 1970, p. 43.

might frighten the wild animals away, and orders them to stop at once. Moreover, he immediately bans these happy songs, ordering the farmers to leave the fields and join his military expedition against the neighbors. At the end of this act, Qaraqāsh's son, who accompanies his father, appears as a contrast to Qaraqāsh, representing, as the playwright himself indicates,[38] the human dimensions in the figure of the despot. While all the characters in the play may be regarded as simple illustrations of the dramatist's political and social ideologies, the son is an intricate and complicated character: as a noble spirit, he falls in love with a beautiful peasant girl and insists on marrying her, despite the girl's attempt to remind him of the huge social barrier that separates them. He asks the vizier to persuade his father to agree to this unequal marriage.

The fourth act opens with the slogan:

حين تحسّ الجماهير بالسّكّين الّتي تقطع لحمها لا يبقى لها مفرّ من التّفكير في شيء ما تفعله إذا أرادت أن تواصل الحياة

> When the masses feel the knife cutting their flesh, they have no choice but to think of something to do if they want to continue living.[39]

In this act, the play reaches its peak with the inevitable development of reality, as the dramatist perceived it in the late 1960s: the people finally rebel and the peasants kill the tyrant, proclaiming themselves as the only just ruler. In this act, the character of Qaraqāsh incorporates Brecht's Azdak and the myth of Qarāqūsh, to both of whom were ascribed a series of absurd and stupid judgments. The woman who lost her son in the war is accused of treason, since she is not happy with her sacrifice, and Qaraqāsh's verdict is as follows:

تقفين على ساق واحدة ستّة أيّام
في شمس اللّيل ودرب التّبّانات الظّهريّة
وقبيل اليوم السّادس، تلدين
سبعة أولاد
سابعهم يؤخذ للخدمة في الجنديّة
والستّة أيضا للخدمة في الجنديّة!

> You will stand on one leg for six days
> In the sun of the night and the Milky Way of the noon
> And before the sixth day you will give birth to
> Seven children
> The seventh of them will be called up to the army
> And the other six will be called up also![40]

38 See al-Qāsim 1993.
39 Al-Qāsim 1970, p. 61.
40 Al-Qāsim 1970, p. 66.

Like his other sentences,[41] this one accords with the "world upside down" situation created by the despot: the bereaved woman is condemned simply because she insists on her right to mourn her son. Similarly, in *The Caucasian Chalk Circle*, when an innkeeper accuses a stableman of assaulting his daughter-in-law, Azdak condemns the girl for assaulting the man. "Do you imagine you can go around with a bottom like that and get away with it in Court? This is a case of deliberate assault with a dangerous weapon." He confiscates a dun-colored horse he has always fancied, and orders the girl to go with him to the stable, "so that the Court may investigate the scene of the crime."[42] The similarity between the two plays is also evident in what seems to be at first glance a contradiction between the abundance of scenes of men being dragged to the gallows and the pacifist messages of both plays and the insistence that wars should and can be abolished. Despite such messages, both plays indicate that social injustices can be removed only by revolution.

Al-Qāsim, like Brecht, reflects his social and political interests and especially his Marxist preoccupations in his satirical attack on bourgeois society and its standards. He preaches Marxism as a sociopolitical order designed to remedy all the grievances of society. It is not only a local and national struggle, but a universal and social one as well.[43] Brecht also seems to have exerted a strong influence on al-Qāsim with regard to the characters in the play. Reminiscent of Azdak is the soldier who substitutes for Qaraqāsh while he goes to eat: "I have not read the books of law," he says to the defendant brought before him, "and the illiterate justice is responsible for removing injustice from you."[44] Like Azdak, the rogue turned judge in *The Caucasian Chalk Circle*, this soldier too is a contradictory character who escapes the rigid formulation of his social and political significance. After hearing the defendant's tale of the destruction of his fields by the military and the death of his son in the war, he pronounces his verdict:

نعلم أنّ العدل الوارد في النّصّ الرّسميّ
يقضي أن تشنق
لكنّ العدل الأمّيّ
يقضي أن تأخذ من أموال الدّولهْ
ما يكفل قوتك، حتّى أغراسك
عجلات العربات الحربيّهْ
وسنابك خيل الجند
ويضيف العدل الوارد في الأنظمة الأمّيّهْ

[41] For example, see al-Qāsim 1970, pp. 71–3.
[42] Brecht 1969, pp. 76–7.
[43] Kanazi 1989, pp. 135–7.
[44] Al-Qāsim 1970, pp. 66–70.

أنّ الحزن على ابنك حقّ لك
لا لوزير يحزن بدموع الحبر المسكوب على الاوراق
ولأنّي أمّيّ أجهل تأريخ الآثار
ولأنّي أمّيّ أجهل جغرافيّة الأقطار
أحكم لك!

We know that the justice included in the formal texts
Rules that you should be hanged
But the illiterate justice
Rules that you will take from the state treasury
All which will guarantee your nourishment, till your plants forget
The war vehicles' wheels
And the soldiers' horses' hoofs
The justice included in the illiterate regimes adds
That the grief at your dead son is your own right,
Not of a vizier grieved with ink tears on the paper
And since I am an illiterate ignorant of the history of antiquities
And since I am an illiterate ignorant of the geography of lands
I judge in your favor![45]

The last six lines were chosen by the dramatist to be the motto of the play. It is only natural that on returning to his seat Qaraqāsh accepts the recommendation of the aristocracy and condemns the soldier who replaced him to death, since he "incites the dregs of people against us." The manner in which the soldier dispenses justice reminds us of Brecht's attitude toward the character of Azdak, the rogue turned judge in *The Caucasian Chalk Circle*, an antihero elevated to the role of judge, who is reminiscent of Švejk, the ribald, drunken antihero in the picaresque novel *The Good Soldier Švejk* (1923) by Jaroslav Hašek (1883–1923). Brecht said about Azdak:

> First I had only his lousy jurisdiction, which made poor people come off well. I knew I mustn't suggest that the normal laws should be bent for justice to prevail, but to indicate that with careless, ignorant, even bad jurisdiction, something emerges for those who really needed law. That's why Azdak had to have the self-seeking, amoral, parasitical features of the lowest, most degenerate of judges. But I still needed an elementary cause of a social kind. I found it in his disappointment that with the overthrow of the old masters, what ensued was not a new era but an era of new masters. So he goes on enforcing bourgeois law, only dilapidated, sabotaged, adapted to serve the unqualified self-interest of the judicature.[46]

45 Al-Qāsim 1970, pp. 68–9.
46 Hayman 1984, p. 82.

The end of the play confirms Brecht's inspiration: the vizier who was sent by Qaraqāsh's son to mediate between the prince and his father tries to sound him out on the matter of a prince marrying a peasant girl. He asks the despot what his judgment would be if a prince in his land should fall in love with a commoner. Qaraqāsh's prompt reaction is that such a couple ought to be beheaded, and he unhesitatingly condemns the lovers to death. When he discovers that he is unwittingly responsible for the death of his own son, who kills himself after he learns of his lover's death (in another evident allusion to Sophocles' *Antigone*!), he is driven by shock and grief to declare a new war in which his people will be compelled to take part. However, the people are unable to stand any more of the despot's crimes, and an open revolt ensues in which both Qaraqāsh and his minister are killed. A popular regime is soon set up amid universal jubilation, and one of the farmers takes Qaraqāsh's seat, with the soldiers throwing away their helmets and joining the farmers in singing and dancing. One of the farmers shouts:

عاش الملك العادل!

Long live the righteous king!

And all the farmers and soldiers shout:

نحن الملك العادل! نحن الملك العادل!

We are the righteous king! We are the righteous king![47]

The similarity between this scene and the concluding scene of *The Caucasian Chalk Circle* is striking.

4. APOCALYPTICISM

The mention of the false god (*al-ṭāghūt*) at the beginning of the play is intended to construct the literary and intertextual context in which the play should be interpreted. The despot's character alludes to the aforementioned figure of the *Dajjāl* (the "Deceiver"), namely, the False Christ/Antichrist and Armillus from the Christian and Jewish traditions—that evil personage endowed with supernatural powers who will come forth before the end of time and rule in heresy and tyranny for a limited period of either forty days or forty years, and who is to be followed by the universal conversion of humanity to Islam. His appearance is one of the proofs of the end of time, and he will die at the hands of the Mahdī (the "Rightly Guided") or Jesus. The allusion to the Antichrist is generally an omen of the coming revolution, which

[47] Al-Qāsim 1970, pp. 82–4.

will annihilate oppression and tyranny, and launch a new era. The significant allusions of this topos to "The Signs of the Day of Judgment" are accompanied in contemporary Arabic poetry and prose by the hyperbolic presentation of an actual or possible rejected reality—be it personal, political, social, ethical, national, rhetorical, or even aesthetic-critical.[48] Use is made of this topos in the play, especially in scenes that combine realistic but unacceptable conditions and present them as "world upside down." Exploited in order to challenge a state of affairs demanding immediate reform, the topos is intended to forewarn against a dangerous deviation from the desired reality, which must be restored. Hence, a non-existent, reversed, rejected reality is created, illustrating the dangers of this deviation unless it is swiftly corrected. Like the identification of the Antichrist with a specific pope or political figure in the Middle Ages,[49] the Islamic allusions in the play indicate that the Israeli regime was perceived by the playwright, shocked by the 1967 War, as the Antichrist of the 1960s. Moreover, as in Palestinian literature in general, the topos is used here to indicate that a world in which vices have become virtues needs urgent reform. As this topos is inherent in the literary imagination of Arab poets and writers, it immediately comes to the fore when they witness a deviation from the desired reality, as they regard it. The signs of Judgment Day, portended by the "world upside down," are no longer in the distant future, but are in the here and now. Thus, the hyperbolic presentation of an actual or possible rejected and horrible reality, in a way that reminds the reader or spectator of these signs, powerfully challenges a situation that demands immediate reform, as manifested in Cassius' words in Shakespeare's *Julius Caesar*:

> Why all these things change from their ordinance,
> Their nature, and pre-formed faculties,
> To monstrous quality; why, you shall find,
> That heaven hath infused them with these spirits,
> To make them instruments of fear and warning,
> Unto some monstrous state.[50]

Like archetypes, the allusions to the "world upside down" are, in some respect, the product of the "collective unconscious" of Arab poets and writers, both Muslim and Christian, bequeathed by the Arab and Islamic heritages. One of the advantages of this topos is that it conceals the writer's own confusions and shifting opinions as he slowly faces reality.[51] Another

48 Snir 1994b, pp. 51–75.
49 Emmerson 1981, p. 7.
50 *Julius Caesar*, Act I, Scene 3, ll. 66–71.
51 Hill 1971, p. 66.

advantage is its vagueness and ambiguity: it can encompass attacks on more than one target. The poets and writers who use its symbolism have presumably no consciously evasive purpose in mind. Like those who used the symbolism of the Antichrist in seventeenth-century England,[52] they draw on allegorical habits of mind inherited from the past. Nevertheless, its imprecision allows differing interpretations to be put upon it, either by different people or by the same person appealing to different groups. Vagueness and ambiguity also have advantages as camouflage: in Egypt in the 1960s, for example, critics of the local "world upside down" were in fact attacking the regime. Nevertheless, even the supporters of the regime could hardly object to a denunciation of this "world upside down," as long as it was not too clearly defined. Like sin, everyone was against it.[53] Using the topos of the "world upside down," al-Qāsim attempts to destroy the foundations of the political and social world in which the Palestinians are living. He calls for the overthrow of the tyrant, who exploits the people and uses them for the sake of increasing his own wealth and glory. Some saw in the figure of Qaraqāsh a symbol of the imperialist powers;[54] others referred to him as a symbol of the Israeli military establishment,[55] or even as standing in for Moshe Dayan, the noted Israeli hero of the 1967 War.[56]

Qaraqāsh, written in a period during which the dramatist believed that Communism would cure all ills, may be described as a political play. It was written in order to ignite the people and inflame them to act against a political and social order perceived to be rotten. In the play, as in his poems, al-Qāsim builds a dialectic between good and evil—between the oppressed people and the tyrannical regime. The emphasis is on the people's power to overcome all misery, all insanity of judgment, and emerge victorious. "In fulfillment of the tradition of the fables of old," as the Egyptian critic ʿAlī al-Rāʿī (1920–1999) states, "a prince loves a peasant girl. Although the result is not at all happy, the young prince's desire that the castle should lower itself a little and the cottage rise a little is achieved, even though the union may be in death."[57] The Brechtian inspiration in this vision is clear, as it is apparent on other levels of the play in general. This inspiration, added to that of the ancient Arabic and Islamic heritages, seems to illustrate some of the main origins of inspiration for contemporary Palestinian theater in general.

52 Hill 1971, pp. 44–5.
53 Cf. Hill 1971, p. 45.
54 Al-Naqqāsh 1991, p. 121.
55 Sayegh 1990, p. 223.
56 Badawi 1992, p. 366; Jayyusi and Allen 1995, p. 18.
57 Badawi 1992, p. 366.

5. CONCLUSION

Palestinian theater, like Palestinian literature in general, has flourished as a direct reaction against the suppression of freedom. The reunification of the Palestinians in Israel with their brothers in the West Bank and Gaza Strip after the 1967 War and the unification of the Palestinian cultural movements within and outside Israel have promoted the emergence of this theater. Its thematic pivot is still, like Palestinian literature in general, the tragic events of 1948 and their after-effects. The professionalization of Palestinian theater has taken a line parallel to the escalation of resistance and has lived up to historical challenges, defying the hardships imposed by censorship, geographical isolation, and lack of education. The theatrical processes and institutional structure have been influenced as much as the content and style by the particular circumstances in which Palestinian theater has functioned. Its main purpose has been to reflect the political aspirations of the Palestinian people. Therein lie both its strength and its weakness: it is a political instrument called upon to raise the level of national consciousness, to incite resistance and revolution, to record the trials and experiences of the nation as a whole, and to prepare for and project a better future. It also has the duty of being a social critic, conducting an exacting self-examination and exposure of the ills and problems of a traditional society trying to meet the challenges of progress and development. It is a part of the dynamic cultural Palestinian movement with the projected vision of self-help and education directed to and rooted in the masses of the Palestinian people. However, as one Palestinian critic indicates, "lacking all types of abstract and material security under occupation, it also lacks the assurance of objective criticism, for most people look to it for its didactic quality."[58] Arab critics, and even leftist Israeli and Western intellectuals, have been willing to accept unconditionally anything that is Palestinian as a positive contribution. This indulgent attitude of panegyric has caused Palestinian writers, poets, and critics themselves to demand greater honesty and responsibility from their readers and critics.[59]

Contemporary Palestinian theater is developing under the impact of the Arab heritage, ancient folklore, and contemporary Arabic literature, but also under the influence of Western theater. A major influence on this theater is still exerted by the Brechtian theater, especially with regard to the essence, contents, and techniques of the epic theater, which appeals less to the spectator's feelings than to their reason. Nor can one overlook the impact of the Hebrew theater—prominent Palestinian actors are graduates

[58] Ashrawi 1976, p. 58.
[59] Ashrawi 1976, p. 58.

of Israeli-Hebrew schools of theater and take part in Israeli-Hebrew performances. Furthermore, owing to the nature of theatrical activity, which obliges direct contact with the people, the relation between the Palestinian dramatic movement in Israel and Hebrew dramatic activities is stronger than in any similar relationship in any other cultural domain. Palestinian theater has been adopted in its full Western image and practice, but the dramatic impulse in Palestinian peasant culture is still very popular. The two traditions currently exist side by side, and are interwoven: various plays have combined elements from peasant culture, and some theater troupes perform in villages and attract large audiences. Essentially, however, the theater is a city activity (mainly in East Jerusalem, Haifa, Nazareth, and Ramallah), and its audience is the middle class, the educated, and the politically aware working class. Nevertheless, the Palestinian theme and the revolutionary orientation of most plays have taken Palestinian drama away from the bourgeoisie and the elite and have made it available to a larger segment of society.

Like other cultural and literary activities and productions, drama has become a serious means of political education, functioning as a channel presenting some of the most basic dilemmas of Palestinian nation-building. It has raised questions of identity without concealing its affinity with Palestinian, rather than pan-Arab or pan-Islamic, characteristics; it has given expression to the tradition–modernity dilemma, stating its preference for modernity, without however discarding tradition as a source of inspiration and reliance. Through its activities, Palestinian theater has promoted the *ṣumūd* ("steadfastness") principle as a solution to the inevitable confrontation between pride and survival and between the hopes for an independent future and the pressures of occupation; and it has enhanced the two-front struggle of Palestinian women, both as symbols of changing Palestinian values and as a channel in which Palestinian female actors may enjoy equal rights.[60]

The presence of contemporary Palestinian theater in the consciousness of the Israeli-Jewish culture is an undoubted fact, in contrast to the minor presence of the other genres of Palestinian culture. This is why Palestinian theater, which since the early 1970s has reflected the Israeli–Palestinian Conflict in the most radical way, has become, paradoxically, a central field in which a true attempt is being made to diminish the alienation between the two cultures. This is doubly evident in the setting of the Western orientation of Israeli culture and its repugnance toward Arabic culture, although the Hebrew literary establishment is not able publicly to express this, owing to its general views concerning the need for a proper attitude toward the culture of

[60] On the *ṣumūd* in Palestinian theater, see Abusultan 2021.

others. Thus, there is a sort of "cognitive dissonance"[61] in the attitude toward Palestinian culture, which is the reason for the manifestation of ensuring a Palestinian "seat" in various activities of Israeli culture as a way to prove that the majority maintains its liberal and tolerant nature toward Palestinian culture. This "seat," however, is not without obvious racism that characterizes nearly all of what is written in Hebrew about Arabic literature—one only has to read it carefully in light of the comments made by the Nigerian Chinua Achebe (1930–2013) about Joseph Conrad's (1857–1924) *Heart of Darkness* (1899), considered to be an anti-imperialistic and anticolonial novel highly critical of the white men in Africa at the turn of the nineteenth century (1899).[62] This, perhaps, may not be said about Palestinian theater inside Israel, whose presence in Israeli culture is absolutely not fictitious. The Palestinian theatrical efforts to create a true dialogue with Israeli culture are in full progress. In *Avanti Popolo*, the actor-soldier Khālid, played by Salīm Ḍaw (b. 1950), expresses his wish to play roles other than Shylock:

> I told them I would like to play another role. I would like a role with strength, with glory. I would like to be admired by the public. I would like the public to love me. I would like to stand on the center of the stage and all the girls in the hall would look at me and say: this is the knight of my dreams, standing on the stage with his white horse. This may sound stupid, but that's what I feel. I wish that each girl in the hall would think that she could be happy only if I took her in my arms and put her in front of me on the saddle, rode with her to Wonderland, and defended her with my body and sword until my last day.[63]

It is not only the Egyptian actor-soldier Khālid, or the Israeli-Palestinian actor Salīm Ḍaw, who refuses to play roles in Israeli theater without being able to influence their nature. It is also the very essence of Palestinian theater inside Israel: closely associated with Arabic heritage and inspired by Western culture, it also desires to dialogue with Israeli and Jewish culture but not at the price of erasing its own national particularity.

[61] Festinger 1957, pp. 1–31.
[62] Achebe 1988 [1977], pp. 251–61.
[63] Bukaee 1990, p. 40.

Chapter 3

Chronicle: The Ongoing *Nakba*[1]

The butterfly effect cannot be seen,
The butterfly effect will never fade away.
– Maḥmūd Darwīsh

1. INTRODUCTION

Poetry was the principal channel of literary creativity and served as the chronicle and public register of the Arabs (*al-Shiʿr Dīwān al-ʿArab*), recording their very appearance on the stage of history. No other genres could challenge the supremacy of poetry in the field of *belles lettres* across more than 1,500 years of literary history. The high status poetry enjoyed among the Arabs was reflected in a passage by the eleventh-century scholar Ibn Rashīq al-Qayrawānī (d. 1063 or 1071), which concludes with the statement that "they used not to wish one another joy but for three things: the birth of a boy, the coming to light of a poet, and the foaling of a noble mare."[2] Only in the second half of the twentieth century was poetry pushed to the margins,[3] and fiction, especially the novel, brought to the forefront.[4] In the early 1970s, the Egyptian magazine *al-Ṭalīʿa* issued a feature called

1 This chapter uses material that first appeared in Snir 2004–2005, pp. 17–85; Snir 2008, pp. 123–66; Snir 2015.

2 Ibn Rashīq al-Qayrawānī 1963, p. 65; al-Suyūṭī n.d., II, p. 473. The translation is according to Lyall 1930, p. xvii, with minor modifications. See also Nicholson 1969 [1907], p. 71.

3 Muḥammad ibn Ismāʿīl refers to the marginaliztion of Arabic poetry in relation to politics as being a metaphor for the rupture between poetry and culture in the contemporary Arab world (*Fikr wa-Fann* 72 [2000], pp. 44–8).

4 Cf. Adūnīs on the value of contemporary poetry: "Our success has been substantially and paradoxically due to our marginality" (Adūnīs 1993, p. 180). The poet Muḥammad ʿAlī Farḥāt (b. 1945) sees this development as corresponding to the disappearance of the "spirit of the countryside" ("*al-rūḥ al-rīfiyya*") and the dominance of the town in the Arab world (*al-Wasaṭ*, March 2, 1992, p. 51). On the dichotomous roles played by town and country in modern Arabic poetry, see Moreh 1984, pp. 161–85.

al-riwāya mir'āt al-sha'b (the novel is the mirror of the people),[5] and more than twenty years later, upon his nomination as head of the prose committee of the Supreme Council for Culture in Egypt, the critic 'Alī al-Rā'ī (1920–1999) asserted: "This is the time of the novel ... the novel is the new chronicle of the Arabs" ("*al-riwāya dīwān al-'arab al-jadīd*").[6] "Glory to the Arabic novel!" declared al-Rā'ī, "the best of its writers have made it a mouthpiece of the nation, the new annals of the Arabs, and a reservoir of the hopes and agonies of our great but torn nation."[7] A book published in 2001 by the Egyptian Ṭāhā Wādī (1937–2008) bears the title *al-Qiṣṣa Dīwān al-'Arab* (*Fiction Is the New Annals of the Arabs*), and the author explains that the narrative genres have become the new Arab chronicle because "they truly reflect their general and personal reality, the social and subjective one."[8]

This change in the status of literary genres is not exclusive to Arabic literature. It is a worldwide phenomenon, and has much to do with the hermetic nature of modernist poetry, which has become self-regarding and employs obscure imagery and highly subjective language. Several reasons have been given for this phenomenon, such as it being a poets' way of passing a negative judgment on the complexities of modern life—on the relatively inaccessible sciences, on the multiple belief systems people are asked to discriminate among, on the separation of arts from everyday life. Also modernist poets have played down poetry-as-communication or poetry-as-message and concentrated on exploiting poetry-as-medium. They tend to write not about public matters but about themselves and for themselves—or for small coteries equally sensitive.[9] Obscurity is a well-known trait in ancient Arabic literature, especially poetry,[10] but the nature of that obscurity is different—the difficulties in understanding the traditional *qaṣīda* with its conventional form and strict theme sequence was largely owing to linguistic, rhetorical, and stylistic reasons and mainly due to the affectation and mannerism that began to influence Arabic literature beginning in the Abbasid

5 *Al-Ṭalī'a*, August 1971, pp. 10–57.

6 *Al-Akhbār*, August 11, 1993, p. 11. Cf. the special volume of *Fuṣūl* 12.1 (Spring 1993) titled *Zaman al-Riwāya* (*The Time of the Novel*), as well as Jabrā 1989, pp. 11–26. See also the words by Iḥsān Abbās (1920–2003): "'*aṣrunā huwa 'aṣr al-riwāya dūna adnā rayb*" (Abbās 1996, p. 230).

7 Al-Rā'ī 1991, p. 19. Cf. Ouyang 2012, pp. 15–16.

8 Wādī 2001, p. 9. On the novel as "the new chronicle of the Arabs," see Snir 2017, pp. 223–6.

9 Preminger 1974, pp. 582–3. Cf. Eliot 1950, p. 248. On obscurity in modern Arabic literature and the reasons for it, see Adūnīs 1971, pp. 43–7, 124–5; Adūnīs 1972, pp. 158–9, 276–84; Adūnīs 1978, pp. 290, 297; 'Abd al-Ṣabūr 1971, pp. 37–44; Lu'lu'a 1973, pp. 151–4; Ismā'īl 1978, p. 194.

10 Cf. Arazi 1986, pp. 473–505.

period.[11] In the second half of the twentieth century, however, canonical Arabic poetry underwent a radical change with the emergence of a new sensitivity—the public, clear, and unambiguous style was replaced by a more personal, obscure, and ambiguous one. Additionally, the role of the reader in the concretization of meaning has become crucial, and the matter-of-fact interpretation dictated by the author gradually disappeared in favor of many subjective reader-oriented interpretations. The awareness that it is the reader who makes sense of a text at both a cognitive and emotional level is now very common. In fact, the same person reading the same text in another time and place may understand it differently from the first time and place he or she read it. Furthermore, the process of reading itself becomes significant, or, as Stanley Fish (b. 1938) put it: "A reader's response to the fifth word in a line or sentence is to a large extent the product of his responses to words one, two, three, and four."[12] It is not only the rational process of constructing meaning that happens gradually but also that of aesthetic experience. "In art," as Viktor Shklovsky (Shklovskij) (1893–1984) put it, "the process of perception is an aesthetic end in itself and must be prolonged. Art is a device for experiencing the process of becoming; that *that* has already become is of no importance for art."[13]

The marginalization of poetry, within the already marginalized role of literature in the age of mass media and the Internet, has consigned it to being an intimate activity of the lonely reader, far removed from the declarative traditional tone of neoclassical poetry. Yet, although the relationship between poet and reader has undergone an essential change, poetry still functions as a register of the experiences of human beings, recording their miseries, feelings, hopes, and trials, if in new ways. Moreover, poetry as a means of expressing the agonies and miseries of a collective is still being written. One example is the poetry used by the Palestinians to chronicle their *Nakba* (the catastrophe of 1948) and its unending agonies. The present chapter deals with a chronicle of the Palestinian people in the mid-1980s against the backdrop of the Israeli invasion of Lebanon in 1982 and the period prior to the outbreak of the first *Intifāḍa* in the West Bank and Gaza Strip in December 1987; in fact, that chronicle is undertaken by a single poet, Maḥmūd Darwīsh (1941–2008), mainly in one collection, *Ward Aqall* (*Fewer Roses*) (1986), and more specifically in one poem, "Sa-Ya'tī Barābiratun Ākharūn" ("Other Barbarians Will Come"). The *Nakba* is always there as a kind of background without which this poetry cannot exist, but its main concern is a dialogue

11 Ḍayf 1983, pp. 275–406.
12 Fish 1980, p. 73.
13 Shklovskij 1966, p. 14.

with other texts and the interplay not only between reality, poetry, and myth but also between poetry, meta-poetry, and meta-myth.

2. "I AM THE LAST ARABS' SIGH"

In one of the first poems in *Ward Aqall*, "Idhā Kāna lī an U'īda al-Bidāya" ("If I Were to Start All Over Again"),[14] the persona asks himself what he would do if he were given the chance to start his life all over again:

إذا كان لي أن أعيد البداية أختار ما اخترت: ورد السّياج
أسافر ثانية في الدّروب الّتي قد تؤدّي وقد لا تؤدّي إلى قرطبة.
أعلّق ظلّي على صخرتين لتبني الطّيور الشّريدةُ عشًّا على غصن ظلّي
وأكسر ظلّي لأتبع رائحة اللّوز وهي تطير على غيمةٍ متربهْ
وأتعبُ عند السّفوحِ: تعالوا إليّ اسمعوني. كلوا من رغيفي
اشربوا من نبيذي، ولا تتركوني على شارع العمر وحدي كصفصافة متعبهْ.
أحبُّ البلاد الّتي لم يطأها نشيد الرّحيل ولم تمتثل لدم وامرأهْ
أحبُّ النّساء اللّواتي يخبّئن في الشّهوات انتحار الخيول على عتبهْ
أعود، إذا كان لي أن أعود، إلى وردتي نفسها وإلى خطوتي نفسها
ولكنّني لا أعود إلى قرطبهْ.

If I could start all over again I'd choose what I have chosen: roses on the fence.
I'd travel again on the roads that may or may not lead to Cordova.
I'd hang my shadow on two rocks for fugitive birds to build a nest on my shadow's bough.
I'd break off my shadow to follow the scent of almonds as it wafts on a cloud of dust
And feel tired at the foot of the mountains; come and listen to me. Have some of my bread,
Drink from my wine and do not leave me on the road of years on my own like a tired willow tree.
I love the countries untrod by migration's song, and held captive to neither blood nor woman
I love women who in their desires conceal the suicide of horses at the threshold
I will return, if I can return, to my own rose and to my own step, but I will never go back to Cordova.

Andalusian Cordova here is the place from which the persona was exiled, the mythological homeland to which he is longing to return. But reaching this homeland may always remain an illusion: the persona in Darwīsh's poetry is not only a man expelled from his homeland but a poet who records the feelings and aspirations of his tribe—a single person from a *jamā'a*, a collective

[14] Darwīsh 1987a, p. 9. The translation is based on Al-Udhari 1984, p. 23. For another English translation, see Darwish 2003, p. 5. For a German translation, see Darwisch 1996, p. 11.

that imposed on him the task of representation. The personal and public voices are always co-mingled, and the persona-poet's distress is the synecdoche for that of an entire people.

Darwīsh is only one among numerous other Arab and Muslim authors who, ever since the nineteenth century, have been invoking the image of al-Andalus—Muslim Spain—in their work.[15] As such, they are part of a much wider phenomenon: a conscious effort on the part of contemporary Arab poets and writers to highlight the al-Andalus experience and the benefits that Western civilization has gained through its interaction with Arab civilization.[16] Furthermore, when poets recall the cultural achievements of the Arabs in al-Andalus—from the time Arabs and Berber troops crossed the Straits of Gibraltar into Iberia in 711 and overthrew the Visigoths, commencing nearly eight hundred years of Muslim rule on the peninsula—they do so to remind their audience that their bitter state in modern times is only a transitory period, a temporary clouding of the skies between a glorious past and a splendid future. Though the Andalusian period was one of political fragmentation and local dynasties (known as *Mulūk al-Ṭawāʾif*, "Party Kings"), it was also a period of great cultural efflorescence that lasted continuously in one form or another up until the fall of Granada in 1492 to the Christians. Inspired by nostalgia, the picture that most frequently appears in modern Arabic literary writings is that of al-Andalus as the lost paradise (*al-firdaws al-mafqūd*) or God's paradise on earth (*jannat Allāh ʿalā al-arḍ*).

For Maḥmūd Darwīsh, the main Andalusian sites (Cordova, Granada, Toledo, and Seville) are icons whose meanings go far beyond the historical, external, or sensuous dimensions of these places. Cordova, as the famous center of Andalusian learning and culture, is not just the historical city but also a trope for the "Palestinian" experience, signifying the lost paradise. As one Palestinian scholar says: "If circumstances prevented the poet from reaching Jerusalem and he was forced to go to Cordova, the idea is that his creative journey stopped as well and remains a dream with a chance of ever being fulfilled."[17] In Darwīsh's poetry, Andalusian sites have the same emotional resonance as "tears, dance and the long embrace of a woman.

15 On al-Andalus in Arabic and Muslim culture, see ʿUthmān 1988, pp. 5–72; Montávez 1992; Noorani 1999, pp. 237–54; Snir 2000, pp. 263–93; Anidjar 2002; Shannon 2007, pp. 308–44; Elinson 2009; Eksell 2011, pp. 103–26; Jarrar 2011, pp. 361–93; Brann 2013, pp. 119–34; Calderwood 2014, pp. 27–55; Arslan 2016, pp. 278–97; Calderwood 2018; Cruz 2018, pp. 103–23; Parrilla 2018, pp. 229–42; López-Calvo 2019, pp. 274–8; Civantos 2020, pp. 598–619; Brann 2021, pp. 172–94.

16 For the argument that traces the beginnings of the Renaissance in Europe to al-Andalus, see Chejne 1980, pp. 110–33; Recapito 1998, pp. 55–74.

17 See al-Juʿaydī 2000, p. 17.

Al-Andalus is a universal aesthetic and artistic property, but Jerusalem is an aesthetic, spiritual and juristic property."[18] In his *Mazāmīr* (*Psalms*),[19] Darwīsh says:

أداعب الزّمن
كأمير يلاطف حصانا
وألعب بالأيّام
كما يلعب الأطفال بالخرز الملوّن

إنّي أحتفل اليوم

بمرور يوم على اليوم السّابق

وأحتفل غدا
بمرور يومين على الأمس
وذكرى اليوم القادم

وهكذا ... أواصل حياتي!

عندما سقطت عن ظهر حصاني الجامح
وانكسرت ذراعي
قبل ألف سنة!
أوجعتني إصبعي الّتي جرحت

وعندما أحييت ذكرى الأربعين لمدينة عكّا
أجهشت في البكاء على غرناطة
وعندما التفّ حبل المشنقة حول عنقي
كرهت أعدائي كثيرا
لأنهم سرقوا ربطة عنقي.

I flirt with Time
As a prince caresses a horse.
And I play with the days
As children play with colored beads.

Today I celebrate
The passing of a day from the previous one
And tomorrow I shall celebrate
The passing of two days from yesterday.
I drink the toast of yesterday

18 Al-Ju'aydī 2000, p. 36.
19 Darwīsh 1988, pp. 396–7.

In remembrance of the day to come
And thus do I carry on my life!

When I fell from my indomitable horse
And broke an arm
My finger, wounded a thousand years ago,
Caused me pain!

When I commemorated the passing of forty days in the city of Acre,
I burst out weeping for Granada
And when the rope of the gallows tightened around my neck
I felt a deep hatred for my enemies
Because they stole my tie.[20]

One of the prominent themes in Darwīsh's poetry after the Israeli invasion of Lebanon in 1982 is the use of al-Andalus as a mirror for Palestine.[21] His series of poems titled "Aḥada 'Ashara Kawkaban 'alā Ākhir al-Mashhad al-Andalusī" ("Eleven Stars at the End of the Andalusian Scene"), from the collection *Aḥada 'Ashara Kawkaban*, is one long repetition of the equation al-Andalus = Palestine = paradise lost. Apart from clear allusion to the advent of the miseries of the "present" following the end of the "Andalusian scene," the title also "justifies" this end by evoking the biblical and Qur'ānic story of Joseph and his brothers (see below). Significantly, Darwīsh published the collection in 1992, that is, five hundred years after the end of Arab rule in al-Andalus when on January 2, 1492 the combined armies of Castile and Aragon captured the city of Granada, which was followed by a royal edict that decreed the expulsion of all non-Catholics from the peninsula. The fourth star-poem is called "Anā Wāḥid min Mulūk al-Nihāya" ("I Am One of the Kings of the End"):

... وأَنا واحِدٌ مِنْ مُلوكِ النِّهاية. أَقْفِزُ عَنْ
فَرَسي في الشّتاء الأخيرِ، أنا زَفْرَةُ الْعَرَبيِّ الأخيرَة [...]
لَمْ يَبْقَ لي حاضِرٌ
كَيْ أَمُرَّ غدًا قُرب أَمْسي. سَتَرفَعُ قَشْتالَةُ
تاجَها فَوْقَ مِئْذَنَة الله. أَسْمَعُ خَشْخَشَةً للْمَفاتيحِ في
بابِ تاريخنا الذَّهَبيِّ، وداعًا لِتاريخنا، هَلْ أَنا
مَنْ سَيُغْلِقُ باب السَّماءِ الأَخيرَ؟ أَنا زَفْرةُ الْعربَيِّ الأخيرَة.

[20] Darwish 1980, p. 50.

[21] One of the first uses of al-Andalus as a mirror for Palestine appeared in 1910, when the Damascene *al-Muqtabas*, edited by Muḥammad Kurd 'Alī (1876–1953), wrote: "We fear that the new settler will expel the indigenous [population] and we will have to leave our country en masse. We shall then be looking back over our shoulder and mourn our land as did the Muslims of Andalusia" (*al-Muqtabas*, March 15, 1910, as quoted in Yazbak 1998, p. 221).

... and I am one of the Kings of the end. Jumping from
My horse in the last Winter, I am the last Arab man's sigh ...
There is no present remaining for me,
So I could pass near my past. Castile is raising her
Crown over Allāh's minaret. I hear the rattling of keys in
The door of our golden history, good-bye our history, will it be me
Who will close the last gate of heaven? I am the last Arab man's sigh.[22]

As against the glory of the past, which elicits the image of al-Andalus in the present, the only remaining hope in this long poor "present" that has been enduring for more than five hundred years is survival. Al-Andalus is a mere mirage:

إِلَى أَيْنَ نَذْهَبُ بَعْدَ الحُدُودِ الأخِيرَةِ؟ أَيْنَ تَطِيرُ العَصَافِيرُ بَعْدَ السَّمَاءِ
الأَخِيرَةِ أَيْنَ تَنَامُ النَّباتَاتُ بَعْدَ الهَوَاءِ الأخِيرِ؟

Where should we go after the last border? Where do the birds fly after the last
Sky? Where do the plants sleep after the last breeze?[23]

For the time being:

قطعنا ثلاثين بحرًا وستّين ساحلْ
وما زال في العمر وقتٌ لنشرُد

Thirty seas have we passed, and sixty shores
And our days of wandering continue.[24]

Each abode is a temporary shelter in a "series of moveable shelters."[25] "My bundle is my village,"[26] declares one woman in Athens airport. The men are despairing:

وَقُلْنَا لِزَوْجَاتِنَا: لِدْنَ مِنَّا مِئَات السِّنِين لِنُكمل هَذَا الرَّحِيلْ
إِلَى سَاعَةٍ مِنْ بِلادٍ، وَمِتْرٍ مِنَ المُسْتَحِيلْ.

We said to our wives: yield us offspring for hundreds of years so we can
complete this journey.
Toward an hour of a land, and a meter of the impossible.[27]

The airport becomes a crossroads of repressed desires and frequent frustrations:

22 Darwīsh 1992, pp. 15–16.

23 Darwīsh 1987a, p. 17. For a translation of the entire poem, see Darwish 2003, p. 9. For a German translation, see Darwisch 1996, p. 19.

24 Darwīsh 1986, p. 43.

25 Darwīsh 1987, p. 73; Darwish 1995, p. 90.

26 Darwīsh 1987a, p. 23.

27 Darwīsh 1987a, p. 21. For another translation, see Darwish 2003, p. 11.

مَطَارُ أَثِينَا يُوزِّعُنَا لِلْمَطَارَاتِ. قَالَ الْمُقَاتِلُ: أَيْنَ أُقَاتِلُ؟ صَاحَتْ بِهِ حَامِلٌ: أَيْنَ أُهْدِيكِ طِفْلَكِ؟ قَالَ الْمُوَظَّفُ: أَيْنَ أُوَظِّفُ مَالِي؟ فَقَالَ الْمُثَقَّفُ: مَالِي وَمَالَكَ؟ قَالَ رِجَالُ الْجَمَارِكِ: مِنْ أَيْنَ جِئْتُمْ؟ أَجَبْنَا: مِنَ الْبَحْرِ. قَالُوا: إِلَى أَيْنَ تَمْضُونَ؟ قُلْنَا: إِلَى الْبَحْرِ. قَالُوا: وَأَيْنَ عَنَاوِينُكُمْ؟ قَالَتِ امْرَأَةٌ مِنْ جَمَاعَتِنَا: بُقْجَتِي قَرْيَتِي. فِي مَطَارِ أَثِينَا انْتَظَرْنَا سِنِينًا. تَزَوَّجَ شَابٌّ فَتَاةً وَلَمْ يَجِدَا غُرْفَةً لِلزَّوَاجِ السَّرِيعِ. تَسَاءَلَ: أَيْنَ أَفُضُّ بَكَارَتَهَا؟ فَضَحِكْنَا وَقُلْنَا لَهُ: يَا فَتًى، لَا مَكَانَ لِهَذَا السُّؤَالِ.

> Athens Airport distributes us to airports. Where will I fight? Asked the fighter.
>   A pregnant
> Woman shrieked to him: where will I bear your child ...
> Where did you come from? Asked the customs officials. We responded:
> From the sea. And where are you heading? They asked. To the sea. We said ...
> A young lad married a maiden, but they could not find any place for a hasty
>   marriage.
> Where will I pierce her maidenhood? He wondered.
> But we laughed and said: O lad, there is no place for such a question.[28]

A Palestinian man has been shunted about from emigration to exile, from sea to desert, from detention camp to slaughter:

هكذا يواجه الفلسطينيّ أسئلة أخرى مضافة إلى أسئلة الحرّيّة والاستقلال، يواجه سؤال المكوث الإنسانيّ العادي على أرض البشر: إلى أين يذهب؟ أين يلد؟ أين ينام؟ أين يعمل؟ أين يتعلّم؟ أين يحبّ؟ أين يكتب الشعر؟ أين يدفن؟

Thus, the Palestinian man confronts other questions besides those of freedom and independence, the questions of normal human existence on the face of the earth: Where to go? Where to give birth? Where to sleep? Where to work? Where to learn? Where to love? Where to write poems? And where to be buried?[29]

Meanwhile:

نَسِيرُ إِلَى بَلَدٍ لَيْسَ مِنْ لَحْمِنَا، لَيْسَ مِنْ عَظْمِنَا شَجَرُ الْكَسْتَنَاءِ
وَلَيْسَتْ حِجَارَتُهُ مَاعِزًا فِي نَشِيدِ الْجِبَالِ. وَلَيْسَتْ عُيُونُ الْحَصَى سَوْسَنًا
نَسِيرُ إِلَى بَلَدٍ لَا يُعَلِّقُ شَمْسًا خُصُوصِيَّةً فَوْقَنَا

> We go toward a land not of our flesh. The chestnut trees are not of our bones
> And its stones are not a goat in the mountain hymn, the gravel's eyes are not
>   roses
> We go toward a land where a personal sun does not shine above us.[30]

---

[28] Darwīsh 1987a, p. 23. For another translation, see Darwish 2003, p. 12. For a German translation, see Darwisch 1996, p. 25.
[29] *Al-Karmil* 18 (1985), p. 216.
[30] Darwīsh 1987a, p. 19. For a translation of the entire poem, see Darwish 2003, p. 10. For a German translation, see Darwisch 1996, p. 21.

What an irony, after being expelled from Beirut and Tripoli, thousands of miles away, to find refuge in Aden, a place named for the Garden of Eden. "We went to Aden," says the poet:

ذَهَبْنَا إِلَى جِنَّةِ الفُقَرَاءِ الفَقِيرَةِ، نَفْتَحُ نَافِذَةً فِي الحَجَرِ
لَقَدْ حَاصَرَتْنَا القَبَائِلُ، يَا صَاحِبِي، وَرَمَتْنَا المِحَنُ،
وَلَكِنَّنَا لَمْ نُقَايِضْ رَغِيفَ العَدُوِّ بِخُبْزِ الشَّجَرِ

We went to the poverty-stricken paradise of the poor people, so as to open a window in the stone.
The tribes besieged us, O my friend, and cast us into tribulations,
Nevertheless we didn't exchange the bread of the trees for the enemy's loaf.[31]

Rather than surrender, they prefer death on the battlefield—"We will write for the thousandth time on the last air: we shall die, but they will not overtake us"[32]—but without losing sympathy for the victims among their enemies:

رَأَيْنَا وُجُوهَ الَّذِينَ سَيَقْتُلُهُمْ فِي الدِّفَاعِ الأَخِيرِ عَنِ الرُّوحِ آخِرُنَا
بَكَيْنَا عَلَى عِيدِ أَطْفَالِهِم. وَرَأَيْنَا وُجُوهَ الَّذِينَ سَيَرْمُونَ أَطْفَالَنَا
مِنْ نَوَافِذِ هَذَا الفَضَاءِ الأَخِيرِ. مَرَايَا سَيَصْقُلُهَا نَجْمُنَا.

We saw the faces of those who will be killed in the last defense of the spirit by the last of us.
We wept for their children's holiday. And we saw the faces of those who will throw our children
From the window of this terminal emptiness—mirrors our star will polish.[33]

There is not only despair but self-flagellation: "There is no more hope to be placed in the Arabs. A nation which does not deserve to live. A nation in the image of its rulers."[34] When the fighters were about to leave Beirut in 1982, the question remained whither?

- هل سنخرج حقًّا؟
- سنخرج حقًّا.
- إلى أين؟
- إلى أيّ مكان عربيّ يقبل بنا.
- ألا يقبلون حتى استقبالنا خارجين؟
- بعضهم لا يقبل حتى جثثنا، وأميركا طلبت من بعضهم الموافقة على استقبالنا.
- أميركا؟
- نعم، أميركا.

---

[31] Darwīsh 1987a, p. 47. For a translation of the entire poem, see Darwish 2003, p. 24. For a German translation, see Darwisch 1996, p. 49.
[32] Darwīsh 1987a, p. 35. For a translation of the entire poem, see Darwish 2003, p. 18. For a German translation, see Darwisch 1996, p. 37.
[33] Darwīsh 1987a, p. 17. For a translation of the entire poem, see Darwish 2003, p. 9. For a German translation, see Darwisch 1996, p. 19.
[34] Darwīsh 1987, p. 81; Darwish 1995, p. 100.

- هل تعني أنّ هذا البعض يريدنا أن ننتحر ونبقى في بيروت؟
- هذا البعض يتحمّل صمودنا، ولا يدعونا إلى الانتحار أسوة بالكولونيل اللّيبيّ ولا يريد لنا أن نبقى في بيروت، أو في أيّ مكان على الأرض، يريد لنا أن نخرج أن نخرج من العروبة ومن الحياة.
- إلى أين؟
- إلى العدم!

– Is it true we are leaving?
– We are leaving.
– Where to?
– To any Arab place which will take us.
– Won't they be willing to accept us when we leave?
– Some of them won't even take our corpses. The United States is asking some of them to agree to receive us.
– The United States?
– Yes, the United States.
– Do you mean that [the Arabs] want us to commit suicide and stay in Beirut?
– They can't stand our steadfastness. They aren't telling us to commit suicide, like the Libyan Colonel [Libya's late president Muʿammar Qadhdhāfī (1942–2011)]; they just don't want us to stay in Beirut, or any other place on earth. They want us to leave, to leave Arabism and leave life.
– To leave it for what destination?
– Nothingness![35]

A substantive change has taken place over the years in the attitude of the Arabs:

كان ما يصيب فلسطين يصيب الشّارع العربيّ بعدوى الحزن والصّخب والغضب. كان الشّارع العربيّ يُسقط الحاكم لأيّ مساس بهذا القلب الجماعيّ. الآن يتسابق الحكام ليرشوا الشّارع، ليدفعوه الى التخلّي عن هذا الإجماع. السّلاح العربيّ الرسميّ يتصدّى، علانيّة، للخطوة والفكرة الفلسطينيتيّن وتحمّلهما المسؤوليّة عن بؤس الأمّة وعبوديتها: لولا فلسطين، البعيدة المنال، الوهميّة، المتخيّلة، المبكّرة إلى موعدها البعيد، المتقدّمة على الوحدة العربيّة، لولاها لكنّا أكثر حرية وأوفر رخاء ورفاهيّة!

There were times when a blow to Palestine filled the Arab street with gloom, turmoil and rage. The Arab street would overthrow the ruler for any injury whatsoever to this collective heart. Now, the rulers are in a race to bribe the street in order to make it renege on this consensus. The official Arab weaponry has been turned publicly against Palestinian action and idea and is making them fully responsible for the wretchedness and subjugation of the Arab nation. Were it not for Palestine—the unattainable, the mirage, the imaginary, the one arriving early for its delayed appointment, the one!

[35] Darwīsh 1987, p. 105; Darwish 1995, pp. 132–3.

moving before Arab unity—our freedom would be fuller and our prosperity and comfort greater.[36]

Moreover:

لأنّ فلسطين تطوّرت من وطن إلى شعار ليس للتّطبيق، بل للتّعليق على الأحداث، ولتزويق خطاب الانقلاب، وحّل الأحزاب ومنع زراعة القمح، واستبدال الكدح بالرّبح السّريع، وإلى تطوير صناعة الانقلابات، الثّقيلة منها والخفيفة، إلى أن يعقد القران على آخر حفيدات الخليفة.

Because Palestine has been transformed from a homeland into an empty slogan, a commentary on events, adorning the rhetoric of revolutions, dismantling political parties and preventing the sowing of wheat, the exchange of labor for quick profits, and the development of the industry of revolutions, heavy and light, until the marriage of the last female granddaughters of the Caliph.[37]

The various conferences that convene to discuss the Palestinian tragedy are a source of bitter irony. At one of them, the persona takes the floor to ask:

يا سيّداتي ويا سادتي الطّيّبين: أأرض البشر لجميع البشر
كما تدّعون؟ إذا أين كوخي الصّغير وأين أنا؟

Good ladies and gentlemen: is the earth of Man for every Man
As you claim? Where thus is my little hut, and where am I?

The best that the Arabs could supply is

ثلاث دقائق أخرى، ثلاث دقائق حرّيّة واعترافا. فقد وافق المؤتمر
على حقّنا في الرجوع ككلّ الدّجاج وكلّ الخيول إلى حلم من حجر.
أصافحهم واحدا واحدا، ثمّ أحني لهم قامتي، وأواصل هذا السّفر
إلى بلد آخر، كي أقول كلاما عن الفرق بين السّراب وبين المطر.

Three minutes of freedom and recognition. The conference affirmed
Our right to return, like all chickens and horses, to a dream made of stone.
One by one, I shake their hands, and bow my head, and continue this journey
To another land, to say something about the difference between the mirage
and the rain.[38]

"The Empire of Arabic Words," as described by the Syrian poet Nizār Qabbānī (1923–1998), becomes greater and greater "and our defeats grow bigger ... and our hopes dwindle."[39] Even the Palestinian revolution itself has clearly gone off course:

لعلّ المحاكمة الّتي تستحقّها الثّورة هي أنّها كانت خالية، وما زالت خالية، من تقاليد محاكمة أعضاء القيادة على جرائمهم المدوّية، واقتصرت المحاكمة على تتبّع جنايات أخلاقيّة يرتكبها شهداء

36 Darwīsh 1987, pp. 83–4; Darwish 1995, p. 105.
37 Darwīsh 1987, pp. 39–40; Darwish 1995, p. 49.
38 Darwīsh 1987a, p. 25. For a translation of the entire poem, see Darwish 2003, p. 13. For a German translation, see Darwisch 1996, p. 27.
39 *Al-Mustaqbal*, May 29, 1983, pp. 6–7.

المستقبل خلال بحثهم عن متعة عابرة في سيجارة حشيش أو امرأة تغوي، قبل أن يتحوّلوا إلى منصّة للخطابة

> Perhaps it is appropriate to judge the revolution for its absence of a tradition for judging its leadership's crimes, which cry out to heaven. Instead, the judging was limited to following the moral crimes of the future martyrs while pursuing the transitory pleasures of a hashish cigarette or seductive women, before their bodies become a podium for speeches.[40]

But, as the poet describes in an earlier collection, there will be harder days ahead as, for example, mentioned in another poem, which opens with the following line:

هُنَالِكَ لَيْلٌ أَشَدُّ سَوَادًا هنالك وَرْدٌ أَقَلُّ

> There will be blacker night. There will be fewer roses.

And concludes with the line:

وَلَكِنَّنِي سَأُتَابِعُ مَجْرَى النَّشِيدِ، وَلَوْ أَنَّ وَرْدِي أَقَلُّ.

> Still, I will follow the path of song, even though I have fewer roses.

In another poem, Darwīsh asks his friend to "tear the arteries of my ancient heart with the poem of the gypsies who are going to al-Andalus / and sing to my departure from the sands and the ancient poets."[41] The Palestinian miseries as illustrated in the image of the Andalusian paradise lost are the major stimuli behind the collection *Ward Aqall*, whose poems were written during and in the wake of the 1982 Israeli invasion of Lebanon.

3. "OH, FATHER, I AM JOSEPH"

Ward Aqall, which includes fifty poems, is very coherent and cohesive—like a fifty-verse *qaṣīda*, each poem echoes the same ideas. At the same time, each poem is a microcosm of the entire collection. The Palestinian poet Salmān Maṣālḥa (b. 1953) understood this peculiarity of the collection immediately upon its publication, and he composed a poem that consists of only the titles of the poems.[42] In order to emphasize the collection's cohesion and organic unity, several techniques were employed by Darwīsh on various levels—rhetorical, metrical, graphical, rhythmical, poetic, metapoetic, and mythical:

[40] Darwīsh 1987, pp. 26–7; Darwish 1995, p. 31.
[41] Darwīsh 1985, p. 23.
[42] *Al-Ittiḥād*, July 24, 1987.

Titles: The titles are complete independent clauses from the grammatical point of view (*jumal mufida*), either a nominative one, with a subject and predicate (*jumla ismiyya*: *mubtada'* + *khabar*), or a verbal one, with a verb and subject (*jumla fi'liyya*: *fi'l* + *fā'il*). The title of one poem, "Maṭār Athīnā" ("Athens Airport") (p. 23), is not a complete grammatical clause, but even this title may be read as the predicate of an omitted subject—"[Hādhā] Maṭāru Athīnā." Moreover, it may be understood as a subject whose verb has been omitted, since the function of an airport is to serve as a spatial and temporal transitive point; the first complete independent sentence of the poem reflects this aspect of the airport: "*Maṭār athīnā yuwazzi'unā li-l-maṭārāt*" ("Athens airport disperses us to other airports"). Each title consists of between two and six words—all of which are taken from the first part of the first line. Only the titles of six poems are not precisely the first words of the poems, but the changes herein are minor. An examination of the few deviations reveals what was important to the poet from the standpoint of the poem and the structure of the title.

First, he wanted very short and condensed titles, for example, in "Yaḥiqqu Lanā an Nuḥibba al-Kharīfa" ("We Have the Right to Love Autumn") (p. 25) the first words are "*Wa-Naḥnu* Yaḥiqqu Lanā an Nuḥibba *Nihāyāti hādhā* al-Kharīfi." Three words were omitted because the title would have been too long. In another poem, "Ilāhī Limādhā Takhallayta 'annī?" ("My God, Why Hast Thou Forsaken Me?") (p. 81), the first words of the poem are "*Ilāhī Ilāhī* Limādhā Takhallayta 'annī?" One word was omitted. In "Astaṭī'u al-Kalāma 'ani al-Ḥubbi" ("I Can Talk about Love") (p. 99), the first words are "*Wa-Hā-Anadhā* 'Astaṭī'u al-Kalāma 'ani al-Ḥubbi." In "Nu'rrikhu Ayyāmanā bi-l-Farāshi" ("We Write the History of Our Days with Butterflies") (p. 105), the first words are "Nu'rrikhu Ayyāmanā bi-Farāshi *al-Ḥuqūli*."

Second, the internal music of the poem was important to the poet, and in one case he prefers to add a word to the first lines of the poem that is not essential for conveying the meaning: in "Ṣahīlun 'alā al-Safḥi" ("Neighing at the Foot of the Mountain") (p. 37), the first words are "Ṣahīlu *al-Khuyūli* 'alā al-Safḥi." The title is much more poetic and condensed, and there is no need to mention *al-Khuyūl*, since *Ṣahīl* conveys the same meaning, but without this word the first line would have been devoid of the musical dimension it has now: the line may be divided into two parts—as if they were two hemistichs of a classical verse in a *qaṣīda* (*ṣadr* and *'ajuz*). In addition, the same line is repeated in line 4; in line 9, there is a variation of the line but with the same musicality. This line thus serves as a sort of *lāzima*, a kind of key sentence that combines the various elements of the poem into a single entity, as can be seen in the following transliterated version:

(1) **Ṣahīlul**Khu**yūli** alāl-Saf**ḥi**, immāl**hubūṭu** wa-immāl**ṣu'ūdu**.
(4) **Ṣahīlul**Khu**yūli** alāl-Saf**ḥi**, immāl**hubūṭu** wa-immāl**ṣu'ūdu**.
(9) **Ṣahīlul**Khu**yūli** alāl-Saf**ḥi**, immāl**ṣu'ūdu** wa-immāl**ṣu'ūdu**.

The alternation of the short and long vowels of i/ī and u/ū may be seen as a kind of simulation of the movement of the horses at the foot of the mountain.

Meter: All the poems use "free verse" (*shi'r ḥurr*),[43] but what is highly peculiar in this collection is that a single foot (*taf'īla*), that of the *mutaqārib* meter (U — —), is used throughout all the poems. This is a rare phenomenon in Arabic poetry. Ever since ancient times, poets have generally used various meters for different poems included in the same poetry collection (in the case of the classical *qaṣīda*), and various feet (in the case of collection of poems using *shi'r ḥurr*) when they were writing poetry on the same theme. Here, Darwīsh uses the same single foot for all the poems, as if to direct the attention of the reader to the peculiarly unified character of the collection. Of course, this unity of the meter enabled Salmān Maṣālḥa to compose a poem from the titles of the collection's poems, serving as a kind of summary of the collection.

Graphic appearance: The poems share approximately the same graphic design; the length and number of lines are very similar. Of the total, forty-three poems have ten lines; four poems have eleven lines; two poems have thirteen lines; and one poem has nine lines. Most of the poems pretend to be prose paragraphs, far away from the traditional structure of the *qaṣīda* or even the familiar structure of the *shi'r ḥurr* with its short lines.

Rhymes: Various rhyme schemes are used, but in all cases the rhyming is functional and by no means dictates the meaning, as we frequently find in traditional poetry when a "successful" rhyme may tempt the poet to use it even if it does not help express the desired meaning. Darwīsh's rhymes are very simple, and sometimes the reader feels that they emerge naturally and effortlessly. None of the rhymes may be attributed to a kind of *ḥashw* ("stuffing") so frequently found in classical and neoclassical poems. From the point of view of their various rhyme schemes, the poems in the collection may be divided into the following groups:

[43] Called also *shi'r al-taf'īla*, the essential concept of which entails a reliance on free repetition of the basic unit of conventional Arab prosody (i.e., the use of an irregular number of a single foot [*taf'īla*] instead of a fixed number of feet). The poet varies the number of feet in a single line and the rhymes at the end of the lines according to his need.

Mono-rhyme poems: Eight poems pretend to be a one-rhyme classical *qaṣīda*; three of them have one united rhyme (pp. 19 [*nā*], 25 [*ar*], 103 [*minā*]). In two poems, one united rhyme is used (pp. 35 [*ru*], 45 [*lu*]) but the last line of each poem is separated from the other lines. In two cases, the poems are strophic but with one rhyme (pp. 99 [*dī*], 101 [*lā*]). In one poem, the united rhyme (*dah* with one case of *hā*) is broken by the last line—which does not share the same rhyme—in order to emphasize the voice of the poem (the last word is *waṭan* ["homeland"]) (p. 13). Thirteen poems use rhyme schemes with only two different rhymes:

ABBABBBBBA (p. 5).
AABBAABBAA (pp. 21 [*ar* / *il*], p. 31 [*mu* / *ihim*]).
ABABABABAB (pp. 27 [*ah* / *mā*], p. 29 [*ad* / *am*], 57 [*at* / *ah*]).
ABBABBAAA (p. 37 [*du* / *ar*]).
AABAABAABB (p. 43 [*a'* / *ah*]).
ABA/BAB/ABA/B (p. 47 [*ar* / *an*]).
ABABABABA/B (p. 91 [*ah* / *aq*]).
AABABBAABA (p. 49 [*iī* / *lak*]).
AABBAAB/BBA (p. 51 [*aā* / *qā*]).
ABAABBABBA (p. 61 [*a'a*]).
ABBABBBBBA (p. 69 [*ah* / *an*]).
AB/BA/AB/BA/BA (p. 83 [*ab* / *lah*]).
ABBBAABAAB (p. 97 [*sī* / *ad*]).

Trio-rhyme poems: Eight poems use rhyme schemes with three different rhymes:

ABABABABCA (p. 7).
AABCAACAAA (p. 15).
ABACBABAAAA (p. 55).
AABA/AACAAA (p. 73).
ABACADAABA (p. 75).
ABBABBBCA (p. 81 [A = Maryam]).
AAA/BBA/CCA/A (p. 85).
ABBBBBCBBB (p. 93).

Quadro-rhyme poems: Seven poems use rhyme schemes with four rhymes:

ABCBCBBBDB (p. 9).
ABBBBBCDBB (p. 17).

AAA/BBB/CCD/D (p. 39).
A/BCDDDDDD/D (p. 65).
ABCABADAAA (p. 71).
ABBBBCDEBB (p. 79).
ABCCCC/CCDD (p. 89).

Casual rhymes: Two poems use only casual rhyming:

ABCBDEBFBFBF (p. 53).
ABCBCDCEF/A (p. 59).

Unique scheme: One poem has three stanzas, each of them beginning with the same sentence ("*'alā hādhihi al-arḍ mā yastaḥiqqu al-ḥayāt*"), and the end of each stanza rhymes with this sentence ("*āt*"). Each stanza is a kind of long line divided by the computer into three or four lines according to the format of the page (p. 11).

No rhymes: Seven poems are without any rhyming; six of them are structured like prose poems printed like prose text, when the computer generally decides the number of lines according to the format of the page, but unlike them they have the same foot of the *mutaqārib* meter (U — —) (pp. 23, 33, 41, 63, 77, 87). In one poem, the lines are printed like free verse but without rhyming at all (p. 95).

Poetic, meta-poetic, and mythical dimensions: All the poems are linked to one another by the persona, who is a representative of a collective but who is at the same time a persona suffering on behalf of other members of this collective because he has been chosen as their poetic proxy. It means that not only the reality is represented but also the manner of representation is also questioned, including issues related to the value of poetry and its relationship to universal questions. Two poems in the collection provide the persona with mythical foundations through two biblical myths, the first of them being "Yu'āniqu Qātilahu" ("He Embraces His Murderer"), which appears as poem number 15 in the collection:

يعانق قاتله كي يفوز برحمته: هل ستغضب منّي كثيرا إذا ما نجوتُ
أخي ... يا أخي! ما صنعتُ لتغتالني؟ فوقنا طائران فصوّب إلى
فوق! أطلق جحيمك أبعد مني ... تعال إلى كوخ أمّي لتطبخ من أجلك
الفول. ماذا تقول؟ وماذا تقول؟ مللت عناقي ورائحتي. هل تعبت من
الخوف فيّ؟ إذن، إرم هذا المسدّس في النّهر! ماذا تقول: عدوّ على
ضفّة النّهر صوّب رشّاشه في اتّجاه العناق؟ إذن أطلق النّار نحو العدو
لننجو معا من رصاص العدوّ، وننجو من الإثم. ماذا تقول؟ ستقتلني كي

يعود العدو إلى بيته / بيتنا وتعود إلى لعبة الكهف، ماذا صنعتَ بقهوة
أمّي وأمّك؟ ماذا جنيتُ لتغتالني يا أخي. لن أحلّ وثاق العناق
لن أتركك!

He embraces his murderer in order to win his compassion: Will you be much angry if I survive?
My brother, oh my brother! What did I do that you want to kill me? Two birds are overhead—shoot
Upward! Shoot your hell far away from me. Come to my mother's hut so she may cook for you broad beans.
What do you say? What is that you say? You grow tired of my embrace and my smell. Are you tired of
The fear within me? So throw your revolver in the river! What do you say? There is an enemy on
The riverbank aiming his machine gun at our embrace? So shoot toward the enemy so that
We may avoid the enemy's bullets and avoid falling into sin. What do you say? You will kill me so
The enemy can go to his own home / our home and you can return to the game of the cave. What
Have you done with the coffee of my mother and your mother? What crime did I commit that you want to kill me, oh my brother? I will never unleash the tie of the embrace,
I will never leave you![44]

Embracing his brother, Cain, who is about to slay him, Abel is not ready to relent, striving desperately to elicit his brother's mercy.[45] The intertextual allusion to the ancient myth is reinforced by the sentence "Two birds are overhead"—an allusion to the Qur'ānic story about Cain and Abel, when God sent a crow to scratch in the earth and show Cain how he might hide his brother's shame.[46] In the poem, a rhetorical question is repeated in two modes: "*mā ṣana'tu li-taghtalanī?*" (line 2) and "*mādhā janaytu li-taghtalanī?*" (line 9)—the murder foretold has no rationale at all. At the same time, the speaker is eager to hear his brother reply, and so repeats the question "*mādhā taqūlu?*" four times in this short poem, but his brother utters no reply and the poem concludes with an exclamation mark—the speaker has been slain by his brother and his last cry—"I will never leave you!"—is in fact also a curse, the Curse of Cain.

44 Darwīsh 1987a, p. 33. For a freer translation that omits several sentences, see Darwish 2003, p. 17. For a German translation, see Darwisch 1996, p. 35.

45 On the story of Cain and Abel in ancient sources, see Busse 1998, pp. 68–70. On this story as an archetypal conflict in classical and modern Arabic literature, see Günther 1999, pp. 309–36.

46 Al-Mā'ida 30–34.

In a certain way, *Chronicle of a Death Foretold* by Gabriel Garcia Marquez (1927–2014) is here recalled, the story of a murder everyone knows about before it happens—with the exception of the murdered man, Santiago Nasar.[47] But unlike in Marquez's novel, in Darwīsh's poem the victim does know of his impending murder and demands an explanation for it—in fact, he is more concerned with plumbing the murderer's motives than in preventing the murder itself. As in Marquez's novel, everyone knows the murder is going to happen but no one intervenes to stop it. Why not? The more that the reader learns, the less he understands, and as the story races toward its inexplicable conclusion, an entire society is placed on trial. Elsewhere, Darwīsh mentions a "knight who stabs his brother / with a dagger in the name of the homeland."[48]

In another poem, number 37 in the collection, "Anā Yūsuf Yā Abī" ("Oh, Father, I Am Joseph"), the persona, Joseph, complains to his father that his brothers want to kill him:

أنا يوسف يا أبي. يا أبي، إخوتي لا يحبّونني، لا يريدونني بينهم يا
أبي. يعتدّون عليّ ويرمونني بالحصى والكلام. يريدونني أن أموت لكي
يمدحوني. وهم أوصدوا باب بيتك دوني. وهم طردوني من الحقل. هم
سمّموا عنبي يا أبي. وهم حطّموا لعبي يا أبي. حين مرّ النّسيم ولاعب
شعري غاروا وثاروا عليّ وثاروا عليك، فماذا صنعتُ لهم يا أبي؟
الفراشات حطّت على كتفيّ، ومالت عليّ السّنابل، والطير حلّق فوق
يديّ. فماذا فعلتُ أنا يا أبي، ولماذا أنا؟ أنت سمّيتني يوسفا، وهمو
أوقعوني في الجبّ، واتّهموا الذّئب؛ والذّئب أرحم من إخوتي، أبت!
هل جنيتُ على أحد عندما قلتُ إنّي رأيت أحد عشر كوكبا، والشّمس
والقمر، رأيتهم لي ساجدينْ.

Oh, Father, I am Joseph. Oh, Father, my brothers neither love me nor want me in their midst, oh
Father, they assault me and cast stones and words at me. They want me to die so
They can eulogize me. They closed the door of your house and left me outside. They expelled me from the field. Oh, Father, they
Poisoned my grapes. They destroyed my toys, oh, Father. When the gentle wind played with my
Hair they were jealous, they flamed up with rage against me and against you. What did I do to them, oh, Father?
The butterflies landed on my shoulder, the wheat spikes bent down toward me and the birds hovered over
My hands. What have I done, oh, Father? And why me? You named me Joseph and they

[47] Marquez 1983.
[48] Darwīsh 1985, p. 136.

Threw me into the well and accused the wolf, and the wolf is more merciful than my brothers, oh, Father!
Did I wrong anyone when I said: "I saw eleven stars, and the sun and the moon; I saw them bowing down before me."[49]

The persona addresses his father stating "I *am* Joseph," as if the father does not know his own son, and he complains about the brothers who assault him—the dialectical tension is thus between the son, the father, and the brothers. The father somehow shares responsibility for the persona's fate because *he* named him Joseph and by doing so caused his misery.[50] The last words of the poem employ the fourth verse from *Surat Yūsuf*, in which Joseph addresses his father Jacob (both of them revered in Islam as prophets):

إِذْ قَالَ يُوسُفُ لِأَبِيهِ يَا أَبَتِ إِنِّي رَأَيْتُ أَحَدَ عَشَرَ كَوْكَبًا، وَالشَّمْسَ وَالْقَمَرَ رَأَيْتُهُمْ لِي سَاجِدِينَ

When Joseph said to his father, "Father, I saw eleven stars, and the sun and the moon; I saw them bowing down before me."

The singer Mārsīl Khalīfa (Marcel Khlife) (b. 1940), who earned a cult following in the Arab world and the diaspora through his nationalistic songs during the Lebanese Civil War, set the poem to music and sang it.[51] Besides the repetition of sentences, only minor changes were introduced to the lyrics: *ʿindamā* instead of *ḥīna*; *aqfalū* instead of *awṣadu*; *katifi* instead of *katifayya*; *ṣanaʿtu* instead of *faʿltu*; and *wahum* instead of *wahumū*. One sentence was omitted: "*wa-hum ḥaṭṭamū luʿabī, yā abī*" ("They destroyed my toys, oh, Father"). But the song does not follow the order of narration of the original poem, and so the division of lines in the poem is:

عندما مرّ النّسيم ولاعب شعري،
غاروا وثاروا،
عندما مرّ النّسيم ولاعب شعري،
غاروا وثاروا، غاروا وثاروا، عليّ وثاروا عليك،
فماذا صنعتُ لهم يا أبي؟
أنا يوسف يا أبي،
أنا يوسف يا أبي، يا أبي،

49 Darwīsh 1987a, p. 77. For another translation, see Butt 2021, pp. 233–4. For a German translation, see Darwisch 1996, p. 79. On the story of Joseph (Yūsuf) in the ancient sources, see Busse 1998, pp. 88–92; Tottoli 2002, pp. 28–31. On this story as employed in modern Arabic literature, see Hartman 2002; al-Musawi 2020, p. 169.
50 For a study of the poem, see Ḥamza 2004, pp. 52–6.
51 The song was released on the album *Rakwat ʿArab* (*Arabic Coffeepot*) (Nagam Records, 1995). Khalīfa divided the song into four stanzas with short musical intervals between them; the duration of the song is 6 minutes and 30 seconds, and the division is as follows: musical prologue (21 seconds); first stanza (1 minute and 8 seconds); musical interval (7 seconds); second stanza (1 minute and 9 seconds); musical interval (13 seconds); third stanza (2 minutes); musical interval (19 seconds); and fourth stanza (1 minute and 32 seconds).

إخوتي لا يحبّونني، لا يريدونني بينهم،
آه يا أبي.

يعتدّون عليّ ويرمونني بالحصى والكلام،
يريدونني أن أموت لكي يمدحوني،
وهم أقفلوا باب بيتك دوني،
وهم طردوني من الحقل،
وهم سمّموا عنبي يا أبي، يا أبي، يا أبي، يا أبي،
أنا يوسف يا أبي،
أنا يوسف يا أبي، يا أبي،
إخوتي لا يحبّونني، لا يريدونني بينهم،
آه، يا أبي.

الفراشات حطّت على كتفي، ومالت عليّ السّنابل،
والطّير حلّق فوق يديّ،
فماذا صنعتُ أنا يا أبي، يا أبي، ولماذا أنا؟
فماذا صنعتُ أنا يا أبي، أبي، ولماذا أنا؟
أنت سمّيتني يوسفا، يا أبي، يا أبي،
أنت سمّيتني يوسفا، يا أبي، يا أبي،
أنت سمّيتني يوسفا، يا أبي، يا أبي،
أنت سمّيتني يوسفا، يا أبي، يا أبي،
وهم أوقعوني في الجبّ، واتّهموا الذئب،
والذئب أرحم من إخوتي،
أبت! أبت، يا أبت!
أبت! أبت، يا أبت!
آه
أبت! أبت، يا أبت!
أبت! أبت، يا أبت!

هل جنيتُ على أحد عندما قلت أنّي
رأيتُ أحد عشر كوكبا، والشّمس والقمر، رأيتهم لي ساجدينْ،
رأيتُ أحد عشر كوكبا، والشّمس والقمر، رأيتهم لي ساجدينْ،
رأيتُهم لي ساجدينْ،
رأيتُهم لي ساجدينْ، آه
لي ساجدينْ، آه
ساجدينْ.

In September 1996, the chief prosecutor of Beirut charged Khalīfa with blasphemy for allegedly "insulting Islam" by singing the Qur'ānic verse,[52] but

[52] While some Muslim clerics maintain that all singing of the Qur'ān is forbidden, others have had no qualms about making lyrical recordings of the Qur'ān, and tapes of clerics singing Islam's holy book can be bought in many places. Also, Qur'ānic verses, whether in the original Arabic, or translated into Persian, have been routinely used in Iranian revolutionary songs since 1978. According to early Islamic tradition, listening to the recital of the Qur'ān

following the protests of many Lebanese Muslim and Christian poets, writers, and journalists, the Lebanese Prime Minister Rafīq al-Ḥarīrī (1944–2005) ordered that the lawsuit against Khalīfa be dismissed.[53]

Darwīsh's poem depicts a relationship between the persona and the collective similar to that presented in "He Embraces His Murderer," as well as showing a similar degree of astonishment as to why the persona's life should be in danger; the same kind of questions are presented here: "*fa-mādhā fa'ltu anā yā abī?*" (line 5) and "*hal janaytu 'alā aḥadin?*" (line 9). The latter is nearly the same wording as the second hemistich of a famous verse by the ascetic poet Abū al-'Alā' al-Ma'arrī (973–1057 CE), which he wished to have inscribed on his grave: "*hādhā janāhu abī 'alayya wamā janaytu 'alā aḥad*" ("This wrong was done by my father to me, but never by me to another").[54] Because al-Ma'arrī's ascetic proclivity made him angry at his father for having sired him, he therefore abstained from sexual congress so as not to spawn any offspring of his own. Darwīsh stresses the evil inflicted on Abel and Joseph by their own fathers—and both of them, Adam and Jacob, are considered in Islam as prophets—through an allusion to al-Ma'arrī's verse.

The two aforementioned myths, together with the above series of poems titled "Aḥada 'Ashara Kawkaban 'alā Ākhir al-Mashhad al Andalusī," which evokes the story of Joseph by recalling the Andalusian lost paradise, are in fact presenting the same theme: the cause of the Palestinians' suffering is not only due to external threats—for example, for the persona, some of his own "friends" even "desire my death in order to say: he was one of us, he was ours."[55] Echoing the desperate cry from "Oh, Father, I Am Joseph"—"They want me to die so / They can eulogize me"—the mission is to protect the martyrs from such eulogy-lovers:

accompanied by music is considered to be a sin of disobedience against God (Kister 1999, p. 61). On the issue of setting verses of the Qur'ān to music, see Baybars 1970, pp. 118–27.

53 Following the case, *Al Jadid* (Los Angeles) published an issue dealing with the freedom of artists, intellectuals, and the media in Lebanon (11 [September 1996]). Among the articles in this issue were "Arab Artists, Intellectuals, Condemn Charges against Khalife as Attack on Liberty, Civil Freedom," by Elie Chalala; "We Turn the Page from City to City," by Marcel Khalīfa; "Marcel Khalife and the Modern Inquisition," by Paul Sha'ūl; and "Lebanese Media Restrictions Stir Broad Opposition," by Michelle A. Marzahn. On the case, see also 'Abd al-Raḥmān 1996, pp. 4–5; *Al Jadid* (Los Angeles) 28 (1999), pp. 7–9, 16. Cf. Snir 2017, pp. 126–9.

54 Ḥusayn 1944, p. 184. Cf. Ḥusayn 1974, pp. 189–90, 306–7.

55 Darwīsh 1987a, p. 41. For another translation into English, see Darwish 2003, p. 21. For a German translation, see Darwisch 1996, p. 43.

عندما يذهب الشّهداء الى النّوم أصحو وأحرسهم من هواة الرّثاء،
أقول لهم: تُصبحون على وطن من سحابٍ ومن شجر، من سراب وماء.
أهنئُهم بالسّلامةِ من حادثِ المُستحيل.

When the martyrs go to sleep, I wake to guard them from the eulogy-lovers;
I say to them: I hope you awaken in a homeland of clouds and trees, of mirage and water.
I wish them well-being from the impossible.[56]

Here the poet-persona in fact confronts the "eulogy-lovers" on the meta-poetic level, one of the main discursive levels in *Ward Aqall.* He addresses his complaint to God, just as Jesus did on the cross:[57]

إلَهي، لِمَاذَا تَخَلَّيْتَ عَنِّي؟ [...]
لِمَاذَا وَعَدْتَ الجُنُودَ بِكَرْمِي الوَحِيدِ. لِمَاذَا؟
وَأَنْزَلْتَ شَعْبَيْنِ مِنْ سُنْبُلَه،
وَزَوَّجْتَنِي فِكْرةً فامْتَثَلْتُ؛ امْتَثَلْتُ تَمَامًا لِحِكْمَتِكَ المُقْبِلَهْ؟
أَطَلَّقْتَنِي؟ أَمْ ذَهَبْتَ لِتُشْفِي سِوَايَ / عَدُوِّي مِنَ المِقْصَلهْ.

My God, my God, why hast thou forsaken me? ...
Why did you promise the soldiers my only vineyard, why? ...
You created two peoples from a single stalk,
You betrothed me to an idea, and I obeyed; I completely obeyed your future wisdom.
Have you divorced me? Or have you hastened to save another, my enemy, from the guillotine?[58]

Against this main theme of the collection, it is obvious why the intertextual allusions and the meta-poetic and meta-mythical dimensions of the collection come to the fore. The following section traces these allusions and dimensions in one poem from the collection.

4. "WILL HOMER BE BORN AFTER US?"

Text and Translation

(0) سيأتي برابرة آخرون

(1) سيأتي برابرة آخرون. ستخطف إمرأة الإمبراطور. سوف تدُقّ الطّبولْ
(2) تُدَقُّ الطّبول لتعلو الخيول على جثث النّاس من بحر إيجا إلى الدّردنيلْ
(3) فما شأننا نحن؟ ما شأن زوجاتنا بسباق الخيول؟

[56] Darwīsh 1987a, p. 43. For another translation into English, see Darwish 2003, p. 22. For a German translation, see Darwisch 1996, p. 45.
[57] Matt. 27:46.
[58] Darwīsh 1987a, p. 81. For a German translation, see Darwisch 1996, p. 83.

(4) ستخطف إمرأة الإمبراطور. سوف تدُقُّ الطّبولْ. ويأتي برابرة آخرونْ
(5) برابرة يملأون فراغ المدائن أعلى قليلا من البحر، أقوى من السّيف وقت الجنونْ
(6) فما شأننا نحن؟ ما شأن أولادنا بسلالة هذا المجونْ؟

(7) وسوف تدُقُّ الطّبولْ. ويأتي برابرة آخرون. وتخطف إمرأة الإمبراطور من بيته
(8) ومن بيته تولد الحملة العسكريّة حتّى تعيد عروس الفراش إلى تخته
(9) فما شأننا نحن؟ ما شأن خمسين ألف قتيل بهذا الزّواج السّريعْ؟

(10) أيولد هومير من بعدنا والأساطير تفتح أبوابها للجميعْ؟

(0) Other Barbarians Will Come

(1) Other Barbarians will come. The Emperor's wife will be abducted. Drums will beat.
(2) Drums will be beaten so that the horses will trample down people's corpses from the Aegean Sea to the Dardanelles.
(3) But what have we got to do with it? What have our wives got to do with this horse race?

(4) The Emperor's wife will be abducted. Drums will beat. And other Barbarians will come.
(5) Barbarians that will fill the vacuum of the cities, somewhat higher than the sea, stronger than the sword in time of madness.
(6) But what have we got to do with it? What have our children got to do with the offspring of this impudence?

(7) And drums will beat. And other Barbarians will come. The Emperor's wife will be abducted from his house.
(8) And from his house the military expedition will be born to bring back the mattress-bride into his Highness's bed.
(9) But what have we got to do with it? What do fifty thousand victims have to do with this quickie marriage?

(10) Will Homer be born after us, and the myths open their gates to all?[59]

Rhetorical Structure

The poem, which uses the same *mutaqārib* meter as the other poems in the collection,[60] consists of ten lines with the following rhyme scheme: AAA/

59 Darwīsh 1987a, p. 39. For other translations, see Darwish 2003, p. 20; Butt 2021, pp. 226–7. For a German translation, see Darwisch 1996, p. 41.

60 Because of the meter, the poet used إمرأة in the Arabic text instead of امرأة, as it grammatically should have been.

BBB/CCD/D—each line ending with a silent vowel (*taskīn*). The lines are arranged in three stanzas, and the last line is isolated as if to form a kind of fourth stanza. Each of the three main stanzas has the same structure:

The first line of each of stanza consists of the same three verbal sentences but in a different order. The three sentences are as follows: "Other Barbarians will come" (a); "The Emperor's wife will be abducted" (b); "Drums will beat" (c).

The second line of each stanza consists of a direct link to the last component of the first line in each stanza (c, a, b, respectively), and then of an action that develops from that link (c).

The third line of each stanza consists of two questions, the first of them identical in all stanzas (e); the second has the same structure and the same broad meaning (f).

The separate last line (g), which is isolated from the main body of the poem, does not have a direct connection to the three stanzas; it is connected by a rhyme with the last line of the third stanza. We can present the rhetorical structure of the poem as follows (the letters illustrate the aforementioned components in each line, and the numeral is a variation of the component):

(a)(b)(c)
(c1)(d1)
(e)(f1)

(b)(c)(a)
(a1)(d2)
(e)(f2)
(c)(a)(b)
(b1)(d3)
(e)(f3)

(g)

Verbs

The use of verbs in the poem betrays a dynamic motion by means of two modes: *taswīf* (henceforth **S**) in order to express the remote future and *muḍāri'* (henceforth **M**) in order to express events in the present or near future. As one reads, the number of verbs denoting the remote future decreases while the number denoting the present and the near future increases as if to reflect the movement of the barbarians toward the persona and the collective that he represents. The first word of the title, which is also the first word of the first line—*sa-ya'tī* (**S**)—alludes to the style of religious texts about the coming of prophets and the Day of Judgment.[61] Together with the second word, it might be understood as future-oriented or as an eschatological myth.[62] In order to show the balance between future and present, what follows is a scheme of the verbs in the poem and their temporal denotation:

(1) *sa-ya'tī* (**S**) / *sa-tukhtafu* (**S**)/ *sawfa taduqqu* (**S**)
(2) *tudaqqu* (**M**) / *li-ta'lū* (**M**)
(3) no verbs

(4) *sa-tukhtafu* (**S**) / *sawfa taduqqu*(**S**) / *wa-ya'tī* (**M**)
(5) *yaml'ūna* (**M**)
(6) no verbs

(7) *sawfa taduqqu* (**S**) / *wa-ya'tī* (**M**) / *wa-tukhtafu* (**M**)
(8) *tuladu* (**M**) / *tu'īda* (**M**)
(9) no verbs

(10) *'a-yuladu* (**M**) / *taftaḥu* (**M**)

In the first stanza, three of the five verbs are in *taswīf*; in the second, only two of four; in the third, only one of five; and neither of the two verbs in the last line denote the remote future. The event in the poem starts off by being in the remote future, but as one reads this future becomes the present. The third line in each stanza is without any verbs at all, as if to show that events that will happen in the remote future have already marked the present. However, although the use of the verbs in the poem reflects the movement of the barbarians toward the persona, the reader is led to the conclusion that the barbarians will not come. The poem has thus two motions: on the thematic, grammatical, and rhetorical levels, the barbarians are advancing, but it is clear that what has already come is only the catastrophe that the emperor wants the people to believe the barbarians are to blame for.

[61] Cf. 'Abd al-Bāqī 1945, p. 6, s.v.; Wensinck and Mensing 1936–1969, I, pp. 9–10. s.v.; Post 1981, pp. 6–7, s.v.

[62] Sivan 1988, p. 9.

Intertextuality

The title of the poem makes several allusions, the most famous of them being to the barbarians who brought about the destruction of the Roman Empire. The barbarians are perceived in the general public discourse as agents of destruction who are teeming at the gates of civilization in order to destroy it. However, due to the marginal status of poetry in the public discourse, it is evident that the poem's mainspring is not a dialogue at the public level but on the meta-poetic one. In this sense, Darwīsh is following in the footsteps of ʿAlī Aḥmad Saʿīd (Adūnīs) (b. 1930), who stated that the readership of the revolutionary Arab poet consists not of consumers (*mustahlikūn*) but of producers (*muntijūn*).[63] Darwīsh's poem thus conducts a dialogue on the meta-poetic level with other texts, the most famous of these being "Waiting for the Barbarians" (1904) by the Greek poet Constantine P. Cavafy (1863–1933):

> What are we waiting for, assembled in the forum?
>
> The barbarians are due here today.
>
> Why isn't anything going on in the Senate?
> Why are the Senators sitting there without legislating?
>
> Because the barbarians are coming today.
> What's the point of senators making laws now?
> When the barbarians are here, they'll do the legislating.
>
> Why did our emperor get up so early,
> And why is he sitting enthroned at the city's main gate,
> In state, wearing the crown?
> Because the barbarians are coming today
> And the emperor's waiting to receive their leader.
> He's even got a scroll to give him,
> Loaded with titles, with imposing names.
>
> Why have our two consuls and praetors come out today
> Wearing their embroidered, their scarlet togas?
> Why have they put on bracelets with so many amethysts,
> Rings sparkling with magnificent emeralds?
> Why are they carrying elegant canes
> Beautifully worked in silver and gold?
>
> Because the barbarians are coming today,
> And things like that dazzle the barbarians.

[63] Adūnīs 1972, pp. 95–6.

Why don't our distinguished orators turn up as usual
To make their speeches, say what they have to say?

Because the barbarians are coming today;
And they're bored by rhetoric and public speaking.

Why this sudden bewilderment, this confusion?
(How serious people's faces have become.)
Why are the streets and squares emptying so rapidly,
Everyone going home lost in thought?

Because night has fallen and the barbarians haven't come.
And some of our men just in from the border say
There are no barbarians any longer.

Now what's going to happen to us without barbarians?
They were, those people, some kind of solution.[64]

Cavafy's barbarians have not come; moreover, some even say that "there are no barbarians any longer," a fact that creates a problem: how will life be without those who were "some kind of solution"? The voice of Darwīsh's poem is very clear: the poem's *other* barbarians—other than Cavafy's barbarians—will not come either, thus leaving the emperor without any solutions. The dialogue that Darwīsh's poem conducts with Cavafy's poem is not only on the meta-poetic level but also on the meta-mythical level. This myth of the barbarians is used by those who have the power to create myths, the poets included, in order to deceive people and divert their attention from true poetry and formative myths. A clear distinction is established between two kinds of poetry and two sorts of myths.[65]

Another intertextual allusion is to the novel *Waiting for the Barbarians* by John Maxwell Coetzee (b. 1940), which also addresses issues of power and justice through the allegory of a war between oppressors and oppressed. The novel is set in an isolated outpost where the magistrate, the novel's narrator, has been a loyal servant of the empire, ignoring constant reports of a threat from the "barbarians" who inhabit the uncharted deserts beyond the village. But when military personnel arrive with captured "barbarians,"

64 Cavafy 1998, pp. 14–15.

65 For an interesting dialogue with Cavafy's poem and Darwīsh's "reading" emphasizing the meta-poetic level, see a poem by the Syrian poet Nūrī al-Jarrāḥ (b. 1956) titled "The Arrival of the Barbarians to Contemporary Trojans" (*al-Jadīd*, September 1, 2021, available at: https://aljadeedmagazine.com, last accessed September 4, 2021). Al-Jarrāḥ's poem may be read against the background of his critical attitude to Darwīsh's personal behavior and poetry (see Snir 2015, pp. 141–5).

we witness an episode that manifests the cruel and unjust attitudes of the empire. Determined to find enemies, Colonel Joll interrogates the prisoners, assuming that acts of the empire, while excessive in force, are necessary to the security of the people. Powerless to prevent the persecution, after the prisoners are released the magistrate finds himself involved in an affair with one of the victims, a girl orphaned by the torturers, begging in the streets, temporarily blinded and crippled as a result of the torture inflicted upon her. The magistrate befriends her and eventually invites her to sleep in his room; the relationship, however, is not based on sexual intimacy but on a deeper psychic, emotional need. They both partake in a relaxing cleansing ritual in which the magistrate washes the girl's body—a symbolic way of washing his hands of the terrible deeds of the oppressors. After the girl's eyesight returns and she regains some use of her feet, the magistrate decides to return the girl to her people. His relationship with the girl—a quixotic act of rebellion—brands him an enemy of the state, and he becomes the newest object of the empire's suspicion.

The narrator, however, is not satisfied with contemplating the events solely on the fictional plane; he is also interested in how these events will be viewed by history:

> What has made it impossible for us to live in time like fish in water, like birds in air, like children? It is the fault of Empire! Empire has created the time of history. Empire has located its existence not in the smooth recurrent spinning time of cycle of the seasons but in the jagged time of rise and fall, of beginning and end, of catastrophe. Empire dooms itself to live in history and plot against history.[66]

The process of perception that the reader passes through in reading the novel is, as Viktor Shklovskij put it, "an aesthetic end in itself"—especially in how Coetzee shows compassion for victims and villains alike. When the narrator is reflecting on the events he witnesses, the reader finds that he too is a witness to the suffering in his own society:

> "When some men suffer unjustly," I said to myself, "it is the fate of those who witness their suffering to suffer the shame of it."[67]

[66] Coetzee 1983, p. 133.
[67] Coetzee 1983, p. 139.

The narrator's conclusion at the end of the story is also relevant to the reader:

> I wanted to live outside the History. I wanted to live outside the History that Empire imposes on its subjects, even its lost subjects. I never wished it for the barbarians that they should have the history of Empire laid upon them. How can I believe that that is cause for shame?[68]

Coetzee's novel—published some years before the publication of Darwīsh's poem—followed in the footsteps of Cavafy's poem and uncovers the use of the myth to deceive and oppress people. The person who tries to confront this process is considered an enemy of the empire, thus deserving to be numbered among the barbarians.

A third intertextual allusion, mainly limited probably to Arab readers, is the destruction of Baghdad by Hulagu in 1258, which has wrongly been engraved on collective Arab memory as the fundamental reason for the destruction of the Arabs' great medieval civilization and the cause of the cultural stagnation of the Arab world until the nineteenth century. Because Hulagu became part of the myth of the anticivilization barbarians, emphasis has been laid by Arab historians and educators on the killing of many of the men of letters in Baghdad and the destruction of cultural institutions and libraries by the Mongol army—even throwing books into the Tigris and using them as a bridge to cross the river. This narrative of the demonic, cruel, and uncivilized Mongols was originally formulated by European Orientalists[69] and later adopted by the Arabs—it can be already found, for example, in a manifesto of Arab nationalists disseminated from Cairo by the Arab Revolutionary Committee at the beginning of the First World War. The manifesto mentioned Genghis and Hulagu who "slaughtered your upright and pure ancestors, destroyed their flourishing civilization, trampled with hooves of their horses on the books of their libraries, or else stopped up the course of the Tigris with the great number of these books which they flung into it." The Turks, according to the manifesto, are descendants of Genghis and Hulagu—"they have destroyed what the ancestors left standing, and have thus prevented Arab civilization from recovering its scattered elements and returning to its former

[68] Coetzee 1983, p. 154.
[69] For example, see D'Ohsson 1834–1835, I, p. 387 (quoted by Browne 1951, II, p. 427); Nicholson 1956, p. 129; Goldziher 1966, p. 141. Cf. Browne 1951, II, p. 463.

glory."[70] Later, this narrative could be found in history books,[71] literary histories,[72] and both poetry and prose.[73]

Arab officials also used the narrative of the destruction of Baghdad by Hulagu for their own ends, as did, for example, Egyptian president Jamāl ʿAbd al-Nāṣir (Gamal Abdel Nasser) (1918–1970) in his *Falsafat al-Thawra* (*The Philosophy of the Revolution*).[74] Also, a Swiss writer on Middle Eastern affairs quotes "a high Syrian government official" as saying "in deadly earnest" that if the Mongols had not burned the libraries of Baghdad in the thirteenth century, "we Arabs would have had so much science, that we would long since have invented the atomic bomb. The plundering of Baghdad put us back centuries."[75] This is, of course, an extreme example, but the thesis that it embodies, as Bernard Lewis elucidates, was not confined to, and was not invented by, romantic nationalist historians. Deriving ultimately from the testimony of contemporary sufferers, it was developed by European Orientalists who saw in the Mongol invasions the final catastrophe that overwhelmed and ended the great Muslim civilization of the Middle Ages. This judgment of the Mongols "was generally accepted among European scholars, and was gratefully, if sometimes surreptitiously, borrowed by romantic and apologetic historians in Middle Eastern countries as an explanation both of the ending of their golden age, and of their recent backwardness."[76]

Yet it is clear that this thesis is quite unjustified, as the signs of the stagnation had appeared long before Hulagu arrived in Baghdad. The successive blows by which the Mongols hewed their way across western Asia, culminating in the sack of Baghdad and the toppling of the independent caliphate, scarcely did more, as H. A. R. Gibb writes, "than give finality to a situation that had long been developing."[77] Even some modern Arab intellectuals and historians feel that this description of the sacking of Baghdad was much exaggerated. Constantine Zurayk (1909–2000), for example, says that "the Arabs had been defeated internally before the Mongols defeated them and

[70] See al-Aʿẓamī 1932, IV, p. 113 (English translation: Haim 1962, p. 86).

[71] For example, see Ghanīm 1938, p. 153; Ḥasan 1967, IV, p. 160; al-Ṣayyād 1968, p. 42; Majīd 1972, p. 291; al-Ālūsī 1987, p. 136.

[72] For example, see Zaydān 1913, III, p. 10; al-Iskandarī and al-ʿInānī 1931, p. 290; ʿAdiyy 1954, I, p. 360; al-Fākhūrī 1954, IV, p. 470; al-Ghazzāwī 1960, pp. 300–1; al-Zayyāt 1960, p. 400; al-Faqqī 1976, pp. 8–9; al-Jundī 1979, I, p. 544; Ḍayf 1983, pp. 240–1.

[73] For example, see Ḥijāzī 1982, pp. 410, 430; al-Ruṣāfī 1986, II, pp. 192–202; al-Qāsim 1987, p. 540; Darwīsh (Zakī) 1989, pp. 67–8; Ḥabīb 1990, pp. 35–41. Cf. ʿIzz al-Dīn 1973, pp. 31–2; Darwīsh 1991, pp. 30–1.

[74] ʿAbd al-Nāṣir n.d. [1955], pp. 45–6, 61.

[75] Hottinger 1957 (as quoted by Lewis 1973, p. 179).

[76] Lewis 1973, p. 179.

[77] Gibb 1962, p. 141. Cf. Smith 1963, p. 40; Wiet 1966, p. 243; Lewis 1968, p. 12; Lewis 1973, pp. 179–98.

that, had those attacks been launched against them when they were in the period of growth and enlightenment, the Mongols would not have overcome them. On the contrary the attacks might have revitalized and re-energized them."[78]

The above allusions use both the linear (the barbarians and Roman Empire; Hulagu) and ironic (Cavafy; Coetzee) modes of intertextuality,[79] but in Arabic literary texts we generally find the barbarians as agents of destruction and devastation, and only rarely do we find them in texts using the ironic mode of intertextuality.[80] Significantly enough, this was also the reading of Darwīsh's "Other Barbarians Will Come" when it was decided that it would be included in the anthology *100 Poets against the War*—first published online in January 2003. The anthology contains a selection from the poems submitted by peace protesters across the world, and features the work of some of the leading contemporary poets and peace activists. The aim was to protest against the American plans to invade Iraq. Darwīsh's poem was given in a translation that does not preserve the structure of the original poem, but still the message was clear:

> Other barbarians will come along.
> The emperor's wife will be abducted.
> Drums will roll.
> Drums will roll and horses will trample a sea of corpses
> All the way from the Aegean to the Dardanelles.
> And why should we care?
> What on earth have our wives got to do with horse races?
>
> The emperor's wife will be abducted.
> Drums will roll.
> And other barbarians will come along.
> The barbarians will take over abandoned cities,
> Settling in just above sea-level,
> Mightier than the sword in an age of anarchy.
> And why should we care?
> What have our children got to do with the progeny of the rabble?
> Drums will roll.
> And other barbarians will come along.
> The emperor's wife will be abducted from the palace.

78 Zurayk 1956, p. 48. See also Gharāyiba 1961, pp. 185–6; Abū al-Khashab n.d., pp. 141–54. Cf. von Grunebaum 1962, p. 255; Lewis 1973, p. 182.

79 On the linear and ironic modes of intertextuality, see Somekh 1991, pp. 53, 61.

80 For example, see the figure of Hulagu in the poem "al-Kutub" ("The Books") by Mīshīl Ḥaddād (1919–1997), first published in *al-Sharq* (Shfaram), January–April 1985, p. 3; incorporated into Ḥaddād 1985, p. 9. On the poem, see Snir 1988a, pp. 9–16.

From the palace a military campaign will be launched
To restore the bride to the emperor's bed.
And why should we care?
What have fifty-thousand corpses got to do with this hasty marriage?

Will Homer be born again?
Will myths ever feature the masses?[81]

In an article published twelve years after the publication of Darwīsh's poem and titled "Barbarians at the Gates,"[82] Edward Said (1935–2003) wrote about the military actions that the United States had been conducting against Iraq "in the guise of sanctioned police action authorised by the United Nations." Said, whose *Orientalism* (1978) undoubtedly inspired Darwīsh's poetry in the 1980s, considered the American actions as part of a "history of reducing whole peoples, countries and even continents to ruin by nothing short of holocaust ... This starts with the native American peoples, 90 per cent of whom were massacred during the first two centuries of this country's life, all in the name of progress, doing God's work and eradicating barbarians." However, in one place Said alludes to the same power relations that structure Darwīsh's poem. Speaking about the Iraqi regime as a government of unprincipled tyranny that has led "the most modern, secular and advanced of Arab countries" into ruin, he says that "neither Saddam Hussein nor his military and political supporters in Iraq are bearing the major brunt of the suffering imposed by the US: it is innocent Iraqi people who are paying the price." Said's conclusion is that serial American aggression embodies "the clash of civilisations, or rather the clash of untrammelled barbarism with civilisation, with a vengeance."

In an article published after Said's death by the Arab-American poet and critic Naomi Shihab Nye (b. 1952),[83] a new dimension to Said's conception is presented. She relates that Said supported a single state solution for Palestine and Israel, writing that "the question is not how to devise means for persisting in trying to separate" Israelis and Palestinians, "but to see whether it is possible for them to live together as fairly and peacefully as possible." She draws attention to the fact that his favorite poem, "Waiting for the Barbarians" by Constantine Cavafy, includes the lines:

> What are we waiting for, assembled in the forum? The barbarians are due here today. Why isn't anything happening in the Senate? Why do the Senators sit there without legislating?

81 Swift 2003, pp. 142–3. The poem was translated by Sarah Maguire with Sabry Hafez.
82 *Al-Ahram Weekly*, March 11–17, 1999.
83 Nye 2004.

Nye thus understands the act of "waiting for the barbarians" as useless—the two sides should be engaged in legislating the single state solution instead of waiting, which only complicates the problem. Unlike the traditional interpretation of Cavafy's poem, the barbarians are conceived by Said, according to Nye, as a destructive force.

The linear mode of intertextuality also uses the myth of the barbarians as a kind of reversal of the well-known Western conception of the Arabs as barbarians. Before the occupation of Iraq by the Americans, Palestinian historian Elias Sanbar (b. 1947), editor-in-chief of *Revue d'études palestiniennes* and translator of some of Darwīsh's works into French, argued that the Americans and Israelis created the barbarians in the image of the Arab and thus "it is certain that the deterioration in Palestine will be permanent ... until this fall when the declared war against Iraq is unleashed. Then Ariel Sharon will hitch his vehicle onto the American convoy, send his provincial legions to be posted at the steps of the Empire 'waiting for the Barbarians' who, refuting the eponymous poems by Cafavy and Darwish this time, will surely arrive by virtue of having been created."[84] Sanbar's argument is supported by the Zionist discourse, two examples of which suffice to show that in this sense Zionism has adhered to the same conception; and the span of time separating them proves that the same attitude remains at the heart of the Zionist toward the Arabs. In 1896, Theodor Herzl (1860–1904), the founder of modern Zionism, wrote about the desire to establish in Palestine a national home for the Jews: "We should there form a portion of the rampart of Europe against Asia, an outpost of civilisation as opposed to barbarism."[85] More than one hundred years later the historian Benny Morris described the Arabs and Muslims as "barbarians," arguing that "due to the nature of Islam and Arab people, it was a mistake to think that it would be possible to establish here a quiet state that would live in harmony with its neighbors."[86]

[84] Elias Sanbar, available at: http://www.autodafe.org/correspondence/chroniques/elias2.htm, June 2002. It should be noted that only Cafavy's poem is called "Waiting for the Barbarians" and that neither this nor Darwīsh's poem illustrate Sanbar's point of view—it seems that Coetzee's novel is much more suitable as an illustration of the message he wished to convey.

[85] Herzl 1936, p. 30.

[86] See the interview with Israeli writer Ari Shavit (b. 1957) on www.haaretzdaily.com, January 9, 2004. In response to the interview, the Palestinian intellectual Salīm Tamārī (b. 1945) refers to the "barbarians" as including also the Mizrahi people inside Israel (www.haaretzdaily.com, January 16, 2004). On how the Israeli establishment created the "barbarians" in the image of the Oriental Jews, see Rejwan 2006a, pp. 111–36.

Helen of Troy vis-à-vis "The Emperor's Wife"

The Arabic text of Darwīsh's poem encourages one to read it in the ironic mode of intertextuality. It is the third line of each stanza that links the irony with one of the components of the first line ("The Emperor's wife will be abducted"). In the first reading, this sentence might evoke the myth of Helen of Troy.[87] Yet, unlike her, the reader gradually becomes aware that Darwīsh's Helen is only a one-night stand for the emperor. This transformation is expressed in the choice of words.

In the first stanza, "the Emperor's wife" ("*imra'at al-imbarāṭūr*") of the first line is contrasted to "our wives" ("*zawjātunā*"). But then "What have our wives got to do with this horse race?" gives a hint of the emperor's interests as being against the interests of the people. For the emperor, it is only entertainment—for *us,* it is our beloved wives.

In the second stanza, "the Emperor's wife" is contrasted with the "our children" ("*awlādunā*"). The impression that there is no balance between the emperor's desires and the sacrifice of the people is reinforced. "What have our children got to do with the offspring of this impudence?" For the emperor, it is only impudence—for *us,* it is our dear children.

In the third stanza, it is only "casual sex" ("*zawāg sarī'*") with the "mattress bride" ("*'arūs al-firāsh*") that brings about this catastrophe of 50,000 men killed, "but what have we got to do with it? What have 50,000 men killed got to do with this quickie marriage?"[88] For the emperor, it is only casual sex—for *us,* it is a massacre. The birth of the military campaign ("*wa-min baytihi tuladu al-ḥamla al-'askariyya*") was a kind of frustration that the emperor could not make love to his new "bride."[89]

[87] The daughter of Leda and Zeus, Helen, was reputed to be the most beautiful woman in the world. When she reached marriageable age, she was wooed by the most illustrious men of Greece. She married Menelaus and lived happily with him for a number of years and bore him a daughter, Hermione. After a decade or so of married life, Helen was abducted by—or ran off with—Paris, the son of King Priam of Troy. As a result, the Greek leaders mobilized a vast coalition army, placed it under the command of Agamemnon (of Mycenae), and set off to wage what became known as the Trojan War. After the fall of Troy, Menelaus took Helen back to Lacedaemon (Sparta), where they lived an apparently happy married life once more. At the end of their mortal existence, they were reunited in Elysium.

[88] Cf. the poem "Maṭār Athīnā" ("Athens Airport"), where *zawāj sarī'* means, though ironically, "sexual intercourse," but it is used here in a sense full of compassion toward two young refugees (Darwīsh 1987a, p. 23; Darwisch 1996, p. 25; Darwish 2003, p. 12).

[89] Cf. Snir 2002, p. 192.

Through the process of reading, one discovers that the barbarians are not so terribly barbaric and at the same time that the possible abduction of the emperor's wife is only a pretext, if that. The real suffering is endured by the people, who have no interest in the sexual life of the emperor. Like in Cavafy's poem and Coetzee's novel, the barbarians are only an excuse for committing greater crimes against civilization. The changing of the three components in the first line of Darwīsh's poem undermines the usual sequence of cause and effect: is it because the emperor's wife will be abducted by the barbarians that war will be declared? Or will war be declared before they come and will they be a kind of excuse for the war, which will be declared only so as to provide entertainment for the emperor?! The reader is led to the conclusion that the emperor and the barbarians are in fact two sides of the same coin.

Before the publication of the poem, Darwīsh published an article in *al-Karmil* (which he edited) under the title "Fī Intiẓār al-Barābira" ("Waiting for the Barbarians").[90] Serving as an epigraph to the article are Constantine Cavafy's lines:

> Now what's going to happen to us without barbarians?
> They were, those people, some kind of solution.

The article begins with the question: "When will they strike?" They, the barbarians, never did arrive in Cavafy's poem, but they "settled down in our reality and consciousness for a long time in order to enable the Arab establishment to solve its problems with us." We, the collective in the poem and in the article, are the victim, whose body became a theater of war between two murderers, between two kinds of terror, internal and external—we are a space that has nothing to do but wait for the new strike. Here, the myths of the barbarians, Hulagu, Cain and Abel, and Joseph and his brothers, as well as the aforementioned intertextual allusions are intermingled and find their manifestation in the myth of Ayyūb, the biblical Job. Both the article and the poem are unquestionably indebted to Said's *Orientalism*, especially in their attempt to illustrate the discourse of power, but they should also be read as trying to engage his main arguments. The article concludes as follows:

> But what could you do, when the big terror and the small terror disagree regarding you? How would you cry when the spears of the enemies are broken on your waist? And when your body is the battleground between your big murderer and your small murderer, where could you send the call? This question should not be put because you are betrayed, oppressed, Job. You must close the gap between the cry and the body, you must listen alone to your silence,

[90] *Al-Karmil* 18 (1985), pp. 4–9. The article was later incorporated into Darwīsh 1987b, pp. 169–75.

> and from this small gap the airplanes of the barbarians will pass, and you might be accused, you will be accused if you cry from pain and from betrayal that you take part in the conspiracy against your small murderer. You should support him, you should embrace him, you should help him plunge his dagger into your liver so that he might defend himself against your big murderer—these are the obligations of brotherhood. Don't mention the name of he who assassinated you, and thus the severed part of your corpse struck a number of foreign passersby, so that America will not hear the deep secret. Don't say anything. Help your brother to kill you, or say that you are killing yourself. Nobody killed you. Nobody killed nobody. Say that he had conducted a remedial operation on your liver and that you died from excess surrender. Say again that you are the murderer of yourself. You are the cost of everything. You are the cost of nothing. Say that you are the murderer of yourself in order to save one oil well, and a weapons deal, or to save a revolutionary sentence from inflation. You don't have any part in what is divided in you and in your corpse, because you are the victim of the victim. Nobody killed you. You are the murderer. Say it and don't regret; soon both murderers will embrace each other over you, and you are the cost which does not look for any result. You should stand now, with all your wounds, and apologize to the dagger that injured your body and injured the form of your spirit, because it could disgrace the murderer, could disgrace him somehow. Have the barbarians already arrived? Have the barbarians already arrived? They were some kind of solution.

Between the lines, the reader may sense a certain disappointment that the barbarians did not come. The repeated question "Have the barbarians already arrived?" ("*hal waṣal al-barābira*?") may be read in Arabic as a kind of wish: "if only they came." They could have been some kind of solution not only for the complicated reality, but also for the poet recording the chronicle of the collective. The conclusion of the article intermingles with the doubt imbued in the last line of the poem.

5. CONCLUSION

On May 1, 1964, a young Maḥmūd Darwīsh, only twenty-three at the time, stepped onto the stage of one of Nazareth's larger movie houses and, to an unsuspecting but eager crowd, proceeded to read his latest poem, in which the imperative "*sajjil Anā 'Arabī!*" ("Write it down: I am an Arab!") is repeated in every stanza:

سجّل
أنا عربيّ
ورقم بطاقتي خمسون ألف
وأطفالي ثمانية
وتاسعهم سيأتي بعد صيف

فهل تغضب
سجّل
أنا عربيّ
وأعمل مع رفاق الكدح في محجر
وأطفالي ثمانية
أسلّ لهم رغيف الخبز
والأثواب والدفتر
من الصخر
ولا أتوسّل الصّدقات من بابك
ولا أصغر
أمام بلاط أعتابك
فهل تغضب
سجّل
أنا عربيّ
أنا اسم بلا لقب
صبور في بلاد كلّ ما فيها
يعيش بفورة الغضب
جذوري
قبل ميلاد الزّمان رست
وقبل تفتّح الحقب
وقبل السّرو والزّيتون
وقبل ترعرع العشب
أبي من أسرة المحراث
لا من سادة نجب
وجدّي كان فلّاحا
بلا حسب ولا نسب
يعلّمني شموخ الشّمس قبل قراءة الكتب
وبيتي كوخ ناطور
من الأعواد والقصب
فهل ترضيك منزلتي
أنا اسم بلا لقب
سجّل
أنا عربيّ
ولون الشّعر فحميّ
ولون العين بنّيّ
وميزاتي
على رأسي عقال فوق كوفيّة
وكفى صلبة كالصّخر
تخمش من يلامسها
وعنواني
أنا من قرية عزلاء منسيّة
شوارعها بلا أسماء
وكلّ رجالها في الحقل والمحجر
يحبّون الشّيوعيّة

فهل تغضب
سجّل
أنا عربيّ
سلبت كروم أجدادي
وأرضا كنت أفلحها
أنا وجميع أولادي
ولم تترك لنا ولكلّ أحفادي
سوى هذي الصّخور
فهل ستأخذها
حكومتكم كما قيلا؟
إذن
سجّل برأس الصّفحة الأولى
أنا لا أكره النّاس
ولا أسطو على أحد
ولكنّي إذا ما جعت
آكل لحم مغتصبي
حذار حذار من جوعي
ومن غضبي

Write it down!
I am an Arab
And my identity card number is fifty thousand.
I have eight children
And the ninth is coming after the summer.
Makes you angry, doesn't it?

Write it down!
I am an Arab
And I work at a stone quarry with comrades of toil
And I have eight children
And I extract for them a loaf of bread,
Clothes and notebooks
From the rocks.
I do not beg at your door for charity
Nor do I humble myself
On the threshold of your court.
Makes you angry, doesn't it?

Write it down!
I am an Arab.
I am a name without a title.
I am patient in a country where everything
Boils with flare.
My roots
Were sunk before the birth of time
And before the advent of the ages

And before the cypress and olive trees
And before the grass had started growing.
My father descends from the family of the plow,
Not from a privileged class,
And my grandfather
Was a farmer
Without a dynasty.
He taught me the glory of the sun before how to read books
And my house is a watchman's hut
Made out of branches and sticks.
My status pleases you, doesn't it?
I am a name without a title!

Write it down!
I am an Arab
And the color of my hair: black.
And the color of my eyes: brown.
And my distinguishing features:
On the head *'iqāl* on *kūfiyya*[91]
And my hand is solid like a rock,
Scratching anyone who touches it,
And my address:
I come from a village deserted and isolated.
Its streets have no names
And all its men work in the fields and the stone quarry.
Makes you angry, doesn't it?

Write it down!
I am an Arab.
You have stolen my ancestors' vineyards
And the land I used to cultivate,
Along with my children
And you left us and my grandchildren,
With nothing but these rocks,
So will your government take them too,
As it has often been said?

Therefore,
Write it down! At the top of the first page:
I do not hate people
Nor do I encroach on anyone,
But if I become hungry

[91] *Kūfiyya* (*kaffiyeh*) is traditional Arab headgear, consisting of a square kerchief diagonally folded and worn under the *'iqāl* (a headband made of camel's hair to hold the *kūfiyya* in place).

I shall eat the flesh of the one who violated me—
Beware, beware of my hunger
And of my anger![92]

The tension among the audience was palpable from the moment Darwīsh began reading, and when he finished the reaction was tumultuous. Within days, the poem "Biṭāqat Huwiyya" ("Identity Card") had spread throughout the country and the Arab world—its straightforward language and forceful images imprinted themselves easily on the minds of the very same people it spoke of. In August 1982, in a Beirut that was being bombarded from the air by Israeli fighter jets and besieged on the ground by Israeli Army tanks, Darwīsh's mind went back to that May Day gathering in Nazareth eighteen years earlier:

> لأوّل مرّة يأذنون لنا أن نغادر حيفا شريطة أن نعود في اللّيل، لنذهب الى محطّة الشّرطة الواقعة على طرف الحديقة، حديقة البلديّة، ليقول كلّ واحد منّا على طريقته: سجّل – أنا موجود. سجّل!! إيقاع جديد قديم أعرفه. سجّل – أنا، أعرف هذا الصّوت البالغ من العمر خمسًا وعشرين سنة. يا للّزمن الحيّ، يا للزّمن الميّت، يا للزّمن الحيّ الخارج مِن الزّمن الميّت. سجّل أنا عربيّ، قلت ذلك لموظّف قد يقود ابنه إحدى هذه الطّائرات قلتُها باللّغة العبريّة لأستثيره. وحين قُلتها باللّغة العربيّة مسَّ الجمهور العربيّ في النّاصرة تيَّار كهربائيّ سِرّي أفلت المكبوت من قمقمه. لم أفهم سرّ هذا الاكتشاف، كأنّني نزعت الصّاعق عن ساحة ملغومة ببارود الهويّة، حتى صارت الصّرخة هي هويّتي الشّعرية الّتي لا تكتفي بأن تشير إليَّ بل تطاردني.

[92] Darwīsh 1988, pp. 73–6. For other translations of the poem, see Darwish 1980, pp. 10–12; Asfour 1988, pp. 199–200; Athamneh 2017, pp. 5–198; Cohen-Mor 2018, pp. 297–9. For a French translation, see Laâbi 1970, pp. 33–5. The influence of the poem has sometimes traversed the national field and spread into the religious sphere, as we find, for example, in "Sajjil Anā Islāmī" ("Write It Down! I Am an Islamist") by the Moroccan poet Muḥammad Bin'Amāra (b. 1945) (Bin'Amāra 1989, pp. 311–18). On the poem, see also Cohen-Mor 2019, p. 5. See also Silverman 2019, which explores the Hebrew "afterlife" of the poem focusing on two realms: translation and Mizrahi poetry. The dissertation is overloaded with errors in translation and transliteration, in addition to misunderstanding of major issue in Arabic poetics and Mizrahi conceptions but, ironically, devotes around fifteen pages (pp. 167–83) in order to present a theory about "sublimation through translation" based on a slip of a pen in a Hebrew translation of the poem in *Mahmud Darwish: Fifty Years of Poetry* (Snir 2015). Silverman was fully aware that it had been a mere slip of a pen based upon a correspondence he had held with the translator (my email to him from December 25, 2018, in response to his email from a previous day) but, according to him, "it is though precisely its uncanny presence as an error, which justifies its discussion here" (p. 177, n. 360). The fact that the error had been corrected in subsequent editions of the translation (2nd edn in May 2015 and 3rd edn in July 2016), more than three years *before* Silverman "discovers" the error, by no means bothered him; moreover, in a previous translation of the same poem, ten years before, the word is translated correctly (Snir 2005c, p. 49). This is further evidence of the sad fact that the demise of Arabic literature by Jews is being accompanied as well by the gradual demise of its scholarship among the Jews (see below, Chapter 7).

> For the first time [since 1948] they [the Israeli authorities] had given us permission to leave Haifa, but we had to be back at night to report to the police station next to the park, that is, the city park—for each of us to say in his own way, "Write it down!—I exist! Write it down!" An old familiar rhythm that I recognize instantly. "Write it down"—I recognize the voice, then 25-years-old. Oh, what a dead time! Oh, for a living time to emerge from this dead time. "Write it down: I am an Arab!" I said that to a government official whose son may very well be flying one of these jets overhead! I said it in Hebrew, to provoke him, but when I put it in a poem the Arab audience in Nazareth was electrified, as if a secret current had sprung the genie from the bottle. At first I didn't quite understand the secret of this discovery—as if, in a yard full of bombs, with the gunpowder of my identity, I had succeeded in defusing the thunderbolt. This cry of mine soon turned into my poetic identity—not satisfied with alluding to me, it pursues me even now![93]

The poem was written against the background of the extensive Israeli-Zionist efforts "to rob that [Palestinian] minority of its Arab personality, culture and identity";[94] or in the forceful words of the Palestinian Anton Shammās (b. 1950), the Israeli policy aimed at "initially phasing out the Arab personality in Israel and then, as a follow-up, demanding that this personality accommodate itself to the state." What Israel wanted to raise were "people whose tongue had been amputated ... with no cultural past, and no future. Just an improvised present, and a free-floating personality."[95]

In the 1980s, Darwīsh had no need to assert his Arab or Palestinian identity—it was a solid, unshakable identity that the daily sufferings and miseries only served to consolidate and strengthen. After being crowned as the unchallenged Palestinian national poet, he wanted to widen his poetic identity.[96] This was the time when he felt totally convinced that the poetry of declarations and slogans had exhausted itself.[97] His concern now was

[93] Darwish 1987, pp. 139–40. The translation is according to Darwish 1995, pp. 173–4, with minor modifications. Cf. Darwīsh and al-Qāsim 1990, p. 151.

[94] Sulaiman 1984, p. 200.

[95] Hareven 1981, pp. 44–5.

[96] On Darwīsh's poetry and the politics of Palestinian identity, see also Abu Eid 2016. On Palestinian collective memory, national identity, and the role of education and the "other" and relevant references, see Nasser 2005; Hovsepian 2008; Litvak 2009.

[97] Already in 1969 Darwīsh published an article titled "Anqidhūnā min Hādhā al-Ḥubb al-Qāsī" ("Save Us from This Crude Love!"), in which he voiced strong dissatisfaction with the injustice Arab critics were doing to Palestinian literature by avoiding objective criticism and in their readiness to accept unconditionally anything that was Palestinian—poetry of slogans included—as a positive contribution to the spirit of the nation. Asking the Arabs not to allow affection for the Palestinian cause to be a decisive criterion when assessing literary works, he points out that Palestinian poetry should not be looked upon as if it had suddenly

not solely to narrate reality—in order to engrave new verses in *Dīwān al-'Arab*—but to explore other realms in which reality and poetry intermingled. The persona was no longer only a witness at the time of the events, but also an outsider who was looking upon them from a point of view that was not unspecified in time and space. *Ward Aqall* reflects this attempt of the poet to be a witness of his time and place and at the same time to wonder about poetry's place in reality, its relationship with the myth, and about the place this poetry will eventually occupy, if at all, in the future. The process of reading and the role of the reader in his efforts to concretize the meaning became much more dominant in Darwīsh's poetry, and instead of the imperative *sajjil* the question "But what have we got to do with it?" became the *lāzima*. The poet has many more questions than answers; even if each question somehow conceals an answer, this answer depends on the readers' responses as well as each reader's own answer and personal preferred meaning.

Yet the reader may remain merely a *consumer* and be satisfied by reading the poems as he read Darwīsh's previous poems, tracing the footsteps of the persona in his experience as a refugee. This is the story of the *Nakba* from the viewpoint of the victim, and through the process of reading the reader identifies with the persona. But the poem is also addressed to the community of poets, the *producers*, whose texts may conduct a dialogue with Darwīsh's texts. The process of reading is thus also a process of poetic dialogue whose core is poetic and aesthetic: this is the purpose and value of the poetry written on the *Nakba* and its continuous aftereffects. In this sense, the reader assumes not only the role of a poet but also that of a critic who is interested in the internal connections in the poems and their relationship to the myth as well as the process of the creation of myths.

This interplay between reality, poetry, and meta-poetry, and between myth and meta-myth, as well as the role of the reader in the concretization of meaning and the significance of the reading process, grant the poems of *Ward Aqall* their peculiar significance. "Other Barbarians Will Come" illustrates this peculiarity of the collection—the question "Will Homer be born after us, and the myths open their gates to all?" is imbued with all the above components and dimensions—and the reader is expected to take part in a poetic and critical discourse that asks whether the poetry of Darwīsh could be considered the equivalent of that of Homer. Can Darwīsh sing the

come from nowhere—"it is only a stream originating from and pouring into the big river of Arabic literature" (*al-Jadīd*, June 1969, pp. 2–4).

poetry of Palestine and the days of its lost paradise as Homer sang the story of Troy?!

At the same time, despair and frustration are deeply ingrained in the poems of *Ward Aqall* and other poems written in the 1980s. Suicide is sometimes seen as a possible solution to the persona's crises. For example, receiving a pistol as a present, he hastened to hide it "for fear of a rage that cannot be contained."[98] Yet,

وَضَعَ المُسَدَّس بين رؤياهْ
وحاول أن ينام
إن لم أجد حلمًا لأحلمهُ
سأطلقُ طلقتي
وأموت مثل ذبابةٍ زرقاءَ
في هذا الظّلامْ وبلا شهيَّهْ

If I find no dream to dream,
I will fire my bullet
And I will die like a blue-tailed fly
In this darkness, and without appetite.[99]

But because there is no dream to dream—"The Time Has Come for the Poet to Kill Himself" (the title of one of Darwīsh's poems):

لا لشيء، بل لكي يقتل نَفْسَهُ [...]
آن للشّاعر أن يخرج منّي للأبد.

Not for a reason, but rather in order to kill himself ...
The time has come for the poet to leave me forever.[100]

The persona wishes to renounce his poetic abilities, and between the lines the reader may feel a sense of the end of the road. Wandering in Beirut, the poet looks at the balcony of the Lebanese poet Khalīl Ḥāwī (1925–1982) and muses:

إلى أين أذهب في هذا الغروب؟ [...] هناك شرفة الشّاعر الّذي رأى سقوط كلّ شيء، فاختار موعد نهايته. أمسك خليل حاوي بندقية الصّيد، واصطاد نفسه، لا ليشهد على شيء، بل لكي لا يشهد شيئا ولا يشهد على شيء. لقد سئم هذا الحضيض، سئم الإطلال على هاوية لا قاع لها [...] كان وحيدا بلا فكرة، ولا امرأة، ولا قصيدة، ولا وعد [...] لا أريد أن أطلّ على شرفته. لا أريد أن أرى ما فعله نيابة عنّي.

Where will I go after this twilight? ... Here is the balcony of the poet who saw all things fall, and chose the time of his end. Khalīl Ḥāwī grasped his hunting rifle and hunted himself, not in order to witness something, but in order not

98 Darwīsh 1987, p. 7; Darwish 1995, p. 5.
99 Darwīsh 1976, pp. 73–4.
100 Darwīsh 1986, pp. 75–8.

> to see anything, and not to bear witness to anything. He was bored with this garbage, hated to observe the bottomless abyss ... He was alone, without an idea, without a woman, without poetry, and without promise ... I don't want to look at his balcony. I don't want to see what he did instead of me.[101]

In his hours of distress, the poet is aware of the fact that poetry has no value:

> [إنّ] الجرحى والعطاشى والباحثين عن الماء والخبز والملجأ لا يطالبونكم بالغناء، والمقاتلين لا يكترثون بغنائكم. غنّوا إذا شئتم، أو فاصمتوا إذا شئتم. فنحن هامشيّون في الحرب وفي وسعنا أن نقدّم خدمات أخرى للنّاس، فإن تنكة من الماء تساوي وادي عبقر. المطلوب منا الآن هو الفاعليّة االإنسانيّة لا الجماليّة الإبداعيّة.

> The wounded and the thirsty, and those who seek water and bread do not want melodies from you, and the fighters pay no attention to your songs. Sing if you want, or be quiet. We are marginal in war. We have the ability to offer other services to people: a small can of water is equal to the 'Abqar valley.[102] What is demanded of us now is not creative aesthetics but human action.[103]

And in order to emphasize that poets "are marginal in war," Darwīsh uses his craft as a poet, and offers his services for the people "who seek water," and provides them with "spiritual" water: he dedicates several pages in his *Dhākira li-l-Nisyān* (1987) to the issue of water, as if to provide the thirsty people with what they need, quoting classical sources and history books mixed with a description of his own experiences with water in these difficult hours, such as with the climax of quoting from one of Ibn Sīda's books the synonyms and adjectives of the word:

> لي. ولمن اكتوى مثلي. بجروح الماء قدم "ابن سيدة". اسماء الماء، ونعوته، هذا غيض من فيضها:
>
> ماء. ماءة. مويه. أمواه. ماهة. بَلال. رجع. أبيض. أسود. عتيق. عدّ. كِرِع. غِمْر. عُلْجُوم. بلاق. زَغْرُب. السّعْبر. الطّيْس. السّغبر. الرّيْب. الجوار. الخْضرم. القَلَيْذم. العُبام. الهُر. الهرهور. الهرهار. الهراهر. اليهمور. الزّمزم. الزُّمزوم. القاموس. الجراجر. اليهيري. الضّحضاح. الكوثر. الأهيغ. الجبجاب. الهلاهل. الطّرطيس. البثق. الحائر. الحفل. الأزيب. الثّمد. المشفوه. المضفوف. الرّقراق. الرّقّ. الفَراش. الطّسل. الضَّهْل. السَّمَل. البَرْضُ. النُّطْفة. الرَّزَغ. الصُّبّة. الشَّوْل. الرّفض. الخِبْط. الصّبابة. القصملة. الصّلاصل. الضُّلْضُل. الذُّفاف. الذُّفّ. الذُّفَف. القطرب. الزَّرْجُون. المَزّة. المجّة. النُّقْمة. النُّغبة. المُكْلَة. النُّشفة. الغُرْفة. القُرحة. الحُسوة. المُزْعة. السُّؤر. الوَشَل. الجحقة. الهلاَل. الرَّشْف. الطَّمْلة. الدَّعْث. الحيْل. الطَّلْح. النُّقاخ. الزُّلال. الفُرات. الرُّضاب. الفضيض. الشّريب. الشّروب. الهُجهج. المُخْضِم. الزُّعاق. الذّعاق. النّمير. المَسُوس. الباضع. الغريض. البُسْر. الحنبريت، القَرَاح.
>
> وغيرها وغيرها وغيرها.[104]

[101] Darwīsh 1987, pp. 123–4; Darwish 1995, pp. 153–4.

[102] The legendary dwelling place of the demons, according to Arab tradition, which maintains, like the Greek theory of the muses, that poetry has its source in divine forces.

[103] Darwīsh 1987, pp. 51–2; Darwish 1995, pp. 62–3. Cf. Van Leeuwen 1999, pp. 265–6.

[104] Darwīsh 1987, pp. 30–1.

The translator of the book tried to give English parallels for these synonyms as follows:

> For me, and others like me who have burned with the wounds of water, Ibn Sida has set out the names of water and its attributes. What follows is only a drop from that flood:
> Water, waters, waterfall, rapids, cataract, cascade, snow, ice, hail, backwater, backwash, aqueduct, canal, droplet, drop, drizzle, cloudburst, rain, shower, torrent, soaker, spate, flood, deluge, mist, dew, steam, condensation, humidity, moisture, vapor, evaporation, aquifer, aquiclude, reservoir, freshet, brook, runnel, rill, rivulet, stream, creek, river, tributary, confluence, inlet, reach, slough, swamp, marsh, fen, puddle, pond, pool, tarn, lake, lagoon, cove, current, wave, eddy, whirlpool, undercurrent, billow, ripple, chop, surge, swell, spray, spurt, spout, squirt, splash, gurgle, gush, run, flow, meander, drip, ooze, seep, percolate, trickle, drop, leak, soak, drench, douse, dunk, dribble, inundate, saturate, irrigate, sprinkle, slosh, wash, dunk, dive, plunge, submerge, splatter, immerse, freeze, thaw, damp, wet, sodden, sopping, hydrous, aquatic, aqueous, watery.
> And many others.[105]

Darwīsh, who believes that poetry cannot be of any benefit, is at the same time a very prolific writer and on other occasions expressed a deep belief in the power of words. Alluding to the power of words and stories, Darwīsh says: "Whoever tells his story will inherit the earth of the story."[106] In his long poem "The Tragedy of Narcissus: The Comedy of Silver"[107] from the collection *Arā Mā Urīdu* (*I See What I Want*) (1990), he repeats four times the sentence:

والأرض
تورَثُ
كاللّغة!

And the land
Is inherited
Like language![108]

In a poem titled "A Traveler Said to a Traveler: We Will Never Return as ..." from his collection *Limādhā Tarakta al-Ḥiṣana Waḥīdan* (*Why Have You Left the Horse Alone?*), Darwīsh emphasizes the same meaning:

[105] Darwish 1995, p. 36.
[106] *Mashārif* (Haifa) 3 (1995), p. 86. Cf. Snir 2015, p. 60.
[107] Darwīsh 1990, pp. 47–78.
[108] Darwīsh 1990, pp. 52, 54, 63, 67. Cf. Williams 2014, pp. 57–62.

قلتُ: لم أتعلّم الكلمات بعدُ
فقال لي: أكتبْ لتعرفها
وتعرفَ أين كنتَ، وأين أنتَ
وكيف جئتَ، ومن تكون غدًا،
ضع اسمكَ في يدي واكتبْ
لتعرف من أنا، واذهبْ غماما
في المدى ...
فكتبتُ: من يكتبْ حكايته يرثْ
أرض الكلامِ ويملك المعنى تماما!

I said: I have not learnt the words yet
Thus, he said to me: Write in order to know them
And know where you were, and where you are
And how you came, and who you will be tomorrow,
Put your name in my hand and write
That you will know who I am, and walk on clouds
Throughout the space ...
Thus, I wrote: Who writes his story will inherit
The land of the words, and will master meaning totally![109]

Darwīsh here refers to the significance of the relationship between teller and listener that is expressed in the figure of Scheherazade from *Alf Layla wa-Layla*, who has been sentenced to death by the king but is able to stave off her execution by telling him stories, ending each of them at an exciting point, thus delaying her death. Referring to narrative seduction and the power of fiction, Ross Chambers argues that "to tell a story is to exercise power."[110] And we find such a power in Scheherazade's stories as we find it in James Joyce's (1882–1941) short story "The Dead" from *Dubliners* (1914), where Gretta's narration about her dead lover avoids the violent passion of her husband Gabriel, which would lead him "to crush her body against him, to overmaster her."[111]

The same paradox is known from the mystical experience: it is ineffable,[112] and the mystic himself inclines to be silent regarding his divine experience,

[109] Darwīsh 1995a, p. 49. For other translations, see Darwish 2006a, pp. 111–12; Darwish 2014, p. 57.
[110] Chambers 1984, p. 50.
[111] Joyce 1991, p. 248
[112] On the impossibility or difficulties of expressing the mystical experience through human language, see Knox 1951, p. 249; Scholem 1954, pp. 4–5; al-Ghazālī 1956, p. 96; Eliade 1959, p. 10; Scharfstein 1993. On the psychological aspects of ineffability, see Tart 1969, p. 16: "Most often, because of the uniqueness of the subjective experience associated with certain ASC [altered states of consciousness] (e.g., transcendental, aesthetic, creative, psychotic, and mystical states), persons claim a certain ineptness or inability to communicate the nature or essence of the experience to someone who has not undergone a similar experience." See also Tart 1969, pp. 23, 40–2, 405–6. On ineffability in poetry, see Cariou 2014, pp. 27–58.

because it is an intimate experience with the divine beloved. At the same time, paradoxically, mystics are very prolific. This conflict between the mind (*'aql*) and the heart (*qalb*) brings us to the meta-poetic dimension. It is sometimes argued that those mystics who speak about their experiences are "weak"—they could not help but surrender to the temptation of disclosing what happened to them. The greatest of the mystics resist the temptation of speaking, and thus we will never know about them. Can we say the same about poets? That is, those who speak are the weak poets? Moreover, ever since Theodor Adorno argued that "to write poetry after Auschwitz is barbaric,"[113] all kinds of artists, not just poets, have been debating whether poetry has any value vis-à-vis reality. Should we also see poetry through the eyes of Walter Benjamin?

> There is no document of civilisation which is not at the same time a document of barbarism. And just as such a document is not free of barbarism, barbarism taints also the manner in which it was transmitted from one owner to another. A historical materialist therefore dissociates himself from it as far as possible. He regards it as his task to brush history against the grain.[114]

Darwīsh, whose interest in Ṣūfī texts had been mainly limited to cultural and literary allusions,[115] started in the mid-1980s to present in his poetry a persona whose poetic experience is sometimes intermingled with the mystical one, culminating in his long poem "al-Hudhud" ("The Hoopoe").[116] Thus, it is no wonder that in his exchange of open letters with Palestinian compatriot Samīḥ al-Qāsim (1939–2014) he used a mystical "pretext" in order to explain his desire to write poetry even if he was very much aware that poetry has in fact no "real" value. Speaking about the generic relationship of poetry to prose, Darwīsh asserts the dominance of fiction over poetry, "if television has left to it any remnant." But if the poet himself is also writing prose, he should not mix the two activities, because poetry is "an explosive desire." Just as the mystic cannot help but speak of his experience because love overflows his heart (sometimes emanating in ecstatic shouts called *shaṭaḥāt*), so too the poet cannot resist this desire; he must "put himself in the wind and madness, because the poet cannot be but a poet."[117] Nevertheless, for Darwīsh it is not only overflowing emotions but also a rational choice—mind and heart are in harmony:

113 Adorno 1967, p. 34.
114 Benjamin 1969, p. 256.
115 See, for example, Neuwirth 1999, pp. 153–78.
116 First published in *al-Karmil* 38 (1990), pp. 33–43; incorporated in Darwīsh1990, pp. 79–99 (English translation: Darwish 2003, pp. 31–51; Hebrew translation with clarifying notes: Snir 1996a, pp. 47–61). On the poem, see Butt 2021, pp. 70–81.
117 Darwīsh and al-Qāsim 1990, p. 72.

إذا كان لي أن أعيد البداية أختار ما اخترت: ورد السّياج
أسافر ثانية في الدّروب الّتي قد تؤدّي وقد لا تؤدّي إلى قرطبة.

If I could start all over again I'd choose what I have chosen: roses on the fence
I'd travel again on the roads that may or may not lead to Cordova.

Chapter 4

Bilingualism: Palestinians in Hebrew[1]

A flag loses contact with reality and flies off.
A shopwindow is decorated with
dresses of beautiful women, in blue and white.
And everything in three languages:
Hebrew, Arabic, and Death.
– Yehuda Amichai

1. INTRODUCTION

In the Israeli feature film *Avanti Popolo* first shown in 1986,[2] which deals with the war of June 1967, one crucial scene has two hungry, thirsty, and exhausted Egyptian soldiers, Khālid and Ghassān, wandering about in the Sinai Desert trying to find their way back to the Suez Canal. The date is June 11, and a ceasefire has just come into effect. Khālid and Ghassān are soon spotted by soldiers of the enemy army whom they beg for some water. They are drunk after finding two bottles of whiskey in a jeep of a dead Swedish soldier of the UN forces. When the Israelis keep refusing, Khālid hits upon a desperate measure as a last resort. Just before the war, he had been rehearsing Shakespeare's *The Merchant of Venice* in which he had been given the part of Shylock, and he now breaks out into Shylock's famous monologue:

> I am a Jew! Hath not a Jew eyes? Hath not a Jew hands, organs, dimensions, senses, affections, passions? Fed with the same food, hurt with the same weapons, subject to the same diseases, healed by the same means, warmed and cooled by the same winter and summer as a Christian is?

1 This chapter uses material that first appeared in Snir 1991a, pp. 245–53; Snir 1992, pp. 6–9; Snir 1995, pp. 163–83; Snir 1997, pp. 141–53; Snir 2001a, pp. 197–224.

2 *Avanti Popolo*, written and directed by Rafi Bukaee; significantly, this was also the film's Hebrew title.

> If you prick us, do we not bleed? If you tickle us, do we not laugh? If you poison us, do we not die?[3]

The Israeli soldiers are shocked by this. One of them asks: "What is he saying?" And another replies: "He's got the roles mixed up. Give him something to drink!"[4] The Israeli soldiers cannot free themselves from the two drunken Egyptian soldiers, and the relationship between them becomes more grotesque when, listening to the French Monte Carlo radio station, Khālid hears that the popular Italian song "Avanti Popolo" is going to be broadcast.[5] He snatches the transistor from the Israeli soldier and, standing as a conductor, asks the Israeli soldiers to sing with him the song accompanying the song heard from the radio:

> Avanti popolo, alla riscossa
> Bandiera rossa, bandiera rossa
> Avanti popolo, alla riscossa
> Bandiera rossa trionferà.[6]

The scene ends with the Israeli and the Egyptian soldiers disappearing into the setting sun. The shadow of the Israeli–Egyptian war, Shylock's monologue, and the Socialist anthem together with the grotesque presentation of several scenes provide the film with several, even contradictory, frames of meaning. That diversity contributed to the success that *Avanti Popolo* had both with the Jewish-Israeli public and with the critics, and it was even chosen to represent Israel for the Oscar competition for foreign films.[7] Its significance, however, had less to do with the way it dealt with the 1967 War or even Arab–Israeli relations in general, than it did with the subtext it contained, which no Israeli could fail to pick up. This was the direct allusion the audience was reading into the story of Khālid and Ghassān to the situation of the Palestinians in Israel, that is, to the skewed balance of power that exists between the country's Jewish majority and its Palestinian minority in political, economic, and cultural terms.[8] *Avanti Popolo* was important

[3] Shakespeare 1964, Act III, Scene 1, ll. 52–60.

[4] Bukaee 1990, p. 52. Bukaee says that the idea of creating an Arab Shylock came to him when he read an article on Arik [Ariel] Sharon (1928–2014), a former Israeli Minister of Defense, later Prime Minister: "I was stunned by his incapacity to perceive the other side, his inability to understand that there are other people who deserve to exist with dignity in this world" (Gertz 2000, pp. 109–10).

[5] In fact, the title of the song is "Bandiera Rossa" ("The Red Flag"), which for a time was the official anthem of the Italian Socialist Party and also of the Communist Party.

[6] Bukaee 1990, pp. 56–8.

[7] The decision provoked a public outcry, and the Council for Films and Plays that had made the decision was dissolved and was replaced with another one (Gertz 2000, p. 110).

[8] Cf. Shammās 1990, p. 14.

because it proved to be a landmark in helping reveal the voice of Palestinian culture to a traditionally patronizing or simply indifferent and dismissive Israeli-Jewish public. This had much to do with the casting of two Israeli-Palestinian actors, Salīm Ḍaw (b. 1950) and Suhayl Ḥaddād (b. 1951), in the two main roles of, respectively, Khālid and Ghassān. It is part of the achievement of Israeli-Jewish director Rafi Bukaee (1957–2003) that he decided to let Ḍaw and Ḥaddād "play themselves," so to speak, and even had them translate the Hebrew text of his original script into their own Palestinian Arab dialect, whereas realistically, the context of the story would have required the two soldiers to speak Egyptian Arabic. For one, this means that watching the movie offers an experience totally different from reading the original Hebrew script. When he plays Khālid, Ḍaw is actually playing himself in the guise of an Egyptian soldier who was still rehearsing the part of Shakespeare's Shylock only a few days before he was recruited. Moreover, Ḍaw and Ḥaddād, who found a subversive Palestinian message in the written original Hebrew scenario,[9] not only translated, but also had an active part in shaping a number of scenes. For example, Ḍaw objected to the final scene in the original script, which had Khālid being killed by his own side (i.e., Egyptian soldiers), and told Bukaee that he would not take part in the movie unless that scene was changed.[10] Now, when Khālid finds his death after reaching the Suez Canal, he is killed in the cross-fire between Egyptian and Israeli soldiers.

The movie showed also that in their mental make-up it is impossible for many Palestinian intellectuals living in Israel to escape the impact of a number of often contradictory sources—Palestinian and Arab, of course, but also Israeli, either narrowly Zionist or more generally Western, and even Jewish. Where else in the Arab world, for example, would an Arab actor be given lines like these:

> You know what they call me in the theater? "The Jew!" You know what my friends said when I was recruited into the army? They said: "What a cruel world, Jew is going to fight Jews!" The Merchant of Venice! They made me Shylock![11]

In Bukaee's *Avanti Popolo*, Ḍaw utters these lines in his own dialect—the Palestinians viewing themselves as the "Jews" of the Arab world, first of all because they are the "victims of yesterday's victims," but then also because they have been forcibly located at a crossroads of conflicting cultures. By thus

[9] Horowitz 1993, p. 131.
[10] Schorr and Shuv 1990, p. 87.
[11] Bukaee 1990, p. 39.

evoking "a Palestinian framework of feeling,"[12] the film conveys a subversive message that pulls at the political and cultural props with which the Jewish majority underpins its hegemonic control. This is a message that castigates all attempts to "absorb" the Palestinian minority into Israel's wider, Hebrew-based Westernized culture.[13] It is firmly grounded, of course, in a collective memory that can never forget that until the *Nakba* of 1948, Israel was Palestine and the Jews a minority.[14] Culturally, Israel's Palestinian minority has always remained part of the Middle East's majority Arab-Muslim culture, a reality that finds its reflection even in Hebrew literature, where a Jewish majority still leans on patterns of expression typical of a minority under threat.[15]

If, against this background, we find a small number of Palestinian authors and poets writing and publishing in Hebrew, the first question that comes up is: why do they do it? Then also, for whom do they write? What difference, if any, is there between their literary writings in Arabic and those in Hebrew? How are their works perceived/received in either literary system? Literary bilingualism is not uncommon in societies where a minority culture, as part of the acculturation process,[16] evolves alongside or within a majority culture.[17] In Israel, however, this minority culture is under constant threat from the majority culture—Arabic is not only the mother tongue, it is the very embodiment of the minority's struggle to defend and preserve its religious and cultural heritage.[18] This explains why the phenomenon has remained

[12] Shohat 1989, p. 249. On the relationship between reality and fiction in the film, see Gertz 2000, pp. 129–31.

[13] See Snir 1990, pp. 244–68. On Israeli society as a European transplant society and the pressures upon the Arab minority as well as the Oriental Jews to Westernize, see Smooha 1984, pp. 28–9; and Smooha's contribution in Ram 1993, pp. 181–2. See also Shafir 1996, pp. 227–44 (also in Pappé 1999, pp. 81–96); Silberstein 1999, pp. 15–45.

[14] This awareness was expressed even in the 1950s, as illustrated by the poem "Harvesting of Skulls" (*al-Jadīd*, January 1957, pp. 25–30).

[15] Cf. Hever 1991, pp. 129–47; Grossman 1992, p. 199.

[16] The concept of "acculturation" describes a largely one-way process in which a minority acquires and absorbs mainstream cultural norms, values, and social habits from the dominant group (see, e.g., Gordon 1964).

[17] On the general issue of minority discourse, see Deleuze and Guattari 1975 (English translation: Deleuze and Guattari 1986); Lloyd 1987, pp. 19–26; *Cultural Critique* 7 (Spring 1987) (special issue: *The Nature and Context of Minority Discourse*); Deleuze and Guattari 1990, pp. 59–69. On Palestinian literature in Israel as minority literature, see Caspi and Weltsch 1998; Taha 2000, pp. 219–34.

[18] On Arabic as a minority language in Israel, sociocultural data, and the language situation, see Talmon 2000, pp. 199–220. An attempt to describe and analyze the main features of the Hebrew language of the Arabs in Israel is presented in Shehadeh 1997, pp. 49–71. For the impact of Hebrew on Arabic in Israel, see Amara and Mar'i 1999; Dana 2000, pp. 113–206; Amara and Mar'i 2010; Mar'i 2013.

limited to writers belonging to the Druze and Christian minorities,[19] and took on some significance only in the 1980s, when Anton Shammās, who is a Christian (b. 1950), and the Druze Na'īm 'Arāyidī (1948–2015)[20] began to make a name for themselves in Hebrew.[21] Others soon joined them or became better known,[22] while a number of Palestinian actors began appearing on the Hebrew stage and in the cinema, apart from the growing number of Palestinian journalists in the Israeli-Hebrew media.[23]

19 The Druze minority is somewhat different from both the Muslim and Christian Palestinian minorities, as it has been subjected to an exhaustive process of co-optation by the state. The Druze are a Muslim sect whose origins go back to the early eleventh century. Numbering about one million, Druze are found today in Lebanon, Syria, Jordan, and Israel. It was their traditional ethno-religious particularism that the Zionists exploited in their efforts to co-opt the Druze and so alienate them from Palestine's other Arabs. This divide-and-rule policy proved "successful," and, as a recent study has it, the fissured identity of Israel's Druze today bespeaks a sense of tragedy within the community itself; see Firro 1999, pp. 242–50. Note especially the following: "[T]he self-image of the Druzes in Israel is part reconstruction, part invention—traditional features of Druze particularism were transformed into a new kind of 'particularism' made to fit the political field created in 1948 by the reality of the Jewish state ... most Druzes ... find it 'easier' to present themselves as the Jewish majority and the state wants to see them than as Arabs or Palestinians" (Firro 1999, pp. 246–7. Cf. Firro 2001, pp. 40–53). On the status of Hebrew among the Druze in Israel, see Shenberg 1998, pp. 21–9. On "co-opting the educational system" and the official attempts to "create" a separate "Israeli-Druze consciousness," see Firro 1999, pp. 225–41. On the *taqiyya* ("simulation") among the Druze, see Layish 1985, pp. 245–81.

20 For biographical and bibliographical details, see Moreh and 'Abbāsī 1987, pp. 122–4, 155–6.

21 At the end of August 2021, Israel's population (9,391,000) included 6,943,000 Jews (74%); 1,982,000 Arabs (Muslims, Christians, and Druzes) (21%), and other 466,000 (5%) (according to Israeli Central Bureau of Statistics, September 5, 2021, available at: https://www.cbs.gov.il/EN/Pages/default.aspx, last accessed September 5, 2021).

22 *Be-Or Ḥadash* (Manṣūr 1966) (English translation: *In a New Light* [Manṣūr 1969]) by 'Aṭāllāh Manṣūr (b. 1934) is the first Hebrew novel written by an Arab. Among the other writers are Rāshid Ḥusayn (1936–1977), Muḥammad Watad (1937–1994), Fārūq Mawāsī (1941–2020), Nazīh Khayr (1946–2008), Sihām Dā'ūd (b. 1952), Muḥammad Ḥamza Ghanāyim (1953–2004), Fāḍil 'Alī (b. 1953), Salmān Maṣalḥa (b. 1953), Maḥmūd Zaydān (b. 1955), Asad 'Azzī (b. 1956), Mas'ūd Ḥamdān (b. 1959), Ṣāliḥ Azzām (b. 1965), Usāma Abū Ghūsh (b. 1966?), Ayman Kāmil Ighbāriyya (b. 1968), Sayyid Qashshū'a (Sayed Kashua) (b. 1975), and Ayman Siksik (b. 1984). About the well-known among them, see Moreh and 'Abbāsī 1987, pp. 65–6, 69, 80–1, 82–3, 155–6, 158, 160, 169–70, 218–19, 221–3. See also Manṣūr 1992, pp. 63–6. On novels by Manṣūr, Shammās, and Qashshū'a as representatives of three generations of Hebrew writing by Arab authors, see Kayyal 2008, pp. 31–51. On interfaces of linguistic, sociological, psychological, and political aspects and on patterns of language usage in the writings of Shammās, Maṣalḥa, Kashua, and Siksik, see Tannenbaum 2014, pp. 99–117.

23 Prominent among them are Makram Khūrī (b. 1945), Yūsuf Abū Warda (b. 1953), Muḥammad Bakrī (b. 1953), Salwā Naqqāra-Ḥaddād (b. 1959), Khawla Ḥājj-Dibsī (b. 1969), in addition to Salīm Ḍaw (b. 1950) and Suhayl Ḥaddād (b. 1951). See Shohat 1989, pp. 237–73; Shammās 1990, pp. 7–17; Snir 1995b, pp. 49–59. See also an interview with Khawla Ḥājj-Dibsī (available at: https://www.mekomit.co.il, February 15, 2022, last accessed February 22, 2022). Among the journalists, the outstanding case is that of the

Of special interest is the case of Sayed Kashua (Sayyid Qashshū'a) (b. 1975),[24] who never wrote in Arabic and has acquired a significant status in Israeli culture and in the press since the late 1990s. Among his novels exploring the marginal and liminal position occupied by Palestinian citizens of Israel, we can mention *Aravim Rokdim* (*Dancing Arabs*) (2002),[25] *Va-Yehi Boker* (*Let It Be Morning*) (2004),[26] and *Guf Sheni Yaḥid* (*Second Person Singular*) (2010).[27] In 2015, Kashua published a new book, which is a collection of his personal weekly columns in Hebrew for the *Haaretz* newspaper: *Ben Haaretz* (English title: *Native*, lit. *Son of Haaretz* (= the Land)) (2015).[28] His last book is *'Akov Aḥar Shinuyyim* (*Track Changes*) (2017).[29] In 2007, a prime-time situation comedy that he wrote, *'Avoda 'Arabit* (*Arab Labor*), was presented on Israel's commercial Channel 2 television. The series, which dealt with Israeli prejudices through the eyes of a Muslim-Arab family, was popular with the Jewish audience but was considered by the Arabic local press as an act of treachery.[30] In June 2014, Kashua was invited to deliver a prestigious commencement address to the graduating class at the Hebrew University. Though the invitation was unprecedented—the first time the university had brought in an Arab to speak at graduation—one can hardly rule out that the invitation had been dictated by the aforementioned cognitive

Druze Rafīq Ḥalabī (b. 1947): after serving for six years as the Head of the News Section for Channel 1 on Israeli television, he was one of the candidates for the position of the director of the channel. On his career as a Hebrew journalist, he says: "I am struggling for my right to contribute to Israeli culture. It was not a coincidence that I studied at the university Hebrew language, in order to master all its secrets, and that language indeed has become my additional mother tongue" (*Kolbo* [Haifa], January 17, 2003, p. 48). Rafīq Ḥalabī is now the mayor of Dāliyat al-Karmil.

24 On Sayed Kashua's novels and how he articulates his identity, see Elkad-Lehman 2008, pp. 119–54; Shimony 2013, pp. 146–69; Suleiman 2017, pp. 152–66; Grumberg 2018, pp. 1–30. See also the interview with Kashua in *Yediot Aḥronoth* (*7 Days*), January 11, 2002, pp. 20–6, as well as the reviews by Haya Hofman in *Yediot Aḥronoth* (supplement), February 1, 2002, pp. 26–7; 'Ilit Karp (b. 1962) in *Kolbo* (Haifa), February 15, 2002, p. 90; Yoram Melcer (b. 1963) in *Maariv* (literary supplement), February 13, 2004. On the duality of Arab-Israeli identity and the politics of survival in Kashua's *Let It Be Morning*, see Agsous 2018, pp. 1–14; Soman et al. 2021, pp. 1–10.

25 Kashua 2002; a monodrama based on the novel was performed in September 2005 by Norman 'Īsā (b. 1967) in a joint production of the Haifa Municipal Theater and the Arab-Hebrew Theater in Jaffa. On the novel, see Rottenberg 2008, pp. 99–114.

26 Kashua 2004 (English translation: Kashua 2006).

27 Kashua 2010 (English translation: Kashua 2013). See Ebileeni 2017, pp. 222–37.

28 Kashua 2015 (English translation: Kashua 2016). See Lital Levy's review of the book in *Middle Eastern Literatures* 20.3 (2017), pp. 306–8.

29 Kashua 2017 (English translation: Kashua 2020). See Priyanka Lindgren's review in *World Literature Today* 94.4, available at: https://www.worldliteraturetoday.org/2020/autumn/track-changes-sayed-kashua, last accessed July 23, 2021.

30 See *International Herald Tribune*, January 7, 2008; *Haaretz*, February 12, 2008.

dissonance. Nevertheless, Kashua seemed to be, from a very early stage of his career as a Hebrew writer, aware of the role he was required to play in the Israeli-Hebrew culture, sometimes even provocatively implicitly alluding to his unique position, such as he did in his speech at the graduation, as reported by the *The New Yorker*:

> Standing before the students and their families, Kashua decided to say a few words about the political climate. These were agitated days. A week earlier, three Israeli teenagers had been kidnapped while hitching a ride in a settlement south of Jerusalem. Kashua recounted how his son told him about it, garbling the news reports and the results of that summer's World Cup soccer tournament. In a recent game, the Netherlands had grabbed five goals; now, his son said, "Palestine grabbed three." His line drew nervous laughs, and Kashua quickly reassured the crowd: "It's my fervent hope ... the boys will be back home, safe and sound." But he confessed to feeling "a stabbing in the chest," and asked, "Does the hope that they will return home imply some sort of declaration that the settlements can be considered legitimate?"[31]

Most Israeli-Palestinian intellectuals have adopted a cynical approach toward the phenomenon of Palestinians writing in Hebrew, admitting that nothing can be done against the backdrop of the rejection of Arab cultural values in Israeli society. A response to such an approach can be found in two novels by another Israeli-Palestinian writer in Hebrew, Ayman Siksik (Sikseck) (b. 1984), *El Yafo* (*To Jaffa*) (2010) and *Tishrin* (*Blood Ties*) (2016).[32] The first, which was translated into Arabic and published in Cairo,[33] has a motto from "I Write in Hebrew" by the Israeli-Palestinian poet Salmān Maṣālḥa (b. 1953):

> I write in Hebrew
> Which is not my mother tongue,
> In order to lose myself in the world.
> He who doesn't get lost, will never
> Find the whole.

As I argued in my studies on this issue, the relationship between those writers and the Hebrew literary system is not balanced; few have expressed such a "one-way" relationship more eloquently than Anton Shammās:

> חָד-סטריות הִיא מִכְּלָלֵי הַמִּשְׂחָק. עֲמִיתַי
> יוֹצֵא מֵהַשִּׁירָה הָעִבְרִית וְתוֹלֶה שֶׁלֶט
> ”תכף אָשׁוּב.“ אֲנִי לֹא, אני לא. אני

[31] *The New Yorker*, September 7, 2015.
[32] See Siksik 2010; Siksik 2016. On the novel, see Fahmawi-Watad 2022, pp. 1–23.
[33] Siksik 2014.

שׁוֹלֵחַ גְּלוּיוֹת בַּבֹּקֶר, לִידִידַי הַיְּקָרִים
בִּמְיֻחָד, כְּדֵי לְהוֹדִיעַם שֶׁאֲנִי שׁוֹלֵחַ לָהֶם
גְּלוּיוֹת בַּבֹּקֶר.

One-wayness is one of the rules of the Game. Amichai
Comes out of the Hebrew poetry and hangs a sign
"Will be back soon." I don't, I don't. I
Send postcards in the morning, to my very dear friends
In order to notify them that I send them
Postcards in the morning.[34]

Typical of the literary activities of Palestinians who write in Hebrew is their membership in two different, even "hostile" literary systems—the Arabic into which they were born and usually created their first works, and the Hebrew into which they were thrown more or less against their will, even if later they are seen to embrace it in an act of conscious aesthetic preference. Most of them possess a natural skill and ability of expression in Hebrew and master the modernist techniques and literary style that enable them to write fluently in the language, sometimes about the same experience in both Hebrew and Arabic.[35] Significant also is the fact that they went through the formal Israeli educational system purposely set up by the Ministry of Education to produce an "Arab-Israeli" intelligentsia willing and able to identify with the Jewish-Zionist state. Both ʻArāyidī and Shammās, for example, were students at Tichon Erony Hey (Municipal High School 5) in Haifa, which the government established so as to undermine the educational influence of the privately run Christian Arab Orthodox College.[36]

[34] Shammās 1979, p. 13.

[35] For example, most of the poems in ʻArāyidī 2002a are Hebrew versions of poems previously published in ʻArāyidī 1994 and ʻArāyidī 1999. See also ʻArāyidī 1986, pp. 47–50 and the Arabic version in ʻArāyidī 1984, pp. 8–17. Three poems in ʻArāyidī 1976, pp. 45, 61, 69, are Arabic versions of poems first published in ʻArāyidī 1975, pp. 19, 24 and ʻArāyidī 1972, p. 36. See also Shammās 1974, p. 27; and the Arabic version in Shammās 1974b, p. 258.

[36] The Arab Orthodox College is funded and run independently by Haifa's Christian-Arab community. It is part of that community's efforts to retain some form of cultural autonomy, in that the College provides its Arab students with an education that tries to steer clear of the Zionist indoctrination imposed by Israel's Ministry of Education. On the education system among the Palestinian Arabs in Israel as well as the attempts to impose on them Jewish, Hebrew, and Zionist culture in order to achieve their assimilation into Hebrew culture and abandon the Arab-Palestinian identity, see Al-Haj 1995; Amara 1999; Amara and Marʻi 1999; Bäuml 2002, pp. 418–31.

In his quasi-autobiographical novel, *Arabeskot* (*Arabesques*) (1986),[37] Shammās describes with delightful irony how Palestinian schoolchildren are forced to adopt the symbols of the conqueror. During ceremonies that marked both the end of the first elementary school year and the first anniversary of the founding of the public school in the village, all children were sent out to collect laurel branches that decorated an enormous Star of David that one of the teachers had put together from six wooden planks in order to make a good impression on the Jewish school inspector. Its placement, however, frightened the children taking part in the program and the people sitting in the first row of chairs, who thought it might come toppling down on them.[38] Several years later, Shammās was to write:

> I sometimes wonder whether we were not seared by the star, whether it wasn't a branding iron after all—a branding iron to all the Arabs who were left, for some reason or another, inside the borders of Israel, in the year of our Lord Balfour 1948, henceforth to be referred to as the Green Liners. And when you brand someone, you are actually telling him two equally painful things: first, that he belongs to you, that he must abide by your laws, wander only in the regions that you had put under his disposal and keep away from the ones that are out-of-bounds; second, you're telling that this searing of the skin is just a searing of the skin—you are not after his heart. When he, too, realizes that you do not seek his utter loyalty, then you both break even, confining yourselves to a position lacking any mutual anticipation. You both acquiesce in the rules of the game: "Don't call us and we won't call you."[39]

Palestinian intellectuals and writers claim that the official Israeli government policy of education is aimed at "initially phasing out the Arab personality in Israel and then, as a follow-up, demanding that personality accommodate itself to the state." What Israel wanted to raise were "people whose tongue had been amputated ... with no cultural past, and no future. Just an improvised present, and a free-floated personality."[40]

[37] Shammās 1987 (English translation: Shammās 1988. All translations from the novel are based on Eden's translation with only minor corrections). The novel's epigraph is: "Most first novels are disguised autobiographies. This autobiography is a disguised novel" (Clive James, *Unreliable Memoirs*). For a bibliographic list of reviews and studies written on the novel, see Kritz 1990, pp. 363–73. On the novel, see also Balaban 1989, pp. 418–21; Brenner 1993, pp. 431–45; Brenner 1999, pp. 85–108; Feldman 1999, pp. 373–89; Szyska 2001, pp. 217–32; Shamir-Tulipman 2004, pp. 173–222; Ginsburg 2006, pp. 187–204; El-Hussari 2013, pp. 423–33.

[38] Shammās 1987, p. 212 (Shammās 1988, p. 237). Cf. Shiḥāda 1997, pp. 139–40.

[39] In Silberstein 1991, p. 219.

[40] Hareven 1981, pp. 44–5.

2. RETERRITORIALIZATION

From the moment they decided to begin publishing in Hebrew, Palestinian bilingual writers in Israel have rebelled against the exclusive "ownership" the Jews appear to reserve for themselves over the modern Hebrew language, and have protested against the ethnocultural norm that identifies each Hebrew author as a Jew (i.e., refuses to make room for authors writing in Hebrew who are not Jewish). What these Arab authors are after is to pry modern Hebrew away from the one function for which it was created (i.e., to be the language of Zionism), and instead to make it the language of *all* Israel's citizens.[41] To enact this new connection between identity, language, and territory, they focus on "un-Jewing" Hebrew, that is, on a "deterritorialization" and simultaneous "reterritorialization" of the language.[42] Shammās has put this in explicit terms as follows:

> What I'm trying to do—mulishly, it seems—is to un-Jew the Hebrew language ... to make it more Israeli and less Jewish, thus bringing it back to its Semitic origins, to its place. This is parallel to what I believe the state should be. As English is the language of those who speak it, so is Hebrew; and so the state should be the state of those who live in it.[43]

In another place he argues that "to my mind, the only achievement of the Jewish National Movement/Zionism was the desire, and later the power, to reterritorialize the Hebrew language."[44]

As early as the mid-1970s, Shammās was already describing himself and his colleagues as the young generation that "bursts through the fence, overcomes the barrier of Hebrew and tries to reach other domains." This generation has the benefit of two worlds: "Knowing Hebrew introduces it, whether through Hebrew literature or through world literature translated

[41] In other words, "the institution of statehood that secures Hebrew also challenges its identification with Judaism and the Jews" (Wisse 2000, p. 326).

[42] Cf. Hever 1987, pp. 47–76 (reprinted in JanMohamed and Lloyd 1993, pp. 264–93); Hever 1989, pp. 30–2; Hever 2001, pp. 175–204. J. L. Kraemer's instructive remark on the culture-bearers of humanism in Islam is very useful here: "The culture bearers were in many respects marginal people. And they performed the cultural role that marginal people often carry out within the framework of majority culture that differs from their own ... marginal people tend to undermine the politically dominant culture so as to escape from their own marginality. In doing so they often become innovators" (Kraemer 1984, pp. 17–18).

[43] Shammās 1989, p. 10. Cf. Mariani 1991, pp. 75–9; *Kol Ha-'Īr* (Jerusalem), February 27, 1987, p. 58. Reflecting on his failure, Shammās said in the early 1990s: "I wrote in the language of the territory. I approached the territory and told her, Territory, come on—is your language Hebrew? Great! I'll write in it. Are you going to give me part of yourself?" (Lavie 1996, p. 85. Cf. Cooke 2001, pp. 36–7).

[44] Shammās 1994, p. 168.

into Hebrew, to unfamiliar experiences; while knowing Arabic introduces it to the recent achievements of modern Arabic literature."[45]

The achievements in Hebrew literature by the Palestinian bilingual writers, especially 'Arāyidī and Shammās, are beyond any doubt.[46] They have, for example, contributed in both poetry and prose several Hebrew descriptions of Israeli country scenery that equal the best descriptions by Jewish writers.[47] Yet they have been unable to divorce the Jewish heritage from the Hebrew language. This is perhaps not as surprising as their conscious aesthetic preference of the Hebrew language, which demands that they absorb at least part of the Jewish cultural and religious heritage. This comes through clearly in their works, although these cannot be labeled as Jewish literature.[48] If one can call this their failure to un-Jew the Hebrew language, we can compare it with the failure of the national territorial ideologies in the Arab world to separate the Arabic language from Islam. For example, the "Phoenician" ideology advocated by the Lebanese poet Sa'īd 'Aql (1912–2014) comes to mind, who through his literary activities tried to create a non-Islamic Lebanese culture, with roots in the ancient Phoenician culture.[49] Shammās' love for 'Aql's works and his sympathetic attitude toward 'Aql as a person suggests perhaps that in this particular "Phoenician" ideology he found the inspiration for his own ideological stance regarding the "un-Jewing" of the Hebrew language.[50] Like 'Aql, who tried to sever the link between Arabic culture and Islam, Shammās strove to purify Hebrew literature of its Jewish features and relics. However, just as Arabic is holy for Muslims by virtue of it being the language of the Qur'ān, so the holiness of Hebrew is inexorably bound up with the Jewish religion. Similarly, some even claim that one cannot separate English from Christianity.[51]

While thus wanting to expand the boundaries of the Hebrew literary canon, bilingual Palestinian writers also seek to exchange the Jewish values of the state for those of a true democracy. For the contradiction between

45 Shammās 1976, pp. 1–7; reprinted in Hochman 1988, pp. 425–30. Cf. Brumm 1995, p. 82; Snir 2005c, pp. 60–1.

46 Cf. Avraham Balaban's evaluation of *Arabeskot* as quoted in Elad-Bouskila 1999, pp. 147–8. Dan Laor, on the other hand, considers it a failure (Elad-Bouskila 1999, p. 148) (a version of Elad-Bouskila 1999 was also published in Elad-Bouskila 1999a, pp. 32–62).

47 For example, see Shammās 1987, pp. 56–7 (Shammās 1988, pp. 63–4).

48 On the general issue of Jewish literature, see Yudkin 1982; Wirth-Nesher 1994; Wisse 2000; Shaked 2006. For a fresh approach toward a theorizing of Jewish literatures, whose main component is contiguity and not continuity, see Miron 2005. On the relevance of the term "Jewish literature" to modern Arabic literature written by Jews, see Snir 2005a, p. 518. On this topic, see also Muehlethaler 2020, pp. 45–52; and below, Epilogue.

49 Cf. Jargy 1961, pp. 93–101; Bawardi 2016, esp. pp. 12–17, 57–88, 137–41.

50 For example, see Shammās 1982–1983, p. 21; Shammās 1985, pp. 30–1.

51 For example, see Ozick 1989, p. 13.

the democratic ideal of a state that respects the identities and upholds the rights of all its citizens and the current exclusive Israeli-Jewish cultural identity, they present a somewhat utopian solution, advocating one single Israeli nationality to be shared by all those who live within the boundaries of Israel, Jews as well as Arabs. Shammās received extensive media coverage following an open debate on this topic with the Jewish-Hebrew writer A. B. Yehoshua (1936–2022), for whom the only authentic Judaism is that of the Jews in Israel.[52] In *Arabesques*, Shammās expresses this debate through the confrontation between the narrator and a fictional character named Yehoshua Bar-On, apparently a thinly veiled stand-in for Yehoshua.[53] It should be noted, however, that while Yehoshua's insular opinions represent the vast majority of the Israeli-Jewish public, Shammās does not enjoy the same position within the Palestinian minority, where his opinions are considered exceptional. Some of his Arab-Palestinian colleagues have even mocked them.[54]

Given the bilingual writers' advocacy of a new Israeli identity, it is not surprising that one of the last Canaanite thinkers, the Hebrew poet and intellectual Aharon Amir (1923–2008), had a special interest in Arab-Palestinian authors writing in Hebrew. Because he wanted Hebrew to become the *lingua franca* of the region, Amir considered them forerunners in a process whereby Israel was to become a Jewish-Arab melting pot.[55] In response to one of the essays on the topic,[56] Amir wrote that the "un-Jewing of the Hebrew language" does not need any assistance from Shammās and 'Arāyidī, for it has been going on anyway ever since the "desacralization" of Hebrew deprived it of its religious-worship holiness and made it a language of everyday life, a practical tool for dialogue and communication. This is also the reason why religious believers avoid using Hebrew for the needs of everyday life. According to Amir, Shammās and 'Arāyidī are indeed pioneers, and this is the

52 For example, see Shammās 1986, pp. 26–7; Yehoshua 1989, pp. 197–205. Cf. Grossman 1992, pp. 193–211; Brenner 1999, pp. 97–8; Elad-Bouskila 1999, p. 158, n. 53; Silberstein 1999, pp. 139–45. Recently, Yehoshua has not ruled out the possibility that Christian, Muslim, and Druze Arabs will want to penetrate deeper into Israeli-Jewish nationality without converting their religions, but that can be done only after a true separation between religion and nationality in Israel and when comprehensive peace prevails in the Middle East "after 50 or 100 years" (Yehoshua 2003, pp. 27, 78).

53 Shammās has never denied that. Cf. Parmenter 1994, p. 95.

54 For example, see Darwīsh and al-Qāsim 1990, p. 179. Cf. Shammās' own words following the publication of his first collection of Hebrew poems, *Hard Cover* (Shammās 1974): "Some of the Arab readers consider my book a kind of attraction, others see it as a mask, and Arabs do not like theatre" (*Davar*, June 21, 1974).

55 See interview with Aharon Amir in *Apirion* 14 (Spring 1989), p. 28, as well as his words in *Ḥadashot*, October 6, 1989, p. 6. Cf. 'Arāyidī 1991, p. 41; Elad-Bouskila 1999, pp. 148–9.

56 Snir 1992, pp. 6–9.

achievement for which they will be remembered even without checking in detail the quality of their work. In his eyes, Shammās and ʿArāyidī do not want Israel to become "a melting pot of nationalities," but in time, and as simply as possible, "a territorial-national society, profane and democratic—almost the only one of its kind in the whole Middle East—that knows how to bring close and love her beloved sons, including the 'exceptional' ones among them."[57] Nevertheless, even within the circle of Yonathan Ratosh (1908–1981), the major ideologist of the Canaanite movement, there were doubts that Muslim Arabs, as opposed to non-Muslims, could be imagined as wanting to exchange their original cultural identity for a Hebrew one.[58] This explains why Ratosh himself was full of appreciation for the Christian minority in Israel and envisaged a federation with the Druze Mountain (Jabal al-Durūz) in Syria.[59] There is, of course, no sign of any desire among Palestinians, at least the Muslims among them, to exchange their cultural identity in this way—that thought is simply unrealistic. According to the Israeli critic Hanan Hever (b. 1953), Shammās' "Israeli" dream differs from the Canaanite vision, since he is not calling for a liberation from the fetters of Judaism through an aggressive severing of historical roots. Shammās' vision "represents a utopia emerging from the detailed critical confrontation between the cultural demands of past and present."[60] However, the difference between Shammās' ideas and those of the Canaanite ideology is one of means, not essence.[61]

57 Amir 1992, pp. 37–41. On the controversy that developed about this topic, see especially Oren 1992, pp. 63–4.

58 The exceptions prove it. The Hebrew novels published by Israeli-Muslim-Palestinian writers do not seem to have any literary pretensions, for example, Usāma Abū Ghūsh, *Ke-Yehudi ben Yehudim* (*As a Jew Among Jews*) (Raʿanana: Institute for Israeli Arab Studies, 1995) or Sayed Kashua's novels, such as *Aravim Rokdim* (*Dancing Arabs*) (Ben-Shemen: Modan, 2002). A monodrama based on the novel was performed in September 2005 by Norman ʿĪsā in a joint production of the Haifa Municipal Theater and the Arab-Hebrew Theater in Jaffa. The novel was also adapted into a movie (2014) by Israeli director Eran Riklis (b. 1954). Another novel by Kashua, *Va-Yehi Boker* (*Let It Be Morning*) (Kashua 2004) (English translation: Kashua 2006) was adapted into a movie, in 2021, by Israeli director Eran Kolirin (b. 1973). In June 2021, the film was selected to compete in the Un Certain Regard section at the 2021 Cannes Film Festival. However, the Palestinian cast of the film opposed the categorization of the film as "Israeli," and withdrew from the Cannes Film Festival in protest. The film was selected as the Israeli entry for the Best International Feature Film at the 94th Academy Awards. On Sayyid Qashshūʿa's novels and how he articulates his identity, see Elkad-Lehman 2008, pp. 119–54; Mendelson-Maoz 2019, pp. 137–64.

59 See Ratosh 1967, pp. 33–4. Cf. Porath 1989, pp. 74, 91, 189, 252, 266, 340–1, 346, 355.

60 Hever 1987, pp. 75–6.

61 One should, however, be careful not to associate Shammās' Canaanite conception with the "Canaanite" narrative in the national Palestinian movement (Eshed 2003, pp. 20–3). While Shammās' conception adopted the Hebrew Canaanite vision, the Palestinian one is part of the Palestinian nation-building movement.

Palestinian bilingual writers—Muslim, Christian, and Druze—have many traits in common. Yet, one can discern two trends or models represented by Na'īm 'Arāyidī, on the one hand, and Anton Shammās, on the other.

3. "I MELT OUT OF LOVE"

Na'īm 'Arāyidī belongs to the group of bilingual writers whose exposure to Hebrew language and culture has effected a change in their cultural preferences. Talking about the anxiety experienced by any person in whom two different cultures conflict, he states that "true exposure to the other culture totally changes all the paths of thinking and of the soul. On the one hand, you do not want to assimilate. On the other, you do want to resemble."[62] This theme comes most strongly to the fore in 'Arāyidī's poetry, but also appears in his prose.[63] 'Arāyidī's exceptional position in the cultural habitat in which he works is marked by his negative attitude toward local Arabic literature, on the one hand, though he writes in Arabic as well, and by his veneration of Hebrew literature, on the other.[64] The problem, he says, is "not learning the new language [Hebrew], but forgetting the old one [Arabic]."[65] The fact that he published his main literary work, a novel called *Tvila Katlanit* (*Fatal Christening*), in Hebrew only serves to underscore this attitude even more. Still, 'Arāyidī complains of the attitude of the canonical center of Hebrew literature: "No one wants to hear my voice / And no one wants to understand me."[66] Therefore, one finds him expressing a sense of having missed an opportunity:

לוּ הָלַכְנוּ
בְּדַרְכֵּנוּ
וְדִבַּרְנוּ בִּשְׂפָתֵנוּ
וְרָכַבְנוּ עַל גָּמָל
וְרָעַבְנוּ וְצָמֵאנוּ
וְעָשִׂינוּ אַהֲבָה
וַחֲסַל

[62] Grossman 1992, p. 218. Cf. the double allegiance of North African writers in French torn between two cultures (Joyaux 1980, pp. 121, 126. See also Snir 2017, pp. 112–16).

[63] For example, see 'Arāyidī 1988, pp. 109–21; 'Arāyidī 1992.

[64] 'Arāyidī 1985, pp. 10–11; 'Arāyidī 1986a, p. 33; 'Arāyidī 1989, p. 79; 'Arāyidī 1991, pp. 41–3; Grossman 1992, pp. 218–19. Cf. the sharp reaction of the Palestinian-Israeli writer Riyāḍ Baydas (b. 1960) to 'Arāyidī's views in *al-Jadīd* 11/12 (November–December 1985), pp. 11–17. See also Bukaee 1990, p. 9.

[65] 'Arāyidī 1991, p. 43.

[66] 'Arāyidī 1975, pp. 33–6.

If we only had gone
In our way
And had spoken our language
And rode a camel
And felt hunger and thirst
And had made love
And that's all.[67]

One can also find, especially in his poetry, feelings of bitterness, as in "Once I'll Talk":

פַּעַם אֲנִי אֲדַבֵּר
אֲדַבֵּר
וְאֶת מְחִיר דְּבָרַי
אוּכַל לְשַׁלֵּם

עוֹד תִּרְאוּ
אִם יִשָּׁבֵר לִי
אוֹמֵר אֶת הַכֹּל
אֶת כֹּל שֶׁהָיָה
טָמוּן בִּשְׁבָרַי

אֲנִי אוֹמֵר —
יֵשׁ לִי מָה לוֹמַר
וְדַי.

Once I'll talk
I'll talk
And the cost of my words
I'll be able to pay

You'll see
If I shall be broken
I'll say it all
All that was
Hidden in my broken pieces

I shall say—
I do have something to say
And that's enough.[68]

67 'Arāyidī 1986, p. 42.

68 'Arāyidī 1972, p. 25. When the collection that included the poem appeared, 'Arāyidī was jailed and accused of being a Jewish-Arab spy and terrorist working in the service of Syrian intelligence. Commenting on the book, Mark Geffen (1917–1989) quotes the aforementioned poem, and, mentioning the accusation, he added: "Certainly, in a democratic regime the poem is by no means considered to be a 'forensic item,' only the days to

'Arāyidī finds refuge from his identity crisis in a longing for his childhood home and family origins:

חָזַרְתִּי אֶל הַכְּפָר
בּוֹ יָדַעְתִּי לִבְכּוֹת בָּרִאשׁוֹנָה
חָזַרְתִּי אַל הָהָר
בּוֹ הַנּוֹף הוּא הַטֶּבַע
וְאֵין מָקוֹם לַתְּמוּנָה
חָזַרְתִּי אַל בֵּיתִי הֶעָשׂוּי אֲבָנִים
אוֹתָן חָצְבוּ אֲבוֹתַי מִסְּלָעִים
— — — — — — —
חָזַרְתִּי אֶל הַכְּפָר הַגְּפָנִים
בּוֹ הָיִיתִי בגלגולי הַקּוֹדֶם
שׁוֹרֶשׁ מִנֵּי רִיבּוֹא הגפנים
עַל הָאֲדָמָה הַטּוֹבָה
עַד שֶׁבָּאָה הָרוּחַ הַזֹּאת
ותדפני רָחוֹק ותחזירני
בגלגולי כְּחוֹזֵר בַּתְּשׁוּבָה.

I went back to the village
Where I first learned to cry
I went back to the mountain
Where the scenery is nature
And there's no place for a picture
I went back to my house-of-stone
Which my ancestors quarried out of rocks
— — — — — — — — — — —
I went back to the village
Where I was in my previous life
A root out of the thousands of vines
On the good earth
Until this wind came
And blew me away and brought me back
In my transmigration as a penitent.[69]

come will reveal if it really consists of a confession of the young man" (*'Al Hamishmar*, December 15, 1972). See also the reference of David Lazar (1902–1974) to the contradiction between the poems in the collection, which could be interpreted as heralding a new Jewish-Muslim "golden age" similar to the Andalusian period, and his involvement in espionage (*Maariv*, December 17, 1978). 'Arāyidī was convicted by the courts only of negligence when it came to preventing an offense and was sentenced to six-and-half months in prison, which was the period he had been imprisoned during the full course of the trial.

69 'Arāyidī 1986, pp. 7–8. For a French translation of the poem, see Araydi 1990, pp. 8–10. On the poem as symbolizing 'Arāyidī's special status in Israeli culture and how "he perceives his return home to his village as an exile from exile," see Lavie 1996, pp. 55–7. Seventeen years later, 'Arāyidī published the poem "Back, Again, to the Village," in which his identity

He also funnels a great part of his literary energy into writing about the love he has for the land and its scenery in a way so intense that it is difficult to find a contemporary parallel even in the works of Jewish poets and writers whose sense of ownership and love of the land are never in doubt among the Hebrew-reading public. Unlike them, ʻArāyidī feels he must "prove" his love again and again to the Hebrew-reading public. His attitude toward the virginal scenery, not yet destroyed by the hands of man, is erotic:

אֲהוּבָתִי הַגְּלִילִית
עַל הַר הַכַּרְמֶל
נוֹתֶנֶת לִי שֶׁעוּר
בְּאַהֲבַת הַמּוֹלֶדֶת.

My Galilean beloved
On Mount Carmel
Gives me a lesson
In the love of the land.[70]

This love is not unrequited: "Haifa shall embrace me and carry me on her back."[71] It is mixed with his Druze religious belief in reincarnation and appears as a pantheistic experience:

הָזַעְתָּר שֶׁעַל הַכַּרְמֶל הָיָה
לְגִלְגּוּלִי הַקֹּדֶם

The wild thyme of the Carmel was
My previous life.[72]

The descriptions of the scenery and nature mingle with those of the beloved until it is no longer clear whether her beauty is intended to expose the beauty of the land, or the other way round:

הַכַּרְמֶל מְנַמְנֵם עַל גְּרוֹנִי לְלַטְּפֵנִי
כִּשְׁתִיקַת אֲהוּבָה שֶׁהָיְתָה
כְּזִכְרוֹנוֹת,
כְּרִקּוּד הַלְּבָנָה.
עָנָן אָפֹר וּבוֹדֵד בֵּין יָדַי
כְּהַר שֶׁל פִּטְמוֹת —
כָּל הַיֹּפִי הַזֶּה הוּא יָפְיֵךְ
וְהַיָּם יַעֲשֶׂה צוּרֹתָיו בַּסְּלָעִים

crisis is much more acute (published with its French translation in *Poésie & Art* 5 [2003], pp. 23–4; republished in ʻArāyidī 2006, pp. 34–5).

70 ʻArāyidī 1986, p. 27.

71 ʻArāyidī 1986, p. 49.

72 ʻArāyidī 1986, p. 38.

— — — — — —

בְּרַגְלַי כּוֹכָבִים אֲהַלֵּךְ
כַּרְמֶלִי נְקֵבָה,
וְלֹא יָדַעְתִּי לִשְׁכֹּחַ אֶת הַגָּלִיל

— — — — — —

הַזִּכְרוֹנוֹת הָלְכוּ חָלְפוּ לָהֶם
וְרַק הַצָּמוֹת,
וְעֵינֶיהָ הַיְּרֻקּוֹת
וּפִטְמוֹת כִּלְהָקוֹת לְהַנִיקֵנִי
וּלְהַשְׁלִיכֵנִי הֲלוֹם
בֵּין הָאֳרָנִים הָאֵלֶּה

— — — — — —

קָשָׁה הַפְּרֵדָה
וְהַשָּׁמַיִם מַמְטִירִים פְּגִישׁוֹת עַד אֵין סְפֹר
וּמַדּוּעַ לֹא אֶמְצָא לוּא רַק אַחַת
שֶׁתְּמַלְּאֵנִי בַּמַּיִם עַל פְּנֵי הַיָּמִים.

The Carmel naps on my throat to caress me
As the silence of a lover that was
As memories,
As the dance of the moon.
A gray and lonesome cloud within my hands
As a mountain of nipples—
All this beauty is yours
And the sea will make its figures on the rocks

— — — — — — — — — — —

With feet of stars I'll walk
My Carmel is a female
And I knew not to forget the Galilee.

— — — — — — — — — — —

The memories have passed by
And only the braids,
And her green eyes
And flocks of nipples to suckle me
And to throw me over here
Among these pines.

— — — — — — — — — — —

Farewell is hard
And the sky rains with innumerous appointments
And why won't I find just one
To fill me with water over the days.

Sometimes it may even seem that love of the land is only a substitute for the love of a woman, while the words of the Hebrew *Song of Songs* echo in the background:

הַכַּרְמֶל מַמְטִיר נְשִׁיקוֹת
עַל גּוּפִי הַשְׁחַרְחַר
קוֹץ וְדַרְדַּר
וַאֲנִי נָמוֹג מִתּוֹךְ אַהֲבָה.

The Carmel rain's kisses
Upon my black body
Thorn and thistle
And I melt out of love.[73]

Against the background of his identity crisis and his fissured soul, it is easy to understand 'Arāyidī's constant yearning to serve as a bridge between the two "hostile" cultures. 'Arāyidī never misses an opportunity to emphasize his position as being at a Hebrew–Arabic crossroads between the two cultures.[74] "I'm living on a fence," he says, "one foot here, one foot there, always trying to close my legs, sometimes with the literary establishment's help, sometimes despite their protest."[75] In a recent poem, titled "On the Question Why I Write in Hebrew," he justifies his Hebrew writing as follows:

כְּדֵי לִבְרֹא אֶת הָעוֹלָם מְחַדֵּשׁ
שֶׁיִּהְיוּ הַדְּבָרִים אַחֶרֶת, מַמָּשׁ
אַחֶרֶת, וְלִרְאוֹת כִּי טוֹב.

In order to create again the world
So that things will be different, very
Different, and to see that it is good.[76]

This desire to serve the cause of peace is also found in his work as a critic and researcher in both Arabic and Hebrew literature.[77] 'Arāyidī's ambition is also reflected in the dichotomy he represents between the pure and virginal nature and the modernization that threatens the human soul. Thus, for instance, his loneliness and double alienation and estrangement are reflected in symbols that join old and new and fluctuate between two poles: simplicity

[73] 'Arāyidī 1986, pp. 47–50. Cf. his Arabic poem "Allegory" published in 'Arāyidī 1978, pp. 44–9.

[74] He wrote a poem in memory of Itzhak Rabin soon after his murder on November 4, 1995.

[75] Lavie 1996, p. 56.

[76] 'Arāyidī 2006, p. 24. The words וְלִרְאוֹת כִּי טוֹב are based on the repeated formula in Genesis 1: "וַיַּרְא אֱלֹהִים, כִּי-טוֹב" ("and God saw that it was good").

[77] See 'Arāyidī 1980; 'Arāyidī 1985; 'Arāyidī 1989a. In 2004, Éditions Stavit in Paris published a selection of his and the Hebrew poet Miron Izakson's (b. 1956) poetry translated into French under the title *Nés en Israël*. Referring to the publication of this book, in which the poetry appears in the original (Arabic or Hebrew) as well as in French translation, 'Arāyidī said: "In this difficult period, such cultural connection of poetry in three languages could and must create a dialogue between peoples and nations" (*Yediot Aḥronoth*, literary supplement, March 28, 2003, p. 28).

and modernization, village and city. ʿArāyidī and others who identify with his attitude toward Hebrew language and culture present a sort of glorification of Hebrew that can be summarized by the word "love," which frequently recurs in their works.

4. "HEBREW, ARABIC, AND DEATH"

Unlike ʿArāyidī, Anton Shammās felt from the beginning of his literary career that the path he had decided to follow could well undermine his native identity. While at school Hebrew was forced upon him as a "step-mother language," he remained aware of the importance of his native Arabic, as Jean Sulivan put it, as "an arsenal, a vocabulary, a system of signs that permits the individual to be part of the tribe."[78] He has always kept the feeling "that this whole thing is a sort of cultural trespassing and I might, one day, be punished for it."[79] When he gives one of his collections of poetry the title *Shetaḥ Hefker* (*No-Man's Land*) (1979), the reader quickly understands that this is the cultural area in which he now lives and acts. The opening poem in the collection reads as follows:

אָבִי מֵת בַּקַּיִץ, והחיץ
בֵּינֵינוּ הוֹלֵךְ מֵאָז וְנֶהֱרָס.

עַכְשָׁו, בִּסְתָו, הוּא נִצָּב כְּדֶלֶת
בִּקְצֵה שֶׁטַח הַהֶפְקֵר שֶׁל חַיַּי —
הַגְּבוּל לְפָנָיו.

כָּךְ אֲנִי מְסַפֵּר לַיֶּלֶד
שֶׁנִּרְמֵס בַּתֵּכִי,
כָּךְ אֲנִי מְסַפֵּר לַיֶּלֶד
הַנִּצָּב לְפָנַי.

אָבִי נִצַּב כְּדֶלֶת,
וְאַחַד מִשְּׁלָשְׁתֵּנוּ נִכְנַס.

My father died in the summer, and the isolation
Between us has been ever since demolished.

Now, in the autumn, he stands as a door
At the edge of the no-man's land of my life—
The frontier is ahead of him.

78 Sulivan 1994, p. 59. Jean Sulivan is the pseudonym of Joseph Lemarachand (1913–1980), a French priest, novelist, and essayist.

79 Hareven 1981, p. 31. Cf. Hever 1987, p. 72. On Shammās' attitude toward Hebrew, see also Shammās 2003, pp. 111–28.

This I tell the boy
Who is trampled down inside me
This I tell the boy
Standing in front of me.

My father stands as a door,
And one of us three goes in.[80]

The lines that conclude the collection refer to the same no-man's land:

אֲנִי לֹא יוֹדֵעַ.
שָׂפָה מֵעֵבֶר מִזֶּה,
וְשָׂפָה מֵעֵבֶר מִזֶּה.
וַאֲנִי הוֹזֶה בִּשְׁטַח הַהֶפְקֵר.

I do not know.
A language beyond this,
And a language beyond this.
And I hallucinate in no-man's land.[81]

For Shammās, the latter is not just some poetic statement, but a metaphor that, in his own eyes, enfolds his own location within the Hebrew culture: hallucination in a territory in which he will never be at home.

Whereas ʻArāyidī continues to write in both Arabic and Hebrew and takes pride in being part of both cultures and "bridging" between them,[82] Shammās abandoned writing in his mother tongue in the mid-1970s, after he had begun to feel "in exile inside Arabic which is my blood tongue," saying he had experienced suffocation and loneliness by creating in it.[83] Being certainly aware that "writing about one's earliest memories against the mother tongue or against the tongue in which they occurred involves a process of reassessment and rewriting,"[84] he justified continuing to write only in Hebrew as a mission: "As an Arab it is important to say what I want to say

80 The poem was first published in *Iton 77* 14 (March–April 1979), p. 5.

81 Shammās 1979, pp. 5, 46. Cf. Shammās' poem "At Don's Party," written in 1981 and published in *Banipal* 3 (October 1998), p. 17: "I'm sitting on the upper stair, second floor. / The dog rubs his warm shoulder / Against mine / (which is not warm at all). / Wagging his tail, looking toward the door — / "Please, let me in!" // I wish I could say that. // And for his own sake, I hope // The Door leads somewhere, / And that there's a room beyond it, / A solid floor."

82 ʻArāyidī published several poetry collections in Arabic, among them ʻArāyidī 1994; ʻArāyidī 1994a; ʻArāyidī 1999; ʻArāyidī 2002. In 1998, he also published four books for children (on his literary work in this field, see Yaḥyā 2003, pp. 148–64).

83 Hareven 1981, pp. 45–6; Shammās 1986a, p. 45. Cf. Lavie 1996, p. 85: "I can't write literature in Arabic anymore. I don't want to."

84 Miletić 2008, p. 32.

to the Jews."[85] It may also be that he made a conscious choice of aesthetic preference. Indeed, he considers himself like

> a guest who comes to your [home] for dinner, and at the end of the meal you find him in the kitchen, washing dishes with the almost Harold Pinterish glee of someone who may, unintentionally, break one of your precious pieces. This also means that maybe, maybe, he will stay for the night.[86]

Shammās went as far as portraying in Hebrew the "Arabesques" of his family, which for him was "a significant labor of love."[87] *Arabesques*, with its frequent use of pseudo-Proustian modes and its obvious undermining of the authority and unity of the narrator's voice, the latter a phenomenon very uncommon in Arabic literature at the time, is the most sophisticated literary work so far written in Hebrew by an Arab author.[88] The novel has already been translated into a number of other languages,[89] but not yet into Arabic, though there have been Palestinian calls, albeit few, that the task be undertaken.[90] This is doubly astounding, as Shammās himself is one of the best translators between the two languages and, more than anyone else, has contributed to what little acceptance Palestinian literature has found among a Jewish reading public[91] and the familiarity some Hebrew literature has gained among an Arab-Palestinian reading public.[92]

As in the case of ʿArāyidī, it is only natural that, in order to ease the identity crisis that he experienced, a typical feature in Shammās' work should be his search for roots. *Arabesques* in its cyclical concept of time and simultaneity joins past and present together, much as in the Oriental iconography of the Arabesque.[93] First presenting his family's origins beginning at the turn of the nineteenth century, Shammās denies that these have any national significance:

85 Aviv 1986, p. 39. Cf. Elad-Bouskila 1999, pp. 150–2.

86 Shammās 1985, p. 31.

87 Amazia Porath in *Yediot Aḥronoth* (December 29, 1989), p. 22. Interviewed for the *New York Review of Books*, on April 17, 1988, Shammās said he wrote the novel in Hebrew because "you cannot write about the people whom you love in a language that they understand; you cannot write freely" (according to Ramras-Rauch 1989, p. 202).

88 Cf. Hever 1987, pp. 51–4; Alcalay 1993, pp. 275–9.

89 Among them, besides English, are French (Arles: Actes Sud, 1988), Spanish (Madrid: Mondadori, 1988), Dutch (Amsterdam: Bert Bakker, 1989), German (Munich: Piper Verlag, 1989), Italian (Milan: Mondadori, 1990), and Portuguese (Lisbon: Dom Quixote, 1991).

90 For example, see Salmān Maṣālḥa's review of the novel (*al-Ittiḥād*, October 10, 1986).

91 Especially through his translations of the works of Imīl Ḥabībī (1921–1996). Cf. Snir 1993a, pp. 21–39; Ginossar 1997, pp. 546–82.

92 See, for example, his translations in Avidan 1982 and Shammās 1984, which include twelve stories from modern Hebrew literature.

93 Cf. Joyaux 1980, p. 125; Hever 1987, pp. 59–64.

מכפר נידח בדרום מערב סוריה, ח'בב שמו, [אבי המשפחה הראשון נדד] לכפר נידח בגליל, שבו עתיד הייתי אני להיולד. אבי המשפחה הראשון יותר משאהב את הנדודים חס על נפשו, שאותה ביקשו בני המשפחה היריבה בכפרו [...] כפר ילדותי, בנוי על חרבות "מפשטה", הכפר היהודי הראשון שישבה בו לאחר חורבן בית שני משמרת הכוהנים "חרים."

From a remote village in southwestern Syria, called Khabab, he [the family's patriarch eventually reached] the remote village of Fassūṭa in Galilee, where I was destined to be born. But it seems that our ancestor was driven less by wanderlust than by his family's fear for his life, which was avidly sought by the Muslim clan in the village ... Our village is built on the ruins of the Crusader castle of Fassov, which was built on the ruins of Mifshata, the Jewish village that had been settled after the destruction of the Second Temple by the Ḥarim, a group of deviant priests.[94]

A deep nostalgia for the places of his childhood usually appears in Shammās' poetry intermingled with the pain and emptiness of the present:

בֵּית יַלְדוּתִי מִתְחַבֵּט בְּתוֹכִי
אֲנִי מִתְחַבֵּט בְּתוֹךְ הַבַּיִת הָרֵיק,
וּמְנַסֶּה לְשַׁכְנֵעַ אֶת עַצְמִי
שֶׁהִנְנִי אָדָם מְבֻגָּר.

My childhood home is struggling within me,
I am struggling within the empty house,
Trying to convince myself
That I'm a grown-up man.[95]

Sometimes, it seems that he wants to forget or deny his past in order to better accept his new identity, but the past refuses to be forgotten:

אֲנִי מְדַקְלֵם שֵׁמוֹת שֶׁהִכַּרְתִּי, בַּנִּגּוּן הַשִּׁכְחָה הָרָגוּעַ
וְרַק הַבַּיִת שֶׁבּוֹ נוֹלַדְתִּי הוֹלֵךְ אַחֲרַי כַּיֶּלֶד פָּרוּעַ.

I recite names I knew, with the tranquil melody of oblivion.
And only the house in which I was born walks behind me as a wild child.[96]

In a rational awareness that the utopian solution to his identity crisis is accepted neither by Arab-Palestinians nor by Israeli-Jews, he makes his true goal a more modest one:

יֵשׁ לִי מְגָרָה וּבָהּ שִׁירֵי
עֶרֶשׂ. וְהִיא נְעוּלָה. אֲנִי עוֹמֵד מוּלָהּ
וְגָדֵל, מִתּוֹךְ תִּקְוָוה שֶׁיּוֹם אֶחָד אַגִּיעַ

[94] Shammās 1987, pp. 14–15 (Shammās 1988, pp. 10–11).
[95] Shammās 1979, p. 44.
[96] Shammās 1979, p. 15.

לַמְּפַתֵּחַ אוֹתוֹ תָּלְתָה אִמִּי
עַל וָו מוֹתָהּ.

I have a drawer with cradlesongs
And it's locked. I stand in front of it
And grow, hoping that one day I'll reach
The key which my mother hung
On the hook of her death.[97]

Despite his choices to make Hebrew his aesthetic preference, to involve himself actively in Israeli culture, and to attempt to become part of it, Shammās remained aware of the futility of his efforts. In one poem, which betrays the inspiration he drew from the Hebrew poet Yehuda Amichai (1924–2000), he says:

מִדֵּי בּוֹקֶר אֲנִי מַבִּיט בְּכַפּוֹת רַגְלַי—
הַשּׁוֹרָשִׁים הַמְּיוּחָלִים לֹא צָמְחוּ עֲדַיִן,
לַמְרוֹת שֶׁרֶטֶט הַשַּׁלֶּכֶת צָפַד בְּעוֹרִי מִזְּמַן.

Each morning I look at my feet—
The longed-for roots have not yet sprung,
Although the vibration of the shedding of leaves has dried up in my skin for long.[98]

Shammās moved to the United States about thirty years ago, and now teaches comparative literature at the University of Michigan. Since *Arabesques* came out in the mid-1980s, he has published no significant literary work in either Hebrew or Arabic, though he continued for a short while to write articles in Hebrew and then also in English. Unlike ʻArāyidī, whose ties with Hebrew literature only became stronger, Shammās seems to have been severing any direct connection with Hebrew literature. In an essay published after one of his visits to Israel describing the growing alienation between himself and the Hebrew literary scene, one can read, between the lines, that he regrets ever having tried to become part of it. He tells us that when he was twelve years old he left the village where he grew up for "Haifa, *the city which I blame till today for ruining my adolescence*." Finding himself now in a small town in the Midwest of the United States, he

> imagines the view seen from my village-childhood window, thirty years ago, *the same view that was obscured from my eyes during my years in Haifa, and even more so during my two decades in Jerusalem. The village that was torn out of me I am rebuilding here, in the (false?) quiet of the Midwest, in the refuge of the longing to that private village, to which I'll never return.* Here, in an obscure and anxiety-arousing

[97] Shammās 1974, p. 27.
[98] Shammās 1979, p. 11.

> way, I feel at home in a way that I have never felt before, although I know that this is not my scenery, to speak in understatement, and that my true homeland is that distant, bilingual homeland, of Arabic and Hebrew. But here I feel protected and unthreatened. I can listen to Arabic music without arousing the fury of my neighbors ... and I can sit in a coffee shop and read an Arabic book or newspaper ... These may seem like little things, but to me they are all that should characterize the "homeland." For me this was the last visit, as far as "homeland" is concerned. *I, who tried during many years to test the boundaries of both the Israeli identity and its patience, now raise tired hands.*[99]

Little wonder that in a special issue of the *Michigan Quarterly Review* on the Middle East he edited in 1992 Shammās decided not to include literary works by Hebrew writers. In his introduction, he explains that, while Arabic literature is very much underrepresented in the United States, "Hebrew literature, for various reasons, has fared wondrously," and he adds that his decision by no means reflects "any disinterest on our side."[100]

If, for Shammās, his "true homeland is that distant, bilingual homeland, of Arabic and Hebrew," one can only guess what it must have meant to him when he decided to "extract" himself from the tragic paradox in which he had been caught: his desire to integrate into Hebrew-Israeli culture, on the one hand, and his deep awareness that such integration would forever be impossible, on the other.[101] This paradox, of course, had been there all the time, but Shammās had known somehow how to conceal it, as, for example, when he created the character of Yehoshua Bar-On in *Arabesques*. Bar-On is writing a book "about the loneliness of the Arab-Palestinian Israeli, which is the greatest loneliness of all."[102] While for the fictional Bar-On this "loneliness" is no more than an idea for another bestseller, it is precisely this loneliness that penetrates the soul of Shammās's narrator (perhaps of the author himself at the time):

> מוכרחים ערבי הפעם, כפתרון כלשהו לשתיקה כלשהי. ערבי שמדבר בשפת החסד, כפי שקרא לעברית לפנים הפלוֹרנטיני הגולה. העברית כשפת החסד לעומת שפת הבִלבוּל שהתרגשה על העולם בהתמוטט מגדל בבל. הערבי שלי יבנה על מגרשי את בִלבוּלו. בשפת החסד. זו לדעתי גאולתו האפשרית היחידה. **בגבולות המותר כמובן**.

> There has to be an Arab this time, as some sort of solution to some sort of silence. An Arab who speaks the language of Grace, as Dante once called it. Hebrew as the language of Grace, as opposed to the language of Confusion that

99 Shammās 1993, p. B3 (my emphasis).
100 *Michigan Quarterly Review* 31.4 (Fall 1992), p. 456.
101 Cf. 'Arāyidī's words: "I know I can never become a real Hebrew author. Never. It's a matter of pride. They won't let me be that, but I won't let myself be that, either" (Lavie 1996, p. 56).
102 Shammās 1987, p. 84 (Shammās 1988, p. 93).

> swept over the world when the Tower of Babel collapsed. My Arab will build his tower of confusion in my plot. In the language of Grace. That's his only possible redemption. *Within the boundaries of what's permissible.*[103]

The significance hidden in the dismissal of the narrator from his role by Bar-On and his replacement by an authentic, if no less stereotypical, Palestinian from Nablus[104] is clear. The narrator's failure to reach salvation finds expression in a desperate episode when the letters he has been writing to his lover, Shlomit, are found by her husband:

> וכשסעד את אביו על ערש מותו כתב לה מכתבים. בעברית. זו היתה הפעם הראשונה שנפרדו, והמכתבים היו מעין סיכום לערגה. ואחרי שליווה את אביו לקבורה בכפר שב לירושלים ונוכח לדעת שתמה הערגה. הבעל גילה את המכתבים, והסוד הנורא ביפיו נתגלה, ושבו הדברים להויתם: עברית, ערבית ומות.

> When his father was on his deathbed and he took care of him, he wrote her letters. In Hebrew. After he had accompanied his father to his burial in the village and returned to Jerusalem, he found out that the letters had proved to be an absolution of sorts. The husband had discovered the correspondence, and the secret, in its terrible beauty, was gone, and the world reverted to its former state of Hebrew, Arabic, and Death.[105]

The words "Hebrew, Arabic, and Death" are based on lines of Yehuda Amichai from his poem "Elegies on the Dead Men in War":

> דֶּגֶל מְאַבֵּד אֶת הַקֶּשֶׁר עִם הַמְּצִיאוּת וְעָף.
> חַלּוֹן רַאֲוָה מְקֻשָּׁט בְּשִׂמְלוֹת נָשִׁים
> יָפוֹת בְּצִבְעֵי תְּכֵלֶת וְלָבָן. וְהַכֹּל
> בְּשָׁלוֹשׁ שָׂפוֹת: עִבְרִית עַרְבִית וּמָוֶת

> A flag loses contact with reality and flies off.
> A shopwindow is decorated with
> dresses of beautiful women, in blue and white.
> And everything in three languages:
> Hebrew, Arabic, and Death[106]

In his poem "Arabic," included in his last collection *Call Me Ishmael Tonight* (2003), the Kashmiri-American poet Agha Shahid Ali (1949–2001) refers to both Amichai's and Shammās' insights about the three languages:

> The only language of loss left in the world is Arabic—
> These words were said to me in a language not Arabic.

[103] Shammās 1987, p. 83 (Shammās 1988, pp. 92–3) (my emphasis).
[104] Shammās 1987, pp. 151–2 (Shammās 1988, p. 168).
[105] Shammās 1987, p. 85 (Shammās 1988, pp. 94–5).
[106] Amichai 1974, p. 92.

Ancestors, you've left me a plot in the family graveyard—
Why must I look, in your eyes, for prayers in Arabic?

Majnoon, his clothes ripped, still weeps for Laila.
O, this is the madness of the desert, his crazy Arabic.

Who listens to Ishmael? Even now he cries out:
Abraham, throw away your knives, recite a psalm in Arabic.

From exile Mahmoud Darwish writes to the world:
You'll all pass between the fleeting words of Arabic.

The sky is stunned, it's become a ceiling of stone.
I tell you it must weep. So kneel, pray for rain in Arabic.

At an exhibition of Mughal miniatures, such delicate calligraphy:
Kashmiri paisleys tied into the golden hair of Arabic.

The Koran prophesied a fire of men and stones.
Well, it's all now come true, as it was said in the Arabic (*sic!*).

When Lorca died, they left the balcony open and saw:
his *qasidas* braided, on the horizon, into knots of Arabic.

Memory is no longer confused, it has a homeland—
Says Shammas: Territorialize each confusion in a graceful Arabic.

Where there were homes in Deir Yassein, you'll see dense forests—
That village was razed. There's no sign of Arabic.

I too, O Amichai, saw the dresses of beautiful women.
And everything else, just like you, in Death, Hebrew, and Arabic.

They ask me to tell them what Shahid means—
Listen: It means "The Beloved" in Persian, "witness" in Arabic.[107]

The poem includes many other religious, cultural, and Hebrew, Arabic, Persian, Spanish, and English literary allusions such as to the Bible and the Qur'ān, the story of Majnūn Laylā, Federico García Lorca's works, and Maḥmūd Darwīsh's poetry.[108] Reading Shahid's poem against the background of the identity crises of the Palestinians writing in Hebrew sheds light on the universal aspects of their existential and cultural dilemma. The failure of the narrator in *Arabesques* to reach salvation parallels the failure of the hero of the very first novel written by a Palestinian in Hebrew, 'Aṭāllāh Manṣūr's (b. 1934), *Be-Or Ḥadash* (*In a New Light*), which had

[107] Ali 2003, pp. 24–5.

[108] David Damrosch refers to several of these allusions, concentrating on the intertextuality between Amichai, Shammās, and Agha Shahid Ali's poetry (Damrosch 2014, pp. 4–10).

come out twenty years before Shammās' novel. Yossī Mizraḥī is an Arab-Palestinian who was adopted in childhood, before 1948, by a Jewish family after his father had been killed. He was brought up and educated on a kibbutz without the members knowing that he was an Arab, and he did all he could to integrate into this new Jewish society. But though an official identity certificate indicated that he was Jewish, and though he spoke only Hebrew and knew no Arabic at all, he still could not be like the others. The kibbutz members are willing to accept him eventually, but only on the condition that the records will not show that he was born an Arab. No wonder that in the end of the novel the hero is disillusioned:

> זאת אומרת שאשאר בקיבוץ, אבל אקבל את זכותי כגנב בלילה! [...] למעשה ניצחתי, אבל טעמו של הנצחון הזה מר [...] פתאום פרצתי בבכי. ריקנות השתלטה עלי. את הכל ראיתי באור חדש.

> This means that I'll stay in the kibbutz, but I shall receive my right as a thief in the night! ... Actually I have won, but this victory is bitter ... Suddenly I burst out in tears. Emptiness overtook me. I saw everything in a new light.[109]

Only in the mid-1990s did Shammās, like Manṣūr's hero, permit himself to say clearly:

> [We] have been constantly pushed from the center, and therefore we try to penetrate into the center by means of literary forms ... Even if anyone of us wrote the masterpiece of Israeli literature, he still would be on the periphery socially and culturally. We get pushed back into the margins, now along with our texts. But the problem is, how wide are the margins? How porous is the border?[110]

5. CONCLUSION

When Palestinian bilingual writers decide to write in Hebrew, they have made a conscious aesthetic and cultural choice. This is doubly significant if we look at the weight they give to the oral familial sources of their literary work, but then see how they make the transition from oral literary transmission to a fiction written in a language whose heritage denies the validity of these sources.[111] As the Israeli-Hebrew critic

[109] Manṣūr 1966, pp. 173–4. Cf. Ramras-Rauch 1989, pp. 195–6; Brenner 1993, pp. 105–6. On the novel, its cultural and social background, the identity of the protagonist, and other related issues, see also Abo-Moch 2006.

[110] Lavie 1996, p. 70.

[111] Cf. al-ʿĪd 1990, pp. 83–4. Cf. al-ʿĪd 1990a, p. 149.

Dan Miron (b. 1934) pointed out regarding Shammās,[112] unlike exiled writers, who desert their ethnic and territorial homeland but cling to their language and literary culture, Palestinians writing in Hebrew remain in touch with their ethnic homeland, but choose to substitute their language, the poetics of their literary writing, and their cultural heritage. Even the poetics of their Arabic-language poetry is based on the central Hebrew poetic school led by Yehuda Amichai (1924–2000) and Natan Zach (1930–2020).[113] Such, for instance, is the case with Shammās' Arabic poem "So We Separated":

נִפְרַדְנוּ כָּךְ: אָמְרָה
מַחֲצִית הַדֶּרֶךְ אֵלֶיךָ אֶעֱשֶׂה בַּחֲלוֹמִי, וְאַתָּה
אֶת הַמַּחֲצִית הַשְּׁנִיָּה

נֶחְבֵּאתִי תַּחַת בְּדִידוּתִי הַקְּרִירָה. כְּמַפְתֵּחַ דִּירָתָהּ
שֶׁתַּחַת אֶבֶן בִּקְצֵה הַמַּדְרֵגוֹת הִיא מַחְבִּיאָה.

So we separated: she said
Half the way to you I'll make in my dream, and you
The other half
I hid underneath my cold loneliness. As the key of her flat
Which she hides under a stone at the end of the stairs.[114]

The poem has no meter familiar from Arabic prosody, avoids rhyme, uses short lines and everyday language, and is reminiscent of the group of sonatas of Yehuda Amichai titled "Here We Loved," from the collection *Acshav u-be-Yamim Akherim* (*Now and in Other Days*), like, for instance, these lines:

אָהַבְנוּ כָּאן. הַמְּצִיאוּת הָיְתָה אַחֶרֶת,
הָעִיתוֹנִים שׁוּב צָעֲקוּ כְּמוֹ פְּצוּעִים.
מֵאֲחוֹרֵי שׁוּרוֹת-עֲנָק שֶׁבַּכּוֹתֶרֶת
אֲנַחְנוּ שְׁנֵינוּ נֶחְבָּאִים.

Here we loved. Reality was different,
Newspapers again screamed like the wounded.

[112] *Ha-'Olam Ha-Ze*, July 9, 1986, p. 26. For comments on Miron's review, see Alcalay 1999, pp. 89–94.

[113] See especially Shammās 1974; Shammās 1974a; Shammās 1979; 'Arāyidī 1986. Cf. Shammās 1985a, p. 19. In a review of Shammās 1979, Mati Shalev refers to the influence of Zach and the Hebrew poetess Yona Wallach (1944–1985) on Shammās, concluding that the "voice is Zach's voice and the hands Wallach's" (*Davar*, June 20, 1980). It is interesting to note that the influence of Hebrew poetry can also be found in Arabic-Palestinian literature (e.g., al-Rifā'ī 1994).

[114] Shammās 1974a, p. 64.

Behind the huge lines in the title
We both hide.[115]

Shammās appropriates the figure of a Russian babushka doll when he describes the Palestinian minority in Israel,[116] and the same figure may represent the situation of the Palestinian bilingual writers within: they are an exceptional minority (writing in Hebrew, in addition to their Arabic writing), within a minority (Christian[117] and Druze)[118] within a minority (Israeli-Palestinians), within a minority (Jews) in the Arab world, not to mention the ambiguous position of the Palestinian minority within the Arab majority in general. In their native environment, they are unique in the conscious aesthetic choice they made to write in Hebrew, while in Hebrew literature they are unique not only because they are outsiders, but mainly because they can be active precisely by their being representatives of a minority. As marginal writers in Arab-Palestinian literature who strive to penetrate the canonical Hebrew literary center, they mainly address the Jewish public. However, in the shadow of the vast cultural cleavage between the Israeli-Jewish majority and its Arab minority, and the lack of any genuine cultural interaction, there are, as Shammās himself puts it, no "intersecting circles between the Hebrew literature and the Arabic one."[119]

Even if we ignore James Joyce's recommendations that "you must write in your own tradition," "borrowed styles are no good," and "in the particular is contained the universal,"[120] the high status Arabic has, especially among Muslim Arabs, assures us that most Palestinian writers would never dream of turning to Hebrew, a language that is considered culturally inferior despite its prestige as the language of the majority. In addition, the general Arab reading public is so much larger than the Hebrew reading public that any comparison between the phenomenon of Arabs writing in Hebrew with that of North Africans writing in French is out of the question.[121] When Palestinian writers move from the Arabic cultural circle into the Hebrew

[115] Amichai 1972, p. 56. On the influence of Amichai on ʻArāyidī, see, for example, Amichai 1972, p. 12; ʻArāyidī 1999, p. 21.
[116] Shammās 1986a, pp. 44–5.
[117] On the special condition of the Christians in Israel as a "minority within a minority," see Munayer 1998.
[118] On the special condition of the Druze in Israel as "minority within a minority," see Slyomovics 1998, p. 67. On the issue of the identity of the Druze in Israel, see Firro 1999, pp. 208–13.
[119] Shammās 1985, p. 32.
[120] Ellmann 1959, p. 520.
[121] Cf. Snir 2017, pp. 112–14. For the fundamental difference between the two phenomena, see the Iraqi poet Fāḍil Sulṭānī's (b. 1948) article in *al-Sharq al-Awsaṭ* (London), September 4, 2001.

one, even if they do not totally abandon writing in Arabic, the attempt originates a lack of legitimation by their own natural cultural environment and at the same time is an outcome of a conscious aesthetic preference for Hebrew culture, often combined with some need to address the Israeli-Jewish public in its own language.[122]

What makes authors like ʻArāyidī and Shammās special in Israeli-Jewish culture is that they insist on writing in Hebrew in a place characterized by cultural confrontation and not pluralism. Moreover, the roots of Jewish nationalism lie in Eastern Europe and the overall orientation of modern Israeli canonical culture is strongly Western. The Hebrew literary establishment, which prides itself on mainly being leftist-liberal-oriented, though it does not like Arabic culture, cannot openly say so, not only because that would mean voicing a disparaging attitude toward the "Other" and would thus not be "politically correct,"[123] but mainly since multiculturalism has become a fundamental component of the new local intellectual discourse, that is, that the Eurocentirc character of our education and culture should be multicultured. To resolve this "cognitive dissonance"[124] and preserve the cozy reassurance of its liberal and tolerant attitude toward the culture of a minority in its midst, the literary establishment gives the minority a "seat" in various institutions of "Israeli" culture,[125] preferably in activities under the heading of "coexistence." The musician ʻĀmir (Amer) Nakhla (b. 1972?), the head of the Musical Conservatory in Shfaram, says that this phenomenon "does not stem from a desire to advance the Arabs, but to exploit them."[126] In the winter of 2002, toward the elections for the Knesset it was even argued that the same practice was used in the political scene, where a "growing part of the younger Arab generation, [feels] that they are nothing but a fig-leaf

122 According to ʻAṭāllāh Manṣūr, his novel was written in order to get even with the Jewish literary critics who had panned his Arabic novel *Wa-Baqiyat Samīra* (*And Samīra Remained*) (Manṣūr 1962). To his astonishment, the critics' attitude toward his Hebrew novel was positive (Manṣūr 1992, p. 65; on the novel, see Abdel-Malek 2005, p. 146).

123 Cf. for example, Yaron Frid's (b. 1965) review of Sayed Kashua's novel *Va-Yehi Boker* (*Let It Be Morning*) (Kashua 2004; English translation: Kashua 2006), in which he "apologizes" for being obliged to present doubts as to Kashua's limited literary ability (*Yediot Aḥronoth*, literary supplement, December 16, 2004, pp. 26–7).

124 According to Festinger 1957, esp. pp. 1–31.

125 An illustration of this might be the positive attitude of the Israeli-Jewish critics toward ʻAṭāllāh Manṣūr's Hebrew novel. The author himself prefers to explain the attitude toward his Arabic novel by stating that it was reviewed by Israeli Arabists, while his Hebrew novel was reviewed by "liberal" critics (Manṣūr 1992, p. 65. Cf. Elad-Bouskila 1999, pp. 141–2). It is ironic that such an attitude to Arabic culture was widespread even among the Jewish Communists; see, for example, Locker-Biletzki 2013, pp. 20–2.

126 See at: www.haaretz.com, June 3, 2004.

for the Israeli pseudo-democracy."[127] Ayman Kāmil Ighbāriyya (b. 1968) is more than any other Palestinian bilingual writer aware of the function these writers play in Israeli culture:

> To be [in Israel] a [Palestinian] author writing in Hebrew is to be the clown of Hebrew literature. This position was occupied alternately by some talented writers who mastered the secrets of Hebrew language: Anton Shammās, Na'īm 'Arāyidī and recently Sayed Kashua. All of them, no matter what they will do, are orderly clowns. It seems that now perhaps it's my role.[128]

Nearly fifteen years later, the Palestinian actor Rā'ida Adon (Adūn) (b. 1972), in an article titled "The Israelis Do Not See Me," argues that nothing has changed:

> When there is only one Arab actor in the Israeli theater, the [Jewish Israelis] loudly declare: "Here, there is coexistence!" And when there is only one female broadcaster in the Israeli television, they scream: "Here, we bestowed upon her!" But I am trying to shout from the other side: We are not only one actor or one singer or one broadcaster. We are many eyes watching and dreaming.[129]

Nevertheless, the fact that Adon insists on participating in the cultural Hebrew activities and on being involved in the public Israeli-Hebrew discourse on various issues,[130] despite her aforementioned protest, only testifies to her collaboration with the colonial discourse. In such a discourse, the encounter between the colonizer and the colonized results in the production of a strategy of "discursive splitting, a certain anomalous containment of cultural ambivalence," according to Homi K. Bhabha (b. 1949). It is a strategy of defense and differentiation:

> Two contradictory and independent attitudes inhabit the *same place*, one takes account of reality, the other is under the influence of instincts which detach the ego from reality. This results in the production of multiple and contradictory belief. The enunciatory moment of multiple belief is both a defence against the anxiety of difference, and itself *productive* of differentiations.[131]

The Israeli-Palestinian scholar Ramzī Sulaymān (b. 1948), himself a poet but *only* in Arabic (although very pleased when his poems were translated into Hebrew!), describes this discourse as steeped with a mentality of *noblesse oblige*: it is possible only when the Palestinian is ready to play the role of the

[127] Ofer Shelach (b. 1960) in *Yediot Aḥronoth* (weekly supplement), January 3, 2003, p. 25.
[128] *Eretz Acheret* 16 (May–June 2003), p. 52.
[129] *Haaretz*, October 11, 2017.
[130] See, for example, her article on the murder of women by their husbands (*Haaretz*, June 1, 2020).
[131] Bhabha 1994, p. 132.

slave who agrees to "represent" the minority according to the wish of the master.[132]

'Arāyidī and Shammās were "chosen" by the Hebrew canonical center as representatives of the minority, not just because they wrote in Hebrew but more so because their poetics were close to that of the Hebrew culture and they were "ready" to represent the minority.[133] It is clear that the way 'Arāyidī and Shammās are assessed in current Hebrew literature cannot be disconnected from the fact that they belong to the minority. What happens is that the dominant Hebrew literary circles adopt exceptional local Arab-Palestinian writers, not only for literary but also for ideological and political reasons, thereby giving them the legitimation they lacked in their natural milieu and creating the illusion that they represent the native cultural circle to which they actually no longer belong.[134]

Arabic literature meanwhile rejects any attempt of significance by Jewish authors in Arabic to be part of it. A salient example is the large body of literary work in Arabic by the Israeli-Jewish Iraqi-born writer Samīr Naqqāsh (1938–2004), who published more than a dozen novels and short-story collections, and won the praise of critics,[135] but who is all but ignored by the dominant circles in Arabic literature. Furthermore, Jewish writers born in Arab countries and writing in Hebrew are also not accepted by the Israeli cultural system as long as they insist on holding on to their original culture. It explains, for example, why Sami Michael (Sāmī Mīkhā'īl) (b. 1926)[136] has been accepted while Shimon Ballas (Sham'ūn Ballāṣ) (1930–2019)[137] has

132 Sulaymān 2005.

133 See Snir 1993b, pp. 52–61; Snir 1993c, pp. 28–9.

134 See Hanan Hever's articles in *Alpayim* 1 (1989), pp. 186–93; *Alpayim* 3 (1990), pp. 238–40.

135 On Samīr Naqqāsh and his work, see Ben-Yaacob 1980, p. 410; Moreh 1981, pp. 251–4; Bezalel 1982, pp. 296–8; Moreh and 'Abbāsī 1987, pp. 236–7; Mudhi 1988, pp. 404–58; Semah 1989a, pp. 21–2; Sarmad 2000, pp. 134–42; Levy 2003, pp. 93–114; Hajjar 2010, pp. 309–36; Elimelekh 2013, pp. 63–75; Elimelekh 2013a, pp. 323–42; Rish 2014, pp. 409–34; Elimelekh 2015, pp. 1–16; Aḥmad 2016; Behar and Evri 2019, pp. 111–31; Elimelekh 2021, pp. 142–60. See also the documentary film *Forget Baghdad: Jews and Arabs—The Iraqi Connection* (2002). On the film, see also below, Chapter 7.

136 On Michael, see Ben-Yaacob 1980, p. 411; Moreh 1981, pp. 221–32; Bezalel 1982, p. 294; Moreh and 'Abbāsī 1987, pp. 226–7; Ramras-Rauch 1989, pp. 179–83; *Bulletin of the Israeli Academic Center in Cairo* 16 (May 1992), pp. 47–50; Hakak 1995, pp. 7–33; Oren 1995, pp. 135–51; Benhabib 2002; Idrīs 2003; Kerbel 2003, pp. 373–4; Berg 2004; Mendelson-Maoz 2014, pp. 47–53, 80–4; Schwartz 2016 (a collection of articles based on the conference "A Tribute to Israeli Author Sami Michael: Between Baghdad and Haifa, 7–9 October 2015, Northwestern University); Snir 2019, pp. 99–102, 124–7, 175–6, 186–8, 232–7; Bashkin 2020, pp. 18–38; Snir 2021b, pp. 188–96. See also the aforementioned documentary film, *Forget Baghdad: Jews and Arabs—The Iraqi Connection.* On the film, see also below, Chapter 7.

137 On Ballas, see Ben-Yaacob 1980, pp. 397–8; Moreh 1981, pp. 187–202; Bezalel 1982, I, p. 283; Moreh and 'Abbāsī 1987, pp. 31–4; Ramras-Rauch 1989, pp. 184–7; Snir 1991,

been rejected.[138] Ella Shohat (b. 1959) writes that "the fact that the 'Orientals' have had closer cultural and historical links to the presumed enemy—the 'Arab'—than to the Ashkenazi Jews with whom they were coaxed and coerced into shared nationhood threatens the conception of a homogeneous nation akin to those on which European nationalist movements were based, while it also threatens the Euro-Israeli self-image, which sees itself as an extension of Europe. The taboo around the Arabness of the Eastern Jews has been clearly manifested in Israeli academic and media attacks on Mizrahi intellectuals who refuse to define themselves simply as Israelis and who dare to assert their Arabness in the public sphere."[139]

Though their achievements in Hebrew writing are no less significant, the Arab-Jewish writers do not receive the attention given to 'Arāyidī and Shammās. That that attention is due to mainly political factors is shown by the fact that, of the dozens of essays written about the works of 'Arāyidī and Shammās, most call attention to the ethnic origin of the authors.[140] Furthermore, the phenomenon has attracted much media attention, to the extent that in a few cases Israeli-Jewish Hebrew writers who published some of their works under an Arabic pseudonym may well have done so to arouse public interest.[141] However, interest vanished the moment their true Jewish

pp. 153–73; Clerk and Siegel 1995, pp. 459–66; Berg 1996, pp. 391–4; Snir 1998, pp. 177–210; Idrīs 2003; Kerbel 2003, pp. 65–6; Abramson 2005, pp. 66–7; Snir 2005a, pp. 325–36, 350–1, 360–2; Rossetto 2012, pp. 103–27; 'Alwān 2014; Bashkin 2020, pp. 18–38; Snir 2021b, pp. 179–88. See also the aforementioned documentary film *Forget Baghdad: Jews and Arabs—The Iraqi Connection.* On the film, see also below, Chapter 7.

138 On this phenomenon in Hebrew, see Snir 1998a, pp. 177–89. See also R. Snir, "The DDT Principle" (Heb.), *Haaretz* (September 15, 1993), p. H8 (A Comment on Sami Michael's *Victoria* [Tel Aviv: Am Oved, 1993]); R. Snir, "The Limits of the 'Right' Discourse" (in Hebrew), *Haaretz* (September 18, 1992), p. B8 (part I); (September 25, 1992), p. B9 (part II), a review of Shimon Ballas' *Otot stav* (*Signs of Autumn*) (Ballas 1992).

139 Shohat 1999, p. 7. Cf. Shohat 1997, p. 102; Shohat 1997a, p. 57.

140 See Kritz 1990, pp. 363–73. In one of the few essays written in Arabic about Shammās' aforementioned novel *Arabeskot* (*Arabesques*) (1986), the Jordanian critic Ibrāhīm Khalīl (b. 1948) argues that the praise it gained had much to do with the fact that it was written in Hebrew (*al-Dustūr* [December 12, 1986], p. 13). In another reaction, the Syrian poet Nūrī al-Jarrāḥ (b. 1956) writes that Shammās' *Arabesques* fails completely to attract the attention of Arab intellectuals and challenges him to decide whether he is Israeli or Palestinian (*al-Nāqid* 16 [October 1989], pp. 34–6). Sharbal Dāghir (b. 1950), a Lebanese poet and critic living in Paris, also criticizes Shammās' choice to write in Hebrew (*al-Nāqid* 2 [August 1988], p. 75). See also Kayyal 2006a, pp. 49–53.

141 See Yosef Sherara (= Yoram Kaniuk), *Aravi Tov* (*A Good Arab*) (Sherara 1984); George Mathias Ibrāhīm (= Israel Eliraz), *Derekh Bet Leḥem (Via Bethlehem)* (Ibrāhīm 1980) and *Har Patuaḥ* (*Open Mountain*) (Ibrāhīm 1984). Cf. *Mifgash-Liqā'* 6 (Spring 1987), pp. 67–72. See also the poetry of Khamīs Tutanjī (= Imanuel Ben-Sabo [b. 1964]) (*Maariv* [May 12, 1989], p. B5; *Kolbo* [Haifa], July 7, 1989, p. 67. Cf. Nāṭūr 1991, pp. 16–25). Ben-Sabo used the name of a Palestinian taxi driver murdered by Jewish terrorists on April 22, 1985.

identity was uncovered.[142] The Israeli-Hebrew writer and poet Israel Eliraz (1936–2016), whose other works prove that his writing under an Arabic pseudonym was by no means done out of any adoption of "Arab" aesthetics and poetical conceptions,[143] is sure that it is no coincidence that the poems he wrote under the Palestinian pen name of George Mathias Ibrāhīm attracted a good deal of attention from the dominant circles in Israeli culture, while poems he published under his real "Jewish" name were rejected.[144]

A peculiar case is the poetry of Dalia Fallah, who since the late 1970s has published her poems in literary supplements and magazines without clear indication whether her name is her real name or a pseudonym. There are some indications that she is an Arab,[145] but the fact that for more than two decades she has insisted on anonymity compels critics to refer to her poetry without any non-literary considerations.[146] Anyhow, the nature of contemporary Hebrew literature, as that of Arabic-Palestinian literature, leaves little hope that the boundaries of Hebrew literature can be expanded. It seems that the desire to create a new Israeli cultural identity is nothing but a daydream.[147]

Identity, as a leading Hebrew critic claimed, "is a genetic disease ... it's a psychological problem ... Poor Ratosh thought that he can turn, with nothing else but words, Jews into Hebrews. This was blindness. He himself remained Halperin until the end of his life."[148] Not only do the bilingual authors fail in changing the "norm" that identifies every Hebrew writer as a Jew, but their own literary and cultural activities serve to confirm it. Unlike some wishful thinking and naïve views,[149] we assume that their fate is to remain marginal

142 Cf. the phenomenon of the pseudotranslations; see Toury 1995, pp. 40–52, esp. p. 44, regarding "manipulating the text's reception by the audience."

143 For example, see his *Hölderlin* (in Hebrew) (Tel Aviv: Ha-Kibbutz Ha-Me'uḥad, 2002).

144 Cf. Eliraz 1987, pp. 68–9. See also the interviews with him in *Davar* (supplement), October 10, 1987, p. 15; and *Yediot Aḥronoth* (weekly supplement), January 11, 2002, p. 26. On ethnic reidentification in modern Hebrew literature, with a discussion of the case of Eliraz, see Lockard 2002, pp. 49–62.

145 For example, the English transliteration of her name "Fallah" (for Fallāḥ), which indicates that the poet is aware of the *shadda* on the *lam* in the Arabic original.

146 Her poems were published in two collections by Am Oved Publishers in 1997 and 2003. On her poetry and the issue of her ethnic identity, see *Proza* 100 (January–March 1988), pp. 66–7; *Haaretz*, January 9, 2004.

147 This is aptly illustrated in Samet 1989. Cf. Alcalay 1995, pp. 15–27.

148 See comments by the literary critic Gershon Shaked (1929–2006) in Aviv 1986, p. 32. Cf. Snir 1991b, pp. 202–5. On the issue of identity and belonging, see below, Chapter 8.

149 Writing on Hebrew works of Palestinians, especially Shammās, L. I. Yudkin says that "Israeli Hebrew literature can no longer be the exclusive province of a club or the expression of a stetl. It is the literature of the State, with a multi-ethnic, pluralist, internally divided and mutually antagonistic population. The European, Western, Ashkenazi impulse which has set the tone in Israeli culture can no longer be seen as the sole determinant of literary concerns and norms" (Yudkin 1992, p. 107).

and exceptional writers in their own natural cultural milieu, but neither can they enter the gates of Hebrew literature with their heads held high as Palestinians. On the contrary, as lone wolves they find themselves in the hell human life becomes when, as Hermann Hesse (1877–1962) indicates, "two cultures and religions overlap,"[150] slowly losing the connection with their roots and being caught in an acute identity crisis; they enter a cultural system that labels them as exceptional (and "entitled" to special benefits for "agreeing" to be representatives of the minority) and at the same time demands that they adapt. As the motto has it that Shammās took from George Bernard Shaw's (1856–1950) *Pygmalion* for the first five chapters of *Arabesques*:

> You told me, you know, that when a child is brought to a foreign country, it picks up the language in a few weeks, and forgets its own. Well. I am a child in your country.[151]

Consciously or unconsciously, in a reversal of Jacques Derrida's ideal, "to speak the other's language without renouncing [their] own,"[152] their original identity begins to erode.[153] Soon preoccupation with the issue of cultural identity starts obscuring other no less important questions. For example, male Palestinian writers in Hebrew are aware of and sensitive to the secondary position of women in their society, and to the oppression of women in a masculine world in general. Still, often in their novels and short stories this awareness seems to take a back seat and instead there emerges "the Arab man" who leaves his traditional, often rural society for Israeli-Jewish society, namely, the town, where he "conquers" its "women." Or should we perhaps see this too as part of their "adoption" of Hebrew-Israeli culture?[154] Anyway,

150 Hesse 1957, p. 22.

151 Shaw 1962, p. 94.

152 Derrida 1986, p. 333. Cf. Gates 1985, pp. 13–15.

153 It is interesting to note that in 1997 the Arab Theater in Israel (al-Masraḥ al-ʿArabī fī Isrāʾīl) presented Shammās' play *Gahssil Wujjak yā Qamar* (*Wash Your Face, O Moon*), which addresses the question of the blurring and loss of identity of the Palestinians inside Israel. The play, which was directed by Daniel Gidron (b. 1942), tells the story of two Israeli-Palestinian burglars (the actors Nūrmān Īsā [b. 1967] and Maḥmūd Qadaḥ [b. 1965]) who break into an Arab apartment in a Jewish neighborhood in Haifa, in the summer of 2012 and discover that they are locked inside some sort of labyrinth. Later, they are joined by three other Palestinians: an old man (Makram Khūrī [b. 1945]) who is looking for the magic word behind a sealed door, a woman (Salwā Naqqāra Ḥaddād [b. 1959]), and a lawyer (Ghassān ʿAbbās [b. 1957]).

154 Cf. "Zionism and masculinity have become inseparable: not only have they constructed one another but also they continue to be one another's lifeline. Zionism provided the blueprint for the *New Jew*'s gender identity ... and masculinity, bravery, and heroism became in turn what the poet Natan Alterman (1910–1970) has called the 'silver platter' on which the Jewish state was given" (Mayer 2000, p. 301). Israeli and Palestinian films offer an alternative to national attitudes by focusing on the realm of women, who "do not themselves

every Palestinian writing in Hebrew since 1948 has shown in his works, to various degrees, a sense of having an inferiority complex. The words of Frantz Fanon (1925–1961) from "The Negro and Language" are appropriate here:

> Every colonized people—in other words, every people in whose soul [an] inferiority complex has been created by the death and burial of its local cultural originality—finds itself face to face with the language of the civilizing nations, that is, with the culture of the mother country. The colonized is elevated above his jungle status in proportion to his adoption of the mother country's cultural standards. He becomes whiter as he renounces his blackness, his jungle. In the French colonial army, and particularly in the Senegalese regiments, the black officers serve first of all as interpreters. They are used to convey the master's orders to their fellows, and they too enjoy a certain position of honor.[155]

To speak a language, certainly to write literature in it, is "to take on a world, a culture."[156] The Black man who wants to be White will be Whiter as he gains, as Fanon indicates, greater mastery of the cultural tool that language is, precisely as he will be Whiter when he sleeps with White women—when his "restless hands caress those white breasts, they grasp white civilization and dignity and make them [his]."[157] The Black man "wants to speak French because it is the key that can open doors which were still barred to him."[158] Likewise, the Palestinian who wants to be "White" will be "Whiter" as he gains greater mastery of the cultural tool that Hebrew language is. He wants—consciously or unconsciously—to speak Hebrew because it is the key that can open for him the doors of Israeli hegemonic culture.[159]

That there are Palestinians who write in Hebrew and have found an Israeli-Jewish readership in no way means that the Jewish national borders that demarcate the literary canon of modern Hebrew have somehow slackened. That would require a change in culture—the creation of a

recognize established borders, who translate received tradition into their own terms and challenge, explicit or implicit, the dominant masculine and national culture that surrounds them" (Gertz 2002, pp. 181–2).

155 Fanon 1967, pp. 18–19.

156 Fanon 1967, p. 38.

157 Fanon 1967, p. 63.

158 Fanon 1967, p. 38.

159 In other cultural fields, where the barrier of language does not exist, the penetration into the hegemonic Israeli culture is much easier, such as in the field of classical (Western) music, not to speak about the possibility that Israeli culture could be a window to success in Western culture. For example, the Palestinian piano player from Nazareth, Salīm 'Abbūd Ashqar (b. 1976), who has no hesitation about his being part of Israeli culture, even admits that he is a sort of a Jew: "We are, too, much closer to Israeli [Jewish] society" (*Yediot Aḥronoth*, February 21, 2003, pp. 8–9, 16).

new, Israeli–Palestinian culture common to both Jews and Arabs. On the way, compromises are needed, and until now the only ones who have made compromises have been the bilingual Palestinian authors.[160] The case of the aforementioned Sayed Kashua is an enlightening illustration: in some of his writings, without seeing his name one would never guess that the writer is a Muslim Arab.[161] As a contributor to the Friday magazine of the Hebrew *Haaretz*, his following article, "Wednesday Night, Jerusalem: Belonging", shows his awareness of the role he plays in Israeli culture:

> Oh, no, I think to myself at the sight of cars in the village that are flying blue ribbons. There were also a few with orange ribbons, but I want to believe that those are cars of Jews whose owners came here to shop, and not to believe what a friend told me about some of his neighbors—who thought it was some new fashion.[162] Never mind about the cars with orange ribbons; that isn't what really bothers me. *What bothers me is Arabs who live under the illusion that they are part of the Israeli game, those who think they actually have the right to express an opinion on internal Jewish issues. Poor guys.* There are hardly any individualists in Jerusalem. Still, in the Holy City one must choose a camp. So in the parking lot of Hama'abada [the Jerusalem Performing Arts Lab] I looked for a car with a blue ribbon and parked to its left. It's a way of taking a stand. "Tipa Pupa, a fantasy for children,"[163] the ads promised ... My little girl releases herself from my grip and runs ahead, to the center of things. I watch her from a distance as she draws with chalk on the asphalt, along with the other children. She even exchanges a few sentences with some of them. *I smile when I think about the perfect Hebrew she speaks ...* "Tipa Pupa" is the name of the play and also the magic words the magician uses to control the action on the stage and the other dancers ... That's all, it's over, and the dancers invite the children onto the stage to dance with them and she makes her way quickly to the stage and takes the hand of a dancer and mimics her movements. I watch her, my little girl, dancing with everyone and looking like everyone. On the way home

[160] In his study pertaining to why Arab soccer in Israel did not become a site for the construction and expression of Palestinian national pride in Israel, Tamir Sorek writes that the Palestinians in Israel distance their national identity from the soccer sphere and channel their expression of nationalism to other spheres. "Most of the Arab fans," he writes, "regard soccer as a channel of integration in Israeli society" (Sorek 2003, p. 435. Cf. Sorek 2006, pp. 162, 181; Sorek 2007). The present writer, however, prefers to see it as another compromise. On this topic, see also Sorek 2001 and the essays published in *Haaretz* by Jerrold Kessel and Pierre Klochendler, such as on October 14, 2004; December 5, 2004; March 6, 2005; May 15, 2005; June 1, 2005.

[161] For example, see *Maariv* (cultural supplement), September 19, 2003, pp. 8, 10.

[162] Blue ribbons were the symbol of the supporters of the disengagement from the Gaza Strip and parts of the West Bank in late 2005. Orange ribbons were the symbol of the settlers.

[163] A play for children by Yossi Yungman.

> she falls asleep and the cars with *the blue ribbons remind me how dumb are the Arabs who do everything to make them feel they belong.*[164]

In 2014, Kashua published an article in *The Guardian* in which he explained his frustration: "Twenty-five years of writing in Hebrew, and nothing has changed. Twenty-five years clutching at the hope, believing it is not possible that people can be so blind ... When Jewish youth parade through the city shouting 'Death to the Arabs,' and attack Arabs only because they are Arabs, I understood that I had lost my little war."[165] It is not surprising that, three years later, Sayed Kashua published a farewell column in *Haaretz*:

> A person with an Arab name can write an impressive piece condemning the occupation, the apartheid and the racism that are built into Israeli society, but he will always be read as an Arab. His ostensibly fierce remarks are liable only to confirm the anxieties lurking in readers' hearts about the Arab: Here's another Arab who's proving, in black and white, that all the fears we have inculcated about them from infancy are justified. And if it's a moderate Arab—a leftist with liberal notions—the Jewish readers will think that it's thanks to them, a consequence of the light they instilled in them. They will also think that this illumination is certainly temporary, the result of years of taming and restraint, a type of enlightenment that can't be trusted if the whip constantly held above the back of the enlightened Arab is set aside for a moment. Over the years, I've wondered about the best way to address the Israeli public, and whether freedom of expression is conceivable for an Arab. Is equality of freedom of expression, according to the liberal-democratic definition, possible when essential components of equality are lacking? Is freedom of expression possible in the face of the knowledge that your boss, whatever his worldview may be, is a Jew? Is freedom of expression possible in the absence of economic equality, in the absence of a fair allocation of status and key positions in the system?[166]

In an essay he published four years later, he argues that "to live under forced exile in the heart of my homeland or to live in voluntary exile as a resident alien—this is my choice. Either way, to be a stranger in a strange land."[167]

164 *Haaretz*, July 15, 2005 (English translation according to www.haaretz.com, July 14, 2005, with some modifications [my emphasis]). Cf. Ayman Siksik, "The Blue that We Cannot Succeed to Be Part of," *Haaretz*, literary supplement, July 22, 2005.

165 See at: https://www.theguardian.com/world/2014/jul/20/sayed-kashua-why-i-have-to-leave-israel, July 20, 2014, last accessed November 8, 2021.

166 *Haaretz*, November 16, 2017.

167 "My Palestinian Diaspora," *The New York Review of Books*, August 8, 2021. It should be noted that Kashua still engages in collaboration with Israeli projects such as writing twenty episodes of a drama for Israeli educational TV about a bilingual school in Jerusalem (available at: https://variety.com, July 12, 2021, last accessed November 9, 2021).

Against the aforementioned background, it is surprising to see how scholars who have been studying the cultural developments within the Arab population in Israel have been still ignoring reality, concentrating on marginal phenomena out of political and ideological motives or sheer blindness. The following are the closing lines of chapter 8, "Journalism, Media, and Arabic Literature," of the publication *Arab Society in Israel: Information Manual* (2009), published by the Abraham Fund Initiatives:

> One of the phenomena from the 1990s has been the tendency of Arab writers to only write in Hebrew in order to approach the wide public Jewish readership and not only the Arab readers. Sayed Kashua (b. 1975) is a good example for that ... [his] novels represent some kind of an autobiography of the struggle of the Arab within Israel in the light of the crisis of their integration into Israeli society following October 2000 events.[168]

The Abraham Fund Initiatives is an organization founded in 1989 with the aim of advancing what is described as

> coexistence, equality and cooperation among Israel's Jewish and Arab citizens by creating and operating large-scale initiatives, cultivating strategic grassroots projects and conducting public education and advocacy that promote its vision of shared citizenship and opportunity for all of Israel's citizens. The Abraham Fund Initiatives views coexistence as the ability of people of different backgrounds and beliefs to live side-by-side in mutual respect. Coexistence is not assimilation. Rather, its objective is to enable individuals and communities to live cooperatively while maintaining their own unique cultural identities. The Abraham Fund Initiatives sees civic equality for Israel's Jewish and Arab citizens as a moral and pragmatic imperative, whereby individual rights and the political, cultural and religious character of the Arab minority must be clearly and unambiguously recognized and respected.[169]

It goes without saying that the vision and the wishful thinking of that organization had motivated the writing of the aforementioned "insight" regarding the tendency of Arab writers to write only in Hebrew. In fact, Arab writers in Hebrew are so few and so marginal in Israeli-Hebrew culture that it is hard not to conclude that most Israeli-Arab intellectuals have adopted a cynical approach, admitting that nothing can be done against the backdrop of the rejection of Arab cultural values in Israeli society. Few have expressed this "one-way" exercise more eloquently than Anton Shammās in his aforementioned lines:

[168] Rekhess and Rodnitzki 2009, p. 23.

[169] From the organization's website at: http://www.abrahamfund.org/main/siteNew/index.php?page=38, last accessed August 8, 2009.

One-wayness is one of the rules of the Game. Amichai
Comes out of the Hebrew poetry and hangs a sign
“Will be back soon.” I don’t, I don’t. I
Send postcards in the morning, to my very dear friends
In order to notify them that I send them
Postcards in the morning.[170]

In 2014, the Department of Arabic Language and Literature at the University of Haifa invited Anton Shammās to participate in a conference about Palestinian literature. His reply did not leave any doubt regarding his attitude to Hebrew literature:

> شكرًا على الدّعوة، الّتي تشرّفني كثيراً. ولكن أرجو أن تتقبّلوا اعتذاري، إذ أنّي لن أستطيع المشاركة في المؤتمر، لسببين أكتفي بذكر الاهمّ من بينهما: الكتابة باللغة العبريّة، والحديث عنها، أمران يتعلّقان بمرحلة من حياتي انقطعت بيني وبينها الوشائج منذ سنوات طويلة، ولن أعود إليها في يوم من الأيّام.

> Thanks for the invitation, which highly honored me. But, please accept my apologies, because I will not be able to take part at the conference for two reasons, and I will mention the more important among them: Writing in Hebrew, and speaking about that, are issues related to a period in my life with which my connections were cut a long time ago, and I will never return to it.[171]

The aforementioned cases of the Druze Na‘īm ‘Arāyidī, the Christian Anton Shammās, and the Muslim Sayed Kashua testify to the refusal of Israeli-Hebrew culture in the second half of the twentieth century and the first two decades of the twenty-first century to accept non-Jewish writers as Israeli authors. Also, I reject arguments that attribute major significance to the aforementioned three authors in Israeli-Jewish culture, for example, that “Kashua creates new political, ethnical, religious and linguistics categories which, due to their surreal possibilities, shocking and shattering established labels, make Israel a country far removed from its statistics, whose people do not fit stereotypes.”[172] At the same time, Arab culture dismisses these authors because of their readiness to be accepted by Israeli-Hebrew culture. From the point of view of the authors themselves, the words of the French-language Tunisian Jewish novelist Albert Memmi (1920–2020), who for many years grappled with the various layers of his own complicated identity, are relevant here:

170 Shammās 1979, p. 13. At the same time, Shammās’ influence was evident during the 1980s and 1990s among leftist Jewish intellectuals, who used his views for their political and ideological purposes. See, for example, Hever 1987, pp. 47–76; Hever 1989, pp. 30–2; Hever 1991; Lavie 1996, pp. 55–96; Silberstein 1999, pp. 127–63; Hever 2001.

171 Email sent to the organizers of the conference, November 9, 2014.

172 Schlesinger 2018, p. 40.

> I saw clearly that my cutting myself off entirely from my own original background did not necessarily allow me to enter any other group. Just as I sat on the fence between two civilizations, so would I now find myself between two classes; and I realized that, in trying to sit on several chairs, one generally lands on the floor.[173]

[173] Memmi 1966, p. 123. Translation according to Memmi 2013, p. 51. The Moroccan scholar Abdelfattah Kilito (b. 1945) refers to similar thoughts when, before publishing one of his books in French, he showed the manuscript to a French friend who implicitly encouraged him to rewrite it in Arabic (Kilito 2020, pp. 57–8).

Part II

Hybridization, Exclusion, and Demise

لا شيء في عرف الوطنيّة اسمه مسلم ومسيحيّ وإسرائيليّ، بل هناك شيء يقال له العراق [...]إنّني أطالب من أبناء وطني العراقيّين أن لا يكونوا إلّا عراقيّين لأنّنا نرجع إلى أرومة واحدة ودوحة واحدة هي دوحة جدّنا سام وكلّنا منسوبون إلى العنصر الساميّ ولا فرق في ذلك بين المسلم والمسيحيّ واليهوديّ [...] وليس لنا اليوم إلّا واسطة القوميّة القويّة التّأثير.

– الملك فيصل

In the vocabulary of patriotism, there is no such thing as a Jew, as Muslim, or a Christian. There is simply one thing called Iraq ... I ask all the Iraqi children of my homeland to be just Iraqis, because we all belong to one origin and one tree, the tree of our ancestor Shem, and all of us are related to the Semitic root, which makes no distinction between Muslim, Christian or Jew ... Today we have but one means [to our end]: influential patriotism.

– King Fayṣal

Throughout the last decades, scholars have pointed out the veritable discursive explosion around the concept of identity: the critique of the self-sustaining subject at the center of post-Cartesian Western metaphysics has been comprehensively advanced in philosophy; the question of subjectivity and its unconscious processes of formation has been developed within the discourse of a psychoanalytically influenced feminism and cultural criticism; and the endlessly performative self has been advanced in celebratory variants of postmodernism. Within the anti-essentialist critique of ethnic, racial, and national conceptions of cultural identity and the "politics of location," some adventurous theoretical conceptions have been sketched in their most grounded forms. What, then, is the need for a further debate about "identity"?

The discussions during the last decades around the concept of identity have been channeled mainly into two major positions, primordialist and non-primordialist. The first position assumes that there is an essential content to any identity that is defined by common origin or common structure of experience. In the words of the Lebanese writer Amin Maalouf (Amīn Maʿlūf), it "presupposes that 'deep down inside' everyone there is just one affiliation that really matters, a kind of 'fundamental truth' about each individual, an 'essence' determined once and for all at birth, never to change thereafter."[1] Although discredited among cultural theorists and sociologists, this view, for obvious reasons, is popular among politicians, particularly with regard to ethnic identity. The second major position, which encompasses non-primordialist views regarding identity, including the instrumentalist and the constructivist views, argues that identities are constructed through the interplay between cultural reproduction, everyday reinforcements, and institutional arrangements. This position emphasizes the impossibility of distinct identities. Any identity depends upon its difference from some other identity—"identity is a structured representation which only achieves its positive through the narrow eye of the negative," writes the Jamaican-born cultural theorist Stuart Hall (1932–2014). "It has to go through the eye of the needle of the other before it can construct itself." While someone's single identity cannot be explored or challenged without a simultaneous investigation of another identity or other identities, investigation is rarely done this way in practice. Most investigations in cultural studies deal with the construction of subaltern or marginalized identities or dominated identities, and rarely are the two ever studied together as mutually constitutive, as theory would seem to dictate. At any event, most of us have gradually become convinced that identity is in general a

[1] Maalouf 2000, p. 4.

temporary and unstable effect of relations that define identities by marking differences—which implies that the multiplicity of identities and differences and the emphasis on connections or articulations between the fragments or differences are inevitable.

Never unified, identities seem to us to be increasingly fragmented and fractured. Never singular, they seem as well to be multiply constructed across different, often intersecting and antagonistic discourses, practices, and positions. In addition, they are subject to a radical historicization and are constantly in the process of change and transformation. Actually, identities arise from the narrativization of the self, but the necessarily fictional nature of this narrativization in no way undermines its discursive, material, or political effectivity. Identities refer to the meeting point between, on the one hand, the discourses and practices that attempt to interpellate, speak to us, or hail us into place as the social subjects of particular discourses and, on the other hand, the processes that produce subjectivities, that construct us as subjects that can be "spoken." All identities seem to be points of temporary attachment to the subject position that discursive practices construct for us.

This second part of the book will investigate the connections between religion, hybridization, and identity beyond the contribution of Jews to Arabic literature since its birth, and the tragic end of Arab-Jewish literature following the escalation of the Arab–Jewish conflict, the establishment of the State of Israel (1948), the Palestinian *Nakba*, and the immigration of most Arab Jews to the new Jewish state. Furthermore, it seems that the only joint "achievement" of this political–ideological conflict is the unspoken agreement between the two national movements—Zionism and Arab nationalism—to perform a total cleansing of Arab-Jewish culture. The national and political struggle over a small piece of territory has not hindered the two national movements from seeing eye-to-eye in this respect, despite the difference between them: one was inspired by European colonialism, and the other was an anticolonial venture. The canonical Arab-Muslim and the Jewish-Zionist cultural and national systems have both excluded the hybrid Arab-Jewish identity and promoted the "pure" Jewish-Zionist identity against the "pure" Arab-Muslim one. As a result, Arab-Jewish culture has become a disease that is to be eradicated, and the few people who cannot be cured are to be quarantined and contained for fear of contamination. That is why, at the present time, we are witnessing the demise of Arab-Jewish culture. A tradition that started more than 1,500 years ago is vanishing before our very eyes. The main factor in the Muslim–Christian–Jewish Arab symbiosis up to the twentieth century, from the Jewish point of view, was that the great majority of the Jews under the rule of Islam adopted Arabic as their spoken language. This symbiosis does not exist in our time because Arabic is gradually disappearing as a language spoken on a daily basis by Jews.

Chapter 5, "Pluralism: Arabs of Mosaic Faith," surveys the literary writing of Jews in Arabic throughout the history of Arabic literature, even before the rise of Islam, and concludes with the demise of this writing today. Judeo-Muslim symbiosis began at the very birth of Islam, in which process the Jews played an important role; the Qur'ān provides a solid testimony to this. Arab Jews had an intimate knowledge of the holy book of Islam and its source texts, and they would play an active role in shaping medieval Arab-Muslim civilization by serving as an intermediate link between Hellenistic-Roman civilization and modern civilization. Medieval Arab-Muslim civilization was to be an admixture of cultural elements; it would invariably manifest pre-Islamic roots alongside the Islamic religion itself, as well as a basis in Greek humanism and in various cultural elements of the ancient heritage of the Near East. Therefore, it is not mere coincidence that the flowering of Jewish culture in the Arab world should occur at the very time that Islamic civilization was at its apogee. Nor is it strange that Jews often preferred writing in Arabic rather than in Hebrew, even when dealing with the most sacred matters of Judaism, which had the effect of making their literature virtually unavailable to Europeans. Arabized Jews had no conscious motivation behind the widespread use of Arabic, as in view of their extensive adjustment under Islam, and the degree to which they identified themselves with its culture, nothing is more natural than that they should use in their writings the language that served them in every other need. But, now, we are witnessing the demise of Arab-Jewish culture. A tradition that started more than 1,500 years ago is vanishing before our eyes—Arabic is gradually disappearing as a language mastered by Jews. The image of an hourglass pops up before us: the grains of sand are quickly running out. We all know that the chapter of Arab-Jewish symbiosis has more or less ended.

Chapter 6, "Spring: 'We Were Like Those Who Dream,'" discusses the flowering of literary Arabic activities of immigrating Arab-Jewish writers in Israel during the 1950s. Among the writers, most of them from Iraq, it was already possible to discern two streams of thought parallel to the dominant trends of the local Arabic literature. The first trend was of the writers and poets close to the Israeli governmental establishment who were steeped in national pride and who were permeated with patriotism and the desire for peace while absent any critique of the authorities. Their work was characterized by an emphasis on Jewish-Arab brotherhood, the yearning for peace, and praise for the accomplishments of the state, "whose flowering land is flowing with milk and honey." Not a drop of criticism against the authorities was heard. The second trend, that of the leftist poets and writers, did not agree that Israeli patriotism implied absolute identification with the authorities. This was so despite their awareness that anti-establishment activity might harm not only their chances for integration into Israeli society, but also their income and even their livelihoods. In contrast to the writers supported by the Israeli governmental establishment, these writers and poets devoted all their literary energies to intellectual struggle, focusing their attention on three central concerns: the manner in which new immigrants were absorbed; the inequality between the Oriental Jews and the Ashkenazi residents; and the fate of the Arab minority. The difference in worldview between the two trends can be seen in the concept of "spring" so frequently used by both sides. According to the writers supported by the establishment, their hopes had been realized in the Jewish, independent Israel of the 1950s, as we find in the opening two words of the poet Salīm Sha'shū'a's first poem in the collection *The World of Light*, "The Spring Has Arrived." In contrast, the struggle was still in full force for the Communist writers, and their eyes gazed toward the future, as seen from the name of David Semah's collection *Till Spring Comes*. All the Jewish writers in Arabic in the 1950s preached coexistence, peace, and brotherhood, and believed in their realization. But while this belief arose among the establishment writers in the wake of the decisive victory of the Jews in the struggle for control of the Land of Israel, it emerged among the Jewish leftist writers from a sense of sympathy with the defeated side.

Until the 1950s, in the 1960s, and especially since the 1970s, only a few among the emigrant-authors insisted on remaining true to their cultural origins and continued to write in Arabic, though they realized that they were working in a void and their books hardly found any readership inside or outside Israel. *Chapter 7*, "Demise: The Last of the Mohicans," deals with the activities of one of the most prominent among them, Isḥāq (Isaac) Bār-Moshe (formerly Khaddūrī [Khedhourie]), whose literary works consist of two main branches with different generic, thematic, and stylistic preferences: for the expression of his general social, existential, and philosophical views, he employed the genre of the short story, with an obvious inclination toward psychological insights. His short stories generally reflect universal concepts and tend to reveal the inner nature of human beings; they are mostly well removed from any specific time and place, and when read in translation hardly point to the ethnic, religious, or national identity of the author. Bār-Moshe's novels—the semi-autobiographical novels or memoirs—are used for the recollection of the author's life in Iraq and for expressing his views regarding the last stage of the Iraqi-Jewish community. The fictional framework is constructed on solid historical material in a way that enables the reader to see the books as an alternative history to the events described from the point of view of an Iraqi Jew living in Israel. Bār-Moshe, whose literary career began in the early 1970s, was one of the last Jewish writers in Arabic. Despite the richness of his literary works, Bār-Moshe was pushed to the margins of Israeli literature and had a very limited readership. The canonical Hebrew establishment did not express any interest in his works—none of his writings have attracted the attention of outstanding literary critics. He has generally been considered to be an ethnic voice giving expression to views and issues that, at most, are relevant to only a limited section of Israeli society. This is in evident contrast, at least as seen above from the point of view of his short stories, to the universal nature of his work. His marginal status in Israeli culture as well as the feeling that for non-literary consideration his work has been left without serious attention from Arab critics and scholars are presumably the reasons why his literary voice was not heard in the years leading up to his death.

Chapter 8, "Identity: Inessential Solidarities," is theoretically oriented, discussing the issue of Arab-Jewish identity and the changes in the concept of identity and belonging among the Arabized Jews during the twentieth century. The main argument is that, due to some processes that the Arabized Jews had experienced and because of some global developments, they gradually developed a negative sensitivity toward the notion of stable identity, whatever identity that may be, asserting instead their particular singularities and searching for alternative forms of identification, mostly various kinds of inessential solidarities and feelings of belonging. From a sample of partial investigations, however, I have a solid basis for the hypothesis that these developments have occurred, if in different rhythms and intensity, among all communities of Arabized Jews. In order to present the changes of the notion of identity among the Arabized Jews, I will use the aforementioned term "interpellation" coined by Louis Pierre Althusser (1918–1990) when theorizing the constitutive process by which individuals acknowledge and respond to ideologies. Thus, I see the Arabized Jews as experiencing during the twentieth century at least four major processes of collective interpellation, and two of them were at the same time intense exclusionary operations and erasures as well: the first is hailing the Iraqi Jews as Arabs; the second is hailing the Iraqi Jews as "Zionists" (= first exclusion); the third is hailing the Iraqi Jews as "Arabs" (= second exclusion); and the fourth, and last one, is hailing the Iraqi Jews as one side in a binary monolithic category. The quotation marks around "Zionist" and "Arabs" in the second and third processes (the first and the second operations of exclusion) mean that, in each case, the hailing ascribed to them a specific identity while at the same time ignoring whether the subjectivities of the interpellated people were at all ready to positively respond to such a hailing. I have focused my investigations on the ways by which the Arabized Jews articulated their cultural preferences, defined their identities, and expressed their identification and belonging before and after their immigration. In other words, I am interested more in their subjectivities and less in the identities ascribed to them.

Chapter 5

Pluralism: Arabs of Mosaic Faith[1]

My heart beats with love for the Arabs,
My mouth proudly speaks their language.
Do they and I not share a common source?
The distant past drew us together,
When al-Samaw'al set in the book of faithfulness
An emblem to the Arabs in al-Ablaq
– Anwar Shā'ul

1. INTRODUCTION

The most significant Jewish contacts with other civilizations are considered to be the symbioses with the Greek civilization of ancient times and with the Romanic and Germanic peoples of Western and Central Europe in the modern period, as well as with Arab-Muslim civilization. The ancient Greek and modern European symbioses were, however, essentially with cultures at variance with the Jewish religious culture, whereas because Islam is from the very flesh and bone of Judaism, as S. D. Goitein (1900–1985) indicated, "never has Judaism encountered such a close and fructitious symbiosis as that with the medieval civilization of Arab Islam."[2] The main factor in the Arab-Jewish symbiosis was that the great majority of Jews under the rule of Islam adopted Arabic as their language. By the tenth century, Jews from Spain to Iraq were speaking Arabic. They also adopted Arab ways of thinking and forms of literature as well as Muslim religious notions. Medieval Jewish piety leaned heavily on Sufism (Islamic mysticism), and only under

[1] This chapter uses material that first appeared in various publications, such as Snir 2004, pp. 143–63; Snir 2005a; Snir 2006a, pp. 283–323; Snir 2006b, pp. 43–60; Snir 2015b; Snir 2019.

[2] Goitein 1955, p. 130.

Arab-Muslim influence did science and scholarly methods of thinking, in the Greek sense of these terms, for the first time become known and practiced by the vast majority of Jews.

Modern Arab-Jewish culture should be viewed against the background of Jewish symbiosis with Arab-Muslim culture and the status of Jews in the Arab-Muslim world from the seventh century AD, and also in light of the process of modernization in the Middle East and North Africa from the second half of the nineteenth century. Modernization, and the social, political, and economic transformations associated with it, the master theme of contemporary social science, should not be referred to as a mere change—"it is the transformation of society."[3] The Jewish communities in the various Arab countries shared in that transformation and sometimes even helped in effecting it. Jews began interacting increasingly in the local life of different places in various ways and at a different paces.[4] However, the Jews of Arab lands never had the chance to completely undergo that process of transformation and to fully enjoy the benefits thereof. That process was soon to be overshadowed by national conflict in the Middle East.

The purpose of the present chapter is to outline Jewish involvement in Arab culture in modern times against this historical background and to analyze the present demise of Arab-Jewish culture.

2. HISTORICAL BACKGROUND

In the sixth century AD, when Arabic reached its full development with the appearance of poetry of high standing, Jewish communities were flourishing throughout the Arabian Peninsula. Jews as an integral part of Arab society participated in the making of the local culture, and Jewish tribes had distinguished poets. The personal integrity of one such poet, al-Samaw'al ibn 'Ādiyā', became proverbial, and he has since been commemorated by the saying "*awfā min al-Samaw'al*" ("more loyal than al-Samaw'al"). The incident referred to was his refusal to yield weapons entrusted to him, even when a Bedouin chieftain laid siege to his castle and murdered his son.[5] Describing the noble qualities of his own Arab-Jewish tribe, al-Samaw'al composed a poem, the opening verse of which was:

[3] Goldscheider and Zuckerman 1984, pp. 4–5.

[4] See the various contributions in Goldberg 1996. The observations of the editor on pp. 29–30 on Jewish involvement in ideological movements as well as on shared identities of Muslims and Jews are very important.

[5] See al-Maydānī 1988, II, pp. 441–2. On the poet and his loyalty, see also Meisami and Starkey 1998, II, pp. 685–6.

إذا المَرءُ لَم يدنَس مِنَ اللُؤمِ عِرضُهُ   فَكُلُّ رِداءٍ يَرتَديهِ جَميلُ

When a man's honor is not defiled by baseness,
Then every cloak he cloaks himself in is comely.[6]

This poem, which even today is highly regarded in the Arabic literary tradition, testifies to the existence of a past in which no one would consider that being an Arab and at the same time a Jew was paradoxical. There were also female poets among the Jewish poets of the pre-Islamic period, such as Sāra al-Qurayẓiyya, whose elegy for 350 noblemen of her tribe killed in a battle in 492 CE is frequently cited in ancient Arab sources.[7] Moreover, we can find some clear Jewish impact on Arabic verse in that period—the poetry of the famous pre-Islamic poet Imru' al-Qays (*c.* 497–545 CE), for example, shows empathy toward the Jews and even absorbed Jewish ideas and different concepts from local Jewish tradition.[8]

When Islam in the seventh century CE became the dominant faith and defining legal and social framework, Jews (together with Christians and in Persia Zoroastrians as well) were considered to be protégés (*Ahl al-Dhimma* [People of the Pact]) of the new community. Jews were not only well-acquainted with the emerging Islamic literature, but were also deeply inspired by it, and gradually became thoroughly Arabicized. As interference normally occurs when a target culture is either in a state of emergence, vacuum, or at a turning point in its history,[9] the Jews had in turn the ability to influence the rising Islamic civilization. To borrow words said on the role of Christians in Muslim society, the seventh century was a peculiar juncture when the characteristic institutions of the dominant community were "in the process of formation, radical modification, or destruction by forces which the marginal community [might] or [might] not have helped generate but which it [was] able to accelerate and focus."[10] The Jews were thus by no means passive agents for the new Muslim society. Judeo-Muslim symbiosis began at the very birth of Islam, in which process the Jews played an important role; the Qur'ān provides solid testimony for this. Arab Jews had an intimate knowledge of the holy book of Islam and its source texts,[11]

6 For the poem, see Abū Tammām n.d., I, p. 36. See also the text, together with an English translation, in Arberry 1965, pp. 30–3.

7 On Arab-Jewish poets in the pre-Islamic period, see al-Iṣbahānī 1964, XXIV, pp. 97–128. On Sāra al-Qurayẓiyya, see al-Iṣbahānī 1964, XXII, pp. 102–5; Bitton 1999, pp. 43–6.

8 See Tobi 2017, pp. 194–390.

9 Sebeok 1986, I, p. 462. Cf. al-'Aẓm 1992, p. 159.

10 Haddad 1970, p. 3.

11 On knowledge of the Qur'ān among Jews, see Lazarus-Yafeh 1992, pp. 143–60. See also a testimony on a literary debate held in Rayy in northern Persia testifying to the familiarity

and they would play an active role in shaping medieval Arab-Muslim civilization by serving as an intermediate link between Hellenistic-Roman civilization and modern civilization. Medieval Arab-Muslim civilization was to be an admixture of cultural elements; it would invariably manifest pre-Islamic roots alongside the Islamic religion itself as well as a basis in Greek humanism and in various cultural elements of the ancient heritage of the Near East. Therefore, "it is not mere coincidence that the flowering of Jewish culture in the Arab world should occur at the very time that Islamic civilization was at its apogee."[12] Nor is it strange that Jews often preferred writing in Arabic rather than in Hebrew, even when dealing with the most sacred matters of Judaism, which had the effect of making their literature virtually unavailable to Europeans. Arab Jews had no conscious motivation behind the widespread use of Arabic, as in view of their extensive adjustment under Islam, and the degree to which they identified themselves with its culture, "nothing is more natural than that they should use in their writings the language which served them in every other need."[13]

The Jews of Mesopotamia, for example, who looked back to Exile to Babylon, for centuries spoke Aramaic, in which language they produced the Talmud. However, after the Arab conquest, especially under the Abbasid Caliphate,[14] the then-thriving Jewish community underwent a rapid process of Arabization and integration into the surrounding Arab-Muslim society, the majority of them congregating in the new metropolis of Baghdad. Facilitating their integration was their high level of achievement and resulting prosperity in commerce, education, and culture. By the ninth century, a Jewish physician, Māsarjawayh of Basra, was already translating medical writings from Greek and Syriac into Arabic and also writing original medical works.[15] Also, it was Mesopotamia where the first Arabic-influenced Hebrew poetry originated.[16]

As with Mesopotamia, in all other lands conquered by the Arabs the Jews adopted Arabic as their language. From the ninth century, Judeo-Arabic

of Jews with both Arabic *belles lettres* and the Qur'ān in Yāqūt 1991, II, pp. 240–1. Cf. Tobi 2004, pp. 59, 63–4.

12 Stillman 1979, p. 61. For an overview of 1,400 years of intertwined destiny of Judaism and Islam, see Stillman 2011, pp. 10–20.

13 Halkin 1956, pp. 220–1. On Arabic as a unifying element among the various religious and ethnic groups in the Muslim Empire and as a universal medium of intellectual expression among both Muslims and non-Muslims, see Chejne 1969, pp. 13–16.

14 "Arabic had become the *lingua franca* of the caliphate. This wide use of this language also served to lower ethnic and cultural barriers. In fact, it had a unifying effect. Politically and ideologically, 'Abbāsid society no longer focused on *Arab* culture. Instead, the emphasis was now on *Arabic* culture" (Pietruschka 2005, p. 32).

15 See Steinschneider 1902, p. 13; *Encyclopaedia Judaica*, X (1971), p. 411.

16 Tobi 2004, pp. 31–64.

literature flourished, that is, texts in Jewish dialects of vernacular Arabic that combined Hebrew and Aramaic lexical items with Arabic and that were generally written in Hebrew script.[17] Large portions of this literature were scientific, philosophical, and theological in nature. The works of, for example, Sa'īd ibn Yūsuf al-Fayyūmī, known as Sa'adia Gaon (882–942), were almost all written in Judeo-Arabic. He translated the Bible into Arabic, the language in which he also composed his commentary, the *Sharḥ*.[18] Born in Egypt, after a stay in Palestine he left for Mesopotamia where in 928 CE he was appointed Head of the Babylonian Academy at Sūra, a position he held (with a six-year intermission) until his death. He applied his knowledge of Arabic poetry and poetics to Hebrew poetics in order to halt a decrease in Hebrew writings; he also used Arabic literary criticism for the purpose of increasing the value of Hebrew poetry in the eyes of his own Jewish generation.[19]

Another famous scholar of the period, the Fatimid vizier of Jewish origin Ya'qūb ibn Killis (930–991), was not only a gifted administrator but a lover of *belles lettres*, and wrote books on Islamic law and the Qur'ān. According to the Mamluk historian al-Maqrīzī (d. 1442), Ibn Killis held weekly Tuesday *majlis* sessions at home, and provided stipends for scholars, writers, poets, jurists, theologians, and master artisans participating in them. On Fridays, he would convene sessions at which he would read his own works.[20] Speaking about the literary Arabic activities in Egypt, the Cairo Genizah has shown its importance as a fruitful source for the study of both liturgical and secular Hebrew poetry. But the Genizah also contains hundreds of poetry fragments written in the Arabic language written in both Hebrew and Arabic script. These fragments are very important for the study of Arabic literature and poetry, and Islamic studies in general, as well as a source for the study of the dissemination of knowledge among medieval Muslim and Jewish elites.[21]

One of the greatest scholars in Jewish history, the physician and philosopher Maimonides (Mūsā ibn Maymūn) (1135–1204), wrote most of his works in Judeo-Arabic; the most influential of these was *Dalālat al-Ḥā'irīn* (*The*

17 As the education at the time was religious, people generally used the script of their religious writings, even when writing in a language in which they had not been educated (Goitein 1967, I, p. 16. Cf. López-Morillas 2000, p. 42).

18 On the particular nature of Sa'adia Gaon's translation, see Blau and Hopkins 2000, pp. 4–14; Kearny 2010–2011, pp. 55–75.

19 On Sa'adia Gaon and his attitude to Arabic poetics, see Tobi 1995, pp. 35–53; Tobi 2000, pp. 59–77; Tobi 2004, pp. 65–175.

20 Cohen and Somekh 1990, pp. 283–314.

21 For an initial survey of Arabic poetry in the Cairo Genizah, see Ahmed 2018, pp. 212–33.

Guide of the Perplexed).[22] Also, the distinguished Jewish-Iraqi philosopher and physician Saʿd ibn Manṣūr ibn Hibat Allāh ibn Kammūna, better known as Ibn Kammūna al-Isrāʾīlī (1215–1284) was well versed in science, philosophy, *belles lettres*, and especially in mathematics and logic. Ibn Kammūna, who came from a learned Jewish family of Baghdad, in 1280 published *Tanqīḥ al-Abḥāth li-l-Milal al-Thalāth* (*Examination of the Inquiries into the Three Faiths*),[23] which focused on Islam but dealt also with Christianity and his own faith, Judaism. His critical remarks on Islam led zealous Muslims to make an issue of the fact that a Jew dared to write about their faith, and several years later he was to escape a mob riot.[24] Despite it being known that he had suffered for being a Jew, some reports seemingly expressed an ambiguous attitude toward him, and referred to Ibn Kammūna as Muslim, or even Shiite.[25]

Also, in Syria there were Jews who wrote poetry in Arabic; the Islamic sources mentioned, for example, Ibn al-Baqaqī (died 1302), who participated in a polemic on free will (*qadar*). He composed a poem of eight verses in which he refers to the Qurʾānic question attributed to the polytheists (*mushrikūn*): "*Law shāʾa Allāh mā ashraknā wa-lā abāʾunā*'" ("Had God willed, we would not have been idolaters, neither our fathers").[26] The poem, which was considered as aiming to slander Islam, stirred up many angry responses, among them a poem of 124 verses by the well-known theologian Ibn Taymiyya (1263–1328).[27]

From the mid-tenth to the mid-thirteenth centuries, Jewish culture in al-Andalus (Muslim Spain) had even more than elsewhere the closest of connections with Arab-Islamic culture through direct translation, imitation, adaptation, and borrowing. The atmosphere created allowed the elements of separate cultures to be actively exposed to one another and also to fuse together. New hybrid literary forms, therefore, came into being where Arabic was the *lingua franca*.[28] In "A Father's Admonition"

[22] On Maimonides and his connection with Arab culture, see Meisami and Starkey 1998, II, pp. 494–5. On the text of *Dalālat al-Ḥāʾirīn* against the background of the end and the disappearance of the medieval Andalusian Arab-Jewish context, and at the same time as "a rhetorical event to be read, a language that maintains but also negotiates and disrupts the localization and divisions established by the end," see Anidjar 2002, pp. 10–56 (the quotation is from p. 7).

[23] See Perlmann 1971.

[24] On Ibn Kammūna, see Nemoy 1964, pp. 507–10.

[25] Ibn Kammūna 2003, p. 2.

[26] *Al-Anʿām* 148 (English translation according to Arberry 1979 [1964], p. 139).

[27] See al-Subkī 1992, vol. 10, pp. 352–66; Ibn Taymiyya 1998, vol. 4, pp. 563–8.

[28] Menocal 1987, p. 65. For references on the hybrid character of al-Andalus, see pp. 69–70, n. 10. See also Menocal 2002.

for his son, Yudah ibn Tibbon (1120–1190) wrote: "Thou art well aware how our foremost men only attained to high distinction through their proficiency in Arabic writing."[29] In the case of Hebrew secular poetry, Arabic poetic models were used that undoubtedly brought about the most perfect expression of Arab-Jewish symbiosis in al-Andalus. The form of most of the secular Hebrew poetry in al-Andalus was on the model of the *qaṣīda*, which uses one unchangeable rhyme throughout the poem and one quantitative meter dividing each verse into two hemistichs.[30] Hebrew literature, grammar, and philosophy also reached a peak during this era. There is no other way of understanding the Jewish achievements and their imitating of the rhetorical embellishment of Arabic poetry and prose at the time, except in the light of their being informed with a knowledge of Arabic literature and Muslim philosophical thinking. There was in fact an elite class of Jewish courtiers and officials who were as polished in the Arabic language, literature, and culture as they were learned in the Hebrew and Jewish religious tradition. At least some of the members of that elite were even more assimilated to Arabic culture than Hebrew culture and more at home in literary standard Arabic (*fuṣḥā*) than in Hebrew, although one cannot, of course, reduce the difference between the Arabic poetry and Hebrew poetry of the time to purely one of language.[31]

Moses ibn Ezra (1055–1138), whose poetry has been described as the one that "most resembles that of an Arabic poet,"[32] wrote a number of prose works in Arabic, among them *Kitāb al-Muḥāḍara wa-l-Mudhākara* (*Book of Conversation and Deliberation*), which is "the most important medieval book about Hebrew poetry."[33] Jewish-Hebrew poets also adopted strophic forms (*muwashshaḥ*), with the last strophe (*kharja*) often written in vernacular Arabic.

Some Jewish poets became famous in both Hebrew and Arabic, such as Ismā'īl ibn Naghrīla (Shmuel ha-Nagid) (993–1056), the Zirid vizier, who held office in Granada during the mid-eleventh century, and the poet and philosopher Ibn Gabirol (1021–1058). Being thoroughly Arabized, Jews used not only Hebrew but also Arabic for liturgical purposes, such as for

29 Abrahams 1926, I, 59. Cf. Ibn 'Aqnin 1964, pp. 490–3.

30 See Goldstein 2004, III, pp. vii–xxxviii.

31 See Schippers 1994. For a critical review of this book, see Rowson 1996, pp. 105–11. For a critical examination of modern research on medieval Andalusi Hebrew literature, see Rosen and Yassif 2002, pp. 241–94.

32 Scheindlin 2000, p. 252.

33 Scheindlin 2000, p. 259.

hymns and religious ceremonies particularly on the New Year, Passover, Pentecost, and the Ninth of Av.[34]

There were also outside the mainstream of Jewish society in the Middle East communities that enjoyed reading or writing Arabic. The Karaites in Egypt wrote even the Hebrew Bible in Arabic characters; present in Karaite manuscripts were vestiges of the works of Muslim Ṣūfī mystics that had been previously transposed into Hebrew characters.[35] The Jews' reading and writing of Arabic poetry was not restricted to al-Andalus: Yehuda al-Ḥarīzī (Yehuda Alharizi) (1165–1225), who translated the *maqāmāt* of al-Ḥarīrī (1054–1122) into Hebrew under the title *Maḥberot iti'el* (*Iti'el's Notebooks*), wrote after leaving Christian Spain poems in Arabic for circulation throughout the Middle East. In the eighteenth *maqāma* in his book titled *Taḥkemonī*, he alludes to the acknowledged primacy of Arabic poetry, stating that "the golden Poesy was the Arabs' legacy."[36]

Nevertheless, when it came to poetry, most of the Andalusian Jewish poets wrote in Hebrew, not Arabic, at least according to the available sources. There are various explanations given for this. Samuel Miklos Stern (1920–1969), for example, thinks that the chief reason for this was love of the Hebrew language as a holy language and the desire to clothe the expression of new ideals in Jewish poetry in the national language. This means that the Hebrew poets did not seek to address themselves to the larger Muslim public because they considered it their function to be at the service of their own particular Jewish society.[37] Joshua Blau (1919–2020) argues that being much less attracted by the ideal of *'arabiyya*, the veritable Arabic language, than their Muslim fellow citizens, the Jews generally attained only a limited mastery of classical Arabic. Consequently, they could venture to write Arabic when composing scientific and religious tracts, but their superficial knowledge did not suffice for writing poetry.[38] According to Rina Drory (1947–2000),

[34] See Tobi 2002, pp. 203–21. Cf. Tobi 1996, pp. 213–25. For the history of Jewish paraliturgical song in the context of Arabo-Islamic culture, see Rosenfeld-Hadad 2019.

[35] See Fenton 1995, pp. 301–34; Fenton 2002, pp. 5–19; Fenton 2004, pp. 82–94; Epafras 2013, pp. 163–96. For a joint venture, if very limited, in which Jews and Muslims in contemporary Israel practice Sufism together, see Randall 2019. These activities, in the framework of "Derekh Avraham Jewish-Sufi Order," try to create pathways of engagement between two faith traditions in a geographical area beset by conflict.

[36] Alḥarizi 2001, pp. 175–89. Cf. Sadan 2002, pp. 105–51; Decter 2020, pp. 351–68. On al-Ḥarīzī and the story of the adaptation of the Arabic Ḥarīrīan *maqāmāt* and (according to the author) his "failure," see Katsumata 2002, pp. 117–37.

[37] Stern 1963, p. 254. Cf. Patai 1977, pp. 103–4; López-Morillas 2000, pp. 42–4.

[38] Blau 1981, pp. 22–3. For a critical approach to this conception, see Drory 2000, pp. 173–7, esp. n. 18. For Blau's response, see the revised edition of his above study (Blau 1999, pp. 230–9. See also Blau 2017, pp. 27–39, 326–9, 335n). For more on the linguistic

Arabic served for lucid, straightforward expression, while Hebrew served for festive and exalted writing, often at the expense of clarity and specificity: "Writing in Hebrew was designed to demonstrate the author's command of the language and to produce a text that would arouse admiration for its beauty and elegance; writing in Arabic was intended to produce a clear and understandable text."[39]

One should, however, distinguish between the use of language for practical purposes, such as composing scientific texts or theological polemical tracts, and the use of language for "non-practical" aesthetic purposes, that is, texts in which the author gives free rein to his/her artistic imagination and expresses his/her inner feelings and emotions. One would not expect a Jewish writer whose inner aesthetic preferences were rooted in the spiritual values of the Jewish culture alone to express his/her innermost feelings in Arabic. Also, in the eleventh through the thirteenth centuries, Jews in al-Andalus became so integrated into Arab culture that many were able to achieve widespread recognition for their Arabic poetry. Information about Jewish poetry in Arabic has as a rule not come from Jewish traditional circles, which considered such activity to be harmful to Jewish cultural identity. Nor could it come from Muslim traditional circles unless it was about Jewish converts to Islam or on a creative level of achievement within Arab culture that Muslim sources were unable to ignore. That we know something at all about Jews who distinguished themselves in Arabic poetry without converting to Islam (some very few!) may only testify to the recognition of the high quality of their poetry. But we can assume that literary writing in Arabic was much more widespread than the available sources indicate. We cannot rule out that many poets who wrote in Arabic were forgotten or caused to be forgotten since both Jewish and Muslim circles did not have any desire that they would be remembered unless they produced literary masterpieces that could not be forgotten.

It would be hard, however, to find in the works of the Arabized Jews a specifically *Jewish* contribution to Arab *belles lettres*; Jews were simply "members of the vast subject population of the Middle East which was assimilated to Arab ways of thinking and expression."[40] The most outstanding of the assimilated Jewish poets known to us is Ibrāhīm ibn Sahl al-Ishbīlī al-Isrā'īlī (1208–1259), who only wrote in Arabic and became famous for his panegyrics and love poems. Regarding some of Ibn Sahl's verses that were

situation in al-Andalus, see Wasserstein 1991, pp. 1–15; Sáenz-Badilios 1997, pp. 49–75; López-Morillas 2000, pp. 33–59.

[39] Drory 2000a, p. 198.

[40] Goitein 1955, p. 127.

said to refer to his worldly love, Raymond P. Scheindlin (b. 1940) thinks that they could just as well be about his conversion to Islam:

تسَلّيتُ عن موسى بحبّ محمّدٍ   هديتُ ولولا اللهُ ما كنتُ أهتدي
وما عن قِلًى قد كان ذاك وإنّما   شريعةُ موسى عُطّلتْ بمحمّدِ

I have found comfort for Moses in the love of Muḥammad,
This is right guidance from God; but without Him I would have strayed.
I did not change out of hatred, but simply
Because Moses's law has been replaced by Muḥammad's.[41]

Although there were no great female poets in Arab cultural circles in al-Andalus, literate Jewish women were not as rare as we tend to assume.[42] In the twelfth century, Qasmūna, a cultured Jewish woman steeped in Arabic literature (it has been suggested that she be identified as the daughter of Shmuel ha-Nagid)[43] composed Arabic poetry sufficiently lofty to be transmitted by some Arab sources. Examples of her poetry are the verses that she composed when she looked into a mirror one day and became aware that, though beautiful, she was not yet married:

أرى روضة قد حان منها قطافها   وليس يُرى جانٍ يمدّ لها يدا
فوا أسفي يمضي الشّباب مضيّعًا   ويبقى الّذي ما إن أسمّيه مفردا

I see a garden whose harvest time has come;
No harvester can be seen to extend a hand.
Alas! Youth passes and is wasted,
While one remains—I will not name him—who is alone.[44]

In the Andalusian Jewish communities, the process of Arabization led to fundamental changes in the attitude of at least some elements to the issue of language. The Jews spoke Arabic for generations, and it is logical to suppose that they "came to think in and view the world through the medium of that language." To speak a language, as Frantz Fanon (1925–1961) argues, "is to take on a world, a culture."[45] And just as language structures reality through

[41] Al-Kutubī 1951, I, p. 42 (English translation: Scheindlin 1992, pp. 188–200). Cf. Meddeb and Stora 2013, pp. 952–4. On Ibn Sahl and the issue of his conversion, see also the introduction by Iḥsān ʿAbbās (1920–2003) to Ibn Sahl's *Dīwān* (Ibn Sahl al-Andalusī 1967, esp. pp. 33–7). See also Schippers 2001, pp. 119–35. For other references, see Snir 2005a, pp. 495–6.

[42] On the role of Arab-Jewish female poets in Arabic literature as well as in Hebrew culture, see Bitton 1999, pp. 7–16; Rosen-Moked 2003.

[43] Bellamy 1983, pp. 423–4.

[44] See al-Suyūṭī n.d.1, p. 75; and al-Maqqarī 1968, V, p. 73. For an English translation and a discussion of these verses, see Nichols 1981, pp. 155–8. On Qasmūna, see also Wasserstein 1993, pp. 120–2; Bitton 1999, pp. 46–51; Rosen-Moked 2003, pp. 2–3; Elmeligi 2019, p. 141. For more references, see Snir 2005a, p. 380, n. 16.

[45] Fanon 1967, p. 38.

pre-existent cognitive ingredients and thereby informs the experience of its speakers, the literary culture of Jews in al-Andalus also represents, as R. Brann states, their instinctive, creative refraction of the language, forms, and substance of Arabo-Islamic learning in the forms of subcultural adaptation:

> The Jews' Arabization fully integrated them into the pluralistic Andalusi scene. Arabic language and culture not only surrounded the Jews in the speech and writings of their Muslim (and Christian) neighbors so as to influence them as cultural others; but also and more pertinently, Arabic was the linguistic medium central to the Andalusi-Jewish experience. Indeed, it was the agency responsible for their intellectual and social integration, which along with their full participation in the political economy of al-Andalus and their inspired attachment to the country they called Sefarad marked them as Andalusis.[46]

The factors that made possible the Jews' involvement in al-Andalus in Arab culture were also effective in modern times, even if to a much lesser degree in the twentieth century due to the national and political conflict in the Middle East. Wherever Jews lived in Arab lands, they adopted the culture of the surrounding society; being part of Arab-Muslim society and speaking its language, the popular aspects of that cultural involvement became natural to them. For example, *ḥumaynī* poetry—written in a mixture of classical Arabic and Yemeni dialects of Arabic and consisting of strophic love poems set to music—had been written by Muslim Arabs since the fourteenth century. However, in the seventeenth century *ḥumaynī* poetry acquired an intercultural dimension as Yemeni Jews began to reinterpret these poems and write their own, and the story of *ḥumaynī* poetry became a story of the interrelationship between Arab and Jewish cultures.[47] Also, a survey of the developments of Arab theater in the nineteenth century and the sources of popular culture that helped its emergence reveals Jewish participation as a vital link between the traditional live theater and the modern theater. One such link can be found in the first-known printed Arabic play, which is by the Algerian-Jewish dramatist Abraham Daninos (1797–1872), that is, *Nazāhat al-Mushtāq wa-Ghuṣṣat al-ʿUshshāq fī Madīnat Ṭiryāq fī al-ʿIrāq* (*The Pleasure Trip of the Enamored and the Agony of Lovers in the City of Ṭiryāq in Iraq*). The play, published in 1847, was written under Western influence but has many similarities with *Ḥikāyat Abī al-Qāsim al-Baghdadī* (*The Tale of Abū al-Qāsim al-Baghdadī*) by Abū al-Muṭahhar al-Azdī (composed about

[46] Brann 2000, pp. 441–2. On the connection of Hebrew literature with Arab culture in al-Andalus, see also Scheindlin 1986; Scheindlin 1991; Scheindlin 1992, pp. 188–200.

[47] See Wagner 2009, which chronicles the origins and development of this genre of Arabic literature, but at the same time also tracks the ways in which *ḥumaynī* poetry has influenced Jewish literature and has bound together Arabic and Jewish traditions of poetry and song.

1010),[48] which is one of the few extant textual versions of a medieval Arabic dramatic variation on the *maqāma*.[49] Another such link may be found in the theatrical activities of the Shiḥaybar brothers, Anṭwān and Ilyās, as well as those of the Cohen (Kūhīn) brothers, Zakī (1829–1904) and Salīm, at the Jewish School (al-Madrasa al-Isrā'īliyya) in Beirut in the late nineteenth century.[50]

The influence of Arab-Muslim culture can be seen in almost every kind of popular Judeo-Arabic literature. Due to a classicist bias that viewed the artistic work of the late Middle Ages and early modern times as essentially decadent,[51] this literature has not obtained the same amount of scholarly attention as has medieval Judeo-Arabic literature. However, it has gradually come to be appreciated for its own sake and judged on its own terms, and scholarly interest has recently been directed to various branches of the popular Judeo-Arabic literature, uncovering its richness and aesthetic merits in addition to its didactic qualities.[52] For example, attention has been turned toward the surge of creativity in the Judeo-Arabic poetry of North Africa from the sixteenth century, the religious poems of praise and prayers, as well as poems on exile and redemption including the Messianic, Sabbatean, liturgical, and paraliturgical poems. Another genre was the "Matruz"—embroidered poetry based on bilingual texts created by combining Hebrew and Judeo-Arabic in various structures in the same text, often in the same stanza, or even in the same verse. This poetry is found in printed books and in many hundreds of manuscripts scattered in public and private libraries throughout the world.[53] In Iraq, folktales of the Jews were put into writing in three languages: Hebrew, Aramaic, and Judeo-Arabic. Although the Judeo-Arabic folk literature of the Babylonian Jews is evidenced in the age of the Gaonim, most Judeo-Arabic folktales were only written down during the last two

48 See Selove 2017.

49 Moreh and Sadgrove 1996, pp. 45–67; the text of Daninos's play appears on pp. 1–42 of the Arabic part.

50 Moreh and Sadgrove 1996, pp. 68–117; the texts of the plays appear on pp. 43–305 of the Arabic part. See also Schulze 2001, pp. 25–6.

51 Cf. Snir 2017, pp. 190–1.

52 For example, see Schine 2018, pp. 392–418.

53 See Chetrit 1994 (for a review of the book by A. Schippers, see *Arabic and Middle Eastern Literatures* 3.1 [January 2000], pp. 112–16); Zafrani 1980. On the musical heritage of the Jewish communities in Algeria, see Seroussi and Karsenti 2002, pp. 31–50. The Algerian scholar Fawzī Sa'd Allāh complains that many of the Algerian musicians and singers were forgotten because they did not support Zionism (*al-Ḥayāt*, October 11, 2004, p. 19). On the Tunisian singer Ḥabība (Ḥbība) Msika (Messika) (1899/1903–1930), see Tobi and Tobi 1998, pp. 187–210; Tsur 2003, pp. 80–91. On the state of research in the field of Judeo-Arabic literature in North Africa and references to the studies of the main scholars in the field, see Tobi 1996, pp. 213–25.

hundred years; they are translations and adaptations from Jewish and non-Jewish literary sources and are also based on the oral traditions of the Jews of Iraq.[54] The interference between Arab-Muslim culture and Jewish popular culture was not one-sided and, for example, Jewish influence is to be found in the stories of *Alf Layla wa-Layla* (*A Thousand and One Nights*), forty of them being identified as being of Jewish origin.[55] Also, marriage ceremonies of Jews of Babylon were accompanied by songs and refrains, some of which were in Hebrew but most in the local Judeo-Arabic dialect. Three kinds of professional ensembles mainly played these wedding songs: the *Chalghi* at the *Ṣebaḥiyī* ceremony; the *Abū Shbaḥot* at the Seven Blessings ceremony; and the *Daqqāqāt* female ensembles at the *Ḥinna* ceremony.[56]

It should be noted that the involvement of Jewish women in popular Arab culture was not different from the involvement of non-Jewish women: sometimes it was even more intense. For example, Jewish female actors played dominant roles in the flowering of modern Egyptian theater in the early twentieth century, when the dramatic activities were still flavored with popular dimensions.[57] Conversely, Jewish involvement in canonical Arab culture barely included female authors. This should be mainly attributed to the minor general participation of Arab women in the canonical culture during the nineteenth century and the first half of the twentieth century.[58] There was, however, the Jewish Lebanese journalist Esther Lazari-Moyal (Istīr Azharī-Mūyāl) (1873–1948),[59] one of the first feminist activists in Arab journalism. She was active in feminist associations, such as Jam'iyyat Bākūrat Sūriyā (Association of the Renaissance of Syria) and Nahḍat al-Nisā' (Ladies' Awakening), both of which were among the first of such associations, and represented Lebanon at an international women's conference held in Chicago in 1893. A year later, she married the Egyptian-Jewish doctor, writer, and journalist Shimon Moyal (Shim'ūn Mūyāl) (1866–1915).[60] After a while, the couple moved to Cairo, where she established and edited the bi-monthly

54 See Avishur 1992. The northern Kurdish-inhabited part of Iraq did not go through the linguistic Arabization of the country after the Arab conquest; therefore, the folktales of the Kurdistani Jews are usually told in neo-Aramaic, but most of the folk songs are in Kurdish and only occasionally in Arabic in addition to Persian and Turkish (see Sabar 1982, pp. xxxii–xxxiii).

55 On the relationship of *Alf Layla wa-Layla* with the Jews, see al-Badrī 2000.

56 See Avishur 1990–1991. Cf. Chetrit et al. 2003; Rosenfeld-Hadad 2011, pp. 241–71.

57 See 'Alī 2001, pp. 155–6.

58 Snir 2000b, pp. 119–49.

59 On Esther Lazari-Moyal, see *Encyclopaedia Judaica*, XII (1971), pp. 493–4; Baron 1994, pp. 20–1, 52, 75, 105, 176; Moreh and Sadgrove 1996, p. 81.

60 On Shimon Moyal, see Gaon 1937, II, p. 381; Yehoshua 1974, pp. 122–5; Moreh and Sadgrove 1996, p. 80; Jacobson 2011, pp. 165–82.

al-ʿĀʾila (*The Family*); the first issue appeared on May 1, 1899. It survived for several years and dealt with issues regarding family and social problems in Egypt in general and with world news. In his study on the history of Arab press and journalism, Philip de Ṭarrāzī (1865–1956) describes her as one of the best female journalists of her time.[61] The role of women in canonical Arab culture noticeably increased toward the 1940s, but it came too late for Jewish feminist involvement, since the role of Jews in Arab culture would then be sharply on the decline.[62]

As Jewish involvement in the popular culture of Arab lands is self-evident, the next sections of this chapter will investigate Jewish involvement in canonical Arab culture, and be mostly limited to Egypt and Iraq and the printing of books and periodicals.[63] There was a real connection between the nature of the Jews' involvement in the canonical Arab culture and the development of Arabic Jewish press and journalism: wherever Jews tried to socially, politically, and especially culturally integrate into society, such as by their writing of Arabic *belles lettres* (e.g., in Iraq, Egypt, and to a lesser extent in Lebanon and Syria), there were active Jewish owners of Arabic newspapers and periodicals as well as editors and journalists writing in literary standard Arabic. But, wherever the Jews showed no interest in the outer cultural activities of the relevant society (e.g., North Africa), only periodicals in Judeo-Arabic dialects written in Hebrew characters are to be found (in addition, of course, to newspapers in other languages). Of these periodicals, more than a few appeared in both Hebrew and Judeo-Arabic, with the addition of the Hebrew part being predominantly an expression of Zionist tendencies. Among the total number of newspapers founded by Jews, those that appeared in literary standard Arabic were few compared with those in local Jewish dialects. It should also be noted that Hebrew newspapers and periodicals were intended to be circulated among Jewish communities throughout the Arab world, and through them Arab Jews became updated on Zionist developments as well as about the Jews in Palestine, Europe, and the United States.[64]

3. "A CARBON COPY OF *IBN AL-BALAD*"

In his studies on Arabic *belles lettres* of the nineteenth century and the first quarter of twentieth century, the Jesuit scholar Louis Cheikho (Shaykhū)

[61] See Ṭarrāzī 1933, IV, p. 287.
[62] On feminist Arab-Jewish activities, see Bashkin 2008, pp. 58, 60; Snir 2019–2020, pp. 133–61.
[63] See Moreh 1973a.
[64] On Arabic press by Jews, see Abramson 2005, pp. 697–704.

(1859–1927) subsumed Arab authors under two rubrics: Muslim authors (*al-Udabā' al-Muslimūn* or *Udabā' al-Muslimīn* or *Udabā' al-Islām*) and Christian authors (*Udabā' al-Naṣārā* or *al-Udabā' al-Naṣārā*).[65] No mention was made either of Jewish authors as a specific category or of individual Jewish authors. While Cheikho was known for his effort to prove the dominant role of Christians in the development of Arabic literature from its very beginnings in the pre-Islamic period,[66] the fact that he did not give Jewish activity in Arabic literature any mention is not a coincidence and cannot be only ascribed to his own "Christian" particularism.

As only very few of them identified with classical language and culture, Jews were virtually inactive in Arabic *belles lettres* in the nineteenth century and in the first two decades of the twentieth. They did not participate in the cultural revival (*Nahḍa*) of the Arabic language and culture in which Syrian Christians played so prominent a role. The only exception to this were the activities of the Egyptian Ya'qūb Ṣannū' (James Sanua) (1839–1912). In fact, he was the only Jewish author to play a significant role in Arab culture in the nineteenth century, especially in the fields of theater and journalism.[67] In retrospect, he has come to be considered the father of Egyptian theater and one of the founders of satirical and humorous journalism in the Arab world. Dubbed "Le Molière Egyptien," Ṣannū' was an integrated Jew totally committed to the cause of Egyptian nationalism, his activities devoid of any Jewish cultural content or religious identity. As was attributed to Jewish literary personalities risen to prominence in Arab culture and incorporated into the Arabo-Islamic canon,[68] it was argued that Ṣannū' had converted to Islam.[69] Ṣannū' made his young literary debut with Arabic poems, and went

65 Cheikho's studies were generally published in the magazine *al-Mashriq*, which he founded in Beirut in 1898. The studies were collected and published in three volumes by al-Maṭba'a al-Kāthūlikiyya li-l-Ābā' al-Yasū'iyyīn in Beirut and titled *al-Ādāb al-'Arabiyya fī al-Qarn al-Tāsi' 'Ashar: min al-Sana 1800 ilā 1870* (*Arabic Literature in the Nineteenth Century: From 1800 to 1870*) (Cheikho 1924); *al-Ādāb al-'Arabiyya fī al-Qarn al-Tāsi' 'Ashar: min al-Sana 1870 ilā 1900* (*Arabic Literature in the Nineteenth Century: From 1870 to 1900*) (Cheikho 1926); and *Ta'rīkh al-Ādāb al-'Arabiyya fī al-Rub' al-Awwal min al-Qarn al-'Ishrīn* (*Arabic Literature in the First Quarter of the Twentieth Century*) (Cheikho 1926a. See also Cheikho 1967).

66 He tried to prove that the Jewish pre-Islamic poet al-Samaw'al ibn 'Ādiyā' was in fact Christian (see the introduction of Ibn 'Ādiyā' 1909), pp. 4–5.

67 In at least one incident, religious reasons seemed to have played a role in Egypt excluding both Syrian Christians and Jews (among them Ṣannū' himself) from a new organization; see Philipp 1985, p. 103.

68 See Snir 2005a, pp. 497–507. Cf. the multifarious and often dialectical forces that made space for poets contemporary to Muḥammad and for their poetry in the Arabo-Islamic literary canon (Klasova 2019, pp. 40–111).

69 In modern times, only a few Arab Jews converted to Islam out of a genuine conviction of this religion's superiority. The Iraqi Aḥmad Sūsa (Ahmed Sousa), born as Nissīm Sūsa

on to compose thirty-two comedies and romantic plays, in addition to the plays he translated from French.[70]

Other Jewish figures involved in the Egyptian general culture were of limited importance to Arab society; some themselves considered their activities as more relevant to Jewish culture than to the Arab. There is, for example, the case of the Karaite journalist, writer, poet, and translator Murād Faraj (Morad Farag) (1866–1956). He was a prolific writer of scholarly works in Arabic on literary, theological, and biblical topics as well as on modern Egyptian and Karaite law, and on comparative philological topics; he edited *al-Tahdhīb* (*The Edification*) (1901–1905), the organ of the Karaite community and took part in editing another Karaite periodical, *al-Irshād* (*The Guidance*) (1908–1909). In 1912, for the general Egyptian reader he published *Maqālāt Murād* (*The Essays of Murād*; French title: *Essais sur la morale*) dealing with various social, cultural, and moral topics. He published his *Dīwān Murād* in four volumes (I, 1912; II, 1924; III, 1929; IV, 1935),[71]

(1900–1982), was one of the more famous of these. On Sūsa, see Baṣrī 1994, II, pp. 524–25. See also Sūsa's account about his way to Islam in Sūsa 1936, as well as the first volume of his autobiography that his daughter published after his death (Sūsa 1986). The figure of Aḥmad Harūn Sawsan, the protagonist-narrator in Shimon Ballas' Hebrew novel *Ve-Hu Akher* (*And He Is Other*; English title: *The Other One*) (Ballas 1991; a second edition of the novel was published by Ha-Kibbutz Ha-Me'uḥad in 2005), is based on the figure of Sūsa (for an English translation of the novel, titled *Outcast*, see Ballas 2007. A section of the novel [pp. 95–105 of the original] was published in English translation [by Alcalay and Shelach] in *Fascicle* 1 [Summer 2005]. For the last pages of the novel in English translation, see *The Literary Review* 37.2 [1994], pp. 188–94. A section of the novel [pp. 7–13 of the original] was published in Arabic translation [by Anṭwān Shalḥat (b. 1956)] in *Ariel* 4 [Summer 1995], pp. 63–8. On the novel, see Zeidel 2009, pp. 229–43). Among other Arab Jews who converted to Islam in modern times are Salīma Murād (1905–1974) and Laylā Murād (1918–1995). On the conversion of Jews to Islam in the Middle Ages and modern times, see Lewis 1984, pp. 92–102; and the special issue of *Pe'amim: Studies in Oriental Jewry* 42 (1990). Among the articles is one by N. Kazzaz on conversions among the Jews of Iraq in modern times (pp. 157–66). See also Stroumsa 1995, pp. 179–97; García-Arenal 1997, pp. 227–48. Two other famous Jewish converts to Islam in the twentieth century were not of Arab origin but underwent a process of Arabization with their conversion: Muḥammad Asad, Austrian-born Leopold Weiss (1900–1992), and Maryam Jameela (Jamīla) (1934–2012), American-born Margaret Marcus. On Asad, see Gerholm 1988, pp. 263–77; Parker 1992, pp. 28–9; Rahim 1995, pp. 45–6; Kramer 1999, pp. 225–47. On Jameela, see Esposito 1995, III, pp. 59–60.

70 On Ṣannūʿ (his name is transcribed sometimes in scholarly publications wrongly as Ṣanūʿ), see Ṭarrāzī 1913, II, pp. 254–7, 281–6, III, pp. 8–9; *The Encyclopaedia of Islam*, I (1960), pp. 141–2 (by J. M. Landau); Gendzier 1966; Moosa 1974, pp. 401–33; Sadgrove 1983, pp. 95–173, 225–63; al-Khozai 1984, pp. 123–68; Badawi 1985, pp. 132–45; Moreh 1987, pp. 111–29; Ayalon 1995, pp. 44–5, 48–9; Sadgrove 1996, pp. 89–124; Meisami and Starkey 1998, II, p. 688; Fahmy 2011, pp. 43–59, 63–6, 74–5; Mestyan 2016, pp. 97–118.

71 In the opening of his second volume, there appear three verses by Aḥmad Shawqī (1868–1932), in which he praises Faraj's poetry ("I found the poetry of Murād a meadow of new herbage, no hill resembles it in beauty and fragrance"). In one of the verses, he refers

as well as another volume, *al-Qudsiyyāt / Heqdeshiyyōt* (*The Holy Works*) (1923), which included poetry and prose on Jewish subjects.[72]

Faraj was considered to be the poet laureate of the Karaite community. Apparently, his Jewish faith prevented him from being innovative in poetry; instead, he tried his best to prove that the Arabic language and Arabic literature, in their very traditional forms, were not the sole monopoly of Muslims. To support his argument, he published *al-Shuʿarāʾ al-Yahūd al-ʿArab* (*The Arab Jewish Poets*; French title: *Les poètes Israèlites Arabes*) (1929) in which he dealt with medieval Arab-Jewish poets. Among his studies is also a comparative Arabic–Hebrew etymological dictionary, *Multaqā al-Lughatayn al-ʿArabiyya wa-l-ʿIbriyya* (English title: *The Unity of the Two Semitic Languages Hebrew and Arabic: An Etymological Comparative Dictionary*) (1930–1950) in which he translated part of the Pentateuch into Arabic. By using the common Semitic root of Hebrew and Arabic words he tried to prove the similarity between both languages in order to refute the claim that rejects their common roots.[73] He did not conceal his Jewish religious identity—in fact, his poems frequently used biblical personalities and events as well as Jewish and Zionist motifs.[74] In 1936, in appreciation of his activities in the field of Arabic studies, Faraj was elected a member of the Academy of Arabic Language in Cairo.[75] Another member of the Academy was Rabbi Chaim Nahum Effendi (Ḥayim Nāḥūm) (1872–1960), the chief *Ḥakhām*, who was one of its founding members in 1932; he was known not only for his knowledge of Hebrew and Aramaic but also for his erudition in Arabic.[76]

Although one can hardly point to other Jewish figures of major importance in literary Egyptian life in the twentieth century, other Jewish intellectuals participated in various literary and intellectual activities,[77] sometimes even after 1948, such as in the literary salon of ʿAbbās Maḥmūd al-ʿAqqād (1889–1964).[78] Among the members of al-Madrasa al-Ḥadītha (The New School), a literary circle playing an important role in the development of

to Murād's Jewish faith by way of alluding to an ancient Muslim tradition concerning *Banū Isrāʾīl* (Faraj 1924, II, opening page).

72 On *al-Qudsiyyāt / Heqdeshiyyōt*, see Ilan 2019, pp. 7–31.

73 For an earlier essay on the topic, see Faraj 1912, pp. 255–60.

74 Faraj also translated into Arabic the novel *Ahavat Tsiyon* (*The Love of Zion*) (1853) written by Avraham Mappu (1808–1867), one of the first *Haskala* intellectuals in Eastern Europe (al-Gamil 1979, I, p. 166). Following the escalation of the conflict in Palestine, the Zionist motifs in Faraj's writings disappeared. On other translations of Mappu's novel, see García Arévalo 2015, pp. 67–83; Kayyal 2016, pp. 29–35.

75 On Faraj, see Nemoy 1976, pp. 87–112; Nemoy 1979–1980, pp. 195–209; Somekh 1987, pp. 130–40; Stillman 1991, pp. 228–30; Zohar 2013, pp. 235–40, 338–45.

76 Somekh 1987, p. 133. See also Zohar 2013, pp. 337–46.

77 See, for example, ʿAwaḍ 1966, pp. 10–12.

78 Manṣūr 1983, pp. 303–36.

Egyptian fiction in the 1920s, one finds the physician Shālūm Dāwud ibn Mas'ūda, who was considered to be the "philosopher" of the circle.[79] Also involved in the general Egyptian culture was the writer and dramatist Maurice (Mūrīs) Shammās (Abū Farīd) (1920–2013), mainly in theatrical activities. After his immigration to Israel, he became involved in promoting Arab music, mainly in the Dār al-Idhā'a al-Isrā'īliyya (Israeli Broadcasting House), the Israeli Arabic broadcasting station. In 1979, he published a collection of ten short stories titled *al-Shaykh Shabtāy wa-Ḥikāyāt min Ḥārat al-Yahūd* (*Sheik Shabtay and Stories from the Jews' Neighborhood*), most of which were based on autobiographical experiences. Apparently, the Egyptian–Israeli peace treaty made him feel that he should recount his memories of Jews who had lived in Egypt as true Egyptians: "The Jew in the Jews' neighborhood," he writes in the introduction, "was a carbon copy of *ibn al-balad* [a native son] who was living in the popular neighborhoods of Cairo."[80] He dedicated the book to the then Israeli prime minister, Menahem Begin (1913–1992), and the then president of Egypt, Anwar al-Sādāt (1918–1981), in appreciation of their efforts for peace.[81] He also published a collection of poems titled *Sab' Sanābil Hazīla* (*Seven Lean Stalks*) (1989) and an autobiography, *'Azza Ḥafīdat Nafratītī* (*'Azza Nefertiti's Granddaughter*) (2003).[82]

Jews were numbered among the pioneers of Egyptian cinema and music, as was, for example, the producer, director, and scriptwriter Togo Mizraḥī (1901–1987), who was also the owner of Aflām Togo Mizraḥī (Togo Mizraḥī's Films). In his early career, he used the name Aḥmad al-Mashriqī (lit. "the Oriental"). From about 270 films made in Egypt between 1923 and 1946, he produced thirty; he wrote the scripts and directed most of his productions.[83] In the field of music, the composer of Karaite origin Da'ūd Ḥusnī (1870–1937)[84] is often mentioned as playing a major role in renovating Egyptian music in the twentieth century; he also set to music several songs for Umm Kulthūm (1903–1975), the most popular Arabic singer of the twentieth century. A Jewish banker from Alexandria Jāk Rūmānū (Romano)

[79] Fawzī 1968, pp. 34, 63. Cf. Somekh 1987, p. 134.

[80] Shammās 1979, p. 6. On the collection, see *October* 138 (June 17, 1979); Beinin 1998, pp. 231–3.

[81] Al-Sadat thanked him in a letter published in the Egyptian journal *October* 140 (July 1, 1979).

[82] On Shammās, see Snir 2019, pp. 107–10, 187–8, 258–60, 318.

[83] On Togo Mizraḥī, see *al-Ṭalī'a*, March 1973, p. 155; Somekh 1987, p. 132; 'Alī 1993, pp. 78–9; Darwish 1998, p. 16; 'Alī 2001, pp. 147–9; Qāsim 1997, pp. 238–44; Starr 2017, pp. 209–30; Starr 2020. On the role of Jews in the development of Egyptian cinema, see Sagi-Bizāwī 2003, pp. 83–98. See also Qāsim 2002, pp. 17–90.

[84] On Da'ūd Ḥusnī, see Somekh 1987, pp. 131–2; 'Alī 1993, pp. 79–82; Beinin 1998, pp. 81–2; Perlson 2000, pp. 52–3; 'Alī 2001, pp. 159–60.

was so appreciated for his brilliant singing that Ḥāfiẓ Ibrāhīm (1871–1932) (one of the most well-known Egyptian poets of the first half of the twentieth century) published in 1908 two poems praising his singing.[85] Among the professional female singers, called *'awālim*, one could find also Jewish singers—groups of Muslim, Christian, and Jewish *'awālim* commonly lived together and worked under an experienced female performer, or *usta*, who taught them the trade.[86] The greatest Egyptian-Jewish singer was Laylā Murād (1918–1995), who made movies and was dubbed the "Cinderella of the Egyptian screen." In 1946, a year after marrying Egyptian actor and director Anwar Wajdī (1904–1955), she publicly announced her conversion to Islam. In 1955, she retired from public life, but her death forty years later prompted a new interest in her as a cultural icon.[87]

An academic, Israel Wolfensohn (Abū Dhu'ayb, as he called himself in Arabic or Ben-Ze'ev in Hebrew) (1899–1980) reached prominence as a teacher of Semitic languages at Egyptian universities, and wrote an Arabic book on the history of Jews in Arab countries during the pre-Islamic era. After his immigration to Palestine, he promoted the study of Arabic in Jewish schools during the British Mandate period. In 1941, he was appointed Inspector of Arabic in the National Commission's Department of Education.[88]

On the whole, however, the participation of Jews in Egyptian-Arab culture was relatively minor and limited.[89] S. Somekh, the director of the Cairo school of the Alliance Israélite Universelle (AIU), lamented in 1912 the indifference of most Jews to Arab culture: "They have neglected the Arab culture and language, some because of their exotic origin, the majority out of contempt for all things native."[90] In the interwar period, Arabic increasingly lost ground and was relegated to the low rank of a language spoken by the poor inhabitants of the Jewish quarter in Cairo (*Ḥārat al-Yahūd*), the provincial towns, and the Karaites.[91] The Arabic edition of the weekly

85 Ibrāhīm n.d. [1937], I, pp. 221–2. Cf. Shalash 1986, pp. 86–7.

86 See Gitre 2019, p. 104.

87 On Laylā Murād, see 'Alī 1993, p. 76; al-Najmī 1993, pp. 235–9; Beinin 1998, pp. 83–5, 232–3; 'Alī 2001, pp. 160–1; Darwish 1998, p. 24; Sagi-Bizāwī 2003, pp. 90–2.

88 On Ben-Ze'ev, see 'Alī 2001, pp. 124–5; Hartwig 2009, p. 251; Abd El Gawad 2016, pp. 287–308; Mendel 2020, pp. 44, 47–56, 64–70.

89 On Jewish cultural and literary activities in Egypt, see also Somekh 1989, pp. 9–14. On Jewish press in Egypt, see 'Abd al-Raḥmān 1979; Naṣṣār 1980; Laskier 1992; Snir 2019, pp. 21–9.

90 Krämer 1989, p. 168.

91 Krämer 1989, p. 28. On the Karaites as an Arab-Jewish community, see Beinin 1996, pp. 5–9. See also al-Khatib 2020, who, based on the thesis that the Egyptian Jews were instrumentalized both by the ideology of political Zionism and by Egyptian nationalism, examines the relationship between the Karaite Egyptian community and the Sephardic Jews between 1915 and 1952. Cf. al-Khatib 2020a, pp. 39–51.

Israël, founded in 1920 by Albert Mūṣayrī (Mosseri) (1867–1933) and his wife Mazal-Mathilde Mūṣayrī (Mosseri) (born Mani) (1894–1981), had to be abandoned in 1933.[92] The weekly *al-Shams* (*The Sun*; French title: *al-Chams*), founded in 1934 by Sa'd Ya'qūb Mālikī (1898–1988), had only a limited number of readers. A book on the Jews of Egypt published in 1938 by Maurice Fargeon (1906–1996), an active member of the Ligue Contre L'Antisémitisme (LICA),[93] makes almost no mention of the participation of Jews in Arab culture.[94] Although in the late 1930s and in the 1940s certain Jewish circles devoted more attention to it, Arabic was never able to replace French or Italian as the language of the intellectual circles among the Egyptian Jews.[95] The tendency among the Jews to strengthen their attachment to the Egyptian nation and culture seemed to be a superficial reaction to the cry raised in Egyptian public life to replace foreigners with Egyptians in places of employment.[96] The childhood experience of the writer André Aciman (b. 1951), whose family lived in Egypt until the 1960s, might serve as a sort of epitome of this situation: as a Jewish child living in Alexandria, he found mastering Arabic to be a real struggle.[97] Sometimes one senses the predominantly English or French cultural tendency with various Egyptian-Jewish immigrant writers, such as Jacqueline Kahanoff (1917–1979), born in Cairo to a father of Iraqi descent and a mother from a Tunisian home, and Yitzhak Gormezano-Goren (b. 1941). In the writings of both authors, there is a sort of sense of superiority over native Arab culture,[98] although some saw them as striving to encourage a multicultural atmosphere, such as Kahanoff's Levantinism. The term "Levantine" is employed by her not as a derogatory epithet for the shallow emulation of Western mannerisms but as a fertile blend for the emergent Israeli society—the potential for what we would now call "multiculturalism," a disparate society that can be united by its diversity. Writing on Kahanoff's Levantinism, the Iraqi-Jewish journalist

92 On the Mosseri family, see *Encyclopaedia Judaica*, XII (1971), p. 441; Gaon 1937, II, pp. 388–9. On the journalistic activities of the family, see Laskier 1992, pp. 18–72.

93 On LICA, see Laskier 1992, pp. 57–68.

94 Fargeon 1938.

95 Krämer 1989, pp. 26–9, 168–72. It should be noted that most of the intellectuals among Egyptian Jews had somehow excluded themselves from Arab culture and language long before Arab and Islamic Egyptianness was defined in a way that excluded them. Cf. Zohar 2013, pp. 309–10.

96 Shamir 1987, p. 53. Cf. Krämer 1987, pp. 68, 71–4.

97 Aciman 1994, pp. 215–92. On the Jews of Alexandria and the cosmopolitan atmosphere in the city, see Youssef 2018, ch. 2. On Alexandrian cosmopolitanism, see Hanley 2017; Snir 2017, pp. 242, 267–8.

98 For example, Kahanoff 1978, p. 26; and Ohana 2005 (on Kahanoff, see Beinin 1998, pp. 50–1, 54–6). See also Gormezano-Goren 1979, pp. 9–14. Cf. Beinin 1996, pp. 13–17; Drori 2020, pp. 43–53.

Nissīm Rajwān (Rejwan) (1924–2017)[99] said that, whatever else it was made to mean, the appellation "Levantine" suited Kahanoff superbly—both in the geographical and cultural sense:

> How else can one describe a Jewish woman who was born in Cairo of an Iraqi father and a Tunisian mother, got her schooling in a French school in the Egyptian capital yet *managed to speak not a word of Arabic*, studies in Paris, lived and worked in the United states, wrote a novel in English, married a Cairo-born Jew of Russian extraction, and came to Israel in the mid-1950s to find herself defending the cause of the Levantine underdog?[100]

However, the view that the emerging "Levantine" Israeli culture, as illustrated in the exemplary conception of Kahanoff, would eventually become "a way to connect with the country's Arab environment without provoking radical antagonism"[101] seems unjustified against the backdrop of her sense of the inherent superiority of her culture over Arab culture.[102]

4. "WE ARE ARABS BEFORE WE ARE JEWS"

In modern times, Jews were nowhere as open to participation in the wider Arab culture or as at home in literary standard Arabic as in the first half of the twentieth century in Iraq. The Jewish community had lived in the Tigris–Euphrates Valley without interruption for two-and-a-half millennia, and traced their domicile in Iraq to the Babylonian Exile. The reasons and circumstances that paved the way for Iraqi Jews to be much more open than in other Arab countries to participation in the wider canonical culture of the local society are still not completely clear, but we know that since the early Islamic era Jews in the territories that would later be part of Iraq had been taking part in Arab cultural gatherings whose cultural atmosphere and

99 On Rejwan, see Ben-Yaacob 1980, p. 404; *The Literary Review* 37.2 (1994), pp. 170–9; Somekh 1995, pp. 108–13; Alcalay 1996, pp. 46–60. See also his autobiographical books (Rejwan 2004; Rejwan 2006; Rejwan 2006a).

100 Rejwan 2006a, pp. 68–9 (my emphasis).

101 Sasson Somekh, *Haaretz, Books*, February 22, 2006.

102 And see also Tal 2017, pp. 237–54, where he insightfully notes that such a reading of Kahanoff, "namely, a carrier of the message of Levantinism as a bridge between Orient and Occident—seems to tell us more about Kahanoff's readers than about Kahanoff herself" (p. 238). On Kahanoff's Levantinism and how, together with the artist Marcel Janco (1895–1984), she fostered the myth of natural occupancy of the new land by appropriating for themselves a sense of nativeness, just as each eliminated the indigenous Palestinian Arab presence through their own selective cultural assimilations, see Slyomovics 2013, pp. 27–47.

openness may be described to have been multicultural.[103] With the advent of modern times, the Iraqi-Jewish community seemed on the whole to be isolated from the main trend of canonical Arab culture. The start of the involvement of Jews in the outer Arab society in Iraq was the outcome of the process of secularization of Jews that started in the second half of the nineteenth century. Much earlier than their Muslim or even Christian compatriots, the Iraqi Jews were aware of the need to master European secular culture, especially its science, as the means to achieve modernization, while defining their religious faith as a matter of personal belief. When they started down the road to secularization, there were attempts to develop a secular Hebrew literature.[104] Under the aegis of secular education, Jews adhered less to a strict religious life to the point that in the twentieth century the intellectual elite was predominantly secular,[105] or, as Emile Marmorstein (1901–1983), headmaster of the Shammāsh School for boys in Baghdad in the 1930s, observed in 1953: "Baghdad between the two wars resembled the Jewish communities of Eastern Europe some 50 or 60 years ago but for the absence of zeal, both religious and irreligious."[106] At the same time, the tendency toward Western culture and the adoption of secular values made Jews more open to the modern Arabic culture that was developing during the same period.[107]

Paradoxically, the secularization process in the Iraqi-Jewish community, which was accelerated by the AIU's educational activities, at the end brought about an eruption of new involvement in Arab culture. But what happened in Iraq was a unique phenomenon among the Arab-Jewish communities. The AIU was active also among other Arab Jews from the mid-nineteenth century, but they were not as open as the Iraqi Jews to participation in the wider culture of their local society. Norman A. Stillman (b. 1945) argues that AIU education did not create secularizing tendencies *ex nihilo*: "The Tanzimat reforms, the protégé élite, and the emergence of a new Jewish middle class linked to European economic and political interests had all fostered secularity." He is also undoubtedly correct in arguing that "in contradistinction to European Jewry, Middle Eastern Jewish secularity did not generally entail a radical break with religion; nor did it lead to

103 It was during the time of the Abbasid caliph al-Manṣūr (754–775), who founded the city of Baghdad and propagated an open and multicultural policy toward religious minorities.

104 Most Hebrew literature written in Babylon focused on religious matters, in addition to liturgical poetry. On the emergence of modern Hebrew literature in Babylon from 1735 to 1950, see Hakak 2003.

105 Sami Michael mentioned jokes among Jews in Baghdad directed at the Chief Rabbi (Goldberg 1996, p. 28 [introduction]. Cf. Marmorstein 1988, p. 366; *al-Burhān*, October 24, 1929, pp. 2, 4; November 19, 1929, p. 3).

106 Preface in Drower 1989, VI, pp. 8–11. Cf. Goldberg 1996, pp. 28–9 (introduction).

107 Cf. Tobi 1996, pp. 215–16.

anti-religiosity or the founding of anti-traditionalist movements parallel to the German Jewish reform."[108] Zvi Yehuda argues that "Iraqi Jewry, in contrast to German Jewry in the early nineteenth century, continued to preserve its social and religious frameworks even after modernization. Evolution of an independent modern educational system helped the Jewish community in Iraq to undergo modernization without accompanying assimilation."[109] Nevertheless, the Iraqi-Jewish openness to the surrounding Arab culture, especially in the 1920s and 1930s, brought the intellectual secular elite of this community into a position that was not very dissimilar to the position of the European-Jewish intellectual elite. H. Z. Hirschberg's argument that education in AIU schools in Eastern Jewish communities created among Jews a "pseudo-European superiority," producing a type of person uprooted not only from the spiritual soil of his community but also from the surrounding local environment[110] can by no means be applied to the Baghdadi Jews. Also, entirely baseless, certainly as regards the Iraqi Jews, is the argument that "the Jews of the Orient have for the most part just begun to enjoy the ambiguous fortunes of modernization with their settlement in the twentieth-century State of Israel."[111]

It seems that the cultural barriers between Jews and the wider Arab society broke down in Baghdad in such an intensive manner, much more than in other Arab lands,[112] due to the close relationship between the Jews of Baghdad and European intellectuals, apart from their exposure to the AIU agents of modernity. Baghdadi Jews functioned as correspondents and representatives for European Hebrew newspapers. In 1884, Rabbi Shlomo Bekhor Ḥuṣīn (1843–1892) founded the first Jewish printing house, and in 1889 he submitted a request to the Ottoman authorities to establish in Baghdad a Jewish newspaper in Arabic and Hebrew, but his request was rejected.[113] Ḥuṣīn himself was a highly fertile writer and published around 150 essays in Hebrew periodicals, such as *Ha-Maggid*, *Ha-Zphira*, and *Ha-Levanon*.[114]

108 Stillman 1996, p. 65.
109 Yehuda 1996, p. 143.
110 Hirschberg 1969, I, p. 220.
111 Mendes-Flohr and Reinharz 1980, pp. 4–5. Cf. Stillman 1996, p. 72, n. 31.
112 The case of the Jews in North Africa is different; therefore, the model of modernization that should be applied to them cannot be that of the Jews of Iraq, mainly because of the close relationship with French culture; see Abitbol 1985, pp. 31–53. A special case of a North African intellectual inspired by the Eastern European *Haskala* was Mordechai Ha-Cohen (1856–1919) from Tripoli, Lybia. See his *Higgid mordechai* (*Mordechai Narrated*) (ed. H. Goldberg) (Ha-Cohen 1978), p. 7.
113 *Ha-Zphira*, 16.109, p. 446.
114 On Ḥuṣīn's journalistic activities, see Hakak 2005. See also Hakak 2003, pp. 211–26.

Also, wealthy Jews used to send their sons to be educated in European institutions, where they were inspired by the atmosphere of the European Enlightenment (*Aufklärung*; *Haskala*). This was especially the case with regard to the need felt by the Jews to learn the language of the country within which they lived and benefit from the advantages offered through participation in the cultural and social activities of the wider society. Such was the case with, for example, Sāsūn Ḥiskīl (Sassoon Eskell) (1860–1932), an Iraqi-Jewish statesman known as Sassoon Effendi. He was instrumental in the creation and the establishment of the Kingdom of Iraq post-Ottoman rule, and served as the first minister of finance in the kingdom and a permanent Member of Parliament until his death. He had been educated in London and then in the Diplomatic Academy of Vienna, as well as in Constantinople where he received higher education in economics and law. In an interview with a correspondent of the Hebrew newspaper *Ha-ʻOlam* (*The World*), published in Vilna, Lithuania, Sassoon Effendi, at the time one of the representatives of Baghdad in the Ottoman Parliament, expressed views inspired by ideas prevalent among European Jews: "Mr. Sassoon wants to be assimilated, and since he does not see any positive aspect which would unite the Jews, beside religion, he would agree to be assimilated even with the Arabs."[115] It is no coincidence that in the second half of the nineteenth century in Vienna, where Sassoon studied, many Jews spoke High German, adopted German names, and dressed and acted like other Austrians.[116]

But much more significant were the activities of Jewish-European travelers who visited Baghdad, bringing to the Jews the conception of enlightenment, inspiring and pushing them toward modern civilization. Although these travelers came from a European society where the categories of East/West and Arab/European mostly prevailed, the view that European Jews did not follow the Kantian conception of enlightenment, positioning "themselves as guides and supervisors and hence did not permit the Iraqi Jews to independently manage their affairs,"[117] cannot be applied to all of them. Immanuel Kant argues that:

> Enlightenment is mankind's exit from its self-incurred immaturity. Immaturity is the inability to make use of one's own understanding without the guidance of another. Self-incurred is this inability if its cause lies not in the lack of understanding but rather in the lack of the resolution and the courage to use it without

[115] *Ha-ʻOlam*, March 10, 1909. On Ḥiskīl, see Baṣrī 1983, I, pp. 28–37; Baṣrī 1993, II, pp. 29–30; Baṣrī 2006, p. 102; al-Rabīʻī 2016, p. 141; al-Rabīʻī 2017, I, pp. 100–2.

[116] Rozenblit 1992, p. 234.

[117] Bashkin 2004, pp. 100–1.

the guidance of another. *Sapere aude!* Have the courage to use your own understanding! is thus the motto of enlightenment.[118]

It is no coincidence that in Beirut, on February 15, 1859, the Christian intellectual Buṭrus al-Bustānī (1819–1883) delivered "A Speech about the Culture of the Arabs,"[119] in which he expressed the Kantian conception. Al-Bustānī referred to his fellow countrymen as the "generation of knowledge and light," and called upon them to wake up.

One the Jewish-European travelers to Baghdad was the Austrian-Jewish scholar Jacob Obermeyer (1845–1935), who lived in Baghdad from 1869 to 1880.[120] He wrote reports on the Iraqi-Jewish community that were published in Hebrew periodicals, such as *Ha-Maggid*, and read by hundreds of local Jews.[121] The importance of Obermeyer for our argument lies in his reformist conceptions through which he tried to modernize the religious framework of the local Jewish community and introduce some leniencies in Jewish law. The strong opposition he faced from the leaders of the Jewish community testified to the revolutionary nature of the conceptions the European immigrants tried to implant in the Baghdadi Jews. In his reformist eagerness, Obermeyer even challenged the Baghdadi religious leader Chacham Yoseif Chaim (1832–1909), who forcefully condemned Obermeyer's innovations. When Obermeyer attacked the positions of Chacham Yoseif Chaim in reports he sent to *Ha-Maggid*, the communal leaders united in putting him into *cherem* (exclusion from communal participation). The proclamation was read aloud in every synagogue in Baghdad. Although he retracted his criticism and begged for forgiveness, it seemed that Obermeyer, together with other Jewish immigrants, had already started a process that would enable the Iraqi Jews to be much more open to participation in the wider culture of their local society.[122]

When in the wake of the First World War the State of Iraq was created, the Jews were inspired by a cultural vision with the eloquent secularist dictum "*al-dīnu li-llāhi wa-l-waṭanu li-l-jamīʿ*" ("Religion is for God, the Fatherland

118 Kant 1996, pp. 58–64. The quotation is from p. 58. For the original text, see Hinske 1973, pp. 452–65.

119 Al-Bustānī 1859. On this speech and its importance, see Sheehi 2004, pp. 19–45. See also Abu-Lughod 1963, pp. 135–6.

120 On Obermeyer, see *Encyclopaedia Judaica*, XII (1971), pp. 1309–10.

121 See, for example, *Ha-Maggid* 20 (1876), no. 6, p. 48.

122 On Obermeyer's criticism and the reaction of the community's leaders, see Obermeyer 1907, pp. 43–6. Cf. Sassoon 1949, pp. 153–6; Ben-Yaacob 1979, pp. 196–202. On other European immigrants in Baghdad in the nineteenth century, see the historical novel *Der Uhrmacher* by Barbara Taufar (Taufar 2001). For a more detailed presentation of my arguments concerning the process of opening the minds of Iraqi Jews to the wider European Enlightenment, see Snir 2005a, pp. 468–74.

is for everyone")[123]—it was employed as part of the Arabization vision of secular Jewish intellectuals who sought to remind people of the close symbiotic contact that Jews had with the wider Arab-Muslim culture. They rallied as a matter of course behind the efforts to make Iraq a modern nation-state for all its citizens—Sunni and Shi'i Muslim Arabs, Kurds and Turcomans, Assyrian and Aramean Christians, Yazidis, and Jews alike.[124] The vision and hopes of European Zionists to establish a Jewish nation-state in Palestine, as promised in 1917 by the Balfour Declaration,[125] was for the Iraqi Jews at the time a far-off cloud, totally undesired.[126] Their real national vision, at least the vision of the intellectual secular elite, was Iraqi and Arab.[127] It was, as previously mentioned, a vision that for the Jews had its roots in the nineteenth century with the start of the processes of Westernization and secularization, a time when cultural barriers between them and the wider local society had begun to crumble. As a result of these processes, in the 1930s most of the Jewish population lived in Baghdad, filling most of the civil service jobs under the British and the early monarchy. The Civil Administration of Mesopotamia, in its annual review for the year 1920, stated that the Jews of the City of Baghdad were "a very important section of the community, outnumbering the Sunnis or Shias."[128] According to the Iraqi-Jewish scholar Elie Kedourie (1926–1992), Baghdad at the time "could be said to be as much a Jewish city as an Islamic one."[129] The aforementioned Iraqi-Jewish journalist Nissīm Rajwān (Rejwan) thought that just as it has often been said that New York is a Jewish city, so "one can safely say the same about Baghdad in the first half of the 20th century."[130]

[123] Shā'ul 1980, pp. 119, 223; Darwīsh 1981, p. 202.

[124] Retrospectively and after the establishment of the State of Israel, it would be more convenient for Jewish-Iraqi immigrants, especially from the economic and intellectual elite, to justify their involvement in Iraq before 1948 by citing the Talmudic principle *dina demalkhuta dina* ("the law of the land is the law") (Babylonian Talmud, *Nedarim* 28a). Cf. Kazzaz 1991, pp. 70–1.

[125] The letter sent on November 2, 1917 by British Foreign Minister Arthur James Balfour to Lord Rothschild in which "his Majesty's Government view with favor the establishment in Palestine of a national home for the Jewish people."

[126] Elie Kedourie argued that even in the 1940s "the Zionist cause did not seem to me as a matter of any political wisdom. The expectancies which Zionism was creating were too high and unrealistic" (*Davar ha-shavu'*, April 7, 1988, p. 9).

[127] Therefore, studies about the pre-1948 relationships between Arabs and Jews (e.g., Khazzoom 2003, p. 498) seem to use an anachronistic dichotomy that never existed in the Arab lands. On the same issue, David Semah says: "The Jews of Iraq never referred to non-Jewish Iraqis as 'Arabs,' but used the words 'Muslim' and 'Christian' ... When they spoke about "Arabs" (*al-'Arab*) they had in mind only Bedouins" (Semah 1993, p. 5).

[128] Rejwan 1985, p. 210.

[129] Kedourie 1989, p. 21.

[130] *Midstream*, February–March 2001, p. 14.

In the 1930s, the Jewish community supported religious schools with elementary studies in Arabic, schools of the AIU (by 1930, 7,200 pupils were attending the ten AIU schools),[131] Jewish schools that followed the government syllabus, and the Shammāsh School, founded in 1928 to teach the English curriculum. Several Jewish secondary schools that gave religious instruction were also founded in order to prevent the flow of Jews to the government schools, where they received a completely secular Arab education. Communal solidarity weakened as, having acquired aspirations for full social, intellectual, and political participation in the local society, Jews preferred the government schools. Many did so even if there was a Jewish school in their area. As long as the government needed them to fill government posts, Jews attended and completed secondary school education in numbers far exceeding their proportion in the local population.[132]

The governmental schools placed emphasis on Arabic in preparation for the administered examinations required for entrance to high schools. The "communal dialects"—speech variations of Arabic according to the religious community that characterized the Muslims, Christians, and Jews in Baghdad[133]—were not at all an impediment to cultural interaction. Due to the high educational standard of Jewish schools in general, 90 percent of the Iraqi candidates for the London Matriculation Examination were Jews.[134] As a result of the growing Iraqi national and patriotic awareness among the Jews and the organized governmental educational efforts to create a specifically Iraqi-Arab national community for all religious and ethnic groups,[135] Jewish educational institutions put heavy emphasis on teaching Arabic, which, according to the writer Isḥāq (Isaac) Bār-Moshe

131 The Alliance Israélite Universelle educational system was established in the 1860s among Jewish communities in Islamic countries as a Westernizing and secularizing enterprise. On the role the Alliance played in the field of Jewish education in the Middle East, see Cohen 1973, pp. 105–56. On the AIU educational system in Iraq, see Yehuda 1996, pp. 134–43.

132 On the educational institutions of the Jews in Iraq, see al-Barāk 1985; Mudhi 1988, pp. 35–44; Meir 1989, pp. 21–271.

133 See Blanc 1963; Jabbari 2013, pp. 139–50; Bār-Moshe 2019; al-Bazzaz and Ali 2020, pp. 68–85.

134 Landshut 1950, p. 44. Mahdī al-Sammāk indicates that, in the academic year 1944–1945, out of seventy students accepted to the Royal School of Medicine in Baghdad, ten were Jews. He hints that Jewish students were sometimes preferred in academic institutions not only because of their educational level, but because of the financial abilities of their families, who used to bribe the officials (al-Sammāk 2001, I, pp. 61–2).

135 On the Iraqi patriotic process, see Simon 1997, pp. 87–104.

(1927–2003),[136] became a "decisive fact of life."[137] The physician and writer Salmān Darwīsh (1910–1982) spoke for an entire generation of Jewish intellectuals when he wrote in his memoirs that the Arabic language and Arabic literature "have penetrated our very bloodstream."[138] More than once, the fluent Arabic style of Jews was deemed superior to the average among their Muslim and Christian counterparts. The Syrian writer and educator ʿAlī al-Ṭanṭāwī (1909–1999), who taught in Baghdad in the 1930s, relates how after the excellence of Jews in Arabic studies had provoked at least one school administration to "guarantee the good of the homeland, and behave toward the Jews as they deserve," it was decided to integrate instruction in literature with instruction in the Muslim religion. Still, this did not prevent the Jews' excelling in the new curriculum.[139] Out of a desire to integrate into the surrounding society as "Arabs of Jewish origin,"[140] Jewish educational institutions in Iraq emphasized instruction in the Arabic language and its heritage. The reputation of their gifted teachers spread; one student of the poet Murād Mīkhāʾīl (1906–1986) described his lessons in the Jewish Shammāsh School as "a ray of sunshine on a rainy day."[141]

Prominent Muslim and Christian intellectuals taught Arabic language and literature in Jewish educational institutions,[142] and non-Jewish students enrolled as well. Some were to later hold important positions in the Iraqi government, such as, for example, the Muslim Tawfīq al-Suwaydī (1892–1968),

[136] On Bār-Moshe, see Moreh 1975, pp. 43–58; Moreh 1981, pp. 233–6; Mudhi 1988, pp. 365–403; *Ha-Kivun Mizraḥ* 7 (2003), pp. 15–21 (interview); Snir 2005, pp. 7–29; Elimelekh 2014, pp. 426–41. See also Idrīs 2003, which is a study of various linguistic, stylistic, and thematic aspects in the writings of Bār-Moshe and of three other Iraqi writers—Samīr Naqqāsh, Sami Michael, and Shimon Ballas.

[137] Bār-Moshe 1983, p. 231.

[138] Darwīsh 1981, p. 200.

[139] *Al-Sharq al-Awsaṭ*, May 24, 1984. About a similar phenomenon in Egypt, see Somekh 1989, p. 14. In the 1940s, prominent Arab intellectuals were teaching Arabic language and literature in Jewish schools in Iraq (Cf. Semah 1989, p. 86). See also a similar case in Syria in which a Muslim journalist was stunned that Jewish students excelled in Arabic exams: "What a humiliation it must be for these Arab students. What a source of heartache it must be for you, dear readers" (Stillman 1991, p. 280).

[140] According to Sami Michael (*Ba-Maḥane*, March 22, 1989, p. 23. Cf. Semah 1989, pp. 88–9).

[141] According to Salim Shaʿshūʿa (*al-Sharq*, April–June 1986, p. 31). Cf. *Ṣadā al-Tarbiya*, February 1986, pp. 29–30. On the study of Arabic in Baghdad Law School, see Moreh and Hakak 1981, p. 86.

[142] Semah 1989, p. 86. Among the teachers in the Shammās School in Baghdad in the late 1940s were the Lebanese writers Muḥammad Sharāra (1906–1979) and Ḥusayn Muruwwa (1908–1987); see Sasson Somekh's memoirs in *al-Jadīd*, November–December 1985, pp. 5–10; Somekh 2007, pp. 156–61; Khabbaza 2010, pp. 102–5; Di-Capua 2013, pp. 21–52.

who became prime minister,[143] or the Christian Assyrian Yūsuf Rizq Allāh Ghunayma (1885–1950), who became minister of finance. Both al-Suwaydī and Ghunayma during the first decade of the twentieth century were educated at an AIU school. Grateful for the good education he had received, Ghunayma later wrote: "It is necessary to set the record straight and thank the principals and all the teachers [of the school] for their dedication; also I remember the love my fellow students showed me."[144]

Among the newly emerging Iraqi intelligentsia of the interwar years were young secular Jews who saw themselves as Arab citizens loyal to the country of their birth. The reality in which they lived and worked was one of close symbiotic contact with the wider Arab-Muslim culture. For most of them, their Arab identity was uppermost; they were "Arab Jews" or "Arabs of the Jewish faith." One cannot ignore the close resemblance between this Jewish intellectual elite with those Viennese Jews of the second half of the nineteenth century who "obtained a secular education and identified with German culture, while simultaneously largely abandoning much of Jewish ritual observance. They prided themselves on being loyal Austrian citizens."[145] Nissīm Rajwān strongly rejects such an analogy:

> Since the idea of ethnic-racial nationalism had no foundation in Arab history or Muslim thought in the first place, there was no need for people to go to any lengths in order to be "accepted" or admitted into the wider society ... the Jews of Baghdad would have been complete idiots even to contemplate seeking such admittance—let alone actually consider it essential. But they were not idiots and they did not try.[146]

But precisely what Rajwān refers to as something of the past—"the idea of ethnic-racial nationalism *had* no foundation in Arab history or Muslim thought"—made that analogy not groundless with regard to the 1920s and 1930s.[147] Therefore, it comes as no surprise to find writings by Baghdadi

143 Cf. the interview with Mīr Baṣrī in *al-Mu'tamar*, no. 328 (November 29–December 5, 2002), p. 6.

144 Ghunayma 1924, p. 178; Ghanimah 1998, p. 140.

145 On the loyalty of Viennese Jews to German culture, see Wistrich 1987, pp. 43–70. Cf. Rozenblit 1992, p. 234. For a comparative approach that tries to face the challenge of the "combined historiography" of the modern Iraqi Jews and modern European Jews, see Miron 2006, pp. 73–98.

146 Rejwan 1985, pp. 53–4.

147 In a review of Dawidowicz 1977, Rejwan—"as a Jew born and brought up as a member of the Jewish community of Baghdad"—referred to the "sons of the Enlightenment" as "the only Jews thus plagued by a preoccupation with their Jewishness"; they "sought virtually to transform Judaism when they themselves failed to be received as equals by the Gentile world" (*Jerusalem Post*, 1980; quoted from Rejwan 2006, pp. 177–9. In a personal electronic communication, Rejwan referred to Elon 2002, which gives "a picture of the rise

Jews, encouraged by their Muslim compatriots, brimming with Iraqi-Arab patriotism and full of confidence toward a common political, national, and cultural future. Sāṭiʿ al-Ḥuṣrī (1880–1968), Director General of Education in Iraq (1923–1927) and Arab nationalism's first true ideologue, argued that "every person who is related to the Arab lands and speaks Arabic is an Arab."[148] Al-Ḥuṣrī sought the "assimilation of diverse elements of the population into a homogeneous whole tied by the bonds of specific language, history, and culture to a comprehensive but still exclusive ideology of Arabism."[149] Palestinian historian Abbas Shiblak (b. 1944) says of that period that

> the Jewish writers and artists of Iraq were in fact part of the general cultural life of the Arab East, maintaining connections and sometimes working relationships with writers and artists in other Arab countries. It is significant that in Iraq (unlike Lebanon, Egypt, or Tunisia for instance) there were few if any Hebrew or Zionist newspapers. The works of the Iraqi-Jewish intelligentsia were Arabic in essence and expression.[150]

It was a "symbiotic contact with the Arab population" in the deep belief that there was no contradiction between the Jews' adherence to their religion and being citizens, with equal rights and responsibilities, in the Iraqi homeland.[151] It is no wonder at all, therefore, that we find even Islamic motifs in the work of Iraqi Jews, and occasionally attempts to blur their Jewish

and decline of German Jewry that is reminding, to me at least, of our Jewry, its rise, and its fall (though, of course, one should take account of the huge contribution of our Zionist friends)." See also Edwin Black's argument that the Iraqi Jews in many ways "resembled the middle-class and affluent, entrenched Jews of Germany who felt more German than Jewish" (www.thejewishweek.com/news, October 21, 2004, available at: http://www.jewishvirtuallibrary.org/the-sudden-end-of-iraqi-jewry, last accessed February 22, 2018).

148 See al-Ḥuṣrī 1965 [1955], p. 12. On al-Ḥuṣrī's definition of the nation, his political theory and the secular concept of Arabic unity, see also Tibi 1990 [1981], pp. 116–98; and Kudryashova 2010, pp. 52–3. Cf. the way George Antonius (1891–1942), one of the first historians of Arab nationalism, defined who is an "Arab": "It gradually came to mean a citizen of that extensive Arab world—not any inhabitant of it, but that great majority whose racial descent, even when it was not of pure Arab lineage, had become submerged in the tide of arabisation; whose manners and traditions had been shaped in an Arab mould; and, *most decisive of all, whose mother tongue is Arabic*" (Antonius 1938, p. 18 [my emphasis]). See also Chejne 1969, pp. 19–22; Cleveland 1971, p. 127; Esposito 1995, I, 113–16; Murre-van den Berg 2016, pp. 176–90; Murre-van den Berg 2016a, pp. 3–38. On the role of al-Ḥuṣrī in using Iraqi schools to inculcate nationalism, see Simon 1986, pp. 75–114. On Arabic language and identity, see the studies in Bassiouney and Walters 2021 and the insights in Walters 2021, pp. 3–10.

149 Cleveland 1971, p. 63.

150 Shiblak 1986, p. 28 (= Shiblak 2005, p. 46; it is a new edition of the original book with minor changes; new preface by Peter Sluglett, pp. 13–26).

151 Eisenstadt 1988, p. 4. Cf. Bezalel 1982, p. 41. The slogan of the majority of Jewish intellectuals in that period was: "Religion to God and the homeland to all" (Shāʾul 1980, pp. 119, 223; Darwīsh 1981, p. 202).

identity.[152] This should not be seen at all as a desire to abandon Judaism, but as a consequence of that same "symbiotic contact" between the Jews and the non-Jews—as an organic and vital part of Iraqi society, the Jews were numbered among the front ranks of the intelligentsia. Thus, Shmuel Moreh (1932–2017) correctly concludes that the Jewish poets and writers in Iraq were the "most active and productive of Jewish writers in all the Arab lands, the most patriotic and the most concerned among them for the future of their country and its development."[153] Even the riots and pogroms against the Jews did not awaken an immediate, sharp, literary response that might have damaged efforts toward integration into Iraqi society.[154]

From the early 1920s, the Jews had every reason to believe that the surrounding local society would not oppose their full integration. For example, presenting al-Samaw'al's aforementioned poem about the noble qualities of his Jewish tribe as the *Iliad* of the Arabs, the newspaper *Dijla* quoted the opening verse as a proof of the true Arabness of Jews in Iraq.[155] On July 18, 1921, one month before his coronation as King of Iraq, Amir Fayṣal (1883–1933), when addressing Jewish community leaders, said:

> لا شيء في عرف الوطنيّة اسمه مسلم ومسيحيّ وإسرائيليّ، بل هناك شيء يقال له العراق [...] إنّني أطالب من أبناء وطني العراقيّين أن لا يكونوا إلّا عراقيّين لأنّنا نرجع إلى أرومة واحدة ودوحة واحدة هي دوحة جدّنا سام وكلّنا منسوبون إلى العنصر الساميّ ولا فرق في ذلك بين المسلم والمسيحيّ واليهوديّ [...] وليس لنا اليوم إلّا واسطة القوميّة القويّة التّأثير.

> In the vocabulary of patriotism, there is no such thing as a Jew, a Muslim, or a Christian. There is simply one thing called Iraq ... I ask all the Iraqi children of my homeland to be just Iraqis, because we all belong to one origin and one tree, the tree of our ancestor Shem, and all of us related to the Semitic root, which makes no distinction between Muslim, Christian or Jew ... Today we have but one means [to our end]: influential patriotism.[156]

152 Cf. Snir 1988, p. 112; Somekh 1989, p. 16; Semah 1989, pp. 84, 88; Marmorstein 1959, p. 198. See also the collections of stories by Shalom Darwīsh, *Aḥrār wa-ʿAbīd* (*Freemen and Slaves*) (Darwīsh 1941); *Baʿḍ al-Nās* (*Some of the People*) (Darwīsh 1948). Cf. Moreh 1981, p. 116.

153 Moreh 1981, p. 98; Semah 1989, p. 120.

154 See Michael 1979, p. 77. Semah's letter is in *Maariv*, January 26, 1989. Even after years, attention is being given by some of the Jewish writers mainly to those Muslims who hastened to the aid of the Jews (see Shāʾul 1980, pp. 247–8. Cf. Somekh 1989, p. 18).

155 *Dijla*, issue no. 8, July 3, 1921; cited from Baṣrī 1993, II, p. 9.

156 The original text was first published in *al-ʿIrāq*, July 19, 1921. For the text of the speech, see *Fayṣal ibn al-Ḥusayn fī Khuṭabihi wa-Aqwālihi* (*Fayṣal ibn al-Ḥusayn in His Speeches and Sayings*), Baghdād: Maṭbaʿat al-Ḥukūma, 1945, pp. 246–9. Cf. Baṣrī 1993, II, p. 9. For a slightly different version, see Ireland 1970 [1937], p. 466. See also Bell 1930, p. 495; Mudhi 1988, p. 21; Stillman 1991, pp. 55–6, 260. For a contemporary vivid description of the ceremony, see Ghunayma 1924, p. 187; Ghanimah 1998, p. 148. In an address Fayṣal had delivered before the Arab Club in Aleppo on June 9, 1919, he had already emphasized

In a poem addressing the British High Commissioner for Palestine, Sir Herbert Samuel (1870–1963), the Iraqi poet Maʿrūf al-Ruṣāfī (1875–1945) wrote: "The two people are but close relatives; in their language is the proof."[157] The poem was composed after al-Ruṣāfī had attended a lecture in Jerusalem on December 13, 1920, on the medieval Andalusian Arab civilization delivered by the Jewish scholar Professor Avraham Shalom Yehuda (1887–1951). The lecture, at the invitation of the Mayor of Jerusalem, Rāghib al-Nashāshībī (1881–1951), was given in literary standard Arabic.[158]

Testifying before the League of Nations' Mandate Commission, the High Commissioner for Iraq declared that he "had never found such tolerance of others races and religions as in Iraq."[159] No wonder that in the late 1930s the Jewish educator Ezra Ḥaddād (1900–1972)[160] declared that "we are Arabs before we are Jews" ("*naḥnu ʿArab qabla an nakūna yahūda*").[161] Yaʿqūb Balbūl (1920–2003)[162] wrote that "a Jewish youth in the Arab countries expects from Zionism nothing other than colonialism and domination."[163]

that "there are no religions or sects, for we were Arab before Moses, Mohammed, Jesus, and Abraham. We Arabs are bound together in life, separated only by death. There is no division among us except when we are buried" (al-Ḥuṣrī 1965, p. 231 [English translation according to al-Ḥuṣrī 1966, p. 113]). In January 1919, Fayṣal signed with Chaim Weizmann (1874–1952), who acted on behalf of the Zionist Organization, the Fayṣal–Weizmann Agreement (for the text of the agreement, see Antonius 1938, pp. 437–9). Although attempts have been made to marginalize Fayṣal's readiness at the time to accept the Zionist programs, even considering the agreement as a failed attempt "to secure by fair or unfair means an Arab endorsement of the Balfour Declaration" (e.g., Tibawi 1974, pp. 315–23), no one, to my knowledge, has gone so far as to doubt Fayṣal's goodwill and sincere intentions.

157 See al-Ruṣāfī 1986, II, pp. 327–31.

158 Al-Ruṣāfī spent several years in Jerusalem (1918–1921) after he had accepted a job at the local Teachers' Training College. On the poem, which later evoked strong protests from Arab nationalists, and the circumstances in which it was written, see Ben Hanania 1959, pp. 186–91; al-Sawāfīrī 1963, pp. 277–9; Yehoshua 1979, pp. 67–77; Yāghī 1981, pp. 181–5; *The Encyclopaedia of Islam*, VI (1991), p. 615 (by S. Moreh). For one of the poems written in response to al-Ruṣāfī's poem titled "In Response to al-Ruṣāfī" by Wadīʿ al-Bustānī (1888–1954), see al-Bustānī 1946, pp. 104–10. Cf. Jubrān 2002–2003, pp. 59–61.

159 Luks 1977, p. 32.

160 On Ḥaddād, see Ben-Yaacob 1980, pp. 379–81; Shohet 1982, p. 123; Baṣrī 1983, I, pp. 78–9; Moreh and ʿAbbāsī 1987, pp. 54–5; Baṣrī 2006, pp. 144–6.

161 Rejwan 1985, p. 219; Rejwan 2004, p. 107.

162 On Balbūl, see Moreh 1981, pp. 97–103; Mudhi 1988, pp. 145–53. Balbūl, with his short story titled "Ṣūra Ṭibqa al-Aṣl" ("True Copy") (Balbūl 1938, pp. 97–103), published the first Iraqi-Jewish short story to use the colloquial language of the local Muslim community. On the story, see Snir 2019, pp. 55–63, 182–3, 212–15; Snir 2020, pp. 109–45.

163 *Al-Akhbār*, July 21, 1938; cited in Maʿrūf 1976, II, p. 70; Rejwan 1985, p. 219. It was argued that notices published by well-known Jews in the Iraqi press during the 1930s declaring that they were loyal to their motherland and that they had no connections with Zionist activities were initiated by the authorities against the background of the anti-Jewish atmosphere created following the disturbances in Palestine (Kedourie 1989, pp. 28–9). The same, of

Albert Hourani (1915–1993) argued in 1947 that "the Iraqi Jews, like the Oriental Jews, are for the most part not Zionists by conviction; some of them indeed profess to Arab nationalism and are hostile to Zionism."[164] In his survey of Jewish communities in the Muslim countries of the Middle East, published in 1950, the German Marxian scholar and sociologist Siegfried Landshut (1897–1968) wrote that, except for a natural interest in developments in Palestine, there has never in Iraq been any feeling of solidarity with the political aspirations of Zionism.[165] The Arabness of the Iraqi Jews, at least of the young secular intellectuals among them, was not in any doubt. Nissīm Rajwān was thus not alone when he spoke about his own literary and intellectual interests:

> It was from quite an early age that I started reading Arabic books and magazines, starting with the numerous historical novels of Jorji Zaydan [1861–1914] and the many translations-adaptations of French and English romances and novels produced by the Egyptian Lutfi al-Manfaluti [1876–1924] and several Syrian and Lebanese literary hacks whose names I don't recall. I was not only an avid reader but also something of a bibliophile. I liked possessing and keeping the books I read, or not read through and by age fourteen or fifteen I had built myself a sizable home library—collected works of the best and most famous Egyptian writers, among them Taha Hussein [1889–1973], Ahmad Amin [1886–1954], Muhammad Hussein Haykal [1888–1956], Ibrahim Abdel Qadir al-Mazini [1890–1949], Tawfiq al-Hakeem [1898–1987], 'Abbas Mahmoud al-'Aqqad [1889–1964] and others. I also collected works by classical Arab writers, such as *Kitab al-Aghani*, *Rasa'il Ikhwan al-Safa*, Ibn al-Atheer's [1160–1233] *History*, *The Muqaddima* (Introduction) of Ibn Khaldun [1332–1406], and the collected poems of such classics as Al-Mutanabbi [915–965], Al-Ma'arri [973–1058], Ibn al-Rumi [836–896] and others. Also prominent on my shelves were bound volumes of carefully collected and kept weeklies like *Al-Risala* of Muhammad Hasan al-Zayyat [1885–1968], Ahmad Amin's *Al-Thaqafa*, and *Al-Riwaya*, and the two leading monthlies, *Al-Hilal* and *Al-Muqtataf*.[166]

Jewish writing in literary standard Arabic (*fuṣḥā*) during the twentieth century began in Iraq, predominantly in the field of journalism, and it developed as a result of the liberalization process that took place in the Ottoman Empire after the Revolution of July 1908 (also known as the Young Turk Revolution) and as a result of secularization and the arrival of modern education in the local community. A year later, in 1909, the first issues of two

course, might be said about the testimonies included in *Iraqi Jews Speak for Themselves* (Baghdad: Dar al-Jumhuriyah Press, 1969).

164 Hourani 1947, p. 104.

165 Landshut 1950, p. 45.

166 Rejwan 2004, pp. 97–8.

newspapers that were edited by Jews, *al-Zuhūr* (*The Flowers*) and *Bayna al-Nahrayn* (*Mesopotamia*), were published. It was argued that the first Iraqi-Jewish author to publish a book in *fuṣḥā* was Salīm Isḥāq (1877–1949), a lawyer who served as a translator in the German embassy in Baghdad before the First World War. The title of the book, which was published in Baghdad in 1909, was said to have been either *al-Inqilāb al-'Uthmānī*[167] or *al-Thawra al-'Uthmāniyya*[168] (both translate to *The Ottoman Revolution*). While both titles refer to the subject of the book, the debate itself suggests that there is still some doubt as to the proper wording of the title. I have not found the book in any library or in any other publications. The Iraqi-Jewish author Mīr Baṣrī (1911–2006), however, mentioned a book published by Isḥāq in 1910 titled *Ḥawādith al-Zamān* (*Time Events*). Baṣrī, who, according to the details he provides about its content, actually read the book said that it was written in Hebrew characters in the Jewish Arabic vernacular infused with *fuṣḥā*. The book concentrates on the reforms of the "Young Turks," especially their 1908 constitution.[169] Isḥāq's subject matter could hardly have been more emblematic: the "Young Turks" seemed to herald a new dawn, especially as their 1908 constitution promised full emancipation for ethnic and religious minorities.

Iraqi-Jewish writers and poets from the 1920s produced in literary standard Arabic works secular in essence that quickly became part of mainstream Arabic literature and gained the recognition of Arab writers and scholars. As did other Arab authors at the time, they wrote in standard Arabic even when it came to dialogue in fiction, although the strong impact of popular literature in the vernacular, be it Jewish or non-Jewish, was undeniable.[170] Drawing on Arab literary modernism and various Western literary trends that they had become familiar with, Jewish authors extensively wrote poetry, but it was as short-story writers that they were to make their most significant

[167] Moreh 1973, p. 46.

[168] Moreh 1981, p. 24.

[169] Baṣrī 1993, II, pp. 72–5. On Salīm Isḥāq, see also Baṣrī 1983, I, pp. 59–60. Isḥāq, who translated the *Rubā'iyyāt* (*Quatrains*) of the Persian poet 'Umar al-Khayyām (Omar Khayyam) (1048–1131) into Hebrew, was praised by Aḥmad Ḥāmid Ṣarrāf (1900–1985), who translated the *Rubā'iyyāt* into Arabic as follows: "I do not know anyone in Iraq more knowledgeable than he is in European and Oriental languages, philosophy, history, law, and Sufism" (Ṣarrāf 1960, p. 320).

[170] Iraqi Jews had their own Iraqi vernacular, which they used in their own houses and in their daily contacts with each other, while at the same time managing to speak with their Muslim neighbors in the latter's own colloquial Arabic (see Blanc 1963; Jabbari 2013, pp. 139–50; Bār-Moshe 2019; al-Bazzaz and Ali 2020, pp. 68–85). On Jewish-Iraqi literature in the vernacular, see Avishur 1995, p. 242.

contribution to Iraqi literature.[171] That they were attracted to that genre may well have been because of their desire to participate in the makings of changes to the society in which they lived. At the turn of the century, Arabic prose in general was already undergoing a process of gradual development toward becoming a powerful medium for the depiction of everyday life and the vicissitudes of ordinary people. Jewish authors were well aware of the Western techniques of the genre that had found their way into the experiments then being made throughout the Arab world, especially in Egypt and Iraq.[172] Their inspiration mainly came from English and French short stories available in Arabic translation. Jews themselves were among the major translators of Western literature into Arabic—prominent translators included Anwar Shā'ul (1904–1984),[173] Yūsuf Makmal (1914–1986),[174] and Na'īm Ṣāliḥ Ṭuwayq (1916–1989).[175] One should, however, be careful not to refer to the Jews of Iraq at the time as having "hybrid cosmopolitan cultural identities that simultaneously made Jews an integral part of Iraq and ultimately excluded them from it."[176] Non-Arab cultural identities such as English and French, not to speak of Hebrew, developed only after the emigration of Jews from Iraq and as a result of it. While in Iraq, Arab cultural identity of the Jewish secular intellectuals did not face any rivalry from other cultural identities; we do not know of any outstanding Iraqi Jew during the first half of the twentieth century in Iraq who wrote *belles lettres* in English, French, or Hebrew; even the cultural identity of those who were active in the field of Iraqi-English press was decisively Arab.

More than once, the literary work and fluent Arabic style of the Jews were deemed superior to the average among their Arab counterparts.[177] Furthermore, although Iraqi Jews while in Iraq never adopted Zionism, their

171 On the development of the art of the short story among Iraqi Jews, see Snir 1988, pp. 108–29; Snir 2002, pp. 182–203; Snir 2005a.

172 On the influence of Egyptian literature on the crystallization of the Iraqi-Jewish short story, see Aḥmad 1969, pp. 87–8. On the general Egyptian cultural influence on Iraq in the first half of the twentieth century, see Amīn 1956, pp. 10–11; Bār-Moshe 1988, pp. 107–8.

173 On Shā'ul, see Marmorstein 1959, pp. 187–200; Aḥmad 1969, pp. 237–56; Ben-Yaacob 1980, pp. 381–2; Moreh 1981, pp. 81–7; Bezalel 1982, I, pp. 307–8; Moreh and 'Abbāsī 1987, pp. 113–15; Mudhi 1988, pp. 191–230; Samra 1993, pp. 125–41; *The Encyclopaedia of Islam*, IX (1997), 370; Aḥmad 2001, I, pp. 253–61. For a list of Shā'ul's short stories published in newspapers and magazines, see Mudhi 1988, pp. 497–501. Shā'ul wrote also the script to *'Alyā wa-'Iṣām* (*'Alyā and 'Iṣām*), one of the first Iraqi films (see Qāsim 2002, p. 1013).

174 See Mudhi 1988, p. 173. On translated Western literature in Iraq in general, see Mudhi 1988, pp. 99–103.

175 On Ṭuwayq, see Mu'allim 1983, pp. 154–8; Moreh and 'Abbāsī 1987, p. 142; *Nehardea* (Hebrew) 8 (1990), p. 40.

176 Y. Beinin in his Foreword to Rejwan 1985, p. xxi.

177 Aḥmad 1969, p. 242; Moreh 1978, II, p. 61; Snir 1988, pp. 125–6.

writings began, early in the 1940s, to gain attention in the Land of Israel as well.[178] Murād Michael (Mīkhā'īl) (1906–1986)[179] is considered by Iraqi literary historians to have been the first Iraqi writer to publish a short story in the Western sense, "Shahīd al-Waṭan wa-Shahīdat al-Ḥubb" ("The Homeland's Martyr and the Love's Female Martyr").[180] Michael was also a talented poet whose poetry was admired even by Jamīl Ṣidqī al-Zahāwī (1863–1936) and Ma'rūf al-Ruṣāfī (1875–1945), who were among the greatest Arab poets of their days.[181] Michael's first poem, which was published in 1922, was an ode of praise and love for his beloved Iraqi nation and state.[182] The admiration for the aforementioned Anwar Shā'ul (1904–1984) was not only limited to the echoes of praise for his works in the Arab world. It was also expressed in the fact that he had been invited to read an elegy for a deceased Iraqi leader in one of the mosques of Baghdad, and in his participation in the Iraqi delegation, along with his friend Mīr Baṣrī (1911–2006), to the Conference of Arab Writers, which took place in 1969 in Baghdad.[183] Anwar Shā'ul, as a writer of poetry and prose, was very active in the literary life of Iraq. He was also the editor of two journals, *al-Miṣbāḥ* (*The Candelabrum*) (1924–1929)[184] and *al-Ḥāṣid* (*The Reaper*) (1929–1938).[185] *Al-Miṣbāḥ* was founded by Salmān Shīna (1898–1978), a lawyer who later became a member of the Iraqi parliament.[186] As the editor of *al-Miṣbāḥ* in its first year of publication, Shā'ul wrote under the pseudonym Ibn al-Samaw'al, an allusion to the aforementioned pre-Islamic Jewish poet al-Samaw'al ibn 'Ādiyā'. His awareness that his Arab cultural activities were extensions of those of al-Samaw'al would accompany him throughout his career in Iraq.

In the first two issues of *al-Miṣbāḥ*, Shā'ul published in two parts one of the very first short stories by an Iraqi Jew, "Bayna Anyāb al-Baḥr" ("Between the Tusks of the Sea").[187] Using the pseudonym of Fatā Isrā'īl (Youth of Israel), the author indicates through his communal identity that he belonged

178 See Yehushua Ben Hananya, "Jewish Writers and Poets in Iraq" (in Hebrew), *Hed Hamizrah*, September 29, 1943, p. 12; October 13, 1943, pp. 6–7; October 29, 1943, p. 7; November 12, 1943, pp. 6–7.

179 On Murād Mīkhā'īl, see Moreh 1981, pp. 73–5; Mudhi 1988, pp. 105–11; *Modern Poetry in Translation* 19 (2003), pp. 138–45.

180 Published in *al-Mufīd*, I, nos. 15, 16, and 22 (March–April 1922).

181 Moreh 1982, pp. 37–8; Mīkhā'īl 1988, pp. 15–17.

182 *Dijla*, issue no. 130, April 11, 1922. For the text of the poem, see also Mīkhā'īl 1988, pp. 181–2.

183 Shā'ul 1980, pp. 120–4, 270–4, 335–7. Cf. Semah 1989, p. 88; Somekh 1989, p. 17.

184 On *al-Miṣbāḥ*, see Shā'ul 1980, pp. 76–9; Bashkin 1998.

185 On *al-Ḥāṣid*, see Shā'ul 1980, pp. 148–73. On Jewish press in Iraq, see al-Ma'āḍīdī 2001.

186 On Shīna, see Baṣrī 1983, I, p. 76; *The Encyclopaedia of Islam*, IX (1997), pp. 442–3; Baṣrī 2006, pp. 141–2.

187 See *al-Miṣbāḥ* I.1 (April 10, 1924), p. 6; I.2 (April 17, 1924), p. 7.

to the wider fabric of Iraq's new society. It did not, of course, express any Jewish nationalist tendency—Zionism was not yet in the picture in Iraq. The second journal, *al-Ḥāṣid*, was the most influential Iraqi literary journal during the 1930s. This time, he was not only an editor but also an owner; his experience with *al-Miṣbāḥ* proved to him, to borrow words from a similar case in Israel eighty years later, that "the absolute freedom of expression of the editor exists fully only if one condition is met: that the editor is also the publisher."[188] Shā'ul did his best to be a faithful son of the Iraqi nation and Arab culture; the journal concentrated on social problems and in general attempted to modernize local journalism and literature. As a Jewish writer living in symbiotic contact with the general Arab-Muslim culture, Shā'ul's work had striking Arabic and Iraqi patriotic motifs to the point that these sometimes blurred his own religious identity.[189] He seemed to be justifiably confident that his religion did not pose an obstacle to his integration into Iraqi society, as seen when, in December 1929, at the al-Kaylānī mosque in Baghdad he read an elegy for the deceased Iraqi leader 'Abd al-Muḥsin al-Sa'dūn (1879–1929).[190]

In fact, Shā'ul can be described as the first Jewish writer who tried to adopt an Arab version of the *Haskala*, the Jewish-European Enlightenment. Although the term *Haskala* remains, as Shmuel Feiner (b. 1955) writes, ambiguous and elusive since every change in traditional religious pattern was dubbed *Haskala*,[191] we can find many similarities between Shā'ul and the European Jews identified as *Maskilim*. Like them, from the start Shā'ul assumed the position of a socially critical agent who, convinced that his victory would greatly benefit the Iraqi-Jewish community, was waging all-out war against ignorance. Like his Jewish-European precedent counterparts, who struggled to entrench their new ideas in society, he was vilified and misunderstood; in his essay "al-Majnūn al-Tā'ih" ("The Wandering Madman"),[192] he alludes to the social price he had to pay for adopting a stance considered to be suspicious, but, like the *Maskilim*, he saw the battle as "the war of progress and light against backwardness and darkness."[193] Shā'ul's "acceptance of suffering and pain in this cultural war was seen as an integral part of

[188] Hanoch Marmari, "A Fine and Fragile Balance," a talk delivered on April 1, 2004, at the conference of the Israel Communication Association, Netanya Academic College (published on www.haaretzdaily.com, April 16, 2004). Marmari resigned from his position as editor of the Israeli daily *Haaretz* following differences of opinion with the publisher.

[189] On the tendency among Iraqi-Jewish authors to blur their religious identity to the point that striking Islamic motifs are found in their works, see Snir 1994c, pp. 161–93.

[190] Shā'ul 1980, pp. 119–24.

[191] Feiner 2001, pp. 184–219. In the following section, I will rely on Feiner's conceptions.

[192] *Al-Miṣbāḥ*, October 1, 1925, pp. 3–4.

[193] Feiner 2001, p. 191.

the maskilic experience," and he saw himself as a prophet "engulfed by the holy spirit."[194] He understood that Jews should learn Arabic, just as Jews in Europe learned the languages of the countries where they were living, because it would help them "earn a decent living, as doctors, professors, or the like."[195] The aforementioned dictum "Religion is for God, the Fatherland is for everyone" bore in fact the same maskilic outlook found in the slogan adopted by Judah Leib Gordon (1830–1892): "Be a man in the street and a Jew at home."[196] Gordon too was regarded as trying to promote assimilation and imitation of other cultures. In short, as did the *Maskilim*, Shā'ul considered himself to be part of an intellectual, variegated elite adopting a general liberal rationalist orientation, a member of a new secular intelligentsia who had themselves gone "through the experience of transition from a world of 'old' knowledge and values to the 'new' world of Haskala."[197]

Apart from their involvement in local literature, Jews played a vital role in other branches of Iraqi cultural life far in excess of their proportion of the local population. For example, a great number of talented Jewish musicians rose to prominent positions, distinguishing themselves as singers, composers, and players of traditional instruments. To name only few of them: the composer Ṣāliḥ al-Kuwaytī (1904–1986) and his brother the oud player and singer Dāwūd (1905–1976);[198] the *maqām*[199] singers Salmān Moshe (1880–1955), Yūsuf Ḥūraysh (1889–1975), and Salīm al-Shibbath (1908–1981); the singer Salīma Murād (1905–1974);[200] and the oud player and singer Ezra Aharon (1903–1995).[201] The *maqām* orchestra that represented Iraq at the First Congress of Arabic Music (Cairo, 1932) was entirely Jewish. Also, the orchestra of the Baghdad Broadcasting House consisted of five Jews and one Muslim. Both ensembles performed with the well-known

[194] Feiner 2001, p. 196.
[195] Feiner 2001, p. 197.
[196] Feiner 2001, p. 204.
[197] Feiner 2001, p. 218.
[198] On the Kuwaytī brothers' music and performances and the role of Jewish composers, instrumentalists, and vocalists in Iraqi music in general during the 1930s–1940s, in light of the processes of modernization and Westernization, at a time when Iraq was forming itself as a nation-state, see Dori 2021.
[199] The Iraqi *maqām* is "an intricate composition with many interwoven parts—vocal and instrumental, ready-made pieces and improvisations, texts in classical Arabic as well as in dialect and other languages [...] It also contains sets of expressions, short phrases, and vocal devices that give each *maqām* its special imprimature" (Shiloah 1992, p. 200).
[200] On Salīma Murād, see Sālim 1986, pp. 24–5; Baghdādī 1998, pp. 106; Baṣrī 1999, pp. 102–5; Zuhur 2001, p. 326; Zubaida 2002, pp. 219–22; Obadyā 2005, pp. 21–46.
[201] On the contribution of Jews to the Iraqi *maqām*, see al-Rajab 1961. See also the numerous details on Jewish musicians within the website "Iraqi Maqam – المقام العراقي (available at: https://iraqimaqam.blogspot.com, last accessed February 9, 2022).

Muslim recitalist Muḥammad al-Qabānjī (al-Qebbantchi) (1901–1989).[202] As well as the involvement in the development of the Arab musical tradition by artists, such as those just mentioned, Jewish traditional circles carried on with the Babylonian-Jewish liturgical musical traditions that played a vital role in their day-to-day lives.[203]

5. CONCLUSION

Pioneers of modernization and Westernization, the Iraqi Jews, for example, even participated in the National Arab Movement,[204] all in the belief that their community would endure and prosper, as the writer Shālūm (Shalom) Darwīsh (1913–1997)[205] was to put it, "to the days of the Messiah."[206] Little did they foresee at the time that political developments in Palestine would abruptly foreshorten such Messianic hopes. King Fayṣal's death in 1933, which was very much mourned by the Jews in Iraq at the time,[207] and events in Palestine would have an insidious effect. By the mid-1930s, although being very marginal in the life of local Jewish communities, Zionist activity was officially banned, the importation of Hebrew books and newspapers from Palestine was interdicted, and the last of the Hebrew-language teachers who had come from Palestine were expelled.[208] The Iraqi government

202 For pictures of both ensembles, see *The Scribe* 72 (September 1999), p. 50. Jewish instrumental ensembles in Morocco also performed for non-Jewish circles; it was even related that "each Sultan had his Jewish musician" (Shiloah 1992, p. 202). On the prominent place of Jewish musicians in classical Algerian music during the twentieth century, see Shiloah 2002, pp. 51–64. For more on the contribution of Jews to Islamic and Arab music, see Hirshberg 1996; Beinin 1998, pp. 81–5; Manasseh 1999; Perlson 2000; Kojaman 2001; Kartomi 2002, pp. 90–110; Seroussi 2006, pp. 596–609; Dardashti 2008, pp. 311–28; Shiloah 2011, pp. 272–83.

203 The Babylonian Jewry Heritage Center (BJHC) in Or-Yehuda has produced several audio and video cassettes, providing glimpses into the rich Iraqi-Jewish musical traditions, such as "The Musical Tradition of Iraqi Jews" (1987); "The Jewish Wedding in Baghdad" (1987); "Men's Folk Songs" (1995).

204 Cf. Eisenstadt 1988, p. 4; Zimhoni 1988, p. 8.

205 On Darwīsh, see Marmorstein 1964, pp. 91–102; Moreh 1981, pp. 111–18; Mudhi 1988, pp. 231–312; Ballas 1989, pp. 27–60; Snir 1997a, pp. 128–46; Aḥmad 2001, I, pp. 261–80; Ballas 2003, pp. 169–92. For a list of Darwīsh's short stories published in newspapers and magazines, see Mudhi 1988, pp. 502–6.

206 Darwish 1980, p. 83. Cf. Michael 1979, p. 77. See also the poem "Fī Dhimmat al-Ta'rīkh" ("For the Benefit of History"), written in 1951 in Tehran by the Iraqi-Jewish poet Ibrāhīm Obadyā (1924–2006) in Obadyā 1990, pp. 61–8.

207 See Schlaepfer 2016a, pp. 185–204.

208 On October 2, 1934, the *Manchester Guardian* published a letter written by Isaac Levy, the Jewish owner of the Al Rashid bookstore in Baghdad, referring to the issue of censorship targeted at the Jewish community of Baghdad during this period. Levy was sentenced to one year of hard labor (for a reading between the lines in the case, see Goldstein-Sabbah 2016, pp. 283–300).

forbade the teaching of Hebrew and Jewish history under the pretext of preventing the dissemination of Zionist ideology. The Public Education Law of 1940 exposed Iraqi Jews to the complications of the political conflict between Zionism and Arab nationalism. Distinctions made by early Arab nationalists between the Jewish religion and political Zionism began to blur, especially after 1936, with the infiltration of Nazi propaganda and when Iraqi support for the Palestinians coalesced with pan-Arab foreign policy.[209] During this period, al-Samaw'al, the aforementioned pre-Islamic Arab-Jewish poet that not only for Jewish intellectuals but also for non-Jewish intellectuals had been an emblem of Muslim–Jewish–Christian cooperation,[210] was dropped from the list of heroes included in the local school curriculum. As Iraqi foreign policy publicly adopted the Palestinian Arab cause, the definition of Arabism became ever narrower and excluded Jews. Because of Palestine, no matter how vociferous their loyalty as Iraqi Arabs and denials of Zionist partisanship were, Jews became targets of anti-Zionism and even anti-Semitism. The *Farhūd* in Baghdad and other Iraqi cities in June 1941, when 149 Jews were killed and Jewish property was looted,[211] led to obfuscation of the Jewish role in Iraqi society by implying doubts about the Jews' loyalty. Torn by centrifugal and centripetal forces, these vents pushed Jews, whether as a committed way of struggle or as a kind of escapism, into joining opposition groups, particularly the Communist Party[212] and the Zionist movement.[213]

[209] Zionist activists in Arab lands, as did Zionism itself, claimed that it was a liberation movement for all Jews; therefore, both "Jewish" and "Zionist" were taken to be synonymous terms. In its February 21, 1924 issue, the scientific and literary weekly *al-ʿĀlam al-Isrāʾīlī* (*The Jewish World*; French title: *L'Univers Israélite*), published in Beirut, stated that "every Jew wherever he lives is a Zionist."

[210] In the mid-1930s, the Iraqi Ministry of Education went as far as to found an elementary school for Jewish children, the al-Samaw'al School; the headmaster of the school was Muslim while most of the teachers were Jews. It was closed down in the late 1930s (Meir 1989, p. 123).

[211] On the *Farhūd,* see Cohen 1966, pp. 2–17; Cohen 1973, pp. 28–32; Kedourie 1974, pp. 283–304; Rejwan 1985, pp. 217–44; Silverfarb 1986, pp. 118–41; Snir 2005a (index); Moreh 2012; Yehuda 2017, pp. 249–81 (providing the names of the 141 Jews killed in Baghdad and the eight Jews killed in other cities); Goorji 2021, pp. 325–9.

[212] According to Iraqi criminal files, 245 Jews joined the Communist Party in the 1940s. Most of them were from Baghdad, and the great majority joined the party in 1946. Quite a few were still students, some of whom were female; see al-Barāk 1985, pp. 245–52. On Jewish Communist activity in Iraq, see Batatu 1978, pp. 650–1, 699–701, 1190–2; Shiblak 1986, p. 59 (= Shiblak 2005, p. 80); Bashkin 2012, pp. 141–82; Schlaepfer 2016.

[213] On Zionist activity in Iraq, see Cohen 1969; Meir 1973; Masliyah 1989, pp. 216–37; Kazzaz 1991, pp. 223–316; Akira 1994; pp. 1–35; Meir 1993; Gat 1997; al-Mashhadānī 1999 (the same book was published in another version under a slightly different title; see al-Mashhadānī 2001).

There is no better illustration of the tragic demise of Jewish involvement in Arabic literature than the fate of the few who preferred to stay in Iraq after the establishment of the Jewish nation-state in Palestine. They refused to leave the homeland they loved for an alternative of being forced into giving up the Arab cultural values of their inner aesthetic preference. Among them were Mīr Baṣrī (1911–2006)[214] and the aforementioned Anwar Shā'ul, who in the 1950s and even into the 1960s carried on with their literary activities, still adhering to their Arab and Iraqi patriotism.[215] In 1959, Shā'ul published a poem in praise of Iraqi Prime Minister 'Abd al-Karim Qāsim (1914–1963) in which he referred to him as "al-Awḥad" ("The Unique"), an epitaph generally reserved only to God.[216] In April 1969, less than two years after the June 1967 War, Shā'ul and Baṣrī participated in the Iraqi delegation to the Conference of Arab Writers held in Baghdad. The faith of the Jews was strong enough for their religion not to pose an obstacle to integration. In the words of the Jewish poet from the Jāhiliyya period, al-Samaw'al ibn 'Ādiyā', "if a man's honor is not stained by baseness, any garment he wears will be glorious."[217] But their faithfulness did not serve them in the hour of distress, and the society into which they had so longed to be integrated vomited them out from her midst.[218] The deep sense of insult brought the poet Ibrāhīm Obadya (1924–2006), who had dedicated his collection of poems *Wābil wa-Ṭall* (*Rain and Dew*) (1946) to King Fayṣal II, to dedicate his collection *Zahara fī Kharīf* (*Flower in Autumn*) (1950) to a nightclub dancer in protest.

Despite the feeling that their Arab-Iraqi patriotism was not appropriately rewarded, the Jews who remained in Iraq persisted in clinging to it. While the citizens of Iraq watched him on their television screens, Anwar Shā'ul expressed this before the Conference of Arab Writers in Baghdad in April 1969:

قلبي بحبّ بنـي العروبـة يخفـق   وفمي بضـادهم يشيد وينطـقُ
أولسـت منهـم منبتـا وأرومـة   قد ضمّنا الماضي البعيد الأوثقُ
إذ خطّ في سفر الوفـاء سمـوأل   أمثولـة عربيّـة والأبلـقُ
واليوم نحو المجـد نقطع دربنـا   وإلى الغـد الهانـي معا نتشـوّق
فعلى الفـرات طفولتي قد أزهـرت   وبدجلة نهـل الشّبـاب الرّيـق

214 On Baṣrī, see Moreh 1981, pp. 155–9; Bezalel 1982, I, pp. 285–6; Mudhi 1988, pp. 157–72; Shohet 1982, p. 124; Semah 1989, pp. 83–122; Badawi 1992, p. 517; Meisami and Starkey 1998, I, p. 141; Muḥsin 2010.

215 See Shā'ul 1955; Baṣrī 1955; Baṣrī 1966.

216 *Al-Zamān*, June 1, 1959.

217 Abū Tammām n.d., I, p. 36.

218 Cf. Sami Michael in *Moznaim*, July–August 1986, p. 16. On the arrest of Baṣrī, see Shā'ul 1980, pp. 329–33; Semah 1989, p. 92.

حييت يا وطن العروبة من حمى   الحسن في أرجائه يترقرق

— — — — — — —   — — — — — — —

ربطت مصائرنا الحياة بموطن   هو ماؤنا وهواؤنا والرّونق
موسى وعيسى والنّبيّ محمّد   رسل الهدى، خلت العصور وقد بقوا

My heart beats with love for the Arabs,
  My mouth proudly speaks their language.
Do they and I not share a common source?
  The distant past drew us together,
When al-Samaw'al set in the book of faithfulness
  An emblem to the Arabs in al-Ablaq.[219]
Today we march toward glory,
  We long together for a happy tomorrow.
My childhood flowered on the waters of the Euphrates,
  The days of my youth drank of the Tigris.
O Homeland of Arabism, blessed be you as a shelter
  The glory shines in its spaces
  — — — — — — — —
Our fates have been bound in radiant homeland
  It is our water, our air, and [our] glamour.[220]

In the early 1970s, Baṣrī, Shā'ul, and other men of letters like Salmān Darwīsh (1910–1982) also reached the conclusion that, despite their continuing Iraqi patriotism, the coffin of Babylonian Jewry had been sealed.[221] Two decades previously, the majority of their comrades had already sensed the deterioration of the status of the Jews in the land of the Tigris and Euphrates. They had decided to abandon it, notwithstanding the great hardship of separation from a land so dearly beloved.

In early January 1969, Mīr Baṣrī, who refused to leave Iraq even after the establishment of Israel, seeing himself as "an Arab Iraqi of Jewish religion,"[222] was detained and imprisoned for almost two months due to his having given an interview to a supposed American spy, who was in fact a young scholar who had written a PhD dissertation at Harvard University[223] and then come to Baghdad to do research for a book she would subsequently publish.[224] The imprisonment of Baṣrī, who was at the time the Chairman of the Jewish Council, together with Shā'ul Nājī Khedhourie (Khaḍḍūrī) (1907–2005), the son of the Community President, Chief Rabbi Sassoon

219 Al-Ablaq was al-Samaw'al's fortress in Taymā', north of al-Madīna; see al-Qazwīnī 1960, pp. 73–4.
220 Shā'ul 1980, pp. 335–6.
221 Semah 1989, pp. 86, 120.
222 Semah 1989, p. 88.
223 Marr 1966.
224 Marr 1985.

Khedhourie (Khaḍḍūrī) (1886–1971),[225] was intended to silence the leaders of the Jewish community and stifle their protests prior to the public hangings in late January 1969 of Jews accused of being spies for Israel and other countries. Commenting on the hardships he had to endure at the hands of his Iraqi compatriots, Baṣrī wrote a poem titled "The Imprisonment of the Body and the Soul," some verses of which are:

أيّ جرم جنيتـه في حياتـي
لأجازى جزاء باغ وعات؟
أوقوفـي منـاضـلا وثبـاتي
لـعراقي ودجـلتي وفراتـي

What sin have I sinned in my life,
For which I am so cruelly and harshly punished?
Is it my struggle and my stand on the side of
my Iraq, and of the Tigris and the Euphrates?[226]

When in the 1970s Shā'ul, Baṣrī, and others finally left Iraq after they realized that their situation had become untenable, it was clear that the 1920s vision of Muslim–Christian–Jewish cultural coexistence in the Middle East had reached its sad end. In the wake of the current situation in Baghdad, after the American occupation in April 2003, it is hard to imagine that as recently as the 1920s Baghdad encapsulated a chance for a future when nationalist ideologies would have given way to cultural cooperation and religious tolerance. Sami Michael (Sāmī Mīkhā'īl) (b. 1926) describes this period as follows:

> On a surprisingly warm spring day I once sat in a park in cold Copenhagen and could almost feel the leaves sprout on the trees that were awakening from the long winter ... Over a period of about 30 years—between the end of the First World War and the elimination of this Diaspora in the 1950s—changes occurred that caused a storm in the life of Iraqi Jewry, greater than anything else that had happened during the prior 1,000 years. Dizziness, intoxication, astounding productivity, a spiritual outburst, a process of accelerated secularization, education and the expansion of the physical boundaries of Baghdad created a frenetic climate, like the spring in that park in Copenhagen.[227]

225 On Chief Rabbi Khedhourie, see the study of his son Shā'ul Nājī Khedhourie (Khaḍḍūrī) (1907–2005) (Khaḍḍūrī 1999).

226 For the entire poem, which was written on April 20, 1969, see Baṣrī 1991, pp. 149–52. See also Baṣrī 1983, p. 11. On the events that prompted the writing of these verses, see Shā'ul 1980, pp. 329–33; Baṣrī 1991a, pp. 139–44; Basri 1994a, p. 16; Muḥsin 2010, pp. 150–4. On Baṣrī's struggle against Zionism, see the June 9, 1950 letter of Mordechai ben Porat (1923–2022), who helped to organize the mass immigration of Iraqi Jews to Israel between 1949 and 1951, in Yehuda 1980, pp. 212–17.

227 In a review of Sasson Somekh, *Baghdad, etmol* (*Baghdad, Yesterday*) (Tel Aviv: Ha-Kibbutz Ha-Me'uḥad, 2004), published in *Haaretz*, February 13, 2004 (literary supplement) (English translation according to *Haaretz* [English version], January 25, 2004).

Jewish-Iraqi intellectuals at the time were literary pioneers who stood "on the threshold of emancipation with the highest hopes in their hearts." Therefore, their attitudes must be examined in the light of the generous prospects of the 1920s rather than in the gloom of subsequent decades "in which their visions have been almost completely shattered."[228]

The encounter of the Arab-Jewish immigrants in Israel following its establishment as a state with a powerful Zionist-Hebrew culture was a severe shock emphatically driving home to them, especially those of them who came from Iraq, that their Arab vision of the 1920s was not what they thought but rather merely an illusion.[229] Being Arab Jews who upon arriving in Israel still tried as Jews to adhere to their Arab cultural heritage, they were Orientalized, marginalized, and stigmatized as stagnant and backward in conformity with the binary ethnic classifying division of Ashkenazim/Mizrahim,[230] which from 1948 started to reflect in a simplified way the heterogeneity of the various Jewish communities immigrating to the Jewish state.[231] Being forced to pass through the Israeli-Zionist "melting pot" in order to adapt to the European and Western nature of the new society created in Israel, that binary ethnic division ignored, for example, the fact that the Iraqi Jews' vision of the 1920s was in essence a Western–Arab identity project with the Jews acting as agents of modernization and secularization in the Iraqi traditional society. The attitude of the Zionist movement toward the Arabic language and Arab culture, which was rooted in the very conceptions of its first leaders, contributed to the Orientalization and the stigmatizing process, and accelerated

[228] The quotation is from Marmorstein 1959, p. 199.

[229] The term "Hebrew culture" is used here to refer to the native culture that emerged in Palestine from the first *'Aliyya* in the late nineteenth century. On the emergence of this culture, see Even-Zohar 1990, pp. 175–91.

[230] Before the establishment of the State of Israel, the Jewish community in Palestine was composed of *Ashkenazim* (lit. Germans—Jews of European origin); *Sephardim* (Spaniards—the offspring of Jews expelled from Spain in 1492; however, since the expulsion, those of them who settled in the Middle East mixed with other Jewish Oriental communities); *Mista'revim* (*Musta'ribūn*) (Arabized—those indigenous Jews who had lived in Palestine and adopted Arab ways of life and spoke Arabic); and *Edot Mizraḥ* (Eastern Communities—Jews who immigrated from Arab and Muslim countries). After the establishment of Israel, the considerable differences between these groups blurred and Israeli society polarized around two primary groups: *Ashkenazim* and non-*Ashkenazim*. For the latter, the term *Mizrahim* was recently in use. For a brief history of Oriental–Ashkenazi relations, see Smooha 1978, pp. 48–61.

[231] On *Mizrahim* as an Israeli invented ethnic category filled with negative cultural connotations and as a symbolic vehicle by which cultural differences capable of masking socio-economic inequality are explained, see Lewis 1985, pp. 149–51; Shohat 1999, pp. 5–20. For an attempt to pinpoint the roots of the Westernizing of the emerging Israeli society in the earlier history of the Jewish encounter with Orientalism and Western colonialism, see Khazzoom 2003, pp. 481–510.

the process through which the Arab Jews started to internalize the negative attitude of the canonical Hebrew center to Arab culture.[232]

In 1957, the aforementioned Sāṭiʿ al-Ḥuṣrī referred to the relationship of Arabism to Islam, mentioning that Arab culture was not born with the emergence of Islam and that there were Arabs before there were Muslims. However, when speaking of the religious identity of these ancient Arabs, he mentioned only the Christians.[233] Because of the conflict in the Middle East, al-Ḥuṣrī, who in the 1920s helped King Fayṣal to promote his conception that there was no distinction in Iraq between Muslims, Christians, or Jews, stopped seeing the Jews as a potential part of the Arab nation. No wonder that the literature Arab Jews produced in Arabic was almost entirely relegated to the margins of Arabic literature. The political and national reasons that were behind that process were also behind the paucity of scholarly attention this literature has been given throughout the years.[234] In the 1950s and the 1960s, it was still possible to find a few scholars in the Arab world dealing with Jewish writing as part of the general Arabic literary legacy, but the June 1967 War made it even more unlikely that Jewish literati in Baghdad or Cairo would somehow be singled out for the contribution they may have made to the development of Arabic literature.

For example, in a biographical dictionary of Iraqi personalities in the twentieth century published in the mid-1990s,[235] the author Ḥamīd al-Maṭbaʿī (1942–2018) omitted *all* the Iraqi-Jewish writers and poets. He mentioned only a few Jews: the aforementioned Aḥmad Nissīm Sūsa[236]—probably because he converted to Islam; the legal scholar and judge Dāwud Samra (1878–1960), without mentioning that he was a Jew;[237] and in the entry on the singer Nāẓim al-Ghazālī (1912–1963) he mentions his Jewish wife, the aforementioned Salīma Murād, but without mentioning that she was a Jew.[238] To show the sheer method of exclusion, the case of Anwar Shā'ul is instructive. Shā'ul is not mentioned in the dictionary, but three

232 The encounter of the Arab Jews in Israel with the Zionist master narrative created new terms to identify them in Israeli society; the most accepted has been the aforementioned *Edot Mizraḥ* or *Mizraḥī*. The term "Arab Jew" was marginalized. As the present study does not see any essential difference between an Arab-Jewish poet living and working in Baghdad and the same poet living and working in Israel, the term "Arab Jew" is generally used here unless I refer to the opinions of others.

233 See al-Ḥuṣrī 1966a, pp. 241–50.

234 In his *A History of the Jews in Baghdad* (Sassoon 1949), David Solomon Sassoon (1880–1942) did not mention at all the literary activities of the Iraqi Jews in Arabic.

235 See al-Maṭbaʿī 1995–1996.

236 Al-Maṭbaʿī 1995–1996, I, pp. 12–13.

237 Al-Maṭbaʿī 1995–1996, II, p. 77.

238 Al-Maṭbaʿī 1995–1996, II, pp. 228–9.

other pioneers of the Iraqi short story are mentioned: Dhū al-Nūn Ayyūb (1908–1988),[239] 'Abd al-Ḥaqq Fāḍil (1915–1992),[240] and Maḥmūd Aḥmad al-Sayyid (1903–1937).[241] Ignoring Shā'ul and mentioning them is sufficient evidence for the exclusion of the Iraqi-Jewish writers. But the author allotted an entry to 'Abd al-Ilāh Aḥmad (1940–2007), pointing to his most famous book in Arabic on the art of the Iraqi short story—*Nash'at al-Qiṣṣa wa-Taṭawwuruhā fī al-'Irāq 1908–1939* (*The Rise of the Short Story and Its Development in Iraq 1908–1939*).[242] In this book, Aḥmad allotted only four chapters to authors whom he considers pioneers of the Iraqi short story: al-Sayyid (pp. 193–236), Ayyūb (pp. 257–89), Fāḍil (pp. 290–315), and Shā'ul (pp. 237–56). It means that Ḥamīd al-Maṭba'ī used the book of 'Abd al-Ilāh Aḥmad as a source, mentioned three authors that Aḥmad thought were so important that they should be studied in separate chapters, but ignored the fourth author only because he was a Jew. Another aspect of the dictionary might provide additional evidence for the exclusivist method: the aforementioned Mīr Baṣrī is one of the famous Iraqi scholars in the field of *tarjamāt* (biographies of personalities).[243] He, of course, is not mentioned—not as a writer and not as a scholar. But a close examination of al-Maṭba'ī's dictionary reveals beyond any doubt that he used Baṣrī's numerous studies in the field without mentioning any of them in the list of the sources of his dictionary.[244]

The above exclusion is a symptom of a wide phenomenon: from the late 1940s, in the wake of national and political conflict in the Middle East, Arab-Jewish culture underwent a process of marginalization, negligence, and gradual dropping into utter oblivion brought about by both the Muslim-Arab and Jewish-Hebrew canonical cultural systems. Both the Muslim-Arab and the Jewish-Zionist canonical cultural and national systems, each as a result of their own narrowed reasons and particularist considerations, have generally refused to accept the legitimacy of the Arab-Jewish hybridity. They have excluded the hybrid Arab-Jewish identity and highlighted the so-called "pure" Jewish-Zionist identity against the "pure" Arab-Muslim one—Arab-Jewish culture has become a disease that is to be contained; the few still infected people are to be quarantined for fear of further contamination.

Moreover, both sides also have doubted even the very existence of such Arab-Jewish hybridity from the historical point of view. For example, the

239 Al-Maṭba'ī 1995–1996, I, p. 72.
240 Al-Maṭba'ī 1995–1996, I, p. 122.
241 Al-Maṭba'ī 1995–1996, I, pp. 197–8.
242 Al-Maṭba'ī 1995–1996, I, p. 119.
243 See Snir 2005a, p. 187, n. 210; Muḥsin 2010, pp. 162–78.
244 Al-Maṭba'ī 1995–1996, I, p. 238. For a similar way of exclusion directed against the Jewish composer Ṣāliḥ al-Kuwaytī, see Dori 2021, pp. 324–9.

Isrā'īliyyāt, a term used by classical Muslim authors to denote material ascribed to Jews (*Banū Isrā'īl*), became a flash point for charges of Jewish, or Zionist, religio-cultural infiltration.[245] This is in evident contrast to solid sources according to which until the twentieth century Arabness referred to a common shared culture and language with religious differences (i.e., the distinction in Arab lands had always been between Muslims, Jews, and Christians, and not at all between Arab and Jew). Moreover, in the formative period of Islamic civilization, when cultural contact between Jews and Muslims was more likely to have been marked by curiosity and interest than by outward antagonism, Muslim scholars were well aware that Jewish scripture and lore deeply penetrated their own tradition and thus engaged in a sharp discussion as to the potential impact of this borrowing.[246] Modern Western intellectual discourse for its part has highlighted the Judeo-Christian cultural heritage, despite the fact that for half a millennium the creative centers of Jewish life were to be found under Islam and not under Christianity and to now speak about a Judeo-Muslim heritage is undoubtedly historically no less justified.[247]

Following the escalation of the national conflict in Palestine, the distinctions made by early Arab nationalists between the Jewish religion and political Zionism began to blur, especially after 1936, with the advent of Nazi propaganda and when Iraqi support for the Palestinians was joined with pan-Arab foreign policy. On June 1–2, 1941, following the attempted *coup d'état* by the pro-Nazi Rashīd 'Ālī al-Kaylānī (1892–1965), they were victims of the aforementioned *Farhūd*, when 149 of them were killed and Jewish property was looted. Following the obfuscation of their role in Iraqi society by implying doubts about their loyalty, and as their life became increasingly intolerable, Jews, especially young men, were forced to choose new directions for their future. Whether as a committed way of struggle or as a kind of escapism, the shift in their thinking pushed them into joining the Zionist movement or the Communist underground. While the first struggled for the establishment of an independent Jewish state, the latter fought against the corrupt, dictatorial regime and for equal rights for all minorities. The Communist underground also struggled against Zionism, and several of its Jewish members in 1946 founded the magazine *al-'Uṣba* (*The League*), which was an organ of 'Uṣbat

[245] On the *Isrā'īliyyāt* and relevant references, see McAuliffe 1998, pp. 345–69; Rubin 1999; Tottoli 1999, pp. 193–210; Tottoli 2021, pp. 1–42. For an updated discussion of the history and development of *Isrā'īliyyāt* as a concept with additional references, see Pregill 2021, pp. 256–302. On the rejection of the *Isrā'īliyyāt* in contemporary literature, see Tottoli 2002, pp. 180–3.

[246] Lassner 1993, p. 121.

[247] Cf. Lewis 1984, pp. 67–106; Lewis 1984a, pp. 3–13.

Mukāfaḥat al-Ṣahyūniyya (The League for the Struggle against Zionism).[248] In the early 1950s, most of the Jewish-Iraqi poets, writers, and intellectuals emigrated from Iraq to Israel;[249] a much smaller number decided to seek their future in the West—such as, for example, Elie Kedourie (1926–1992)[250] and Naïm Kattan (Naʿīm Qaṭṭān) (1928–2021).[251] Only a few chose to stay in Iraq, the most outstanding among them being Anwar Shāʾul (1904–1984)[252] and Mīr Baṣrī (1911–2006).[253]

248 Al-Maʿāḍīdī 2001, pp. 64–6. On the League in general, see Akira 1989, pp. 1–26; Akira 2006, pp. 211–25.

249 On the Jewish-Iraqi emigration to Israel, its causes, and its motives, see Mudhi 1988, pp. 58–91; Gat 1997.

250 In 1947, Kedourie left for London, and later became a renowned professor of political science at the London School of Economics; on him, see Kedourie (Sylvia) 1998; Rejwan 2004, pp. 122–3, 150–68.

251 Kattan left Baghdad for Paris and then went to Canada to start a career as a writer and critic in French; he published an autobiographical novel on his life in Iraq, *Adieu babylone* (Kattan 1975), which was also published in English and Arabic translations: *Farewell, Babylon* (Kattan 1980) and *Wadāʿan Bābil* (Kattan 1999). On Kattan and his work, see *al-Ḥayāt* (London), November 11, 1994, p. 16; *The Scribe* 66 (September 1996), p. 34; Mahdī 1995, pp. 14–37; Benson and Toye 1997, pp. 588–9; Malinovich 2019, pp. 19–36; Drori 2020, pp. 43–53; Snir, forthcoming. See also interviews conducted with him by his son, the writer Emmanuel Kattan (b. 1968) (Kattan 2017).

252 On Anwar Shāʾul and his work, see Marmorstein 1959, pp. 187–200; Aḥmad 1969, pp. 237–56; Ben-Yaacob 1980, pp. 381–2; Moreh 1981, pp. 81–7; Bezalel 1982, I, pp. 307–8; Moreh and ʿAbbāsī 1987, pp. 113–15; Mudhi 1988, pp. 191–230, 497–501; *The Encyclopaedia of Islam*, IX (1997), p. 370.

253 On Baṣrī and his work, see above.

Chapter 6

Spring: "We Were Like Those Who Dream"[1]

But your poem dwells in the tranquil heart,
Sung by the lips of spring.
It is in every soul which longs for tranquility
And in the eyes aching for light,
Love and brotherhood.
– David Semah

1. INTRODUCTION

Toward the end of the 1940s and during the early 1950s, largely in the framework of the mass immigration of Iraqi Jews, many talented writers and poets emigrated from Iraq to Israel. Among them were Murād Mīkhā'īl (1906–1986), Shalom Darwīsh (1913–1997), Ya'qūb Balbūl (1920–2003), Nuriel Zilkha (1924–2015), Ibrāhīm Obadyā (1924–2006), Sami Michael (b. 1926), Zakkay Binyamin Aharon (Binyāmīn Hārūn) (1927–2021), Isḥāq Bār-Moshe (1927–2003), Nīr Shoḥet (1928–2011), Shlomo Zamir (1929–2017), Shimon Ballas (1930–2019), Salīm Sha'shū'a (1930–2013), Sālim al-Kātib (Shalom Katab) (b. 1931), Najīb Kaḥīla (b. 1931), David Semah (1933–1997), Sasson Somekh (1933–2019), Shmuel Moreh (1932–2017), and Samīr Naqqāsh (1938–2004).[2] The harsh material conditions in the new Jewish state, the difficulties of adapting to a new society, and a lack of knowledge of Hebrew took their toll on a number of them. They underwent an "experience of shock and uprooting," as Somekh says, and under these conditions "it became difficult to think about literature."[3]

[1] This chapter uses material that first appeared in Snir 1991, pp. 153–73; Snir 2006c, pp. 92–123; Snir 2019.

[2] On these writers and poets, see Moreh 1973; Moreh 1981; Moreh and Hakak 1981, pp. 83–132; Moreh and 'Abbāsī 1987; Snir 2005a.

[3] *Iton 77*, January–February 1988, p. 32.

Nevertheless, and in spite of the difficulties in adapting to the new and fundamentally different Hebrew-Jewish society, the fact that they arrived to a state where Arabic was considered an official language, apart from Hebrew, gave them, at least in the beginning, the hope that they would be able to continue their literary careers. Also, following the events of 1948, the greater part of the Arab urban intelligentsia abandoned the territories of Palestine, while those who remained inside the boundaries of the State of Israel were generally from the poorer or the uneducated village population.[4] This cultural vacuum was partially filled by the immigrating Jewish writers and poets.

And, indeed, not a few of the Jewish immigrants continued to create in Arabic while adhering to the poetics they had grown accustomed to in Iraq, which was suffused with literary English and French inspiration. A significant thematic change appeared in their work: alongside the conventional subjects that had preoccupied them in Iraq—love, social and ethical problems, the status of women, fate and its illusions, death and thoughts on life—subjects touching on the pressing social and political circumstances of Israel in the 1950s became dominant in their work. Furthermore, as far as Arabic writing by Jews in Israel was concerned, those works that dealt with traditional themes were marginal. It was precisely its preoccupation with issues of urgency that granted importance, however limited, to Jewish writing in Arabic during these years.

Following the efforts of the Israeli establishment to paint Jewish immigration from the Arab world in Zionist colors,[5] Arab-Jewish intellectuals with split personalities had to cope with the new situation. Many hastened to present themselves as Israeli and Zionist while referring to their Arab identity as a mark of disgrace. Israeli patriotism quickly permeated the writing of most of the immigrant authors and poets, though this should not be understood as an absolute identification with the political establishment among all of them. For some, the immigration to a new homeland did not bring a total change in their fundamental worldviews. Others underwent a process of growing identification with the establishment, which was largely a result of the change in their status in a Jewish state, the reverse of their status in Iraq as a minority within an Arab majority. Characterizing the writing of the

[4] See Snir 1990, pp. 247–8.

[5] An example is the Babylonian Jewry Heritage Center in Or-Yehuda (BJHC) founded in 1972; its museum, opened sixteen years later, has adopted the memorialization practices used in Yad Vashem, the Holocaust Martyrs' and Heroes' Remembrance Authority, Israel's national Holocaust memorial. On the success of the BJHC and its museum in presenting the history of Iraqi Jewry as an integral part of the Zionist narrative, see Meir-Glitzenstein 2002, pp. 165–86.

poets who immigrated to Israel as opposed to those who remained in Iraq, Shmuel Moreh says:

> The Jewish poets who came to Israel from Iraq in 1950 and 1951 wrote poetry full of national pride for Israel and her achievements. Whereas in Iraq their poetry was marked by melancholy, in Israel it became optimistic and throbbing with the emotion of being a part of the people and state. In contrast, the poetry of those who remained in Iraq, like Anwar Shā'ul and Meir Baṣrī, became more melancholic and pessimistic, and contained complaints on the vicissitudes of the time, on the dispersion of friends and on their fears and suspicions.[6]

It is more correct to say that the immigration to Israel, which many undertook unwillingly and as a result of a physical threat to their lives, shifted their allegiance from Iraqi patriotism to loyalty to the new Jewish state. Furthermore, the generalization that the writing of those who remained in Iraq became pessimistic and melancholy apparently derives from a projection of their wretched ends onto their feelings in the 1950s and 1960s.

Having internalized the negative attitude of the canonical cultural center to Arab culture, the immigrating authors learned to reject their own roots in order to get closer to the heart of the Israeli Zionist collective. The negative impact of all this on youth growing up in Arab-Jewish families has since been very apparent. Trying to conform to the *Sabra* norm,[7] children were made to feel ashamed of the Arabness of their parents. In his autobiographical story, "Pictures from the Elementary School,"[8] the Syrian-born writer Amnon Shamosh (1929–2022)[9] confesses that as a child he forbade his mother to speak Arabic in public. "For our parents," the Moroccan-born poet Sami Shalom Chetrit (b. 1960) says, "all of us were agents of repression."[10] The Iraqi-born Yehouda Shenhav (Shenhav-Shahrabani) (b. 1952), a Tel Aviv University professor and one of the activists of the social movement Ha-Keshet Ha-Demokratit Ha-Mizrahit (Mizrahi Democratic Rainbow Coalition),[11] described his own experience:

6 Moreh 1981 (English introduction), p. 23.

7 Sabra, a prickly pear that was believed to be indigenous to the Middle East, has become the term applied to native Israeli Jews, symbolizing their being, as is the sabra fruit, hard on the outside but sweet on the inside. In Zionist ideology, the Sabra was of especially lofty, heroic status, frequently portrayed as the brave, altruistic defender of Israel. With the increasing questioning of Zionist mythology, the image of the Sabra has undergone extensive transformation—post-Zionists now question the validity of the heroic image of the Sabra (Medoff and Waxman 2009, p. 174).

8 Shamosh 1979, pp. 79–87.

9 On Shamosh, see Shaked 1993, IV, pp. 172–3; and Zenner 1988, pp. 25–35.

10 *Yediot Aḥronoth*, August 8, 2003, p. 54.

11 On this movement, see Snir 2015b, pp. 203–7, and the references.

> On the first Thursday of every month, the Egyptian singer Umm Kulthūm [1903–1975] would begin to sing and I would begin to tense up. As the Oriental tones filled the house my mother would gradually make the radio louder and louder and I would not know where to bury myself. I would try to turn the radio off and she would turn it back on and make it even louder. I had become a foreign agent in my own house.[12]

Among the immigrants who continued writing in Arabic, it was soon possible to discern two groups generally operating in parallel with the dominant trends among the local Palestinian minority at the time: those who preferred to be active under the aegis of the cultural and literary establishment and those who joined the Communist Party or expressed sympathy with it.[13] The Histadrūt, the General Workers' Union, played an important role in encouraging and cultivating what was called "positive" literature and culture within the Palestinian minority through establishing literary prizes and literary competitions, as well as through the founding of the Arab Book Fund.[14] Those literary and cultural activities dealt with the yearning for peace and "Arab-Jewish brotherhood,"[15] but avoided dealing with controversial problems, such as the government's policy toward the Palestinian minority and the way Jews from Arab lands were absorbed into Israel. Consequently, the works produced by these immigrants tended to emphasize more traditional themes, such as male–female relations, social and ethical problems, the status of women, fate and its illusions, and universal questions of existence.

In the opposing camp stood the leftist Jewish writers who continued to work within the framework of the Communist Party, whose intellectuals had not abandoned Palestine following 1948. The establishment 's ban on Communist writers, Jews and Arabs, inspired the Association of Arabic Language Poets to refuse to collaborate with them.[16] The jour-

[12] A lecture at the School for Peace Neve Shalom / Wāḥat al-Salām, Israel, March 2000; and *School for Peace Annual Review 1999–2001*, January 2001. For Shenhav-Shahrabani's views, see Shenhav 1999, pp. 605–30; Shenhav 2002, pp. 27–56; Shenhav 2002a, pp. 521–44; Shenhav 2003; Evri 2020a, pp. 65–85.

[13] On their activities, see Snir 1991, pp. 153–73.

[14] See, for example, *Fī Mahrajān al-Adab* (*In the Festival of Literature*) (Aggassi 1959). It was published by the Arab Book Fund and contained works that earned prizes in a literary competition put on by the Histadrūt in 1958. The introduction of the book by the Iraqi Jew Iliyāhū Aghāsī (Eliyahu Aggassi) (1909–1991) illustrates the efforts to produce "positive" culture. On Aghāsī, see Moreh 1973, pp. 28–9; Ben-Yaacob 1980, pp. 390–4; Moreh and 'Abbāsī 1987, pp. 24–5; Kayyal 2016, p. 19.

[15] While in Iraq, Arab cultural and national identity encompassed Jews side by side with Muslims and Christians; in Israel, since the 1950s, the Jewish identity has become in itself a cultural and national identity. Thus, because of the political conflict, the natural Iraqi hybrid Arab-Jewish identity turned into a sharp dichotomy of Jewish versus Arab.

[16] See *al-Jadīd*, December 1955, pp. 40–3.

nals of the two camps were fiercely competitive, but the Communist journals stood out, particularly *al-Ittiḥād* and *al-Jadīd*, for their quality and wide circulation. They did not hesitate to deal with subjects considered taboo by the governmental press, which the Arab public perceived as the trumpet of the ruling party, even attributing to it the hatred of Arabs.[17] In contrast to those writers who were supported by the Israeli governmental establishment, a preoccupation with political and social problems was dominant in Communist writing. Besides this thematic difference, it was possible to discern, in their poetry, a significant formal difference: while those writers close to the establishment in general clung strictly to conservative Arabic poetics, the Communists were already inclined, in the early 1950s, toward the modernism of "free verse," despite the fact that this new poetics had hardly been digested by Arab poets in Israel.[18] The Jewish poets had already absorbed this poetics in Iraq, where it had first flourished, and where it was also identified with Communist writers.[19]

2. "IN THE WORLD OF LIGHT"

The work of the writers and poets close to the governmental establishment was steeped in national pride and was permeated with patriotism and the desire for peace while absent any critique of the authorities. One of the prominent figures among them was the poet and jurist Salīm Sha'shū'a, whose volume of poetry *Fī 'Ālam al-Nūr* (*In the World of Light*) (1959) represents these writers well.[20] The book's name reflects the character of the poems, which praise the exodus from the dark of exile to the light of redemption in Israel while underscoring the dichotomy between the wretchedness of the past and the joyous life of the present. The author provides no critique in these poems, not even allusive, of the establishment, or any protest of social, economic, or political conditions. The reverse is true. Notwithstanding the difficult travails of absorption of the new immigrants, and the severe problems of the Arab minority, the poet depicts, like others close to the Israeli governmental establishment, an idyllic picture of a paradise on earth. This gave the book's critics their pretext for a scathing critique.[21] Its national patriotism is expressed also in the dedication of the volume to the then

17 See Snir 1990, pp. 249–53.
18 Snir 1990, p. 248.
19 Moreh 1976, pp. 267–8. On the acquaintance of Somekh with Badr Shākir al-Sayyāb (1926–1964), see *al-Anbā'* (weekly supplement), December 10, 1982, p. 4.
20 Cf. Moreh and Hakak 1981, p. 97.
21 See, for example, *al-Jadīd*, July 1958, pp. 23–4.

president of the state, Yitzḥak Ben Zvi (1884–1963), whose picture figures alongside the dedication above the following lines of verse:

من لآلي الشّعر يا مولاي قد صنعت عقودا
وبها رصّعت تأريخا طريفا وتليدا
فإذا قدّمتها اليوم لمولاي نشيدا
فهي فيض من شعوري خطّه الحبّ قصيدا

From the pearls of my poetry, your exalted glory, I made these verses,
And interwove them with stories of the heritage of fathers and sons.
Now I present them to you today as a hymn to your honor,
Behold the bounty of my feeling, transformed to poetry by love.

Thus, Sha'shū'a conforms to the custom of the medieval Arab court poets, who glorified and praised their patrons. Like one who felt the rush of history's wings above his head, the poet composed a rhetorical introduction to the volume. As there is no better way to characterize this type of writing from these years, it is important to quote it in full:

أخي القارئ الكريم
في هذه البلاد
حيث تكّد الأيدي، وتجّد العقول، وتتفتّق الأذهان،
في هذه البلاد حيث تنبثق الفكر كالأشّعة، فتتألّق الخواطر كالأهّلة، وتسمق شجرة المعرفة، وتعبق الحكمة، وتنطلق الرّوحانيّة. يلتقي الشّرق بالغرب، فتتجسّم الفكرة بالصّورة، ويخترع الغرب ويبتدع الشّرق، دنيا جديدة شيّقة. ويطلع فجر وتشرق شمس وتتدفّق أضواء في عالم النّور.
في هذه الدّنيا حيث ترتفع المصانع، وتصطخبا لمعامل، ويتصاعد الدّخان وتفوح البخور.
في هذه الدّنيا الجديدة، حيث الجنائن الغلب والحدائق الغنّ الّتي كانت قبل عقد من الزّمن، صحارى قاحلة، يقف الإنسان اليوم معجبا بأخيه الإنسان. الإنسان الّذي يزرع. الإنسان الّذي يبني. الإنسان الّذي يفّكر. هذا الإنسان الّذي لم تعقه الطّبيعة دون الّذي يريده، تجده هنا في إسرائيل يعمل وينتج، حيث يخلق القلم وتتفنّن الرّيشة ويبدع الإزميل! وقفت أنصت وملء عينيّ هذا الجمال، في البطاح، في الرّوابي وفي الوديان. جمال الأرض الطّيبة! وجمال الأيدي المنتجة! وجمال العقول المبدعة! هذا الجمال أحسّه كلّما تأمّلت وحيثما تملّيت، فلا عجب إذا أستلهمه قصائدي مختارا أو غير مختار، قصائد كتبتها في عالم النّور، وأنا أسير في قافلة الأخوّة العربيّة اليهوديّة المناضلة من أجل السّلام والمحّبة بين شعبينا العربيّ والعبريّ السّاميين. هذه القصائد بين يديك، لعلّك أن تجد فيها ما تقرأه وما تعجببه وما يحبّب لك هذه الأخوّة الّتي تنبثق من ربوع إسرائيل. وغايتي—كّل غايتي—أن نكتسح—أنا وأنت—الأشواك الّتي قد تقف في طريق أخوّتنا المسالمة، لنعيش معا في عالم النّور.

My brother the Reader! In this land in which hands labour, brains strive and thoughts grow weary. In this land, in which ideas are distinguished like rays of the sun and thoughts sparkle like moons, the Tree of Knowledge blooms, Wisdom spreads her pleasant scents and spirituality bursts forth, East meets West and the Idea crystallizes in Form. The West discovers and the East invents a new and astounding world. The dawn rises, the sun shines and its rays break forth in a world of light. In this new world, in which gardens are overgrown and orchards bloom, where ten years ago was arid desert, Man stands today and reveres his fellow Man. Man who sows, Man who builds, Man who thinks, this

> Man before whom Nature is no obstacle to the realization of his desires. Here you will find us working and creating in Israel, where the Pen creates, the paint-brush is productive and the scalpel (of the sculptor) makes wonders! I stood and hearkened, my eyes full of this beauty, the plains, the hills and the valleys. The beauty of the good earth! The beauty of hands which create! The beauty of brains which invent! I sense this beauty at every moment and in every place I look and in which I take pleasure. It is no wonder, then, that here, willingly or unwillingly, I have sought my inspiration for my poems—these very poems which I have written in the world of light, while I walk in the columns of that Arab-Jewish brotherhood which strives for peace and love between our two peoples under Hebrew and Arab skies.
>
> Perhaps you will find something pleasing among these poems placed before you to endear to you that noble brotherhood which spreads across Israel. I hopefully await the day when you and I shall triumph over the thorns which may perhaps stand in the path of our brotherhood and pursuit of peace, so that we may live together in a world of light.[22]

These are beautiful phrases on the meeting of East and West, the flowering of the desert, the blossoming of the new state, Jewish–Arab brotherhood, and the yearning for peace, but they absolutely ignore the severe problems of Israeli society. Sha'shū'a is satisfied with a vague reference to the thorns that "may perhaps (*sic!*) stand in the path of our brotherhood and pursuit of peace." The same patriotic tone characterizes the poems of this volume as well, as in the introductory poem.[23] This poem, written for an Independence Day celebration in the 1950s, bears the title "Victory Is among Its Followers" and is based on the following words:

قـدم الرّبيع مهنّئا بقدومـه [...]
شعبا يقود النّصر حيث يريده
فالنّصر من أتباعه وجنـوده

> Spring has come saluting in its arrival ...
> A people who leads victory to every place it wishes:
> Victory is among its followers and one of its soldiers.

The Israeli Defense Forces reap only victories because victory is one of their soldiers. In this poem, which draws an analogy between the spring and human happiness,[24] the Jews return to their ancestral inheritance and make the desert bloom with the aid of the divine light, Torah and Talmud. Nonetheless, the poem is not militaristic, as its ultimate goal is peace and

[22] Sha'shū'a 1959, pp. 7–8.
[23] Sha'shū'a 1959, pp. 9–13. Two other poems are based on this poem: Sha'shū'a 1976, pp. 59–66; Moreh 1982, pp. 78–81.
[24] Cf. "The Spring in Israel" (Sha'shū'a 1959, pp. 44–8).

coexistence between Jews and Arabs. In the poem "Cooperation," which the poet recited at the first national conference of the cooperative association convened by the Arabic Department of the Histadrūt in Nazareth on October 1, 1958, the poet says:

إنّنا سنبني بالتّعاون عالما
والسّلم يصبح غاية في ذاته
ألخير من أهدافه والعدل من
أوصافه والحبّ من آياته

Through cooperation, we shall yet build a world
Whose purpose is peace,
Whose goals count goodness among them, whose plans
Include justice, and whose signs include love.[25]

The poet continued to explore these same motifs and ideas through his work of the 1960s and 1970s, as we see in the volume *Ughniyyāt li-Bilādī* (*Songs to My Homeland*) (1976). It is most noteworthy that the yearning for peace is one of the most striking characteristics of the Iraqi-born poets in the 1950s. Thus, for instance, the poet Sālim al-Kātib (Shalom Katab) says in a poem dedicated to "the mothers of the world, to the mothers of Israel, to my mother":

أين السّلام، يا أمّاه
أين السّكون؟!

ما أبهى شعبنا يا أمّاه
والشّعوب
لو احتضنه الهدوء
وفي سمائها الصّافية الزّرقاء
رفرفت طيور السّلام

Where is peace, woe my mother?
Where is tranquility?!

How glorious our people would be
And all peoples
If tranquility would envelope them
And in their clear blue skies
The doves of peace would flutter.[26]

In the poem "Peace and the Dawn," written in December 1951 and dedicated "to humanity which yearns for light and for peace," the same poet says:

[25] Sha'shū'a 1959, p. 18.
[26] Al-Kātib 1959, pp. 52–3; Moreh 1982, pp. 112–13.

الدّيك يصيح
والفجر الجميل
يأبى النّزوح
لكنّه يزول
مع موكب الصّبح
ولحنه الشّادي
«لحن السّلام»
يأبى أن يزول

The rooster cries
And the beautiful dawn
Refuses to vanish
But it melts
With the oncoming morning
Still its sweet melody,
The melody of peace,
Refuses to vanish.[27]

Even the harshest critics of this poetry did not ignore the "yearning for peace and human brotherhood"[28] with which it was anointed. For many of the Jewish writers, Israel symbolized the focal point of peace and brotherhood:

وطني
عرين العدل،
مأوى الحقّ،
سوق البرّ
بند السّلم صدر بنوده

My homeland
Pasture of peace
Shelter of truth
Market of justice
The banner of peace at the head of its banners.[29]

The work of those close to the establishment was characterized by an emphasis on Jewish–Arab brotherhood, the yearning for peace, and praise for the accomplishments of the state "whose flowering land is flowing with milk and honey."[30] Not a drop of criticism against the authorities could be heard.

27 Al-Kātib 1959, pp. 62–3; Moreh 1982, pp. 113–14.
28 See *al-Jadīd*, December 1958, pp. 42–3.
29 Sha'shū'a 1976, p. 63; Moreh 1982, p. 79.
30 From a poem by Zakkay Binyamin Aharon that earned the third prize in the 1958 competition (Aggassi 1959, pp. 106–7).

3. "TILL SPRING COMES"

The leftist poets and writers who emigrated from Iraq did not agree that Israeli patriotism implied absolute identification with the authorities. This was so despite their awareness that anti-establishment activity might harm not only their chances for integration into Israeli society, but also their income and even their livelihoods.[31] The argument that literary anti-establishment activity derived only from bitterness over harsh living conditions in Israel[32] is difficult to accept. The Jewish Communist writers arrived in Israel with an ideology already formed. In Iraq, as in other Middle Eastern states,[33] Jewish intellectuals after the Second World War inclined to either Communism or Zionism. With the outbreak of the war, the Communist underground in Iraq strengthened, and Jews joined "out of feelings of Iraqi patriotism"[34] and the belief that Communism was the only force capable of withstanding Nazism. "From a small, childish, one-dimensional framework," this underground grew in strength to "a tidal wave."[35] The underground struggled not only against the corrupt, dictatorial regime and for equal rights for all minorities, but also against Zionism. In Baghdad, in 1946, several of its Jewish members even founded the magazine *al-Uṣba* (*The League*), the magazine of 'Uṣbat Mukāfaḥat al-Ṣihyūniyya (The League for the Struggle against Zionism).[36] Opposition to Zionism was not exclusive to Communist Jews, but extended also to community institutions and their leaders, and this opposition included the dispatching of an anti-Zionist telegram to the League of Nations from the General Council of the Iraqi Jewish community.[37] Still, it is possible that there were also those, particularly among the youth, who saw no real contradiction between Zionism and Communism as liberation movements acting against British occupation.[38]

Immigration to Israel did not chill the fervor of the Communist writers for this ideology: thus, for instance, Sami Michael, persecuted as a Communist in Iraq, fled to Iran and from there to Israel with no Zionist motives

[31] See Ballas' story in *al-Jadīd*, December 1955, pp. 26–34 (= Moreh 1981, pp. 191–202). Cf. *Maariv*, April 25, 1989, p. B9. On the opportunism of others, see Sami Michael's story in *al-Jadīd*, February 1955, pp. 24–9 (= Moreh 1981, pp. 225–32); Semah's letter in *Maariv*, January 26, 1989.

[32] Moreh 1958, p. 31.

[33] Cf. Memmi 1966, p. 167; Memmi 2013, p. 89.

[34] Semah's letter in *Maariv*, January 26, 1989.

[35] According to Sami Michael (*Ba-Maḥane*, March 22, 1989, p. 23).

[36] Moreh 1973, p. 111; Moreh and Hakak 1981, p. 89.

[37] According to Shalom Darwīsh, who composed the telegram (Yehuda 1980, pp. 82–5).

[38] Conversations with Semah, May 2, and June 6 and 14, 1989.

whatsoever.[39] His worldview found expression not only in his participation on the editorial board of the Communist journal *al-Ittiḥād*, but in his literary work as well. The latter, who published under the pen name "Samīr Mārid," emphasized social and national injustice, supported the battle against the bourgeoisie, and praised Communism.[40] These ideas were also expressed in his Hebrew works, such as his novels *Ḥasūt* (*Shelter*) (1977) and *Ḥofen shel 'Arafel* (*A Handful of Fog*) (1979). Shimon Ballas' case is similar. He joined the Communist Party as an Iraqi patriot while still a student, and his immigration to Israel was "of necessity, not ideology," as he was never and still is not a Zionist.[41] He followed conditions in Israel by reading the European and American press while serving as an aide to the Iraqi-Jewish senator Ezra Ben Menaḥem Daniel (1874–1952). In Israel, he joined the party and published in its journals in Arabic under the pen name "Adīb al-Qaṣṣ."[42]

In contrast to the establishment writers, these writers and poets devoted all their literary energies to intellectual struggle, focusing their attention on three central concerns: the manner in which new immigrants were absorbed; the inequality between the Oriental Jews and the Ashkenazi residents; and the fate of the Arab minority. The manner in which new immigrants were absorbed was a searing insult to these writers. Even the passage of time would not let them forget how a new culture and values were imposed on them while their pasts were derided,[43] and in this context their party activity was a means to an end—a change in this condition. Later, this sense of insult was even expressed by those who did not hold leftist views, as we find with the writer Eli 'Amīr (b. 1937), the author of *Tarnegol Kapparot* (*Scapegoat*) (1983). 'Amir focuses this sense in the dwarfing of the father figure in the eyes of his children, which "brings you to want revenge."[44] Social protest, touching on relations within Jewish society, comes to more prominent expression in the Hebrew works of these writers of a later period, and especially in the novel.[45]

39 *Ba-Maḥane*, March 22, 1989, p. 23. See also *Moznaim*, July–August 1986, p. 16. On the way of life in the underground in Iraq, see his novel *Ḥofen shel 'Arafel* (1979).

40 See, for example, his story "Muḥarrir Aūrūba" ("The Liberator of Europe") in *al-Ittiḥād*, monthly supplement, vol. 9, no. 1 (49), pp. 17–27 (Cf. Moreh 1981, pp. 222–3). See also his story "Fī Ziḥām al-Madīna" ("In the Tumult of the City") (*al-Jadīd*, November 1955, pp. 26–9), whose title is the same as that of Anwar Shā'ul's collection of short stories published in Baghdad in the same year.

41 *Maariv*, April 25, 1989, p. B9.

42 Conversation with Ballas, June 14, 1989. His novel *Ḥeder Na'ūl* (*A Locked Room*) (Ballas 1980) describes the way of life of members of the Communist press in Israel.

43 See Ballas' words in *Maariv*, April 25, 1989, p. B9.

44 *Haaretz*, February 8, 1985, p. 16; *Maariv*, April 25, 1989, p. B9.

45 See, for example, Moreh and Hakak 1981, pp. 116–23; Hakak 1981, pp. 111–18.

By formulating their literary protest on the national question in Arabic, the Communist writers assisted their Arab colleagues, in whose work this issue was central. These Jewish writers attempted to imply: let us not do to the Palestinians, especially as they are a minority in our midst, what the Muslims did to the Jewish minority in the land of the Tigris and Euphrates; let us stand alongside them as did those Arabs who stood beside us in our most difficult hours in Iraq.[46] The literary activity of two young writers of the same age, Sasson Somekh and David Semah, represents this facet of anti-establishment writing in the 1950s. Somekh immigrated to Israel in 1951 after graduating from the Shammāsh School without knowing Hebrew at all.[47] He had already published in Iraq, and in Israel he continued to do so in Communist and other journals, such as the monthly *al-Fajr* of Mapam. He even had a cultural column, called "Tel Aviv Letter," in *al-Jadīd*. At the same time, he translated poetry, mastered Hebrew, and was one of the first to reconcile himself to the advantage of writing in Hebrew. Semah also immigrated to Israel in 1951. He did so after completing his studies at the Alliance School in Baghdad without knowing Hebrew. He began publishing in Arabic in the Communist press, and in 1959 his first volume of poetry appeared, which aroused great interest in leftist Arabic literary circles in Israel.[48] While still in their twenties, the two poets responded to *al-Jadīd*'s call to encourage local Arabic literature by founding the "Club of the Friends of Arabic Literature in Israel," which later became the "Hebrew-Arabic Literary Club."[49] This club, whose activity encompassed the transit and immigrant camps as well, set itself the goal of becoming a "bridge between Hebrew and Arabic literatures" while working for mutual understanding "despite the borders of bloodletting."[50] Not without hesitation regarding the fundamental dilemmas of literary language and target audience,[51] the club helped to bring the Arabic reading public in Israel news of what was happening in Arabic, Hebrew, and world literature, as well as specific topics from Arab history.[52] The work of

46 See even in the 1980s a letter of a Jewish reader titled "A Call to My Jewish Brothers of Iraqi Origin" (*al-Ittiḥād*, June 2, 1986, p. 5).

47 *Moznaim*, October–November 1983, p. 49; *Iton 77*, January–February 1988, p. 32.

48 Conversations with Semah, May 2, and June 6 and 14, 1989. See also *al-Jadīd*, February 1959, p. 20; March 1959, pp. 45, 55.

49 See *al-Jadīd*, March 1954, pp. 54–5. On the club's activities, see *al-Jadīd*, January 1956, p. 54; February 1956, p. 16.

50 *Al-Jadīd*, November 1954, p. 45. Cf. Moreh 1958, p. 31; *al-Jadīd*, February 1956, p. 16. See also Somekh's words in *al-Anbā'* (weekly supplement), December 10, 1982, p. 4.

51 See, for example, *al-Jadīd*, November 1954, pp. 45–6, and also Somekh's words in *Iton 77*, January–February 1988, p. 32, as well as Sami Michael in *Yediot Aḥronoth*, February 15, 1985, p. 20; *Iton 77*, July–August 1985, p. 50.

52 See, for example, in *al-Jadīd*: Semah's articles in April 1956, pp. 6–10; January 1959, pp. 22–7; November 1959, pp. 27–32, as well as Ballas' surveys in January 1956, pp. 16–18;

Somekh, Semah, and their colleagues was characterized by protest against the Jewish establishment, and for equal rights and social justice. This protest also found expression in solidarity gatherings.[53] The impulse behind their literary activism was not party politics, but rather, in Somekh's words, "a spontaneous inclination toward the brotherhood of peoples," which in turn characterized the activity of the Communist Party, "the only party shared by both Arabs and Jews."[54] Their work was a sensitive seismic register of Arab minority sentiment in Israel, and occasionally an expression of its collective conscience in the shadow of the military administration's restrictions and political censorship. Thus, for instance, David Semah's poem "Sawfa Ya'ūdu" ("He Shall Return") was one of the first poems to be written about the massacre of scores of innocent men and women at Kafr Qāsim on October 29, 1956.[55] As with a famous Hebrew poem by Saul Tchernichovski (1875–1943), "The Rabbi's Daughter and Her Mother,"[56] the poet chose to represent the tragic events in the form of a dialogue between a mother and daughter on the father who was killed. The girl does not understand why her father has not returned:

لقد كدت أنساه! ما لونه
أتلمع من لهفة عينه؟
أراحِ يحلّق فوقِ الغيوم
ويبحث عن ساطعات النّجوم
لينظم عقدا يطوّق جيدي
ويهديه لي يوم عيدي!

I have nearly forgotten him! What is the color of his face?
Are his eyes sparkling with longing?

March 1956, pp. 23–6; translation of poetry by Semah in February 1956, p. 14; Sami Michael's article in December 1955, pp. 35–9.

53 Such as, for example, Semah's participation in the solidarity gathering with the Algerian people (*al-Jadīd*, April 1958, pp. 51–5). The poems he recited there are included in his collection (Semah 1959, pp. 13–16, 49–50).

54 *Iton 77*, January–February 1988, p. 33; and conversations with Semah, May 2, and June 6 and 14, 1989.

55 It was completed, according to Semah, approximately two weeks after the massacre. The poem was published for the first time in *al-Ittiḥād*, December 31, 1956, and was included later with slight revisions in Semah's collection (pp. 41–5). In January 1957, *al-Jadīd* published literary reactions to the massacre, among them a poem by the Palestinian poet Tawfiq Zayyād (1932–1994), which he claimed to have been written on November 3, 1956 (Yinnon 1981, p. 238). On Zayyād as a Communist and national leader, see Sorek 2020. On Palestinian responses to the massacre and its aftermath, see Robinson 2003, pp. 393–416. On collective memory and the commemoration of the massacre among Palestinians in Israel, see Sorek 2015, pp. 41–65.

56 Tchernichovski 1950, pp. 736–7. Semah was then very fond of his poetry much more than he was of Hayyim Nahman Bialik's (1873–1934) (conversations with Semah, May 2, and June 6 and 14, 1989).

Has he gone to fly above the clouds,
Seeking sparkling stars,
To string around my neck like a necklace of pearls
A birthday gift?

The mother calms the daughter with the promise of the father's return, rose bouquet in hand, forever. Not only shall he return, but also with a bit of money to redeem the wretched family. The poet ties the national woe of the Arab minority to its social and economic woes, as the death of the family patriarch, caused only by his being Arab, has brought the family to the threshold of hunger and caused a deterioration in the condition of the ailing daughter. Slowly, the certainty of the father's return, which the mother displays to her daughter, is undermined. It becomes clear that he was killed after leaving for work without a permit, an allusion to the restrictions endured by the Palestinian population in Israel of the 1950s. The daughter herself, who becomes aware of the circumstances of his death from the whispering of the neighbors' children, is stunned by the knowledge that her father "will never return." To calm her, the mother confronts her with the certainty of future redemption, and a vision of sweeping revolution:

تقرّب يوم الصّراع
فقد هبّت العاصفة
على الكون حانقة جارفة
تطوّح بالظّلم والظّالمين
وبالسّارقين طعام الجياع
وبالسّجن تذهب والسّاجن
وبالسّالبين حليب الرّضاع
وبالسّافكين الدّماء
لتنقذ أطماعهم من ضياع
فشدّوا القوى أيّها الكادحون
فليس لكم ما تخسرون

The day of the final struggle is near
The storm already blows
Over the world, raging and sweeping
Striking oppression and oppressors
Those who steal the bread of the hungry
The prison and the prisoners
Those who steal milk from babies
Those who spill blood
To save their lust from oblivion
Gather courage! O you are the workers
You have nothing to lose.

The revolution seen by the mother in her vision will bring a total change of the existing order, and it is described in standard Communist terminology: the masses, the workers, the red flag, the struggle against social oppression, the crushing of oppressors and shedders of blood, and the call to the proletariat, who "have nothing to lose," to storm the old regime. The allusion is to the concluding words of Karl Marx and Friedrich Engels' *Communist Manifesto*: "The proletariat has nothing to lose but its chains."[57] A new era will follow the removal of oppression and injustice:

وإذ ذاك سوف يعود
أب وصديق ودود
وحتّى أبوك، عساه يعود
وفي كفّه باقة من ورود
تضمّخ أنفاسنا بالعطور

And then they will return again,
Father and beloved friend
Even your father might return
A bouquet of roses in his hand
To anoint our souls with fragrance.

The worldview presented in this poem is based on a clear dualism between the oppressive rulers and the oppressed masses, the belief that social justice is a necessary condition for peace among peoples, and the hope for a better tomorrow. This is also expressed in the poem that Semah dedicated to the Palestinian Communist poet Tawfīq Zayyād (1932–1994), which is addressed to "my brother, Tawfīq":[58]

لنـــا وطــن لشعبينـــا سمـاه   وأرضه والنّسائم والزّهور
إذا حصدوا جماجم في ثراه   فإنّ حصـــادنا أمـل ونـور

We have a homeland—its skies
  And earth and winds and flowers belong to both our peoples,
If they reap skulls in its dust,[59]
  Then our harvest is hope and light.

57 Somekh concluded one of his poems in memory of the October Revolution with similar words (*al-Jadīd*, November 1959, pp. 48–9).

58 Semah recited this poem in the festival of poetry held in Acre on July 11, 1958, when Zayyād was in prison. It was later published in *al-Jadīd*, July 1958, pp. 39–40, and portions of it were incorporated into Semah's above-mentioned collection (pp. 55–7).

59 An allusion to Zayyād's poem "The Harvest of Skulls," which was written on the massacre at Kafr Qāsim (*al-Jadīd*, January 1957, pp. 25–30).

Semah's poem on the massacre at Kafr Qāsim, no lesser in poetic and tragic affect than those written by the best Palestinian poets,[60] represents one facet of the literary activism of the leftist Jewish writers: an immediate reaction of protest, chiefly in poetry, to what struck them as injustice toward the Arab-Palestinian minority. Another facet of their work is expressed in the strong longing for a utopia of social justice and peace among peoples, as we find in a poem that Semah dedicated to Somekh and the latter's response.[61] The editorial board of *al-Jadīd* introduced the two poems with the following words:

> حبّ الحياة في ظلّ السّلام أثار ويثير أرقّ العواطف وأعذب الأماني. وقد أنطق هذا الحبّ شاعرين فتساجلا، ورأى أحدهما نشيد السّلام "في القلب الوديع" ورآه الثاني في "قلوب لظّها الألم المريع" ولكنّهما اجتمعا في تخليد حبّهما للسّلام وللعاملين في سبيله.

> The love for life in the shadow of peace has inspired, and continues to inspire, the most tender feelings and the sweetest hopes. This love has moved two poets to speak in the form of poetic debate. One of them saw the poem of peace "in a tranquil heart," while the other saw it in "hearts seared by awful pain." But they both join forces in immortalizing their love for peace and for those who labor toward it.

Semah's poem, "Laḥn al-Salām" ("Song of Peace"), while written in the classical *kāmil* meter, conceals within it modernist principles of form, such as varying line length, changing and functional rhyme, and enjambment. The poem not only presents a dualism on the realistic level of good and bad, but also a clear distinction, on the literary level, between the poetry of those bearing grudges and animus, and true poetry. According to Semah, Somekh writes the latter:

أمّا نشيدك، فهو في القلب الوديع
يشدو به ثغر الرّبيع
هو في النّفوس الصّابيات إلى الأمان
في الأعين المتطلّعات إلى الضّياء
وإلى المحبّة والإخاء.

But your poem dwells in a tranquil heart,
Sung by the lips of spring.
It is in every soul which longs for tranquility
And in the eyes aching for light,
Love and brotherhood.

60 Cf. for example, the poems of the Palestinian poet Maḥmūd Darwīsh (1941–2008) on this event (Darwīsh 1988, pp. 207–20).

61 The two poems were published in *al-Jadīd*, March 1954, pp. 18–19. They were reprinted with some changes in Semah 1959, pp. 83–8.

Unlike poetry that successfully camouflages itself, whose antagonism is quickly revealed and then withers and melts away, Somekh's poetry has chosen to dwell in the tranquil heart, and it belongs to all seekers of peace, love, and brotherhood. The poet is convinced that this poem will overcome all of time's reversals:

سيذوب في أعماقه، وقع السّياط على الظّهور
وقع السّياط على ظهور الكادحين
ورنين أقداح الطّغاة الظّالمين
لمّا تمادوا في الغرور
ستذوب فيه أنّة القتلى الّذين
دفعوا إلى الموت اللّعين.

In its depths shall fade
The ring of lashes on the backs of nations
On the backs of the workers
And the trill of the arrows of oppressors
Whose pride was vaunted.
In it the sigh of the slaughtered shall yet fade,
Those who were driven to the accursed death.

The strength of this poetry is concealed in its eternal and hope-inspiring human values:

لحن رأيت به عروقْ!
فإذا جرت فيه الدّماء
وجرت دموع الأبرياء
منحته أسرار البقاء.
لحن تضجّ به القلوب المتعبة
والأنفس الملتهبة
عذب، تدفّق في حليب المرضعات
الصّارخات من الألم
هو خالد في كلّ فم
نشوان لا يدري الخفوت
هو لا يموت.

This is a poem in which I saw veins!
And when its blood flows
And the tears of the innocent
It finds the secret of eternity.
This is a poem in which throb the hearts of the weary
And burning souls.
It is sweet, poured in the milk of nursing mothers
Shrieking in pain.
This poem is immortal, sung by every mouth,
It is drunk and knows not dumbness,
It transcends death.

Not only do blood and tears not destroy this poetry, which flows in mothers' milk, but they strengthen it until it realizes its principles.

Sasson Somekh responded with a poem called "Tilka al-Qulūb" ("These Hearts"), which is written in the same meter as Semah's poem. Like Semah's poem, it incorporates modernist elements of "free verse," such as varied line length, functional rhyme, and enjambment. It uses as its motto Semah's lines "but your poem dwells in the tranquil heart / sung by the lips of spring." However, Somekh rejects the idea that his poem dwells in a tranquil heart:

لا! ليس في القلب الوديع!
لا ما هناك!
يشدو بأنغام السّلام
إعصار عنف واضطرام
إعصار حقد وانتقام
إعصار حبّ لا ينام!
بل في قلوب لظّها الألم المريع
بل في عيون لاهبات.

No! [my poem] does not dwell in a tranquil heart!
Not there!
The poem of peace is sung
By a violent, burning storm
A resentful, vengeful storm
A storm of sleepless love.
My poem is sung by hearts seared by pain,
In burning eyes.

How is it possible to know tranquility, when everywhere one sees just hunger, oppression, and misery?

تلك القلوب:
أوتستطيع إلى الوداعة من سبيل؟
وهي الّتي في كلّ يوم تجتني بؤسا جديد
أوتستطيع إلى الوداعة من سبيل
أمّ سقت بدموعها اللّيل الطّويل؟
تبكي المصير
والطّفل يبكي الجوع
والقطّ الصّغير
لحس الصّحون الفارغات.

These hearts:
Can they reach tranquility?
While every day they pluck new miseries
Can a mother reach tranquility
When she waters the long night with her tears?
Weeping over Fate

And the child wails in hunger,
And a small cat
Licks empty plates.

The poet describes the gloom of the present, but points also to the hope for salvation: in the shadow of the tent smolders a spark. The cold winds try to smother it, but the spark ignites into a giant flame:

لكنّما، قبس يلوح، كما يلوح
في ذلك المصباح
تبغي خنقه هوج الرّياح
عبثا! فسوف يشبّ نارا
تحرق البؤس الثّقيل
وتزيح أكداس الظّلام
ولدي هو النّور الكبير!
ولدي سيبني الغد، لا للزّمرة المتعتعين
لا للطّغاة
بل للبناة
للكادحين!

But a live coal pops up, it appears
In that lamp
The violent winds wish to extinguish it
In vain! It will yet burn like fire
Which will burn this awful wretchedness
And remove the darkness.
My child is the great light!
My child, yet to build the morrow, not for those who stammer,
Not for the oppressors,
But for the builders,
For the workers!

As is customary in Arabic Communist literature, the poet believes that the new generation will build the morrow, which stands in total contrast to the gloom of the present world:

لا! ليس في القلب الوديع!
بل في قلوب مثقلات بالمحبّة والإخاء
لا تستطيع سوى الشّقاء
في عالم ما زال للأشرار
في أرجائه عبث كبير
ما دامت الأبطال فيه مشرّدين وفي السّجون
ما دام يعلو للمشانق كلّ داع للسّلام
ما دامت الحشرات والأمراض تذرى
كي تبيد الآمنين
ما دام زنج يشنقون

ما دام عرب من قراهم يطردون
ما دام في الدّنيا عبيد
لم يروا غير التّراب
لا ليس في القلب الوديع!

No! [My poem] does not dwell in a tranquil heart!
But in hearts loaded with love and brotherhood
Their fate is only misery
In a world in which evil men still
Act recklessly and abusively
As long as its heroes are refugees and in prisons
And those who talk of peace go to the gallows
As long as the spread of insects and disease
Destroys those who are tranquil[62]
As long as blacks go to the gallows
As long as Arabs are banished from their villages
As long as there are still slaves in the world
Who see nothing but dust!
No! [My poem] does not dwell in a tranquil heart!

The above lines convey a worldview whose universality rejects the narrow confines of nationalism and preaches equality of rights for all peoples, and justice and equality in all human societies. The two poems, on the surface contradictory, actually complement one another. Semah's poem was written out of a naïve pacifism, while his friend tries to rouse him from his innocence. Semah confesses that his intellectual world was still unformed at that time, while Somekh, the active figure among the Communist Jewish writers of the 1950s, was ideologically mature.[63] The two poems paint reality in very gloomy colors indeed, in contrast to the utopian future of the redeemed world of Communist teaching, in which social justice will be realized for all. "We were like those who dream,"[64] Somekh says years later, but there is no doubt that their faith was strong in their ability to change reality, as expressed also in another poem by a Jewish poet, who signed it only with the letter "N":

قف يا أخي! لا تشكُ ظلما ثمّ تسكت كالبهائـــم
ناضل فلا يرجى التّخلّص والتّحرّر من مظالم
إن سارت الدّنيـــا وأنت بعقر دارك بتّ نائـــم [...]

62 This and the preceding line were omitted in the later version of the poem.

63 Conversation with Ballas (June 14, 1989); conversations with Semah, May 2, and June 6 and 14, 1989. See, for example, his poem in memory of the October Revolution in *al-Jadīd*, November 1955, pp. 48–9.

64 In his letter to me of April 17, 1989. Semah and Ballas confirmed this in my conversations with them mentioned above.

إن القلــــوب إذا تآلفــت شوقها للعيــش حــرّا
لا بدّ إلاّ أن تحقّق من ليـــــالي الظّلــم فجــرا

Stand, my brother! Rather than sleep on corruption and remaining silent like a beast.
Struggle! It is impossible to be free from injustice,
If the world goes on its way while you sleep at home ...
If the hearts strive together for freedom,
They will undoubtedly bring the dawn beyond the nights of oppression.[65]

4. THE SHIFT TO HEBREW

Unlike local Palestinian poets and writers,[66] most of the Arab-Jewish writers who immigrated to Israel became familiar with Hebrew literature without relinquishing their attachment to Arabic culture.[67] Sooner or later, they were confronted with the stark choice of which language they should write and communicate in, that is, whether to adapt to their new cultural surroundings and make the required and conscious shift in their aesthetic preference in the hope of finding a new audience, or whether to continue to write in Arabic, their beloved mother tongue. Hebrew literature by Arab-Jewish writers was known before this: for example, there was the work of Sulaymān Menaḥem Mānī (1850–1924), who even published a story on Sephardic life in Palestine.[68] Still, Hebrew writing by Arabized Jews adopting the new poetics of Hebrew literature emerged only in Israel. In the 1950s, for example, Nīr Shohet (1928–2011)[69] was already publishing short stories in Hebrew; in 1957, Zakkay Binyamin Aharon (1927–2021) published *El Ḥofo shel Ra'ayon* (*To the Edge of an Idea*), a collection of poems.[70] Shelomo Zamīr (1929–2017)[71] published *Ha-Kol mi-Ba'ad la-'Anaf* (*The Voice through the Branch*) (1960), which earned him the Shlonsky Prize along with Amir

[65] *Al-Jadīd*, July 1958, p. 55.
[66] On the issue of Palestinian writers' attitudes toward Hebrew literature, see Snir 1990, pp. 257–65; Snir 2001, pp. 197–224.
[67] Moreh and Hakak 1981, pp. 97–106, 112–15, 116–24. On the interactions between Hebrew culture and Arabic literature and the involvement of Iraqi-Jewish writers, see Snir 1998, pp. 177–210.
[68] *Ha-Tsvi* I (1885), pp. 31–4; Yardeni 1967, pp. 45–53. Most Hebrew literature written in Iraq focused on religious matters (as did liturgical poetry). The beginnings of Hebrew writing in Iraq were mainly in the field of translation (see, e.g., Shā'ul 1980, pp. 92–4). On the emergence of modern Hebrew literature in Iraq from 1735 to 1950, see Hakak 2003.
[69] On Nīr Shohet, see Ben-Yaacob 1980, pp. 398–400; Bezalel 1982, I, p. 309; Moreh and 'Abbāsī 1987, pp. 127–9.
[70] On Zakkay Binyamin Aharon, see Ben-Yaacob 1980, pp. 430–2; Bezalel 1982, I, p. 281; Moreh and 'Abbāsī 1987, pp. 239–40; Snir 2005a, pp. 276–85.
[71] On Shelomo Zamīr, see Snir 2005a, p. 249.

Gilboa (1917–1984) and Abba Kovner (1918–1987). In 1964, Shimon Ballas (1930–2019) published *Ha-Ma'abara* (*The Immigrant Transit Camp*), the first Hebrew novel to be written by an Iraqi émigré.[72]

Most of the immigrating Arab-Jewish writers who succeeded in adapting to writing in Hebrew adopted the Zionist narrative in their literary work, with the prominent among them being the aforementioned Sami Michael (b. 1926).[73] In the early 1950s, when he was still publishing only in Arabic, Michael tried his hand at Hebrew—he started to write a novel that took place in a *ma'abara*, that is, an immigrant transit camp. In 1954, he published a chapter of the novel, titled "Ḥarīq" ("Fire"), but only in Arabic translation.[74] He was unable to find a publisher for the Hebrew novel but continued to write and publish in Arabic—it seems that he was one of the first Arab-Jewish writers to understand the delicate position of the Arab-Jewish authors in a Hebrew-speaking society against the background of two clashing national narratives. This is why I consider one of the stories he published in the 1950s, "al-Fannān wa-l-Falāfil" ("The Artist and the Falafel"),[75] as one of the most significant and insightful literary contributions by any Arab-Jewish writer in the last stage of Arabic literature written by Jews before its total demise. The story is about a hungry deaf-mute child who begs passersby for money by way of drawing American cowboys on the sidewalks of Haifa streets. This boy-artist "did not blame 'bad luck' as most mature people do when they stumble on hard times, but rather he would try to find the cause that deprived him." The story illustrates the complicated picture of the new Arab-Jewish experience in Israel after its establishment, where the local society was torn between Jews and Palestinians, between Ashkenazim and Mizrahim, and between rich and poor, while the author's panoramic view of Israeli society does not ignore other sections of society. For example, Michael, as an Arab-Jewish author, did not ignore the misery of the Holocaust's survivors—one of the characters in the story is a survivor who sells thermometers and who can barely function because of his uncontrollable shivering; he is like a ghost for he does not engage with others around him and is given very little attention

[72] Ballas 1964.

[73] For an earlier discussion of the shift to Hebrew among Arab-Jewish writers, see Snir 2021b, pp. 162–214.

[74] *Al-Jadīd*, December 1954, pp. 39–43. On this chapter, see Snir 2005a, pp. 313–18. Later Michael revealed that he had completed this Hebrew novel, titling it *Ge'ūt ha-Naḥal* (*The Rise of the Stream*), and that he had tried to publish it with Am Oved but had been rejected (*Haaretz* [Books – Special Issue], October 17, 2005).

[75] The story was first published in *al-Jadīd*, December 1955, pp. 30–6. For an English translation, see Snir 2019, pp. 232–7. For an earlier English translation, see Snir 2015b, pp. 235–40. For a Hebrew translation, see Snir 2005a, pp. 544–8. For an analysis of the story, see Snir 2005a, pp. 381–2.

by other people. Also, the author chose as the stage of his story the city of Haifa in northern Israel, where he had been living since his emigration from Iraq, a city that still boasts a mixed population of various religions—Jews, Muslims, Christians, Druzes, Bahais, and others—despite the collapse of the urban life that the city had developed in Mandate Palestine following Israel's War of Independence in 1948.

The starving boy-artist is wandering the streets of Haifa in order to display his artistic creativity. He paints on the asphalt images of the unarmed American cowboy—a romantic, heroic symbol, independent and strong, that seems to fly above the ground. His paintings are surrealistic, just as the term "artist" that is used to describe him is unrealistic. Separating his cowboy from the mundane, the boy-artist makes it his own special possession that the curious stares of the crowd cannot harm. He is very hungry, but at the same time finds it difficult to believe that he cannot assign responsibility for his miserable situation. He looks for some sort of causation, an explanation for his hunger, but he seems to discover that there is no true explanation to be found. The core of the story is that the crowd enjoys seeing this deaf-mute boy wrapped in rags in the process of his artistic creation. While casting his art under their feet, a few people would say in a knowing tone: "He's an orphan and his aunt is disabled." In spite of this, no one finds even some measure or other of gallantry in the child's art, the gallantry of a person bent over the sidewalk for the sake of his aunt. Furthermore, they throw coins on the ground not out of compassion for the disabled aunt and not out of compassion for the hungry child, and even not out of a desire to reward the artist for his art, but as recompense to the *clown* who provided them with entertainment on one of their winter evenings. The boy-artist is aware that the crowd sees him as being akin to a clown, and the narrator takes care to provide the readers with a great deal of sympathy for him, turning their attention to the gap between society and the individual. Nature is also portrayed as sympathetic with the boy and, at the same time, antagonistic to the people around him as illustrated by a strong gust of cruel wind that is received "with great displeasure, for it took the street away from them." Because of the reality of destitution, food must come before artistry or self-expression, and this is undoubtedly why the boy is willing to put up with being on display to passersby as little more than a charming freak show: "The crowd enjoys seeing this ragamuffin deaf-mute creating art under their feet."

As Jean-Paul Sartre (1905–1980) indicated in his one-act play *Huis Clos* (*No Exit*) (1944), "hell is other people"—the "Other," that by which we define ourselves and that which is not ourselves, is, or can be, a source of our distress. We construct a hell for ourselves, Sartre says, if we refuse to take responsibility for our own actions, leaving us at the mercy of others.

Constantly worried about where the next meal is coming from and obsessed with the smell of falafel before him, the creativity of the boy-artist is contrasted to his own survival. He goes "wild with rage" because he cannot eat his wares, the drawings, like the boy who sells chocolate or the woman selling falafel, who is presented by the author in a sensual way ("the face of the woman with the very red fingernails"), thus mixing food preparation and sexual desire. On the other hand, the mother and daughter who are selling flowers, like the Holocaust survivor, are sad and neglected and in danger of being toppled ("He saw someone walk backward and almost fall on the vessel with the flowers"). In this story that examines what is traditionally seen as mundane, Michael's marked pessimism is mixed with an insight that although the world is often arbitrary and unkind, and although we cannot always find reasons for what happens to us, we cannot accept this reality. Yet the kindness of others is one way in which we can overcome our situation, and Michael ruminates on why people are not generous toward those less fortunate than them, describing the cynical people who throw coins to the artist because they view him as a clown designed for their entertainment. While Michael is certainly condemning the reductionist viewpoint that turns human beings into tools for individuals' satisfaction, his message is far more complicated than that: the movie-goers' feet trampling the horse and rider, that is, the indifference of the middle class, do not upset the artist. Art and its inspiration can overcome physical harm to the art itself, and its ultimate value is a way for the artist to express himself rather than as a means for getting money. The kindness of strangers and the solidarity among the oppressed and marginalized are what is really important, and this can be seen when the artist tries to help the mother and daughter who are selling flowers. Although the artist has no "friends" on the street, they all seem to have a kind of symbiotic and supportive relationship, and this insight would serve Michael's next literary contributions in Hebrew, as we will see below.

In the late 1950s, after six years of devoted adherence to Communism, Michael ceased publishing in Arabic. At about the same time, he left the Communist Party—he could no longer face, he says, the constant self-justification involved in his Communist activities. It was the first step in a long process of adapting himself to mainstream Israeli society. Then came the issue of language: as a Jew writing in Arabic, he was confronted with the need for self-justification. About his first years in Israel, he says, "I continued to read the world's literature in English, spoke a broken Hebrew on the street, and bemoaned my fate, silently, in Arabic." After he had consolidated his position as a writer of the short story in Arabic, the question was whether he should adapt to the new cultural surroundings and make the required shift in his aesthetic "preference" in the hope of finding a new audience, or to continue writing in Arabic in a country where Arabic was now the language of the enemy. In the process of adopting the Hebrew language, he says, the fluency of his Arabic writing was impaired: "I activated a forgetting mechanism."[76]

Michael entered a period of silence during which he joined the Israel Hydrological Service in the Ministry of Agriculture, where he worked for twenty-five years surveying water sources located mainly on the Syrian border. He also studied Arabic literature and psychology at the University of Haifa. Ending his literary silence, his first published novel was a Hebrew one, *Shavīm ve-Shavīm Yoter* (*Equal and More Equal*) (1974).[77] The novel, whose nucleus was the aforementioned chapter titled "Ḥarīq" ("Fire") written in the 1950s, exposed the humiliating attitude of the authorities to immigrants from Arab countries. It raised a storm of protests, bringing to the fore the ethnic question and generating public controversy through its representation of the oppression of Oriental immigrants. It brought to Hebrew literature the motif of the DDT spray with which these immigrants were disinfected, a motif immediately adopted as a symbol of the humiliation of the immigrants in Israeli society.[78] Mainstream literary critics, however, referred to the novel, as to other Hebrew works by writers from Arab countries, as inferior protest literature with no real literary value.

In his subsequent novels, Michael continued to deal with the margins of Israeli society. In *Ḥasūt* (*Refuge*) (1977),[79] he deals with Jewish–Christian–Muslim relationships against the background of the 1973 Arab–Israeli War (also known as the Yom Kippur War, hereafter the 1973 War).[80] The plot takes place in Haifa and in Jenīn in the West Bank, and all the major figures are members of the Israeli Communist Party. *Ḥofen shel 'Arafel* (*A Handful of Fog*) (1979)[81] is about the pluralistic Iraqi society of the 1940s prior to the mass emigration of the Jews. *Ḥatsotsra ba-Wadī* (*A Trumpet in the Wadi*) (1987)[82] depicts relationships between Jews and Arabs in Haifa in light of the Lebanon War of the 1980s. The novel was adapted for the stage at the Haifa Municipal Theater, and a film based upon the novel won first prize at the Haifa Festival.

76 See www.haaretz.com, July 30, 2006. On this period in Michael's life, see Snir 2005a, pp. 319–20.
77 Michael 1974.
78 Cf. Snir 2005a, p. 349. See also May 2018, pp. 251–5.
79 Michael 1977.
80 See Shaked 1979, pp. 138–49; Shamir-Tulipman 2004, pp. 56–109.
81 Michael 1979.
82 Michael 1987. An Arabic version of one chapter from the novel, translated by 'Āyida Tūmā (b. 1964), was published before its publication in Hebrew (*al-Sharq*, March 1987, pp. 79–87).

Michael wrote for children and youth as well, and among his books targeted at this audience are *Sūfa Bein ha-Dekalīm* (*Storm among the Palms*) (1975),[83] *Paḥonīm ve-Ḥalomot* (*Tin Shacks and Dreams*) (1997),[84] *Ahava Bein ha-Dekalīm* (*Love among the Palms*) (1990),[85] and *Shedīm Ḥumīm* (*Brown Devils*) (1993).[86] His writing for children was inspired by the contradictions he experienced when it came to child–adult relationships: while in Iraq, the child's opinions were ignored, but the child in Israel is the all-important center of the family. Much more than in his writings for adults, in his books for children Michael showed a strong tendency to adapt himself to mainstream Israeli society. Some of Michael's works were adapted to the theater, and he also wrote original plays, among them *Shedīm ba-Martef* (*Demons in the Basement*) (1983) and *Te'omīm* (*Twins*) (1988), both of which were performed at the Haifa Municipal Theater.[87] Apart from his original writings, Michael translated into Hebrew the Cairene trilogy of the Egyptian Nobel laureate Najīb Maḥfūẓ (1911–2006).

It was, however, the publication of his best-selling novel *Victoria* (*Victoria* [the name of the heroine]) (1993),[88] more than any other of his works, that established Michael as a well-known writer. The novel soared to the top of the Israeli best-seller list, selling more than 100,000 copies; for fifty weeks, it stayed at the top of the list of the newspaper *Haaretz*'s weekly books supplement. It was translated into many languages, including English, Dutch, German, Greek, Arabic, and French. Named for its female heroine who, as her name suggests, succeeds in gaining a victory over the challenges of her life, the novel describes the life of the Iraqi Jews before and after their emigration. It was argued that the accent with which Michael wrote is that of the margins, a minority accent, even as he was entering the mainstream.[89] Because the novel challenged traditional values of the Jewish family in Iraq, and because it was permeated by a sensual atmosphere steeped in sexual encounters, including episodes of incest and pedophilia, it raised a great deal of protest. It especially raised the ire of Iraqi-Jewish intellectuals, who accused the author of serving the interests of the Ashkenazi establishment. They especially protested against descriptions giving a picture of Jewish life in Iraq in which, for example, on mattresses spread out on the roofs "recalcitrant women were raped night after night, despite their curses," and "tigresses

[83] Michael 1975.
[84] Michael 1997.
[85] Michael 1990.
[86] Michael 1993.
[87] On these plays, see Urian 2001, p. 30; Urian 2004, pp. 185–8.
[88] Michael 1993a.
[89] Oren 1995, pp. 146–7.

won tigers; together they shook the roof and its tens of inhabitants" and all that when others heard everything and saw much.[90] Some mainstream critics described, however, the novel as exotic, fantastic, and sensational with a plot flavored with elements of *A Thousand and One Nights*, and an attempt was even made to classify it with Gustave Flaubert's (1821–1880) *Madame Bovary* (1856) and Leo Tolstoy's (1828–1910) *Anna Karenina* (1877).

Here, some explanation is needed in order to clarify the attitude of some mainstream critics toward literary works, such as *Victoria*, especially when exaggerated praises are showered on them. In various publications, I have referred to such praises attributed to Palestinian and Mizrahi authors in Israeli-Jewish society as politically correct gestures, in fact, nothing more than a way out of the aforementioned Israeli-Jewish-Ashkenazi mainstream's cognitive dissonance, and as a tool to preserve the cozy reassurance of the canonical center's liberal and tolerant attitude toward the culture of the margins.[91] This is doubly evident in the setting of the Western orientation of Israeli culture and its repugnance toward Arabic and Mizrahi culture, although the cultural Hebrew establishment is not able publicly to express this, owing to its general views concerning the need for a proper liberal and pluralistic attitude toward the cultures of others. To resolve this cognitive dissonance, the establishment assigns to apparent "chosen" representatives of the Palestinian and Mizrahi voices "seats" in the local cultural arena. A survey of Israeli media in general and cultural magazines, printed and electronic, in particular would show that the interest in Arabic and Mizrahi literature and culture is generally not a truly aesthetic tendency but a politically correct enterprise. When the Israeli media is in need of presenting the view of the "Other," it usually turns to the same writers and intellectuals, who seem to be on call playing the role of decorative tokens in Israeli culture. Whenever an academic, cultural, social, or political activity requires an "authentic Oriental speaker," their names emerge and they are "forever 'burdened' with the glorious weight of that representation."[92] Also, Ha-Markkaz le-Shilūv Moreshet Yahadūt Sepharad ve-ha-Mizraḥ (The Center for the Integration of the Heritage of the Oriental and Sephardi Jewry), which was established in 1977 in the Ministry of Education, has been frequently cited

[90] On *Victoria*, see Snir 2005a, pp. 318–22.

[91] On such cognitive dissonance, see Snir 2001, pp. 220–2. Cf. Snir 2005a, pp. 436–41. The fact that the novel was translated into Arabic by Samīr Naqqāsh (Michael 2005), the greatest of the modern Jewish writers in Arabic, illustrates the gap between Michael as a mainstream writer in Israel and the marginalized status of Naqqāsh, who had to find his livelihood in translating a novel, which he rejected because of its Zionist message.

[92] Following Ella Shohat's words referring to Edward Said (1935–2003) as a "Palestinian speaker" in the United States (Shohat 1992, p. 121).

to point out that the Israeli establishment is tolerant toward Arab-Jewish culture. However, its main orientation has been Zionist, and it has hardly dealt with modern Arab-Jewish culture at all.[93]

Sami Michael's aforementioned Arabic story "The Artist and the Falafel" created during the 1950s a "Communist" interpellating machine for the Arabic readers, Muslim, Christian, and Jewish alike: to the artist, in fact, to all intellectuals, the space of artistic and cultural creativity and thought is the place of joint and shared belonging. The artist feels most at home on the streets—his physical home is not described at all. However, the artist's sense of belonging is also defined strongly by the fact that he does not belong with the crowds and the people who stop to watch him draw on the pavement. Belonging, thus, might be best described in negative terms of where one does not belong. Michael is creating a sense of otherness around the very idea of belonging, setting up the identity of the artist as fundamentally not belonging to the crowds. Michael started with this story a process of interpellation in Israeli society—it is not without connection that, besides his literary creations, in the past two decades Michael has been heavily involved with various peace movements; he has been a determined advocate for Palestinian human rights even in the midst of the second *Intifāḍa* in the Occupied Territories. In 2002, he was elected President of the Association for Civil Rights in Israel (ACRI). His unique position as an Arab-Jewish writer in Arabic who shifted to writing only in Hebrew as well as his adoption of Zionism's main conceptions, although he does not see himself as a Zionist, have made him a kind of celebrity in the local intellectual arena with a hectic schedule consisting of lectures and public appearances and even a nomination for the Nobel Prize in Literature. He is a very popular guest in the Israeli media, generally playing the role of the voice of the Eastern "Other" in Israeli society. However, in most of these appearances, against his will, he seems to be considered as a token representative of the "Oriental voice." Ironically, Michael's "The Artist and the Falafel" might be read now as reflecting his own contemporary role in Israeli society: a clown who provides the canonical local Ashkenazi elite with entertainment and amusement, but who has never been considered a true part of it. Furthermore, the story might be considered as heralding,

[93] For an evaluation of the center's activities during the first twenty-five years of its existence, see the various contributions in the two special issues of *Pe'amim: Studies in Oriental Jewry*, namely, 92 (Summer 2002) and 93 (Autumn 2002). It seems to be no coincidence that none of the contributors are Arabized Jews who still adhere to their original culture and that none of the contributions in either issue deal with modern Arab-Jewish culture. Also worthy of note is that the advisory board of the journal does not include a scholar in the field of Arab-Jewish secular literature.

already in the 1950s, the Israeli-Jewish-Ashkenazi mainstream's cognitive dissonance toward the Mizrahi and Palestinian cultures, and, at the same time, signaling the tools to be used to preserve the cozy reassurance of the canonical center's liberal and tolerant attitude toward the culture of the margins. During the last seventy years, we may find in Israeli-Jewish society and culture numerous manifestations of the balance of power alluded to in Michael's story written around seventy years ago.

As a result of the political and national Arab–Israeli Conflict in the Middle East, on the one hand, and Israel's Western-oriented Ashkenazi cultural hegemony, on the other, the refusal inside Israel to tolerate any aspect of Arab culture gaining a foothold in mainstream society is still quite powerful. Israeli society, according to Yossi Ginosar (1945–2004), a former high official in the Israeli General Security Services (*Shabak*), "has not humanized Arab society yet ... there is a deep abhorrence of its essential perspectives throughout Israeli social classes."[94] Recent indications of interest in Arab culture among Israeli-Jewish intellectuals have generally been only a theoretical tool in the discussion around the future of Israel in the Middle East. Literary Arabic writing by Jews is a phenomenon, which, as we have seen, will gradually disappear in the next few years. Paradoxically enough, even Jewish advocates of the inclusion of Arab culture as a fundamental component of Israeli society do not see this culture as part of their own cultural world; those among them who immigrated to Israel from Arab countries without becoming proficient in the standard Arabic language or who were not born in Arab countries do not, as a rule, bother with Arabic anymore. The fact that an Israeli-Jewish manager of a McDonald's fired a female Arab employee for "speaking Arabic to another Arab employee"[95] without arousing any public protest only serves to undercut the legal status of Arabic in Israel despite its being an official language.[96]

Against the background of the aforementioned cognitive dissonance, Shimon Ballas (1930–2019) is perhaps the only Arab-Jewish writer who has successfully adapted to writing in Hebrew while still trying to adhere to Arabic cultural preferences: "I am an Arab Jew," says Ballas. "I write in Hebrew, and I belong here. This does not mean, however, that I have given up my cultural

94 *Yediot Aḥronoth* (Saturday supplement), January 9, 2004, p. 24.

95 *Al-Ahram Weekly Online*, March 10, 2004.

96 Arabic is currently considered an official language in Israel, but several members of the Knesset recently submitted a draft law that would establish Hebrew as Israel's only official language. The draft law would change the accepted definition of Israel as a "Jewish and democratic state" and would make democratic rule subservient to the state's definition as "the national home for the Jewish people." On the status of Arabic language in Israel and its politics from a sociolinguistic point of view, see Mendel 2014; Suleiman 2017.

origins, and my cultural origins are Arab."[97] Born as "a Jew by chance," in his words, in the Christian quarter of Baghdad (al-Dahhāna), Ballas grew to adopt a secular cosmopolitan worldview. He was educated at the AIU School, where he mastered Arabic and French, the latter serving as his window to world literature. He attributes his membership in the Iraqi Communist Party, which he obtained when he was sixteen,[98] as being triggered by reading *The Iron Heel* (1907) by Jack London (1876–1916) in French. Yet, Arabic literature, especially by Jubrān Khalīl Jubrān (1883–1931) and Ṭāhā Ḥusayn (1889–1973), proved to be his major inspiration. Besides publishing essays on movies and engaging in the translation of texts, he wrote short stories and a detective novel—*al-Jarīma al-Ghāmiḍa* (*The Mysterious Crime*)—all of which he burned before immigrating to Israel in 1951, something he would later deeply regret.[99] His immigration was by no means motivated by any form of Zionist ideology; he had been chosen for a scholarship to study at the Sorbonne, but this dream would materialize only about twenty years later when Paris became for him a second home. In Israel, the *ma'abara* experience and his activities in the Communist Party would inspire his literary production. He served for six years as Editor of Arab Affairs for the party's Hebrew organ, *Kol ha-'Am* (*The Voice of the People*) and published Arabic short stories and essays under the pen name of "Adīb al-Qāṣṣ" (lit. "Adīb [Man of Letters] the Storyteller"). In one story, "Aḥabba al-Ḥayāt" ("He Loved Life"),[100] although the protagonist is facing the very real possibility of being deprived of his livelihood, he does not surrender his principles. After leaving the Communist Party in 1961, Ballas devoted himself to literary writing, academic research, and translation. His major scholarly study, on the Arab–Israeli Conflict in Arabic literature, was based on his PhD thesis written at the Sorbonne. It was published in French[101] and later translated into Hebrew[102] and Arabic.[103] He also published an anthology of Palestinian stories (1970) in Hebrew translation,[104] served as the Chair of the Department of Arabic Language and Literature at the University of Haifa, and edited the academic Arabic-language journal *al-Karmil: Studies in Arabic Language and Literature*.

Ballas' first novel, *Ha-Ma'abara* (*The Immigrant Transit Camp*) (1964), was originally completed in Arabic and titled *Mudhakkirāt Khādima* (*Memories*

97 *New Outlook*, November–December 1991, pp. 30–2.
98 According to al-Barāk 1985, p. 249, Ballas joined the party on December 6, 1946.
99 Personal communication in Haifa, April 4, 2001.
100 *Al-Jadīd*, December 1955, pp. 26–34.
101 Ballas 1980a.
102 Ballas 1978.
103 Ballas 1984a.
104 Ballas 1970a.

of a Maid). Ballas, however, decided not to publish it and to switch over to writing in Hebrew.[105] He devoted himself to a thorough reading of the Bible and the Mishnah, the postbiblical collection and codification of Jewish oral laws; later, he concentrated on the writings of Shmuel Yosef Agnon (1888–1970), Nobel Prize laureate writer and one of the central figures of modern Hebrew fiction, in addition to other prominent Hebrew literary works, though by moving from Arabic to Hebrew he felt forced to unlearn his Arabic and refashion his identity.[106] Explaining his switch to Hebrew, he says that he felt that in Arabic he was facing a contradiction and was isolating himself from the society in which he was living.[107] *Ha-Ma'abara* depicts the tragedy of the Arab-Jewish immigrants who were uprooted from their homes in the Arab world and reduced to poverty and thrown back on insufficient resources. Ballas' approach was to skirt the material deprivation and focus on the cultural impoverishment of those Arabized Jews, whose most esteemed moral and cultural values were rejected. Thrown into a hostile environment that felt contempt for their original culture, these Arabized Jews were labeled as exceptional, thus becoming victims of an organized and institutionalized process of adaptation to a culture in which their original cultural assets were considered to be inferior and to be "weapons" of the enemy.[108] Surprisingly, the novel was very well received by critics, some of whom praised the author as representing those Arabized Jews who had preserved Hebrew down through the generations, even though Ballas, like most Iraqi immigrants, had arrived in Israel knowing no Hebrew at all. It seems that the positive responses were nothing more than a way out, for the establishment, of the aforementioned cognitive dissonance and a tool that it could use to preserve the cozy reassurance of its liberal and tolerant attitude toward the cultures of those on the margins. There is no better proof for this assertion than the following fact: shortly after the publication of *Ha-Ma'abara* Ballas completed its sequel, *Tel Aviv Mizraḥ* (*Tel Aviv East*);[109] however, due to the patronizing and dismissive attitude of the literary establishment its publication was delayed some thirty years and first saw print only in 1998. In 2003, Ballas published the trilogy *Tel Aviv Mizraḥ* (*Tel Aviv East*),[110] which consisted of *Ha-Ma'abara* and *Tel Aviv Mizraḥ*, in addition

105 According to a conversation with Ballas in Haifa, June 14, 1989.

106 Cf. Lavie 1996, p. 73.

107 He would return to literary Arabic writing in order to cooperate in translating (or better composing Arabic versions of) two of his Hebrew short stories included in Ballas 1997; another story, originally written in Hebrew, was rewritten in Arabic by Ballas and published in July 2003 on www.elaph.com.

108 *Maariv*, April 25, 1989, p. B9.

109 Ballas 1998a.

110 Ballas 2003.

to the new instalment, *Yalde Ḥuts* (*The Outsiders*), which describes the lives of the heroes until the murder of Prime Minister Yitzḥak Rabin in 1995.[111]

Other works by Ballas also testify to his Arab cultural preferences. In *Ve-Hu Akher* (*And He Is Other*) (1991),[112] he presents his views on the fate of Iraqi Jews via the story of several non-Zionist intellectuals. One of them, to whom the title of the novel alludes, is Aḥmad Hārūn Sawsan, whose character is based on the real-life Iraqi Jew who converted to Islam, Aḥmad Nissīm Sūsa (1900–1982). The novel, which fictionalizes the life of Sūsa, who ended up writing works used in anti-Jewish propaganda by the late Iraqi president Ṣaddām Ḥusayn's (1937–2006) regime, begins during the Iran–Iraq War of the mid-1980s, with the protagonist writing a memoir in which he tries to explain why he wrote his enormous work on the history of the Jews. What unfolds is Sūsa's life story, the primal scene being his marriage to a non-Jewish American woman, Jane, while a visiting engineering graduate student in the United States in the 1930s. The marriage results in Sawsan's older brother and acting family patriarch, Daniel, disowning him and having him excommunicated from his hometown Jewish enclave at al-Ḥilla. That trauma sets off a chain of events that ruins Sawsan's marriage and makes for a too-pat justification for all of his subsequent actions. The title of the novel is based on a conversation between Sawsan and his friend, the poet As'ad Nissīm, whose figure is reminiscent of Anwar Shā'ul. Nissīm is critical of Sawsan and the radical positions that he takes against the Jewish religion. To illustrate his point, he mentions the story from the Talmud[113] of Elisha ben Avuya (first half of the second century AD)—a great sage of his time who achieved a unique level of Torah knowledge but eventually became a heretic—studying Greek and wishing to transcend the parameters set by the Torah. This "crime" was considered so terrible that his colleagues no longer referred to him by name but called him "Akher" ("Other"). According to Nissīm, Sawsan, like Elisha ben Avuya, went too far in his efforts to assimilate into Arab-Muslim society.[114] However, it seems that Ballas considered as

111 On the connections between the historical realities of Iraqi-Jewish immigrants and the literary representation of their world in this trilogy, see Ahmed and Elsharkawy 2015, pp. 430–45.

112 Ballas 1991.

113 Talmud Bavli, Ḥagiga 15a–b.

114 Ballas 1991, p. 117. A second edition of the novel was published by Ha-Kibbutz Ha-Me'uḥad in 2005. An English translation (by Ammiel Alcalay and Oz Shelach) titled *Outcast* was published by City Lights Books in San Francisco (Ballas 2007). A section of the novel (pp. 95–105 of the original) was published in English translation (by Alcalay and Shelach) in *Fascicle* 1 (Summer 2005). A chapter of the novel translated into Arabic by the critic and translator Anṭwān Shalḥat (b. 1956) was published in *Ariel, Majalla li-l-Funūn wa-l-Ādāb fī Isrā'īl* 4 (1995), pp. 63–8.

inevitable the solution Sawsan found to his identity crisis in Iraq: "Islam was not only the religion of the majority [in Iraq], but it was also the foundation of Arab civilization. Therefore, if you belong to the [Iraqi] homeland and [Arab] nation you must reject the dual identity."[115] A number of critics commented that this novel could have been written by an Iraqi author and the fact that it was in Hebrew was not particularly significant.

A year later, Ballas published *Otot Stav* (*Signs of Autumn*) (1992),[116] which consists of three novellas, each symbolizing a necessary component in the longed-for Ballasian utopia. Based on autobiographical material, the first novella, "Iyya" ("Iyya" [the name of the heroine]) (1992)[117] depicts the Iraqi Jews in the late 1940s, before their departure from their homeland, as viewed by a Muslim maid named Zakiyya, nicknamed "Iyya." The second novella, "Signs of Autumn," centers on the cosmopolitan Ḥusnī Manṣūr, who is based on the figure of the Egyptian Ḥusayn Fawzī (1900–1988), who was well known for his books that make use of the mythical figure al-Sindbād (Sinbād) from *Alf Layla wa-Layla* (*A Thousand and One Nights*). The third novella, "In the Gates of Kandinski," is about Ya'qov Reshef, an immigrant Jewish painter from Russia, who is torn between the values of his new society and his idealistic aspirations. Failing to pass through "the Gates of Kandinski," he dies two days before the beginning of the new year. The three protagonists of *Otot Stav* illustrate three components of Israeli culture, each of them related to the town where the events of each novella take place: Baghdad, Paris, and Tel Aviv.

Although it concentrates on the role of Arab culture in mainstream Israeli society, Ballas' literary project is much more comprehensive, accompanying readers into fresh fictional realms: *Ash'ab mi-Baghdad* (*Ash'ab from Baghdad*)[118] centers on the historical and legendary figure of Ash'ab, a versatile musician of medieval Arab cultural heritage who caught the imagination of the Arabs.[119] In *Hitbaharūt* (*Clarification*) (1972),[120] the protagonist is an Iraqi Jew who does not participate in the 1973 War.[121] Iraqi characters also appear in his short stories, including those in the collection *Mūl*

115 See at: www.elaph.com, April 17, 2004.
116 Ballas 1992.
117 The novella was originally published in Hebrew in Ballas 1992, pp. 7–50. For an English translation, see Snir 2019, pp. 266–94 (trans. Susan Einbinder). For an earlier English translation, see Alcalay 1996, pp. 69–99. An Arabic version approved by the author was published in Ballas 1997, pp. 57–110 (trans. Mahā Sulaymān and Shimon Ballas). On the novella, see Snir 2005a, pp. 330–5; Snir 2019, pp. 135–7, 174–5, 188–9.
118 Ballas 1970.
119 On Ash'ab in classical Arabic literature, see Kilpatrick 1998, pp. 94–117.
120 Ballas 1972.
121 On the presence of symbolism in the novel, see Ballas 2009, pp. 111–13.

ha-Ḥoma (*In Front of the Wall*) (1969).[122] In the novel *Ḥoref Aḥaron* (*Last Winter*) (1984),[123] the focus is on Middle Eastern exiles in Europe, especially Henri Curiel (1914–1978), a Jewish Communist of Egyptian origin assassinated in Paris.[124] *Solo* (*Solo*) (1998)[125] is also based on the life of an Egyptian Jew—the aforementioned dramatist and journalist Yaʻqūb Ṣannūʻ (James Sanua) (1839–1912), considered the father of Egyptian theater and Arabic humoristic journalism. *Ḥeder Naʻūl* (*A Locked Room*) (1980) describes life among members of the Communist Party in Israel. Some other works Ballas published, such as the self-referential novel *Ha-Yoresh* (*The Heir*) (1987)[126] and *Lo bi-Mkoma* (*Not in Her Place*) (1994),[127] which has some feminist implications, deal only indirectly with the issue of Arab immigrants involved with the Communist Party generally by alluding to the question of identity. Later, Ballas went on to publish other novels, including *Tom ha-Bikkūr* (*The End of the Visit*) (2008)[128] and *Be-Gūf Rishon* (*First Person Singular*) (2009).[129] Experiencing alienation and estrangement, most of Ballas' protagonists—or rather, antiheroes—are outsiders living on the margins of society and unwilling to compromise on their principles.[130] Preaching a new connection between identity, language, and territory, Ballas demystifies the Hebrew language, attempting to "un-Jew" it—that is, to divorce it from Jewishness in a process of what the French theorists Gilles Deleuze (1925–1995) and Félix Guattari (1930–1992) call "deterritorialization" and "reterritorialization."[131] The Zionist master narrative, in his view, is an Ashkenazi ideology that developed in a different cultural milieu and came to stake its claim in the Middle East without embracing the Middle Eastern environment.[132] Zionism, according to Ballas, is based on the European colonialist conception of the Arab East, and so its "attitude toward the Jews from Arab countries, the Arabized Jews, was no different from the attitude toward the Arabs."[133]

[122] Ballas 1969.
[123] Ballas 1984.
[124] On Henri Curiel, see Schrand 2004, pp. 103–36; Dammond 2007, pp. 300–2.
[125] Ballas 1998.
[126] Ballas 1987.
[127] Ballas 1994.
[128] Ballas 2008.
[129] Ballas 2009.
[130] Cf. Taha 1997, pp. 63–87.
[131] Deleuze and Guattari 1990, pp. 59–69.
[132] *The Literary Review* 37.2 (1994), pp. 67–8.
[133] *Haaretz Magazine*, July 4, 2003, p. 50. On the Zionist project as a colonial enterprise in the Middle East, in addition to being a national liberation movement of European Jews, and the role of Ballas and other Arab-Jewish and Mizrahi intellectulas, see Haramati 2020. The theoretical premise of Michal Haramati's research is based upon contemporary developments of postcolonial theory, especially among Latin-American social scientists, named by

Ballas is now considered by a new generation of critics and scholars to be a prophetic voice who, ever since the mid-1960s, has boldly challenged the Ashkenazi and Western-oriented reluctance to accept the legitimacy of Arab culture in the Hebrew literary canon. Only after redrawing the new boundaries for Hebrew literature so as to encompass not only cosmopolitan and humanistic values but Arab values as well, according to Ballas, will Israeli society be able to boast an original culture in which are expressed the aspirations of all its citizens—Jewish, Muslim, and Christian.

Shimon Ballas' literary contribution is represented by the novella "Iyya," which was originally written in Hebrew and immediately translated into Arabic. The novella presents the story of a Baghdadi Muslim maid named Zakiyya (nicknamed "Iyya") within a Jewish family that she "adopted" as her own during the flight of the Iraqi Jews to Israel. The story starts off as if right in the middle of a narrative, *in medias res* as it were, and the plot sequence is circular with flashbacks to Iyya's marriage and previous life experience. An important feature of the novella's narrative is that the nature of the characters' relationships is not made clear, something that is only further obscured by the complex web of interactions between the characters. The story is also punctuated by dialogues in which there are frequent changes in speaker, with it sometimes being difficult to trace the relevant personal pronoun to its antecedent. This style of narration, especially the frequent dialogue interruptions, adds a sense of immediacy to the text. The events are generally told from Iyya's point of view in a stream-of-consciousness-style narrative of remembrances (such as her miserable life before joining the Jewish family and her abusive husband) and interior monologues (such as her bargaining with God or the acceptance of the fate of never having another husband). Often, her present thoughts interrupt the narration of the events: for example, as the Jewish family is preparing to leave the country, the reader has the privilege of being aware of Iyya's inner thoughts about one of the members of the family: "There [in Israel] he won't have to burn papers and hide them from his pursuers. Let them go, let them go!"—Iyya struggles to reconcile her desire to remain with the Jewish family with her understanding that the family will be safer abroad. The mixed feelings about the departure of the family are well-represented in the character of the maid that will remain in Baghdad—paradoxically, she is a Muslim but will remain the

some "the decolonial turn." The decolonial perspective is especially useful for conceptualizing the social and political struggles of ethnic groups that have been oppressed by colonial power relations. The research uses the decolonial terminology to examine autonomous Mizrahi and Sephardic political organizations in Israel, in order to elicit decolonial aspects in their activity and discourse, and examine the conditions that limited their decolonial potential, as well as their activity at large.

link, the very preserver of the Jewish connection to Baghdad, even after the Jews are gone. There can be nothing worse, in her view, than leaving one's homeland, and she cannot understand the decision to "abandon everything and go." Moreover, she views Israel as backward, assuming that everyone there is a poor farmer or a menial laborer: "A beautiful and educated girl, splendid and upright, how would she [Sophie] do farm work? Like those sunburned barefooted girls?"—Iyya is clearly not able to fathom an identity for the Jewish family in Israel away from the relative luxury and refinement of Baghdad (compared with what was expected for them in the new Jewish state). Furthermore, she asks: "How would Baghdad look without Jews?"

The text gives the reader a sense of the cultural cohesiveness in Baghdad as a place of diversity and cooperation, each group being a necessary part of the whole with the Jews being an integral part of the local Baghdadi and even national Iraqi identity. Iyya cannot imagine Sarah performing the chores that she normally performs, such as washing clothes: "How will they manage there? Sarah doing laundry? In a tent?" As the kitchen is her private space, her refuge and, at the same time, her source of strength as well, we do not see any other characters inside it, enforcing her role as the glue that keeps the family together—"On leaving the kitchen, she suddenly felt weak." Musings over her identity frequently attack Iyya: she may even be considered to be an allegory for Baghdad itself—she is "more Jewish than Muslim and a Muslim among Jews." She keeps silent over others' accusations that the Jews are a cursed race condemned to be degraded, but she does not feel the Jewish identity enough to take sides, seeing her relationship with the Jewish family as that with her own family, and not as one with an employer. Although she admits that she is essentially a servant, Iyya does not feel comfortable working for someone else. It seems that the idea of family is more important for her than earning money and being a part of her actual family that has failed her, namely, her mother, father, and husband: "She realized that all she had to say was now meaningless to them." The Jewish family is leaving, and she encounters difficulties in letting go of them, identifying more strongly with the Jewish family than with her own sister's household.

Ballas uses a very disjointed, stream-of-consciousness method to write the story, which occurs over a short time span, even though it discusses events occurring throughout the lifetime of the maid. The use of this very fluid, uncensored method helps create this sense of richness in her life and gives profound meaning (rooted in the "everydayness" of the prose) to the relationships between the characters. Iyya feels that she is incapable of protecting Sarah's family—"I, a panic-stricken, miserable woman?" Even though she is a Muslim and is of the majority, her identification as a woman clearly ascribes to her a marginalized otherness, perhaps a result of her history of domestic abuse. She compares her plight with the plight of the children of the Jewish family and the violent looters with her "beast" of a husband. Iyya goes out often, always saying "defensively" that she needs fresh air, moving basically independently in the streets, running errands, and meeting people. It is understood that women should stay inside, and Iyya feels that she needs to defend her decision to go outdoors. She is possibly motivated by her traditional upbringing and her mother telling her to obey her husband as if he were her master—he used to prevent her from going outside. The freedom of the outdoors versus the horrible conditions inside closed doors is a contrast that is frequently deployed by the author to illustrate Iyya's past, as can be seen when she would return to the "wretched room" with her mother. The closing of the novella seems to be deliberately ambiguous, but it is undoubtedly symbolic, with Iyya receiving a Qur'ān from one of the sons of the Jewish family before their departure.

Unlike the authors whose works are discussed above, Elī 'Amīr (b. 1937)[134] is a novelist and not a professional short-story writer. However, it is important here to mention his literary activities, as he is one of the major Arab-Jewish authors in Hebrew and has inspired many others. After emigrating from Iraq to Israel in 1950, 'Amīr was sent with his family—his parents and six siblings—to settle in a cloth tent in a *ma'abara.* Although he had finished the eighth grade in Baghdad, he was sent to the fourth grade in Israel: "The Ashkenazim thought that we had just come down from the trees," he says.[135] Eventually, he was sent to receive his education in the kibbutz Mishmar ha-'Emek, which he later would describe as "the most important and decisive" experience of his life.[136] Occupying positions in the Ministry of Absorption and serving as an emissary of the Sephardi Federation in the United States, he was subsequently appointed Director General of 'Aliyyat ha-No'ar (Youth Immigration) in the Jewish Agency, which would later become part of the Ministry of Education. This Zionist path, in which 'Amīr, as a young *'oleh ḥadash* ("new immigrant") comes to be in charge of the fate of young immigrants, would induce him to adopt enthusiastically the Zionist master narrative, which considers the Jewish exodus from Iraq as the new exodus of the Children of Israel.

Arab-Muslim culture has been an integral part of 'Amīr's background; he also majored in Arabic language and literature at the Hebrew University

134 His original name in Iraq was Fu'ād Ilyās Nāṣiḥ Khalaschī. On 'Amīr and his work, see Berg 1996, pp. 391–4; Snir 1993e, p. B9; Snir 1997a, pp. 128–46; Kerbel 2003, pp. 42–3; Abramson 2005, pp. 19–20; Snir 2006, pp. 110–14; Benhabib 2007, pp. 100–18; Morad et al. 2008, pp. 193–9; Snir 2021b, pp. 197–203.

135 *Jerusalem Post Magazine*, March 18, 1988, p. 4.

136 *Haaretz*, February 8, 1985, p. 16.

of Jerusalem. Although he never wrote in Arabic, he has occasionally displayed his talent as a traditional *ḥakawātī* ("storyteller") on televised Arabic-language programs. He made his literary debut in the mid-1970s with a part of his memoirs, a sort of short story titled "Tarnegol Kappara" ("Rooster of Atonement"), which was included in a reader for students edited by Abraham Stahl (1933–2000).[137] Eight years later, it would serve as the nucleus for his first quasi-autobiographical novel with a slightly different title, *Tarnegol Kapparot* (*Rooster of Atonements*) (1983).[138] Described as "casually turning a flashlight into a dark corner of a field and catching the eyes of a ferocious beast,"[139] the novel immediately proved to be a best-seller: it was published in eighteen editions (about 70,000 copies) and was successfully adapted to the small screen by the veteran Israeli filmmaker Dan Wolman (b. 1941). The protagonist Nūrī, a young boy of Iraqi origin, is sent from the *ma'abara* to receive his education in the fictional Kiryat Oranīm, a kibbutz in the Yizrael Valley established by Polish pioneers. Nūrī's struggle to become one of "them"—the arrogant and aristocratic *Sabra* youth (native-born Israeli Jews)—epitomizes the conflict between East and West, and between the original values of the Oriental immigrants and the Ashkenazi values enforced upon them. When he came to the kibbutz accompanied by "the whole of Jewish Baghdad," Nūrī attempted to reassure himself that the painful process through which he would acquire his new identity would not come at the expense of his original one. 'Amīr considers the novel to be a way of "settling accounts with myself and with Zionism,"[140] but the Zionist narrative dominates it, and the fate of Nūrī is dictated by Ashkenazi (Western) values. The Polish-born Israeli-Hebrew writer Aharon Megged (1920–2016) said that the novel is "one of the significant treasures of Jewish culture, like the stories of the Jewish villages in Poland and Russia."[141]

Heavily colored by "invented tradition,"[142] 'Amīr's second novel, *Mafriyaḥ ha-Yonīm* (*The Pigeoneer*; English title: *Farewell, Baghdad*) (1993),[143] has at its core the desire of Arabized Jews to return to their ancient homeland. Referring to the relationship of past to present, 'Amīr says that "it is a mixture that can hardly be reduced to its original components ... I told my story through my anxiety about the fate of Israeli society."[144] The panoramic

137 Stahl 1978, pp. 90–101.
138 'Amīr 1983 (English translation: Amir 1988).
139 *The Jerusalem Post*, March 11, 1988, p. 15.
140 *Ba-Ma'rakha*, 281, March 1984, pp. 12–13.
141 *Yediot Aḥronoth*, March 19, 1993, p. 27.
142 See Hobsbawm 1992; Hobsbawm and Ranger 1992 [1983].
143 'Amīr 1993 (English translation: Amir 2010a; Arabic translation: Amir 2018a).
144 *Ba-Ma'rakha*, 281, March 1984, p. 12.

novel, a kind of *Bildungsroman* based on the author's childhood in Iraq, is related through the eyes of the protagonist Kabī as he attains the age of puberty. Highlighting the historical events on the eve of the mass emigration, it depicts the complicated relationship of Jews to their Muslim neighbors and is steeped in sensual descriptions touching on almost every aspect of Jewish life in the colorful exotic streets and alleys of Baghdad. Described as "one of the most important achievements of Hebrew literature in recent years,"[145] the novel is populated by dynamic figures reflecting the diversity of characters in a kind of *A Thousand and One Nights* Baghdad. The events of the plot are flavored with the music of the Egyptian singer and composer Muḥammad ʻAbd al-Wahhāb (1901–1991) and the Jewish singer Salīma Murād Bāsha (1905–1974), erotic bellydancing with the dancer Bahiyya, seductive prostitutes, adventurous sailing on the Tigris, summer nights on rooftops, rich cousins, smells of spices, and the sexual dreams of the adolescent narrator whose fantasies include Rachelle, his uncle's wife, the teacher Sylvia, and Amīra, Abū Edwar's daughter, who will end up, like him, in a kibbutz. Within the rich and varied social mosaic of the novel, each character represents a particular way of approaching the national and existential issues faced by the Iraqi Jews.[146] However, one may raise doubts concerning the implied author's tendency to depict the figure of the teacher Salīm Afandī as a typical Communist—he is presented as a *carpe diem* hedonist—since all the evidence shows that Salīm Afandī by no means reflects the nature of contemporary Iraqi-Jewish Communist activists. It should be noted that the Communist option in Iraq was even more popular among the Jews at the time than was the Zionist underground.

The novel expresses the tragedy of the first generation of Iraqi immigrants. While in Iraq, Kabī's father, Salmān, dreamed of growing rice in the Ḥula Valley of northern Israel, but soon after he kissed the sacred soil of the "Promised Land" his dreams were shattered by reality. Likewise, ʻAmīr's own father collapsed after the immigration; that is the reason, says the author, why it was only in his second autobiographical novel that he returned to his childhood: "The confrontation with the figure of the father was difficult[147] ... When writing this Hebrew novel, I imagined myself listening in one ear to my father telling it to me in Arabic."[148] Unlike the father, the

145 *Moznayim*, February–March 1993, p. 70.

146 Cf. *Moznayim*, February–March 1993, p. 69.

147 *Yediot Aḥronoth*, March 19, 1993, p. 27. Alluding to the manner in which Jewish immigrants from Arab countries were absorbed into Israel in the 1950s, ʻAmīr focuses on the dwarfing of the figure of the father in the eyes of his children; it "brings you to want revenge" (*Haaretz*, February 8, 1985, p. 16; *Maariv*, April 25, 1989, p. B9).

148 Personal communication, May 23, 2000.

mother in the novel, Umm Kabī, who initially opposed emigration, shows a marvellous ability to adjust. Still, the disappointment of the father is mingled with a glimmer of hope—the birth of his first *Sabra* son signifies, in its own way, a new beginning.[149]

'Amīr surprised his readers with a third novel, *Ahavat Sha'ūl* (*Sha'ul's Love*) (1998),[150] which departed from his own fictionalized experiences and the autobiographical alter egos of Nūrī and Kabī. Appealing to mainstream Israeli readers, it touches on Ashkenazim, Sephardim of the Old Yishuv, Oriental Jews, the Israeli Army, and the Holocaust, and its plot verges on the melodramatic. One critic wrote that "Amir compensates his heroes and readers with plenty of tasty food, sexual encounters serenaded by Hebrew joyous songs, journeys which are full of love of the land and encomiums to the gathering of the Jewish immigrants."[151] Also noteworthy in the novel is the implied author's view regarding the territorial price Israel should pay for peace in the Middle East.

After seven years, 'Amīr returned to telling his own story and published *Yasmīn* (*Yasmin* [the name of the heroine]) (2005), a sequel to his previous two autobiographical novels. The protagonist is Nūrī, the young boy from *Mafriyaḥ ha-Yonīm*, who is now serving as a governmental advisor on Arab affairs. With the publication of this new novel, 'Amīr fulfilled his dream of composing a trilogy similar to that of Najīb Maḥfūẓ, whom he highly admires, having said as much in his essay on their meeting in Cairo.[152] This trilogy covers what 'Amīr once described as "the via dolorosa of being an Israeli and devoting myself to this society."[153] However, *Yasmīn*—a love story between a Jewish man and an Arab-Christian woman—seems to be much closer to *Ahavat Sha'ūl* than to the other two parts of 'Amīr's trilogy, especially in his strong desire for it to appeal to mainstream readers, even if the novel is critical of the Israeli establishment, especially following the 1967 War.[154] In a review of the novel, the poet and scholar Yochai Oppenheimer (b. 1958) shows how "the author even tends to make the reader forget about

149 Considering the novel to be Zionist, the critic Yosef Oren (b. 1940) thinks that its last chapters channeled this work along an ethnic, ideological, and even didactic path, and that it would have been much better had those chapters not been included (Oren 2006, pp. 111–30. On the novel, see also Abramovich 2007, pp. 1–19).

150 'Amīr 1998.

151 *Yediot Aḥronoth*, February 20, 1998, p. 28.

152 *Yediot Aḥronoth*, December 3, 1999, p. 26.

153 Israeli Radio, February 16, 1991.

154 Avraham Burg (b. 1955), former Knesset speaker and former head of the Jewish Agency, considers the novel to be a kind of an elegy on the missing of the opportunity to let Arabized Jews build bridges between the new Israel and the old, ancient Middle East (Burg 2007).

the trauma of the banishment from Iraq and about the difficult experience of adjusting to a new country." The emotional tension that was characteristic of his previous work is "given no expression in this novel, which has no characters that inspire any rage or genuine pity in the reader's heart." Stating that in *Yasmīn* 'Amīr graphically illustrates what critic Fredric Jameson (b. 1934), following Friedrich Wilhelm Nietzsche (1844–1900), terms the "prison-house of language,"[155] Oppenheimer argues that the enlightened occupier, who proclaims words of "heresy" regarding the consensus, "is no different, in this respect, from the benighted occupier who proclaims messianic visions." The "prison-house" also relates to the selection of a shop-worn format that "turns literary creations into a constant, harmless chaperon of the occupation, into a means of generating excitement that does not require any commitment and relates to the complexity of the conflict between two nations and to the human tragedy involved." Also, his clinging to the clichés of the political discourse does create a "realistic" novel, as the back cover announces, but it is a realistic novel that "lacks a suitable independent artistic stance."[156]

Propagating the central myths of Zionism—the kibbutz, the *'aliyya*, and the Israeli Army—'Amīr has been considered since the mid-1990s as one of the most established Hebrew writers. One of his novels, *Mafriyaḥ ha-Yonīm*, was even published in a shortened version (by Rina Tsdaka [1939–2019]) for a young audience as part of the Israeli-Hebrew school curriculum. 'Amīr's novels are steeped in an awareness of the injustice done to the Oriental Jews, but at the same time they deal with the mitigating circumstances under which the Zionist vision was pursued. The founders of the kibbutz had themselves rebelled against their original culture with the aim of "overturning the pyramid," as Dolek, in charge of the fertilizer section in *Tarnegol Kapparot*, puts it. Dolek himself had abandoned his doctoral studies in physics. 'Amīr expresses his appreciation of the way that the kibbutz absorbed the newcomers and the values it represents. "No other immigrant society in the modern era has registered," says 'Amīr, "a comparable success or social revolution in absorbing nearly two million immigrants in difficult economic conditions and while fighting five wars."[157] Attempting to bridge the gap between East and West, he is trying in his novels to fulfil Jacques Derrida's (1930–2004) ideal for someone "to speak the other's language without renouncing his own."[158] Yet, more than any

155 See Jameson 1972.

156 Oppenheimer 2005. Yosef Oren considers the novel to be political-didactic in nature with a social-Zionist conception; see Oren 2006, pp. 149–65.

157 *Jerusalem Post Magazine*, March 18, 1988, p. 4.

158 Gates and Appiah 1986, p. 333.

other author of Iraqi origin, his writings illustrate the adoption of the Zionist master narrative.

In 2018, ʿAmīr published his last novel so far, another quasi-autobiographical novel entitled *Naʿar Ha-Ofanayim* (*Bicycle Boy*), in which he returns to his protagonist Nūrī from the aforementioned *Tarnegol Kapparot* (*Rooster of Atonements*) (1983).[159] Now Nūrī leaves the kibbutz upon his father's request to come and help the family in the transit camp, but soon after his return he was asked again to move to Jerusalem to try to assist the whole family to relocate to Jerusalem. Working distributing newspapers, he found a job as a delivery boy at the Prime Minister's Office from which he has the ability to overlook significant occurrences in the life of the young Jewish state. The events of the novel occurred during the first half of the 1950s, and more precisely between 1953, when the author was sixteen, and 1956, before the start of the Suez Crisis. Here, the narrator is much more sophisticated; in fact, if we compare him with the author himself, as he has been expressing his views in the media, we can safely say that ʿAmīr himself functions as the narrator of this novel. In other words, the gap between the narrator and the implied author is very small. We can see it, for example, when the narrator uses terms, such as *ʿAravim Yehudim* ("Arab-Jews") (p. 396), or when Nūrī wonders "why we don't learn at school on the Jews' life in the Arab countries" (p. 394)—both issues started to be used in the public Hebrew discourse only in the 1980s. The teacher in the school where Nūrī studies asks one of the students to read aloud a eulogy that the Israeli Chief of Staff Moshe Dayan (1915–1981) gave for Roi Rotberg (1935–1956), a kibbutz security officer killed on April 29, 1956 near the Gaza Strip. ʿAmīr quotes the whole text of the eulogy, some of whose sections reflect the implied author of the novel, such as when Dayan refers to the murderers of the young officer:

> Let us not cast the blame on the murderers today. Why should we declare their burning hatred for us? For eight years they have been sitting in the refugee camps in Gaza, and before their eyes we have been transforming the lands and the villages, where they and their fathers dwelt, into our estate. It is not among the Arabs in Gaza, but in our own midst that we must seek Roi's blood. How did we shut our eyes and refuse to look squarely at our fate, and see, in all its brutality, the destiny of our generation?[160]

[159] ʿAmīr 2018. ʿAmīr published a chapter of a new Hebrew novel he was in the process of writing with the title "Umm Kulthūm Eats *Kubba Burghul*" (*Haaretz*, September 5, 2021).

[160] See at: https://en.wikipedia.org/wiki/Death_and_eulogy_of_Roi_Rotberg, last accessed July 23, 2020.

5. CONCLUSION

The vacuum created in Arabic literature in Israel after the founding of Israel encouraged Arab-Jewish poets and writers, especially those who had emigrated from Iraq, to engage actively in this field, particularly in the then dominant genre of poetry. Under the contemporary circumstances, their work was characterized by a preoccupation with sociopolitical issues and questions related to the tensioned relationship between the Jewish majority and the Palestinian minority. Very quickly, two currents arose among the Jews who were writing in Arabic, which thematically encompassed the basic currents in local Arabic literature. In both, the sharp, black-versus-white dichotomy was striking. For those who were sponsored by the Israeli governmental establishment, this dichotomy had a nationalist character; it contrasted the dark past of a minority degraded in exile with the joyous present of Jewish independence in the new homeland. For the Communists, the dichotomy was social and universal, between a dark present filled with oppression and a utopian future ruled by justice, which did not prevent nostalgic allusions to their past in Iraq from appearing in their work. The difference in the worldviews may be seen in the concept of "spring" so frequently used by both sides in their poetry. According to the establishment writers, their hopes had been realized in the Jewish, independent Israel of the 1950s, as we find in the first two words of Salīm Sha'shū'a's first poem in the collection *The World of Light*, "The spring has arrived."[161] In contrast, the struggle was still in full force for the Communist writers, and their eyes gazed toward the future, as seen from the title of Semah's collection *Till Spring Comes*.

All the Jewish writers in Arabic in the 1950s preached coexistence, peace, and brotherhood out of a belief in their realization soon in the developing young state. But while this belief arose among the establishment writers in the wake of the decisive victory of the Jews in the struggle for control of the land, it emerged among the Jewish leftist writers out of a sense of sympathy with the defeated side. The Palestinian leaders of the Communist Party preferred to emphasize the obligations of the Arabic literature in Israel to "carry the banner of Jewish-Arab brotherhood," in the words of Palestinian author Emil Ḥabībī (1921–1996). They stressed Jewish–Arab cooperation in times past and in the present and future, as they also praised the contribution of Jewish writers in this field.[162] Nevertheless, when historically speaking of the development of Palestinian Arabic literature, there is no doubt that the contribution of Jewish writers was marginal. There is no justification at

[161] Sha'shū'a 1959, p. 9.
[162] Quoted by al-Qāsim n.d., p. 24. Cf. the editorial in *al-Jadīd*, November 1954, p. 5.

all for the attempts to emphasize the importance of that contribution[163]—such attempts were also met with scorn from Palestinian Arabs, who saw them as vain boasts.[164] The Jewish contribution, and principally that of the Communists among them, was, however, very important because it stimulated the Arab literary climate in Israel thematically and poetically, and because it was a cry for a just coexistence which sprang from the throats of a few amid the majority. It also signaled to the Arab minority, and in its own language, that not all the Jews were at peace with the injustice caused to the Palestinians.

The 1960s marked the beginning of the end for the Arabic literature of the Arab Jews in Israel: the majority of the writers who belonged to the Communist Party left it after their faith in Communism was undermined following the exposure of Stalinist crimes, the border conflicts between the Soviet Union and China, the increased radicalism within the Communist Party in Israel, and the Soviet Union's blind support for the Arab states. On the other hand, with the failure to create a "positive" and meaningful Arab culture, the establishment gradually relinquished its support for those who had taken shelter in its shade. A few succeeded in adapting to Hebrew writing, while others severed themselves from literary activity in Arabic. It was sad to see those few who were unable to accept this reality, like the talented writer Samīr Naqqāsh, who arrived in Israel at the age of thirteen and developed most of his talents there.[165] With astounding devotion, he continued to write even when there was almost no one interested in his or his comrades' writing. "Their voices were lost," said Sasson Somekh,[166] who had already understood in the 1950s that there was no hope for Jewish participation *as Jews* in Arabic literature.

The demise of Arab-Jewish writing in Arabic may be illustrated by Almog Behar's (b. 1978) story "Anā min al-Yahūd" ("I Am One of the Jews") (2006).[167]

[163] Moreh 1958, pp. 27, 39; Moreh and Hakak 1981, p. 97; Moreh 1988, p. 168; Moreh, *Encyclopaedia Judaica*, XIII, pp. 1040–3.

[164] See, for example, *al-Jadīd*, July–August 1969, pp. 40–1.

[165] On his writing, see Semah 1989, pp. 21–2.

[166] Somekh 1989, p. 19.

[167] The Hebrew story with the Arabic title was first published in *Haaretz*, literary supplement, April 22, 2005. It was republished in Behar 2008, pp. 55–64; Behar 2017, pp. 78–82. For an English translation, see Snir 2019, pp. 309–16. An earlier English translation was published on www.haaretz.com (April 28, 2005). An Arabic translation, by Muḥammad 'Abbūd, was published on his blog at: http://aboud78.blogspot.com (June 7, 2006). It was republished in Behar 2008, pp. 65–76; Behar 2017, pp. 83–8. For a short film based on the story, see at: https://www.facebook.com/anaminelyahud, last accessed August 5, 2019. For a theatrical production based on the story, see at: http://www.arab-hebrew-theatre.org.il/show.php?id=6594, last accessed August 1, 2020. On Behar and characteristics of his works, see Miccoli 2014, pp. 15–36.

Behar was born in Ra'anana, Israel, to an Iraqi-born mother and a father who was born in Copenhagen. He was expected to grow up, like many of his status, as a *Sabra*—a native-born Israeli Jew—which was to distance him from any dimension of Arab-Jewish identity and culture. But, in a conscious twist of fate he decided to create for himself an Arab-Jewish identity or, better still, to reclaim the identity of his Iraqi-Arab mother and her original family. In fact, Behar is one of the only members of the new generation of Arabized Jews to decide to consciously adopt Arab-Jewish identity and invest their energies into acquiring the culture that Israeli-Jewish society decided to abandon. Behar's efforts are by no means a part of the fictional Arab-Jewish identity that was invented somewhere in the late 1980s and the early 1990s mostly for the aim of identity politics.[168]

"Anā min al-Yahūd" is an exceptional autobiographical meta-fictional Hebrew story with an Arabic title that might be a good illustration of the demise of Arab-Jewish cultural hybridity. The story was selected in April 2005 as the winner of the short-story competition held by the literary supplement of the Hebrew daily newspaper *Haaretz*—despite its literary quality, there can be no doubt that its selection for the first prize was due *also* to the aforementioned cognitive dissonance and to the emergence, during the late 1980s, of Arab-Jewish identity as a new "fashion trend" that the leftist *Haaretz* was encouraging at the time mainly on its cultural and literary pages. The *Arabic* title of the *Hebrew* story is understandable for every Hebrew-speaking Israeli: the Arabic words correspond to the same Hebrew words, indicating the common Semitic origins and the similarity of both languages. But, the title at the same time shocks the readers who are not used to such titles for Hebrew literary works. The plot is somehow surrealistic: as the narrator walks down the street in Jerusalem, he loses his Hebrew-Israeli accent and begins to speak in the Arabic accent of his Iraqi-Arab-Jewish grandfather Anwar:

> Suddenly that beautiful voice, which had been entirely in my past, started coming out of me and not as a beggar and not asking for crumbs, but truly my voice, my voice strong and clear.

No matter how hard he tries to extricate himself from this accent, which emerged after two generations of forgetting, and throw it away into one of the public trash cans, he cannot manage to do it:

> I tried and tried to soften the glottal *'ayyin*, the way my mother had in her childhood, because of the teachers and the looks from the other children, but strangers passing by just rooted me to the spot; I tried to soften the pharyngeal

168 See Snir 2015b, pp. 225–6.

> fricative *ḥet* and pronounce it gutturally like *kaf*; I tried to make the *tsadī* sound less like an *samekh* and I tried to get rid of that glottal Iraqi *qūf* but the effort failed.

The "return to his roots," which is accompanied by reviving the pre-1948 Palestinian reality in Jerusalem, only exacerbates the narrator's estrangement. The Jews suspect him of being an Arab, and the Arabs alienate themselves from him. Policemen start to head assertively toward him on the streets, stopping him and inquiring as to his name and identity. Because of the suspicion that he is not a Jew but an Arab, he wants to pull out his identity card before every passing policeman on the street and point out the nationality line and tell them: "*Anā min al-Yahūd, Anā min al-Yahūd.*" But the policemen check him slowly, going over his body with metal detectors, eager to defuse any suspicious object. Suddenly, explosive belts begin to form on his heart, "swelling and refusing to be defused, thundering and thundering." But at the same time, he is suffering from a sort of schizophrenia; the self-denial of his new situation reflects the tragedy of the demise of Arab-Jewish hybridity: "And my heart did not know I had returned to my heart, it didn't know, and my fears didn't know they had all returned to me, they did not know."

Then this "plague" begins to strike other Israelis, who also begin to speak in the accents of their parents and grandparents. The narrator's life companion wonders about his voice, but suddenly she gets infected and her lips connect to form a jumble of her father's Yemenite Arabic accent and her mother's Istambouli Ladino accent. This *dybbuk*, this malicious possessing spirit, soon starts to haunt Ashkenazim as well. The security authorities begin to keep track of who has been infected by whom with the forbidden accents, "and that there is already concern that the country will be filled with Arabs, many, many Arabs, and that they have therefore decided to reinforce the radio with announcers whose Hebrew is so pure that we will feel alien in our speech." His parents, who consciously tried to rid themselves of their Arabic accents, stand staunchly against him and against the plague, remembering the years of effort they had invested into acquiring their clean Israeli accent, and they begin to hint strongly to him to cease and desist. But his ears are not open to hearing them, and his language becomes deaf, and their accent becomes alien to him and distant. His deceased grandfather also starts to complain, asking him whether there is any end to this story:

> How I have come to trouble your life, I am the generation of the desert and how have you arisen to renew me. You are the generation for which we waited so that there would be no difference between its past and the past of its teachers,

> because our past was already very painful and we remained in the desert for the birds of prey to eat us for your sake.

And also:

> Build extensions in your heart, my grandson, he would say to me, make many departments, and lodge me in one of the hidden departments, and live in the rest of them. Or move into the silence department, because the change that you thought is occurring is too simple, and what is going to change if a different accent is spoken? Will I live again; will you live my new life?

Upon the advice of his dead grandfather, the narrator chooses silence, only to discover that this too does not provide security, and again he is taken to jail. He starts to write stories and poems of opposition to Hebrew in Hebrew because he has no other language in which to write. In his silence, he shows to his parents his writings, trying to convince them that his estrangement is a reflection of their alienation because "you too are the same exile, the same silence, the same alienation between heart and body and between thought and speech; perhaps you will know how the plot will be resolved." But his parents' response is a total denial: "This is not our son ... we don't have this accent ... his grandfather Anwar died before he was born." The last sentence of the story, a variation on the aforementioned sentence that reflects his schizophrenic situation, reflects the tragedy of the demise of Arab-Jewish hybridity:

> And my parents did not know that I had returned to their heart, they did not know, and they did not know that all of their fears had returned to me, they did not know.

The reader is led to the conclusion that the estrangement of the narrator in Israeli society is due to some sort of historical blindness. The direct intertextual allusion is to *Blindness* (1995) by the Portuguese writer José Saramago (1922–2010), in which suddenly a man loses his sight while he is waiting in his car at a traffic light. The mysterious epidemic of "white blindness" spreads to the whole nation. The novel ends when people start to regain their sight:

> Why did we become blind, I don't know, perhaps one day we'll find out, Do you want me to tell you what I think, Yes, do, I don't think we did go blind, I think we are blind, Blind but seeing, Blind people who can see, but do not see.[169]

In Behar's story, too, initially one person is affected in one of his capacities, the capacity for speech, though he is not rendered mute but only loses his Hebrew accent and begins to speak in his grandfather's Iraqi accent. But, unlike Saramago's novel, which is full of hope, Behar's story is full of despair.

[169] Saramago 2013, p. 309.

The "plague" or the *dybbuk*—the return of the narrator to his Arab roots—is by no means a start of a revolution, but only "the last visit of health before death."

It is possible to compare Behar's story with novels detailing the immigrant experience, such as *My Antonia* (1918) by the American writer Willa Cather (1873–1947), *Bread Givers* (1925) by American-Jewish author Anzia Yezierska (1885–1970), and *The Fortunate Pilgrim* (1965) by the American author of Italian descent Mario Puzo (1920–1999). Unlike these novels, which feature members of the younger generation as the driving force behind the adaptation to a new society and culture, and portray them as going against tradition, in Behar's story the young man rebels by going back to tradition. It is instructive, from both a literary and a symbolic point of view, to note the intertextual links of Behar's story with "The Metamorphosis" (1915) by Franz Kafka (1883–1924), which also begins with the protagonist being inexplicably changed by some external force. Obviously, the stories do not exactly parallel each other—Kafka's protagonist, the hard-working Gregor, is turned into a bug and left alone by his family, while Behar's unnamed protagonist starts speaking with an accent and watches his "disease" spread all around him. Yet, the ending of both stories is one of rejection by those whom the protagonist loves most; and the changes that occur in the protagonists are not within their control. In a sense, both stories emphasize the same sort of despair and lack of hope for the future as illustrated, for example, by Samīr Naqqāsh's works as in the novella "Prophecies of a Madman in a Cursed City."[170] Behar provides no real resolution, instead echoing in his final sentence the same ambiguity of identity that carries through the story.[171] Shortly before the story was published, Almog Behar published his poem "My Arabic Is Mute," which seems to be the nucleus of his story, and the reader is requested to remember the encounter between the Arabic language and the policeman in the last lines of the poem and compare it to the cases of interpellation[172] mentioned in Chapter 8 below:

הָעֲרָבִית שֶׁלִּי אִלֶּמֶת
חֲנוּקָה מִן הַגָּרוֹן
מְקַלֶּלֶת אֶת עַצְמָהּ
בְּלִי לְהוֹצִיא מִלָּה
יְשֵׁנָה בָּאֲוִיר הַמַּחֲנִיק
שֶׁל מִקְלְטֵי נַפְשִׁי
מִסְתַּתֶּרֶת

[170] See Snir 2019, pp. 110–22, 173–4, 179–80, 196–202, 295–308.
[171] On the story, see also Mendelson-Maoz 2014, pp. 112–20.
[172] See also Snir 2015b, pp. 4–8.

מִבְּנֵי-הַמִּשְׁפָּחָה
מֵאֲחוֹרֵי תְּרִיסֵי הָעִבְרִית.
וְהָעִבְרִית שֶׁלִּי גּוֹעֶשֶׁת
מִתְרוֹצֶצֶת בֵּין הַחֲדָרִים
וּמִרְפְּסוֹת הַשְּׁכֵנִים
מַשְׁמִיעָה קוֹלָהּ בָּרַבִּים
מְנַבֵּאת בּוֹאָם שֶׁל אֱלֹהִים
וְדַחְפּוֹרִים
וְאָז מִתְכַּנֶּסֶת בַּסָּלוֹן
חוֹשֶׁבֶת אֶת עַצְמָהּ
גְּלוּיוֹת עַל שְׂפַת עוֹרָהּ
כְּסוּיוֹת בֵּין דַּפֵּי בְּשָׂרָהּ
רֶגַע עֵירֻמָּה וְרֶגַע לְבוּשָׁה
הִיא מִצְטַמְצֶמֶת בַּכֻּרְסָא
מְבַקֶּשֶׁת אֶת סְלִיחַת לִבָּהּ.
הָעֲרָבִית שֶׁלִּי פּוֹחֶדֶת
מִתְחַזָּה בְּשֶׁקֶט לְעִבְרִית
וְלוֹחֶשֶׁת לַחֲבֵרִים
עִם כָּל דְּפִיקָה בִּשְׁעָרֶיהָ:
"אַהְלָן, אַהְלָן".
וּמוּל כָּל שׁוֹטֵר עוֹבֵר בָּרְחוֹב
שׁוֹלֶפֶת תְּעוּדַת זֶהוּת
מַצְבִּיעָה עַל הַסְּעִיף הַמְּגוֹנֵן:
"אַנָא מִן אַלְ-יַהוּד, אַנָא מִן אַלְ-יַהוּד"
וְהָעִבְרִית שֶׁלִּי חֵרֶשֶׁת
לִפְעָמִים חֵרֶשֶׁת מְאֹד.

My Arabic is mute
Strangled in the throat
Cursing itself
Without uttering a word
Sleeping in the suffocating air
Of the shelters of my soul
Hiding
From family members
Behind the shutters of the Hebrew.
And my Hebrew erupts
Running around between rooms
And the neighbors' porches
Sounding her voice in public
Prophesizing the coming of God
And bulldozers
And then she settles in the living room
Thinking herself
Openly on the edge of her skin

Hidden between the pages of her flesh
One moment naked and the next dressed
She almost makes herself disappear in the armchair
Asking for her heart's forgiveness.
My Arabic is scared
Quietly impersonating Hebrew
Whispering to friends
With every knock on her gates:
"Ahlan, ahlan [Welcome, welcome!]"
And in front of every policeman on the street
She pulls out her ID card
Pointing out the protective clause:
"*Anā min al-Yahūd, Anā min al-Yahūd*" [I am one of the Jews, I am one of the Jews],
And my Hebrew is deaf
Sometimes so very deaf.[173]

[173] The poem was published in 2005 in *Helicon: Anthological Journal of Contemporary Poetry* 68, p. 30. Together with the original poem, an Arabic translation, by Rīmā Abū Jābir (b. 1981), was appended (p. 31). For the poem translated into six languages, see at: https://almogbehar.wordpress.com, last accessed July 6, 2018. On the poem and the story, as well as on the differences between the stages in which people identified themselves as Arab Jews, from the late nineteenth century to the early twenty-first century, see also Behar 2017a, pp. 131–52. The article concludes with the following: "Today, in the beginning of the twenty-first century, the only place left for the Arab-Jew to live or relive a full life, is the literary imagination. We have finally become fiction" (p. 150). However, in his lecture "'Come from the Corner to the Stage of Stages': On Poetry and Translation between Hebrew and Arabic," Behar expressed his desire to write in Arabic, giving the impression that it is not an impossible option for him and his Arab-Jewish colleagues (Behar 2020, pp. 24–5). The fact that in the same lecture Behar fully quotes the aforementioned poem in Arabic translation without paying attention to the fundamental errors it consists of in its Arabic version proves that the desire to write in Arabic by the new generation of Arab-Jewish writers is nothing but a daydream, at least in the near future.

Chapter 7

Demise: The Last of the Mohicans[1]

My adherence to Moses's creed has not
Diminished my love for Muhammad's nation;
Faithful I will stay like al-Samaw'al
Be I happy in Baghdad or miserable.
– Anwar Shā'ul

1. INTRODUCTION

Witnessing the gradual demise of Arab-Jewish culture, most of the Arab-Jewish writers and poets completely severed themselves from any creative activities in their mother tongue. The language of the new society was Hebrew, the language of Zionism, while Arabic became the language of the enemy.[2] The gradual demise of Arabic literature written by Jews was accompanied by a controversy on the cultural preferences of Israeli society.[3] The main factor in the Muslim–Christian–Jewish Arab symbiosis up to the twentieth century, from the Jewish point of view, was that the great majority of the Jews under the rule of Islam adopted Arabic as their spoken language. This symbiosis does not exist in our time because Arabic is gradually disappearing as a language spoken and written on a daily basis by Jews and because, retrospectively and at least regarding the relevant interactions in the field of written Arabic literature during the twentieth century, it was

1 This chapter uses material that first appeared in Snir 2005, pp. 7–29; Snir 2005b, pp. 102–35; Snir 2019; Snir 2021, pp. 173–88.
2 On Arabic as the language of the enemy, see Mendel 2014; Mendel 2020; Mendel 2021, pp. 218–30.
3 On the literary activities of the Iraqi Jews in the 1950s, see Snir 1991, pp. 153–73. On contemporary interactions between Hebrew and Arabic literature and the involvement of Iraqi-Jewish writers, see Snir 1998a, pp. 177–210.

a largely one-way process in which the Jewish intellectuals acquired and absorbed mainstream cultural norms from the dominant group.[4]

Since the start of the 1980s, dozens of Arab-Jewish writers, poets, and intellectuals have passed away, while we cannot see even one new Israeli-Jewish author joining the community of Arabic writers. Following the death of Anwar Shā'ul (1904–1984), Murād Mīkhā'īl (1906–1986), Salīm al-Baṣṣūn (1927–1995), Shalom Darwīsh (1913–1997), and David Semah (1933–1997) at the turn of the twentieth century we can find only those Arabic writers who started their literary careers in Iraq and continued to write after their immigration, such as Ya'qūb Balbūl (1920–2003), Mīr Baṣrī (1911–2006), Ibrāhīm Obadyā (1924–2006), Murād 'Abd Allāh al-'Imārī (1923–2012), Maurice Shammās (1920–2013), Salīm Murād Sha'shū'a (1926–2013), Maryam al-Mullā (al-Baṣṣūn) (1927–2013), and Shmuel Moreh (1932–2017). Only two writers who were born in Iraq started their literary careers in Israel—Isḥāq Bār-Moshe (1927–2003) and Samīr Naqqāsh (1938–2004), who insisted on remaining true to their cultural origins and continued to write in Arabic though they realized that they were working in a void and that their books hardly found any readership inside or outside Israel. They were the last of the Mohicans of a tradition that started more than 1,500 years ago and that has been vanishing before our very own eyes. Since I am preparing a separate monograph on Naqqāsh, I will concentrate here on Isḥāq Bār-Moshe. Bār-Moshe (formerly Khaddūrī [Khedhourie]) was born in 1927 to a religious middle-class family in the overwhelmingly Muslim Qambar 'Alī quarter in Baghdad and passed away in Manchester in December 2003. He was educated at the Rachel Shaḥmūn School and then at al-Ruṣāfa School and al-I'dādiyya al-Ahliyya. He related that from the age of five he read translations of world literature as well as original Arabic literature, his favorite authors being the Iraqi Dhū al-Nūn Ayyūb (1908–1998) and the Egyptians Ibrāhīm 'Abd al-Qādir al-Māzinī (1890–1949) and Tawfīq al-Ḥakīm (1898–1987).[5] In 1949, he attended the Baghdad Law College;

[4] For example, because of the short period of the time called "Iraqi Spring" between the 1920s and 1950s, one can by no means refer to any true mutual cultural dialogue between Arab-Jewish, on the one hand, and Arab-Muslim and Arab-Christian writers, on the other hand; it was a largely one-way process in which the Jewish authors acquired and absorbed mainstream Arabic literary norms—it was in sheer contradiction to the aforementioned medieval cultural dialogue, or, alternately, the modern Jewish–German cultural symbiosis characterized in "a literally astonishing wealth of talent and of scientific and intellectual productivity" (Arendt 1974, p. xvii), or the dialogue between Jewish and Polish artists during the twentieth century (Silber [fortcoming]; based on a presentation given at the Fifth Annual Polish Jewish Studies Workshop Centering the Periphery: Polish Jewish Cultural Production Beyond the Capital, March 6, 2018).

[5] Bār-Moshe 1988, pp. 94–7, 138–9, 223.

however, while still a student in September 1950 he emigrated to Israel. He worked for a time as a clerk at the oil refineries in Haifa, until in 1958 he joined Dār al-Idhā'a al-Isrā'īliyya, the Israeli Arabic broadcasting station, where he served as a commentator and held several positions, among them the head of the political department. In October 1968, he founded the governmental Arabic-language daily *al-Anbā'* and edited it until April 1970. Following the signing of the peace treaty with Egypt, Bār-Moshe served two terms as Attaché for Journalistic and Cultural Affairs at the Israeli embassy in Cairo (1983–1986 and 1988–1991). Then he edited the monthly Arabic cultural magazine *Qaws Quzaḥ* (*Rainbow*) published by the Israeli Foreign Ministry; he also edited the Arabic version of the Journal *Ariel* published by the ministry in several foreign languages. Bār-Moshe was an active member of the Jerusalem lodge of the Freemasons,[6] which has among its objectives religious toleration, assistance to others, brotherly love, and political compromise—these themes from Freemasonry are found in his literary writings, which are far removed from any kind of extremism or radicalism.

Bār-Moshe's literary works consist of two main branches with different generic, thematic, and stylistic preferences: for the expression of his general social, existential, and philosophical views, he employed the genre of the short story, with an obvious inclination toward psychological insights. The stories generally reflect universal concepts and tend to reveal the inner nature of human beings; they are mostly well removed from any specific time and place, and when read in translation one can hardly know the ethnic, religious, or national identity of the author. The novel, the semi-autobiographical novel, or the memoir are used for the recollection of his life in Iraq and for expressing his views regarding the last stage of the Iraqi-Jewish community. The fictional framework is constructed on solid historical material in a way that enables the reader to see the books as an alternative history for the events described from the point of view of an Iraqi Jew living in Israel.

2. EXISTENTIALIST SENSIBILITY

While in Baghdad, Bār-Moshe anonymously published short stories,[7] but in Israel it was only in 1972 that he published his first collection, *Warā' al-Sūr wa-Qiṣaṣ Ukhrā* (*Behind the Fence and Other Stories*).[8] Apart from his own

6 See his article "Historic Freemasonry in the Middle East," available at: www.geocities.com/Athens/Forum/9991/mideast.html August 23, 2003; and at: http://www.mastermason.com/fmisrael/mideast.html, last accessed August 5, 2019.

7 Moreh 1975, p. 43 (for the Hebrew version, see *Shevet ve-'Am* 3 [8] 1978, p. 426).

8 Bār-Moshe 1972. On the collection, see 'Abd al-Raḥmān 'Abbād, "Some Words on 'Behind the Fence and Other Stories'," *al-Anbā'*, August 18, 1972, p. 4; Mudhi 1988, pp. 369–403.

literary writing, he published Arabic translations of literary works by Hebrew writers,[9] which contributed to his mastering of some modernist techniques of the genre. Inspired by stream-of-consciousness literature, especially that of Virginia Woolf (1882–1941), who since the 1940s has had a great literary impact on Arab writers,[10] most of his stories probe the complexity of the human soul in an attempt to understand the psychological motives behind people's actions. Detailed interior monologues appear frequently in his writings, which also reveal a spiritual drive in a way reminiscent of that of the medieval Muslim mystics. Most of his protagonists, or better antiheroes, are outsiders living in their own world of misery or on the margins of society, not willing to compromise their principles. Some of them suffer from schizophrenia, which leads them to find refuge in a world of imagination and dreams, a world that is sometimes nothing other than another nightmare.[11] Generally stripped of any signifier of space or ethnicity, they are introvert personalities marked by alienation and strangeness with hardly any interest in matters outside their own feelings and thoughts.

Bār-Moshe's stories were part of the general trend in Arabic literature of the 1960s and 1970s that expressed the tragic absurdity of human existence in modern civilization, maintaining that this materialistic civilization obliterates human spiritual values and leaves human beings in an existential limbo.[12] Many of his stories seem to have been inspired by the writings of the Austrian-Jewish writer Franz Kafka (1883–1924), especially by his existentialist sensibility, which reflects the religious confusion in the twentieth century, the strangeness and alienation of the human being in this world, and his wafting between the nihility of existence and divine salvation.[13] The conflicts in Bār-Moshe's stories are generally not because of political or social differences, but rather due to inner emotional disharmony, intellectual discord, and a struggle against the darkest sides of the soul. Sometimes, the battle is against fate or against those forces in society that consider the

[9] For example, the short story "Minzar Ha-Shatkanim" ("The Trappist Monastery") by Amos Oz (1939–2018), whose translation was published in *al-Sharq*, June–August 1973, pp. 75–82. On the translation, see Kayyal 2000, p. 115. When he edited the journal *Ariel*, Bār-Moshe published in several issues translations he made into Arabic of Hebrew literary works, such as those by Amnon Shamosh (1929–2022) (3 [Winter 1994], pp. 23–8), Amos Oz (1939–2018) (5 [Winter 1995], pp. 4–11), Yitzhak Navon (1921–2015) (5 [Winter 1995], pp. 33–39, 45–54), and Nissim Aloni (1926–1998) (7 [Winter 1996], pp. 40–63).

[10] See Snir 1999, pp. 6–7.

[11] See, for example, the story "Infiṣām" ("Schizophrenia") (Bār-Moshe 1972, pp. 73–84. On the story, see Mudhi 1988, pp. 393–5).

[12] See, for example, the story "Dār Saʿīd" ("Saʿīd's House") (Bār-Moshe 1972, pp. 21–30. On the story, see Mudhi 1988, pp. 389–91).

[13] On Kafka's influence on Bār-Moshe, see Mudhi 1988, pp. 366, 392–3.

progress of human civilization as engendering the sacred tradition. Other characteristics of his stories include his focus on ghosts and the irrational, the life hereafter, and death.[14] Some scholars refer to Bār-Moshe's interest in the world of dreams and imagination as a kind of escapism following the suffering of Iraqi Jews in the transit camps: "Everything was new to them—the language, the customs and social atmosphere ... the camp was a new world completely different from the world the emigrants had known in Iraq."[15] However, when Bār-Moshe published his first stories, the transit camps were a phenomenon of the past.

Bār-Moshe's above-mentioned first collection consists of twelve stories, one of which may be referred to as semi-autobiographical and meta-fictional dealing with the literary creative experience, that is "Mu'ānāt Qiṣṣa" ("The Experience of a [Birth] of a Story").[16] This story is about a man's attempt to express his own experiences in literary writing. Unlike the original pragmatic meaning of the Aristotelian "catharsis" (purgation), it seems that, at the time of writing, this story served for Bār-Moshe himself as an act with a cathartic purpose.[17] Like the Egyptian poet Ṣalāḥ 'Abd al-Ṣabūr (1931–1981) in his theory of the creative process,[18] Bār-Moshe indirectly argues that the "catharsis" takes place within the soul of the artist himself.[19] In what seems to be a kind of reflection on the author's own hesitation to write and publish in the 1950s, the hero cannot start writing *his* story, as becomes clear in the following interior monologue:

— I have to start working. My soul is exploding with experiences.
— Start? Where from?
— I don't know yet. But it's unreasonable to go on thinking about the story not knowing how to start and what to do ...

14 See, for example, the stories "al-Ḥāris" ("The Guardian") and "'Awdat Maḥbūb" ("The Return of Maḥbūb") (Bār-Moshe 1972, pp. 85–98, 113–32. On the stories, see Mudhi 1988, pp. 385–9, 395–7).

15 Mudhi 1988, pp. 365–6.

16 Bār-Moshe 1972, pp. 31–50. Mudhi translated the title as "The Suffering of a Story" (Mudhi 1988, p. 369).

17 In reply to Plato's view that art arouses and fans dangerous emotions, Aristotle considers art as beneficial, as it cleanses and purifies the souls of people by wisely regulating the emotions and preventing anarchy in them (Aristotle 1967, p. 25; Aristotle 1968, p. 10). The exact meaning of "catharsis" has been the subject of much debate in the philosophy of art (see Preminger 1974, pp. 106–8).

18 See Snir 1993, pp. 74–88.

19 Though Aristotle himself does not deal with the catharsis of the poet, the philosophy of art has produced theories maintaining that poetry is a catharsis for the author himself. Edmund Wilson (1895–1972), for example, suggests the metaphors of the "wound" and the "bow," where the former refers to the artist's neurosis, and the latter refers to the art which is its compensation (Wilson 1941, pp. 272–95).

– Do you think that you have gained all the experiences needed to start a story?
– Perhaps not. But what I have is enough for the beginning.
– All that you are going to write will be incomplete due to the absence of the needed experiences. Don't you think it's better to continue having more experiences? Don't stop thinking about the story but you have more in front of you. Without more experiences your story won't be a story.
– And if death strikes me?[20]

After many frustrating attempts the hero succeeds and starts to write *his* own story—it is a moment of purgation, the achievement of spiritual satisfaction, and the raising the soul to a higher level:

> His eyes were shining with hope while the first beautiful fascinating sentences accumulated to write for him in the world of fantasies the first desired words which struck his mind as if they were like an axe digging the earth so that the water would burst forth and become a noisy river, the source hidden in the unknown but that flowed vigorously and abundantly, noisy and free, in order to flood the world.[21]

One can hardly ignore the autobiographical dimensions in this story—Bār-Moshe himself had waited until he was forty-five years old before publishing his first collection. The highly optimistic closure of the story may be a hint as to the hopes that the author had set on his literary writing: it is like a hard digging of the earth in search of the hidden source that inevitably will burst forth and flood the world.

Another story in the collection, "al-Rābiya al-Thālitha" ("The Third Hill"),[22] may be reckoned as a sequel to the above story that adds to the optimistic feeling of the implied author (that is "the implicit image of an author in the text")[23] the aspect of the limitation on a human being's activity in this world. The hills that the hero passes through may be deemed as stages in the creative experience. However, when reaching the third hill he realizes he is a prisoner: "The most important thing that you should have is the desire to obey. We want from you complete surrender without any reservations."[24] The hero discovers that human freedom is only relative; real freedom without any restrictions is impossible. The "axe digging the earth," which appears at the end of the story "The Experience of a [Birth] of a Story," seems also to be a prisoner of restrictions on human freedom. The issue of relative individual

20 Bār-Moshe 1972, pp. 39–40. Translations from the story are according to Mudhi 1988, pp. 370–1 with some modifications.
21 Bār-Moshe 1972, p. 50.
22 Bār-Moshe 1972, pp. 57–72.
23 Prince 1987, pp. 42–3.
24 Bār-Moshe 1972, p. 64.

freedom is also the subject of another story, "Sūhā,"[25] titled after the name of the protagonist's girlfriend, whose father refuses to allow her to marry him.

Some of the stories in the first collection deal with the mystical and metaphysical drive in human life. In "al-Dār al-Mayyita" ("The Dead House"),[26] whose implied author is convinced that the world of childhood is a metaphor for the mystical dimensions within human existence, the narrator at exactly 9:00 am receives a telephone call from a childhood friend who many years before had joined him in entering a risky deserted house next to their school. In its dark basement, they had met a female demon that had given them a sense of knowing the unknown. When they had returned, they realized that their journey had not taken any time at all; it was, as it were, as if time itself had stopped. Moreover, at the level of the narration, when the conversation with his friend ends, the narrator realizes that the time is still 9:00 am! The story brings to mind the oxymoronic mystical nature of the *ḥāl* (a mystical "state"),[27] according to medieval Ṣūfī sources: it is an enduring phenomenon, one that occurs, however, outside of human serial time. Accordingly, the Ṣūfī term *waqt* (literally, "time") designates the "present moment," that is, the moment the gift of *ḥāl* is granted to the mystic. *Waqt* then is like a sword, cutting off whatever was beforehand and whatever will be afterward, leaving man in absolute nakedness in the presence of God.[28] The Ṣūfī mystic has been called *ibn al-waqt*—that is, he who gives himself completely over to the present moment and receives what God sends down to him without a single thought about present, past, and future.[29] For the Ṣūfīs, the Prophet's expression "*lī ma'a Allāh waqt*" ("I have a time with God") pointed to their own mystical experience when, as the German Orientalist and scholar of Sufism Annemarie Schimmel (1922–2003) puts it, "they break through created time and reach the Eternal Now in God," when everything created is annihilated. Similarly, for the Indian poet and philosopher Muḥammad Iqbāl (1873–1938) this Prophetic tradition signifies the moment at which "the infidel's girdle," namely, "serial" time, is torn and "the mystic establishes direct contact with God in a person-to-person encounter."[30]

25 Bār-Moshe 1972, pp. 5–20.

26 Bār-Moshe 1972, pp. 151–66.

27 See al-Qushayrī n.d., p. 54; al-Ṭūsī 1960, pp. 66–7; Gardet 1971, pp. 83–5; Trimingham 1971, p. 200; al-Ḥifnī 1980, p. 73; Schimmel 1983, pp. 99–100.

28 Cf. Meister Eckhart's concept of time: "The person who lives in the light of God is conscious neither of time past nor of time to come but only of one eternity ... Therefore he gets nothing new of future events, nor from chance, for he lives in the Now-moment that is, unfailingly, 'in verdure newly clad'" (Scharfstein 1973, p. 151).

29 Schimmel 1983, pp. 129–30. Cf. al-Suhrawardī 1993, pp. 79–80.

30 Schimmel 1983, p. 220.

For Bār-Moshe, following medieval mystic Muslim literature, the mystical and sexual experiences are somehow frequently connected.[31] Some of his stories also include themes from modern Arabic science fiction and fantasy literature, especially with regard to the encounter with the higher essence. The combination of the mystical drive, sexual energy, and phantasy zeal is found in his stories as in the writing of other modern Arab authors. For example, in Bār-Moshe's "al-Sirdāb" ("The Cellar"),[32] which has allusions to the mystical Muslim heritage,[33] the protagonist is obsessed with a desire to go down into the cellar of the family's house, where his grandma had told him a genie dwelled. This obsession is highly reminiscent of the retreat and seclusion striven for by medieval Muslim ascetics (*zuhhād*) and mystics (Ṣūfīs) escaping the world of human passions in order to find refuge in the Divine Essence. After hesitating for many years, the protagonist finally overcomes his dread and goes down into the cellar. There at last he sees the genie, and has the epitome of the mystical sexual encounter with the Divine Truth:

> شعر أنّ عينيه تكاد تخرجان من محجريهما. تحجّر جسمه وتوقّفت حركة جفنيه. ثمّ أحسّ بهدوء عجيب يفيض على روحه ويغسل أفكاره وخواطره وينّظف دمه كّله ويحيل الهواء من حوله إلى شباك رائعة من النّور الخفيف. هذا هو نور الظّلام إذن. التصقت عيناه بهذا البريق الفّضي المنبعث من العينين المجهولتين ثمّ استطاع أن يرى على ضوء عينيها كّل جسمها. هل كان الجسم جسم طفلة أم جسم امرأة كاملة؟ التّناسق الرّائع في جسدها كان يمثّل شيئا يفوق كلّ صور الجمال الّتي يعرفها. أمّا العينان فكانتا ترمقانه بنظرة عميقة مشرقة هادئة، بل كانتا تشّعان فضّة. خيّل إليه أنّها حرّكت إحدى يديها. وفجأة اختفت كما ظهرت. ساد الظّلام الدّامس في السّرداب مرّة أخرى.

> He felt his eyes almost pop out of their sockets. His body turned to stone and the movement of his eyelids stopped. Then he felt that wondrous stillness abound in his soul and purify his thoughts and inner reflections and cleanse all his blood, and turn the air around him into a startling display of glowing light. Actually, this was the light of the gloom. His eyes were glued to the lightning from the silvery void of her mysterious eyes; then he was able to see, to the light of her eyes, the fullness of her body. Was this the body of a child or of a grown woman? The perfect harmony of her body was a thing that was better than all the beautiful pictures he knew. The eyes looked at him with a deep look, shining and serene, radiating a silvery light.[34]

Less than ten years later, the Egyptian science fiction writer Nihād Sharīf (1932–2011) published the story "Imra'a fī Ṭabaq Ṭā'ir" ("A Woman in a

[31] See, for example, Ibn ʿArabī 1966.

[32] Bār-Moshe 1972, pp. 167–78. The story was also published in *al-Sharq*, May 1972, pp. 12–14. On the story, see also Mudhi 1988, pp. 383–5. For an English translation of the story, see Snir 2019, pp. 251–7.

[33] See the chapters dealing with the various stages of the mystical experience in al-Qushayrī 1940, pp. 33–49, 62–4.

[34] Bār-Moshe 1972, p. 177.

Flying Saucer"),[35] which is highly reminiscent of Bār-Moshe's "The Cellar" in its mystical-sexual-phantasy drive: the narrator escapes from the noisy bustle of big city life for a few hours in order to look for some mystical refuge. Unlike Bār-Moshe's protagonist, he drives his car up into the mountains around Cairo, where he suddenly sees a beautiful woman:

> لمحتها تستند بكتفها العاري إلى نتوء صخريّ، وقد راحت تلوّح بأصابع رخصة موسيقيّة الأطراف، لكن ... هل لفظتها سحابة ضباب، فأين أطراف السّحابة وما حجمها؟ أم انبثقت من قلب نافورة دخان تبخّر تكوينها على الفور؟

> I saw her leaning with her naked shoulder on a jutting rock signaling to me with her soft musical-edged fingers. Yet, had she been thrown by a cloud of fog, where was that cloud and where were its edges and what was its size? Or had she been born from the heart of a fountain of smoke and its formation vanished at once?[36]

Genies or any other female demons in Bār-Moshe's stories also serve as a kind of *deus ex machina* to solve complicated mental, psychological, and spiritual disturbances of the suffering heroes. For example, in "Ṭarīq al-Ẓilāl" ("The Path of Shadows"),[37] a female demon appears before the hero while he is walking down a forest path to meet with his lover, Salmā.[38] In another story, which bears the collection's title, "Warā' al-Sūr"("Behind the Fence"),[39] the narrator is a small stone that a worker kicks inside the courtyard of a house. Through the stone's voice, the reader is invited to witness an investigation into the human characteristics and the relationships between characters from different classes in society, such as the owner of the house, the old gardener, the servant, a young man and his girlfriend hiding inside the garden kissing one another, the postman, and the servant-girl and her boyfriend. The stone also listens to a conversation between two men on whether God exists in stones. The story ends with a kind of pantheistic-mystical conception that everything in the world, even inanimate objects, share in the Divine Essence. The mystical and metaphysical tendency that characterizes some of the stories included in Bār-Moshe's first collection will be more dominant in his later collections.

35 Sharīf 1981, pp. 121–33.

36 Sharīf 1981, p. 122. On science fiction literature in Arabic, see Snir 2000a, pp. 263–85; Snir 2002b, pp. 209–29.

37 Bār-Moshe 1972, pp. 99–112.

38 It was suggested that the encounter with the female voice in the densely packed trees in the valley might be considered as a symbol of the possible solution to the hero's sexual needs (Moreh 1975, p. 50 [for the Hebrew version, see *Shevet ve-'Am* 3 (8) 1978, p. 434]. Cf. Mudhi 1988, pp. 380–1).

39 Bār-Moshe 1972, pp. 187–99. The story was also published in *al-Sharq*, June–July 1972, pp. 107–10. On the story, see also Mudhi 1988, pp. 400–3.

3. MYSTICAL AND METAPHYSICAL MOTIFS

Bār-Moshe's second collection, *al-Dubb al-Quṭbī wa-Qiṣaṣ Ukhrā* (*The Polar Bear and Other Stories*) (1973), includes fourteen stories, one of the most prominent of which is the story "Qaryat al-Aḥrār" ("The Village of Free Men"),[40] where the main idea is the desire to be free from the imprisonment of the body. The rejection of the chains of the body is one of the main doctrines of Muslim asceticism (*zuhd*), which was the historical basis of Sufism, and many of its principles were later assimilated into the theories of Muslim mysticism. This collection also refers to the author's interest in meta-fiction as expressed in the story "Riwāyat al-Ḥayāt" ("The Novel of Life"),[41] which deals with the gap between the behavior of the characters in a novel written by a friend of the narrator and their principles. However, unlike with his previous collection, here Bār-Moshe touches on his experiences in Iraq, such as in the story "Abū Naʿīma,"[42] which tells the story of a poor man whose love for a woman called Naʿīma is so desperate that he refuses to be named except after her.

The third collection, *Raqṣat al-Maṭar wa-Qiṣaṣ Ukhrā* (*The Dance of the Rain and Other Stories*) (1974), includes twelve stories, with most of them dealing with the sense of alienation of the individual from the surrounding society, with the mystical drive intruding, sometimes with mysterious and Surrealist implications. A good illustration is the story "al-Ishāʿa" ("The Rumor"),[43] in which a young woman has been disappointed by her lover and shuts herself into her house, abandoning society, and although no one speaks with her various rumors spread about her fate:

> راجت في البلد إشاعة تقول إنّ مريم اختفت. لم يرها أحد منذ أيّام وقد عجب الكثيرون لذلك إلّا أنّهم ربطوا الحوادث ببعضها البعض حتّى توصّلوا إلى نتيجة مفادها أنّ مريم لم تعد هناك. ربّما كان الاستنتاج من قبيل العباطة والتّسرّع في الحكم. ربّما. ولكن مريم لم يرها أحد أيّاما كثيرة. وليس أسهل من انتشار إشاعة. وفيما يخصّ مريم بالذّات لم يكن أسهل من أن تولد هذه الإشاعة عنها وانتشارها.

> There was a rumor in the town that Maryam had disappeared. No one has seen her for days and many wondered, but they linked the events to each other until they came to the conclusion that Maryam was no longer there. Perhaps the conclusion was accidental and hasty judgment. Maybe. But no one saw Maryam for many days. And no easier than spreading rumor. With

40 Bār-Moshe 1973, pp. 155–68.
41 Bār-Moshe 1973, pp. 79–92.
42 Bār-Moshe 1973, pp. 123–38. The story was also published in *al-Sharq*, September 1973, pp. 39–44.
43 Bār-Moshe 1974, pp. 7–28. On the collection, see the review by Salīm al-Baṣṣūn (1927–1995) in *al-Sharq*, October–December 1974, pp. 96–8.

regard to Maryam in particular, it was not easy to generate this rumor about her and spread it.[44]

One can hardly overlook the similarities between this story and texts by the Surrealist writer and poet André Breton (1896–1966), especially when translated into Arabic,[45] or Surrealist Arabic texts, such as those by the Iraqi poet ʻAbd al-Qādir al-Janābī (b. 1944), as in his prose poem "Allāh fī Kalima" ("Allāh in a Word"), which was published about twenty years after the publication of Bār-Moshe's story. One cannot exclude that al-Janābī was inspired by this very story when writing one of his own prose poems, which seems to hold intertextual connections with the story:

العجوزُ الّتي تعيش في الغرفة المقابلة لشقّتنا، والّتي كثيرا ما كانت تتأمّل، في مرآةٍ مشروخة، أحناء جمالها المترهّل، العجوزُ هذه ... لا أظنّها إلّا قد ماتت. منذ ثلاثة أيّام وغرفتها في ظلام يثير أسئلة جدّ متضاربة في أذهان نُزلاء البناية الّتي أسكن. لكن ...، لِم هذا الشّعور المتشائم بأنّ كلّ غيابٍ هو موتٌ نهائيّ؟ العجوز هذه، إمّا انزوت عن أنظارنا لغرضٍ إبداعيّ (ألم تقل لنا أنّها تنادم الكتابة أيّاما لكي تتخلّص من الصّور التي جعلتها ضريرة) وإمّا ذهبت إلى بلد آخر للاستراحة، للتأمّل: ربّ هواءٍ صحيح يتسرّب من نافذة - ذاكرة بعيدة ... إنّها عجوز قبل كلّ شيء.
غيرَ أنّ ليلة أخرى قد مرّت والظّلام هو إزاءُهُ؟ "فليكن"، صرّح أحدُ النّزلاء: "ما دام ليس هنالك من مَعلَم يؤكّد لنا موت عجوز. البابُ مبهمٌ فحسب".
إنّهُ على حقّ: "مبهمٌ فحسب".
إذن،
شيءٌ ما يسري.

The old woman who lives in the apartment facing our apartment, who frequently is contemplating, before a shrouded mirror, the beauty of her sagging beauty, that old woman ... I think that she has passed away. For three days her apartment has been in darkness arousing very conflicting questions in the minds of the tenants of my building. But ... why is this pessimistic feeling that any absence is a final death? That old woman, perhaps she disappeared out of our eyes for a creative purpose (didn't she tell us that she used to occupy herself in writing in order to get rid of the images that had made her blind), or perhaps she went to another country to rest, for contemplation: perhaps a correct air leaks out of a window—a distant memory ... She is indeed an old woman before anything else. But another night has passed and the darkness is the same. "Let it be," one of the tenants declared, "as long as there is no sign referring to a death of an old woman. The door is just vague and that's all."
He is right: "It is just vague and that's all."
Which means,
Something is happening.[46]

44 Bār-Moshe 1974, p. 9.
45 See, for example, Breton 2018.
46 See al-Janābī 1995, p. 27.

People in both the story and the poem are preoccupied with the disappearance of a "strange" woman, but their assumptions and the rumors they spread regarding the circumstances of that disappearance are not only about her—they uncover the attitude of the surrounding society toward the individual.

The first three collections give the impression that Bār-Moshe wishes to present his literary work within the tradition of universal literature written in Arabic with only minor connections with his Arab-Jewish past in Iraq or with the Middle East conflict. The span of time between his emigration from Baghdad and the publication of these collections strengthens that conviction and has enabled critics to present theses about his literary preferences.[47]

In the following years, Bār-Moshe published three more collections of short stories, some of which dealt with the Israeli–Palestinian Conflict. He dedicated his fourth collection, *Aswār al-Quds wa-Qiṣaṣ Ukhrā* (*The Walls of Jerusalem and Other Stories*) (1976), which includes eleven stories, to "my brothers and friends on both sides of the line." The stories deal with various aspects of Jewish–Arab encounters following the 1967 War; most of them express an attempt to understand the feeling and desires of people on either side of the conflict. For example, the first story, "al-La'na al-Ūlā" ("The First Curse"),[48] deals with the psychological motives behind the acts of the Palestinian *fedayeen* who risk their lives in the struggle with Israel. In the second story, "al-Risāla" ("The Letter"),[49] an Israeli soldier whose brother was killed in the war reveals a humanistic sense by helping a Palestinian to send a letter to worried relatives abroad. In both stories, the writer tries to understand the feelings and miseries of Palestinian individuals. Other stories, such as "Aḥmad wa-l-Ṭabīb" ("Aḥmad and the Physician")[50] and "Maktab al-Ustādh Anwar" ("The Office of Mr. Anwar"),[51] try to penetrate into the souls of Palestinian individuals in East Jerusalem, who suffer and feel distress as a result of the 1967 encounter with their Jewish neighbors. One sentence from an interior monologue in a story titled "al-Musaddas" ("The Revolver")[52] will illustrate the stance of the implied author of the entire collection: "The only important point is to observe human relationships and respect the humanity of human beings, in every situation, in every

47 For example, S. Ballas' article in *Haaretz*, July 25, 1975.
48 Bār-Moshe 1976, pp. 7–22.
49 Bār-Moshe 1976, pp. 23–40.
50 Bār-Moshe 1976, pp. 41–59. The story was also published in *al-Sharq*, October–December 1975, pp. 49–59.
51 Bār-Moshe 1976, pp. 103–19.
52 Bār-Moshe 1976, pp. 135–49. The story was also published in *al-Sharq*, August–October 1974, pp. 33–8.

circumstance, by way of any and all means."[53] In his next two collections, *Allāh wa-l-Zahra wa-Qiṣaṣ Ukhrā* (*God and the Flower and Other Stories*) (1982) and *Mā Warā' al-Ḥayāt wa-Qiṣaṣ Ukhrā* (*Beyond Life and Other Stories*) (1985), the writer continues his preaching of this objective with new attempts to understand the psychological structure of ordinary men and women. However, all he published after 1975 was overshadowed by his semi-autobiographical trilogy in which through a personal account he gave expression to the collective experiences of the Iraqi Jews in the twentieth century. The three parts of the trilogy remain as indispensable historical documents for the history of Iraqi Jews in modern times.

4. "IRAQ'S DAYS"

From the middle of the 1970s, Bār-Moshe surprised his readers with the publication of a semi-autobiographical trilogy covering his own life in Iraq and corresponding to the most critical stage of the Jewish-Iraqi community in modern times. The historical and political events that influenced the life of the Iraqi Jews until the mass immigration were for Bār-Moshe a background for a vivid and colorful panoramic description of Jewish life in Baghdad. In rich language, he touches on almost every corner of the culturally Arab-Jewish life in the colorful exotic streets and alleys of Baghdad; its characters, traditions, costumes, daily life; and the complicated relationship of the Jews with their Muslim neighbors. Reading the trilogy, one can hardly ignore the great inspiration that Egyptian literature had on Bār-Moshe,[54] particularly the work of Ṭāhā Ḥusayn (1889–1973) and Najīb Maḥfūẓ (1911–2006). In writing each of the three novels, the author was inspired by Ḥusayn's autobiographical novel *al-Ayyām* (*The Days*) (1926–1927); however, unlike *al-Ayyām*, Bār-Moshe employs the first person, coloring his narrative with a very intimate and subjective tone. The intimate tone is strengthened by the frequent use of dialogues and interior monologues. Inspired by Maḥfūẓ's Cairene trilogy,[55] Bār-Moshe employs a fictional strategy in which the general political events are a necessary framework for the depiction of the characters and their lives. And this was so much so that one may read the

[53] Bār-Moshe 1976, p. 147. On the collection, see Sasson Somekh's (1933–2019) essay in *Iton 77*, April–May 1977, pp. 12–13.

[54] On the role of Egypt in the life of Jewish intellectuals in Iraq, see Bār-Moshe's own testimony in his novel *Ayyām al-ʿIrāq* (Bār-Moshe 1988, pp. 107–8, 223–24). Bār-Moshe also published *Miṣr fī Qalbī* (*Egypt in My Heart*) (Bār-Moshe 1994), a memoir on the years he had spent in Egypt during his diplomatic mission. The book describes his impressions of Egyptian culture. While living in Baghdad in the 1940s, like all Iraqi intellectuals of his generation, he was greatly inspired by its leadership in the Arab world.

[55] Written before the revolution of 1952 and published only in 1956–1957.

trilogy of Maḥfūẓ as a kind of alternative history of Egyptian society in the first half of the twentieth century and Bār-Moshe's trilogy as a kind of history of the Iraqi Jews in the twentieth century. The dialogues in both trilogies are reconstructions in literary standard Arabic (*fuṣḥā*) of what would have been spoken in the Egyptian or Iraqi dialect (*ʿāmmiyya*).

The first book in the trilogy is the memoir *al-Khurūj min al-ʿIrāq: Dhikrayāt 1945–1950* (*Exodus from Iraq: Memories 1945–1950*) (1975).[56] With this, Bār-Moshe was the first author to publish a personal account of the events leading up to the tragic end of the Iraqi-Jewish community, which was descended from the ancient Jewish Babylonian community as described in the Old Testament. The book, Bār-Moshe says, is "a novel if you like, or a collection of short stories, or a personal history, but in the final [analysis] it is perhaps a mixture of all of these things together."[57] Consisting of 123 chapters, each self-contained and recounting some event, the book records true episodes, either experienced by the author himself or by friends of his. Some episodes may seem trivial and minor, while others provide the reader with glimpses that contribute to the study of the short stories the author had previously published: for example, in one episode, which calls to mind the above story "al-Sirdāb" ("The Cellar"), he describes how children were afraid to go down into the cellar of the family's house for fear of meeting the genie that dwelled there.[58]

It is the accumulation of all these types of episodes that gives the book its full impact, especially seen from the viewpoint of the events that preceded the mass immigration of the Iraqi Jews to Israel in the early 1950s, following a wave of harassment and systematic persecution. In all their long history, Iraqi Jews had never experienced such significant discrimination from their Muslim compatriots. Moreover, the reader is led to the conclusion that the Jewish emigration was not at all a result of an inner Zionist drive on the part of the Iraqi Jews but rather the result of sheer stupidity and blindness on the part of the Iraqi authorities at the time (in particular that of the successive governments of Nūrī al-Saʿīd [1888–1958]) and their shortsighted policies

[56] For reviews of the book, see N.R.(*sic!*) in *Jewish Observer & Middle East Review*, June 27, 1975; Nīr Shohet (1928–2011) in *Ba-Maʿracha*, 174 (July 1975), pp. 16–17; Muḥammad Abū Shalabiyya, "Some Observations and Notions about the Book 'Exodus from Iraq,'" *al-Anbāʾ*, July 20–27, 1975; S. Khayyat in *Ba-Maʿracha*, 177 (October 1975), pp. 20, 24; S. G. Haim, "Anatomy of an Exodus," *Times Literary Supplement*, March 12, 1976, p. 296. The book was also published in Hebrew (with the addition of titles to all its chapters): see Bār-Moshe 1977. For reviews of the Hebrew version, see Moshe-Giyora Elimelekh in *Haaretz*, May 29, 1977, p. 14; S. Somekh in *Iton 77*, June–July 1977, pp. 12–13; I. Black in *The Jerusalem Post*, November 11, 1977; as well as a review in *ʿAl Ha-Mishmar*, May 12, 1978.

[57] Bār-Moshe 1975, p. 20.

[58] Bār-Moshe 1975, p. 45.

and cynical opportunism; it seems they used the Jews as a scapegoat for their own problems and failures, in order to protect themselves from the anger of their own people. In a chapter titled "When the Time Stopped,"[59] Bār-Moshe refers to the trial and execution of Shafīq ʿAdas (1900–1948) as a turning point in the modern history of Iraqi Jews. ʿAdas, a wealthy businessman from Basra, is arrested on charges of siding with the clandestine Zionist movement. For their refusal to interfere, the author considers the British as another villain in this injustice, which the Jews understood as a clear sign that Iraq was no longer their homeland.

Eight years later, Bār-Moshe published the semi-autobiographical novel *Bayt fi Baghdad* (*A House in Baghdad*) (1983),[60] which tells the story of three generations of his family and of his own childhood and boyhood. The novel opens in the mid-1920s, when the narrator was two years old, and ends with the events of 1936, when the *coup d'état* of Bakr Ṣidqī took place. Referring to the strong impression that the novel leaves on readers as regards the deep bonds of friendship and goodwill between Jews and Muslims in Iraq, Nissīm Rijwān (Rejwan) (1924–2017),[61] himself an Iraqi Jew, wrote that many readers of the book, including Muslim and Christian Arabs, "will probably find it difficult to believe how closely-knit the lives of the Jews and non-Jews were in Iraq."[62] The period that the author deals with, which is prior to the penetration of Nazi propaganda into Iraq, was colored with a vision of Muslim–Christian–Jewish cooperation. However, throughout the novel the implied author is aware of the inevitable expected failure of this vision. Although the novel concentrates on the life of the Jews in Iraq, some writers in Egypt paid specific attention to the phenomenon of a Jewish author writing about the symbiotic contact of the Jews with Muslims and Christians. In his column in *al-Jumhūriyya*, Ibrāhīm al-Wirdānī (1919–1991), for example, expressed his astonishment at the similarities in the life and mores of the Jewish community, as described in the novel, and those of the average Arab household. Bār-Moshe, according to al-Wirdānī, "frankly, let me enter the Jewish-Arab household in all its detail and made me feel as if I

59 Bār-Moshe 1975, pp. 287–95. This chapter is not numbered within the 123 chapters of the book and appears after chapter 56 and before chapter 57, as if to give the impression of the stopping of the serial time. Against the background of the above discussion of the Ṣūfī *waqt* and the mystical experience as breaking through created serial time, one can think of the author as ascribing "metaphysical roots" to the historical events.

60 The novel was published in Hebrew a year before its publication in Arabic (Bār-Moshe 1982).

61 On Rejwan and his work, see Ben-Yaacob 1980, p. 404; Alcalay 1996, pp. 46–60; Rejwan 2004.

62 *Jerusalem Post Magazine*, September 26, 1984, p. 26.

had actually lived there."[63] Unfortunately, the hybridic Arab-Jewish cultural aspects of the novel, which were praised by al-Wirdānī, were the very reason why the Hebrew version has been totally ignored by the Israeli canonical cultural circles, which still do not recognize the hybridic Arab-Jewish culture as a legitimate option in Israeli society.[64]

In 1988, Bār-Moshe completed his trilogy with *Ayyām al-ʿIrāq* (*Iraq's Days*), which covers the period between the mid-1930s and the mid-1940s. One of the anecdotes in this novel provides further evidence of the motivation for Jewish students to demonstrate excellence in Arabic and the resultant tension that came about between themselves and Muslims. The narrator recalls how a teacher of his praised his style and even held his work up as a model of excellence, but in so doing did not reveal his identity.[65]

A short while before he passed away in December 2003, Bār-Moshe had completed the manuscript of his last book, which was on the events of the *Farhūd*. This book, *Yawmān fī Ḥazīrān* (*Two Days in June*), was published posthumously.[66] In a "clarification" appended to the book, Bār-Moshe explains that this book is part of the historical context of his already published trilogy and that the four books together form *al-Rubāʿiyya al-ʿIrāqiyya* (*The Iraqi Quartet*). One could, however, view *Two Days in June* as an addendum to *Ayyām al-ʿIrāq* (1988), in the last scene of which the narrator walks down al-Rashīd Street in Baghdad in an atmosphere of increasing tension following the start of the German offensive against Poland. When he notices headlines in the *Iraq Times* newspaper on Britain's declaration of war against Germany, he walks faster to try to avoid bursting into tears; when he gets home, he breaks down and weeps, crying until "I started to paint in my imagination a dreadful picture of what would happen, the horror of which put an end to tears, and made the heart as strong as granite."[67]

From the fictional point of view, the last scene of *Ayyām al-ʿIrāq* is a kind of foreshadowing or an advance mention, that is, a narrative "seed" whose importance would not usually be recognized on first appearance. However, in *Ayyām al-ʿIrāq* it is clear to the reader that this foreshadowing is a prelude to the *Farhūd*'s events, which are described in *Yawmān fī Ḥazīrān*, whose 154 pages are divided into 38 chapters that are full of expanded and detailed

[63] See *al-Jumhūriyya*, October 19, 1983, p. 6. See also al-Wirdānī's column in the same daily on September 23, 1983, p. 6; as well as Muḥammad al-ʿAzabī's essay in *al-Jumhūriyya*, November 21, 1983.

[64] For reviews on the Hebrew version, see M. Avi-Shlomo (Mordechai Avishai [1931–2004]) in *ʿAl Ha-Mishmar*, December 17, 1982; Moshe Piamenta (1921–2012) in *Maariv*, May 6, 1983; Ehud Ben-Ezer (b. 1936) in *Haaretz*, July 1, 1983, p. 23.

[65] Bār-Moshe 1988, pp. 265–6.

[66] Bār-Moshe 2004.

[67] Bār-Moshe 1988, pp. 388–9.

dialogues complementary to *Ayyām al-'Irāq*. The latter is the shortest part of the trilogy. It has 389 pages; *Bayt fī Baghdad* (*A House in Baghdad*) (1983) has 420 pages; and "Exodus from Iraq" has 597 pages. It seems that, when Bār-Moshe wrote *Ayyām al-'Irāq* (*Iraq's Days*) (1988), confronting memories of the *Farhūd* was very disconcerting. Even in his last book, *Yawmān fī Ḥazīrān*, he was very cautious in dealing with the horrors of the events and generally preferred to concentrate on general background and related events.[68]

Bār-Moshe wrote his last book from a Zionist perspective. For example, one of the main figures is the narrator's friend Elie Kedourie (Īlī Khaddūrī) who, as a fourteen- or fifteen-year-old at the time, appears to be, despite his youth, an authority on political science and Middle Eastern affairs (undoubtedly, his figure is built in view of his future achievements). In a dialogue with the narrator, Kedourie, whose relationship with the narrator seems to be that of a mentor to admirer (although he was older than the author-narrator by only one year), anticipates even before the *Farhūd* that, as an outcome of the war in Europe and the situation in Palestine, "the upshot of it all will probably be the declaration soon of a Jewish state."[69] This is presumably a view that the "real" Kedourie would never have expressed in early 1941. More than once Kedourie argued that even in the 1940s "the Zionist cause did not seem to me as a matter of any political wisdom. The expectancies which Zionism was creating were too high and unrealistic."[70]

Events in Iraq in 2003 and hopes for the establishment of a new Iraqi state dominate the last chapter of *Yawman fī Ḥazīrān*. Titled "Retrospective Glance—in 2003," the chapter relates how the *Farhūd* was followed by a second *Farhūd*—in the early 1950s, when Iraqi harassment and persecution caused the mass immigration to Israel. The end of the last chapter reads: "The Iraqi people woke up in 2003 when their country had to start everything from the beginning (this time it was a popular *Farhūd* against the *Ba'th* government and the tyrannical family of Ṣaddām Ḥusayn)."[71]

68 We cannot find any references to the *Farhūd*'s events in the Arabic literature of the Iraqi Jews written in Iraq; even after the mass immigration of the Iraqi Jews to Israel in the early 1950s, those who continue to write in Arabic hardly mentioned these events. Only from the 1970s, writers such as Isḥāq Bār-Moshe and Samīr Naqqāsh started to deal with these events in their fiction (Snir 2005a, pp. 201, 214–15, 226, 229). In Hebrew literature, we can find earlier mentions of events (Snir 2005a, pp. 277, 309–10, 430, 432). Muslim and Christian authors have rarely mentioned the *Farhūd* such as the poet Jabbār Jamāl al-Dīn (see at: https://akhbaar.org/home/2016/6/212638.html, June 1, 2016, last accessed December 18, 2021).

69 Bār-Moshe 2004, p. 66.

70 *Davar Ha-Shavu'*, April 7, 1988, p. 9.

71 Bār-Moshe 2004, p. 154.

On the whole, from the literary point of view one should note that the author's work in journalism had an imprint on his style: unlike the tendency of Arab writers of the second half of the twentieth century to present condensed texts, sometimes so ambiguous so as to permit "a variety of interpretations" and "a multiplicity of meanings,"[72] Bār-Moshe avoids any ambiguity and provides readers with lengthy and detailed conversations without leaving anything in doubt. This certainly brings some of his descriptive writing closer to being journalistic reportage and somehow farther from the modernist literary style.[73]

5. CONCLUSION

Arab-Jewish authors who insisted on retaining some connection with their Arab origins, such as writing in Arabic even if they did it from a Zionist perspective, have paid the price of marginalization and being pushed to the remote edges of Israeli society and culture. Isḥāq Bār-Moshe, whose literary career began in the early 1970s, was one of the last Jewish writers in Arabic.[74] Despite the richness of his literary works, he was pushed to the margins of Israeli literature and had a very limited readership. The canonical Hebrew establishment did not express any interest in his works—none of his writings have attracted the attention of outstanding literary critics. He has generally been considered to be an ethnic voice giving expression to views and issues that at most are relevant to only a limited section of Israeli society. This is in evident contrast, at least as seen above from the point of view of his short stories, to the universal nature of his work. His marginal status in Israeli culture as well as the feeling that for nonliterary considerations his work has been left without serious attention from Arab critics and scholars are presumably the reasons why his literary voice was not heard in the years before his death. He tried to publish his memoir *Miṣr fī Qalbī* (*Egypt in My Heart*) in Hebrew, but no publisher expressed any interest in the experiences

[72] The phrases are of the Syrian poet Adūnīs ('Alī Aḥmad Sa'īd) (b. 1930), who speaks in favor of the rejection of clarity and the pre-eminence of ambiguity and obscurity (Adūnīs 2000 [1985], p. 54 [English translation: Adonis 1990, p. 52]). Although Adūnīs speaks about the writing of poetry, since the 1960s the transgeneric phenomena in Arabic literature have been so outstanding that many traits of poetry have become integral components of Arabic prose.

[73] For a review of the trilogy, see M. J. L. Young's essay in *Middle Eastern Studies* 27.3 (July 1991), pp. 528–33.

[74] In addition to the above references, for more on Bār-Moshe's life and works, see Ben-Yaacob 1980, pp. 400–1; Moreh 1981, pp. 233–6; Moreh and 'Abbāsī 1987, pp. 26–8; Berg 1996, pp. 112–20. M. H. Mudhi deals with Bār-Moshe's literary works of the early 1970s only; therefore, his discussion is void of an overall perspective (Mudhi 1988, pp. 365–403).

of an Arab-Jewish writer restoring his direct connections with Arab culture after a break of more than thirty years.[75] As the roots of Jewish nationalism lie in Eastern Europe and the overall orientation of modern Israeli canonical culture is predominantly Ashkenazi- and Western-oriented, no wonder that Arab culture has been rejected by the dominant circles. As I mentioned above, there is no better illustration of this than the structure of Hebrew and comparative literature departments at Israeli universities, where you can hardly find tenured academic scholars of modern Hebrew literature or comparative literature who have knowledge of Arabic or have taken the trouble to study Arabic language and literature. Comparative studies may legitimately be done with Russian, Italian, Japanese, Polish, and, of course, with English, French, and German, but hardly with Arabic literary works in the original.

Bār-Moshe's life and literary work may be regarded as a microcosm for the fate of Arabic literature by Jews. As part of a Eurocentric narrative and adopting the dichotomy between East and West as a given, objective category, the hegemonic Zionist narrative's attitude to Bār-Moshe's work and to Arab-Jewish culture in general is not surprising. "Stripped of our history," as Arab-Jewish scholar Ella Shohat (b. 1959) says in her "Reflections of an Arab Jew,"[76] "we have been forced by our no-exit situation to repress our collective nostalgia." In the documentary film *Forget Baghdad: Jews and Arabs—The Iraqi Connection* (2002),[77] Shohat relates how "when I went to kindergarten in Israel, I was aware that Arabic words sometimes slipped in when I spoke. I was ashamed." The Western-Ashkenazi cultural Israeli center imposed limits upon thought about the Arab-Jewish legacy, as Orientalism imposed limits upon thought about the Orient. Like Orientalism, the Western-Ashkenazi center has "a political vision of reality whose structure promoted the difference between the familiar (Europe, the West, 'us') and the strange (the Orient, the East, 'them')."[78] In order to be incorporated into the narrative, as the historian Gabriel Piterberg (b. 1955) puts it, "the Arab-Jews were forced to negate their memory and culture, just as 'the Exilic Jew' was forced to do according to the general pattern of the Negation of Exile, in order to transform themselves and become eligible to join the Zionist/Israeli imagined community."[79]

75 Bār-Moshe 1994, p. 7.

76 Shohat 2003, pp. 115–21.

77 The film prodiced by Dschoint Ventschr (Zurich) was directed by the Iraqi Shiite exile filmmaker Samīr Jamāl al-Dīn (b. 1955). On the film, see also below, Chapter 8.

78 Said 1985 [1978], p. 43.

79 Piterberg 1996, p. 135. On the unbridgeable gap between the paradigm of Jewish return as expressed in Zionist ideology, and the concrete, lived history of many of Arab Jews who have migrated to Israel, see Ben-Dor 2006, pp. 135–62.

Isḥāq Bār-Moshe made his literary debut in Arabic in Israel in the beginning of the 1970s. These were the years when the Jewish writers, who had remained in Iraq and refused to join the immigration to Israel in the beginning of the 1950s, started to realize that Iraq was no more a place for Jews. Nevertheless, even in these circumstances, they still were hoping that Arabic was a language in which Jews could express themselves as they had done continuously from the pre-Islamic period. However, it was paradoxical that when Bār-Moshe was in the process of writing stories that would be included in his first collection *Warā' al-Sūr wa-Qiṣaṣ Ukhrā* (1972), the Iraqi-Jewish authors sensed that what had been natural during more than 1,500 years was not obvious now and that there were doubts about the Arab-Jewish road of literary cooperation. In February 1969, Anwar Shā'ul wrote in Baghdad the poem "Religion and Patriotism," in which he tried to prove that there was no contradiction between being a Jew and a proud Arab-Iraqi poet:

إن كنت من موسى قبست عقيدتي   فأنا المقيم بظـلّ دين محمّـدِ
وسماحة الإسـلام كانـت موئلـي   وبلاغة القرآن كانت موردي
مـا نـال من حبّي لأمّـة أحمـدِ   كوني على دين الكليم تعبّدي
سأظلّ ذيّاك السّـمـوأل في الوفـا   أسعدت في بغداد أم لم أسعدِ

From Moses I borrowed my creed,
  But under Islam's protection I have lived;
Its generosity is my shelter;
  The Qur'ān's bounty is my undying fountain;
My adherence to Moses's creed has not
  Diminished my love for Muhammad's nation;
Faithful I will stay like as-Samaw'al
  Be I happy in Baghdad or miserable.[80]

It is sad that in the present Israeli Western-oriented culture, the terms "Arab-Jewish" or "Jewish-Arab" refer almost exclusively to activities concerning both Arabs *and* Jews. Thus, when the press mentions, for example, a "Jewish-Arab Musical Youth Orchestra,"[81] it is unreasonable to suppose that this refers to any sort of revival of the Jewish-Arab Baghdadi ensembles of the 1930s. Only few remembered that the orchestra that represented Iraq

[80] Shā'ul 1983, p. 69. According to Shā'ul, those verses contributed to the release of Mīr Baṣrī after he had been detained and charged with spying (Shā'ul 1980, pp. 329–33; see also the details concerning that case in Snir 2005a, pp. 87–8).

[81] A "multicultural" orchestra of Israeli-Jewish, Christian, and Muslim players, directed by Ronen Shapira (b. 1966) and Wisām Jubrān (b. 1970) and supported by UNESCO, whose purpose was to promote peace in the Middle East through music (see *Haaretz*, November 12, 2003).

at the First Congress of Arabic Music (Cairo, 1932) was entirely Jewish.[82] Also, as mentioned above, the orchestra of the Baghdad Broadcasting House consisted of five Jews and one Muslim. Both ensembles performed with the well-known Muslim recitalist Muḥammad al-Qabānjī (al-Qebbantchi) (1901–1989).[83]

In July 2004, less than seven months after Bār-Moshe had passed away, the aforementioned Samīr Naqqāsh, another of the last of the Arab-Jewish Mohicans, passed away. Both of them spent their last years in Manchester—the new exile they had chosen for themselves after the great disappointment they experienced in Israel, the ancient Jewish homeland to which both of them immigrated from their Iraqi fatherland. Despite the differences in the nature of their literary works,[84] both reached a tragic dead-end—their life outside Iraq was essentially cultural exile. Because of their unique position as Jews writing in Arabic, neither the Jewish Hebrew literary arena nor the Muslim or Christian Arabic arena was willing to accept them as legitimate authors. Several years before his death, and without possessing the most elementary means for honorable survival, Naqqāsh expressed his tragic situation as an Arab-Jewish writer in the Israeli Zionist Western-oriented society in the following words:

> I don't exist in this country, neither as a writer, citizen, or human being. I don't feel that I belong anywhere, not since my roots were torn from the ground [in Baghdad].[85]

82 By no means do I overlook the multiplicity of contemporary popular Oriental musical traditions (*muzika mizraḥīt*) and popular manifestations of Arab-Jewish and Mizrahi identities as expressed, for example, in the studies of the poet and scholar Haviva Pedaya (b. 1957), such as *Ha-Mizraḥ Kotev Et 'Atzmo* (*The Mizrah Writes Itself*) (Pedaya 2015); and *Shivato shel Ha-Kol Ha-Goleh: Zehut Mizraḥit, Po'etika, Muzika U-Merchav* (*Return of the Lost Voice: Poetics, Music and Space*) (Pedaya 2016). See also Regev 1996, pp. 275–84; Regev and Seroussi 2004, pp. 191–235; Oppenheimer 2012; Oppenheimer 2014; Francfort 2021. Also, it goes without saying that my arguments have nothing to do with issues of the civil rights struggle as expressed, for example, in Roby 2015. Cf. Roby 2022, pp. 1–42. In addition, my arguments do not deal with the linguistic interactions between Hebrew and Arabic within the intensely politicized space of Israel/Palestine and the relationship through literature between Jewish and Palestinian authors as discussed in Levy 2014.

83 See *The Scribe* 72 (September 1999), p. 50. On the contribution of Arab Jews to Arab music, see Shiloah 1992; Hirshberg 1996; Kojaman 2001.

84 Muḥammad Jalā' Idrīs (b. 1953) referred to the writings of both of them in order to illustrate the influence of Islam on the writings of Jewish writers in Arabic; moreover, he considers the inspiration they drew from Islam as part of a wider influence of Islam on Israeli literature, Hebrew and Arabic (Idrīs 1992, pp. 83–117. Cf. Idrīs 2003).

85 Berg 1996, p. 3.

In one of his last interviews,[86] Bār-Moshe expressed the same feeling. I have been reading and investigating their literary works for more than thirty years—whenever I concentrate on the works of one of them, I have the temptation to regard his whole literature as conveying and encapsulating the life-sensation of the Arab-Jewish authors against the backdrop of the demise of Arab-Jewish culture and identity. But then I think of his compatriot Arab-Jewish Mohican and remember that it is impossible to convey the life-sensation of even their own dark existence among people who never tried to understand their tragedy. As great admirers of Western literature, I assume that both read *Heart of Darkness* (1899) by Joseph Conrad (1857–1924), where he wrote:

> No, it is impossible; it is impossible to convey the life-sensation of any given epoch of one's existence—that which makes its truth, its meaning—its subtle and penetrating essence. It is impossible. We live, as we dream—alone.[87]

But unlike Conrad, the exiled Polish writer regarded as one of the greatest English novelists and at the same time considered as "the first novelist of globalisation,"[88] Bār-Moshe and Naqqāsh were exiled even from their own language. Trying to live as they dream, if we borrow Conrad's words, and although Arabic is one of the languages of globalization, both of them have been forgotten.

In the wake of national and political conflict in the Middle East, Arab-Jewish culture underwent a process of a gradual drop into utter oblivion thanks to both the Muslim-Arab and Jewish-Hebrew canonical cultural systems. Both sides, each for their own narrowed reasons and out of their own particularistic considerations, have generally refused to accept the legitimacy of the Arab-Jewish hybridity. While imposing their interpretative authority over all other cultural groups, the hegemonic cultural Hebrew circles, which pride themselves on being mainly leftist-liberal, refrain from openly and publicly expressing negative views regarding Arab culture, certainly not regarding Arab-Jewish culture. This is presumably for fear that it would mean voicing a disparaging attitude toward the "Other" and would thus not be "politically correct," especially after multiculturalism had become a fundamental component of the new local intellectual discourse and the consensus of opinion, at least publicly, was that the Eurocentric character of Israeli society should be multiculturalized. To resolve this "cognitive dissonance" and preserve the cozy reassurance of its liberal and tolerant attitude toward the culture of the

86 *Ha-Kivun Mizrah* 7 (2003), pp. 15–21.
87 Conrad 1996, p. 43.
88 *The Economist*, November 4, 2017.

minorities in its midst, the literary establishment gives Arab or Arab-Jewish culture "seats" in the local cultural arena—examples are Palestinian writers, such as the Druze Na'īm 'Arāyidī (1948–2015) and the Christian Anṭūn Shammās (b. 1950), who were "chosen" by the canonical center as "representatives" of the Israeli-Palestinian minority,[89] or Arab-Jewish writers, such as Sami Michael (b. 1926) and Eli 'Amīr (b. 1937), as "representatives" of the Mizrahi communities.[90]

It is not too far-fetched to see Arabic literature by Jews as another victim of the conflict played out in Palestine, especially following the disappearance of the distinction between "Jew" and "Zionist" in Arab nationalist discourse and the attitude of the hegemonic Zionist narrative to Arab culture. Since the early 1950s, the literature of twentieth-century Arabized Jews produced in Arabic has entirely been relegated to the margins of Arabic literature. Political, national, and cultural reasons are behind that process and behind the paucity of scholarly attention that has been paid to this literature through the years. Although the literary writing of Arabized Jews in the 1940s gained some attention among Jewish intellectuals in Palestine,[91] scholars outside the Arab world since 1948 have shunned the study of that literature. Now, unfortunately, only rarely can we hear Muslim and Christian authors and intellectuals regret the fact that the Jewish voice in Arab literature has been lost.[92] Moreover, most of them hardly know that such a voice ever existed.

At the same time, the scholarship of Arabic literature has recently been experiencing vital changes that also shed light on the scholarship of

89 See Snir 1992, pp. 6–9; Snir 1995a, pp. 163–83; Snir 1997, pp. 141–53; Snir 2001a, pp. 197–224. Cf. Dekel and Tzelgov 2020, pp. 1–10.

90 See Snir 2005a, pp. 309–76.

91 See, for example, Y. Ben Hananya, "Jewish Writers and Poets in Iraq" (in Hebrew), *Hed Ha-Mizrah*, September 29, 1943, p. 12; October 13, 1943, pp. 6–7; October 29, 1943, p. 7; November 12, 1943, pp. 6–7.

92 The Lebanese writer and critic Ilyās Khūrī (Elias Khoury) (b. 1948) considers the "Jewish-Arab voice" a central voice in Arab culture; therefore, its loss has been a severe blow to that culture (interview with Anton Shammās in *Yediot Aḥronoth*, March 15, 2002, p. 60. Cf. the Arabic version of the interview is in *Mashārif* (Haifa) 17 (Summer 2002), pp. 237–8. It is ironic that, about six years earlier, Khūrī himself threatened to walk out of the hall during a conference on Arabic literature in Carthage (Tunis) when the Israeli writer Sami Michael, himself an Arab Jew in origin, was prepared to come up on the stage to give his lecture. Michael's anger was expressed in his essay "Shylock in Carthage," *The Jewish Quarterly*, Winter 1994–1995, pp. 71–2. Under the title "The Experience of Oriental Jews in Israel: Have We Lost Forever the Jews of Iraq?" the Jordanian writer Ibrāhīm Gharāyiba (b. 1962) laments the failure of the Arabs to have the Arab Jews, especially the Iraqis, as an integral part of Arab society and culture (*al-Ḥayāt*, July 25, 2002, p. 25. The article appeared in English translation in *The Scribe*, the journal of Babylonian Jewry published by the Jewish Exilarch's Foundation in London, vol. 72 [September 1999], p. 25. However, the translation omits some sentences in which the writer argues that the above failure has only served Israeli and Zionist aggression against the Arabs).

Arab-Jewish culture, the basic canonical component of which since the pre-Islamic period has been literature. The rapid development and spread of Internet technologies have done much to change the way culture is perceived and have changed dramatically the way literature in general—Arabic literature included—is created and consumed. The impact of the Internet on Arabic literary writing has been gradually intensifying, and there are signs that Arabic literature is changing in many respects. Where the Internet is available (without strict governmental interventions), there is no censorship, no publishing limitations, no need for literary editors, and no need for financial resources to publish whatever you want. Also, the temporal distance between writing and publishing has now become shorter, if it really exists at all.[93] One of the consequences of these developments is that the scholarship on Arabic literature has frequently been moving into non-academic spaces without sticking to unbiased academic discourse. It is not rare to see now scholars sometimes turning to emotions in order to support perceptions that are scientifically unsubstantiated, creating a discourse directed by ideologically, politically, and socially unrelated motives. In the field of Arab-Jewish identity and culture, the scholarship has deteriorated mainly following the death of the Iraqi-Jewish scholars of Arabic literature who studied, in addition to their main field, the Arabic literature of the Jews. All of them were actually part of the literary Arab-Jewish community both in Iraq and Israel using their direct experience to enrich their own studies. The prominent among them are the aforementioned Shimon Ballas, Shmuel Moreh, David Semah, and Sasson Somekh—all of them were professional scholars of Arabic literature—with doctoral studies in prestigious international academic institutions. They were fluent in Arabic with excellent writing skills in *fuṣḥā* and served as editors of international scholarly collections and professional journals of Arabic literature and Middle Eastern Studies. Conversely, nearly all the scholars who are investigating now the Arabic literature by Jews lack the linguistic active skills in Arabic and the expertise in Arabic literature. When they keep insisting that Jewish-Arab identity is still blooming and that the relevant culture is flourishing among Jews in Israel, they do not act as impartial academics and researchers but adopt post-truth populist strategies.[94] Four examples will suffice here.

[93] See Snir 2017, pp. 274–5.

[94] Those scholars are sometimes encouraged by nostalgic references among Arab intellectuals to "the beautiful time" ("*al-zaman al-jamīl*") when Muslims, Christian, Jews and others were living in harmony in the Arab world during the first half of the twentieth century, which are generally due to a mere longing for a previous secular discourse and, mainly, are used as a weapon against the rise of the Islamist circles considered by the Arab secular elite as a great danger (see below).

The first is the publication of a special issue of the prestigious *Ho! – Literary Magazine* (March 16, 2018) with the title "Arabic Literature and Yiddish Literature: Modern Hebrew Culture's Two Sisters." Unlike the Yiddish section in the volume, the Arabic one, despite the huge energy invested in it by the editors, illustrates in its poor scholarly formation and scientific input the demise of Arabic culture and its scholarship among the Jews—since I hope to discuss this volume in a future review essay, I will not go into detail about this here.

The second example is the controversy surrounding Arab-Jewish identity and culture that has emerged among a research group known as "Jewish Life in Modern Islamic Contexts," which convened during the 2018–2019 academic year at the Herbert D. Katz Center for Advanced Judaic Studies at the University of Pennsylvania in Philadelphia. Summarizing my experience as a member of this research group, I published a short essay in *Haaretz* titled "Arab-Jewish Identity: For a Long Time, There Has Been No Such Thing."[95] Four of the fellows at the group, Yoram Meital, Orit Bashkin, Nancy Berg, and Yoval Evri, responded in an essay,[96] which basically uses fallacious straw-man arguments, attributing to me distorted weaker arguments and misrepresenting my positions, only to "successfully" defeat them. Strangely, one of the authors, Orit Bashkin, published in 2017 a book whose conclusion, "The Death of Arab Jewishness," contradicts the very essence of the essay she co-authored.[97] I published a detailed response to their essay in which I referred in detail to their fallacious straw-man arguments,[98] but, surprisingly (or not), the four scholars responded with another article full (again!) of new fallacious straw-man arguments but this time much more sophisticated in their misleading methods.[99] Suffice it to mention that the very title of *their* response,[100]

95 Snir 2019b.
96 *Haaretz*, May 25, 2019.
97 Bashkin 2017, pp. 221–9.
98 See Snir 2020a, pp. 317–52.
99 *Jama'a: Interdisciplinary Journal of Middle East Studies* 25 (2020), pp. 353–78.
100 Examining *all* the publications of the four scholars, it is beyond any doubt that the response had been written by Bashkin alone, with only minor contributions by the others three scholars—Bashkin is the only one among them whose Arabic-language skills as well as her studies illustrate her ability to produce what seems to be a detailed analytical and knowledgeable response on the topic. On Evri, see below. Meital is a historian who does not have any interest in Arabic literature in addition to his limited Arabic skills. Berg published significant studies on Arab-Jewish literature (see the References), but her Arabic-language skills are very limited; for example, she wrote the Foreword to the English translation of Samīr Naqqāsh's *Nzūla wa-Khayṭ al-Shayṭān: Riwāya 'Irāqiyya* (*Tenants & Cobwebs: An Iraqi Novel*) (Naqqāsh 1986; translation: Naqqāsh 2018), but it seems that she did it without reading the novel in the original.

in its Hebrew wording,[101] includes in its meaning and implications several additional straw-man arguments reiterating their populist semi-academic strategies of their earlier essay:

1. To describe those who argue for the demise of Arab-Jewish identity and culture as only philologists is nothing more than using an *ad hominem* offensive remark that should scarcely be found in respectable scholarly and academic discourses. All the arguments I had presented are by no means referring to any philological considerations but only theoretical, cultural, and literary ones.
2. To attribute to the present writer a malicious joy for the demise of Jewish identity and culture through ironical use of the Hebrew word *tuga*, which opens the title of their response (in the meaning of great sorrow), is nothing more than a post-truth and vile populist strategy.
3. To mistranslate the Hebrew title of their article into English within the abstracts section of the journal as "The Philologists' Sorrow and the *Failure* to Bury Arab-Jewish Identity and Culture," without due respect to the precise meaning of the Hebrew wording is another proof of their aforementioned strategies. Speaking in the original about "faults" while the English version of the title related to "failure" without trying at all to refute any of the arguments I had presented is another *ad hominem* offensive remark.
4. To accuse me of an attempt to bury the identity and culture to which I have dedicated more that forty years of teaching, research, and translating activities cannot be understandable without wondering about the extent of adopting post-truth populist strategies by respectable academics. One needs only a glimpse of my numerous publications on the topic of Arab-Jewish identity and culture to get a total refutation for that evil implication—all the more so in light of my own long struggle during several decades for the survival of this identity and culture.

All the above straw-man arguments exposing the populist semi-academic orientation of the response are implied by the title alone! In order to expose all the false arguments included in the response itself, an article of several dozens of pages is needed, but perhaps it is appropriate to quote here Norman A. Stillman's comment on Bashkin's basic approach as a cultural studies scholar who interprets texts but does not fully take into account the actual events, people, and politics. It is also, according to Stillman, due to her *a priori* ideological assumptions:

101 "תוגת הפילולוגים וכשלי הניסיון לקבור את הזהות והתרבות היהודית-ערבי"

> Bashkin from the very outset acknowledges her intellectual debt to contrarians such Sami Zubaida, Ella Shohat, and Gilbert Achcar, and the ghost of Edward Said often lurks in the background unnamed. Previous historical work on the Jews of the Islamic world is reduced to an oversimplified caricature: "a model of harmonious coexistence" or "a tale of perpetual persecution," and "alongside these ideas, an orientalist [*sic*] interpretation" ([Bashkin 2012, p.] 9). More seriously, there is an element of naïve wishful thinking which constantly views positive examples of Jewish acculturation and patriotism, on the one hand, and the openness of some Arab liberal intellectuals and politicians, on the other, as proving that the dark forces of radical Arab nationalism were not really as powerful as they appeared in retrospect.[102]

The third example is the insistence of scholars lacking knowledge of the Arabic language or whose language skills are very limited on publishing studies on issues that cannot thoroughly be studied without fluency in Arabic. One recent example that encapsulates this very phenomenon is Yuval Evri's Hebrew book *The Return to al-Andalus: Disputes over Sephardic Culture and Identity between Arabic and Hebrew* (2020).[103] Although the book deals with issues related to Arabic culture in al-Andalus as expressed in studies and controversies during the nineteenth and twentieth centuries, the bibliographic list[104] does not include even one Arabic item! Furthermore, major Arabic terms and concepts are mentioned without any awareness of their meaning and significance. For example, the term *al-Nahḍa* is frequently mentioned in the book (see index, p. 329), even appearing in Arabic letters (uncommonly in such studies!) and all that without understanding the complicated implications of the term. Moreover, it was done without paying any attention to the insights of the single scholar, Tarek El-Ariss, whose studies are mentioned several times in the references (pp. 30, 110, 130). Evri totally ignores

102 A review of Bashkin 2012, in *Shofar: An Interdisciplinary Journal of Jewish Studies* 32.2 (2014) pp. 149–51.

103 See also Evri 2018, pp. 337–54. Evri is also one of the editors of issue 72 of *Banipal: Magazine of Modern Arab Literature* that deals mainly with Arabic works by Iraqi-Jewish Writers: *all* the contributors to the issue, the editors included, with the exception of the present writer, are not professional scholars of Arabic literature; moreover, most of them are not fluent in Arabic, certainly not capable of writing in *fuṣḥā*. The opening essay of the issue, "The Iraqi-Jewish Literary Networks," by the poet and scholar Haviva Pedaya (b. 1957) (pp. 16–20), may illustrate how the demise of Arabic literature by Jews is accompanied as well by the demise of its serious scholarship. Ironically, in February 2022, Israel's Council for Higher Education (CHE) recognized the study of Sephardi and Mizrahi Jewry as an academic discipline that merits study and research. The council resolution was based on recommendations by a committee headed by Pedaya (*Haaretz*, February 22, 2022, available at: https://www.haaretz.co.il/news/education/.premium-1.10627977, last accessed February 27, 2022).

104 Evri 2020, pp. 302–26.

recent controversies around the issue of *al-Nahḍa*,[105] referring to Lital Levy, one of the members of the aforementioned Herbert D. Katz Center research group, as an academic oracle on the topic despite her biased arguments on the connection between *al-Nahḍa* and the *Haskala*, the Jewish-European Enlightenment (*Aufklärung*), and without being aware of many relevant other related studies.[106] Jaroslav Stetkevych (1929–2021) has already indicated, in an article published fifty years ago on the confluence of Arabic and Hebrew literatures, that the unquestionable effect of Zionism on Hebrew literature produced a Hebrew-Arabic confluence on various levels, even though the streams of *al-Nahḍa* and the *Haskala* appear to be meeting in a whirlpool of cross-purposes:

> Some essential analogies between the *Haskalah* and the *Nahḍah* were perhaps even stronger than they were during the ensuing Zionist period—but there had been no physical encounter of the two literatures. Only similar forces were operating at great distance.[107]

Levy, who was aware of Stetkevych's article, wonders whether it is possible that "the two movements had any productive encounters before the tragedy of the Arab–Israeli conflict," and whether the Arab Jews have not provided "a bridge, however small, between the *nahḍa* and the *haskala*."[108] But her questioning, reasonable from the limited point of view of Hebrew literature, is by no means in place from Arabic literature's perspective. For lack of space and since I have referred to the topic in previous publications and plan thoroughly to refer to it again in a future study, I will not go into detail here.

The last example is the responses to the exhibition "Juifs d'Orient, une Histoire Plurimillénaire" ("Jews from Islamic Lands, a Multi-Millennial History") held at the Institut du Monde Arabe (Arab World Institute) in Paris.[109] In an open letter titled "Culture Is the Salt of the Earth and We Shall Not Allow It to be Used for Normalizing Oppression," and signed by more than 260 Arab intellectuals, writers, and artists, most of them Palestinian,[110]

[105] See, for example, Snir 2019, pp. 137–92.

[106] Evri quotes six(!) studies by Lital Levy while totally ignoring all other studies by distinguished scholars, including my three books and dozens of articles, that deal with these topics, *al-Nahḍa* included. Being one of the four aforementioned scholars with whom I have engaged in the above controversy, one can hardly disconnect my critical remarks toward his academic practices from his poor scholarship.

[107] Stetkevych 1973, p. 219.

[108] Levy 2013, p. 309. On the same topic, see also Levy 2013a, pp. 128–63.

[109] The exhibition was held between November 24, 2021 and March 13, 2022; see at: https://www.imarabe.org/en/expositions/juifs-d-orient, last accessed January 21, 2022.

[110] Among the signatories are the aforementioned Ella Shohat and Ammiel Alcalay (b. 1956), both of them scholars of Arab-Jewish culture and activists of the Boycott, Divestment, and Sanctions (BDS) movement working "to end international support for Israel's oppression

they called on the Arab World Institute to retract the signals it has sent through the exhibition, "which indicate a trend toward normalization—an attempt to impose Israel as if it were a normal state in the Arab region." The Arab World Institute, according to the open letter, betrays its intellectual mission by adopting this normalization approach that is "one of the worst forms of coercive and immoral political abuse of art as a tool to legitimize colonialism and oppression." It is also

> a betrayal of intellectual and moral honesty because *it deliberately conflates Arab Jews and the Jews of the "Orient," on the one hand, and Israel as a colonial and apartheid regime, on the other.* Israel, in coordination with the global Zionist movement, has not only ethnically cleansed most of the indigenous Palestinian people, colonizing their land and parts of their Arab heritage and culture, it has also appropriated the Jewish component in Arab culture and attempted to Zionize it and Israelize it, as a prelude to extracting it from its authentic roots and using it to serve its colonial project in the region. *The culture of Arab Jews is an integral part of Arab culture, and the process of severing it from its roots is an attempt to destroy part of Arab memory and history.* The continuation of this normalization approach would cause the Institute to lose not only the intellectuals and artists whose creative cultural output it has hosted for decades, but also the Arab public in general.[111]

The exhibition and the open letter from the Arab intellectuals, writers, and artists did not stir any interest among the Arab Jews or their offspring in Israel or outside it. Also, the fact that the open letter was published in Arabic, French, and English but *not in Hebrew* is proof that the signatories to the open letter had by no means any interest in communicating with the communities of Arab Jews and their offspring, which can be approached now only in Hebrew and through Israeli media. Moreover, the open letter, despite its poor scholarly foundations, has not aroused any responses or reactions even from the scholarly community of Arab-Jewish culture or Arab culture in general with the exception of a Hebrew essay by Moshe Behar of the University of Manchester and Zvi Ben-Dor Benite from New York University more than a month after the publication of the letter and in a marginal platform: *Haokets: Critical Platform on Socioeconomic, Political, Media, Cultural and Other Issues in Israel and Beyond.*[112] Although the scholarly foundations of the open letter are very weak to the point that the persons who prepared it seem to have not read the updated studies on the

of Palestinians and pressure Israel to comply with international law," available at: https://usacbi.org/endorsers, last accessed January 21, 2022.

111 See at: https://docs.google.com/forms/d/e/1FAIpQLSfo5DR7RGXkbLw0l82jwaW-N8Qu40lKcx46uR9euvWVnddX-Q/viewform, December 6, 2021, last accessed January 21, 2022 (my emphasis).

112 *Haokets*, January 10, 2022.

topic, let alone investigated it themselves, Behar and Ben-Dor Benite in their response by no means challenged its scholarly foundations but were satisfied to protest only against the *political agenda* of the open letter:

> התנועה הציונית האירופית הועידה למזרחים/ות תפקיד היסטורי אחד: להיות קורבנות של הערבים. המסמך על התערוכה בפריז מועיד לנו תפקיד היסטורי דומה: להיות קורבנות של הציונות. ואולם סך כל ההתפתחויות שיכולנו לתאר כאן בקצרה בלבד מחייב אותנו להצהיר ברורות: יהודי ערב של המאה ה-21 מסרבים להיות יהודים על פי התנאים שהועידה להם הציונות האשכנזית ומסרבים להיות ערבים על פי קווי המתאר שמועידה להם הקבוצה המרשימה של חותמי מסמך הפאן-ערבי, יהיה זה במודע או במובלע.

> The European Zionist movement conferred on the Mizrahim one historical role: to be victims of the Arabs. The document on the exhibition in Paris gives us a similar historical role: to be victims of Zionism. However, the total developments we could describe here only briefly require us to state clearly: The Arab Jews of the twenty-first century refuse to be Jews according to the conditions imposed on them by Ashkenazi Zionism and refuse to be Arabs according to the outline indicated, consciously or implicitly, by the impressive group of signers on the Pan-Arab document.

Nothing in their response refers to the poor scholarship the open letter was based on, although, as indicated above, Muslim and Christian Arab intellectuals in general do not pay any attention to the cultural aspect of Arab-Jewish identity unless it may be used as a tool against Israel and Zionism. The response of Behar and Ben-Dor Benite illustrates that they are interested only in politics or identity politics but not at all in culture, literature, and art.

In one way or another, all four aforementioned examples clearly illustrate that the scholarship on Arabic literature relevant to the issues discussed in the present chapter has been moving into non-academic spaces without at least even trying to stick to unbiased academic discourse, which unfortunately is sometimes turned into mere preaching directed by unrelated ideological, political, social, or even opportunistic motives. Related to the actual gradual demise of Arab-Jewish culture and the deterioration of its scholarship, on the one hand, and the strenuous attempts of some scholars and Israeli Mizrahi intellectuals to argue that this culture is still flowering, on the other hand, is the sheer exaggeration of the importance of some persons' activities and the tendency to attribute to marginal phenomena what seems to be unjustified significance. The case of the Iraqi journalist and publisher Māzin Laṭīf (b. 1973) is instructive in this regard: for more than a decade Laṭīf was very active in spreading the case of the Iraqi-Jewish contribution to modern Iraq together with wide communication with Iraqi-Jewish intellectuals and writers helping them to publish their works, especially through the publishing house he had established in Baghdad, Dār Mesopotamia. He published many essays and several books on the Iraqi-Jewish community and their history, though most of them were not original and were based on studies of other scholars.[113] Among the publications of the publishing house he owned, there appeared also some excellent studies about the Iraqi Jews and their culture.[114] Laṭīf also conducted interviews and dialogues with Israeli scholars and authors such as Shmuel Moreh and Almog Behar.[115] Israeli-Jewish scholars and intellectuals were proud to declare that Iraqi intellectuals are glad to be in touch with them while actually Māzin Laṭīf was the only person with whom they were in touch.[116] The prominence and popularity of Māzin Laṭīf among Iraqi-Jewish intellectuals in Israel is clearly illustrated in an article by Sigal Goorji.[117] The article deals with the publication of a Hebrew novel[118] published in Arabic translation by Laṭīf's publishing house[119] and the reactions and responses to the novel. Goorji argues that the reception of the novel by Iraqi readers exemplifies the emergence of a new dialogue in Iraqi society, one that seeks to read and learn about the Jewish minority that lived in Iraq because it fills a chapter on Iraqi Jews that has been forgotten in Iraqi history. We can find some mentions in the Israeli press of the book and its publication.[120] But the life of this utopian image of the revival of the Jewish presence in Iraqi society and culture was short, very short. On January 31, 2020, Māzin Laṭīf was kidnapped in broad daylight in Baghdad near al-Mutanabbi Street.[121] According to journalist reports it was because of his "activities related to the exposure of the social life and the history of the Jews in Iraq."[122] He was accused of cooperating with Israeli-Zionist organizations, among them the Israeli Mosad.[123] So far his fate is unknown. But what is more interesting is that *all* the Israeli-Jewish scholars who had been in touch with Laṭīf have been ignoring his disappearance as if he never existed. Moreover, the Israeli media has hardly reported on his disappearance, mainly because the aforementioned intellectuals, who had been so eager to be in touch with him and benefit from his generous services, have

113 For example, Laṭīf 2011; Laṭīf 2013.
114 For example, Ḥātim 2014.
115 See, for example, several of them included in Laṭīf 2011; *al-ʿĀlam*, May 24, 2016.
116 Several years ago, he started a dialogue with me and offered to publish books of mine in Baghdad.
117 Goorji 2020.
118 Fattal-Kuperwasser 2015.
119 Fattāl 2017.
120 For example, *Yediot Aḥronoth*, June 4, 2017; *Ynet*, August 22, 2017; *Israel Hayom*, August 31, 2017.
121 See at: https://www.facebook.com/permalink.php?story_fbid=1121504561575002&id=100011464068582, February 3, 2020, last accessed December 24, 2021.
122 See *al-ʿArabī al-Jadīd*, March 18, 2020.
123 See at: https://www.facebook.com/watch/?v=867893124026343, December 10, 2020, last accessed November 29, 2021.

avoided spreading the news of his kidnapping in contrast to their enthusiasm for spreading the news of their communication with him before his disappearance and their publications, which without his assistance would never have been published in Iraq. In fact, I found only a few mentions of Laṭīf's disappearance in Israeli Hebrew media, mainly by the journalist Jacky Hugi (b. 1968), himself of Iraqi origin.[124]

To sum up, one fact can by no means be denied: the vision embedded in the aforementioned dictum "Religion is for God, the Fatherland is for everyone" was the product of a very limited period, a very confined space, and a very singular history. It lived to the age of a sturdy human being, by this rare combination of time, space, and history, before disappearing and being forgotten, at least for the foreseeable future. In this sense, one can hardly forget the 137th psalm of the Book of Psalms, known as "By the Rivers of Babylon," a communal lament about being in exile after the Babylonian captivity, and yearning for Jerusalem:

עַל נַהֲרוֹת בָּבֶל שָׁם יָשַׁבְנוּ גַּם בָּכִינוּ, בְּזָכְרֵנוּ אֶת צִיּוֹן.
עַל עֲרָבִים בְּתוֹכָהּ תָּלִינוּ כִּנֹּרוֹתֵינוּ.
כִּי שָׁם שְׁאֵלוּנוּ שׁוֹבֵינוּ דִּבְרֵי שִׁיר וְתוֹלָלֵינוּ שִׂמְחָה, שִׁירוּ לָנוּ מִשִּׁיר צִיּוֹן.
אֵיךְ נָשִׁיר אֶת שִׁיר ה' עַל אַדְמַת נֵכָר.
אִם אֶשְׁכָּחֵךְ יְרוּשָׁלָם תִּשְׁכַּח יְמִינִי.
תִּדְבַּק לְשׁוֹנִי לְחִכִּי אִם לֹא אֶזְכְּרֵכִי, אִם לֹא אַעֲלֶה אֶת יְרוּשָׁלַם עַל רֹאשׁ שִׂמְחָתִי.
זְכֹר ה' לִבְנֵי אֱדוֹם אֵת יוֹם יְרוּשָׁלָם, הָאֹמְרִים עָרוּ עָרוּ עַד הַיְסוֹד בָּהּ.
בַּת בָּבֶל הַשְּׁדוּדָה, אַשְׁרֵי שֶׁיְשַׁלֶּם לָךְ אֶת גְּמוּלֵךְ שֶׁגָּמַלְתְּ לָנוּ.
אַשְׁרֵי שֶׁיֹּאחֵז וְנִפֵּץ אֶת עֹלָלַיִךְ אֶל הַסָּלַע.

In the King James Version, we find the following translation of the nine verses:

By the rivers of Babylon, there we sat down, yea, we wept, when we remembered Zion.
We hanged our harps upon the willows in the midst thereof.
For there they that carried us away captive required of us a song; and they that wasted us required of us mirth, saying, Sing us one of the songs of Zion.
How shall we sing the Lord's song in a strange land?
If I forget thee, O Jerusalem, let my right hand forget her cunning.
If I do not remember thee, let my tongue cleave to the roof of my mouth; if I prefer not Jerusalem above my chief joy.
Remember, O Lord, the children of Edom in the day of Jerusalem; who said, Rase it, rase it, even to the foundation thereof.
O daughter of Babylon, who art to be destroyed; happy shall he be, that rewardeth thee as thou hast served us.

[124] For example, *Maariv*, July 10, 2020; Galei Zahal: the official radio station of the Israeli Army, February 5, 2021.

Happy shall he be, that taketh and dasheth thy little ones against the stones.

The psalm expresses the yearnings of the Jewish people during their Babylonian Exile for Jerusalem as well as their hatred for the enemies, expressed by violent imagery. The first lines describe the sadness of the Israelites in exile, weeping and hanging their harps on trees. Asked to "sing the Lord's song in a strange land," they refuse. Then the speaker turns to self-exhortation to remember Jerusalem and the psalm ends with prophetic predictions of violent revenge. The psalm is customarily recited on Tish'a Be-'Av, the ninth day of the month of Av—the eleventh month of the civil year on the Hebrew calendar. It is the saddest day of the Jewish year, on which Jews fast, deprive themselves, and pray, commemorating the destruction of the temples in Jerusalem. In fact, the psalm originally lamented only the destruction of the First Temple, totally destroyed by the Babylonians in 586 BC, after Nebuchadnezzar II's successful siege of Jerusalem in 597 BC. The inhabitants of the Kingdom of Judah were deported to Babylonia, where they were held captive until after the Fall of Babylon in 539 BC. The "rivers of Babylon" mentioned in the lament are the Euphrates and the Tigris Rivers—this is the region of Mesopotamia (from the Greek, meaning "between two rivers") located in the eastern Mediterranean and bounded in the northeast by the Zagros Mountains and in the southeast by the Arabian Plateau, corresponding mainly to today's Iraq but also parts of modern-day Iran, Syria, and Turkey.

Around 2,600 years after the destruction of the First Temple, the aforementioned documentary film *Forget Baghdad: Jews and Arabs—The Iraqi Connection* (2002) epitomizes the demise not only of Arab-Jewish identity and culture but also, as previously argued, of its scholarship, certainly among the Jews. The film revolves around the life of five Iraqi Arabized Jews: Mūsa Ḥūrī (1924–2010), Sami Michael (b. 1926), Shimon Ballas (1930–2019), Samīr Naqqāsh (1938–2004), and Ella Shohat (b. 1959).[125] Although it is common to describe the Iraqi Jews in Israel as a unique "Mizrahi" collective well integrated into Israeli-Jewish society and one that is inseparable from the Israeli middle class, in fact as what has been described as a great "success story,"[126] one can easily notice that, except for their common ethnic origins, the five aforementioned intellectuals hardly have anything essential in common. The differences between the common layers of identity that all of the aforementioned intellectuals and authors share, such as Iraqiness and Arabness, are more significant than the differences between the layers of identity such as Israeliness and Hebrewness, that they share with their

[125] On the film, see Tsoffar 2006, pp. 133–43.
[126] See Meir-Glitzenstein 2015, pp. 107–21.

non-Arabized Israeli-Jewish counterparts. For example, what Naqqāsh considered as true basic Arab cultural characteristics is totally different from what is seen by Shohat as being true basic Arab characteristics—in fact, she does not master Arabic at all and cannot read in the original his literary texts! On the other hand, if we compare most of Sami Michael's Hebrew novels with most contemporary Hebrew novels by any leftist writer of his generation, it would probably be hard to find essential differences between their literary, cultural, and ideological narratives.[127]

The corpus of Arab *belles lettres* written by Jews during the twentieth century has hardly become wider during the last two decades. Furthermore, even the Judeo-Arabic tradition (Judeo-Arabic dialects written in Hebrew) waned with the decline of Jewish communities in Arab-controlled lands.[128] Jews do not now write Arabic literature, and if they do so at all their works are not published—no one is interested in such writing anymore. For the last thirty-five years, I have been closely investigating the whole corpus of Arab-Jewish poems, stories, novels, plays, and memoirs written since the 1920s—until the last decades. I was able to also discuss my arguments with Arab-Jewish authors who had highly contributed to the scholarship of the topic, such as the aforementioned Nissīm Rijwān, Shimon Ballas, Shmuel Moreh, David Semah, and Sasson Somekh. Now, as illustrated above, you can hardly find a scholar of Arab-Jewish culture whose scholarship is based on direct knowledge and experience of this culture. Most of the scholars publishing in the field adopt post-truth populist strategies and are more interested in identity politics than in Arab-Jewish culture and identity. At any event, the hidden voice of the implied collective authors of the literary works written after the immigration of the Iraqi Jews to Israel is a sad lament, inspired by but at the same time contradicting the 137th psalm quoted earlier, and it may be summarized as follows:

> By the rivers of *Zion*, there we sat down, yea, we wept, when we remembered *Babylon*.
> We hanged our harps upon the willows in the midst thereof.
> If I forget thee, O *Baghdad*, let my right hand forget her cunning.

[127] On the issue of Arab-Jewish identity and other layers of identity, see Snir 2015b, and the following chapter. On Iraqi identity in general, see Marr 2010, pp. 15–41; Kirmanj 2010, pp. 43–59.

[128] See Hary 2018, pp. 35–69.

Chapter 8

Identity: Inessential Solidarities[1]

In recent decades, national communities have been increasingly eclipsed by tribes of customers who do not know one another intimately but share the same consumption habits and interests, and therefore feel part of the same consumer tribe—and define themselves as such.
– Yuval Noah Harari

1. INTRODUCTION

The poet and scholar Sami Shalom Chetrit (b. 1960) was born in Morocco and immigrated with his family to Israel at the age of three. In his literary and journalistic activities, he has tried to return to his Arabized roots. Illustrating this, for example, is a poem titled "Who Is a Jew and What Kind of a Jew," in which he refers to the demise of the Arab-Jewish cultural option; he tries to express what he sees as the despair in the hearts of both the new generation of Arabized Jews born in Israel and those who have emigrated from Arab lands as children with their parents. In a conversation between an American female friend and the persona, the mask the poet assumes, she asks whether he is a Jew or an Arab. "I'm an Arab-Jew," he responds. "I've never heard of that," she exclaims. The speaker then tries to convince her that just as there is an American Jew or a European Jew, so too one can imagine the existence of an Arab Jew. Still, his American friend cannot seem to accept the existence of the category:

- You can't compare, a European Jew is something else.
- How come?
- Because "Jew" just doesn't go with "Arab," it just doesn't go. It doesn't even sound right.

[1] This chapter uses material that first appeared in Snir 2012, pp. 169–89; Snir 2013, pp. 140–60; Snir 2015a, pp. 299–314; Snir 2015b; Snir 2019, pp. 149–90; Snir 2021a, pp. 123–54.

- Depends on your ear.
- Look, I've got nothing against Arabs. I even have friends who are Arabs, but how can you say "Arab-Jew" when all the Arabs want is to destroy the Jews?
- And how can you say "European-Jew" when the Europeans have already destroyed the Jews?[2]

Chetrit has in fact not returned to his Arabized cultural roots; rather, he has developed his own singularity which does not adhere to any specific stable identity and which is an inessential solidarity.[3] The present chapter deals with the changes in the concept of identity and belonging among the Arabized Jews, especially the Iraqi-Baghdadi among them, during the twentieth century.[4] My main argument is that, due to some processes that the Baghdadi Jews had experienced and because of some global developments, they gradually developed a negative sensitivity toward the notion of stable identity, whatever that identity may be, asserting instead their particular singularities and searching for alternative forms of identification, mostly various kinds of inessential solidarities and senses of belonging.

Although I have based my study in the main on the experiences of Iraqi Jews, one can find the same developments with Jewish immigrants and their offspring from other Arab lands. Furthermore, from a sample of partial investigations I have a solid basis for the hypothesis that the same developments have occurred, if in different rhythms and intensity, among other communities of Arabized Jews as well. In other words, there is no doubt today about the supremacy of singularity and inessential solidarity among the Arabized Jews and—moreover, more and more, we find that Arabized Jews act like the playwright Henrik Ibsen's hero Peer Gynt, who, in the eponymous play, is obsessed all his life with finding his "true identity": "I tried to make time stand still by dancing!"[5] What Peer Gynt was afraid of more than anything else was "to know you can't ever free yourself" and "to be stuck as a troll for the rest of your days."[6] That is why he decides to keep his freedom of choice, "to know that behind you there is always / a bridge, if you have to beat a retreat."[7]

[2] For the entire poem, see Chetrit 2003, pp. 50–3. On the poem, see also Haskin 2015, pp. 801–15.

[3] On Chetrit and the various layers of his own identity and for a review of his scholarship on Arab-Jewish identity and culture, see Snir 2015b, pp. 197–218.

[4] For the ways in which Jews in Baghdad and Baghdadi Jews as a whole self-identified or saw themselves as part of larger transnational Jewish networks and at times ascribed themselves specific identities in Hashemite Iraq in the age of nationalism, see Goldstein-Sabbah 2018; Goldstein-Sabbah 2021.

[5] Ibsen 1998, p. 105.

[6] Ibsen 1998, p. 46.

[7] Ibsen 1998, p. 77. Cf. Bauman 2004, pp. 90–1.

Any discussion referring to the identities of Arabized Jews that involves an attempt to combine the experience of all Arabized Jewish communities together faces the challenge of how to say something meaningful about Iraqi and North African Jewish communities—they always seem to be at opposite ends of the spectrum, an obstacle for any attempt to situate Arabized Jews under the same umbrella, even if the umbrella is by no means a collective one and is rather conceptual by nature—this is the tendency toward inessential solidarity. Apart from the aforementioned Sami Shalom Chetrit, here are some additional examples of Israeli-Jewish intellectuals whose subjectivities have some Moroccan layers of identity, but who have preferred, like Peer Gynt, to keep their freedom of choice, each of them knowing "that behind you there is always / a bridge, if you have to beat a retreat."[8]

The mother of the Israeli novelist A. B. Yehoshua (1936–2022) was an immigrant from Morocco, while the latter's father, the journalist and scholar Ya'acob Yehoshua (1905–1982), was from a Sephardic family from Jerusalem. In an introduction to a book by his father published posthumously, Yehoshua argues, based on his own experience, that identity cannot be stable and that we have the right to change our identity and choose what we deem to be appropriate from both an intellectual and a spiritual point of view. Yehoshua, a pillar of the contemporary Hebrew literary establishment, explains that his father and (especially) his mother, both belonging to families with Arab backgrounds, did their best in order to guide him into the heart of the "Zionist-Ashkenazi world" as a "proper object of identification and imitation." He does not deny that the aim of his attempts to conceal his Arab cultural roots was to distinguish his identity from that of the Jewish immigrants who came from the Arab world:

> I completely reject the view that a son of [Jewish] parents from Poland, Romania, or Hungary has the right to erase the accent of his parents as well as their religious-Jewish-communal identity in order to become an Israeli, while a son [of parents] from the Mizrahi communities cannot do it only because these communities have a basic existential weakness compared to the Ashkenazi communities, and because, from the ethical point of view, you can "abandon" the strong, but it is forbidden to "abandon" the weak.[9]

Yehoshua's conception of the fluidity of identity was expressed indirectly in his literary writings, which have showed a clear tendency to deal with Sephardic and Mizrahi characters. Nothing in these writings, however, prepared the public, more than ten years later, for the novel *Ha-Kalla ha-Meshaḥreret* (*The Liberating Bride*) (2001), which consists of large

[8] Ibsen 1998, p. 77.
[9] Yehoshua 1988, pp. 8–11.

portions of Arabic texts in Hebrew transliteration and translation, while the implied author laments the absence of Arab components in Israeli culture. In one of the episodes that seems to reflect the author's own inner voice, we find the protagonist, Professor Tedeschi, declaring: "We have no hope of rationally understanding the Arabs; therefore, we must go back and study profoundly their poetry."[10] Yehoshua is not a Baghdadi Jew, but his understanding of the notion of identity is typical of the attitude of the Baghdadi-Jewish intellectuals toward identity.[11]

Another example shows Arab-Jewish identity being reclaimed by a Moroccan Jew in order to support worldviews that, to the contrary, do not call for that kind of a connection to such identity. Meir Amor (b. 1955), the son of Moroccan immigrants, is a "refusenik"—he refused to serve in the Israeli Army. This is how he describes his own identity:

> To be an Israeli, you must serve in the army. To serve in the army means to fight Arabs. So fighting Arabs means fighting for your identity. We are Jews, not Moslems, but in Morocco my family lived with Arabs for the past 500 years. Part of my culture is Arab. Because in Israel Arabs are defined as the enemy, having any trace of Arab culture means being on the Arab side. It's contradictory. I am an Arab Jew; I have no complexes about it. Living with Arabs was not paradise, but it was a lot better than living with Christians. Therefore, we should find a way to talk to Palestinians. This is not romanticism, it's in my family life. We speak Arabic, we eat Arab food, we listen to Arab music. I fully represent the effective integration of Mideastern (Sephardi) Jews into Israeli society. I graduated from high school and university, I served in the army and became an officer. But now I have these questions, and that's how I became a refusenik.[12]

The simplified method of argumentation Amor uses in order to explain the different layers of his own identity leaves no doubt that it is a "pick and choose" or recycling. He is a refusenik, and in order to support that political and ideological worldview he uses the necessary components in his own life experience to support his position. Shenhav-Shahrabani, Shohat, and Chetrit do the same, but as professional scholars they do it with more sophistication.

10 Yehoshua 2001, p. 500. The English translation of the novel does not keep the meaning of the original: "It is hopeless to try to understand the Arabs rationally. Back to their poetry, then, for that is all we have to go on" (Yehoshua 2004, p. 515). The original title of the novel before its publication in Hebrew was *Ha-Kalla ha-Meshuḥreret* (*The Liberated Bride*); the English translator, unaware that the author had changed the title before publication, kept the old title.

11 See Yehoshua's last novel, *Ḥesed Sfaradi* (*Spanish Charity*) (Yehoshua 2011). On the concept of identity in Yehoshua's writings, see Snir 2015b, pp. 192–3.

12 Kidron 2004, p. 28.

My third example is Sami Berdugo (b. 1970), a son of Moroccan immigrants. While responding to a question about his own identity, he tries to thwart any attempt to put him into some sort of solid "identity box":

> I agree that there is such a term [Arab Jew]. I do not know if I include myself in it. I can understand and accept the meaning of being an Arab Jew ... Every definition of myself inside a group is difficult for me. I accept the existence of such [a group] but I do not know if I include myself in it ... A Mizrahi Jew; this term is easier for me ... The problem is that the term ["Mizrahi Jew"] has absorbed so many adjacent meanings, so many connotations, so many cultural, political, and social expressions that I do not know if I belong to them ... All my texts deal with identity and searching for identity, and with identity crisis and the attempt to establish an identity, but that identity is so vast. [That identity] is not only Israeli. It is not only Mizrahi, Ashkenazi. It is Israeli, Jewish-Israeli, it is masculine and it is many [other] things. So, trying to reduce it into Mizrahi is wrong.[13]

In a presentation he delivered at Oxford University in December 2008, Berdugo said:

> Look at me; look at me closely. I, standing here in front of you—the fruit of Integration, the perfect example of that Israeli "Combination," a good recipe that can be proudly displayed throughout Israel's territory and within her institutions. This product is trying to portray its Identity, is trying to declare who he is among Israeli and Jewish society, and also outside of it. But this is an odd concept, I must say, because I don't think it's even possible, the act of including me and giving me an Identity, is not a real thing and it is not tangible. There is one clear fact: When I label myself with any identity, with any specific description, I thereby provide victory to the collective, to the State, and for me that means that the general concept has succeeded ... I am lacking an Identity. I am lacking a proper language. I refuse to obey certain instructions in these two dominant creatures. *This is why I create my own rules. You see, I have no other choice. I need to stand up from the depth, from the minus, and conceal myself in the kingdom that I rule in.*[14]

Berdugo's novel *Zeh ha-Devarim* (*This Is the Things* [*sic*]) (2010) leaves no doubt that singularity and not any fixed or stable identity is his only war cry.

The supremacy of singularity and inessential solidarity over collective identity is now shared by members of all communities of Arabized Jews in Israel, certainly by their offspring who have been educated in Israel. When they were young, they were exposed to the dichotomizing methods and terms aimed at venting dismay whenever Arab culture was suggested as a

13 Personal interview conducted with Sami Berdugo by Oshrat Edri (Tel Aviv, May 8, 2009). I thank Oshrat Edri for providing me with the text of the interview.

14 Sami Berdugo, "I Am an Immigration-Integration Product, or Am I?" Oxford Centre for Hebrew and Jewish Studies, December 4, 2008 (my emphasis).

possible component of the new Israeli society. Trying to conform to the Ashkenazi norm of the *Sabra*, children were made to feel ashamed of the Arabness of their parents. Some scholars consider these phenomena to be a "rapid assimilation to prevailing Israeli values and lifestyle," which "removed all meaningful differences on the general level."[15] But that "assimilation" was only on the surface, at least for the intellectuals among the offspring of Arabized Jews. They were aware that the assimilation was to the prevailing *Ashkenazi* values and lifestyle; all the efforts at imitation have never abolished the differences, and the desire of Arabized Jews to belong to the Ashkenazi mainstream collective has only, to use Abdelfattah Kilito's argument, marked their "animality."[16] At the same time, nothing outlandish was seen in viewing Arabized Jews as a main impediment to peace in the Middle East; the same internalized oppression was also partially responsible for the nationalist positions that Arabized Jews had adopted.[17]

Aware of the process of exclusion in Israel and the attempts to remove from them any vestige of Arabness, the intellectuals found refuge in their singularities even if on the surface they pretended to be "true" Israelis. "For our parents," says the Moroccan-born poet Sami Shalom Chetrit, "all of us were agents of repression."[18] Chetrit does not hesitate to be critical of the systems of power that tried to educate Arabized Jews and their offspring. However, we may ask whether he can find refuge in his parents' identity. The answer is, undoubtedly, "no."

The process of identification creates identity, and we recognize ourselves when we are hailed—you identify me, and I become that me that you have identified. I know that it is me who is being called as I unconsciously accept the subject position and my subjectivity is thus created or modified—it is as if I had always already been there. By subjectivity, I mean the inner life processes and affective states as they have been expressed in words, images, institutions, and behaviors through which people actually represent themselves to themselves and to one another. This understanding is accompanied by the awareness that subjects are themselves unfinished and unfinishable as well as by the recognition that, because individuals are members of cross-cutting and often conflicting associations, subjectivity characterizations shift widely between multiple perspectives and no single analytic framework can

15 Dowty 1998, p. 151.

16 "When two languages meet, one of them is necessarily linked to animality. Speak like me or you are an animal ... The paradox of mimicry resides in the fact that the mimic wants to belong but in the end marks his own separation" (Kilito 1994, pp. xxi–xxxi; the quotation is from p. xxvii).

17 Cf. Rejwan 1999, pp. 148–75.

18 *Yedi'ot Aḥronoth*, August 8, 2003, p. 54.

fully account for the inner lives of people and their intersubjective relations.[19] The apparent freedom with which we recognize and accept that position only serves to cement us further into it. The notion of interpellation, as coined by the aforementioned French Marxist philosopher Louis Pierre Althusser, can be considered as "recruitment" as it invites a person into a subject position, but, it is rarely as specific as being addressed by name, but rather is being addressed as a member of an audience or any collective. As previously mentioned, one can immediately see the connection between interpellation and rhetoric—when we recognize that we are being spoken to, we not only engage more deeply with the hailing, we also accept the social role being offered to us: young, white, female, gay, athletic, liberal, etc. In the context of our present study, we have the following social roles: Arab, Jew, Muslim, Israeli, Zionist, as well as Mizrahi, Levantine, Oriental, Sephardi, Black, etc. Speaking about terminology, it should be noted that, while the term "Mizrahi" had been invented by the systems of power, it has also been used as a subversive catchword by militant Middle Eastern and North African Jewish intellectuals and activists to express resistance to the conception of Israel as a Zionist and Western country.[20]

2. NARRATIVIZATION OF THE SELF

The cultural and intellectual contexts within which identities have been studied during the last few decades have changed dramatically and have led us to an appreciation of the profound limits of human understanding. We have started to recognize the embeddedness of human understanding in the very phenomena we are trying to understand, and the comprehension of the enormity of the universe has made us very modest in our scholarly ambitions and goals. A much-cited quotation by the astronomer Timothy Ferris could not leave any scholar indifferent no matter what his field of research:

> [T]he more we know about the universe, the more we come to see how little we know. When the cosmos was thought to be but a tidy garden, with the sky its ceiling and the earth its floor and its history coextensive with that of the human family tree, it was still possible to imagine that we might one day comprehend it in both plan and detail. That illusion can no longer be sustained ... If

[19] Based on Biehl et al. 2007, pp. 1–23 (introduction). For tracing the history of some of the philosophical insights that have shaped current understandings of subjectivity, see Rorty 2007, pp. 34–51.

[20] According to Ella Shohat, one of the first of these radical thinkers, the aim is "to re-link [our]selves with the history and culture of the Arab and Muslim world, after the brutal rupture experienced since the foundation of Israel" (Shohat 1992, pp. 121–43 [the quotation is from p. 141, n. 4]). See also Levy 2009, pp. 127–72.

> we possessed an atlas of our galaxy that devoted but a single page to each star system in the Milky Way (so that the sun and all its planets were crammed on one page), that atlas would run to more than ten million volumes of ten thousand pages each. It would take a library the size of Harvard's to house the atlas, and merely to flip through it, at the rate of a page per second, would require over ten thousand years. Add the details of planetary cartography, potential extraterrestrial biology, the subtleties of the scientific principles involved, and the historical dimensions of change, and it becomes clear that we are never going to learn more than a tiny fraction of the story of our galaxy alone—and there are a hundred billion more galaxies. As the physician Lewis Thomas writes, "The greatest of all the accomplishments of twentieth-century science has been the discovery of human ignorance." Our ignorance, of course, has always been with us, and always will be. What is new is our awareness of it, our awakening to its fathomless dimensions, and it is this, more than anything else, that marks the coming of age of our species.[21]

Throughout the last three or four decades, scholars have pointed out the veritable discursive explosion around the concept of identity: the critique of the self-sustaining subject at the center of post-Cartesian Western metaphysics has been comprehensively advanced in philosophy; the question of subjectivity and its unconscious processes of formation has been developed within the discourse of a psychoanalytically influenced feminism and cultural criticism; and the endlessly performative self has been advanced in celebratory variants of postmodernism and within the anti-essentialist critique of ethnic, racial, and national conceptions of cultural identity; and in the "politics of location" some adventurous theoretical conceptions have been sketched in their most grounded forms. What, then, "is the need," asks Stuart Hall in 1996, "for a further debate about 'identity'? Who needs it?"[22] In 2009, however, the Polish sociologist and philosopher Zygmunt Bauman (1925–2017) still refers to the same "discursive explosion" around the concept of identity that has even "triggered an avalanche."[23]

In the labyrinths of these theoretical and sometimes bewildering discussions about identity, one can notice that most deliberations have been conducted around two models: the first assumes that there is an essential content to any identity, which is defined by common origin or common structure of experience. The second one, which stands in the center of the present study, emphasizes the impossibility of fully separate distinct identities. Any identity depends upon its difference from some other identity—"identity is a

[21] Ferris 1991 [1988], pp. 382–3. I first saw a part of this quotation in Mitchell 1993, pp. 19–20. The first lines inserted before the quotation were inspired by Mitchell's discussion.

[22] Hall 1996, p. 1.

[23] Bauman 2009, p. 1.

structured representation which only achieves its positive through the narrow eye of the negative," writes Hall. "It has to go through the eye of the needle of the other before it can construct itself."[24] Identity is thus always a temporary and unstable effect of relations that define identities by marking differences, which means that the multiplicity of identities and differences and the emphasis on connections or articulations between the fragments or differences are inevitable. While the identity of someone cannot be explored or challenged without a simultaneous investigation of another, this is, however, rarely the case in practice, and most investigations in cultural studies deal with the construction of subaltern, marginalized, or dominated identities, and rarely are the two ever studied together as mutually constitutive, as the theory would seem to dictate. Also, identities arise from the narrativization of the self, and most people identify with their narrating self:

> When they say "I," they mean the story in their head, not the stream of experiences they undergo. We identify with the inner system that takes the crazy chaos of life and spins out of it seemingly logical and consistent yarns. It doesn't matter that the plot is full of lies and lacunas, and that it is rewritten again and again, so that today's story flatly contradicts yesterday's; the important thing is that we always retain the feeling that we have a single unchanging identity from birth to death (and perhaps even beyond the grave). This gives rise to the questionable liberal belief that I am an individual, and that I possess a consistent and clear inner voice, which provides meaning for the entire universe.[25]

Here, it is important to note that science undermines not only the liberal belief in free will, but also the belief in individualism. The literal meaning of the word "individual" is "something that cannot be divided." That I am an "in-dividual" implies that my true self is a holistic entity rather than an assemblage of separate parts. This indivisible essence allegedly endures from one moment to the next without losing or absorbing anything.[26] Science challenges the assumptions that I am an "in-dividual"—that is, I have a single essence which cannot be divided into any parts or subsystems and that my authentic self is completely free and that I can know things about myself nobody else can discover.[27]

Although identities arise from the narrativization of the self, the necessarily fictional nature of this narrativization in no way undermines its discursive, material, or political effectivity, even if the belongingness, the "suturing

24 Hall 1991, p. 21.

25 Harari 2017, p. 271. See also Gazzaniga 2011, ch. 3.

26 Harari 2017, pp. 97–8. This idea is based on conceptions introduced by Deleuze and Guattari 1987. Cf. Lattas 1991, pp. 98–115; Linkenbach and Mulsow 2020, pp. 323–43.

27 Harari 2017, pp. 264, 296–7.

into the story" through which identities arise is, partly, in the imaginary (as well as the symbolic) and therefore, always, partly constructed in fantasy, or at least within the fantasmatic field. Identities refer to the meeting point, that very point of *suture*, between, on the one hand, the discourses and practices that attempt to interpellate, speak to us, or hail us into place as the social subjects of particular discourses, and, on the other hand, the processes that produce subjectivities, which construct us as subjects that can be "spoken." All identities are thus only "points of temporary attachment to the subject position which discursive practices construct for us."[28] Because we are always in the process of being exposed to new interpellating machines and processes, reacting always consciously *and* unconsciously to them with our own complicated and unique singular subjectivities, there is no escape from elusiveness and fluidity. Bauman describes contemporary society as a place in which everything is elusive, and where the disorientation and insecurity caused by living in society cannot be solved by parading past certainties and established systems.[29] In other words, identities deal with the past only on the exterior level, simply because they cannot be but present- and future-oriented projects: they are about questions of using the resources of history, language, and culture in the process of becoming rather than being: not "who we are" or "where we came from," so much as "what we might become," "how we have been represented," and "how that bears on how we might represent ourselves."[30] Yuval Noah Harari refers to such present- and future-oriented projects by discussing the stories we relate to ourselves, and such stories are by no means complete:

> Yet in order to construct a viable identity for myself and give meaning to my life, I don't really need a complete story devoid of blind spots and internal contradictions. To give meaning to my life, a story needs to satisfy just two conditions: first, it must give me some role to play. A New Guinean tribesman is unlikely to believe in Zionism or in Serbian nationalism, because these stories don't care at all about New Guinea and its people. Like movie stars, humans like only those scripts that reserve an important role for them. Second, whereas a good story need not extend to infinity, it must extend beyond my horizons. The story provides me with an identity and gives meaning to my life by embedding me within something bigger than myself. But there is always a danger that I might start wondering what gives meaning to that "something bigger."[31]

[28] The quotations in the last sentences are from Hall 1996, pp. 5–6.
[29] Bauman 2004. See also Bauman 2007.
[30] Hall 1996, p. 4.
[31] Harari 2019, p. 246.

We are "migrant animals in the labyrinths of the metropolis," says the aforementioned Italian social theorist Alberto Melucci (1943–2001). "In reality or in the imagination, we participate in an infinity of worlds. And each of these worlds has a culture, a language, and a set of roles and rules that we must adapt to whenever we migrate from one to another."[32] Moreover, following the recent studies of the human brain and the neural networks that control it, Yuval Noah Harari can write that "when you begin to explore the manifold ways the world manipulates you, in the end you realise that your core identity is a complex illusion created by neural networks."[33]

The recent changes and developments in the attitude to the notions of identity and belonging are thus a natural outcome of the intense globalization, the wide migration, the growing social and political uncertainty and insecurity, the developments in the field of communication, and the cosmopolitan turn, all this in addition to the heritage of postmodernism, poststructuralism, psychoanalysis, and postfeminism. They could not have happened, however, without what has been described as the market triumphalism in our era, which has witnessed "the expansion of markets and market-oriented reasoning into spheres of life traditionally governed by non-market norms."[34] All of us are "*in* and *on* the market," says Bauman, "simultaneously customers and commodities. No wonder that the use/consumption of human relations and so, by proxy, also our identities ... catches up, and fast, with the pattern of car use/consumption, imitating the cycle that starts from purchase and ends with waste disposal."[35] More than seventy years after the Austrian philosophical writer Robert Musil's (1880–1942) *The Man without Qualities* (1930), Bauman suggests the "Man without Bonds" as the hero of our liquid modern society: "If you wish 'to relate' keep your distance; if you want fulfillment from your togetherness, do not make or demand commitments. Keep all doors open at any time."[36]

In his popular book *Sapiens: A Brief History of Humankind* (2014), Yuval Noah Harari writes the following:

32 Melucci 1997, p. 61.

33 Harari 2019, p. 222.

34 Sandel 2009, p. 265. Sandel's hero is Robert F. Kennedy (1925–1968), who tried to confront what he called "the poverty of satisfaction," as in the following quotation: "But even if we act to erase material poverty, there is another great task. It is to confront the poverty of satisfaction—a lack of purpose and dignity—that inflicts us all. Too much and too long, we seem to have surrendered community excellence and community values in the mere accumulation of material things" (March 18, 1968).

35 Bauman 2004, p. 91.

36 Bauman 2003, pp. vii, x.

> In recent decades, national communities have been increasingly eclipsed by tribes of customers who do not know one another intimately but share the same consumption habits and interests, and therefore feel part of the same consumer tribe—and define themselves as such. This sounds very strange, but we are surrounded by examples. Madonna fans, for example, constitute a consumer tribe. They define themselves largely by shopping. They buy Madonna concert tickets, CDs, posters, shirts and ring tones, and thereby define who they are. Manchester United fans, vegetarians and environmentalists are other examples. They, too, are defined above all by what they consume. It is the keystone of their identity. A German vegetarian might well prefer to marry a French vegetarian than a German carnivore.[37]

And in his *21 Lessons for the 21st Century* (2019), Harari emphasizes that:

> hardly anyone has just one identity. Nobody is just a Muslim, or just an Italian, or just a capitalist. But every now and then a fanatical creed comes along and insists that people should believe in only one story and have only one identity. In recent generations the most fanatical such creed was fascism. Fascism insisted that people should not believe any story except the nationalist story, and should have no identity except their national identity.[38]

It is interesting how the Arabized Jews' experiences with the issue of identity and belonging during the twentieth century could provide Harari with good examples for his arguments. The aforementioned refusal of both Muslim-Arab and Jewish-Zionist cultural and national systems to adopt the hybrid Arab-Jewish identity and their insistence on highlighting the so-called "pure" Jewish-Zionist identity against the "pure" Arab-Muslim can hardly escape the definition of fascism.

3. INTERPELLATION AND EXCLUSION

In the modern history of the Iraqi Jews, we may notice some processes that led already around the middle of twentieth century to the creation of embryonic forms of such singular subjectivities, which, some decades later, would be celebrated globally, as we have just showed, among intellectual and academic circles in the West. The following analysis is based on an investigation of the subjectivities and singularities of more than a hundred Iraqi-Jewish intellectuals, writers, and artists.[39] As previously mentioned, I have a solid basis for the hypothesis that the same developments have occurred among

37 Harari 2014, p. 309.
38 Harari 2019, p. 259.
39 On these subjectivities, see my publications on the Iraqi Jews that have come out during the last two decades, especially Snir 2005a.

other communities of Arabized Jews as well. Because the Iraqi Jews have been the topic of my studies during the last two decades, I will concentrate here on them. Also, I will try to trace the exclusionary operations that the Iraqi Jews experienced during the last century. "Once it is understood that subjects are formed through exclusionary operations," says feminist theorist Joan Scott, "it becomes necessary to trace the operations of that construction and erasure."[40] The Iraqi Jews as a whole experienced during the twentieth century at least four major processes of collective interpellation, two of them were at the same time intense exclusionary operations and erasures as well:

1. Hailing the Iraqi Jews as Arabs.
2. Hailing the Iraqi Jews as "Zionist" (= *first exclusion*).
3. Hailing the Iraqi Jews as "Arabs" (= *second exclusion*).
4. Hailing the Iraqi Jews as one side in a binary monolithic category.

The quotation marks around "Zionist" and "Arabs" in the second and third processes (the first and the second operations of exclusion) mean that, in each case, the hailing ascribed to them a specific identity while at the same time ignoring whether the subjectivities of the interpellated people were at all ready to positively respond to such a hailing. I have focused my investigations on the ways in which Iraqi Jews articulated their cultural preferences, defined their identities, and expressed their identification and belonging before and after their immigration. In other words, I am interested more in their subjectivities and less in the identities ascribed to them.

Before elaborating on the four processes, it is essential, as I previously pointed out, to emphasize the necessary connection between interpellation, rhetoric, and identity—after all, Parmenides' question of "the one and the many," of the self's relation to others, is a problem not only for philosophy but also for rhetoric, which interests itself in the speaker or writer's capacity to engage and to move an audience, to have an effect on others.[41] Offering a rhetoric of rationality that hypothesizes no unity of self, no positive identity as such, Kenneth Burke (1897–1993) turns our attention toward the question of the *many in the one*, suggesting that what goes for one's individual "substance" amounts to the incalculable totality of one's complex and to contradictory identifications, which are never reducible to one identity. Starting

[40] Nicholson 1995, p. 12.

[41] The following section is based on Kenneth Burke's (1969) and Diane Davis' (2003) reflections on identity and belonging and their connections with rhetoric, especially Davis 2003, pp. 3–6.

with a "weak" or inessential subject that cannot rest upon itself, Burke argues that there is no identity, no one at all, that has not already been identified, hailed into existence as a subject via the very others to which it would address itself. This rhetoric necessarily presumes an exposed and so radically non-self-sufficient and non-figurable "subject"—we might in fact say that it presumes *love's* subject.[42] We are clearly in the region of rhetoric, says Burke, when considering the identifications whereby a specialized activity makes one a participant in some social or economic class. "Belonging" in this sense is rhetorical.[43] Burke's rhetor is charged with hailing his audience into existence, pulling together a community of readers or citizens by figuring them as such and prompting them to identify with some representable condition of belonging that they are presumed to hold in common. The rhetor's task, adds Carolyn Miller (b. 1938), Distinguished Professor of Rhetoric at North Carolina State University, is "*to construct one out of many, over and over again.*"[44] Barbara Biesecker refers to "the power of persuasive discourse to constitute audiences out of individuals, to transform singularities into collectives, *to fashion a 'we' out of a plurality of 'I's,'* and to move them to collective action."[45]

First Process: The Jews Are Arabs

From the late nineteenth century and even after the 1917 Balfour Declaration, the Jews living in Arab societies had been hailed, in one way or another, as Arabs; they were considered part of the Arab collective, if from the linguistic respect, they spoke Arabic. In the conclusion to his four-volume *Ta'rīkh al-Ṣiḥāfa al-ʿArabiyya* (*History of the Arab Press*), the pioneer scholar of Arabic journalism Philip de Ṭarrāzī (1865–1956) wrote in 1933 about Islam, Christianity, and Judaism as "the leading religions to which the Arabic writers of the world belong."[46] The Balfour Declaration was considered by many Arabized Jews as encapsulating the vision and hopes of only European Ashkenazi Jews. For most of the Iraqi Jews, the idea of establishing a Jewish nation-state in Palestine was at the time a far-off cloud, totally undesired. Sir Arnold Talbot Wilson (1884–1940), the Acting Civil Commissioner in

[42] Cf. Agamben 2003 [1993], pp. 1–3.
[43] Burke 1969, p. 28. Cf. "Belonging can be considered a process whereby an individual in some way feels some sense of association with a group, and as such represents a way to *explain* the relationship between a personalized identity and a collective one. In a purely conceptual way belonging is about the relationship between personal identity and a collective identity" (Delanty et al. 2011, p. 44 [my emphasis]).
[44] Miller 1993, p. 91 (my emphasis).
[45] Biesecker 1997, p. 1 (my emphasis).
[46] Ṭarrāzī 1933, IV, pp. 486–7.

Mesopotamia (1918–1920), wrote in 1936 that he had discussed the declaration with several members of the Jewish community and that they remarked that Palestine was a poor country, and Jerusalem a bad town to live in. Compared with Palestine, Mesopotamia was a paradise. "This is the Garden of Eden," said one of the Jews, "it is from this country that Adam was driven forth—give us a good government and we will make this country flourish—for us Mesopotamia is a home, a national home to which the Jews of Bombay and Persia and Turkey will be glad to come. Here shall be liberty and with it opportunity! In Palestine there may be liberty, but there will be no opportunity."[47]

The real national vision of most of the Iraqi Jews at the time, certainly of the intellectual secular elite, was Iraqi and Arab. It was a vision that had its roots in the nineteenth century with the start of the process of secularization and when cultural barriers between the Jews and the wider local society had begun to crumble. The connection between interpellation, rhetoric, and identity was expressed, for example, by the aforementioned speech of Emir Fayṣal, who, one month before his coronation as King of Iraq, addressed the Jewish community leaders as follows:

> In the vocabulary of patriotism, there is no such thing as a Jew, a Muslim, or a Christian. There is simply one thing called Iraq ... I ask all the Iraqi children of my homeland to be just Iraqis, because we all belong to one origin and one tree, the tree of our ancestor Shem, and all of us are related to the Semitic root, which makes no distinction between Muslim, Christian or Jew ... Today we have but one means [to our end]: influential patriotism.[48]

The aim of Fayṣal was to create "an independent strong Arab state, which will be a cornerstone for Arab unity"—the Jewish citizens were an integral part of that vision. As previously mentioned, Sāṭiʿ al-Ḥuṣrī, Director General of Education in Iraq at the time, argued that "every person who is related to the Arab lands and speaks Arabic is an Arab."[49] The Iraqi Constitution of March 21, 1925 (*al-Qānūn al-Asāsī al-ʿIrāqī*) stated that "there is

[47] Wilson 1936, I, pp. 305–6. Wilson writes afterwards: "Vain words, no doubt, but they concealed perhaps the seeds of economic truth." This comment, however, was presumably added in retrospect, in the light of the escalation in the national conflict in the Middle East and the increasing tension between the Jews and the Iraqi authorities. Elie Kedourie, however, argued that even in the 1940s "the Zionist cause did not seem to me as a matter of any political wisdom. The expectancies which Zionism was creating were too high and unrealistic" (*Dvar ha-shavu*ʿ, April 7, 1988, p. 9).

[48] The original text was first published in *al-ʿIrāq*, July 19, 1921. For the text of the speech, see *Fayṣal ibn al-Ḥusayn fi Khuṭabihi wa-Aqwālihi* (*Fayṣal ibn al-Ḥusayn in His Speeches and Sayings*) (Baghdād: Maṭbaʿat al-Ḥukūma, 1945), pp. 246–9.

[49] See al-Ḥuṣrī 1965 [1955], p. 12.

no difference between the Iraqi people in rights before the law, even if they belong to different nationalities, religions and languages."[50]

The evident inclusive rhetorical expressions toward the Jews and the hailing of them as Arabs should not be surprising, since Arab nationalists at their earliest phases had already considered the Jews living among Arabs as part of the Arab "race." A manifesto of Arab nationalists disseminated from Cairo by the Arab Revolutionary Committee at the beginning of the First World War, and some sections of which were published from Istanbul in French translation in 1916, served as a strong interpellating machine:

> Arabes chrétiens et israélites unissez-vous à vos frères musulmans. N'écoutez pas ceux qui disent qu'ils préfèrent les Turcs sans religion aux Arabes de croyances différentes; ce sont des ignorants qui méconnaissent les intérêts vitaux de la race.[51]

Another manifesto printed in December 1918 in Damascus hailed the children of all three monotheistic religions as Arabs: "You are Arabs before you are Muslims, before you are Christians, and before you are Jews. The land is your land and the fatherland is your fatherland, and you must join together to defend its independence."[52] It is thus not surprising to find the intellectual secular elite of the Jews in Iraq rallying behind the efforts to make it a state for all its citizens—Muslims, Christians, and Jews. On July 20, 1938, the poet Anwar Shā'ul (1904–1984) emphasized the Arabism of the Iraqi Jews and their rejection of Zionism.[53] Considering themselves an integral part of Arab-Muslim culture and the Iraqi nation, Iraqi Jews were full of confidence that Iraq was their only homeland and that the Jewish community in Iraq would endure, as the previously mentioned Iraqi-Jewish writer Shālom Darwīsh (1913–1997) was to put it, "to the days of the Messiah."[54]

Second Process: The Jews Are "Zionist" (= First Exclusion)

The German sociologist and cultural critic Siegfried Kracauer (1889–1966) makes a distinction between two kinds of communities: on the one hand, there are "communities of life and fate," whose members "live together in an indissoluble attachment rather than being welded together solely by ideas or

[50] For the text of the constitution, see al-Ḥusnī 1974, I, pp. 319–34; the quotation is from p. 319.

[51] *La Vérité sur la question syrienne* (Stamboul: Imprimerie tanine, 1916), p. 35. For the full original Arabic text of the manifesto, see al-A'ẓamī 1932, IV, pp. 108–17 (for an English translation, see Haim 1962, pp. 83–8).

[52] Tauber 1995, p. 49.

[53] Darwaza 1993, III, p. 545.

[54] Darwīsh 1980, p. 83.

various principles." Instances of this kind are the family and the nation: they envelop any person born into them just the way they are, from their birth through death and even beyond death. These communities, whose origins and purposes are irrational, devote themselves to an "endless multiplicity of objectives, though they never find their definitive significance in any of them." On the other hand, there are those communities whose accord is based on an idea with which they arise and perish. Their unity "is not an immanent part of organic, growing life, but is fully encompassed by a specific concept that will come to life through them."[55]

For the Jews, Iraqi society was certainly of the first kind: it was a community of life and fate whose members had been living together in an indissoluble attachment. Suddenly, however, that community was denied to them and they were excluded as the "Others"—they were not considered anymore *true* Iraqis and *real* Arabs. It was the Balfour Declaration that started a process that interpellated the Iraqi Jews into Zionism while, at the same time, interpellating the Arab Muslims and Christians as a unified Arab community calling upon themselves to operate exclusionary operations against Jews, regardless of their ethnicity. Because of the escalation of the Arab–Jewish Conflict over Palestine during the late 1940s and the beginning of the 1950s, the Iraqi-Arab identity of the Jews, which had been firmly consolidated during the 1920s and 1930s, underwent a speedy fragmentation in a way that left them no alternative but to emigrate. Among the immigrants to Israel we can hardly find even one, no matter what his political point of view, who did not lament that exclusion. Here, it should be noted that the controversy about whether the Arabized Jews lived in perfect harmony with Muslims and Christians or whether this is only a myth current among left-wing intellectuals is irrelevant. At any event, unlike popular conceptions, the well-known myth of a "Golden Age" and harmonious Muslim–Jewish relations prior to the rise of Zionism as well as the "neo-lachrymose" countermyth, which views Jewish history under Arab Islam as a story of intolerance, persecution, and an unending nightmare of oppression and humiliation, are both highly exaggerated, and no serious professional scholar of Jewish history under Islam holds to either of them.[56]

After the immigration of the Iraqi Jews to Israel, their subjectivities, certainly those of their offspring, were gradually "enriched" by new components of identity, the most outstanding of which were the Zionist, the Israeli, and

[55] Kracauer 1995, p. 144.

[56] See the debate in *Tikkun*: Cohen 1991, pp. 55–60; Stillman 1991a, pp. 60–4; Cohen 2012, pp. 110–37. J. Beinin rejects both approaches and opts instead for a Marxist interpretation of the political events and the question of identity (see especially Beinin 1998, pp. 1–28).

the Hebrew layers of identity. No Arabized Jew who immigrated to Israel could resist the strong interpellating processes administrated by the state, even those in whose subjectivities the Arab component was dominant. The new Zionist-Israeli rhetoric of identity overwhelmingly swept all of them up.

The Zionist and Israeli processes of interpellation lead us to both the third and fourth processes of interpellation that the Iraqi Jews have experienced. These processes were somehow temporally overlapping, though we refer to them here as two different processes—that is, the hailing of them as a population in need of "education" due to their *Arabness* (= primitiveness), and at the same time, the hailing of them, together with all other communities of Arabized Jews in Israel, as a monolithic population.

Third Process: The Jews Are "Arabs" (= Second Exclusion)

The third process of interpellation is thus the second exclusion of the Iraqi Jews, and this time it is in Israel. After their exclusion in Iraq, they realized that they were excluded again, and now precisely because of their Arabness, by none other but their fellow co-religionists. Before their immigration, they had found themselves excluded because of their *Jewish* identity, and now, in Israel, they found themselves excluded because of their *Arab* identity. Both exclusions were based on a kind of unspoken agreement and a substantial identity of interests between both national movements, Zionism and Arab nationalism, seeing *Jewishness* as equated with *Zionism* and later even with *Israeliness* to the point that the three identities have been considered by both movements as virtually synonymous. In order to be part of the new Israeli-Jewish-Zionist collective, the immigrants were encouraged to change their Arab names, to stop using Arabic in public spaces, to train themselves to adopt Israeli-Hebrew culture, to remodel their family patterns, and to "refine" their lifestyles. In retrospect, many of the Arabized Jews would consider this process as a "cultural ethnic cleansing."[57] They were Jews, and they immigrated to the state of the Jews, but they discovered that Israeli society was not for them a community in which they could live together with the others, in Kracauer's aforementioned terms, in "an indissoluble attachment." For most of them, certainly after their very immigration, the bond with the other Jewish majority members was only a bond of religion.

But there was another process, which was simultaneous to and overlapping with that process: the second exclusion was accompanied by labeling the immigrants as one side in an evaluative binary.

[57] See, for example, Rabeeya 2000, p. 27.

Fourth Process: The Immigrants Are Sephardim, 'Edot Mizrah, Mizrahim, etc.

For the purpose of my argument, there is no difference if the monolithic category is Sephardim, *'Edot Mizrah*, Mizrahim, Easterners, Orientals, Levantines, or any derogatory name like Blacks, Franks, or the journalist Arye Gelblum's (1921–1993) description of one community of Arabized Jews as "people whose primitivism is at a peak, whose level of knowledge is one of virtually absolute ignorance, and worse, who have little talent for understanding anything intellectual."[58] Now, it is widely recognized that any such monolithic category is inadequate, but this insight into the inadequateness of the monolithic hailing had been always a matter of fact among all communities of Arabized Jews, certainly among the Iraqis. In their reflections on their study of Middle Eastern Jewries within the context of Israeli society, Harvey E. Goldberg and Chen Bram showed how "analysis based on explicit and implicit binary models skews the understanding of some historical developments." Furthermore, "critical approaches have provided useful insights into how hegemonic structures have excluded Jews defined as 'Eastern,' but have been less successful in documentation and grasping developments reflecting the distinctiveness and creative categories and assumptions of those groups themselves."[59] From my investigations into the identities of the Arabized Jews from Iraq—and I do not have any reason to believe that something fundamentally different happened with Arabized Jews emigrating from other places—it is clear that Goldberg and Bram were too cautious in their critical comments on binary-oriented analytical methods and critical approaches.

Such monolithic categories were never adopted by Arabized Jews in the way they were meant to interpellate and hail them using the systems of power. From the point of view of the Iraqi Jews, this process of interpellation has been the weakest among all four processes. But it has served the aims of the state and of the dominant and hegemonic systems and structures, precisely as any exclusionary operations serve the aims of any state or any system of power. The influence of such a process was highly significant but by no means in the direction the interpellating systems desired, particularly because it coincided with the previously mentioned global processes that created the tendency to escape into inessential subjectivities and to prefer singularities and, also, because it did not take into account the double exclusion of the previous two processes. Unfortunately, for political and ideological reasons, scholars have preferred mostly so far to emphasize only one side of that double exclusion—either that exercised in the Arab countries before

[58] *Haaretz*, April 22, 1949.
[59] Goldberg and Bram 2007, pp. 227–56 (quotations from pp. 242 and 247, respectively).

the Jews' immigration, or that exercised in Israel after their immigration. Measured in their combined effect, the significance of both exclusionary operations cannot be underestimated. Most of the Iraqi Jews realized that what was very convenient for the state might be convenient for them as well as long as they can behave as singularities. What is the difference if I am personally hailed as Mizrahi, Sephardic, Easterner, *'Edot Mizrah*, Iraqi, Frank, Black or any other identity ascribed to me (and personally I have faced *all* those very labels), if I insist in my personal life to behave according to my own singularity without affirming, in my own subjectivity, any stable identity?

4. GLOBALIZATION

The global developments were not fully effective during the middle of the twentieth century, but the contemporary political, social, and cultural circumstances had prepared the Iraqi Jews to gradually develop a negative sensitivity toward the notion of stable identity. If it were only the first exclusion, it would have been sufficient for them to be aware that belonging and identity were not set in stone, and that they were not secured by a lifelong guarantee. What were they to expect after they would be excluded again in their very promised homeland, "promised" by both those who pulled them—the Zionists—as well as by those who pushed them—the Iraqi authorities and the Arab national activists?! Was there any chance for them to think that belonging and identity were set in stone? Following that very double exclusion, and after adapting and adjusting to the new Israeli society, they found themselves, separately and not collectively, preferring to assert their own singularities and at the same time to reject any essential identity. To paraphrase a declaration by writer Sami Michael (b. 1926), each chose to build his own unique "state" that consisted of only one citizen—himself.[60] During less than half a century, they had witnessed a rapid process by which their Iraqi-Arab-Jewish identity was firmly consolidated (1920s–1940s), to be followed by another process that resulted in its speedy fragmentation (1950–1951). Many hoped that their uprooting from Iraq might be a blessing in disguise, dreaming that their immigration to the new Jewish land would

[60] In the aforementioned documentary film *Forget Baghdad: Jews and Arabs—The Iraqi Connection* (2002), Michael says: "When I first arrived here in Israel, I decided to found a state called 'Sami Michael.' [There has been] an ongoing fight between [the State of] Israel and [the state of] myself. Of course, both the state and myself wanted to be [victorious]. But today I can say that I have won" (this is the written translation of his original Arabic text, which appears in the subtitles of the film, with necessary modifications. The exact wording of the original spoken Arabic text was slightly different).

guarantee for them a full integration into a unified new Israeli-Jewish identity without them having to renounce their Arabness. Instead of that, they were left excluded from both old and new identities.

It was thus the absurdity of both exclusionary operations that paved the way to the rejection *tout court* of the notion of fixed identity, simply because each of these operations was aiming at the heart of a *major* component of their identity: in Iraq, precisely when the Jews felt themselves *more Arab and Iraqi than Jewish* they were excluded as the "Other" (Jews) in a way that left them no alternative but to immigrate to the state of the Jews. In Israel, precisely when they should have felt themselves *more Jewish than Arab and Iraqi* they were excluded as the "Other" (Iraqis and Arabs). But, now, unlike the first exclusion, there was no other abode that would serve as a new promised haven. The political circumstances in the Middle East, which were the direct cause of that double exclusion, accelerated among many of the immigrants a tendency, which at the time was globally and universally still in its infancy, to reject in principle the notion of stable and fixed identities, to assert their particular singularities, and to search for alternative forms of identification, mostly various kinds of inessential solidarities and senses of belonging. The local, regional, and global developments, sometimes simultaneous and overlapping, served as a fertile ground for the formation among many of them of such a form of subjectivity that responded to the natural human need for identification and belonging and, at the same time, was flexible enough to provide them with some shield against additional frustrations and disappointments. Singularity has been the preferred option but not by default. It has been a conscious choice that has been able to fit their local, global, and, in most cases, personal circumstances.

I believe that the aforementioned analysis of the subjectivities of the Iraqi Jews is applicable as well, in one way or another, to other immigrants from Arab countries. There are of course significant differences between the Iraqi Jews and other Arabized immigrants with regard to the attitude to Arabic language and culture. But I found that the tendency toward inessential solidarities had *nothing* to do with the Iraqi Jews' well-known Arab cultural preference and that it had mainly to do with the two processes of exclusion, which most, if not all, the Arabized Jews had undergone.[61] Already in the 1950s,

[61] In his study on ethnic demonstration and cultural representation and the case of Mizrahi-*Sabras* in Israel, Baruch Shimoni (b. 1957) refers to his own identity as a "Mizrahi-Sabra, one of the second generation of Israeli Jews from Iraqi Kurdistan." He presents his cultural identity as "an unintended consequence of the efforts invested by the Ashkenazi hegemony to turn [him] into a new Jew, brave and fearless, holding European values—efforts which haven't fully succeeded. By generating concealed processes of self-hate and internalization of oppression, the melting pot strategy applied by the Ashkenazi hegemony pushed the

three decades before the global/local dialectics could be clearly noticed in Israel as well, most of the intellectuals among the Arabized immigrants felt the same dialectics but tripled: global/regional/local—and these dialectics involved their very existence: as members of the Israeli-Hebrew society, they spoke *Hebrew* but they were also part of the *Arabic*-speaking Middle East, and, at the same time, they could not escape the *global* developments. Whoever lived this double exclusion could not have adhered to any notion of a stable identity and, if he wished to survive, he must have thought about the need to be flexible and adapt himself to the changing circumstances, emphasizing his own singularity in which each of the major layers of collective identity, such as Arabness, Jewishness, Hebrewness, Israeliness, Zionism, and Communism, played different roles, in addition of course to various more specific components like gender, profession, hobby, and local environment.[62]

As for the new generation of neo-Arab-Jewish post-Zionist or anti-Zionist intellectuals,[63] those radical Mizrahi leftist scholars, such as Yehouda Shenhav-Shahrabani (b. 1952), Ella Shohat (b. 1959), and Sami Shalom Chetrit (b. 1960) and their followers, it seems that all of them adopted Arab-Jewish or Mizrahi identity as part of identity politics in Israel, which cannot be, at least not exclusively, isolated from what appears to be, during the last decades, a switching of identities with the changing winds of fashion. Following Edward Hallett Carr's (1892–1982) constructive suggestion "to study the historian before you begin to study the facts,"[64] I have studied the "identities" of the three of them in the same way I have studied the subjectivities of the Iraqi-Jewish writers and intellectuals during the last century. It is paradoxical that my investigations have led me to one solid conclusion: all of them have been recycling their identities according to changing circumstances, preferring, in one way or another, to adhere, each in his own way, to various inessential solidarities as well. All of them are moving toward what Giorgio Agamben (b. 1942) has described as the "Coming Community,"

Kurdish-Jewish cultural tradition to the margins of my identity, but failed to accomplish its total removal. Through the long process of my cultural identity development, I have been thinking and acting in a third space in which consciously and unconsciously I mix Israeli-Ashkenazi and Kurdish-Jewish values and practices to produce my hybrid identity. This identity represents imposition and coercion, initiated by Israeli-Ashkenazi Jews, but also a process of self-creation and innovation in which I hybridize the Ashkenazi and my parents' cultural characteristics to produce my identity" (Shimoni 2007, pp. 13–34. The quotation is from p. 30). In my view, Shimoni's discussion of his own identity is part of the aforementioned tendency toward inessential solidarities among Arabized Jews.

62 Zvi Zohar (b. 1949), scholar of Sephardic law and ethics, goes even futher and argues that non-Ashkenazic Jewry is the ground of contemporary Israeli multiculturalism (Zohar 2007, pp. 137–48).

63 For a critical approach toward post-Zionist and anti-Zionist intellectuals, see Gelber 2008.

64 Carr 1965, p. 32.

which is a community of human beings devoid of any stable or fixed identity attached to them. In other words, they are not viewed, and do not see themselves, as belonging to a particular group by virtue of some essential feature of theirs. They do not have any identity in the usual sense of the term: Shenhav-Shahrabani, Shohat, and Chetrit do not think of themselves as having a core essence that is the *sine qua non* of their existence. More than that, even if they speak in favor of Arab-Jewish identity, Arabism and Arabic, they are excellent examples of how the Arabic language has been gradually disappearing as a language spoken on a daily basis and mastered by Jews and of how Arab-Jewish identity has been gradually disappearing as a *Jewish* identity.

Proficiency in Arabic can mainly be traced now to two populations: Jews who emigrated from Arab lands having already mastered the language as native Arabic speakers (and their number, of course, is rapidly decreasing), and those who make a living from their knowledge of Arabic whether in the Israeli governmental, educational, or security services (and their number, of course, is always increasing). The Jewish or Israeli canonical elite, among them these very Mizrahi intellectuals, in their academic activities do not see Arabic language and culture as an intellectual asset, as proven in their daily life and professional practice. What is more interesting is their reluctance to master Arabic or to touch upon Arabic *belles lettres*, especially such *belles lettres* that were written by Jews. Even those who speak of the importance of reviving the hybridic Arab-Jewish option, their cultural identity is more a political or imported academic tool than an ethnic or cultural one. Paradoxically, the way those radical intellectuals refer to the historical Arab-Jewish identity implies conceiving the notion of identity as essential and at the same time playing down the fluidity of the subjectivities of immigrants, regardless of where they are from.[65]

The fact that we can hardly find among those Mizrahi radical intellectuals even one who can write an essay in literary Arabic, not to speak about an Arabic poet or fiction writer, proves that their adoption of Arab-Jewish identity is nothing but a political and ideological tool in their struggle to change the agenda of the Zionist-Jewish state. Moreover, how can they pretend to deal academically with Arab-Jewish culture when most of them have not mastered Arabic. In his review of *God Has Ninety-Nine Names: Reporting from a Militant Middle East* (1996) by the *New York Times* reporter Judith Miller, Edward Said (1935–2003) neatly encapsulates this point when he says the following:

[65] On evidence of the fluidity of identity in the early modern Mediterranean, see Dursteler 2006, pp. 10–21.

> Writing about any other part of the world, Miller would be considered woefully unqualified. She tells us that she has been involved with the Middle East for twenty-five years, yet she has little knowledge of either Arabic or Persian. It would be impossible to be taken seriously as a reporter or expert on Russia, France, Germany or Latin America, perhaps even China or Japan, without knowing the requisite languages, but for "Islam," linguistic knowledge is unnecessary since what one is dealing with is considered to be a psychological deformation, not a "real" culture or religion.[66]

Most of these neo-Arab-Jewish intellectuals refer in practice to the standard literary Arabic (*fuṣḥā*) as a dead language—as Jaroslav Stetkevych (1929–2021) said: "If we don't write in Arabic, we don't think in it either. Not thinking in it implies that we are emotionally unengaged as well."[67] As far as I know, most of them do not want to be emotionally engaged with Arabic to a greater extent than they are with Hebrew. To shed light on the notion of being "emotionally engaged" with Arabic, we can turn, for the sake of comparison, to Gershom Scholem (1897–1982), founder of the academic study of Jewish mysticism, Kabbalah, whose generous definition of a mystic is as being not only a person who attains "an immediate, and to him real, experience of the divine, of ultimate reality," but also a person who "at least *strives* to attain such experience."[68] And we can hardly find Arab-Jewish intellectuals who strive to master Arabic. One of the few exceptions that proves the rule is the aforementioned Yehouda Shenhav-Shahrabani, who in recent years has gradually learned Arabic and started to translate from Arabic literature and even established the *Maktūb* project for translating works of Arabic literature and culture and for making them accessible to Israeli readers. The project, an initiative of translators and scholars of Arabic, both Jews and Palestinians, grew out of the translators' forum that was established at the Van Leer Jerusalem Institute in 2015. The project offers "a hybrid model in which Jewish Israelis and Palestinian Arabs translate together through dialogue and speech, with linguistic flexibility and a multiplicity of versions intended to connect, instead of dividing the linguistic space and breaking the linear and delayed connection between source and translation."[69] However, the fact that this project published many books in Hebrew translation but nobody has presented yet any critical and serious assessment of its conception and literary products, despite its fundamental shortcomings and the

66 See *al-Jadīd* [Los Angeles] 2.10 (August 1996), p. 6.

67 Address delivered in February 1967 at St. Antony's College, Oxford. An article based on the address was published as "Arabism and Arabic Literature: Self-View of a Profession" (Stetkevych 1969, pp. 145–56 [the quotation is from p. 154]).

68 Scholem 1965, p. 5 (my emphasis).

69 Shenhav-Shahrabani and Mendel 2019, p. 13.

level of some of the translations, is another testimony to the aforementioned demise of Arab-Jewish culture.[70]

5. CONCLUSION

Identity is a double-edged sword. Sometimes, the edge of identity is turned against "collective pressure" by individuals who resent conformity; at other times, it is the group that turns the edge against a larger group that is accused of a wish to destroy it. In both cases, "identity" appears to be a war cry used in a defensive war: an individual against the assault of a group, or a weaker group against a stronger totality.

But Is Arab-Jewish Identity Currently a War Cry at All?[71]

First, there were Jews that identified themselves as Arab, but no Jewish group has ever declared itself an Arab-Jewish community. We can only find retrospective allusions to Jewish communities who lived in Arab societies as such. It goes without saying that no Arab-Jewish community currently exists.

Second, all current references to any historical Arab-Jewish identity do not aim to celebrate the past but only to express present and future ideological and political desires and aspirations.

Third, Arab-Jewish identity has been paradoxically reinvented precisely when those who could have been mostly interpellated as Arab Jews were in the process of escaping such recruitment. More than that, the interpellating machine is being now administrated by people who pretend to be such but never had the potentiality of such an identity.

Fourth, most of the individuals who, during the last decades, have been identifying themselves as Arab Jews, have been using such an identity only as a war cry against Zionism.

Fifth, the radical Mizrahi intellectuals have succeeded in provoking "real" Arabized Jews, mostly Iraqis (e.g., Nissim Rejwan [1924–2017], Sami Michael [b. 1926], Shimon Ballas [1930–2019], Shmuel Moreh [1932–2017],

70 On the *Maktūb* project, see also the various contributions in *Journal of Levantine Studies* 9.2 (2019) titled "Translation and the Colonial Encounter Maktoob مكتوب מכתוב," and edited by Yehouda Shenhav-Shahrabani and Yonatan Mendel. For a limited critical approach to the project, and not only because the writer does not have any knowledge of Arabic or Arabic literature, see Benni Ziffer's (b. 1953) essay in *Haaretz*, June 2, 2021, available at: https://www.haaretz.co.il/literature/study/.premium-REVIEW-1.9864452, last accessed November 24, 2021. On Ziffer's tendentious agenda toward Arab culture, see Snir 2019, pp. 128–9.

71 The emphasis here is on Arab-Jewish identity as different from Sephardi/Mizrahi identity as presented, for example, in Behar 2017, pp. 312–31; Picard 2017, pp. 32–60.

and Sasson Somekh [1933–2019]), into "reclaiming" their Arab-Jewish identity and to use it as a war cry against those very radical intellectuals themselves. Those Arab-Jewish "veterans" rightly feel that, now when Arab-Jewish identity has become something to be proud of in certain circles, if there is any credit to be given for having such an identity, *they* deserve it more than anyone else.

Sixth, Muslim and Christian Arab intellectuals in general do not pay any attention to the emergence of the new "fashion" of Arab-Jewish identity in Israel. If they do so, it is mostly only for political reasons and as a tool against Israel and Zionism.

Seventh, nostalgic references among Arab intellectuals to "the beautiful time" ("*al-zaman al-jamīl*") when Muslims, Christian, Jews, and others were living in harmony in the Arab world during the first half of the twentieth century, or attempts to reclaim the aforementioned eloquent secularist dictum "*al-dīnu li-llāhi wa-l-waṭanu li-l-jamī'*" ("Religion is for God, the Fatherland is for everyone"), are generally due to a mere longing for a previous secular discourse and, mainly, are used as a weapon against the rise of the Islamist circles considered by the Arab secular elite as a great danger.[72] So are Arabic novels, short stories, plays, and films in which Jews are at the center of the narratives and plots—they serve to underline the lost pluralism (*ta'addudiyya*) of some Arab societies in the past and to admonish against a darker fate that may await other communities in the Arab world.[73]

And last, but not least: in the preface to his *The Black Atlantic*,[74] Paul Gilroy (b. 1956) mentioned two aspirations that he would like to share with his readers before they embark on the sea voyage that he would like his book to represent. I have three aspirations, two of them are essentially Gilroy's

[72] See, for example, the wishful thinking of the Lebanese scholar Youssef M. Choueiri (b. 1948) that "the emerging Arabness of Arab Jews may find a more receptive ground, or both sides of the divide may start to see common threads of cultural and political attitudes" (Choueiri 2016, p. 328). Cf. a post by the Iraqi poetess Amal al-Jabbūrī (b. 1968) (Amal Al-jubouri, August 1, 2019, available at: https://www.facebook.com/eastwestalmasar/posts/1649515045182047, last accessed December 27, 2020). On such nostalgic tendencies that unfortunately have disrupted the serious academic discourse on Arab-Jewish culture, see Snir 2020a, pp. 317–52. The longing for *al-zaman al-jamīl* is probably also the reason behind the changes in the image of the Jews in Arabic literature (see, e.g., the file dedicated to this issue in *Afkār* 374 [March 2020], pp. 3–30). Another phenomenon is the increasing number of studies on the Jews and their culture in the Arab world, mainly in Iraq (see, e.g., the activities of Ibrāhīm Khalīl al-'Allāf [b. 1945] in detailing the bibliographically relevant data, such as in https://www.ahewar.org/debat/show.art.asp?aid=337988, December 24, 2012, last accessed December 19, 2021, as well as in his blog at: http://wwwallafblogspot com.blogspot.com, last accessed December 19, 2021).

[73] See, for example, the novels about Iraqi Jews discussed in Zeidel 2013; Zeidel 2018.

[74] Gilroy 1993.

adapted to my needs: the first is my hope that the present study articulates transparently the notion of the inescapable intermixture of ideas of all communities and persons and at the same time the dangerous obsessions with essential purity that have been circulating for more than a century inside and outside Zionist-Jewish and Arab-Muslim national politics and cultures. The second is my desire that the study's heartfelt plea against the closure of the categories with which we conduct our cultural and political lives will not go unheard. The history of the Arabized Jews during the last century yields a course of lessons as to the instability and mutability of identities, which are always unfinished, always being remade. My third aspiration is that scholars of Jewish, Muslim, and Arab cultures and identities, who have produced dozens of excellent scholarly studies, will benefit more from the theoretical insights of thinkers and philosophers who have been working on notions of identity and belonging. In this context, fresh identity debates based on genetic studies, such as "Who Are the Jews?"[75] or new controversies around the invention of peoples[76] are irrelevant. There is instead an urgent need, to quote Diane Davis (b. 1963), to "shoot for a thinking of fluidity and a fluidity of thinking."[77] Thinking, as Hélène Cixous (b. 1937) writes, "is trying to think the unthinkable: thinking the thinkable is not worth the effort."[78] After all, we, as scholars dealing with such delicate issues, must find ways to stop trying to regulate only the thinkable and the knowable. And this is why the following words of Georges Bataille (1897–1962) were never so relevant for the academic community as they are today:

> Woe to those who, to the very end, insist on regulating the movement that exceeds them with the narrow mind of the mechanic who changes a tire.[79]

[75] See Balter 2010, p. 1342.

[76] Such as that evoked following the publication of Shlomo Sand's *The Invention of the Jewish People* (Sand 2009. See also a critical review of the book in Shapira 2009, pp. 63–72. For an analysis of Jewish genomes refuting the Khazar claim, see Begley 2010).

[77] Davis 2000, p. 15.

[78] Cixous 1993, p. 38.

[79] Bataille 1988, I, pp. 26–7.

Epilogue

"Trailed Travellers": Between Fiction, Meta-Fiction, and History

I do not know.
A language beyond this,
And a language beyond this.
And I hallucinate in no-man's land.
– Anton Shammās

The Palestinian *Nakba,* the destruction of Palestinian society and homeland in 1948, was by no means an isolated event or series of events but an ongoing process of uprooting, permanent persecution, displacement, and occupation. Against the background of the *Nakba,* the process of nation-building has been the major aim of all branches of Palestinian culture as illustrated above in the fields of theater and poetry. A good example was the rise of the Palestinian theatrical and dramatic movement, particularly the growth of professional theater after 1967. More rooted in Palestinian collective memory is poetry, encapsulated in our present study in the poetry of Maḥmūd Darwīsh, the national Palestinian poet, especially his attempt to provide a chronicle of the ongoing *Nakba* in the mid-1980s against the backdrop of the Israeli invasion of Lebanon and the lead-up to the outbreak of the first *Intifāḍa* in the West Bank and Gaza Strip in December 1987. Apart from Palestinian Arabic culture, the emergence of Palestinian authors writing in Hebrew has been encapsulating the cultural Palestinian dilemma of life as a minority among the Jewish-Hebrew majority in Israel.

Unlike the flowering of Palestinian culture, we are currently witnessing the demise of Arab-Jewish culture—a tradition that started more than 1,500 years ago is vanishing before our very own eyes. The main factor in the Muslim–Christian–Jewish Arab symbiosis up to the twentieth century, from the Jewish point of view, was that the great majority of the Jews under the rule of Islam adopted Arabic as their spoken language. This symbiosis does not exist in our time because Arabic is gradually disappearing as a language spoken and used on a daily basis by Jews. The image of an hourglass is an apposite one: the grains of sand are quickly running out. In the field of *belles lettres*, there is not even one Jewish writer of record who was born after 1948 and who is writing literature in Arabic. Jews who are now fluent in Arabic have probably either been born in an Arab country (and their numbers, of course, are rapidly decreasing) or have acquired the language as part of their training for service in the military or security services (and their numbers, needless to say, are always increasing).

Scholars have tried to refer to the differences between the *Nakba* of the Palestinians compared with the "success" of the Arabized Jews in restarting their life in Israel or in other countries despite their own "Jewish Nakba"—the plight of the Jewish refugee from the Arab world: "There may have been two *Nakbas*, but it must be noted that the Jewish *Nakba* is not only a story of catastrophe, it is also one of triumph over adversity."[1] In an essay reviewing some novelistic reactions and approaches to history and how far modern Sephardic novelists draw parallels with past events, Judith Roumani writes:

> From Morocco, to Egypt, to Iraq, Sephardim over the second half of the twentieth century were forced to flee their ancestral homes in Muslim lands, often taking with them no more than a small suitcase and hardly any money, to start new lives on other continents, in totally different climes and cultures. That they successfully restarted their lives, from Israel to Europe to North and South America, without the aid of the United Nations or any refugee agency, is a tribute to them, and allows one to make comparisons with the fate of the roughly equal number of Palestinian refugees after 1948 ... Sephardic writers themselves have portrayed the end of *convivencia* or symbiosis in aesthetic, novelistic ways. From Didier Nebot's imagining of the expulsion from Spain, an archetype for more recent expulsions, to Naim Kattan's farewell to Iraq, Albert Memmi's and Marco Koskas' departure from Tunisia, and Andre Aciman's reluctant leavetaking from Egypt, emotional pain is sometimes masked under humor, but always present.[2]

Unlike the aforementioned attempt balance between the Palestinian *Nakba* and the Jewish "Nakba," my aim here is more modest and cultural in essence: to look at the contradicting aforementioned processes—the flowering of the Palestinian culture and at the same time the demise of modern Arab-Jewish culture—through the examination of the relationship between fiction, meta-fiction, and history. Because Palestinian culture is discussed in numerous studies published during the last three decades, while the issue

1 Cohen 2016.
2 Roumani 2022, p. 5.

of Arab-Jewish culture has been nearly neglected in the academic scholarly discourse, the focus of the discussion will naturally be on the latter topic with only minor references to Palestinian culture, mainly from comparative points of view.

1. HISTORY AND LITERATURE

Critics often mention four models related to the relationship between literary texts and history. The first is a model that considers literature as aesthetically autonomous and universal, transcending the contingencies of any particular historical time or place and having its own laws. The second model sees literary texts as being produced within specific historical contexts that are necessary to their proper understanding; at the same time, however, this model sees these texts as remaining separate from their contexts. The third one refers to literature, especially realist works, as providing imaginative representations of specific historical events and periods. And finally the fourth model, associated with the new historicist criticism, refers to literary texts as being bound up with other discourses and as a part of a history that is still in the process of being written.[3]

These four models, which characterize various schools of literary studies, are not contradictory—critics belonging to each school can easily present examples of literary works that represent their specific approaches. Here, I will basically rely on the fourth model, but, because the *Nakba* occurred only around seventy-five years ago, on the one hand, and because of the short period of the flowering of the modern Arabic literature by Jews (less than one century!), on the other hand—in addition to the accessible historical and social contexts relevant to the study of both Palestinian literature and Arab-Jewish literature—I will also use elements from the other models in order to emphasize the unique relationship between the modern history of the Palestinians and the Arabized Jews and their relevant identities and cultures. For anyone familiar with the history of Palestinian and Arab-Jewish cultures and identities, there can be no distinction between the literary texts and the other cultural or historical practices among both communities, or, as literary critics Andrew Bennett (b. 1960) and Nicholas Royle (b. 1963) write, the "literary texts are embedded within the social and economic circumstances in which they are produced and consumed."[4] In this regard, as the new his-

[3] Bennett and Royle 2004, pp. 18–26, 113–23.

[4] Bennett and Royle 2004, p. 115. See also White 1978, pp. 91–2; White 1987; Greenblatt 1988, p. 13; Greenblatt 1990, p. 158; Greenblatt 1995, pp. 225–32. On this conception in the history of Arabized Jews, see Snir 2010–2011, pp. 116–17.

toricists argue, the categories of literature and history are not separated and we cannot distinguish between the need for the interpretation of literary texts and the transparency of historical facts—the autonomy of the literary text is rejected, the objectivity of interpretation is unacceptable, and literary production is considered as a practice that is not different from other cultural practices.

Furthermore, as Stephen Greenblatt (b. 1943) argues, culture is a particular network for negotiation for the exchange of ideas that remains aware of the way in which social and cultural codes play themselves out in the discourses of the present, including those of history, identity, and literature. Any reading of a literary text is an issue of a negotiation between text and reader within the context of history or histories that cannot be closed or finalized. As knowledge of the past is mediated by texts, history itself is also always in the making and open to transformation and rewriting—the critical strategies and tools that are relevant to the study of literature are appropriate to the study of history as well. As for the role of the historian or literary critic, the work of each of them at the margins of the text is an attempt to gain insight into cultural transactions, even as their reading is embedded as well within the cultural situation. Any research is implicated in structures and strategies of power—power is omnipresent, as Michel Foucault (1926–1984) argues, and it is always unstable.[5]

For example, the current demise of Arab-Jewish literature coincides with the collapse of Arab-Jewish identity—those who have been trying during the last two decades to reclaim such an identity have been doing so mostly superficially and in general out of ideological and local, sometimes opportunistic, identity politics.[6] The literary works of the Arabized Jews are embedded within the ideological, social, and cultural circumstances in which they have been produced since the 1920s. For lack of space, we cannot explore here in detail all the specific circumstances beyond what has been presented above, but it is interesting to briefly pay attention to some literary layers of several works. It will be done here in the context of the discourses of history and literature with an attempt to offer a reading which reflects the emergence of the new Arab-Jewish identity in the first quarter of the twentieth century and its current demise. Such a reading cannot be closed or finalized, but is the result of a negotiation between the texts, on the one hand, and the writer of these lines, on the other, in his capacity as a critic of Arabic literature and a scholar of Arab-Jewish culture and identity. Looking only at the

[5] Foucault 1980 [1969], pp. 113–38; Foucault 1981, p. 93. Cf. Greenblatt 1995, pp. 229–30; Bennett and Royle 2004, pp. 116–23.

[6] See Snir 2015b, pp. 197–218. Cf. Tal 2017a, pp. 57–77.

first sentences of some short stories by Arab-Jewish authors, I will adopt Greenblatt's suggestion "to look less at the presumed center of the literary domain than at its borders, to try to track what can only be glimpsed, as it were, at the margins of the text."[7]

2. META-FICTIONALITY

Many of the Arab-Jewish stories published during the twentieth century have some meta-fictional layers and dimensions in the sense that the stories refer to themselves and draw attention to the fact that a story is being told. Such is the case with one of the first of these stories, "Bayna Anyāb al-Baḥr" ("Between the Fangs of the Sea") (1924),[8] whose author used the pseudonym Fatā Isrāʾīl (Youth of Israel). The story illustrates the first embryonic and immature stage of the development of the Arabic short story by Jews in its modern Western sense (in fact, this art was at the time in its infancy in Arabic literature as a whole):

> The passengers sat here and there in a scattered manner, toying with whatever they had in hand, oblivious to the entire world. There was *a joker boisterously laughing, a narrator skillfully telling his stories, a secluded individual reading his book*, and *another gazing at the view and admiring the beauties of nature* which steal one's heart and take one's breath away.[9]

While describing the calm and tranquil atmosphere among the tourists on the stern of the ship, the narrator in the story takes a special look at four specific passengers in order to illustrate the tranquility and peacefulness on the ship before the outbreak of the fire: the joker, the narrator, the reader, and the admirer of the beauties of nature; all of them are related in one way or another to the process of composing and receiving the literary text. Nothing in this beginning, in fact nothing in the whole story, is relevant to Arab-Jewish culture and identity—the name of the author indicates his communal identity, but the text itself testifies to his belonging to the wider fabric of Iraqi society without any personal biographical or Jewish religious or nationalist tendency.

Unlike this early story, later stories offer a mixing of fiction and (auto) biographical writing that provokes questions about the relationship between

[7] Greenblatt 1988, p. 4. On the stories discussed below, see Snir 2019.

[8] The story was first published in two parts in *al-Miṣbāḥ* I.1 (April 10, 1924), p. 6; I.2 (April 17, 1924), p. 7. It was republished in Moreh 1981, pp. 51–5. For an English translation, see Snir 2019, pp. 204–6. For a Hebrew translation, see Snir 2005a, pp. 527–8. For a detailed analysis of the story, see Moreh 1981, pp. 49–50; Snir 2005a, pp. 138–45.

[9] My emphasis. In the following quotations from the beginnings of the stories, all emphasized words are mine.

the stories and their authors, narrators, implied authors, as well as their characters. The questions in this context are: Who is speaking in each story? Who is behind the "I" or "we" or "you" or "he" or "she" or "they" in the stories assumed to be directly associated with reality and history in some sense? These questions have various and different dimensions on the level of the narrative: for example, in the case of Anwar Shā'ul's (1904–1984) "Banafsaja" ("Violette") (1928),[10] it is clear that the narrator and the implied author are not connected biographically to the narrated events, but both of them serve as a channel to deliver a social message, that is, the need to improve the status of women in contemporary Iraqi society. The first sentence of the story prepares the ground:[11]

> If *we* have the right to say that God creates people in His own beautiful image, then Violette, that attractive, charming girl, was one of those divine images that Heaven grants to the sons of earth, so that *she* might be a delight for their eyes and recreation for their souls.

The meta-fictional dimension is expressed here by mentioning God, the Creator who "creates people in His own image"—the author does not create all his characters in his own image, but the implied author of the literary work *speaks in his own voice.*

The same may be said about the first sentence of Mīr Baṣrī's (1910–2006) "Mu'allim al-Madrasa" ("The Schoolteacher") (1955),[12] in which the message is social and educational (but also existential, as it is evident at the end of the story)—the traditional style of narration implicitly draws attention to the fact that a story is being told:

> Many years ago, *I* used to know a *teacher* working at a humble elementary school who proved to be a *leader* of that benighted albeit generous working class that extends a helping hand to youth.

10 The story was first published in *al-'Ālam al-'Arabī*, February 3, 1928. It was republished in Shā'ul 1930, pp. 9–13; *al-Ḥāṣid* 45 (June 1932), p. 5; Moreh 1981, pp. 88–92. For an English translation, see Snir 2002a, pp. 195–7; Snir 2019, pp. 209–21. For a detailed analysis of the story, see Snir 2005a, pp. 167–74.

11 It is not accidental that in the following sections the first sentences of the stories are presented. The beginning of a literary work, even more than its title, is the gate to its meaning, in which the author invests his creative energy to make it an independent micro-text written from the point of view of the whole text and structured according to the latter's intended meaning. On the beginnings of literary texts, see Said 1975; Bennett and Royle 2004, pp. 1–8 (and the bibliography on p. 8).

12 The story was published in Baṣrī 1955, pp. 139–42. For a Hebrew translation, see Snir 2005a, pp. 542–3.

A short story by Maryam al-Mullā (al-Baṣṣūn) (1927–2013), "Ma'sātuhu Mathal" ("His Tragedy, a Proverb") (1951),[13] begins with the proverb to which the title alludes and that is in itself a kind of a story:

> "*He* who knows, knows and *he* who doesn't know, a handful of lentils." 'Āmir would recite that popular Iraqi proverb or that saying tens of times every day.

The first sentences in Isḥāq Bār-Moshe's (1927–2003) "al-Sirdāb" ("The Cellar"),[14] written and published in Israel, may be included in such a category of meta-fictional beginnings. Whoever is familiar with the author's biography could ponder as well Bār-Moshe's personal intellectual aspirations and spiritual tendencies:

> "What are miracles? They're anything that goes beyond the usual course of our day-to-day lives. All that *we* see and know becomes habit. What goes beyond the ordinary *we* call a miracle." This is what *he* said to himself when *he* looked at the door of the cellar where some minutes before *he'd* seen a strange and shocking phenomenon.

Miracles are also stories, and the attempt of the narrator to rationally explain them is also meta-fictional. This story, like all the other stories mentioned above, reflect, through the narrator and the implied author in each of them, a solid belief in Arab-Jewish identity, even if we consider the mere fact that they refer to it as natural—the authors wrote them in Arabic, and the reader cannot have any doubts about their identity.

Shmuel Moreh's (1932–2017) "Rāqiṣa min Baghdād" ("A Dancer from Baghdad") (1981)[15] was also published in Israel, but the reader here can easily sense the distance between the narrator and the dancer (that her capacity as narrator within the story provides its meta-fictional dimension!) even from the first sentence of the story:

[13] The story was published in *al-Muṣawwar* (Baghdad) in 1951 (precise issue and date are not available). It was republished in Moreh 1981, pp. 176–8. For an English translation, see Snir 2019, pp. 228–9. For a Hebrew translation, see Snir 2005a, pp. 540–1. Al-Mullā published many stories and poems in Iraq before immigrating to Israel, but there are no details about or references to them; in the last years of her life, she republished most of them on the website www.akhbaar.org, last accessed September 25, 2017. On al-Mullā, see also 'Alwān 2016, pp. 173–242; Snir 2019–2020, pp. 133–61. See also the biographical note by her daughter Nīrān al-Baṣṣūn (Niran Bassoon) at https://www.facebook.com/nb1957/posts/870587766971222, December 23, 2021, last accessed December 25, 2021.

[14] The story was published in Bār-Moshe 1972, pp. 167–78. It was republished in *al-Sharq*, May 1972, pp. 12–14. For an English translation, see Snir 2005b, pp. 118–25; Snir 2019, pp. 251–7. For a Hebrew translation, see Snir 2005a, pp. 552–7. On Bār-Moshe and the story, see also Reuven Snir, "Arabic Literature by Iraqi-Jews in the Twentieth Century: The Case of Ishaq Bar-Moshe (1927–2003)," *Middle Eastern Studies* 41.1 (2005): 7–29.

[15] The story was published in Moreh 1981, pp. 207–13. For an English translation, see Snir 2019, pp. 261–5. See also Mustafa 2008, pp. 197–200.

> *I* stared at *her* for a long time. It's not often *you* see those oriental features in a London cabaret.

The dancer is "from Iraq," as it is mentioned in the title of the story, and the narrator is staring at her "oriental features" not in Baghdad or Jerusalem but in London.

3. THE IMMIGRATION AND "JEWISH LITERATURE"

Like the previously mentioned stories, Shalom Darwīsh's (1913–1997) stories can by no means be isolated from the author's life and experiences in both Iraq and Israel. But unlike the other authors, Darwīsh's contribution to the art of the Arabic short story was significant both before as well as after his immigration to Israel. "Qāfila min al-Rīf" ("A Caravan from the Village") (1948),[16] written and published in Baghdad, starts as follows:

> Now *he* can well remember how *he* tried, for the first time in *his* life, to cross the big street in Baghdad. *His* mother was holding *him* with her right hand and holding her wide, broad cloak with her left; she looked to the right and to the left, before shouting to the group to cross.

Nothing "Jewish" can be found in the story, although some readings of the story based on the religious identity of the author tried falsely to attribute to him "Zionist" motives.[17] Another story by Darwīsh, "Ḥadīth al-Nāqira" ("The Story of the Perforator") (1964),[18] written in Israel, begins as follows:

> In 1953, *I* was still working in the north of the country as Liaison Officer of the Ministry of Religious Affairs.

The temporal and spatial setting of the first story is a "big street in Baghdad" during the first quarter of the twentieth century, while the point of view of the narrator is the late 1940s. The events of the second story occurred during the 1950s in "the north of the country [Israel]." The meta-fictional

16 The story was published in Darwīsh 1948, pp. 1–29. It was republished in Moreh 1981, pp. 119–38. For an English translation, see Snir 2006d pp. 45–61; Snir 2019, pp. 216–27. For a Hebrew translation, see Snir 2005a, pp. 530–9; Darwīsh 2016, pp. 69–82. On the story and relevant bibliographical references, see Snir 1997a, pp. 128–46; Snir 2005a, pp. 174–82. On Shalom Darwīsh, see also Snir 2021c, pp. 169–90.

17 Snir 2015b, pp. 180–1.

18 The story was published in Darwīsh 1976, pp. 71–83. For an English translation, see Snir 2019, pp. 242–50. See also Marmorstein 1964 pp. 92–100. For a Hebrew translation, see *Ha-Kivvun Mizrah* 7 (2003), pp. 35–45; Darwīsh 2016, pp. 184–95. Marmorstein indicated that it had been published in one of the Arabic journals in Israel but without providing any specific references (Marmorstein 1964, pp. 91–102). Unfortunately, I was unable to locate the original publication, but I assume that the story was published in Arabic during 1964. On the story, see Mudhi 1988, p. 303.

dimensions in both stories are illustrated by the narrated memories and the distance between the narrator of each story, and the events in both of them could serve as "historical" documents for the thoughts and feelings as well as for the aspirations and disappointments of the real author Shalom Darwīsh while he was writing them.

Most importantly, taken together the stories represent the shift in Darwīsh's intellectual, social, and cultural tendencies after his immigration to Israel, reflecting as well the shift in literary writing by Jews, at least the Iraqi among them, from Arabic literature with no Jewish agenda at all to Arabic literature that could be investigated as part of "Jewish literature": Before the immigration to Israel, Jewish authors in Iraq wrote as only *Iraqi* and *Arab* authors, but after their immigration their literature could be considered as contributing to the *Jewish* collective. Hence, any research project of "Jewish literature" must pay attention to such a differentiation, the investigation of the relationship between Jewish literature and world literature[19] included. Writing on Jewish literature and world literature, Lital Levy and Allison Schachter emphasize the role of what they call the "nonuniversal global"—"the condition of a global diaspora that is cosmopolitan yet is everywhere marked by its minority status."[20] Here, the study of literary writing of Jews in languages other than Hebrew should consider Hayyim Nahman Bialik's (1873–1934) classification according to which the literature of Iraqi Jews before their immigration to Israel should be classified as "foreign literature with universal meaning" unlike the literature that they wrote after their immigration.[21] Another useful classification is by Dov Sadan (1902–1989),[22] according to which the literature of Iraqi Jews before their immigration is a foreign literature because its authors strove to be integrated into the societies in which they lived.[23]

4. PERFORMATIVITY AND HETEROGLOSSIA

But, more than all the short stories published by Arab-Jewish authors, the stories by four of them are connected directly to the authors' lives and intellectual, ideological, and cultural conceptions, on the one hand, and to the demise of Arab-Jewish culture and identity, on the other. These are Sami Michael (b. 1926), Shimon Ballas (1930–2019), Samīr Naqqāsh (1938–2004),

[19] Levy and Schachter 2015, pp. 92–109.
[20] Levy and Schachter 2017, pp. 1–26.
[21] Bialik 1954, pp. 42–52.
[22] Sadan 1950, pp. 25–6. Cf. Snir 2005a, p. 518.
[23] On the question of whether the literature of Arabized Jews is "Jewish" literature, see also Muehlethaler 2020, pp. 45–52.

and Almog Behar (b. 1978). For lack of space and because I have previously referred in detail in other publications to Michael and Ballas,[24] I will concentrate in the following on Samīr Naqqāsh's "Nubū'āt Rajul Majnūn fī Madīna Mal'ūna" ("Prophecies of a Madman in a Cursed City") (1995)[25] and Almog Behar's "Anā Min al-Yahūd" ("I Am One of the Jews") (2006).[26] An in-depth study of Naqqāsh's and Behar's stories against the backdrop of their personal lives and activities may encourage the readers to treat both of the stories not only as windows to their subjectivities or as meta-fictional texts but also as performative statements.[27] Literary texts are not only descriptive "words on a page" or mere texts related to the fictional worlds, they also perform things in the real world, certainly when they are used to express conceptions of identity and to serve the subjectivities of their authors. This is evident in Samīr Naqqāsh's "Prophecies of a Madman in a Cursed City" (1995) from the first sentence:

> "*Here I am*" is the utterance *I* had gotten into the habit of reciting spontaneously.

Almog Behar's "Anā min al-Yahūd" (2006) starts with the following:

> At that time, *my tongue* twisted around, and with the arrival of the month of Tammuz the Arabic accent got stuck in *my mouth*, deep down in *my throat*.

As soon as the reader starts the process of reading, certainly if he has some biographical information of each of the authors, he may treat the stories as performative: the use of the first person singular in addition to using the phrase "Here I am," in the case of Naqqāsh,[28] and mentioning "my tongue," "my mouth," and "my throat," in the case of Behar, explicitly or implicitly,

24 See especially Snir 2005a, pp. 309–76; Snir 2019.

25 The story was first published in Naqqāsh 1995, pp. 13–27. For an English translation, see Snir 2019, pp. 266–94; See also Alcalay 1994, pp. 206–19. For a Hebrew translation, see *Mifgash-Liqā'* 12 (1989–1990), pp. 4–8. On the story, see Snir 2005a, p. 244.

26 The Hebrew story with the Arabic title was first published in *Ha'aretz* (literary supplement), April 22, 2005. It was republished in Behar 2008, pp. 55–64; Behar 2017, pp. 78–82. An English translation was first published on www.haaretz.com (April 28, 2005). An Arabic translation, by Muḥammad 'Abbūd, was published on his blog at: http://aboud78.blogspot.com (June 7, 2006). For a short film based on the story, see at: https://www.facebook.com/anaminelyahud, last accessed April 1, 2018.

27 See Austin 1962; Bennett and Royle 2004, pp. 233–9.

28 The first person singular used by Samīr Naqqāsh as a window to his own subjectivity in a meta-fictional narrative and, at the same time, as a performative statement, reached its most sophisticated expression in his last novel *Shlūmū al-Kurdī wa-Anā wa-Zaman* (*Shlomo al-Kurdi, Myself, and Time*) (Naqqāsh 2004; French translation: Naqqāsh 2014; Hebrew translation: Naqqāsh 2020). On trauma, memory, and language in Naqqāsh's novel, see Green 2013. On the unsettled space of identity formation in the novel, see Mahmoud 2017, pp. 86–94. On the novel, see also the review of Nancy Hawker in *New Left Review* 25 (2004), pp. 153–60; Mustafa 2008, pp. 58–68.

are useful criteria for performative statements.[29] I cannot present here in detail the performative layers in both texts which are connected to the wider issue of the relationship between the history of the Arabized Jews and their literature, but it would be instructive to notice the connection between the author and the narrator in each story. It is illuminating, especially against the backdrop of the dialectical tension between the entire creative writing corpora of both authors: Samīr Naqqāsh's story could be considered as the swan song of the new Arab-Jewish identity before its total demise, while Almog Behar tries in his story to present a new revival of this identity albeit only an imaginative, innocent, and hopeless one. Behar, one of the last Jewish writers still insisting on reclaiming Arab-Jewish identity, wrote his story in Hebrew and not in Arabic simply because he was not able to write it in that language—Arabic is not his mother tongue, though it is the language of his mother. The fact that he did not write in Arabic his main literary Arab-Jewish manifesto, the story discussed here, epitomizes the demise of Arab-Jewish culture and identity.

In the context of culture and identity, language is not simply an *instrument*, certainly not in the case of Arabic. Apart from Behar, all the other Arab-Jewish authors whose stories have been discussed here were born *into* the Arabic language and, at the same time, have been its *subjects* and *agents*. Unlike them, Behar started by reclaiming Arab-Jewish identity but has been investing all his creative energy *only* in Hebrew. The fact that some of his works were translated into Arabic does not distinguish him from any other Hebrew writer whose works have been translated into Arabic. In this context, the dialectical tensions and interactions between author, narrator, and implied author in his story as well as in Naqqāsh's story are of fundamental importance. Moreover, both stories may be seen as spaces in which the readers encounter multiple voices surging and resurging, overlapping and penetrating one another, in terms of what Mikhail Bakhtin (1895–1975) calls "heteroglossia,"[30] but the dominant voice in this polyphony of voices is that of the end of the road for Arab-Jewish culture and identity.

5. THE DEATH OF THE AUTHOR?!

A lot has been written during the last decades about the "the death of the author," especially following the 1967 essay of the same title by the French literary critic and theorist Roland Barthes (1915–1980)[31] and another essay

[29] Cf. Austin 1962 pp. 56–7.
[30] Bakhtin 1981.
[31] Barthes 1977 [1967], pp. 142–8.

published two years later (1969), "What Is an Author?" by Michel Foucault (1926–1984).[32] Both Barthes and Foucault think that the author cannot be regarded as the origin of the meaning of the literary work, arguing against the traditional literary ascription of authority to the figure of the author or the Author (with capital letter). In their fresh approach to the institution of the author in literature, they reflect what William Kurtz Wimsatt (1907–1975) and Monroe Beardsley (1915–1985) described in their 1946 essay as "The Intentional Fallacy,"[33] that is, the fallacy of defining the meaning of a work using the author's intentions. Here is Barthes:

> We know now that a text is not a line of words releasing a single "theological" meaning (the "message" of the Author-God) but a multi-dimensional space in which a variety of writings, none of them original, blend and clash. The text is a tissue of quotations drawn from the innumerable centres of culture ... His [= the author's] only power is to mix writings, to counter the ones with the others, in such a way as never to rest on any one of them. Did he wish to express himself, he ought at least to know that the inner "thing" he thinks to "translate" is itself only a ready-formed dictionary, its words only explainable through other words, and so on indefinitely ... Once the Author is removed, the claim to decipher a text becomes quite futile. To give a text an Author is to impose a limit on that text, to furnish it with a final signified, to close the writing.[34]

Concluding his essay, Barthes says that "we know that to give writing its future, it is necessary to overthrow the myth: *the birth of the reader must be at the cost of the death of the Author*."[35]

Like Barthes, Foucault puts into question the idea that the author is the presiding authority for the understanding of the text, arguing that there was a time when literary texts were accepted and valorized without referring to the identity of their authors—only more recently literary authorship has been integrally bound up with the question of ownership of texts. Foucault concludes his essay as follows:

> The author—or what I have called the "author-function"—is undoubtedly only one of the possible specifications of the subject and, considering past historical transformations, it appears that the form, the complexity, and even the existence of this function are far from immutable. We can easily imagine a culture where discourse would circulate without any need for an author. Discourses, whatever their status, form, or value, and regardless of

[32] Foucault 1980 [1969], pp. 113–38.
[33] Wimsatt and Beardsley 1946, pp. 468–88.
[34] Barthes 1977 [1967], pp. 146–7.
[35] Barthes 1977 [1967], p. 148 (my emphasis).

> our manner of handling them, would unfold in a pervasive anonymity. No longer the tiresome repetitions:
>
> "Who is the real author?"
> "Have we proof of his authenticity and originality?"
> "What has he revealed of his most profound self in his language?"
> New questions will be heard:
> *"What are the modes of existence of this discourse?"*
> *"Where does it come from; how is it circulated; who controls it?"*
> *"What placements are determined for possible subjects?"*
> *"Who can fulfill these diverse functions of the subject?"*
> Behind all the questions we would hear little more than the murmur of indifference:
> *"What matter who's speaking?"*[36]

Paradoxically, the arguments of Barthes and Foucault, which on the surface remove the author from the process of interpretation, only assert in our case the readings that cannot ignore the real authors of the aforementioned stories by Naqqāsh and Behar. First, in light of the psychoanalysis, the issue of "authorial intention" is ambiguous,[37] certainly in view of the unique circumstances of the literary voices among the Arabized Jews. And, second, Barthes' declaration that the "birth of the reader must be at the cost of the death of the Author," and Foucault's question "What matter who's speaking?" enable us as readers to negotiate with the fictional texts within the context of the unstable history of the Arabized Jews that cannot be closed or finalized. In the present specific historical moment of the demise of Arab-Jewish culture and identity, the author of each of these stories cannot "die" precisely because, as Bennett and Royle write, "the author is, always has been and always will be a *ghost*. Never fully present or fully absent, a figure of fantasy and elusiveness, *the author only ever haunts.*"[38]

But there is another dimension to the relationship between the author and the text in the context of the demise of Arabic literature by Jews. Naqqāsh and Behar are part of this process of demise not only as the authors of the stories but also as the very protagonists of that drama. In *Ulysses* (1922) by James Joyce (1822–1941), we find an early version of the usual modernist conception regarding the relationship between the author and his text:

> When we read the poetry of *King Lear* what is it to us how the poet lived? As for living our servants can do that for us ... peeping and prying into greenroom

[36] Foucault 1980 [1969], p. 138 (my emphasis).
[37] See Bennett and Royle 2004, p. 21.
[38] Bennett and Royle 2004, p. 22 (my emphasis).

gossip of the day, the poet's drinking, the poet's debts. We have *King Lear*: and it is immortal.[39]

But, as we all know, *Ulysses* is not disconnected from Joyce's biography—likewise, in our case, we cannot talk about Naqqāsh's and Behar's stories as simply "representing" or "reflecting" any specific historical developments as we cannot talk about their personalities as mere subjectivities of authors separated from their texts. As the last monuments of a living culture disappearing before our own eyes, they are part of a reality we have been witnessing and of a history that is being now written. Their stories are performative, in the sense that they implicitly "declare" the demise of a culture they are part of and of an identity they have gladly adopted. Barthes' argument that the text is "a multi-dimensional space in which a variety of writings, none of them original, blend and clash" and the "text is a tissue of quotations drawn from the innumerable centres of culture" is extraneous to both stories, at least in our reading. The proximity to the developing events and our perception of the tragic present of Arab-Jewish culture and the inevitable future of the relevant identity make Barthes' words in our case miss the mark. Likewise, Jacques Derrida's statement "Il n'y a pas de hors-text" ("There is no outside text")[40]—in the sense that readers cannot access the "real world" of the literary work but through its language—is also irrelevant, since we cannot ignore this intriguing juxtaposition of the last texts of Arab-Jewish literature and the *real* demise of that literature that we are *now* witnessing.

Naqqāsh's and Behar's texts are part of a *real* world, and the metafictional dimensions in both of them only assert this merger of literature and reality. Such a merger is attributed by scholars to a literary text published more than four hundred years ago: chronicling the demise of Arabic literature in al-Andalus, Miguel de Cervantes' (1547–1616) *Don Quixote* (published in two volumes in 1605 and 1615)—a founding work of modern Western literature and one of the earliest canonical novels—sheds light on an era when al-Andalus' Islamic culture forcibly came to an end. According to Cervantes, he acquired a book and then looked around for a Moor to translate it: this was the Arabic manuscript written by an Arab historian named Cide Hamete Benengeli, who is the fictional Moorish author created by Cervantes and listed as the chronicler of the adventures of Don Quixote.[41] If such a merger between the contemporary Andalusian

[39] Joyce 1922, p. 181.
[40] Derrida 1976, pp. 158, 163.
[41] See Soons 1959, pp. 351–7; El Saffar 1968, pp. 164–77; Forcione 1970, pp. 155–6; Stewart 1997, pp. 111–27; Rothstein 2005, available at: http://www.nytimes.com/2005/06/13/arts/13conn.html. Based on the phonetic rule that Cervantes frequently uses in his invention

literature and demise of Arabic literature seems to be so realistically represented in *Don Quixote* by an author who was witnessing that demise, according to our reading of the novel,[42] such a merger is all the more represented as we discuss texts written *now* chronicling the demise of a literature before our very *own* eyes.

6. "AN ALIENATED HISTORY"

The readers of the aforementioned stories in which the occasional flashes of meta-fictional self-consciousness narrow the distance between the authors and the narrators cannot ignore the personalities and identities of the authors as *the* heroes *and* antiheroes of the birth and *now* the tragedy of the demise of Arab-Jewish culture. This tragedy has been determined and constrained by broader political, ideological, social, and cultural realities. The activities of specifically both Naqqāsh and Behar encourage their readers to rethink the recent Arab-Jewish cultural past, and perhaps the entire history of Arab-Jewish culture since the rise of Islam. Here, the Nigerian Chinua Achebe's (1930–2013) novel *Anthills of the Savannah* (1987) may provide us with an insightful understanding of the last stage of Arab-Jewish culture before its total demise. Pondering the fate of the two protagonists, the narrator wonders:

> Were they not in fact *trailed travellers* whose journeys from start to finish had been *carefully programmed* in advance by *an alienated history*? If so, how many

of names, it was suggested that the name Benengeli is derived from Arabic/Hebrew Ben-Engelis ("Angel's Son") with intertextual allusions, among others, to the symbolic meaning of the Islamic primordial pen and Qur'ānic *Sūrat al-Qalam* (*The Pen*) (López-Baralt 2006, pp. 579–93).

42 Cf. a similar reading by the British-Pakistani novelist and historian Tariq Ali (b. 1943) in his Globalisation Lecture given on December 1, 2010 at SOAS, University of London, available at: https://www.youtube.com/watch?v=NaP0KEwdGro&t=1222s, last accessed December 12, 2017. In her keynote address "The Secret Literature of the Last Muslims of Spain," at the International Conference at the American University of Beirut, "Latin America, al-Andalus, and The Arab World" (April 17, 2018), Luce López-Baralt referred to the "underground authors' manuscripts," written in Spanish but transliterated with Arabic script as a last sign of loyalty to the Arabic language, providing "a first-hand testimony of what it was like to experience the decline of Islamic culture." Those manuscripts were written by the sixteenth-century Moriscos or Moors in the midst of their collective misfortune as a strangled minority. The term "Moor" was first used by Christian Europeans to designate the Muslim inhabitants of the Maghreb, the Iberian Peninsula, Sicily, and Malta during the Middle Ages. The Moors initially were the indigenous Maghrebine Berbers. The name was later also applied to Arabs and Arabized Iberians. The "Moriscos" were former Muslims and their descendants whom the Roman Catholic Church and the Spanish Crown commanded to convert to Christianity or face compulsory exile after Spain outlawed the open practice of Islam by its sizable Muslim population in the early sixteenth century; see at: https://www.youtube.com/watch?v=WhizgnMTtyg, last accessed April 25, 2021.

> more doomed voyagers were already in transition just sitting out, faces fresh with illusions of duty-free travel and happy landings ahead of them?[43]

As these protagonists are supposed to be "trailed travellers" whose journeys "had been carefully programmed" by "an alienated history," we may rethink the past of Arab-Jewish culture by pondering the tragedy of its demise, as illustrated by the figures of its "last Mohicans," as it were, Naqqāsh and Behar: were they not in fact "trailed travellers" whose journeys from start to finish had been carefully programmed in advance by "an alienated history"?

For me, retrospectively, after several decades of investigating Arab-Jewish culture and identity in the context of the general Arab culture, the answer is definitely "yes." But, unlike the assumption in Achebe's novel, there are by no means "more doomed voyagers" already in transition along the Arab-Jewish cultural path, certainly not voyagers "with illusions of duty-free travel and happy landings ahead of them." When the aforementioned Iraqi-Jewish journalist and social activist Nīrān al-Baṣṣūn (Niran Bassoon) (b. 1957) refers to the literary activities of her Iraqi-Jewish parents—the aforementioned Salīm al-Baṣṣūn and Maryam al-Mullā—she does not have any "illusions of duty-free travel and happy landings ahead of them." Her mother's verses that she published on her Facebook page do not leave any doubt that their dear homeland has been lost:

وين أنت يا عراقي الحبيب، لوين رحلت؟
وين دجلة إللي من ميّها الصّافي شربت؟
وين الجزرة إللي على رملها گعدت؟
گصگصوا أوصالك وأنت سكتت
تشرّدوا أحبابك بالغرب وأنت طحت
ودنّسوا الأوباش ترابك وأنت رضخت
دوّرت عليك بكلّ بلاد الرحت
وسألت عنك كلّمن شفت
ما حدا دلاني وين أنت صرت
حبّك بگلبي معشعش گد ما عشت
وراح أبقى مخلصة إلك حتّى لو متت!

Where are you, my beloved Iraq, where did you go?
Where is the Tigris, from which pure water I drank?
Where is the al-Jazra[44] on which sand I used to sit?
Your limbs have been dismembered and you fell silent
Your beloved ones have been displaced in the West while you were overthrown
The bastards desecrated your soil, and you bowed
I looked for you in all the countries I visited

[43] Achebe 1987, p. 220 (my emphasis).
[44] A small island on the Tigris in Baghdad used as a place for recreation.

I asked whoever I saw about you
No one guided me to where you are
Your love will be nested in my heart as long as I live
I will remain loyal to you even if I die![45]

From among the many authors of the Arab-Jewish literature who have been active since the 1920s, only a few are still alive as the last witnesses of the Muslim–Christian–Jewish Arab symbiosis, and their direct testimonies are now irreplaceable. That is why each literary text can also be considered—at least now when many of us have known and still know some of the authors and other Arab-Jewish poets, writers, and intellectuals—as a document, even if literary and fictive, signaling the last stage of Arab-Jewish culture born more than 1,500 years ago in the deserts of pre-Islamic Arabia. The authors, the narrators, and the implied authors of the stories, the few readers who still remain as well, certainly the implied readers, are the last witnesses of the bi-national savage flood—the unspoken "agreement" between the two national movements, Zionism and Arab nationalism, to perform a total cleansing of Arab-Jewish culture. The national and political struggle over a small piece of territory has not hindered the two national movements from seeing eye-to-eye in this respect, although I was very much aware of the difference between them: one was inspired by European colonialism, and the other was an anticolonial venture. This flood is currently sweeping away Arab-Jewish culture toward its speedy anticipated cleansing:

هذا ما رأيناه في صباح الفيضان
نحن الشّهود على الضّفاف.

This is what we saw, the morning of the flood
We, the witnesses on the banks.[46]

As for the scholarship on Arab-Jewish identity and culture, it seems that its fate would be by no means different. From my scholarly experience during the last thirty years, the number of scholars who have been expressing any interest in investigating this topic and, at the same time, have the necessary skills to do that, mastery of Arabic and Hebrew included, have been gradually dwindling. For example, one can hardly expect that the relevant scholarship would turn to the topic of Arab Jews in Palestine as a an attractive subject, contrary to what Menachem Klein has hoped in a recent essay

45 See Niran Bassoon, October 18, 2021, available at: https://www.facebook.com/nb1957/posts/832473224116010, last accessed November 6, 2021.

46 Borrowed from the poem "Shuhūd 'alā al-Ḍifāf" ("Witnesses on the Banks") by the Iraqi poet Sarkūn Būluṣ (1944–2007) (Boulus 1997, pp. 6–9).

on whom he describes as "the twenty-first-century new critical historians."[47] The great significance he attributes to calls of Palestinian leaders during the 1920s encouraging local Oriental Jews to become political partners of the Palestinians seems to be exaggerated. Klein mentioned such a call by Jamāl al-Ḥusaynī (1894–1982), who served as the Secretary to the Executive Committee of the Palestine Arab Congress (1921–1934) and to the Muslim Supreme Council, which had been previously discussed as regards the question of whether every Jew is a Zionist, against the background of the doubts expressed at the time about the loyalty of Oriental Jews to the Zionist movement.[48] Klein justifies the current lack of public interest in the insights of the "new critical historians" with their diversity, or "it may be related to the pure academic style that almost all of them employ." He admits, however, that outside the academic ivory tower "they have made only a modest impact on Israelis interested in reconstructing their 'Arab Jew' identity as a legitimate Israeli identity." Also, he does not ignore the fact repeatedly emphasized above by the present writer that the "milieu of Arab-Jewish life remains a mere memory and only occasionally an object of yearning" for the Israeli Jews who do not have any desire to reverse the Arab-Jewish hybridity. But his concluding insight that "the new critical historians' methods and conclusions have a future" is for me, after dozens of years of investigating the topic and evaluating its scholarship, nothing but a daydream.[49] Klein's arguments should be considered in light of the aforementioned discussions in Chapter 5, and against the background of the cultural vision encapsulated in the eloquent secularist dictum "*al-dīnu li-llāhi wa-l-waṭanu li-l-jamīʿ*" ("Religion is for God, the Fatherland is for everyone"), especially in Iraq and Egypt of the 1920s and 1930s. The calls of Palestinian leaders during the 1920s to local Oriental Jews to become political partners of the Palestinians are nothing but a pale echo of the wishful but totally unsuccessful calls of Arab leaders such as King Fayṣal (1883–1933), who on July 18, 1921, declared, as previously mentioned, that "we all belong to one origin and one tree, the tree of our ancestor Shem, and all of us related to the Semitic root, which makes no distinction between Muslim, Christian or Jew ... Today we have but one means [to our end]: influential patriotism."[50]

Unlike the demise of Arab-Jewish culture and identity and the tendency of most of its scholarship to adopt populist semi-academic strategies, Palestinian

[47] Klein 2017, pp. 146–63.

[48] Klein 2017, p. 146. See Jacobson and Naor 2016, pp. 19–33.

[49] Klein 2017, pp. 158–9.

[50] The original text was first published in *al-ʿIrāq*, July 19, 1921. For the text of the speech, see *Fayṣal ibn al-Ḥusayn fī Khuṭabihi wa-Aqwālihi* (Baghdād: Maṭbaʿat al-Ḥukūma, 1945), pp. 246–9.

culture and its scholarship are flowering and blooming in their various traditional branches as well as in their fresh innovative new spheres despite the absence of ancient roots.[51] Following the aforementioned discussion of the issue of identity in Palestinian culture, it seems that the poetry of Maḥmūd Darwīsh may encapsulate the relevant changes and developments. Together with his previously mentioned hesitations as regards the value of poetry, Darwīsh's attitude toward the concept of identity went through significant changes. In a poem entitled "Ṭibāq" ("Antithesis"), which he dedicated to his friend, the late Palestinian intellectual Edward Said (1935–2003), the speaker conducts a dialogue with Said concerning the issue of identity. Here is a section from the poem that was published in the collection *Fī Ḥaḍrat al-Ghiyāb* (*In the Presence of Absence*):

والهويَّةُ؟ قُلْتُ
فقال: دفاعٌ عن الذّات،
إنَّ الهويّة بنتُ الولادة لكنّها
في النّهاية إبداعُ صاحبها، لا
وراثة ماضٍ. أنا المتعدِّد. في
داخلي خارجي المتجدِّدُ. لكنّني
أنتمي لسؤال الضّحيّة. لو لم أكن
من هناك لدرَّبْتُ قلبي على أن
يُرَبّي هناك غزال الكِنَايةِ
فاحمل بلادك أنّى ذهبتَ وكُنْ
نرجسيًّا إذا لزم الأمر
— منفًى هوَ العالَمُ الخارجيُّ
ومنفًى هوَ العالَمُ الباطنيّ
فمن أنت بينهما؟
لا أعرّفُ نفسي
لئلاّ أضيّعها. وأنا ما أنا
وأنا آخَري في ثنائيّةٍ
تتناغم بين الكلام وبين الإشارة
ولو كنتُ أكتب شعرًا لقُلْتُ:
أنا اثنان في واحدٍ

[51] The word *Filasṭīnī* ("Palestinian") gained acceptance as a description of Palestine's Arabic speakers during the first decade and a half of the twentieth century. Khalīl Baydas (1874–1949) was presumably the first to use the term in 1898, and after the 1908 Ottoman Constitutional Revolution eased press censorship laws, dozens of periodicals appeared in Palestine, and the term *Filasṭīnī* exploded in usage as a result. The newspapers *al-Quds* (1908–1914), *al-Munādī* (1912–1913), *Filasṭīn* (1911–1914), *al-Karmil* (1908–1914), and *al- Nafīr* (1908–1914) used the term about 170 times in more than 110 articles from 1908 to 1914 (based on Emanuel Beška at: https://www.academia.edu/49925414/The_Origins_of_the_term_Palestinian_Filas%E1%B9%AD%C4%ABn%C4%AB_in_late_Ottoman_Palestine_1898_1914, last accessed August 26, 2021. See also Foster 2017 and the detailed references in the study).

كجناحَيْ سُنُونُوَّةٍ
إن تأخّر فصلُ الرّبيع
اكتفيتُ بنقل البشارة!
يحبُّ بلادًا، ويرحل عنها،
يحبُّ الرّحيل إلى أيِّ شيء
ففي السّفَر الحُرّ بين الثّقافات
قد يجد الباحثون عن الجوهر البشريّ
مقاعد كافيةً للجميع
هنا هامِشٌ يتقدّمُ. أو مركزٌ يتراجَعُ.
لا الشّرقُ شرقٌ تمامًا
ولا الغربُ غربٌ تمامًا،
فإنّ الهويّة مفتوحَةٌ للتّعدّدِ
لا قلعة أو خنادق.

And what about identity? I asked.
It is a self-defense, he said.
Identity is born but
At the end, it is a creation by its owner, not
Inheritance of the past. I am the multiple. Inside
Me you can find my self-renewing exteriority. But
I belong to the victim's question. If I had not been
From there, I would have trained my heart to
Rear there the metonymy's deer
Thus, bear your homeland to wherever you go and be
Narcissistic, if it is necessary.
The external world is an exile
And the internal world is an exile
So, who are you between them?
I do not know myself
In order not to lose it. I am what I am.
I am my Other in a doubleness
Concording in harmony between words and hints
And if I were writing poetry I would say:
I am two in one
Like the wings of a swallow
If the spring is belated
I would have been satisfied with delivering the news!
He loves a homeland and leaves her,
He loves the journey to any thing
Because in the free travel between cultures
Researchers looking for the essence of man perhaps will find
Room enough for everybody
Here is a margin advancing, or a center retreating.
The East is not exactly the East
Nor the West exactly the West,

> Because identity is open to multiplicity
> Not a fortress or trenches.[52]

The traditional notion of identity seems to have lost its conceptual strength in Darwīsh's view, and he follows postmodern thinkers who suggest that one can always change one's life, that identity can always be reconstructed, and that one is free to change and produce oneself as one chooses. In other words, identity becomes a freely chosen game, a *theatrical presentation of the self*, in which one is able to present oneself unconcerned about shifts, transformations, and dramatic changes.[53] Darwīsh follows Ilyās Khūrī's notion of identity:

> No one has a single identity, with the exception of the perfect idiot or the fascist. Rather than speak of identity, one should speak of identification. This is also the guiding principle behind my literary work: how to identify with the other, with a multiplicity of identities, exchanged with one another ... Indeed, I am Lebanese ... but my Palestinian identity stems from my identification with the victim. Similarly, tomorrow, I could be a Cambodian, an African ... even a Jew ... I am a human. A human being. That is my identity. Some would say an Arab, because I write in Arabic. But I am no more hers than she is mine. And she is not the most beautiful of languages. She is the language in which I write.[54]

Some verses from Darwīsh's last collections illustrate this process. For example, in a collection published posthumously, he deals directly with the issue of Palestinian identity and belonging, such as in the poem entitled "If I Had Been Born":

لو ولدتَ من امرأة أسترالّية
وأب أرمنيّ
ومسقط رأسك كان فرنسا
ماذا تكون هويّتك اليوم؟
طبعًا ثلاثيّة
وجنسيّتي
فرنسيّة
وحقوقي فرنسيّة
وإلى آخره...
وإن كانت الأم مصريّة
وجدّتك من حلب

[52] Darwīsh 2006, p. 185. See also Rooke 2008, pp. 24–5. On the aesthetics of proper names and diasporic identity in both Darwīsh and Said's writings, see Hamamra and Abusamra 2020, pp. 1065–78. On the formulation and representation in their respective works of the theme of identity, see Alenzi 2015.
[53] Kellner 1991, pp. 153–4, 158 (my emphasis).
[54] Tzelgov 2009, p. 55 (according to Goldberg 2016, p. 337).

ومكان الولادة في يثرب
وأمّا أبوك فمن غزّة
فماذا تكون هويّتك اليوم؟
طبعًا رباعيّة مثل ألوان رايتنا العربيّة
سوداء، خضراء، حمراء، بيضاء
ولكن جنسيّتي تتخمّر في المختبر
وأما جواز السّفر
فما زال مثل فلسطين مسألة كان فيها نظر
ومازال فيها نظر! وإلى آخره

If I had been born to an Australian woman
And Armenian father
And your birth place was France
What is your identity today?
Of course, tripled!
And my citizenship is
French
And my rights are French
And so forth ...
And if the mother is Egyptian
And your grandmother is from Aleppo
And the birth place is Yathrib
And your father from Gaza,
What is your identity today?
Of course, quadrupled like the colors of our Arab flag!
Black, green, red, and white
But my identity is still fomenting in the laboratory
And my passport
Remains, like Palestine,
A question that was examined
And is still examined! And so forth.[55]

Darwīsh passed away while he was still grappling with the two issues that preoccupied him as a poet: the value of poetry and identity. The poem "Athar al-Farāsha" ("The Butterfly Effect") published in his last collection leaves both issues open:

أثر الفراشة لا يُرَى
أثر الفراشة لا يزولُ
هو جاذبيّةُ غامضٍ
يستدرج المعنى، ويرحلُ

[55] Darwīsh 2009, pp. 151–2. This poem is included in a collection published by several friends of Darwīsh's after his death. Khūrī 2014 argues, unjustifiably in my view, that the poem should not have been published.

حين يتَّضحُ السّبيلُ
هو خفَّةُ الأبديِّ في اليوميِّ
أشواقٌ إلى أعلى
وإشراقٌ جميلُ
هو شامَةٌ في الضّوء تومئُ
حين يرشدنا الى الكلماتِ
باطننا الدّليلُ
هو مثل أُغنية تحاولُ
أن تقول، وتكتفي
بالاقتباس من الظّلالِ
ولا تقولُ ...
أَثرُ الفراشة لا يُرَى
أُثرُ الفراشة لا يزولُ!

The butterfly effect cannot be seen,
the butterfly effect will never fade away
It is the gravitational force of a mysterious
Tempting the meaning, then leaving
After the way becomes clear
It is the simplicity of the eternal in the daily
Passion for the sublime
And a beautiful illumination
It is a beauty mark in the light shining
When our internal guide
Directs us into the words
It is like a melody attempting to
Say something but is satisfied by
Citing from the shadows and
Say nothing ...
The butterfly effect cannot be seen,
The butterfly effect will never fade away![56]

In my translation of the title "Athar al-Farāsha" as "The Butterfly Effect," I allude to the concept bearing the same name that has been initially used in theories about weather prediction but now is also used as a popular metaphor for other fields. Using the meaning that "small causes can have larger effects," which is encapsulated in this very concept, the poet argues, in my opinion, that the impact of both poetry and identity on human beings' lives in our current world, in which most traditional significant values have been ignored, "cannot be seen," like the butterfly effect, but both "will never fade away." However, this is *my reading* of the poem. The Swedish scholar Tetz Rooke (b. 1955), for example, translated the title of the collection and the

[56] Darwīsh 2008, pp. 131–2.

specific poem as "The Trace of the Butterfly."[57] As indicated above, while arguing against the traditional literary ascription of authority to the figure of the author or the Author (with capital letter), both Roland Barthes and Michel Foucault think that the author cannot be regarded as the origin of the meaning of the literary work. Their aforementioned arguments, which on the surface remove the author from the process of interpretation, only assert in our case the reading that cannot ignore the real author of a text. First, in light of psychoanalysis, the issue of "authorial intention" is ambiguous,[58] certainly in view of the unique circumstances related to the composing of the poem. And second, Barthes' declaration that the "birth of the reader must be at the cost of the death of the Author" and, at the same time, Foucault's question "what matter who's speaking?" enable us, as readers, to negotiate the fictional texts within the context of the unstable history of Palestinian poetry that cannot be closed or finalized. In this specific historical moment of Palestinian history and culture, the author of this specific poem cannot "die" precisely because, as Andrew Bennett and Nicholas Royle write, "the author is always has been and always will be a *ghost*. Never fully present or fully absent, a figure of fantasy and elusiveness, *the author only ever haunts*."[59] If it is relevant to any author, it goes without saying that it is relevant to Darwīsh as the major contemporary Palestinian poet. It is thus interesting that on the tomb of the poet there is an inscription with the same two lines that open and conclude the poem:

أثرُ الفراشة لا يُرَى
أثرُ الفراشة لا يزولُ!

The butterfly effect cannot be seen,
The butterfly effect will never fade away.

57 Rooke 2008, p. 24. On the nuances of the word *athar* in Darwish's poem focusing on its dual meanings in Arabic as "effect" and "trace," see Suyoufie 2015, pp. 93–124.
58 See Bennett and Royle 2004, p. 21.
59 Bennett and Royle 2004, p. 22 (my emphasis).

References

The definite *al-* only in the beginning of a surname is not taken into consideration in the alphabetical order. It appears in this form throughout the entire book before solar and lunar letters. Titles of Arabic books and articles are transliterated into English. Titles of Hebrew books and articles are translated into English and identified as such at the end of the translated title.

Abbās, Iḥsān. 1996. *Ghurbat al-Rā'ī*. Beirut: Dār al-Shurūq.

'Abd al-Bāqī, Muḥammad Fu'ād (ed.). 1945. *al-Mu'jam al-Mufahras li-Alfāẓ al-Qur'ān al-Karīm*. Beirut: Dār Iḥyā' al-Turāth al-'Arabī.

'Abd Allāh, Ghassān. 1979. *al-Masraḥ al-Filasṭīnī Bayna al-Tajriba wa-l-Aṣāla*. Jerusalem: n.p.

'Abd al-Nāṣir, Jamāl. n.d. [1955]. *Falsafat al-Thawra*. Cairo: Dār al-Ma'ārif.

'Abd al-Raḥmān, 'Awātif. 1979. *al-Ṣiḥāfa al-Ṣahyūniyya fī Miṣr 1897–1954*. Cairo: Dār al-Thaqāfa al-Jadīda.

'Abd al-Raḥmān, Wā'il. 1996. "al-Qur'ān Bayna Shi'r Maḥmūd Darwīsh wa-Alḥān Mārsīl Khalīfa." *Star*, 7 November, pp. 4–5.

'Abd al-Ṣabūr, Ṣalāḥ. 1965 [1964]. *Ma'sāt al-Ḥallāj*. Beirut: Dār al-Ādāb.

——. 1971. *Riḥla 'alā al-Waraq*. Cairo: Maktabat al-Anglo al-Miṣriyya.

——. 1972. *Dīwān*. Beirut: Dār al-'Awda.

Abd El Gawad, Walid. 2016. "Dreifache Vermittlung: Israel Wolfensohn als Pionier der israelischen Orientwissenschaft." In Arndt Engelhardt et al. (eds.). *Ein Paradigma der Moderne: Jüdische Geschichte in Schlüsselbegriffen. Festschrift für Dan Diner Zum 70*. Göttingen: Vandenhoeck & Ruprecht, pp. 287–308.

Abdel-Malek, Kamal. 2005. *The Rhetoric of Violence: Arab-Jewish Encounters in Contemporary Palestinian Literature and Film*. New York: Palgrave Macmillan.

Abitbol, Michel. 1985. "The Encounter between French Jewry and the Jews of North Africa: Analysis of a Discourse (1830–1914)." In Frances Malino and Bernard Wasserstein (eds.). *The Jews in Modern France*. Hanover, NH: Brandeis University Press, pp. 31–53.

Abo-Moch, Huda. 2006. "'In New Light' and the Portrayal of Reality in the Novel" (in Hebrew). MA thesis, the Hebrew University of Jerusalem.

Abrahams, I. (ed.). 1926. *Hebrew Ethical Wills*. Philadelphia: Jewish Publication Society of America.

Abramovich, Dvir. 2007. "Eli Amir's Mafriah Hayonim." *Modern Judaism* 27.1, pp. 1–19.

Abramson, Glenda (ed.). 2005. *Encyclopaedia of Modern Jewish Culture*. London: Routledge.

Abu Eid, Muna. 2016. *Mahmoud Darwish: Literature and the Politics of Palestinian Identity*. London: I. B. Tauris.

Abū al-Khashab, Ibrāhīm ʻAlī. n.d. *Taʼrīkh al-Adab al-ʻArabī fī al-ʻAṣr al-ʻAbbāsī al-Thānī*. Cairo: Dār al-Fikr al-ʻArabī.

Abu-Lughod, Ibrahim. 1963. *Arab Rediscovery of Europe: A Study in Cultural Encounters*. Princeton, NJ: Princeton University Press.

Abū Sālim, François. 2006. "Exclusion—Insertion en Palestine," unpublished essay.

Abusultan, Mahmoud. 2021. "A Palestinian Theatre: Experiences of Resistance, Sumud and Reaffirmation." MA thesis, Bowling Green State University, Ohio.

Abū Tammām. n.d. *al-Ḥamāsa*. Cairo: Muḥammad ʻAlī Ṣubayḥ.

Achebe, Chinua. 1987. *Anthills of the Savannah*. London: Heinemann.

——. 1988 [1977]. "An Image of Africa: Racism in Conrad's 'Heart of Darkness.'" In Robert Kimbrough (ed.). *Heart of Darkness: An Authoritative Text, Background and Sources Criticism*. London: W. W. Norton, pp. 251–61.

Aciman, André. 1994. *Out of Egypt: A Memoir*. New York: Farrar, Straus & Giroux.

ʻAdiyy, Nadīm. 1954. *Taʼrīkh al-Adab al-ʻArabī*. Aleppo: Maktabat Rabīʻ.

Adorno, Theodor W. 1967. *Prisms*, trans. Samuel and Shierry Weber. Cambridge, MA: MIT Press.

Adūnīs (Adonis). 1971. *Muqaddima li-l-Shiʻr al-ʻArabī*. Beirut: Dār al-ʻAwda.

——. 1972. *Zaman al-Shiʻr*. Beirut: Dār al-ʻAwda.

——. 1978. *al-Thābit wa-l-Mutaḥawwil: Ṣadmat al-Ḥadātha*. Beirut: Dār al-ʻAwda.

——. 1990. *An Introduction to Arab Poetics*, trans. Catherine Cobham. London: Saqi.

——. 1993. *Hā Anta, Ayyuhā al-Waqt*. Beirut: Dār al-Ādāb.

——. 2000 [1985]. *al-Shiʻriyya al-ʻArabiyya*. Beirut: Dār al-Adāb.

Agamben, Giorgio. 1999. *Potentialities: Collected Essays in Philosophy*, trans. Daniel Heller-Roazen. Stanford, CA: Stanford University Press.

——. 2003 [1993]. *The Coming Community*, trans. Michael Hardt. Minneapolis: University of Minnesota Press.

——. 2009. *What Is an Apparatus?* trans. David Kishik and Stefan Pedatella. Stanford, CA: Stanford University Press.

Aggassi (Aghāsī), Eliyahu (ed.). 1959. *Fī Mahrajān al-Adab*. Tel Aviv: Maṭbaʻat Davar.

Agsous (Agsous-Bienstein), Sadia. 2018a. "Hegemonic (Israeli) Time and Minority (Palestinian) Space: Sayed Kashua's Chronotopic Approach in *Let It Be Morning*." *Dibur: Literary Journal* 6, pp. 1–14.

Aḥmad, ʻAbd al-Ilāh. 1969. *Nashʼat al-Qiṣṣa wa-Taṭawwuruhā fī al-ʻIrāq 1908–1939*. Baghdad: Maṭbaʻat Shafīq.

——. 2001. *al-Adab al-Qaṣaṣī fī al-ʻIrāq mundhu al-Ḥarb al-ʻĀlamiyya al-Thāniya: Ittijāhātuhu al-Fikriyya wa-Qiyamuhu al-Fanniyya*. Damascus: Ittiḥād al-Kuttāb al-ʻArab.

Aḥmad, Hadīl ʻAbd al-Razzāq. 2016. *Taʼaddud al-Aṣwāt fī al-Riwāya al-ʼIrāqiyyah: Dirāsa Naqdiyyah fī Mustawayāt Wujhat al-Naẓar (1985–2010)*. Amman: Dār Ghaydāʻ lil-Nashr wa-l-Tawzīʻ.

Ahmed, Mohamed A. H. 2018. "An Initial Survey of Arabic Poetry in the Cairo Genizah." *Al-Masāq* 30.2, pp. 212–33.

Ahmed, Mohamed A. H. and Elsharkawy, Ashraf. 2015. "Tel Aviv Mizrah." *Journal of Modern Jewish Studies* 14.3, pp. 430–45.

Akira, Usuki. 1989. "The Anti-Zionist Movement among the Iraqi Jews: Zionism, Arab Nationalism, and Communism in Iraq Immediately after the Second World War." *Journal of the Faculty of Liberal Arts, Saga University* 21, pp. 1–26.

——. 1994. "Zionism, Communism and Emigration of the Iraqi Jews: A Brief Survey of an Ancient Community in Crisis, 1941–1951." *Annals of the Japan Association for Middle East Studies* 9, pp. 1–35.

——. 2006. "Jewish National Communist Movement in Iraq: A Case of Anti-Zionist League in 1946." *Mediterranean World* 18, pp. 211–25.

Alcalay, Ammiel. 1993. *After Jews and Arabs: Remaking Levantine Culture*. Minneapolis: University of Minnesota Press.
——. (ed.). 1994. *The Literary Review* (special issue: *Keys to the Garden in the Middle East*), 37.2. Madison, NJ: Fairleigh Dickinson University Press.
——. 1995. "Exploding Identities: Notes on Ethnicity and Literary History." *Jewish Social Studies* 1.2, pp. 15–27.
——. (ed.). 1996. *Keys to the Garden: New Israeli Writing*. San Francisco, CA: City Lights Books.
——. 1999. *Memories of Our Future: Selected Essays 1982–1999*. San Francisco, CA: City Lights Books.
Alenzi, Suad A. H. S. M. 2015. "I Am Neither There, Nor Here: An Analysis of Formulations of Post-Colonial Identity in the Work of Edward W. Said and Mahmoud Darwish: A Thematic and Stylistic Analytical Approach." PhD thesis, University of Manchester.
Alḥarizi, Yudah. 2001. *The Book of Taḥkemoni: Jewish Tales from Medieval Spain*, trans. D. S. Segal. London: Littman Library of Jewish Civilization.
Ali, Agha Shahid. 2003. *Call Me Ishmael Tonight: A Book of Ghazals*. New York: W. W. Norton.
'Alī, 'Arafa 'Abduh. 1993. *Milaff al-Yahūd fī Miṣr al-Ḥadītha*. Cairo: Madbūlī.
——. 2001. *Yahūd Miṣr: Bārūnāt wa-Bu'asā'*. Cairo: Ītrāk li-l-Nashr wa-l-Tawzī'.
Allen, Roger (ed.). 1978. *In the Eye of the Beholder: Tales of Egyptian Life from the Writings of Yusuf Idris*. Minneapolis, MI: Bibliotheca Islamica.
——. 1987. *Modern Arabic Literature*. New York: Ungar.
——. 2018. "Transforming the Arabic Literary Canon." In Roger Allen (eds.). *New Geographies: Texts and Contexts in Modern Arabic Literature*. Madrid: Ediciones Universidad Autónoma de Madrid, pp. 15–26.
Althusser, Louis. 1971. *Lenin and Philosophy and Other Essays*, trans. Ben Brewster. London: NLB.
al-Ālūsī, Jamāl al-Dīn. 1987. *Baghdād fī al-Shi'r al-'Arabī: Min Ta'rīkhiha wa-Akhbāriha al-Ḥaḍariyya*. Baghdād: Maṭba'at al-Majma' al-'lmī al-'Irāqī.
'Alwān, Khālida Ḥātim. 2014. *al-Riwā'iyyūn al-'Irāqiyyūn al-Yahūd: Dirāsa fī al-Thaqāfa wa-l-Mutakhayyal wa-l-Tajrīb al-Riwā'ī*. Baghdad: Dār Mesopotamia.
——. 2016. *Ḥafriyyāt Unthawiyya: Dirāsa fī al-Qaṣṣ al-Niswī al-'Irāqī al-Yahūdī al-Mughayyab*. Baghdad: Dār wa-Maktabat 'Adnān.
'Alyān, Suhayl. 1992. "al-Masraḥ al-Filasṭīnī, al-Masār wa-l-Intifāḍa." *Balsam*, April, pp. 84–7.
Amara, Muhammad Hasan. 1999. *Politics and Sociolinguistic Reflexes: Palestinian Border Villages*. Amsterdam: John Benjamins.
Amara, Muhammad Hasan and Abd Al-Rahman Mar'i. 1999. *Issues in Language Education Policy in Arab Schools in Israel* (in Hebrew). Givat Haviva: Jewish-Arab Center for Peace.
——. and Abd Al-Rahman Mar'i. 2010. *Language Education Policy: The Arab Minority in Israel*. Dordrecht: Springer.
Amichai, Yehuda. 1972. *Poems 1948–1962* (in Hebrew). Tel Aviv: Schocken.
——. 1974. *Behind All This There Hides Great Happiness* (in Hebrew). Jerusalem: Schocken.
Amīn, 'Abd al-Qādir Ḥasan. 1956. *al-Qaṣaṣ fī al-Adab al-'Irāqī al-Ḥadīth*. Baghdad: Maṭba'at al-Ma'ārif.
Amir, Aharon. 1992. "A Jewish Norm for Hebrew Literature" (in Hebrew). *Moznaim*, September–October, pp. 37–41.
'Amīr (Amir), Elī. 1983. *Rooster of Atonements* (in Hebrew). Tel Aviv: Am Oved.
——. 1988. *Scapegoat*, trans. Dalya Bilu. London: Weidenfeld & Nicolson.
——. 1993. *The Pigeoneer* (in Hebrew). Tel Aviv: Am Oved.
——. 1998. *Sha'ul's Love* (in Hebrew). Tel Aviv: Am Oved.

——. 2005. *Yasmin* (in Hebrew). Tel Aviv: Am Oved.
——. 2010. *What Is Left* (in Hebrew). Tel Aviv: Am Oved.
——. 2010a. *The Dove Flyer*, trans. Hillel Halkin. London: Halban.
——. 2018. *Bicycle Boy* (in Hebrew). Tel Aviv: Am Oved.
——. 2018a. *al-Mṭayyarjī*, trans. ʻAlī ʻAbd al-Amīr. Cologne: Manshūrāt al-Jamal.
And, Metin. 1963–1964. *A History of Theatre and Popular Entertainment in Turkey*. Ankara: Forum Yayinlari.
Anderson, Amanda. 1998. "Cosmopolitanism, Universalism, and the Divided Legacies of Modernity." In Pheng Cheah and Bruce Robbins (eds.). *Cosmopolitics: Thinking and Feeling beyond the Nation*. Minneapolis: University of Minnesota Press, pp. 265–89.
Anidjar, Gil. 2002. *"Our Place in al-Andalus": Kabbalah, Philosophy, Literature in Arab Jewish Letters*. Stanford, CA: Stanford University Press.
Antonius, George. 1938. *The Arab Awakening: The Story of the Arab National Movement*. London: Hamish Hamilton.
Appiah, Kwame Anthony. 2005. *The Ethics of Identity*. Princeton, NJ: Princeton University Press.
——. 2006. *Cosmopolitanism: Ethics in a World of Strangers*. London: Penguin.
Araydi, Naïm. 1990. *Le trente-deuxième rêve*. Paris: Levant.
ʻArāyidī, Naʻīm. 1972. *How We Can Love* (in Hebrew). Tel Aviv: Eked.
——. 1975. *Pity and Fear* (in Hebrew). Tel Aviv: Eked.
——. 1976. *Ka-Iḥmirār al-Arḍ ʻInda al-Maghribayn*. Dalyat al-Karmil: Manshūrāt Sīmfūsardiyya.
——. 1978. *Ka-Iḥtirāq al-Shams*. Acre: Dār al-Aswār.
——. 1980. *The Playing Liquids in the Work of Uri Zvi Grinberg* (in Hebrew). Tel Aviv: Eked.
——. 1984. *Qaṣā'id Karmiliyya fī al ʻIshq al Baḥrī*. Shfaram: al Mashriq.
——. 1985. "Between My Two Cultures" (in Hebrew). *Mifgash-Liqā'* 2 (Summer), pp. 10–11.
——. 1986. *Back to the Village* (in Hebrew). Tel Aviv: Am Oved.
——. 1986a. "The Role of the Intellectual in the Education for Peaceful Co-Existence" (in Hebrew). *Moznaim*, September 1986, pp. 31–3.
——. 1988. *Soldiers of Water* (in Hebrew). Tel Aviv: Maariv.
——. 1989. "To Be a Levantine" (in Hebrew). *Moznaim*, July–August, p. 79.
——. 1989a. "Poetics and Thought in the Poetry of Uri Zvi Grinberg" (in Hebrew). PhD thesis, Bar-Ilan University.
——. 1991. "Hebrew Literature, You Gave Me Pleasure" (in Hebrew). *Moznaim* (January), pp. 41–3.
——. 1992. *Fatal Christening* (in Hebrew). Tel Aviv: Bitan.
——. 1994. *Hunālika Dā'iman Umniya*. Haifa: Dār al-Mashriq.
——. 1994a. *Waḥda*. Acre: Mu'assasat al-Dawālī.
——. 1999. *Qaṣīdatī Jisr wa-Anā al-Khashab*. Kfar Qaraʻ: Dār al-Hudā.
——. 2002. *Aʻtinī Furṣa Ukhrā*. Kfar Qaraʻ: Dār al-Hudā.
——. 2002a. *Penetrating Calm* (in Hebrew). n.p.: Kor'im.
——. 2006. *Leaving the Rage to Others* (in Hebrew). Tel Aviv: Gvanim.
ʻArāyidī, Naʻīm and Izakson, Miron. 2004. *Nés en Israël*. Paris: Éditions Stavit.
Arazi, Albert. 1986. "Une Epitre d'Ibrahim b. Hilal al-Sabi sur les genres litteraires." In Moshe Sharon (ed.). *Studies in Islamic History and Civilization in Honour of Professor David Ayalon*. Leiden: Brill, pp. 473–505.
Arberry, Arthur J. 1965. *Arabic Poetry: A Primer for Students*. Cambridge: Cambridge University Press.
——. 1979 [1964]. *The Koran Interpreted*. Oxford: Oxford University Press.
Arendt, Hannah. 1974. *Rahel Varnhagen: The Life of a Jewish Woman*, trans. Richard and Clara Winston. New York: Harcourt Brace Jovanovich.

Aristotle. 1967. *Poetics.* ed. and trans. G. F. Else. Ann Arbor: University of Michigan Press.
——. 1968. *Poetics.* ed. D. W. Lucas. Oxford: Clarendon.
'Arsān, 'Alī 'Uqla. 1983. *al-Ẓawāhir al-Masraḥiyya 'inda al-'Arab.* Tripoli, Libya: al-Munsh'a al-'Āmma li-l-Nashr wa-l-Tawzī' wa-l-I'lān.
Arslan, C. Ceyhun. 2016. "Translating Ottoman into Classical Arabic: *Nahḍa* and the Balkan Wars in Aḥmad Shawqī's 'The New al-Andalus.'" *Middle Eastern Literatures* 19.3, pp. 278–97.
Arthur, Paige (ed.). 2011. *Identities in Transition: Challenges for Transitional Justice in Divided Societies.* Cambridge: Cambridge University Press.
Asfour, John Mikhail (ed.). 1988. *When the Words Burn: An Anthology of Modern Arabic Poetry 1945–1987.* Dunvegan, ON: Cormorant Books.
Ashrawi, Hanan Mikhail. 1976. *Contemporary Palestinian Literature under Occupation.* Birzeit, West Bank: Birzeit University Publications.
Athamneh, Waed. 2017. *Modern Arabic Poetry: Revolution and Conflict.* Notre Dame, IN: University of Notre Dame Press.
Atkins, Kim. 2008. *Narrative Identity and Moral Identity: A Practical Perspective.* New York: Routledge.
Al-Attabi, Qussay. 2021. "The Polemics of Iltizām: Al-Ādāb's Early Arguments for Commitment." *Journal of Arabic Literature* 52, pp. 124–46.
Auron, Yair. 2012. *Israeli Identities: Jews and Arabs Facing the Self and the Other.* New York: Berghahn.
Austin, J. L. 1962. *How to Do Things with Words.* Oxford: Clarendon.
Avidan, David. 1982. *Idhā'a min Qamar Iṣṭinā'ī.* Acre: al-Surūjī.
Avaes, Mohammad. 2014. "Theatre of the Occupied." *Wasafiri* 29.4, pp. 24–9.
Avishur, Yitzhak. 1990–1991. *The Jewish Wedding in Baghdad and Its Filiations* (in Hebrew). Haifa: University of Haifa Press.
——. 1992. *The Folktales of the Jews of Iraq* (in Hebrew), 2 vols. Haifa: University of Haifa Press.
——. 1995. "Mutations in the Literary Creation and Linguistic Changes among Iraqi Jews in the Modern Era (1750–1950)" (in Hebrew). *Miqqedem Umiyyam* 6, pp. 235–54.
Aviv, Naomi. 1986. "A Fine Israeli Man" (in Hebrew). *Kol Ha-'Īr* (Jerusalem), April 4, pp. 32–9.
'Awaḍ, Luwīs. 1966. *al-'Anqā' aw Ta'rīkh Ḥasan Muftāḥ.* Beirut: Manshūrāt Dār al-Ṭalī'a.
al-'Awdāt, Ya'qūb. 1992. *A'lām al-Fikr wa-l-Adab fī Filasṭīn.* Jerusalem: Dār al-Isrā'.
Ayalon, Ami. 1995. *The Press in the Arab Middle East.* New York: Oxford University Press.
al-A'ẓamī, Aḥmad 'Izzat. 1932. *al-Qaḍiyya al-'Arabiyya: Asbābuhā, Muqaddimātuhā, Taṭawwuruhā wa-Natā'ijuhā.* Baghdad: Maṭba'at al-Sha'b.
al-'Aẓm, Ṣādiq Jalāl. 1992. *Dhihniyyat al-Taḥrīm: Salmān Rushdī wa-Ḥaqīqat al-Adab.* London: Riyāḍ al-Rayyis.
Badawi, M. M. 1985. "The Father of the Modern Egyptian Theatre: Ya'qūb Ṣanū'." *Journal of Arabic Literature* 16, pp. 132–45.
——. (ed.). 1992. *Modern Arabic Literature.* Cambridge: Cambridge University Press.
al-Badrī, Jamāl. 2000. *al-Yahūd wa-Alf Layla wa-Layla.* Cairo: al-Dār al-Dawliyya li-l-Iththithmārāt al-Thaqāfiyya.
Baghdādī, 'Abbās. 1998. *Li-Allā Nansā: Baghdād fī al-'Ishrīnāt.* Beirut: al-Mu'assasa al-'Arabiyya li-l-Dirāsāt wa-l-Nahsr.
Bakhtin, M. M. 1981. *The Dialogic Imagination: Four Essays*, trans. Michael Holquist and Caryl Emerson. Austin: University of Texas Press.
Balaban, Avraham. 1989. "Anton Shammas: Torn between Two Languages." *World Literature Today* 63.3 (Summer), pp. 418–21.
Baladi, Sarya. 2018. "Unfinished Identities: Expressions of Cosmopolitanism in Levantine Literature." *Al Noo:, The Boston College Middle Eastern Studies Journal* 11.2, pp. 45–56.

Balbūl, Ya'qūb. 1938. *al-Jamra al-Ūlā*. Baghdad: Maṭba'at al-Ma'ārif.
Ballas (Ballāṣ), Shimon (Sham'ūn). 1964. *The Immigrant Transit Camp* (in Hebrew). Tel Aviv: Am Oved.
——. 1969. *In Front of the Wall* (in Hebrew). Tel Aviv: Masada.
——. 1970. *Ash'ab from Baghdad* (in Hebrew). Tel Aviv: Am Oved.
——. 1970a. *Palestinian Stories* (in Hebrew). Tel Aviv: Eked.
——. 1972. *Clarification* (in Hebrew). Tel Aviv: Sifriyat Poalim.
——. 1978. *Arabic Literature under the Shadow of the War* (in Hebrew). Tel Aviv: Am Oved.
——. 1980. *A Locked Room* (in Hebrew). Tel Aviv: Zmora-Bitan-Modan.
——. 1980a. *La littérature arabe et le conflit au proche-orient (1948–1973)*. Paris: Éditions Anthropos.
——. 1984. *Last Winter* (in Hebrew). Tel Aviv: Keter.
——. 1984a. *Arabic Literature under the Shadow of the War* (in Hebrew). Shfaram: Dār al-Mashriq.
——. 1987. *The Heir* (in Hebrew). Tel Aviv: Zmora-Bitan.
——. 1989. "al-Ittijāh al-Wāqi'ī fī Qiṣaṣ Shalūm Darwīsh." *al-Karmil: Studies in Arabic Language and Literature* 10, pp. 27–60.
——. 1991. *And He Is Other* (in Hebrew). Tel Aviv: Zmora-Bitan.
——. 1992. *Signs of Autumn* (in Hebrew). Tel Aviv: Zmora-Bitan.
——. 1994. *Not in Her Place* (in Hebrew). Tel Aviv: Zmora-Bitan.
——. 1997. *Signs of Autumn* (in Hebrew). Cologne: Manshūrāt al-Jamal.
——. 1998. *Solo* (in Hebrew). Tel Aviv: Sifriyat Poalim.
——. 1998a. *Tel Aviv East* (in Hebrew). Tel Aviv: Bimat-Kedem le-Sifrut.
——. 2003. *Ruwwād wa-Mubdi'ūn: Dirāsāt fī al-Adab al-'Arabī al-Mu'āṣir*. Cologne: al-Kamel Verlag.
——. 2003a. *Tel Aviv East: A Trilogy* (in Hebrew). Tel Aviv: Ha-Kibbutz Ha-Me'uḥad.
——. 2007. *Outcast*, trans. Ammiel Alcalay and Oz Shelach. San Francisco, CA: City Lights Books.
——. 2008. *The End of the Visit* (in Hebrew). Tel Aviv: Ha-Kibbutz Ha-Me'uḥad.
——. 2009. *First Person Singular* (in Hebrew). Tel Aviv: Ha-Kibbutz Ha-Me'uḥad.
Balter, Michael. 2010. "Who Are the Jews? Genetic Studies Spark Identity Debate." *Science* 328, June 11, p. 1342.
al-Barāk, Fāḍil. 1985. *al-Madāris al-Yahūdiyya wa-l-Īrāniyya fī al-'Irāq*. Baghdad: al-Dār al-'Arabiyya.
al-Barghūthī, 'Abd al-Laṭīf. 1979. *al-Aghānī al-Sha'biyya fī Filasṭīn wa-l-Urdunn*. Jerusalem: Maṭba'at al-Sharq al-'Arabiyya.
Bār-Moshe, Assaf. 2019. *The Arabic Dialect of the Jews of Baghdad: Phonology, Morphology, and Texts*. Wiesbaden: Harrassowitz Verlag.
Bār-Moshe, Isḥāq. 1972. *Warā' al-Sūr wa-Qiṣaṣ Ukhrā*. Jerusalem: Majallat al-Sharq.
——. 1973. *al-Dubb al-Quṭbī wa-Qiṣaṣ Ukhrā*. Jerusalem: Majallat al-Sharq.
——.1974. *Raqṣat al-Maṭar wa-Qiṣaṣ Ukhrā*. Jerusalem: Majallat al-Sharq.
——.1975. *al-Khurūj min al-'Irāq: Dhikrayāt 1945–1950*. Jerusalem: Manshūrāt Majlis al-Ṭawā'if al-Sfārādiyya.
——.1976. *Aswār al-Quds wa-Qiṣaṣ Ukhrā*. Jerusalem: Majallat al-Sharq.
——.1977. *Iraq's Exodus* (in Hebrew), trans. Nir Shohet. Jerusalem: Sephardi Council.
——.1982. *A House in Baghdad* (in Hebrew), trans. Hanita Brand. Jerusalem: Sephardi Council.
——. 1983. *Bayt fī Baghdad*. Jerusalem: Rābiṭat al-Jāmi'iyyīn al-Yahūd al-Nāziḥīn min al-'Irāq.
——. 1988. *Ayyām al-'Irāq*. Shfaram: Dār al-Mashriq.
——. 1994. *Miṣr fī Qalbī*. Nazareth: Ministry of Education and Culture.

——. 2004. *Yawmān fī Ḥazīrān*. Jerusalem: Rābiṭat al-Jāmiʿiyyīn al-Yahūd al-Nāziḥīn min al-ʿIrāq.
Barnes, Djuna. 1961. *Nightwood*. New York: New Directions.
Baron, Beth Ann. 1994. *Women's Awakening in Egypt: Culture, Society, and the Press*. New Haven, CT: Yale University Press.
Barthes, Roland. 1977 [1967]. "The Death of the Author." In *Image—Music—Text*, ed. and trans. Stephan Heathen. New York: Farrar, Straus & Giroux, pp. 142–8.
Bashkin, Orit. 1998. "Al-Miṣbāḥ (1924–1929): A Jewish Iraqi Newspaper" (in Hebrew). MA thesis, Tel Aviv University.
——. 2004. "Why Did Baghdadi Jews Stop Writing to their Brethren in Mainz? Some Comments about the Reading Practices of Iraqi Jews in the Nineteenth Century." In Philip C. Sadgrove (ed.). *History of Printing and Publishing in the Languages and Countries of the Middle East*. Oxford: Oxford University Press, pp. 95–110.
——. 2008. *The Other Iraq: Pluralism and Culture in Hashemite Iraq*. Stanford, CA: Stanford University Press.
——. 2012. *New Babylonians: A History of Jews in Modern Iraq*. Stanford, CA: Stanford University Press.
——. 2017. *Impossible Exodus: Iraqi Jews in Israel*. Stanford, CA: Stanford University Press.
——. 2020. "Unforgettable Radicalism: *Al-Ittihad*'s Words in Hebrew Novels." In Laure Guirguis (ed.). *The Arab Lefts: Histories and Legacies, 1950s–1970s*. Edinburgh: Edinburgh University Press, pp. 18–38.
Baṣrī (Basri), Mīr. 1955. *Rijāl wa-Ẓilāl:Qiṣaṣ wa-Ṣuwar Qalamiyya*. Baghdad: Sharikat al-Tijāra li-l-Ṭibāʿa.
——. 1966. *Nufūs Ẓāmi'a*. Baghdad: Sharikat al-Tijāra li-l-Ṭibāʿa.
——. 1983. *Aʿlām al-Yahūd fī al-ʿIrāq al-Ḥadīth*, vol. I. Jerusalem: Rābiṭat al-Jāmiʿiyyīn al-Yahūd al-Nāziḥīn min al-ʿIrāq.
——. 1991. *Aghānī al-Ḥubb wa-l-Khulūd*. Jerusalem: Rābiṭat al-Jāmiʿiyyīn al-Yahūd al-Nāziḥīn min al-ʿIrāq.
——. 1991a. *Riḥlat al-ʿUmr min Ḍifāf Dijla ilā Wādī al-Tīms*. Jerusalem: Rābiṭat al-Jāmiʿiyyīn al-Yahūd al-Nāziḥīn min al-ʿIrāq.
——. 1993. *Aʿlām al-Yahūd fī al-ʿIrāq al-Ḥadīth*, vol. II. Jerusalem: Rābiṭat al-Jāmiʿiyyīn al-Yahūd al-Nāziḥīn min al-ʿIrāq.
——. 1994. *Aʿlām al-Adab fī al-ʿIrāq al-Ḥadīth*. London: Dār al-Ḥikma.
——. 1994a. "A Young American Lady and I." *The Scribe* 62 (September), p. 16.
——. 1999. *Aʿlām al-Fann fī al-ʿIrāq al-Ḥadīth*. London: Mu'assasat al-Rāfid.
——. 2006. *Aʿlām al-Yahūd fī al-ʿIrāq al-Ḥadīth*. London: Dār al-Warrāq.
Bassiouney, Reem and Walters, Keith (eds.). 2021. *The Routledge Handbook of Arabic and Identity*. New York: Routledge.
Bataille, Georges. 1988. *The Accursed Share: An Essay on General Economy*, trans. Robert Hurley. New York: Zone Books.
Batatu, Hanna. 1978. *The Old Social Classes and the Revolutionary Movements of Iraq*. Princeton, NJ: Princeton University Press.
Bauman, Zygmunt. 1996. "From Pilgrim to Tourist: Or a Short History of Identity." In Stuart Hall and Paul Du Gay (eds.). *Questions of Cultural Identity*. London: Sage, pp. 18–36.
——. 1998. *Globalization: The Human Consequences*. New York: Columbia University Press.
——. 2003. *Liquid Love: On the Frailty of Human Bonds*. Cambridge: Polity.
——. 2004. *Liquid Modernity*. Cambridge: Polity.
——. 2007. *Liquid Times: Living in an Age of Uncertainty*. Cambridge: Polity.
——. 2009. "Identity in the Globalizing World." In Anthony Elliott and Paul Du Gay (eds.). *Identity in Question*. Los Angeles: Sage, pp. 1–12.

Bäuml, Yair. 2002. "The Attitude of the Israeli Establishment to the Arabs in Israel: Policy, Principles, and Activities: The Second Decade, 1958–1968" (in Hebrew). PhD thesis, University of Haifa.
Bawārdī (Bawardi), Bāsīlyūs Ḥannā. 1998. "Bayna al-Ṣaḥrā' wa-l-Baḥr: Baḥth fī Ta'thīr al-Qawmiyyatayn al-Lubnāniyya-al-Fīnīqiyya wa-l-Sūriyya 'alā al-Adab al-'Arabī al-Mu'āṣir." MA thesis, University of Haifa.
——. 2016. *The Lebanese-Phoenician Nationalist Movement: Literature, Language and Identity*. London: I. B. Tauris.
Baybars, Ḍiyā' al-Dīn. 1970. "Talḥīn al-Qur'ān Bayna Ahl al-Fann wa-Rijāl al-Dīn." *al-Hilāl*, December, pp. 118–27.
Al-Bazzaz, M. A. and Ali, S. A. 2020. "A Sociolinguistic Study of Selected Iraqi-Arabic Dialects with Reference to TV Series." *Journal of Language Studies* 3.3, pp. 68–85.
Beck, Ulrich and Sznaider, Natan. 2006. "Unpacking Cosmopolitanism for the Social Sciences: A Research Agenda." *British Journal of Sociology* 57.1, pp. 1–23.
Begley, Sharon. 2010. "The DNA of Abraham's Children: Analysis of Jewish Genomes Refutes the Khazar Claim."' *Newsweek*, June 3.
Behar, Almog. 2008. *Wells' Thirst* (in Hebrew). Tel Aviv: Am Oved.
——. 2008a. *I Am One of the Jews* (in Hebrew). Tel Aviv: Babel.
——. 2009. *A Thread Drawing from the Tongue* (in Hebrew). Tel Aviv: Am Oved.
——. 2017. *The Baghdad Book: A Selection of Poems, Stories, Dreams* (in Hebrew), available at: https://almogbehar.wordpress.com, last accessed August 3, 2020.
——. 2017a. "We Can't Understand Ourselves without the Arabic: Dreams in Cambridge (2009)." *Journal of Levantine Studies* 7, pp. 131–52.
——. 2020. "'Come from the Corner to the Stage of Stages': On Poetry and Translation between Hebrew and Arabic." Judith Lee Stronach Memorial Lectures on the Teaching of Poetry, published by the Bancroft Library, University of California, Berkeley.
——. 2021. *Rub Salt into Love* (in Hebrew). Tel Aviv: Ha-Kibbutz Ha-Me'uḥad.
Behar, Almog and Evri, Yuval. 2019. "Samir Naqqash and His Polyglotic Literature in the Age of National Partition." *Journal of Levantine Studies* 9.2, pp. 111–31.
Behar, Moshe. 2017. "The Birth of the Mizrahi–Ashkenazi Controversy." *Journal of Modern Jewish Studies* 16.2, pp. 312–31.
Behar, Moshe and Ben-Dor Benite, Zvi (eds.). 2012. *Modern Middle Eastern Jewish Thought: Writings on Identity, Politics, and Culture, 1893–1958*. Waltham, MA: Brandeis University Press.
Beinin, Joel. 1996. "Egyptian Jewish Identities: Communitarianisms, Nationalisms, Nostalgias." *Stanford Electronic Humanities Review* 5.1, pp. 1–23.
——. 1998. *The Dispersion of Egyptian Jewry: Culture, Politics, and Formation of a Modern Diaspora*. Berkeley: University of California Press.
Bell, D. B. E. 1930. *The Letters of Gertrude Bell*. London: Ernest Benn.
Bellamy, James A. 1983. "Qasmūna the Poetess: Who Was She?" *Journal of the American Oriental Society* 103.2, pp. 423–4.
Ben-Dor, Zvi. 2006. "Invisible Exile: Iraqi Jews in Israel." *Journal of the Interdisciplinary Crossroads* 3.1, pp. 135–62.
Benhabib, Doli. 2007. "From Arab Diaspora to Eretz Israel: Literary Portraits of Mizrahi Female Immigrants in the 1940s and 1950s." In Peter Y. Medding (ed.). *Sephardic Jewry and Mizrahi Jews*. Oxford: Oxford University Press, pp. 100–18.
Ben Hanania, Yehoshua (= Yaacob Yehoshua). 1959. "The First Cultural Attaché in Arab Countries before the Foundation of Israel" (in Hebrew). In *Hommage à Abraham: recueil littéraire en l'honneur de Abraham Elmaleh à l'occasion de son 70ème anniversaire, 1885–1955*. Jerusalem: Ahva, pp. 186–91.
Benjamin, Walter. 1969. "Theses on the Philosophy of History." In Hannah Arendt (ed.). *Illuminations*, trans. Harry Zohn. New York: Schocken, pp. 253–64.

Bennett, Andrew and Royle, Nicholas. 2004. *An Introduction to Literature, Criticism and Theory*. Harlow: Pearson Longman.
Benson, Eugene and Toye, William (eds.). 1997. *The Oxford Companion to Canadian Literature*. Oxford: Oxford University Press.
Ben-Yaacob, Abraham. 1979. *The Jews of Iraq in Modern Times* (in Hebrew). Jerusalem: Kiriath-Sepher.
——. 1980. *The Jews of Iraq in the Land of Israel from the First Emigrations to the Present Day* (in Hebrew). Jerusalem: Rubin Mass.
Ben Ze'ev, Na'ama. 2020. "I Came Naïve from the Village': On Palestinian Urbanism and Ruralism in Haifa under the British Mandate." *British Journal of Middle Eastern Studies* 47.2, pp. 264–81.
Berg, Nancy E. 1996. *Exile from Exile: Israeli Writers from Iraq*. Albany: State University of New York Press.
——. 1996a. "The Cavalcade of Hebrew Literature on TV." *Prooftexts* 16, pp. 301–12.
——. 2004. *More and More Equal: The Literary Works of Sami Michael*. Lanham, MD: Lexington Books.
Berkey, Jonathan P. 2001. *Popular Preaching and Religious Authority in the Medieval Islamic Near East*. Seattle: University of Washington Press.
Bezalel, Itzhak. 1982. *The Writings of Sephardic and Oriental Jewish Authors in Languages Other than Hebrew* (in Hebrew). Tel Aviv: Tel Aviv University Press.
Bhabha, Homi K. 1994. *The Location of Culture*. London: Routledge.
Bialik, Hayyim Nahman. 1954. *Writings on Literature* (in Hebrew). Tel Aviv: Dvir.
Biehl, João et al. (eds.). 2007. *Subjectivity: Ethnographic Investigations*. Berkeley: University of California Press.
Biesecker, Barbara A. 1997. *Addressing Postmodernity: Kenneth Burke, Rhetoric, and a Theory of Social Change*. Tuscaloosa: University of Alabama Press.
Bin'Amāra, Muḥammad. 1989. *Min al-Shi'r al-Islāmī al-Ḥadīth: Mukhtārāt min Shu'arā' al-Rābiṭa*. Amman: Dār al-Bashīr.
Bitton, Michèle. 1999. *Poétesses et lettrées juives: une mémoire éclipsée*. Paris: Éditions Publisud.
Blanc, Haim. 1963. *Communal Dialects in Baghdad*. Cambridge, MA: Harvard University Press.
Blau, Joshua. 1981. *The Emergence and Linguistic Background of Judaeo-Arabic: A Study of the Origins of Middle Arabic*. Jerusalem: Ben-Zvi Institute for the Study of Jewish Communities in the East.
——. 1999. *The Emergence and Linguistic Background of Judaeo-Arabic: A Study of the Origins of Neo-Arabic*. Jerusalem: Ben-Zvi Institute for the Study of Jewish Communities in the East.
——. 2017. *Arabic Linguistics* (in Hebrew). Jerusalem: Bialik Institute.
Blau, Joshua and Hopkins, Simon. 2000. "Ancient Bible Translation to Judeo-Arabic" (in Hebrew). *Pe'amim: Studies in Oriental Jewry* 83, pp. 4–14.
Boulus, Sargon. 1997. *Zeugen am Ufer*, trans. Khālid al-Ma'ālī and Stefan Weidner. Berlin: Das Arabische Buch.
Brann, Ross. 2000. "The Arabized Jews." In Maria Rosa Menocal et al. (eds.). *The Cambridge History of Arabic Literature: The Literature of al-Andalus*. Cambridge: Cambridge University Press, pp. 435–54.
——. 2013. "Andalusi 'Exceptionalism.'" In Suzanne Akbari and Karla Mallette Akbari (eds.). *Sea of Languages: Rethinking the Arabic Role in Medieval Literary History*. Toronto: University of Toronto Press, pp. 119–34.
——. 2021. *Iberian Moorings: Al-Andalus, Sefarad, and the Tropes of Exceptionalism*. Philadelphia: University of Pennsylvania Press.
Brecht, Bertolt. n.d. *Dā'irat al-Ṭabāshīr al-Qawqāziyya*, trans. 'Abd al-Raḥmān Badawī. Acre: Abū Raḥmūn.

——. 1962. *Dā'irat al-Ṭabāshīr al-Qawqāziyya*, trans. 'Abd al-Raḥmān Badawī. Cairo: al-Dār al-Miṣriyya li-l-Ta'līf wa-l-Nashr.
——. 1962 [1944–1950]. *Der Kaukasische Kreidekreis*. Berlin: Suhrkamp Verlag.
——. 1969. *The Caucasian Chalk Circle*, trans. James and Tania Stern, with W. H. Auden. London: Methuen.
Brenner, Rachel Feldhay. 1993. "In Search of Identity: The Israeli Arab Artist in Anton Shammas's *Arabesques*." *PMLA*, May, pp. 431–45.
——. 1999. "'Hidden Transcripts' Made Public: Israeli Arab Fiction and Its Reception." *Critical Inquiry* 26, pp. 85–108.
Breton, André. 2018. *al-Abadiyya Tabḥathu 'an Sā'at Yad*, trans. Mubārak Wasāṭ. Cologne: Manshūrāt al-Jamal.
Browne, Edward G. 1951. *A Literary History of Persia*. Cambridge: Cambridge University Press.
Brumm, Ann- Marie. 1995. "Three Interviews." *Edebiyât* 6, pp. 81–98.
Bsīsū, Mu'īn. 1988. *al-A'māl al-Masraḥiyya*. Acre: Dār al-Aswār.
Bukaee, Rafi. 1990. *Avanti Popolo* (Hebrew). Jerusalem: Kinneret.
Burg, Avraham. 2007. *Victory over Hitler* (in Hebrew). Tel Aviv: Yediot Ahronoth.
Burke, Kenneth. 1969. *A Rhetoric of Motives*. Berkeley: University of California Press.
Busse, Herbert. 1998. *Islam, Judaism, and Christianity: Theological and Historical Affiliations*, trans. Allison Brown. Princeton, NJ: Markus Wiener.
al-Bustānī, Buṭrus. 1859. *Khuṭba fī Ādāb al-'Arab*. Beirut: al-Maṭba'a al-Amīrkāniyya.
al-Bustānī, Wadī'. 1946. *Dīwān al-Filasṭīniyyāt*. Beirut: Maktabat al-Bustānī.
Butt, Aviva. 2021. *Salim Barakat, Mahmud Darwish, and the Kurdish and Palestinian Similitude: Qamishli Extended*. Newcastle upon Tyne: Cambridge Scholars Publishing.
Cachia, Pierre. 1990. *An Overview of Modern Arabic Literature*. Edinburgh: Edinburgh University Press.
Calderwood, Eric. 2014. "The Invention of Al-Andalus: Discovering the Past and Creating the Present in Granada's Islamic Tourism Sites." *Journal of North African Studies* 19.1, pp. 27–55.
——. 2018. *Colonial al-Andalus Spain and the Making of Modern Moroccan Culture*. Cambridge, MA: Harvard University Press.
Cariou, Morgane. 2014. "Le topos de l'ineffable dans les catalogues poétiques." *Revue de philologie, de littérature et d'histoire anciennes* LXXXVIII.2, pp. 27–58.
Carr, E. H. 1965. *What Is History?* Harmondsworth: Penguin.
Caspi, Mishael Maswari and Weltsch, Jerome David. 1998. *From Slumber to Awakening: Culture and Identity of Arab Israeli Literati*. Lanham, MD: University Press of America.
Cavafy, Constantine P. 1998. *Collected Poems*, trans. Edmund Keely and Philip Sherrard. London: Chatto & Windus.
Cervantes, Míguel de. 1972. *The Selected Works*, ed., and trans. Samuel Putnam. London: Chatto & Windus.
——. 2003. *Don Quixote*, trans. Edith Grossman. New York: HarperCollins.
Chambers, Ross. 1984. *Story and Situation: Narrative Seduction and the Power of Fiction*. Chicago: University of Chicago Press.
Cheikho (Shaykhū), Louis. 1924. *al-Ādāb al-'Arabiyya fī al-Qarn al-Tāsi' 'Ashar: Min al-Sana 1800 ilā 1870*. Beirut: al-Maṭba'a al-Kāthūlīkiyya li-l-Ābā' al-Yasū'iyyīn.
——. 1926. *al-Ādāb al-'Arabiyya fī al-Qarn al-Tāsi' 'Ashar: Min al-Sana 1870 ilā 1900*. Beirut: Maṭba'at al-Ābā' al-Yasū'iyyīn.
——. 1926a. *Ta'rīkh al-Ādāb al-'Arabiyya fī al-Rub' al-Awwal min al-Qarn al-'Ishrīn*. Beirut: Maṭba'at al-Ābā' al-Yasū'iyyīn.
——. 1967. *Shu'arā' al-Naṣraniyya Ba'da al-Islām*. Beirut: Dār al-Mashriq.
Chejne, Anwar G. 1969. *The Arabic Language: Its Role in History*. Minneapolis: University of Minnesota Press.

——. 1980. "The Role of al-Andalus in the Movement of Ideas between Islam and the West." In Khalil I. Semaan (ed.). *Islam and the Medieval West: Aspects of Intercultural Relations*. Albany: State University of New York Press, pp. 110–33.

Chetrit, Joseph. 1994. *The Written Judeo-Arabic Poetry in North Africa* (in Hebrew). Jerusalem: Misgav Yerushalayim.

——. et al. 2003. *The Jewish Traditional Marriage in Morocco*. Haifa: University of Haifa Press.

Chetrit, Sami Shalom. 2003. *Poems in Ashdodian* (in Hebrew). Tel Aviv: Andalus.

Choueiri, Youssef M. 2016. "Arab Nationalism: Arabness, Arab Jews, and the Arab Spring." In Josef Meri (ed.). *The Routledge Handbook of Muslim–Jewish Relations*. London: Routledge, pp. 317–30.

Civantos, Christina. 2020. "Writing on Al-Andalus in the Modern Islamic World." In Maribel Fierro (ed.). *The Routledge Handbook of Muslim Iberia*. New York: Routledge, pp. 598–619.

Cixous, Hélène. 1993. *Three Steps on the Ladder of Writing*. New York: Columbia University Press.

Clerk, Jayana and Siegel, Ruth (eds.). 1995. *Modern Literature of the Non-Western World: Where the Waters Are Born*. New York: HarperCollins.

Cleveland, William L. 1971. *The Making of an Arab Nationalist: Ottomanism and Arabism in the Life and Thought of Sati' al-Husri*. Princeton, NJ: Princeton University Press.

Coetzee, M. 1983. *Waiting for the Barbarians*. Harmondsworth: Penguin.

Cohen, Edy. 2016. "There Was a Jewish Nakba, and It Was Even Bigger than the Palestinian One." *The Tower Magazine* 39 (June 2016), see at: http://www.thetower.org/article/there-was-a-jewish-nakba-and-it-was-even-bigger-than-the-palestinian-one, last accessed January 28, 2022.

Cohen, Hayyim. 1966. "The Anti-Jewish Farhud in Baghdad." *Middle Eastern Studies* 3.1, pp. 2–17.

——. 1969. *Zionist Activity in Iraq* (in Hebrew). Jerusalem: Jewish Agency.

——. 1973. *The Jews of the Middle East 1860–1972*. Jerusalem: Israel Universities Press.

Cohen, Mark R. 1991. "The Neo-Lachrymose Conception of Jewish-Arab History." *Tikkun* 6, pp. 55–60.

——. 2012. "Historical Memory and History in the Memoirs of Iraqi Jews." In Eli Yassif Yassif et al. (eds.). *Ot le-Tova: Essays in Honor of Professor Tova Rosen*. Be'er Sheva: Ben-Gurion University of the Negev, pp. 110–37.

Cohen, Mark R. and Somekh, Sasson. 1990. "In the Court of Ya'qūb ibn Killis: A Fragment from the Cairo Genizah." *Jewish Quarterly Review* 80.3/4, pp. 283–314.

Cohen-Mor, Dalya (ed.). 2018. *Cultural Journeys into the Arab World: A Literary Anthology*. Albany: State University of New York Press.

——. 2019. *Mahmoud Darwish: Palestine's Poet and the Other as the Beloved*. New York: Palgrave Macmillan.

Conrad, Joseph. 1996. *Heart of Darkness*. New York: Palgrave Macmillan.

Cooke, Miriam. 2001. *Women Claim Islam: Creating Islamic Feminism Through Literature*. London: Routledge.

Creswell, Robyn. 2019. *City of Beginnings: Poetic Modernism in Beirut*. Princeton, NJ: Princeton University Press.

Cruz, Anna C. 2018. "In Memory of al-Andalus: Using the Elegy to Reimagine the Literary and Literal Geography of Cordova." In Nizar F. Hermes and Getchen Head (eds.). *The City in Arabic Literature: Classical and Modern Perspectives*. Edinburgh: Edinburgh University Press, pp. 103–23.

Dammond, Liliane S., with Yvette M. Raby. 2007. *The Lost World of the Egyptian Jews: First-Person Accounts from Egypt's Jewish Community in the Twentieth Century*. New York: Lincoln.

Damrosch, David. 2014. "Foreword: Literary Criticism and the Qur'an." *Journal of Qur'anic Studies* 16.3, pp. 4–10.

Dana, Joseph. 2000. *Hebrew and Arabic over Generations* (in Hebrew). Haifa: Institute for Hebrew–Arabic Comparative Research.

Dardashti, Galeet. 2008. "The Buena Vista Baghdad Club: Negotiating Local, National, and Global Representations of Jewish Iraqi Musicians in Israel." In Julia Brauch et al. (eds.). *Jewish Topographies: Visions of Space, Traditions of Place*. Aldershot: Ashgate, pp. 311–28.

Darwaza, Muḥammad 'Izzat. 1993. *Mudhakkirāt Muḥammad 'Izzat Darwaza: Sijjil Ḥāfil bi-Masīrat al-Ḥaraka al-'Arabiyya wa-l-Qaḍiyya al-Filasṭīniyya Khilāla Qarn min al-Zaman; 1305–1404H/1887–1984*. Beirut: Dār al-Gharab al-Islāmī.

Darwisch, Mahmud. 1996. *Weniger Rosen*, trans. Khalid Al-Maaly and Heribert Becker. Berlin: Das Arabische Buch.

Darwīsh (Darwish), Maḥmūd (Mahmoud). 1969. "Anqidhūnā min Hādhā al-Ḥubb al-Qāsī." *al-Jadīd*, June, pp. 2–4.

——. 1969a. "Min Maḥmūd Darwīsh ilā al-Nuqqād wa-l-Udabā' al-'Arab: Anqidhūnā min Hādhā al-Ḥubb al-Qāsī." *al-Ṭalī'a*, September, pp. 113–16.

——. 1969b. "Anqidhūnā min Hādhā al-Ḥubb al-Qāsī." *al-Ādāb*, August, pp. 5–6.

——. 1980. *The Music of Human Flesh*, trans. Denys Johnson-Davies. London: Heineman.

——. 1985. *Ḥiṣār li-Madā'iḥ al-Baḥr*. Beirut: Dār al-'Awda.

——. 1986. *Hiya Ughniyya Hiya Ughniyya*. Acre: Dār al-Aswār.

——. 1987. *Dhākira li-l-Nisyān*. Acre: Dār al-Aswār.

——. 1987a. *Ward Aqall*. Acre: Dār al-Aswār.

——. 1987b. *Fī Waṣf Ḥālatinā*. Beirut: Dār al-Kalima.

——. 1988. *Dīwān*. Acre: Dār al-Aswār.

——. 1990. *Arā Mā Urīdu*. Casablanca: Dār Tubqāl.

——. 1991. "Hudna ma'a al-Maghūl Amāma Ghābat al-Sindiyān." *Filisṭīn al-Thawra*, February 24, pp. 30–1.

——. 1992. *Aḥada 'Ashara Kawkaban*. Beirut: Dār al-Jadīd.

——. 1995. *Memory for Forgetfulness*, trans. Ibrahim Muhawi. Berkeley: University of California Press.

——. 1995a. *Limādhā Tarakta al-Ḥiṣana Waḥīdan*. Beirut: Riyāḍ al-Rayyis.

——. 2003. *Unfortunately, It Was Paradise: Selected Poems*, ed. and trans. Munir Akash and Carolyn Forché, with Sinan Antoon and Amira El-Zein. Berkeley: University of California Press.

——. 2006. *Fī Ḥaḍrat al-Ghiyāb*. Beirut: Riyāḍ al-Rayyis.

——. 2006a. *Why Did You Leave the Horse Alone?* trans. Jeffrey Sacks. Brooklyn, NY: Archipelago Books.

——. 2008. *Athar al-Farāsha*. Beirut: Riyāḍ al-Rayyis.

——. 2009. *Lā Urīdu li-Hādhī al-Qaṣīda an Tantahiya*. Beirut: Riyāḍ al-Rayyis.

——. 2014. *Why Did You Leave the Horse Alone?* trans. Muhammad Shaheen. London: Hesperus Press.

Darwīsh, Maḥmūd and al-Qāsim, Samīḥ. 1990. *al-Rasā'il*. Haifa: Arabesque.

Darwish, Mustafa. 1998. *Dream Makers on the Nile: A Portrait of Egyptian Cinema*. Cairo: American University in Cairo Press.

Darwīsh, Salmān. 1981. *Kull Shaya' Hādi' fī al-'Iyāda*. Jerusalem: Rābiṭat al-Jāmi'iyyīn al-Yahūd al-Nāziḥīn min al-'Irāq.

Darwīsh, Shalom. 1931. *Ba'da Mawt Akhīhi*. Baghdad: Maṭba'at al-Ma'ārif.

——. 1941. *Aḥrār wa-'Abīd*. Baghdad: Maṭba'at al-Rashīd.

——. 1948. *Ba'ḍ al-Nās*. Baghdad: Sharikat al-Tijāra wa-l-Ṭibā'a al-Maḥdūda.

——. 1976. *Bayḍat al-Dīk*. Jerusalem: Majallat al-Sharq.

——. 1980. "The Relations between Communal Institutions and the *He-Ḥaluts*

Underground Movement in Baghdad" (in Hebrew). In Zvi Yehuda. *From Babylon to Jerusalem* (in Hebrew). Tel Aviv: Iraqi Jews' Traditional Cultural Center, pp. 82–5.
——. 2016. *Free Men and Slaves* (in Hebrew), trans. Benyamin Rish. Bnei Brak: Translator's Publication.
Davenport, John J. 2012. *Narrative Identity, Autonomy, and Mortality: From Frankfurt and MacIntyre to Kierkegaard*. New York: Routledge.
Davis, Diane. 1999. "'Addicted to Love'; Or, Toward an Inessential Solidarity." *Jac: A Journal of Composition Theory* 19.3, pp. 633–56.
——. 2000. *Breaking Up [at] Totality: A Rhetoric of Laughter*. Carbondale: Southern Illinois University Press.
——. 2003. "Inessential Solidarity." PhD thesis, European Graduate School.
Dawidowicz, Lucy S. 1977. *The Jewish Presence: Essays on Identity and History*. New York: Holt, Rinehart & Winston.
Ḍayf, Shawqī. 1983. *'Aṣr al-Duwal wa-l-Imārāt*. Cairo: Dār al-Ma'ārif.
Debord, Guy. 1995 [1967]. *The Society of the Spectacle*, trans. Donald Nicholson-Smith. New York: Zone Books.
——. 2000 [1967]. *The Society of the Spectacle*, trans. Ken Knabb. London: Rebel Press.
Decter, Jonathan. 2020. "The (Inter-Religious?) Rededication of an Arabic Panegyric by Judah al-Ḥarīzī." *Journal of Arabic Literature* 51, pp. 351–68.
Dekel, Yael and Tzelgov, Eran. 2020. "The Hope of Salman Masalha: Re-Territorializing Hebrew." *Comparative Literature and Culture* 22.1, pp. 1–10, doi.org/10.7771/1481-4374.3713.
Delanty, Gerard et al. (eds.). 2011. *Identity, Belonging and Migration*. Liverpool: Liverpool University Press.
Deleuze, Gilles and Guattari, Félix. 1975. *Kafka: Pour une littérature mineure*. Paris: Les Éditions de Minuit.
——. and Guattari, Félix. 1986. *Kafka: Towards a Minor Literature*, trans. Dana Polan. Minneapolis: University of Minnesota Press.
——. and Guattari, Félix. 1987. *A Thousand Plateaus: Capitalism and Schizophrenia*, trans. Brian Massumi. Minneapolis: University of Minnesota Press.
——. and Guattari, Félix. 1990. "What Is a Minor Literature?" In Russell Ferguson et al. (eds.). *Out There: Marginalization and Contemporary Cultures*. New York: New Museum of Contemporary Art, pp. 59–69.
Derrida, Jacques. 1976. *Of Grammatology*, trans. Gayatri Chakravorty Spivak. Baltimore: Johns Hopkins University Press.
——. 1986. "Racism's Last Word." In Henry Louis Gates. Jr. and Kwame Anthony Appiah (eds.). *"Race," Writing and Difference*. Chicago: University of Chicago Press, pp. 329–38.
DeYoung, Terri. 1992. "Language in Looking-Glass Land: Samīḥ al-Qāsim and the Modernization of *Jinās*." *Journal of the American Oriental Society* 112.2, pp. 183–97.
Di-Capua, Yoav. 2012. "Arab Existentialism: An Invisible Chapter in the Intellectual History of Decolonization." *American Historical Review* 117.4, pp. 1061–91.
——. 2013. "Homeward Bound: Ḥusayn Muruwwah's Integrative Quest for Authenticity." *Journal of Arabic Literature* 44, pp. 21–52.
——. 2015. "The Intellectual Revolt of the 1950s and the 'Fall of the Udabā''." In Friederike Pannewick and Georges Khalil (eds.). *Commitment and Beyond: Locating the Political in Arabic Literature since the 1940s*. Wiesbaden: Reichert Verlag, pp. 89–104.
——. 2018. *No Exit: Arab Existentialism, Jean-Paul Sartre, and Decolonization*. Chicago: University of Chicago Press.
DiMeo, David. 2016. *Committed to Disillusion: Activist Writers in Egypt from the 1950s to the 1980s*. Cairo: American University in Cairo Press.
D'Ohsson, C. 1834–1835. *Histoire des Mongols depuis Tchinguiz-Khan jusqu'a Timour Bey ou Tamerlan*. The Hague: Les Frères Van Cleef.

Dori, Dafna. 2021. "The Brothers Al-Kuwaity and the Iraqi Song 1930–1950." PhD thesis, Uppsala University.

Dostoevsky, Fyodor. 1993. *Crime and Punishment*, trans. Richard Pevear and Larissa Volokhonsky. New York: Vintage.

Dowty, Alan. 1998. *The Jewish State: A Century Later*. Berkeley: University of California Press.

Drori, Danielle. 2020. "Tightrope Walkers: Jacqueline Shohet Kahanoff and Naïm Kattan as 'Translated Men.'" *Dibur: Literary Journal* 8, pp. 43–53.

Drory, Rina. 2000. *Models and Contacts: Arabic Literature and Its Impact on Medieval Jewish Culture*. Leiden: Brill.

——. 2000a. "The Maqama." In Maria Rosa Menocal et al. (eds.). *The Cambridge History of Arabic Literature: The Literature of al-Andalus*. Cambridge: Cambridge University Press, pp. 190–210.

Drower, E. S. 1989. "Evergreen Elijah: Ritual Scenes from Jewish Life in the Middle East." In Jacob Neusner and Ernest S. Frerichs (eds.). *Approaches to Ancient Judaism*. Atlanta, GA: Scholars Press, pp. 8–11.

Du Gay, Paul. 2009. *Organizing Identity: Persons and Organizations "After Theory."* Los Angeles: Sage.

Dursteler, Eric R. 2006. *Venetians in Constantinople: Nation, Identity, and Coexistence in the Early Modern Mediterranean*. Baltimore, MD: Johns Hopkins University Press.

Ebileeni, Maurice. 2017. "Literary Trespassing in Susan Abulhawa's *Mornings in Jenin* and Sayed Kashua's *Second Person Singular*." *Comparative Literature* 69.2, pp. 222–37.

Eisenstadt, Shmuel N. 1988. "Modernization without Assimilation: Notes on the Social Structure of the Jews of Iraq" (in Hebrew). *Pe'amim: Studies in Oriental Jewry* 36, pp. 3–6.

Eksell, Kerstin. 2011. "The Legend of Al-Andalus: A Trajectory across Generic Borders." In Kerstin Eksell and Stephan Guth (eds.). *Borders and Beyond: Crossings and Transitions in Modern Arabic Literature*. Wiesbaden: Harrassowitz Verlag, pp. 103–26.

Elad-Bouskila, Ami (ed.). 1993. *Writer, Culture, Text: Studies in Modern Arabic Literature*. Fredericton, NB: York Press.

——. 1999. "Arabic and/or Hebrew: The Languages of Arab Writers in Israel." In Kamal Abdel-Malek and David C. Jacobson (eds.). *Israeli and Palestinian Identities in History and Literature*. New York: St. Martin's Press, pp. 133–58.

——. 1999a. *Modern Palestinian Literature and Culture*. London: Frank Cass.

El-Hussari, Ibrahim A. 2013. "Arabesques: An Arabic Tale in Hebrew Letters Posing a Challenge for a Dialogue and Mutual Recognition in Honor of Peace." *International Journal of Arts & Sciences* 6.2, pp. 423–33.

Eliade, M. 1959. *The Sacred and the Profane*. New York: Harcourt Brace Jovanovich.

Elimelekh, Geula. 2013. "The Search for Identity in the Works of Samīr Naqqāsh." *Middle Eastern Studies* 49.1, pp. 63–75.

——. 2013a. "Kafkaesque Metamorphosis as Reflected in the Works of Samir Naqqash." *Journal of Semitic Studies* 58.2, pp. 323–42.

——. 2014. "Fantasy as 'Recovery, Escape and Consolation' in the Short Stories of Isaac Bar Moshe." *Middle Eastern Studies* 50.3, pp. 426–41.

——. 2015. "Samīr Naqqāsh: Between the Sacred and the Demonic." *Studia Orientalia Electronica* 3, pp. 1–16.

——. 2021. "Samīr Naqqāsh: From One Universe to Another—Iraq to Israel." In Meir Hatina and Yona Sheffer (eds.). *Cultural Pearls from the East: In Memory of Shmuel Moreh, 1932–2017*. Leiden: Brill, pp. 142–60.

Elinson, Alexander E. 2009. *Looking Back at al-Andalus: The Poetics of Loss and Nostalgia in Medieval Arabic and Hebrew Literature*. Leiden: Brill.

Eliot, T. S. 1950. *Selected Essays*. New York: Harcourt.

Eliraz, Israel. 1987. "To Search by Poems New Territories" (in Hebrew). *Mifgash-Liqā'* 6, pp. 68–9.

Elkad-Lehman, Ilana. 2008. "A Suitcase and a Fence: On *Aravim Rokdim* [*Dancing Arabs*] and *Va-Yehi Boker* [*Let It Be Morning*] by Sayed Kashua" (in Hebrew). In Ilana Elkad-Lehman (ed.). *Israeli Identities: The Familiar and the Unknown* (in Hebrew). Jerusalem: Carmel, pp. 119–54.

Ellmann, Richard. 1959. *James Joyce*. New York: Oxford University Press.

Elmeligi, Wessam. 2019. *The Poetry of Arab Women from the Pre-Islamic Age to Andalusia*. London: Routledge.

Elon, Amos. 2002. *The Pity of It All: A History of the Jews in Germany, 1743–1933*. New York: Metropolitan Books.

El Saffar, Ruth Snodgrass. 1968. "The Function of the Fictional Narrator in *Don Quijote*." *MLN* 83.2, pp. 164–77.

Emmerson, Richard Kenneth. 1981. *Antichrist in the Middle Ages*. Seattle: University of Washington Press.

Encyclopaedia Judaica. 1971. Jerusalem: Macmillan.

Epafras, Leonard Chrysostomos. 2013. "The Condition of Jewish Minority in Medieval Egypt: A Study of Jewish Sufi's Tractate al-Maqalat al-Hawdiyya." *Al-Jami'ah Journal of Islamic Studies* 51.2, pp. 163–96.

Eshed, Eli. 2003. "In the Beginning There Was Palestine" (in Hebrew). *Mit'an* 8, pp. 20–3.

Esposito, J. L. (ed.). 1995. *The Oxford Encyclopedia of the Modern Islamic World*. New York: Oxford University Press.

Even-Zohar, Itamar. 1990. "The Emergence of a Native Hebrew Culture in Palestine, 1882–1948." *Poetics Today* 11.1, pp. 175–91.

Evri, Yuval. 2018. "Return to al-Andalus beyond German-Jewish Orientalism: Abraham Shalom Yahuda's Critique of Modern Jewish Discourse." In Ottfried Fraisse (ed.). *Modern Jewish Scholarship on Islam in Context: Rationality, European Borders, and the Search for Belonging*. Berlin: Mouton de Gruyter, pp. 337–54.

——. 2020. *The Return to Al-Andalus: Disputes over Sephardic Culture and Identity between Arabic and Hebrew* (in Hebrew). Jerusalem: Magnes Press.

——. 2020a. "Translation and the Colonial Encounter: Conversation between Yuval Evri and Yehouda Shenhav-Shahrabani on Bi-National Team Translation." *ReOrient* 6.1, pp. 65–85.

Fahmawi-Watad, Aida. 2022. "Identity of Writing and the Writing of Identity: Ayman Sikseck's Novel *Tishrin*." *Journal of Modern Jewish Studies* 21, pp. 1–23, online, April 4, 2022, available at: https://www.tandfonline.com/doi/full/10.1080/14725886.2022.2031141, last accessed February 9, 2022.

Fahmy, Ziad. 2011. *Ordinary Egyptians: Creating the Modern Nation through Popular Culture*. Stanford, CA: Stanford University Press.

al-Fākhūrī, Ḥannā. 1954. *al-Jadīd fī al-Adab al-'Arabī*. Beirut: Maktabat al-Madrasa wa-Dār al-Kitāb al-Lubnānī li-l-Ṭibā'a.

Fanon, Frantz. 1967. *Black Skin White Masks*, trans. Charles Lam Markmann. New York: Grove Press.

Faraj, Murād. 1912. *Maqālāt Murād*. Cairo: Maṭba'at Ibrāhīm Rosenthal.

——. 1924. *Dīwān Murād*. Cairo: Matba'at al-I'timād.

Fargeon, Maurice. 1938. *Les juifs en Egypte depuis les origins jusqu'à ce jour*. Cairo: Imprimerie Paul Barbey.

al-Faqqī, Muḥammad Kāmil. 1976. *al-Adab fī al-'Aṣr al-Mamlūkī*. Cairo: al-Hay'a al-'Āmma li-l-Kitāb.

Fattāl (Fattal-Kuperwasser), Tsionit. 2015. *The Pictures on the Wall* (in Hebrew). Kiryat Gat: Korim Publishing.

——. 2017. *al-Ṣuwar 'alā al-Ḥā'iṭ*, trans. 'Amr Zakariyā Khalīl. Baghdad: Dār Mesopotamia.

Fawzī, Ḥusayn. 1968. *Sindbād fī Riḥlat al-Ḥayāt*. Cairo: Dār al-Maʿārif.
Fayṣal ibn al-Ḥusayn fī Khuṭabihi wa-Aqwālihi. 1945. Baghdad: Maṭbaʿat al-Ḥukūma.
Feiner, Shmuel. 2001. "Towards a Historical Definition of the Haskalah." In Shmuel Feiner and David Sorkin (eds.). *New Perspectives on the Haskalah*. Portland, OR: Littman Library of Jewish Civilization, pp. 184–219.
Feldman, Yael S. 1999. "Postcolonial Memory, Postmodern Intertextuality: Anton Shammas's *Arabesques* Revisited." *PMLA* 114.3, pp. 373–89.
Fenton (Yinnon), P. B. 1995. "A Treatise on Perfection, Providence and Prophecy from Jewish Ṣūfī Circle." In Daniel Frank (ed.). *The Jews of Medieval Islam: Community, Society, and Identity*. Leiden: Brill, pp. 301–34.
——. 2002. "Karaites and Sufis: The Traces of Sufism in Karaite Manuscripts" (in Hebrew). *Peʿamim: Studies in Oriental Jewry* 90, pp. 5–19.
——. 2004. "Two Akbarī Mss. in Judeo-Arabic" (Hebrew). In Yosef Tobi (ed.). *Contacts between Arabic Literature and Jewish Literature in the Middle Ages and Modern Times*, vol. III (in Hebrew). Tel Aviv: Afikim, pp. 82–94.
Ferris, Timothy. 1991 [1988]. *Coming of Age in the Milky Way*. London: Vintage.
Festinger, Leon. 1957. *A Theory of Cognitive Dissonance*. Stanford, CA: Stanford University Press.
Firro, Kais M. 1999. *The Druzes in the Jewish State: A Brief History*. Leiden: Brill.
——. 2001. "Reshaping Druze Particularism in Israel." *Journal of Palestine Studies* 30.3, pp. 40–53.
Fish, Stanley E. 1980. "Literature in the Reader: Affective Stylistics." In Jane P. Tompkins (ed.). *Reader-Response Criticism: From Formalism to Post-Structuralism*. Baltimore, MD: Johns Hopkins University Press, pp. 70–100.
Foster, Zachary J. 2017. "The Invention of Palestine." PhD thesis, Princeton University.
Forcione, Alban K. 1970. *Cervantes, Aristotle and the Persiles*. Princeton, NJ: Princeton University Press.
Foucault, Michel. 1980 [1969]. "What is an Author?" In Donald F. Bouchard (ed.). *Language, Counter-Memory, Practice: Selected Essays and Interviews by Michel Foucault*. Ithaca, NY: Cornell University Press, pp. 113–38.
——. 1981. *The History of Sexuality: An Introduction*, trans. Robert Hurley. Harmondsworth: Penguin.
Francfort, Didier. 2021. "Musiques orientales et questions nationales en Israël de 1948 aux années 2000." *Revue d'histoire culturelle: XVIIIe–XXIe siècles* 2, available at: http://revues.mshparisnord.fr/rhc/index.php?id=1354.
Frayn, Michael. 1974. *Constructions*. London: Wildwood House.
Frosh, Stephen and Baraitser, Lisa. 2009. "Goodbye to Identity?" In Anthony Elliott and Paul Du Gay (eds.). *Identity in Question*. Los Angeles: Sage, pp. 158–69.
al-Gamil, Yosef ben Ovadia. 1979. *History of Karaite Jewry*. Ramla: Ha-Moʿaza Ha-Arzit shel Ha-Yehudim Ha-Karaim Be-Yisrael.
Gaon, Moshe David. 1937. *The Jews of the East in Land of Israel* (in Hebrew). Jerusalem: Author's Publication.
García-Arenal, Mercedes. 1997. "Jewish Converts to Islam in the Muslim West." *Israel Oriental Studies* 17, pp. 227–48.
García Arévalo, T. M. 2015, "Sobre Ḥikāyat al-Ḥūb wa-l-Waṭan, la versión judeo-árabe de 'Amor en Sion' de Abraham Mapu. Estudio preliminar." *Miscelánea de Estudios Árabes y Hebraicos. Sección Hebreo* 64, pp. 67–83.
Gardet, L. 1971. "Ḥāl." *Encyclopaedia of Islam*, 2nd edn. III, pp. 83–5.
Gat, Moshe. 1997. *The Jewish Exodus from Iraq 1948–1951*. London: Frank Cass.
Gates, Henry Louis Jr., 1985. "Editor's Introduction: Writing 'Race' and the Difference It Makes." *Critical Inquiry* 12, pp. 1–20.
Gates, Henry Louis Jr. and Appiah, Kwame Anthony (eds.). 1986. *"Race," Writing and Difference*. Chicago: University of Chicago Press.

Gazzaniga, Michael S. 2011. *Who's in Charge? Free Will and the Science of the Brain.* New York: Ecco.

Gelber, Yoav. 2008. *The New Post-Zionist Historians.* New York: American Jewish Committee.

Gendzier, Irene L. 1966. *The Practical Visions of Ya'qub Sanu'.* Cambridge, MA: Center for Middle Eastern Studies of Harvard University.

Gerholm, Tomas. 1988. "Three European Intellectuals as Converts to Islam: Cultural Mediators or Social Critics." In Tomas Gerholm and Yngve Georg Lithman (eds.). *The New Islamic Presence in Western Europe.* London: Mansell, pp. 263–77.

Gertz, Nurith. 2000. *Myths in Israeli Culture: Captives of a Dream.* Portland, OR: Vallentine Mitchell.

——. 2002. "Space and Gender in the New Israeli and Palestinian Cinema." *Prooftexts* 22, pp. 157–85.

Ghanīm, Muḥammad. 1938. *Maḥāsin al-Sulūk fī Ta'rīkh al-Khulafā' wa-l-Muluk.* Cairo: Maṭba'at al-'Ulūm.

Ghanimah, Yusuf Rizk-Allah. 1998. *A Nostalgic Trip into the History of the Jews of Iraq,* trans. A. Dallal. Lanham, MD: University Press of America.

Gharāyiba, 'Abd al-Karīm. 1961. *al-'Arab wa-l-Atrāk.* Damascus: Damascus University.

al-Ghazālī, Abū Ḥāmid. 1956. *al-Munqidh min al-Ḍalāl,* ed. Jamīl Ṣalība and Kāmil 'Ayyād. Damascus: Maṭba'at al-Taraqqī.

Ghazoul, Ferial J. 2006. "From the Spokesman of the Tribe to a Tribune of the Dispossessed." In Andreas Pflitsch and Barbara Winckler (eds.). *Poetry's Voice: Society's Norms: Forms of Interaction between Middle Eastern Writers and Their Societies.* Wiesbaden: Reichert Verlag, pp. 1–10.

al-Ghazzāwī, 'Abbās. 1960. *Ta'rīkh al-Adab al-'Arabī fī al-'Irāq.* Baghdad: al-Majma' al-'Ilmī al-'Irāqī.

Ghunayma, Yūsuf Rizq Allāh. 1924. *Nuzhat al-Mushtāq fī Ta'rīkh Yahūd al-'Irāq.* Baghdad: Maṭba'at al-'Irāq.

Gibb, Hamilton A. R. 1962. *Studies on the Civilization of Islam.* London: Routledge.

Gilroy, Paul. 1993. *The Black Atlantic: Modernity and Double Consciousness.* Cambridge, MA: Harvard University Press.

Ginossar, Yaira. 1997. "The Acceptance of Emil Habiby in Contemporary Israeli Literature: Hebrew Literary Supplements on *Saraya, Daughter of the Ghoul*" (in Hebrew), *Iyunim bi-Tkumat Israel* 7, pp. 546–82.

Ginsburg, Shai. 2006. "'The Rock of Our Very Existence': Anton Shammas's *Arabesques* and the Rhetoric of Hebrew Literature." *Comparative Literature* 58.3, pp. 187–204.

Gitre, Carmen M. K. 2015. "The Dramatic Middle East: Performance as History in Egypt and Beyond." *History Compass* 13.10, pp. 521–32.

——. 2019. *Acting Egyptian: Theater, Identity, and Political Culture in Cairo, 1869–1923.* Austin: University of Texas Press.

Goitein, Shelomo Dov. 1955. *Jews and Arabs: Their Contacts through the Ages.* New York: Schocken.

——. 1967. *A Mediterranean Society: The Jewish Communities of the Arab World as Portrayed in the Documents of the Cairo Genizah.* Berkeley: University of California Press.

Goldberg, Amos. 2016. "Narrative, Testimony, and Trauma: The Nakba and the Holocaust in Elias Khoury's *Gate of the Sun.*" *International Journal of Postcolonial Studies* 18.3, pp. 335–58.

Goldberg, Harvey E. (ed.). 1996. *Sephardi and Middle Eastern Jewries: History and Culture in the Modern Era.* Bloomington: Indiana University Press.

Goldberg, Harvey E. and Bram, Chen. 2007. "Sephardic/Mizrahi/Arab-Jews: Reflections on Critical Sociology and the Study of Middle Eastern Jewries within the Context of

Israeli Society." In Peter Y. Medding (ed.). *Sephardic Jewry and Mizrahi Jews*. Oxford: Oxford University Press, pp. 227–56.
Goldscheider, Calvin and Zuckerman, Alan S. 1984. *The Transformation of the Jews*. Chicago: University of Chicago Press.
Goldstein, Miriam. 2004. "Adaptations of the Arabic *Qaṣīda* in Andalusian Hebrew Poetry." In Yosef Tobi (ed.). *Contacts between Arabic Literature and Jewish Literature in the Middle Ages and Modern Times*, vol. III (in Hebrew). Tel Aviv: Afikim, pp. vii–xxxviii.
Goldstein-Sabbah, Sasha Rachel. 2016. "Censorship and the Jews of Baghdad: Reading Between the Lines in the Case of E. Levy." *Journal of the Middle East and Africa* 7.3, pp. 283–300.
——. 2018. "Baghdadi Jewish Networks in Hashemite Iraq: Jewish Transnationalism in the Age of Nationalism." PhD thesis, University of Leiden.
——. 2021. *Baghdadi Jewish Networks in the Age of Nationalism*. Leiden: Brill.
Goldziher, Ignác. 1966. *A Short History of Classical Arabic Literature*. Hildesheim: Georg Olms Verlag.
Goorji, Sigal. 2020. "Fiction Produces Reality: *The Pictures on the Wall* and the Longing for a 'Golden Age' in Iraq" (in Hebrew). *Jama'a: Interdisciplinary Journal of Middle East Studies* 25, pp. 73–90.
——. 2021. "Shmuel Moreh's *Baghdad Mon Amour*: Autobiographical Works as Historical and Cultural Documents." In Meir Hatina and Yona Sheffer (eds.). *Cultural Pearls from the East: In Memory of Shmuel Moreh, 1932–2017*. Leiden: Brill, pp. 315–32.
Gordon, Milton. 1964. *Assimilation in American Life*. New York: Oxford University Press.
Gormezano-Goren, Y. 1979. *An Alexandrian Summer* (in Hebrew). Tel Aviv: Am Oved.
Green, Rachel Elizabeth. 2013. "Towards a Poetics of the Black Hole: Trauma, Memory and Language in Samir Naqqash's 'Shlomo al-Kurdi, Myself, and Time.'" PhD thesis, University of Texas at Austin.
Greenblatt, Stephen J. 1988. *Shakespearean Negotiations: The Circulation of Social Energy in Renaissance England*. Oxford: Clarendon.
——. 1990. *Learning to Curse: Essays in Early Modern Culture*. New York: Routledge.
——. 1995. "Culture." In Frank Lentricchia and Thomas McLaughlin (eds.). *Critical Terms for Literary Study*. Chicago: University of Chicago Press, pp. 225–32.
Grossberg, Lawrence. 1996. "Identity and Cultural Studies: Is That All There Is?" In Stuart Hall and Paul Du Gay (eds.). *Questions of Cultural Identity*. London: Sage, pp. 87–107.
Grossman, David. 1992. *Present Absentees* (in Hebrew). Tel Aviv: Ha-Kibbutz Ha-Me'uḥad.
Grumberg, Karen. 2018. "'The Whole Content of My Being Shrieks in Contradiction against Itself': Uncanny Selves in Sayed Kashua and Philip Roth." *Shofar: An Interdisciplinary Journal of Jewish Studies* 36.3, pp. 1–30.
Günther, Sebastian. 1999. "Hostile Brothers in Transformation: An Archetypal Conflict in Classical and Modern Arabic Literature." In Angelika Neuwirth et al. (eds.). *Myths, Historical Archetypes and Symbolic Figures in Arabic Literature*. Beirut: Orient-Institut der DMG, pp. 309–36.
Guo, Li. 2020. *Arabic Shadow Theatre 1300–1900: A Handbook*. Leiden: Brill.
Ḥabīb, Shafiq. 1990. *al-'Awda ilā al-Ātī*. Nazareth: Maṭba'at al-Ḥakīm.
Ḥabībī, Imīl (Emile). 1974. *al-Waqā'i' al-Gharība fī Ikhtifā' Sa'īd Abī al-Naḥs al-Mutashā'il*. Haifa: Dār al-Ittiḥād.
——. 1980. *Luka' ibn Luka'*. Nazareth: Manshūrāt Dār 30 Ādhār.
——. 1985. *Sudāsiyyat al-Ayyām al-Sitta; al-Waqā'i' al-Gharība fī Ikhtifā' Sa'īd Abī al-Naḥs al-Mutashā'il wa-Qiṣas Ukhrā*. Haifa: Dār al-Ittiḥād.

Habiby, Emile. 1982. *The Secret Life of Saeed, the Ill-Fated Pessoptimist*, trans. Trevor Le Gassick. New York: Vintage.
Ha-Cohen, Mordechai. 1978. *Mordechai Narrated* (Hebrew), ed. H. Goldberg. Jerusalem: Ben-Zvi Institute for the Study of Jewish Communities in the East.
Ḥaddād, Mīshīl Iskandar (ed.). 1985. *Fī al-Nāḥiya al-Ukhrā*. Shfaram: Dār al-Mashriq.
Ḥaddād, Mīshīl Iskandar and Qaʻwār, Jamāl. 1954. *Ẓalām wa-Nūr*. Nazareth: Maktabat al-Jalīl.
Haddad, Robert M. 1970. *Syrian Christians in Muslim Society: An Interpretation*. Princeton, NJ: Princeton University Press.
Haim, Sylvia G. 1962. *Arab Nationalism: An Anthology*. Berkeley: University of California Press.
Al-Haj, Majid. 1995. *Education, Empowerment, and Control: The Case of the Arabs in Israel*. Albany: State University of New York Press.
Hajjar, Osman. 2010. "Exile at Home: Samir Naqqash—Prophesy as Poetics." In Angelika Neuwirth et al. (eds.). *Arabic Literature: Postmodern Perspectives*. London: Saqi, pp. 309–36.
Hakak, Lev. 1981. "The Contribution of Iraqi Jews to Hebrew Literature in Israel" (in Hebrew). In Menahem Zohori et al. (eds.). *Studies on Jewish Themes by Contemporary Jewish Scholars from Islamic Countries* (in Hebrew). Jerusalem: World Hebrew Union and World Jewish Congress, pp. 111–18.
——. 1995. "Sami Michael's Literary World" (in Hebrew). *Yahadut Bavel* 1, pp. 7–33.
——. 2003. *Budding of Modern Hebrew Creativity in Babylon* (in Hebrew). Or-Yehuda: BJHC.
——. 2005. *The Collected Essays of Rabbi Shlomo Bekhor Ḥuṣīn* (Hebrew). Tel Aviv: Ha-Kibbutz Ha-Me'uḥad.
Halkin, Abraham S. 1956. "The Judeo-Islamic Age: The Great Fusion." In Leo W. Schwarz (ed.). *Great Ages and Ideas of the Jewish People*. New York: Modern Library, pp. 214–33.
Hall, Stuart. 1991. "The Local and the Global: Globalization and Ethnicity." In Anthony D. King (ed.). *Culture, Globalization and the World-System: Contemporary Conditions for the Representation of Identity*. Binghamton, NY: Department of Art and Art History, State University of New York at Binghamton, pp. 19–40.
——. 1993. "Culture, Community, Nation." *Cultural Studies* 7, pp. 349–63.
——. 1996. "Introduction: Who Needs 'Identity'?" In Stuart Hall and Paul Du Gay (eds.). *Questions of Cultural Identity*. London: Sage, pp. 1–17.
Hamamra, Bilal Tawfiq and Abusamra, Sanaa. 2020. "'What's in a Name?' The Aesthetics of Proper Name and Diasporic Identity in Darwish and Said." *Interventions: International Journal of Postcolonial Studies* 22.8, pp. 1065–78.
Hämeen-Anttila, Jaakko. 2008. "Building an Identity: Place as an Image of Self in Classical Arabic Literature." *Quaderni di Studi Arabi* 3, pp. 25–38.
Ḥamza, ʻAbd al-Laṭīf. 2000. *Thalāth Shakhṣiyyāt fī al-Ta'rīkh: Ibn al-Muqaffaʻ, Ṣalāḥ al-Dīn, Qarāqūsh*. Cairo: al-Hay'a al-Miṣriyya al-ʻĀmma li-l-Kitāb.
Ḥamza, Ḥusayn. 2004. "*Anā Yūsuf Yā Abī*: Maḥmūd Darwīsh Bayna Marjaʻiyyat al-Naṣṣ wa-l-Ta'wīl." *al-Sharq*, March, pp. 52–6.
Handal, Nathalie. 2015. "Introduction." In Naomi Wallace and Ismail Khalidi (eds.). *Inside/Outside: Six Plays from Palestine and the Diaspora*. New York: Theater Communication Group, pp. 16–61.
Hanley, Will. 2008. "Grieving Cosmopolitanism in Middle East Studies." *History Compass* 6.5, pp. 1346–67.
——. 2013. "Cosmopolitan Cursing in Late Nineteenth-Century Alexandria." In Derryl N. MacLean and Sikeena Karmali Ahmed (eds.), *Cosmpolitanisms in Muslim Contexts: Perspectives from the Past*. Edinburgh: Edinburgh University Press, pp. 92–104.
——. 2017. *Identifying with Nationality: Europeans, Ottomans, and Egyptians in Alexandria*. New York: Columbia University Press.

Hanna, Nelly. 2003. *In Praise of Books: A Cultural History of Cairo's Middle Class, Sixteenth to the Eighteenth Century*. Syracuse, NY: Syracuse University Press.
Haramati, Michal. 2020. "Auto-Emancipation: Decolonial Perspectives on Autonomous Political Mizrahi and Sephardic Organizations in Israel 1948–1967." PhD thesis, University of the Basque Country.
Harari, Yuval Noah. 2014. *Sapiens: A Brief History of Humankind*. London: Harvill Secker.
——. 2017. *Homo Deus: A Brief History of Tomorrow*. New York: HarperCollins.
——. 2019. *21 Lessons for the 21st Century*. New York: Vintage.
Hareven, Alouph (ed.). 1981. *One out of Every Six Israelis* (in Hebrew). Jerusalem: Van Leer Institute.
Hartman, Michelle. 2002. *Jesus, Joseph and Job: Reading Rescriptings of Religious Figures in Lebanese Women's Fiction*. Wiesbaden: Reichert Verlag.
Hartwig, Dirk. 2009. "Die 'Wissenschaft des Judentums' und die Anfänge der kritischen Koranforschung: Perspektiven einer modernen Koranhermeneutik." *Zeitschrift für Religions- und Geistesgeschichte* 61.3, pp. 234–56.
Hary, Benjamin. 2018. "Judeo-Arabic in the Arabic-Speaking World." In Benjamin Hary and Sarah Bunin Benor (eds.). *Languages in Jewish Communities Past and Present*. Berlin: Mouton de Gruyter, pp. 35–69.
Ḥasan, Ibrāhīm Ḥasan. 1967. *Ta'rīkh al-Islām*. Cairo: Maktabat al-Nahḍa.
Haskin, Mimi. 2015. "Are You an Arab or a Jew?" (Sami Shalom Chetrit)—The Jewish-Arabic Position in Hebrew Literature." *Us-China Law Review* 12, pp. 801–15.
Hayman, R. 1984. *Bertolt Brecht: The Plays*. London: Heinemann.
Herzl, Theodor. 1936. *The Jewish State: An Attempt at a Modern Solution of the Jewish Question*, trans. S. D'avigdor. London: Central Office of the Zionist Organization.
Hesse, Hermann. 1957. *Steppenwolf*, trans. Basil Creighton. New York: Holt, Rinehart & Winston.
Hever, Hannan. 1987. "Hebrew in an Israeli Arab Hand: Six Miniatures on Anton Shammas's *Arabesques*." *Cultural Critique* 7, pp. 47–76.
——. 1989. "Israeli Literature's Achilles's Heel." *Tikkun* 4.5, pp. 30–2.
——. 1991. "Minority Discourse of a National Majority: Israeli Fiction of the Early Sixties." *Prooftexts* 11, pp. 129–47.
——. 2001. *Producing the Modern Hebrew Canon: Nation-Building and Minority Discourse*. New York: New York University Press.
al-Ḥifnī, 'Abd al-Mun'im. 1980. *Mu'jam Muṣṭalaḥāt al-Ṣūfiyya*. Beirut: Dār al-Masīra.
Ḥijāzī, Aḥmad 'Abd al-Mu'ṭī. 1982. *Dīwān*. Beirut: Dār al-'Awda.
al-Hilālī, Muḥammad Muṣṭafā. 1977. "Qarāqūsh al-Muftrā 'Alayhi." *al-Dawḥa*, March, pp. 132–4.
Hill, Christopher. 1971. *Antichrist in Seventeenth-Century England*. London: Oxford University Press.
Hinske, Norbert (ed.). 1973. *Was ist Aufklärung? Beiträge aus der Berlinischen Monatsschrift*. Darmstadt: Wissenschaftliche Buchgesellschaft.
Hirschberg, H. Z. 1969. "The Oriental Jewish Communities." In Arthur J. Arberry (ed.). *Religion in the Middle East: Three Religions in Concord and Conflict*, vol. I. Cambridge: Cambridge University Press, p. 220.
Hirshberg, J. 1996. *Music in the Jewish Community of Palestine 1880–1948: A Social History*. Oxford: Oxford University Press.
Hobsbawm, Eric. 1987. *The Age of Empire 1875–1914*. London: Weidenfeld & Nicolson.
——. 1992. *Nations and Nationalism since 1780: Programme, Myth, Reality*. Cambridge: Cambridge University Press.
Hobsbawm, Eric and Ranger, Terence (eds.). 1992 [1983]. *The Invention of Tradition*. Cambridge: Cambridge University Press.

Hochman, Rami. 1988. *Jews and Arabs in Israel* (in Hebrew). Jerusalem: Hebrew University of Jerusalem.
Hoffman, Adina. 2009. *My Happiness Bears No Relation to Happiness: A Poet's Life in the Palestinian Century*. New Haven, CT: Yale University Press.
Horowitz, Danny. 1993. *Like a Troubled Bridge: Conversations with the Actors Muḥammad Bakrī, Salwā Naqqāra-Ḥaddād, Makram Khūrī, Khawla Ḥājj and Salīm Ḍaw* (in Hebrew). Beit Berl: Institute for Israeli Arab Studies.
Hottinger, Arnold. 1957. "Patriotismus und Nationalismus bei den Araben." *Neue Zurcher Zeitung*, May 12.
Hourani, Albert H. 1947. *Minorities in the Arab World*. London: Oxford University Press.
Hovsepian, Nubar. 2008. *Palestinian State Formation: Education and the Construction of National Identity*. Newcastle upon Tyne: Cambridge Scholars Publishing.
Hugo, Victor-Marie. 1937. *The Hunchback of Notre Dame*. Reading, PA: Spencer.
——. 1956 [1831]. *Notre-Dame de Paris*. Paris: Librairie Gründ.
——. 1989. *Aḥdab Notre Dame*, trans. Ramaḍān Lāwand. Beirut: Dār al-'Ilm li-l-Malāyīn.
Ḥusayn, Kamāl al- Dīn. 1993. *al-Turāth al- Sha'bī fī al-Masraḥ al-Miṣrī*. Cairo: al-Dār al-Miṣriyya al-Lubnāniyya.
Ḥusayn, Ṭāhā. 1926. *Fī al-Shi'r al-Jāhilī*. Cairo: Dār al-Kutub.
——. (ed.). 1944. *Ta'rīf al-Qudamā' bi-Abī al-'Alā'*. Cairo: Dār al-Kutub al-Miṣriyya.
——. 1974. *al-Majmū'a al-Kāmila, vol. 10—Abū al-'Alā' al-Ma'arrī*. Beirut: Dār al-Kitāb al-Lubnānī.
al-Ḥusnī, 'Abd al-Razzāq. 1974. *Ta'rīkh al-Ḥukūmāt al-'Irāqiyya*. Beirut: Maṭba'at Dār al-Kutub.
al-Ḥuṣrī, Abū Khaldūn Sāṭi'. 1965. *Yawm Maysalūn: Ṣafḥa min Ta'rīkh al-'Arab al-Ḥadīth*. Beirut: Manshūrāt Dār al-Ittiḥād.
——. 1965 [1955]. *al-'Urūba Awwalan!* Beirut: Dār al-'Ilm li-l-Malāyīn.
——. 1966. *The Day of Maysalūn: A Page from the Modern History of the Arabs—Memoirs*, trans. Sidney Glaze. Washington, DC: Middle East Institute.
——. 1966a. *Fī al-Lugha wa-l-Adab wa-'Alāqatihimā bi-l-Qawmiyya*. Beirut: Manshūrāt Dār al-Ṭalī'a.
Ibn 'Ādiyā', al-Samaw'al. 1909. *Dīwān al-Samaw'al*, ed. Louis Cheikho. Beirut: al-Maṭba'a al-Kāthūlīkiyya li-l-Ābā' al-Yasū'iyyīn.
Ibn 'Aqnin, Joseph. 1964. *Divulgatio Mysteriorum Luminumaque Apparentia*, ed. and trans. A. S. Halkin. Jerusalem: Mekize Nirdamim.
Ibn 'Arabī, Muḥyī al-Dīn (Muhyiddin). 1966. *Tarjumān al-Ashwāq*. Beirut: Dār Ṣādir.
Ibn Kammūna. 2003. *al-Tanqīḥāt fī Sharḥ al-Talwīḥāt*, ed. Hossein Ziai and Ahmed Alwishah. Costa Mesa, CA: Mazda.
Ibn Mamātī, al-As'ad. n.d. *al-Fashūsh fī Ḥukm Qarāqūsh*. Beirut: al-Maktaba al-Ḥadītha.
Ibn al-Nadīm. 1970. *The Fihrist*, ed. and trans. Bayard Dodge. New York: Columbia University Press.
——. 1985. *al-Fihrist*. al-Dawḥa, Qatar: Dār Qaṭrī ibn al-Fujā'a.
Ibn al-Rāfidayn (Salmān Dabbī). 1990. *Hāy Hiya al-Qiṣṣa Tafaḍḍalū Isma'ūhā!* Shfaram: Dār al-Mashriq.
Ibn Rashīq al-Qayrawānī. 1963. *al-'Umda*. ed. Muḥammad Muḥyī al-Dīn 'Abd al-Ḥamīd. Cairo: al-Maktaba al-Tijāriyya al-Kubrā.
Ibn Sahl al-Andalusī. 1967. *Dīwān*. Beirut: Dār Ṣādir.
Ibn Taymiyya. 1998. *Majmū'at al-Fatāwā*, ed. Āmir al-Jazzār and Anwar al-Bāz. al-Riyāḍ: Maktabat al-'Abīkān.
Ibrāhīm, George Mathias (= Israel Eliraz). 1980. *Via Bethlehem* (in Hebrew). Tel Aviv: Sifriyat Poalim.
——. 1984. *Open Mountain* (in Hebrew). Tel Aviv: Sifriyat Poalim.
Ibrāhīm, Ḥāfiẓ. n.d. [1937]. *Dīwān*, ed. Aḥmad Amīn et al. Beirut: Dār al-'Awda.

Ibsen, Henrik. 1998. *Peer Gynt: A Dramatic Poem*, trans. Christopher Fry and Johan Fillinger. Oxford: Oxford University Press.

al-ʿĪd, Yumnā. 1990. "*Arabesques*: al-Tawẓīf wa-l-Huwiyya." *al-Karmil* 35, pp. 69–92.

——. 1990a. *Tiqniyyat al-Sard al-Riwāʾī fī Ḍawʾ al-Manhaj al-Bunyawī*. Beirut: Dār al-Fārābī.

Idrīs, Muḥammad Jalāʾ. 1992. *Qaḍāyā al-Adab al-Muqārin fī Iṭār al-Dirāsāt al-Sāmiyya*. Cairo: al-Markaz al-Qawmī li-l-Dirāsāt al-ʿArabiyya wa-l-Islāmiyya.

——. 2003. *Muʾaththirāt ʿArabiyya wa-Islāmiyya fī al-Adab al-Isrāʾīlī al-Muʿāṣir*. Cairo: Dār al-Thaqāfa al-ʿArabiyya.

Idrīs, Yūsuf. n.d. [1954]. *Arkhaṣ Layālī*. Cairo: al-Dār al-Qawmiyya li-l-Ṭibāʿa wa-l-Nashr.

Ilan, Nahem. 2019. "Murād Farag as a 'Zionist Prophet' According to his Book *Al-Qudsiyyāt/Heqdeshiyyōt*." In Dov Schwartz (ed.). *Religious Zionism: History, Thought, Society*. Brighton, MA: Academic Studies Press, pp. 7–31.

Innes, Christopher. 1999. "Modernism in Drama." In Michael Levenson (ed.). *The Cambridge Companion to Modernism*. Cambridge: Cambridge University Press, pp. 130–56.

Iraqi Jews Speak for Themselves. 1969. Baghdad: Dar al-Jumhuriyah Press.

Ireland, Philip Willard. 1970 [1937]. *ʿIraq: A Study in Political Development*. New York: Russell & Russell.

al-Iṣbahānī, Abū Faraj. 1964. *Kitāb al-Aghānī*. Cairo: n.p.

al-Iskandarī, Aḥmad and al-ʿInānī, Muṣṭafā. 1931. *al-Wasīṭ fī al-Adab al-ʿArabī wa-Taʾrīkhihi*. Cairo: Maṭbaʿat al-Thākafa.

Ismāʿīl, ʿIzz al-Dīn. 1978. *al-Shiʿr al-ʿArabī al-Muʿāṣir: Qaḍāyāhu wa-Ẓawāhiruhu al-Fanniyya wa-l-Maʿnawiyya*. Cairo: Dār al-Fikr al-ʿArabī.

ʿIzz al-Dīn, Yūsuf. 1973. *al-Riwāya fī al-ʿIrāq*. Cairo: Maʿhad al-Buḥūth wa-l-Dirāsāt al-ʿArabiyya.

Jabbari, M. J. 2013. "Arabic in Iraq: A Diglossic Situation." *International Journal of Applied Linguistics and English Literature* 2.1, pp. 139–50.

Jabrā, Ibrāhīm Jabrā. 1989. *Taʾammulāt fī Bunyān Marmarī*. London: Riyāḍ al-Rayyis.

Jacobson, Abigail. 2011. "Jews Writing in Arabic: Shimon Moyal, Nissim Malul and the Mixed Palestinian/Eretz Israeli Locale." In Yuval Ben Bassat and Ginio Eyal Ginio (eds.). *Late Ottoman Palestine: The Period of Young Turk Rule*. London: I. B. Tauris, pp. 165–82.

Jacobson, Abigail and Naor, Moshe. 2016. *Oriental Neighbors: Middle Eastern Jews and Arabs in Mandatory Palestine*. Hanover, NH: Brandeis University Press.

Jamal, Amal. 2012. "Manufacturing 'Quiet Arabs' in Israel: Ethnicity, Media Frames and Soft Power." *Government and Opposition* 48.2, pp. 245–64.

Jameson, Fredric. 1972. *The Prison-House of Language: A Critical Account of Structuralism and Russian Formalism*. Princeton, NJ: Princeton University Press.

al-Janābī, ʿAbd al-Qādir. 1995. *Ḥayāt Mā Baʿda al-Yāʾ*. Paris: Manshūrāt Farādīs.

JanMohamed, A. and Lloyd, David (eds.). 1993. *The Nature and Context of Minority Discourse*. Oxford: Oxford University Press.

Jargy, Simon. 1961. "Vers une révolution dans les lettres arabes?" *Orient* 17, pp. 93–101.

Jarrar, Maher. 2011. "'A Tent for Longing': Maḥmūd Darwīsh and al-Andalus." In Ramzi Baalbaki et al. (eds.). *Poetry and History: The Value of Poetry in Reconstructing Arab History*. Beirut: American University of Beirut Press, pp. 361–93.

Jawad, Rania. 2013. "Theatre Encounters: A Politics of Performance in Palestine." PhD thesis, New York University.

al-Jawzī, Naṣrī. 1990. *Taʾrīkh al-Masraḥ al-Filasṭīnī 1918–1948*. Nicosia: Sharq Press.

Jayyusi, Salma Khadra and Allen, Roger (eds.). 1995. *Modern Arabic Drama: An Anthology*. Bloomington: Indiana University Press.

Johansson, Ola and Wallin, Johanna (eds.). 2018. *The Freedom Theatre: Performing Cultural Resistance in Palestine*. New Delhi: LeftWord.

Joyaux, Georges J. 1980. "Driss Chraïbi, Mohammed Dib, Kateb Yacine, and Indigenous North African Literature." In Issa J. Boullata (ed.). *Critical Perspectives on Modern Arabic Literature*. Washington, DC: Three Continents Press, pp. 117–27.
Joyce, James. 1922. *Ulysses*. Paris: Shakespeare.
——. 1991. *Dubliners*. London: Everyman.
al-Ju'aydī, Muḥammad 'Abd Allāh. 2000. "Ḥuḍūr al-Andalus fī al-Adab al-Filasṭīnī al-Ḥadīth." *'Ālām al-Fikr* 28.4, pp. 7–52.
Jubrān, Sulaymān. 2002–2003. "Wadī' al-Bustānī: Shā'ir Filasṭīnī min Lubnān." *al-Karmil: Studies in Arabic Language and Literature* 23/24, pp. 59–61.
Judt, Tony. 2010. *Ill Fares the Land*. New York: Penguin.
al-Jundī, In'ām. 1979. *al-Rā'id fī al-Adab al-'Arabī*. Beirut: Dār al-Rā'id al-'Arabī.
Kahanoff, Jacqueline. 1978. *From the East Sun* (in Hebrew). Tel Aviv: Yariv.
Kanazi, George. 1989. "Ideologies in the Palestinian Literature in Israel" (in Hebrew). *HaMizrah HeHadash* 32, pp. 129–38.
Kant, Immanuel. 1996. "An Answer to the Question: What Is Enlightenment?" trans. James Schmidt. In James Schmidt (ed.). *What Enlightenment? Eighteenth-Century Answers and Twentieth-Century Questions*. Berkeley: University of California Press, pp. 58–64.
Kartomi, Margaret. 2002. "Continuity and Change in the Music-Culture of the Baghdadi-Jews Throughout Two Diasporas in the Colonial and Post-Colonial Periods: An Introduction." *Australian Journal of Jewish Studies* 16, pp. 90–110.
Kashua, Sayed (Sayyid Qashshū'a). 2002. *Dancing Arabs* (in Hebrew). Ben-Shemen: Modan.
——. 2004. *Let It Be Morning* (in Hebrew). Jerusalem: Keter.
——. 2006. *Let It Be Morning*, trans. Miriam Shlesinger. New York: Black Cat.
——. 2010. *Second Person Singular* (in Hebrew). Jerusalem: Keter.
——. 2013. *Second Person Singular*, trans. Mitch Ginsburg. New York: Grove Press.
——. 2015. *Native* (in Hebrew). Jerusalem: Keter.
——. 2016. *Native: Dispatches from an Israeli-Palestinian Life*, trans. Ralph Mandel. New York: Grove Press.
——. 2017. *Track Changes* (in Hebrew). Shoham: Kinneret, Zmora, Dvir.
——. 2020. *Track Changes*, trans. Mitch Ginsburg. New York: Grove Press.
Kassabova, Kapka. 2007. *Geography for the Lost*. Auckland: Auckland University Press.
al-Kātib, Sālim. 1959. *Washwashāt al-Fajr* (*The Whispers of the Dawn*). Tel Aviv: Maṭba'at Davar.
Katsumata, Naoya. 2002. "The Style of the *Maqāma*: Arabic, Persian, Hebrew, Syriac." *Arabic and Middle Eastern Literatures* 5.2, pp. 117–37.
Kattan, Emmanuel. 2017. *Naïm Kattan. Entretiens*. Montreal: Boreal.
Kattan (Qaṭṭān), Naim (Naïm, Na'īm). 1975. *Adieu babylone*. Montreal: Julliard.
——. 1980. *Farewell, Babylon*, trans. Sheila Fischman. New York: Taplinger.
——. 1999. *Wadā'an Bābil*, trans. Ādam Fatḥī. Cologne: Al-Kamel Verlag.
——. 2006. *Farīda*, trans. Ādam Fatḥī. Cologne: Al-Kamel Verlag.
Kayyal, Mahmoud. 2000. "Translational Norms in the Translations of Modern Hebrew Literature into Arabic between 1948 and 1990." PhD thesis, Tel Aviv University.
——. 2006. *Translation in the Shadow of Confrontation: Norms in the Translations of Modern Hebrew Literature into Arabic between 1948 and 1990* (in Hebrew). Jerusalem: Magnes Press.
——. 2006a. *Israeli Culture in Arab Eyes: Stereotyping and Normalization* (in Hebrew). Tel Aviv: Tel Aviv University Press.
——. 2008. "'Arabs Dancing in a New Light of Arabesques': Minor Hebrew Works of Palestinian Authors in the Eyes of Critics." *Middle Eastern Literatures* 11.1, pp. 31–51.
——. 2016. *Selected Issues in the Modern Intercultural Contacts between Arabic and Hebrew Cultures: Hebrew, Arabic, and Death*. Leiden: Brill.

Kazzaz, Nissim. 1991. *The Jews in Iraq in the Twentieth Century* (in Hebrew). Jerusalem: Ben-Zvi Institute for the Study of Jewish Communities in the East.

Kearny, Jonathan. 2010–2011. "The Torah of Israel in the Tongue of Ishmael: Saadia Gaon and His Arabic Translation of the Pentateuch." *Proceedings of the Irish Biblical Association* 33/34, pp. 55–75.

Kedourie, Elie. 1974. *Arabic Political Memoirs and Other Studies*. London: Frank Cass.

——. 1989. "The Break between Muslims and Jews in Iraq." In Mark R. Cohen and Abraham L. Udovitch (eds.). *Jews among Arabs: Contacts and Boundaries*. Princeton, NJ: Darwin Press, pp. 21–63.

Kedourie, Sylvia (ed.). 1998. *Elie Kedourie CBE, FBA 1926–1992: History, Philosophy, Politics*. London: Frank Cass.

Kellner, Douglas. 1991. "Popular Culture and the Construction of Postmodern Identities." In Scott Lash and Jonathan Friedman (eds.). *Modernity and Identity*. Oxford: Blackwell, pp. 141–77.

Kennedy, Ann. 1997. "Inappropriate and Dazzling Sideshows: Interpellating Narratives in Djuna Barnes's Nightwood." *Post Identity* 1.1, pp. 94–112.

Kerbel, Sorrel (ed.). 2003. *Jewish Writers of the Twentieth Century*. New York: Fitzroy Dearborn.

Khabbaza, Albert. 2010. *The Last Tango in Baghdad*. Bloomington, IN: Authorhouse.

Khaḍḍūrī, Shā'ul. 1999. *Rā'in wa-Ra'iyya: Sīrat Ḥayāt al-Khākhām Sāsūn Khaḍḍūrī*. Jerusalem: Rābiṭat al-Jāmi'iyyīn al-Yahūd al-Nāziḥīn min al-'Irāq.

al-Khatib, Taqadum. 2020. *Die Juden in Ägypten (1915–1952): Korrelation von Sprache und Minderheit*. Wiesbaden: Harrassowitz Verlag.

——. 2020a. "A Historical Perspective on the Relationship between the State and Minorities in Egypt: Lessons from the Interwar Jewish Case." *Rowaq Arabi* 25.2, pp. 39–51.

Khazzoom, Aziza. 2003. "The Great Chain of Orientalism: Jewish Identity, Stigma Management, and Ethnic Exclusion in Israel." *American Sociological Review* 68.4, pp. 481–510.

al-Khozai, M. A. 1984. *The Development of Early Arabic Drama (1847–1900)*. London: Longman.

Khūrī (Khoury), Jiryis (Jeries) Na'īm. 1999. "al-Ughniyya al-Sha'biyya al-Filasṭīniyya fī al-Jalīl." MA thesis, University of Haifa.

——. 2014. "'Law Wulidta': Qaṣīda Ḍubiṭat 'Āriya! Muqāraba Naqdiyya li-Naṣṣ Darwīshī," available at: https://www.assawsana.com/portal/pages.php?newsid=175570, last accessed August 3, 2020.

Khūrshīd, Fārūq. 1991. *al-Judhūr al-Sha'biyya li-l-Masraḥ al-'Arabī*. Cairo: al-Hay'a al-Miṣriyya al-'Āmma li-l-Kitāb.

Kidron, Peretz. 2004. *Refusenik! Israel's Soldiers of Conscience*. London: Zed Books.

Kilito, Abdelfattah. 1994. "Dog Words." In Angelika Bammer (ed.). *Displacements: Cultural Identities in Question*. Bloomington: Indiana University Press, pp. xxi–xxxi.

——. 2020. *Fī Jaww min al-Nadam al-Fikrī*. Milan: Manshūrāt al-Mutawassaṭ.

Kilpatrick, Hilary. 1998. "The 'Genuine' Ash'ab: The Relativity of Fact and Fiction in Early *Adab* Texts." In Stefan Leder (ed.). *Story-Telling in the Framework of Non-Fictional Arabic Literature*. Wiesbaden: Harrassowitz Verlag, pp. 94–117.

Kirmanj, Sherko. 2010. "The Clash of Identities in Iraq." In Amatzia Baram et al. *Iraq between Occupations Perspectives from 1920 to the Present*. New York: Palgrave Macmillan, pp. 43–59.

Kishtainy, Khalid. 1985. *Arab Political Humour*. London: Quartet.

Kister, M. J. 1999. "'Exert Yourselves, O Banū Arfida!': Some Notes on Entertainment in the Islamic Tradition." *Jerusalem Studies in Arabic and Islam* 23, pp. 53–78.

Klasova, Pamela. 2019. "Reacting to Muḥammad: Three Early Islamic Poets in the *Kitāb al-Aghānī*." *Al-'Uṣūr al-Wusṭā* 27, pp. 40–111.

Klein, Menachem. 2017. "The Twenty-First-Century New Critical Historians." *Israel Studies Review* 32.2, pp. 146–63.

Knox, Ronald A. 1951. *Enthusiasm*. Oxford: Clarendon.

Kojaman, Yeheskel. 2001. *The Maqam Music Tradition of Iraq*. London: Author's Publication.

Korsgaard, Christine. 1996. *The Sources of Normativity*. Cambridge: Cambridge University Press.

Kracauer, Siegfried. 1995. *The Mass Ornament: Weimar Essays*, trans. Thomas Y. Levin. Cambridge, MA: Harvard University Press.

Kraemer, J. L. 1984. "The Culture Bearers of Humanism in the Renaissance of Islam." Annual Lecture, Irene Halmos Chair of Arabic Literature, Tel Aviv University, pp. 3–19.

Krämer, Gudrun. 1987. "Political Participation of the Jews of Egypt between World War I and the 1952 Revolution." In Shimon Shamir (ed.). *The Jews of Egypt: A Mediterranean Society in Modern Times*. Boulder, CO: Westview Press, pp. 68–82.

——. 1989. *The Jews in Modern Egypt, 1914–1952*. London: I. B. Tauris.

Kramer, Martin. 1999. "The Road from Mecca: Muhammad Asad (Born Leopold Weiss)." In Martin Kramer (ed.). *The Jewish Discovery of Islam*. Tel Aviv: Moshe Dayan Center for Middle Eastern and African Studies, Tel Aviv University, pp. 225–47.

Kritz, Reuven. 1990. *Miscellany* (in Hebrew). Tel Aviv: Pura.

Kudryashova, Irina. 2010. "State-Building in the Arab Middle East: From Ummah to a Nation?." In Krzysztof Kościelniak (ed.). *Change and Stability: State, Religion and Politics in the Contemporary Middle East and North Africa*. Krakow: UNUM Publishing, pp. 47–57.

Kurzweil, Ray. 2005. *The Singularity Is Near: When Humans Transcend Biology*. New York: Viking.

al-Kutubī, Ibn Shākir. 1951. *Fawāt al-Wafayāt*, ed. Muḥammad Muḥyī al-Dīn 'Abd al-Ḥamīd. Cairo: Maktabat al-Nahḍa al-Miṣriyya.

Laâbi, Abdellatif. 1970. *La poésie palestinienne de combat*. Honfleur: Pierre Jean Oswald.

Landau, J. M. 1958. *Studies in the Arab Theatre and Cinema*. Philadelphia: University of Pennsylvania Press.

Landshut, Siegfried. 1950. *Jewish Communities in the Muslim Countries of the Middle East*. London: Jewish Chronicle.

Lane, Edward William. 1954 [1908]. *Manners and Customs of the Modern Egyptians*. London: Dent.

Laskier, Michael M. 1992. *The Jews of Egypt, 1920–1970: In the Midst of Zionism, Anti-Semitism, and the Middle East Conflict*. New York: New York University Press.

Lassner, Jacob. 1993. *Demonizing the Queen of Sheba: Boundaries of Gender and Culture in Postbiblical Judaism and Medieval Islam*. Chicago: University of Chicago Press.

Laṭīf, Māzin. 2011. *Yahūd al-'Irāq: Mawsū'a Shāmila li-Ta'rīkh Yahūd al-'Irāq wa-Shakhṣiyyātihim wa-Dawrihim fī Ta'rīkh al-'Irāq al-Ḥadīth*. Baghdad: Dār Mesopotamia.

——. 2013. *Dawrat al-Qamar al-Qaṣīra li-Yahūd al-'Irāq: al-Buzūgh wa-l-Ufūl fī Ta'rīkh al-'Irāq al-Ḥadīth*. Baghdad: Dār Mesopotamia.

Lattas, Andrew. 1991. "Primitivism in Deleuze and Guattari's 'A Thousand Plateaus.'" *Social 68 Analysis: International Journal of Social and Cultural Practice* 30, pp. 98–115.

La Vérité sur la question syrienne. 1916. Stamboul: Imprimerie Tanine.

Lavie, Smadar. 1996. "Blowups in the Borderzones: Third World Israeli Authors' Gropings for Home." In Smadar Lavie and Ted Swedenborg (eds.). *Displacement, Diaspora and Geographies of Identity*. Durham, NC: Duke University Press, pp. 55–96.

Layish, Aharon. 1985. "*Taqiyya* among the Druzes." *Asian and African Studies* (Jerusalem) 19, pp. 245–81.

Lazarus-Yafeh, Hava. 1992. *Intertwined Worlds: Medieval Islam and Bible Criticism.* Princeton, NJ: Princeton University Press.

Levi, Tomer. 2012. *The Jews of Beirut: The Rise of a Levantine Community, 1860s–1930s.* New York: Peter Lang.

Levy, Lital. 2003. "Exchanging Words: Thematization of Translation in Arabic Writing in Israel." *Comparative Studies of South Asia, Africa and the Middle East* 23.1/2, pp. 93–114.

——. 2007. "Jewish Writers in the Arab East: Literature, History, and the Politics of Enlightenment, 1863–1914." PhD thesis, University of California, Berkeley.

——. 2013. "The *Nahda* and the *Haskala*: A Comparative Reading of 'Revival' and 'Reform.'" *Middle Eastern Literatures* 16.3, pp. 300–16.

——. 2013a. "Partitioned Pasts: Arab Jewish Intellectuals and the Case of Esther Azharī Moyal (1873–1948)." In Dyala Hamzah (ed.). *The Making of the Arab Intellectual Empire: Public Sphere and the Colonial Coordinates of Selfhood.* New York: Routledge, pp. 128–63.

——. 2014. *Poetic Trespass: Writing between Hebrew and Arabic in Israel/Palestine.* Princeton, NJ: Princeton University Press.

——. 2017. "The Arab Jew Debates: Media, Culture, Politics, History." *Journal of Levantine Studies* 7, pp. 79–103.

Levy, Lital and Schachter, Allison. 2015. "Jewish Literature/World Literature: Between the Local and the Transnational." *PMLA* 130, pp. 92–109.

——. and Schachter, Allison. 2017. "A Non-Universal Global: On Jewish Writing and World Literature." *Prooftexts* 36.1/2, pp. 1–26.

Lewis, Arnold. 1985. "Phantom Ethnicity: 'Oriental Jews' in Israeli Society." In Alex Weingrod (ed.). *Studies in Israeli Ethnicity after the Ingathering.* New York: Gordon & Breach, pp. 133–58.

Lewis, Bernard. 1968. *The Middle East and the West.* London: Weidenfeld & Nicolson.

——. 1973. *Islam in History: Ideas, Men and Events in the Middle East.* London: Alcove Press.

——. 1984. *The Jews of Islam.* Princeton NJ: Princeton University Press.

——. 1984a. "The Judeo-Islamic Heritage" (in Hebrew). *Pe'amim: Studies in Oriental Jewry* 20, pp. 3–13.

——. 2003. *What Went Wrong? The Clash between Islam and Modernity in the Middle East.* New York: Perennial.

Lifton, Robert Jay. 1993. *The Protean Self: Human Resilience in an Age of Fragmentation.* New York: Basic Books.

Linkenbach, Antje and Mulsow, Martin. 2020. "Introduction: The Dividual Self." In Martin Fuchs et al. (eds.). *Religious Individualisation: Historical Dimensions and Comparative Perspectives.* Berlin: Mouton de Gruyter, pp. 323–43.

Litvak, Meir (ed.). 2009. *Palestinian Collective Memory and National Identity.* New York: Palgrave Macmillan.

Lloyd, David. 1987. *Nationalism and Minor Literature: James Clarence Mangan and the Emergence of Irish Cultural Nationalism.* Berkeley: University of California Press.

Lockard, Joe. 2002. "Somewhere between Arab and Jew: Ethnic Re-Identification in Modern Hebrew Literature." *Middle Eastern Literatures* 5.1, pp. 49–62.

Locker-Biletzki, Amir. 2013. "The Holidays of the Revolution: Myth, Ritual and Identity among Tel Aviv Communists, 1919–1965." PhD thesis, University of Guelph.

López-Baralt, Luce. 2006. "Islamic Influence on Spanish Literature: Benengeli's Pen in 'Don Quixote.'" *Islamic Studies* 45.4, pp. 579–93.

López-Calvo, Ignacio. 2019. "The Afterlife of al-Andalus: Muslim Iberia in Contemporary Arab and Hispanic Narratives." *Review: Literature and Arts of the Americas* 52.2, pp. 274–8.

López-Morillas, C. 2000. "Language." In Maria Rosa Menocal et al. (eds.). *The Cambridge*

History of Arabic Literature: The Literature of al-Andalus. Cambridge: Cambridge University Press, pp. 33–59.
Luks, Harold P. 1977. "Iraqi Jews during World War II." *Wiener Library Bulletin* 30, NS 43/44, pp. 30–9.
Lu'lu'a, 'Abd al-Wāḥid. 1973. *al-Baḥth 'an Ma'na*. Baghdad: Dār al-Ḥurriyya.
Lyall, Charles James (ed.). 1930. *Translation of Ancient Arabian Poetry*. London: Williams & Norgate.
al-Ma'āḍīdī, 'Iṣām Jum'a Aḥmad. 2001. *al-Ṣiḥāfa al-Yahūdiyya fī al-'Irāq*. Cairo: Dār al-Dawliyya li-l-Ithtithmārāt al-Thaqāfiyya.
Maalouf, Amin. 2000. *On Identity*, trans. Barbara Bray. London: Harvill Press.
MacDonald, Margaret Read (ed.). 1999. *Traditional Storytelling Today*. London: Fitzroy Dearborn.
Mackenzie, Catriona and Atkins, Kim. 2008. *Practical Identity and Narrative Agency*. New York: Routledge.
Mahdī, Sāmī. 1995. *Al-Majallāt al-'Irāqiyya al-Riyādiyya wa-Dawruhā fī Taḥdīth al-Adab wa-l-Fann 1945–1958*. Baghdad: Dār al-Shu'ūn al-Thaqāfiyya al-'Āmma.
Mahmoud, Amel A. 2017. "The Unsettled Space of Identity Formation in Samir Naqqash's *Shlomo al-Kurdi, Myself and Time*." In Jyotsna G. Singh and David D. Kim (eds.). *The Postcolonial World*. London: Routledge, pp. 86–94.
Majīd, 'Abd al-Mun'im. 1972. *Ta'rīkh al-Ḥaḍāra al-Islāmiyya fī al-'Uṣūr al-Wusṭā*. Cairo: Maktabat al-Anglo al-Miṣriyya.
al-Malā'ika, Nāzik. 1983 [1962]. *Qaḍāyā al-Shi'r al-Mu'āṣir*. Beirut: Dār al-'Ilm li-l-Malāyīn.
Malinovich, Nadia. 2019. "Growing up in Interwar Iraq: The Memoirs of Naim Kattan and Heskel Haddad." *Journal of Jewish Identities* 12.1, pp. 19–36.
Manasseh, Sara. 1999. "Women in Music Performance: The Iraqi Jewish Experience in Israel." PhD thesis, Goldsmiths, University of London.
Manṣūr, Anīs. 1983. *Fī Ṣālūn al-'Aqqād Kānat Lanā Ayyām*. Beirut: Dār al-Shurūq.
Manṣūr, 'Aṭāllāh. 1962. *Wa-Baqiyat Samīra*. Tel Aviv: Dār al-Nashr al-'Arabī.
——. 1966. *In a New Light* (in Hebrew). Tel Aviv: Karni.
——. 1969. *In a New Light*, trans. Abraham Birman. London: Vallentine & Mitchell.
——. 1992. "Reach Thy Neighbor: Arabs Writing Hebrew." *Bulletin of the Israeli Academic Center in Cairo* 16, pp. 63–6.
al-Maqqarī, Aḥmad ibn Muḥammad. 1968. *Nafḥ al-Ṭīb fī Ghuṣn al-Andalus al-Raṭīb*, ed. Iḥsān 'Abbās. Beirut: Dār Ṣādir.
Mariani, Philomena (ed.). 1991. *Critical Fictions: The Politics of Imaginative Writing*. Seattle, WA: Bay Press.
Mar'i, Abd Al-Rahman. 2013. *Walla, Beseder: A Linguistic Profile of the Arabs in Israel* (in Hebrew). Jerusalem: Keter.
Marinetti, F. T. 2006. *Critical Writings*, ed. Günter Berghaus; trans. Doug Thompson. New York: Farrar, Straus & Giroux.
Marmorstein, Emile. 1959. "Two Iraqi Jewish Short Story Writers: A Suggestion for Social Research." *Jewish Journal of Sociology* 1.2, pp. 187–200.
——. 1964. "An Iraqi Jewish Writer in the Holy Land." *Jewish Journal of Sociology* 6.1, pp. 91–102.
——. 1988. "Hakham Sasson in 1949." *Middle Eastern Studies*, pp. 364–8.
Marom, Yafit. 2005. "Al-Maydān Theatre in Haifa: From Original Text to Performance" (in Hebrew). MA thesis, University of Haifa.
Marquez, Gabriel Garcia. 1983. *Chronicle of a Death Foretold*, trans. Gregory Rabassa. New York: Alfred A. Knopf.
Marr, Phebe A. 1966. "Yasin al-Hashimi: The Rise and Fall of a Nationalist." PhD thesis, Harvard University.
——. 1985. *The Modern History of Iraq*. Boulder, CO: Westview Press.
——. 2010. "One Iraq or Many: What Has Happened to Iraqi Identity?" In Amatzia

Baram et al. (eds.). *Iraq Between Occupations Perspectives from 1920 to the Present.* New York: Palgrave Macmillan, pp. 15–41.

Maʿrūf, Khaldūn Nājī. 1976. *al-Aqalliyya al-Yahūdiyya fī al-ʿIrāq Bayna Sanat 1921 wa-1952.* Baghdad: al-Dār al-ʿArabiyya li-l-Ṭibāʿa wa-l-Nashr.

al-Mashhadānī, Saʿd Salmān ʿAbd Allāh. 1999. *al-Nashāṭ al-Diʿāʾī li-l-Yahūd fī al-ʿIrāq 1921–1952.* Cairo: Madbūlī.

——. 2001. *al-Diʿāya al-Ṣihyūniyya fī al-ʿIrāq 1921–1952.* Baghdad: Dār al-Shuʾūn al-Thaqāfiyya al-ʿĀmma.

Masliyah, Sadok H. 1989. "Zionism in Iraq." *Middle Eastern Studies* 25, pp. 216–37.

al-Maṭbaʿī, Ḥamīd. 1995–1996. *Mawsūʿat Aʿlām al-ʿIrāq fī al-Qarn al-ʿIshrīn.* Baghdad: Dār al-Shuʾūn al-Thaqāfiyya al-ʿĀmma.

al-Maydānī, Aḥmad ibn Muḥammad. 1988. *Majmaʿ al-Amthāl*, ed. Naʿīm Ḥusayn Zarzūr. Beirut: Dār al-Kutub al-ʿIlmiyya.

Mayer, Tamar. (ed.). 2000. *Gender Ironies of Nationalism: Sexing the Nation.* London: Routledge.

McAuliffe, Jane Dammen. 1998. "Assessing the *Isrāʾīliyyāt*: An Exegetical Conudrum." In Stefan Leder (ed.). *Story-Telling in the Framework of Non-Fictional Arabic Literature.* Wiesbaden: Harrassowitz Verlag, pp. 345–69.

McCrum, Robert. 2010. *Globish: How the English Language Became the World's Language.* New York: W. W. Norton.

McKibben, Bill. 2007. *Deep Economy: The Wealth of Communities and the Durable Future.* New York: Times Books.

Meddeb, Abdelwahab and Stora, Benjamin. 2013. *A History of Jewish–Muslim Relations: From the Origins to the Present Day*, trans. Jane Marie Todd and Michael B. Smith. Princeton, NJ: Princeton University Press.

Medoff, Rafael and Waxman, Chaim I. 2009. *The A to Z of Zionism.* Toronto: Scarecrow Press.

Meir (Meir-Glitzenstein), Esther. 1993. *Zionism and the Jews in Iraq 1941–1950* (in Hebrew). Tel Aviv: Am Oved.

——. 2002. "Our Dowry: Identity and Memory among Iraqi Immigrants in Israel." *Middle Eastern Studies* 38.2, pp. 165–86.

——. 2015. "A Different Mizrahi Story: How the Iraqis Became Israelis." In Fran Markowitz et al. (eds.). *Toward an Anthropology of Nation Building and Unbuilding in Israel.* Lincoln: University of Nebraska Press, pp. 107–21.

Meir, Yosef. 1973. *Beyond the Desert: Underground Activities In Iraq 1941–1951* (in Hebrew). Tel Aviv: Ministry of Defence.

——. 1989. *Socio-Cultural Development of Iraqi Jews from 1830 till Our Days* (in Hebrew). Tel Aviv: Naharayim.

Meisami, Julie Scott and Starkey, Paul (eds.). 1998. *Encyclopaedia of Arabic Literature.* London: Routledge.

Melucci, Alberto. 1997. "Identity and Difference in a Globalized World." In Pnina Werbner and Tariq Modood (eds.). *Debating Cultural Hybridity: Multi-Cultural Identities and the Politics of Anti-Racism.* London: Zed Books, pp. 58–69.

Memmi, Albert. 1966. *La statue de sel.* Paris: Gallimard.

——. 2013. *The Pillar of Salt*, trans. Edouard Roditi. Lexington, MA: Plunkett Lake Press.

Mendel, Yonatan. 2014. *The Creation of Israeli Arabic: Political and Security Considerations in the Making of Arabic Language Studies in Israel.* New York: Palgrave Macmillan.

——. 2020. *Language out of Place: Orientalism, Intelligence and Arabic in Israel* (in Hebrew). Jeruslaem: Van Leer Institute.

——. 2021. "The De-Arabised Israeli Arabic: Between Eradication among Arab-Jews and Ashkenisation in Society." In Reem Bassiouney and Keith Walters (eds.). *The Routledge Handbook of Arabic and Identity.* New York: Routledge, pp. 218–30.

Mendelson-Maoz, Adia. 2014. *Multiculturalism in Israel: Literary Perspectives*. West Lafayette, IN: Purdue University Press.
——. 2019. "Palestine, My Love: Place and Home in the Literary Works of Sayed Kashua" (in Hebrew). *Iyunim: Multidisciplinary Studies in Israeli and Modern Jewish Society* 32, pp. 137–64.
Mendes-Flohr, Paul and Reinharz, Jehuda (eds.). 1980. *The Jew in the Modern World: A Documentary History*. New York: Oxford University Press.
Menocal, Maria Rosa. 1987. *The Arabic Role in Medieval Literary History*. Philadelphia: University of Pennsylvania Press.
——. 2002. *The Ornament of the World*. Boston, MA: Little, Brown.
Mestyan, Adam. 2016. "Muḥammad Yūsuf Najm (1925–2009): A Maker of the *Nahḍa*." *Al-Abhath* 64, pp. 97–118.
Miccoli, Dario. 2014. "Di generazione in generazione: 'Almog Behar e la letteratura mizrahi in Israele." *Annali di Ca' Foscari* 50, pp. 15–36.
Michael (Mīkhā'īl), Sami (Sāmī) (trans.). 1974. *Equal and More Equal* (in Hebrew). Tel Aviv: Bustan.
——. 1975. *Storm among the Palms* (in Hebrew). Tel Aviv: Am Oved.
——. 1977. *Refuge* (in Hebrew). Tel Aviv: Am Oved.
——. 1979. *A Handful of Fog* (in Hebrew). Tel Aviv: Am Oved.
——. 1987. *A Trumpet in the Wadi* (in Hebrew). Tel Aviv: Am Oved.
——. 1990. *Love among the Palms* (in Hebrew). Jerusalem: Domino.
——. 1993. *Brown Devils* (in Hebrew). Tel Aviv: Yedi'ot Aḥronoth.
——. 1993a. *Victoria* (in Hebrew). Tel Aviv: Am Oved.
——. 1997. *Tin Shacks and Dreams* (in Hebrew). Tel Aviv: Am Oved.
——. 2005. *Fīktūryā*, trans. Samīr Naqqqāsh. Cologne: Manshūrāt al-Jamal.
Mīkhā'īl, Murād. 1988. *al-A'māl al-Shi'riyya al-Kāmila*. Tel Aviv: Dār al-Sharq.
Miletić, Tijana. 2008. *European Literary Immigration into the French Language: Readings of Gary, Kristof, Kundera and Semprun*. Amsterdam: Rodopi.
Miller, Carolyn. 1993. "Rhetoric and Community: The Problem of the One and the Many." In Theresa Enos and Stuart C. Brown (eds.). *Defining the New Rhetorics*. Newbury Park, CA: Sage, pp. 79–92.
Miron, Dan. 2005. *From Continuity to Contiguity: Towards a New Theorizing of Jewish Literatures* (in Hebrew). Tel Aviv: Am Oved.
Miron, Guy. 2006. "Between Berlin and Baghdad: The Study of the History of Iraqi Jews and the Challenge of Combined Historiography." *Zion* 61.1, pp. 73–98.
Mitchell, Stephen A. 1993. *Hope and Dread in Psychoanalysis*. New York: Basic Books.
Montávez, Pedro Martínez. 1992. *Al-Andalus, España, en la literatura árabe contemporánea*. Madrid: MAPFRE.
Moosa, Matti. 1974. "Ya'qūb Ṣanū' and the Rise of Arab Drama in Egypt." *International Journal of Middle East Studies* 5, pp. 401–33.
Morad, Tamar et al. (eds.). 2008. *Iraq's Last Jews: Stories of Daily Life, Upheaval, and Escape from Modern Babylon*. New York: Palgrave Macmillan.
Moreh, Shmuel. 1958. "Arabic Literature in Israel" (in Hebrew). *Hamizrah He-Hadash* 9.1/2 (33/34), pp. 26–40.
——. 1967. "Arabic Literature in Israel." *Middle Eastern Studies* 3.3, pp. 283–94.
——. 1973. "The Neoclassical *Qaṣīda*: Modern Poets and Critics." In Gustave E. von Grunebaum (ed.). *Arabic Poetry: Theory and Development*. Wiesbaden: Harrassowitz Verlag, pp. 155–79.
——. 1973a. *Arabic Works by Jewish Writers 1863–1973*. Jerusalem: Ben-Zvi Institute for the Study of Jewish Communities in the East.
——. 1974. *Bibliography of Arabic Books and Periodicals Published in Israel 1948–1972*. Jerusalem: Hebrew University of Jerusalem.

——. 1975. "al-Ṭaba' al-Dhātī li-Qiṣaṣ Isḥāq Bār Moshe's Stories." *al-Sharq*, April/May, pp. 43–58.

——. 1976. *Modern Arabic Poetry 1800–1970*. Leiden: Brill.

——. 1978. "The Intellectual Production of Iraqi Jews in the Arabic Language" (in Hebrew). In Jacob Mansour (ed.). *Arabic and Islamic Studies* (in Hebrew). Ramat Gan: Bar-Ilan University, II, pp. 60–8.

——. (ed.). 1981. *al-Qiṣṣa al-Qaṣīra 'Inda Yahūd al-'Irāq*. Jerusalem: Magnes Press.

——. (ed.). 1982. *Mukhtārāt min Ash'ār Yahūd al-'Irāq al-Ḥadīth*. Jerusalem: Akademon.

——. 1984. "Town and Country in Modern Arabic Poetry from Shawqī to al-Sayyāb." *Asian and African Studies* (Jerusalem) 18, pp. 161–85.

——. 1987. "Ya'qūb Ṣanū': His Religious Identity and Work in the Theater and Journalism, according to the Family Archive." In Shimon Shamir (ed.). *The Jews of Egypt: A Mediterranean Society in Modern Times*. Boulder, CO: Westview Press, pp. 111–29.

——. 1988. *Studies in Modern Arabic Prose and Poetry*. Leiden: Brill.

——. 1992. *Live Theatre and Dramatic Literature in the Medieval Arabic World*. Edinburgh: Edinburgh University Press.

——. 2012. *Baghdād Ḥabībatī: Yahūd al-'Irāq – Dhikrayāt wa-Shujūn*. Haifa: Maktabat Kull Shay'.

Moreh, Shmuel and 'Abbāsī, Maḥmūd. 1987. *Tarājim wa-Āthār fī al-Adab al-'Arabī fī Isrā'īl 1948–1986*. Shfaram: Dār al-Mashriq.

Moreh, Shmuel and Hakak, Lev. 1981. "Literary and Scholarly Works of Iraqi Jews in Iraq and Israel" (in Hebrew). In Shumuel Moreh (ed.). *Studies on the History and Culture of Iraqi Jews* (in Hebrew). Or-Yehuda: Center for the Heritage of Iraqi Jewry, pp. 296–345.

Moreh, Shmuel and Sadgrove, Philip C. 1996. *Jewish Contributions to Nineteenth-Century Arabic Theater*. Oxford: Oxford University Press.

al-Mu'allim, Idwār (ed.). 2020. *Firqat Masraḥ al-Ḥakawātī al-Filasṭīnī: al-Masraḥiyyāt al-Ūlā 1978–1985*. Jerusalem: n.p.

Mu'allim, Izzat Sāsūn. 1983. *Ba'īd ... Wa ... Qarīb: Dhikrayāt wa-Ḥikāyāt min al-Furāt al-Awsaṭ 1911–1983*. Shfaram: Dār al-Mashriq.

Mudhi, M. H. 1988. "The Origin and Development of the Iraqi-Jewish Short Story from 1922 to 1972." PhD thesis, University of Exeter.

Muehlethaler, Lukas. 2020. "Teaching Literatures by Arabized Jews: Medieval and Modern." In Susanne Zepp et al. (eds.). *Disseminating Jewish Literatures: Knowledge, Research, Curricula*. Berlin: Mouton de Gruyter, pp. 45–52.

Muḥsin, Fātin Muḥyī. 2010. *Mīr Baṣrī: Sīra wa-Turāth*. Baghdad: Dār Mesopotamia.

Munayer, S. J. 1998. "The Ethnic Identity of Palestinian Arab Christian Adolescents in Israel." PhD thesis, University of Sussex.

Murre-van den Berg, Heleen. 2016. "The Language of the Nation: The Rise of Arabic among Jews and Christians (1900–1950)." *British Journal of Middle Eastern Studies* 43.2, pp. 176–90.

——. 2016a. "Searching for Common Ground: Jews and Christians in the Modern Middle East." In Sasha Rachel Goldstein-Sabbah and Heleen Murre-van den Berg (eds.). *Modernity, Minority, and the Public Sphere: Jews and Christians in the Middle East*. Leiden: Brill, pp. 3–38.

al-Musawi, Muhsin Jasim. 2020. "Canons, Thefts, and Palimpsests in the Arabic Literary Tradition." *Journal of Arabic Literature* 51, pp. 165–88.

Mustafa, F. 1997. "Comparative Study of Modern and Classic Styles of Story-Telling in Arabic Literature." MA thesis, University of Manchester.

Mustafa, Gharbi M. 2008. "Kurdish Identity in Samir Naqqāŝ's. Shlomo al-Kurdi, wa-anā wa-az-zamān." *Rocznik Orientalistyczny* 61.2, pp. 58–68.

Mustafa, Shakir. 2008. *Contemporary Iraqi Fiction: An Anthology*. Syracuse, NY: Syracuse University Press.

al-Najmī, Kamāl. 1993. *Turāth al-Ghinā' al-'Arabī*. Cairo: Dār al-Shurūq.

Nakhle-Cerruti, Najla. 2019. "La Palestine sur scène: Une approche géocritique du théâtre palestinien (2006–2016)." PhD thesis, Sorbonne Paris Cité University.

——. 2020. "L'apport du Fonds François Abou Salem à la connaissance des débuts de la pratique théâtrale palestinienne dans les années 1970." *Arabica* 67, pp. 611–29.

al-Naqqāsh, Rajā'. 1991. "Al-Ḥubb wa-l-'Adl wa-l-Sulṭān al-Jadīd." In *Samīḥ al-Qāsīm fī Dā'irat al-Naqd*. Kafr Qara': Dār al-Hudā, vol. 7 of the *Completed Works*, pp. 109–22.

Naqqāsh, Samīr. 1986. *Nzūla wa-Khayṭ al-Shayṭān: Riwāya 'Irāqiyya*. Jerusalem: Rābiṭat al-Jāmi'iyyīn al-Yahūd al-Nāziḥīn min al-'Irāq.

——. 1995. *Nubū'āt Rajul Majnūn fī Madīna Mal'ūna*. Jerusalem: Rābiṭat al-Jāmi'iyyīn al-Yahūd al-Nāziḥīn min al-'Irāq.

——. 2004. *Shlūmū al-Kurdī wa-Anā wa-Zaman*. Cologne: Manshūrāt al-Jamal.

——. 2014. *Shlomo le Kurde*, trans. Xavier Luffin. Paris: Galaade Éditions.

——. 2018. *Tenants & Cobwebs*, trans. Sadok Masliyah. Syracuse, NY: Syracuse University Press.

——. 2020. *Shlomo al-Kurdi, Myself, and Time* (in Hebrew), trans. Samira Yosef and Ruth Naqqash Vigiser. Jerusalem: Van Leer Institute.

Nassar, Maha. 2010. "The Marginal as Central: Al-Jadid and the Development of a Palestinian Public Sphere, 1953–1970." *Middle East Journal of Culture and Communication* 3.3, pp. 333–51.

——. 2017. *Brothers Apart: Palestinian Citizens of Israel and the Arab World*. Stanford, CA: Stanford University Press.

Naṣṣār, Sihām. 1980. *al-Yahūd al-Miṣriyyūn wa-Ṣuḥufuhum wa-Majallātuhum 1877–1950*. Cairo: al-'Arabī li-l-Nashr wa-l-Tawzī'.

Nasser, Riad M. 2005. *Palestinian Identity in Jordan and Israel: The Necessary "Other" in the Making of a Nation*. London: Routledge.

Nāṭūr, Salmān. 1991. *Yamshūn 'alā al-Rīḥ*. Nazareth: Jaffa Research Centre.

Nemoy, Leon. 1964. "New Data for the Biography of Sa'd ibn Kammūnah." *Revue des Études Juives* 122, pp. 507–10.

——. 1976. "Mourad Farag and His Book *The Karaites and the Rabbanites*." *Revue des Études Juives* 135.1/3, pp. 87–112.

——. 1979–1980. "A Modern Karaite-Arabic Poet: Mourad Farag." *Jewish Quarterly Review* 70, pp. 195–209.

Neuwirth, Angelika. 1999. "Maḥmūd Darwīsh's Re-staging of the Mystic Lover's Relation: Towards a Superhuman Beloved." In Stephan Guth et al. (eds.). *Conscious Voices: Concepts of Writing in the Middle East*. Beirut: Orient-Institut der DMG, pp. 153–78.

Nevo, Eshkol. 2018. *The Last Interview* (English title: *The Storyteller*) (in Hebrew). Tel Aviv: Kinneret Zmora-Bitan.

Nichols, James Mansfield. 1981. "The Arabic Verse of Qasmūna bint Ismā'īl ibn Bagdālah." *International Journal of Middle East Studies* 13.2, pp. 155–8.

Nicholson, Elin. 2014. "Theatrical Practices of Resistance to Spacio-Cide in Palestine, 2011–12." PhD thesis, University of Manchester.

Nicholson, Linda. 1995. "Introduction." In Seyla Benhabib et al. (eds.). *Feminist Contentions: A Philosophical Exchange*. New York: Routledge, pp. 1–16.

Nicholson, Rashna Darius. 2021. "On the (Im)possibilities of a Free Theatre: Theatre against Development in Palestine." *Theatre Research International* 46.1, pp. 4–22.

Nicholson, Reynold A. 1956. *A Literary History of the Arabs*. Cambridge: Cambridge University Press.

——. 1969 [1907]. *A Literary History of the Arabs*. Cambridge: Cambridge University Press.

Noorani, Yaseen. 1999. "The Lost Garden of al-Andalus: Islamic Spain and the Poetic Inversion of Colonialism." *International Journal of Middle East Studies* 31.2, pp. 237–54.

Nye, Naomi Shihab. 2004. "Meeting Edward Said at the Alamo," *Texas Observer*, January 16.

Obadyā, Ibrāhīm. 1990. *Ṣayḥa min 'Irāq al-'Ahd al-Bā'id*. Jerusalem: Rābiṭat al-Jāmi'iyyīn al-Yahūd al-Nāziḥīn min al-'Irāq.

——. 2005. *Ma'a al-Ghinā' al-'Irāqī: Muṭribūn wa-Muṭribāt wa-Aghānin min al-Turāth al-'Irāqī*. Jerusalem: Rābiṭat al-Jāmi'iyyīn al-Yahūd al-Nāziḥīn min al-'Irāq.

Obermeyer, Jacob. 1907. *Modernes Judentum im Morgen- und Abendland*. Vienna: Karl Fromme.

Ohana, David (ed.). 2005. *Between Two Worlds: Essays and Observations* (in Hebrew). Jerusalem: Keter.

Oppenheimer, Yochai. 2005. "My Gentle Occupier" (in Hebrew). *Haaretz* (Books), February, 9.

——. 2012. *What Is to Be Authentic: Mizrahi Poetry in Israel* (in Hebrew). Tel Aviv: Resling.

——. 2014. *From Ben-Gurion to Shāri' al-Rashīd: On Mizrahi Prose* (in Hebrew). Jerusalem: Ben-Zvi Institute.

Oren, Yosef. 1992. "A Canaanite Future for Hebrew Literature?" (in Hebrew). *Moznaim*, November, pp. 63–4.

——. 1995. *Trends in Israeli Prose* (in Hebrew). Rishon Le-Tsiyon: Yahad.

——. 2006. *Literature and Sovereignty* (in Hebrew). Rishon Le-Tsiyon: Yahad.

Ouyang, Wen-chin. 2012. *Poetics of Love in the Arabic Novel: Nation-State, Modernity and Tradition*. Edinburgh: Edinburgh University Press.

Ozick, Cynthia. 1989. "Unforgivable, Indefensible, Uninnocent." *Jewish Frontier*, July–August, p. 13.

Pamuk, Orhan. 2006. *Istanbul: Memories and the City*, trans. Maureen Freely. New York: Vintage.

——. 2009. *The Museum of Innocence*, trans. Maureen Freely. New York: Alfred A. Knopf.

Pannewick, Friederike and Khalil, Georges (ed.). 2015. *Commitment and Beyond: Locating the Political in Arabic Literature since the 1940s*. Wiesbaden: Reichert Verlag.

Pappé, Ilan (ed.). 1999. *The Israel/Palestine Question*. London: Routledge.

Parker, Mushtak. 1992. "Death of a Muslim Mentor." *The Middle East* 211 (May), pp. 28–9.

Parmenter, Barabara McKean. 1994. *Giving Voice to Stones: Place and Identity in Palestinian Literature*. Austin: University of Texas Press.

Parrilla, Gonzalo Fernández. 2018. "Disoriented Postcolonialities: With Edward Said in (the Labyrinth of) Al-Andalus." *Interventions: International Journal of Postcolonial Studies*, 20.2, pp. 229–42.

Patai, Raphael. 1977. *The Jewish Mind*. New York: Charles Scribner's.

Pedaya, Haviva. 2015. *The Mizrah Writes Itself* (in Hebrew). Tel Aviv: Gama Press.

——. 2016. *Return of the Lost Voice: Poetics, Music and Space* (in Hebrew). Tel Aviv: Ha-Kibbutz Ha-Me'uḥad.

Peled, Mattityahu. 1982. "Annals of Doom: Palestinian Literature 1917–1948." *Arabica* 29.2, pp. 141–83.

Perlmann, Moshe. 1971. *Ibn Kammūna's Examination of the Three Faiths*. Berkeley: University of California Press.

Perlson, Inbal. 2000. "The Musical Tradition of the Emigrants from the Islamic Countries during the First Years of the State of Israel" (in Hebrew). PhD thesis, Tel Aviv University.

Philipp, Thomas. 1985. *The Syrians in Egypt 1725–1975*. Stuttgart: Franz Steiner Verlag.

Picard, Avi. 2017. "Like a Phoenix: The Renaissance of Sephardic/Mizrahi Identity in Israel in the 1970s and 1980s." *Journal of Israeli History* 22.2, pp. 32–60.

Pietruschka, Ute. 2005. "Classical Heritage and New Literary Forms: Literary Activities of Christians during the Umayyad Period." In Sebastian Günther (ed.). *Ideas, Images,*

and Methods of Portrayal: Insights into Classical Arabic Literature and Islam. Leiden: Brill, pp. 17–39.
Piterberg, Gabriel. 1996. "Domestic Orientalism: The Representation of 'Oriental' Jews in Zionist/Israeli Historiography." *British Journal of Middle Eastern Studies* 23.2, pp. 125–45.
Plato. 2000. *The Republic*, trans. Benjamin Jowett. Mineola, NY: Dover Publications.
——. 2006. *Republic*, trans. R. E. Allen. New Haven, CT: Yale University Press.
Porath, Yehoshua. 1989. *The Life of Uriel Shelah (Yonathan Ratosh)* (in Hebrew). Tel Aviv: Maḥbarot Lesifrut.
Post, George E. (ed.). 1981. *Fihris al-Kitāb al-Muqaddas*. Beirut: Maktabat al-Mash'al.
Pregill, Michael E. 2021. "Blurred Boundaries and Novel Normativities: The Jews of Arabia, the Quranic Milieu, and the 'Islamic Judaism' of the Middle Ages." *Al-'Uṣūr al-Wusṭā* 29, pp. 256–302.
Preminger, Alex (ed.). 1974. *Princeton Encyclopedia of Poetics and Poetry*. Princeton, NJ: Princeton University Press.
Prince, Gerald. 1987. *A Dictionary of Narratology*. Lincoln: University of Nebraska Press.
Qabaha, Ahmad. 2022. "To Reverse or to Rehearse Performing Colonial Reality in *Arna's Children*." *Interventions: International Journal of Postcolonial Studies* 24.1, pp. 74–87.
Qabbānī, Nizār. 1974. *al-A'māl al-Siyāsiyya*. Beirut: Manshūrāt Nizār Qabbānī.
Qāsim, Maḥmūd. 1997. *Ṣūrat al-Adyān fī al-Sīnamā al-Miṣriyya*. Cairo: Wizārat al-Thaqāfa.
——. 2002. *Dalīl al-Aflām fī al-Qarn al-'Ishrīn fī Miṣr wa-l-'Ālam al-'Arabī*. Cairo: Maktabat Madbūlī.
al-Qāsim, Nabīh. n.d. *Dirāsāt fī al-Adab al-Filasṭīnī al-Maḥallī*. Acre: Dār al-Aswār.
al-Qāsim, Samīḥ. 1969. "Ḥayātī wa-Qaḍiyyatī wa-Shi'rī." *al-Jadīd*, April/May, pp. 23–9.
——. 1969a. "Ṣafaḥāt min Mufakkira." *al-Jadīd*, July/August, pp. 29–32.
——. 1970. *Qaraqāsh*. Haifa: Dār al-Ittiḥād.
——. 1987. *Dīwān*. Beirut: Dār al-'Awda.
——. 1990. *Samīḥ al-Qāsim fī Dā'irat al-Naqd*. Kafr Qara': Dār al-Hudā.
——. 1993. Unpublished interview by Milḥim Qabalān, January 13.
al-Qazwīnī, Zakariyyā ibn Muḥammad. 1960. *Āthār al-Bilād wa-Akhbār al-'Ibād*. Beirut: Dār Ṣādir & Dār Bayrūt.
al-Qushayrī (al-Qushayri), Abū al-Qāsim. n.d. *al-Risāla fī 'Ilm al-Taṣawwuf*. Cairo: Maṭba'at Ṣabīḥ.
——. 1940. *al-Risāla fī 'Ilm al-Taṣawwuf*. Cairo: Ḥalabī.
Qutbuddin, Tahera. 2005. *al-Mu'ayyad al-Shirazi and Fatimid Da'wa Poetry: A Case of Commitment in Classical Arabic Literature*. Leiden: Brill.
Rabeeya, David. 2000. *The Journey of an Arab-Jew in European Israel*. Philadelphia, PA: Xlibris Corp.
al-Rabī'ī, Nabīl 'Abd al-Amīr. 2016. *Lamaḥāt min Ta'rīkh Yahūd al-'Irāq (859 BC–1973 AD)*. al-Ḥilla: Dār al-Furāt.
——. 2017. *Mu'jam A'lām Yahūd al-'Irāq (859 BC–1973 AD)*. al-Ḥilla: Dār al-Furāt.
Rahim, Hasan Zillur. 1995. "Muhammad Asad: Visionary Islamic Scholar." *Washington Report on Middle East Affairs* (September), pp. 45–6.
al-Rā'ī, 'Alī. 1979. *al-Masraḥ fī al-Waṭan al-'Arabī*. Kuwait City: al-Majlis al-Waṭanī li-l-Thaqāfa wa-l-Funūn wa-l-Ādāb.
——. 1991. *al-Riwāya al-'Arabiyya fī al-Waṭan al-'Arabī*. Beirut: Dār al-Mustaqbal al-'Arabī.
——. 1993. *Masraḥ al-Sha'b*. Cairo: Dār Sharqiyyāt.
al-Rajab, Hāshim Muḥammad. 1961. *al-Maqām al-'Irāqī*. Baghdad: Maṭba'at al-Ma'ārif.
Ram, Uri (ed.). 1993. *Israeli Society: Critical Perspectives* (in Hebrew). Tel Aviv: Breirot.
Ramras-Rauch, Gila. 1989. *The Arab in Israeli Literature*. Bloomington: Indiana University Press.

Randall, Yafiah Katherine. 2019. *Sufism and Jewish–Muslim Relations: The Derekh Avraham Order in Israel*. London: Routledge.
Ratosh, Yonatan. 1967. *[The Year] 1967 and What's Next* (in Hebrew). Tel Aviv: Hermon Press.
Recapito, Joseph. 1998. "Al-Andalus and the Origin of the Renaissance in Europe." *Indiana Journal of Hispanic Literatures* 8, pp. 55–74.
Regev, Motti 1996. "*Musica Mizrakhit*, Israeli Rock and National Culture in Israel." *Popular Music* 15.3, pp. 191–235.
Regev, Motti and Seroussi, Edwin. 2004. *Popular Music and National Culture in Israel*. Berkeley: University of California Press.
Rejwan, Nissim. 1985. *The Jews of Iraq: 3000 Years of History and Culture*. London: Weidenfeld & Nicolson.
——. 1998. *Arabs Face the Modern World: Religious, Cultural, and Political Responses to the West*. Gainesville: University Press of Florida.
——. 1999. *Israel in Search of Identity: Reading the Formative Years*. Gainesville: University Press of Florida.
——. 2004. *The Last Jews in Baghdad: Remembering a Lost Homeland*. Austin: University of Texas Press.
——. 2006. *Israel's Years of Bogus Grandeur: From the Six-Day War to the First Intifada*. Austin: University of Texas Press.
——. 2006a. *Outsider in the Promised Land: An Iraqi Jew in Israel*. Austin: University of Texas Press.
——. 2008. *Arabs in the Mirror: Images and Self-Images from Pre-Islamic to Modern Times*. Austin: University of Texas Press.
Rekhess, Elie and Rodnitzki, Arik (eds.). 2009. *Arab Society in Israel: Information Manual* (in Hebrew). Neve Ilan: Abraham Fund Initiatives.
al-Rifāʿī, Jamāl Aḥmad. 1994. *Āthār al-Thaqāfa al-ʿIbriyya fī al-Shiʿr al-Filasṭīnī al-Muʿāṣir: Dirāsa fī Shiʿr Maḥmūd Darwīsh*. Cairo: Dār al-Thaqāfa al-Jadīda.
Rish, Benyamin. 2014. "Samīr Naqqāsh in His Writings Challenges Existentialist Philosophers with the Ideas of Abū al-'Alāʿ al-Ma'arrī." *Journal of Semitic Studies* 59.2, pp. 409–34.
Robinson, Shira. 2003. "Local Struggle, National Struggle: Palestinian Responses to the Kfar Qasim Massacre and Its Aftermath, 1956–1966." *International Journal of Middle East Studies* 35.3, pp. 393–416.
Roby, Bryan K. 2015. *The Mizrahi Era of Rebellion: Israel's Forgotten Civil Rights Struggle 1948–1966*. Syracuse, NY: Syracuse University Press.
——. 2022. "How Race Travels: Navigating Global Blackness in J. Ida Jiggetts's Study of Afro-Asian Israeli Jewry." *Jewish Social Studies: History, Culture, Society* 27.1, pp. 1–42.
Rooke, Tetz. 2008. "*In the Presence of Absence*: Mahmoud Darwish's Testament." *Journal of Arabic and Islamic Studies* 8.2, pp. 11–25.
Rorty, Amélie Oksenberg. 2007. "The Vanishing Subject: The Many Faces of Subjectivity." In João Biehl et al. (eds.). *Subjectivity: Ethnographic Investigations*. Berkeley: University of California Press, pp. 34–51.
Rosen, Tova and Yassif, Eli. 2002. "The Study of Hebrew Literature of the Middle Ages: Major Trends and Goals." In Martin Goodman (ed.). *The Oxford Handbook of Jewish Studies*. Oxford: Oxford University Press, pp. 241–94.
Rosenfeld-Hadad, Merav. 2011. "*Miṣḥaf al-Shbaḥot*—The Holy Book of Praises of the Babylonian Jews: One Thousand Years of Cultural Harmony between Judaism and Islam." In Michael M. Laskier and Yaacov Lev (eds.). *In the Convergence of Judaism and Islam: Religious, Scientific, and Cultural Dimensions*. Gainesville: University Press of Florida, pp. 241–71.
——. 2019. *Judaism and Islam, One God One Music: The History of Jewish Paraliturgical*

Song in the Context of Arabo-Islamic Culture as Revealed in Its Jewish Babylonian Sources. Leiden: Brill.
Rosen-Moked, Tova. 2003. *Unveiling Eve: Reading Gender in Medieval Hebrew Literature*. Philadelphia: University of Pennsylvania Press.
Rossetto, Piera. 2012. "Space of Transit, Place of Memory: Ma'abarah and Literary Landscapes of Arab Jews." *Quest. Issues in Contemporary Jewish History* 4, pp. 103–27.
Rothstein, Edward. 2005. "Regarding Cervantes, Multicultural Dreamer." *New York Times*, June 13, available at: http://www.nytimes.com/2005/06/13/ arts/13conn.html.
Rottenberg, Catherine. 2008. "Dancing Arabs and Spaces of Desire." *Topia: Canadian Journal of Cultural Studies* 19, pp. 99–114.
Roumani, Judith. 2022. "Mizrahi Jewish Novelists and the End of Jewish Life in the Middle East: Echoes of Voices." *Sephardic Horizons* 6.2, pp. 1–7, available at: https://www.sephardichorizons.org/Volume6/Issue2/Roumani.html, last accessed January 28, 2022.
Rowson, Everett K. 1996. "Arabic Poetics in Hebrew Poetry of the Golden Age." *Prooftexts* 16, pp. 105–11.
Rozenblit, Marsha L. 1992. "Jewish Assimilation in Habsburg Vienna." In Jonathan Frankel and Steven J. Zipperstein (eds.). *Assimilation and Community: The Jews in Nineteenth-Century Europe*. Cambridge: Cambridge University Press, pp. 225–45.
Rubin, Uri. 1999. *Between Bible and Qur'ān: The Children of Israel and the Islamic Self-Image*. Princeton, NJ: Darwin Press.
al-Ruṣāfī, Ma'rūf. 1986. *Dīwān*. Beirut: Dār al-'Awda.
Sabar, Yona. 1982. *The Folk Literature of the Kurdistani Jews: An Anthology*. New Haven, CT: Yale University Press.
Sa'd, Fārūq. 1990. *Qarāqūsh wa-Nawādiruhu*. Beirut: Dār al-Āfāq al-Jadīda.
Sadan, Dov. 1950. *On Our Literature: Introductory Essay* (in Hebrew). Jerusalem: Zionist Organization.
Sadan, Joseph. 2002. "Un intellectuel juif au confluent de deux cultures: Yehūda al-Ḥarīzī et sa biographie arab." In Maribel Fierro (ed.). *Judíos y musulmanes en al-Andalus y al Magreb: Contactos intelectuales*. Madrid: Casa de Velásquez, pp. 105–51.
Sadgrove, Philip C. 1983. "The Development of the Arabic Periodical Press and Its Role in the Literary Life of Egypt (1798–1882)." PhD thesis, University of Edinburgh.
——. 1996. *The Egyptian Theatre in the Nineteenth Century (1799–1882)*. Reading: Ithaca Press.
Sáenz-Badilios, A. 1997. "Philologians and Poets in Search of the Hebrew Language." In Ross Brann (ed.). *Languages of Power in Islamic Spain*. Bethesda, MD: CDL Press, pp. 49–75.
Sagi-Bizāwī, Eyal. 2003. "Jews in the Film Industry in Egypt" (in Hebrew). *Ha-Kivvun Mizrah* 7, pp. 83–98.
Said, Edward W. 1975. *Beginnings: Intention and Method*. New York: Columbia University Press.
——. 1985 [1978]. *Orientalism*. London: Penguin.
——. 1994. *Culture & Imperialism*. London: Vintage.
Sālim, Kamāl Laṭīf. 1986. *Nāẓim al-Ghazālī: Safīr al-Ughniyya al-'Irāqiyya*. Baghdad: Manshūrāt Maktabat al-Ishtirākī.
Samet, Gideon. 1989. *The List of 6,000* (in Hebrew). Tel Aviv: Edanim.
al-Sammāk, Mahdī. 2001. *Mudhakkirāt wa-Khawāṭir Ṭabīb Baghdadī*. Baghdad: Dār al-Shu'ūn al-Thaqāfiyya al-'Āmma.
Samra, Myer. 1993. "'Shaded by the Followers of Muhammad': The Poet Anwar Shaul and the Jews in Iraq." *Australian Journal of Jewish Studies* 7.2, pp. 125–41.
Sand, Shlomo. 2009. *The Invention of the Jewish People*, trans. Yael Lotan. London: Verso.
Sandel, Michael J. 2009. *Justice: What's the Right Thing to Do?* London: Penguin.
Saramago, José. 2013. *Blindness*, trans. Giovanni Pontiero. London: Vintage.

Sarmad, ʻIzz al-Dīn. 2000. "The Period I Lived in Baghdad Has Been All My Life: An Interview with Samīr Naqqāsh" (in Arabic). *al-Thaqāfa al-Jadīda* 294 (May–June), pp. 134–42.
Ṣarrāf, Aḥmad Ḥāmid. 1960. *ʻUmar al-Khayyām*. Baghdad: Maṭbaʻat al-Maʻārif.
Sassoon, David Solomon. 1949. *A History of the Jews in Baghdad*. Letchworth: S. D. Sassoon.
al-Sawāfīrī, Kāmil. 1963. *al-Shiʻr al-ʻArabī al-Ḥadīth fī Ma'sāt Filasṭīn min Sanat 1917 ilā Sanat 1955*. Cairo: Maktabat Nahḍat Miṣr.
——. 1979. *al-Adab al-ʻArabī al-Muʻāṣir fī Filasṭīn min Sanat 1860–1960*. Cairo: Dār al-Maʻārif.
al-Sawāḥirī, Khalīl. 1980. "al-Bidāyāt al-Ūlā li-l-Masraḥ al-Muqāwim fī al-Arḍ al-Muḥtalla." *al-Aqlām*, March, pp. 131–8.
Sayegh, Anis (ed.). 1990. *Encyclopaedia Palaestina*. Damascus: Encyclopaedia Palaestina Corp.
al-Sayyāb, Badr Shākir. 1971. *Dīwān*. Beirut: Dār al-ʻAwda.
al-Ṣayyād, Fu'ād ʻAbd al-Muʻṭī. 1968. *Mu'arrikh al-Maghūl al-Kabīr Rashīd al-Dīn*. Cairo: Dār al-Kātib al-ʻArabī.
Scharfstein, Ben-Ami. 1973. *Mystical Experience*. Oxford: Blackwell.
——. 1993. *Ineffability: The Failure of Words in Philosophy and Religion*. Albany: State University of New York Press.
Scheindlin, Raymond P. 1986. *Wine, Women and Death: Medieval Hebrew Poems on the Good Life*. Philadelphia, PA: Jewish Publication Society.
——. 1991. *The Gazelle: Medieval Hebrew Poems on God, Israel, and the Soul*. Philadelphia, PA: Jewish Publication Society.
——. 1992. "The Jews in Muslim Spain." In Salma Khadra Jayyusi (ed.). *The Legacy of Muslim Spain*. Leiden: Brill, pp. 188–200.
——. 2000. "Moses Ibn Ezra." In Maria Rosa Menocal et al. (eds.). *The Cambridge History of Arabic Literature: The Literature of al-Andalus*. Cambridge: Cambridge University Press, pp. 252–64.
Schimmel, Annemarie. 1983. *Mystical Dimensions of Islam*. Chapel Hill: University of North Carolina Press.
Schine, Rachel. 2018. "Mirror for the Modern Man: The Siyar Ša'biyya as Advice Literature in Tunisian Judeo-Arabic Editions." *Arabica* 65, pp. 392–418.
Schippers, Arie. 1994. *Spanish Hebrew Poetry and the Arabic Literary Tradition*. Leiden: Brill.
——. 2001. "Humorous Approach of the Divine in the Poetry of al-Andalus: The Case of Ibn Sahl." In Gert Borg and Ed de Moor (eds.). *Representations of the Divine in Arabic Poetry*. Amsterdam: Rodopi, pp. 119–35.
Schlaepfer, Aline. 2016. *Les intellectuels juifs de Bagdad (1908–1951)*. Leiden: Brill.
——. 2016a. "*The King is Dead, Long Live the King!* Jewish Funerary Performances in the Iraqi Public Space." In Sasha Rachel Goldstein-Sabbah and H. L. Murre-van den Berg (eds.). *Modernity, Minority, and the Public Sphere: Jews and Christians in the Middle East*. Leiden: Brill, pp. 185–204.
Schlesinger, Juliana Portenoy. 2018. "Sayed Kashua's Chronicles: A New Religion Is in Israel." *Journal of Historical Archaeology & Anthropological Sciences* 3.1, pp. 36–42.
Scholem, Gershom G. 1954. *Major Trends in Jewish Mysticism*. New York: Schocken.
——. 1965. *On the Kabbalah and Its Symbolism*. New York: Schocken.
Schorr, Renen and Shuv, Yael. 1990. "Shylock in the Desert." In Rafi Bukaee (ed.). *Avanti Popolo* (in Hebrew). Jerusalem: Kinneret, pp. 75–96.
Schrand, Irmgard. 2004. *Jews in Egypt: Communists and Citizens*. Münster: Lit Verlag.
Schulze, K. E. 2001. *The Jews of Lebanon: Between Coexistence and Conflict*. Brighton: Sussex Academic Press.

Schwartz, Yigal (ed.). 2016. *A Prince and a Revolutionary: Studies of the Fiction of Sami Michael* (in Hebrew). Beer Sheva and Or Yehuda: Gamma, Heksherim, Dvir.
Sebeok, Thomas A. (ed.). 1986. *Encyclopedic Dictionary of Semiotics*. Berlin: Mouton de Gruyter.
Seekamp, Birgit. 1988. *Die Palästinensiche Kurzprosa der Gegenwart*. Frankfurt: Peter Lang.
Seigneurie, Ken (ed.). 2003. *Crisis and Memory: The Representation of Space in Modern Levantine Narrative*. Wiesbaden: Reichert Verlag.
Selove, Emily. 2017. *Ḥikāyat Abī al-Qāsim: A Literary Banquet*. Edinburgh: Edinburgh University Press.
Semah, David. 1959. *Ḥattā Yajī' al-Rabī'*. Tel Aviv: al-Maṭba'a al-Ḥadītha.
——. 1974. *Four Egyptian Literary Critics*. Leiden: Brill.
——. 1989. "Mīr Baṣrī wa-Nahḍat al-Adab al-'Irāqī." *al-Karmil: Studies in Arabic Language and Literature* 10, pp. 83–122.
——. 1989a. "The Iraqi Novel of Samīr Naqqāsh" (in Hebrew). *Neharde'a* 7, pp. 21–2.
——. 1993. "Between Jews and Muslims" (in Hebrew). *Nehardea* 12, p. 5.
Seroussi, Edwin. 2006. "Jewish Musicians in the Lands of Islam." *Tapasam: A Quarterly Journal of Kerala Studies* 1.3 (2006), pp. 596–609.
Seroussi, Edwin and Karsenti, Eric. 2002. "The Study of Liturgical Music of Algerian Jewry" (in Hebrew). *Pe'amim: Studies in Oriental Jewry* 91, pp. 31–50.
Shafir, Gershon. 1996. "Zionism and Colonialism: A Comparative Approach." In Michael N. Barnett (ed.). *Israel in Comparative Studies: Challenging the Conventional Wisdom*. New York: State University of New York Press, pp. 227–44.
Shaked, Gershon. 1993. *Hebrew Narrative Fiction 1880–1980* (Hebrew). Tel Aviv: Ha-Kibbutz Ha-Me'uḥad.
——. 2006. *Identity: Jewish Literatures in European Languages* (in Hebrew). Haifa: University of Haifa Press.
Shaked, Haim. 1979. "Experience into Fiction: Israeli Writers on Jewish-Arab Relations (the Case of Hasut by Sammy Michael)." In Gustav Stein and Udo Steinbach (eds.). *The Contemporary Middle Eastern Scene: Basic and Major Trends*. Opladen: Leske und Budrich, pp. 138–49.
Shakespeare, William. n.d. *The Complete Works*. London: Spring Books.
——. 1964. *The Merchant of Venice*. London: Methuen.
——. 1971. *Julius Caesar*. London: Longman.
Shalash, 'Alī. 1986. *al-Yahūd wa-l-Māsūn fī Miṣr*. Cairo: al-Zahrā' li-I-I'lām al-'Arabī.
Shamir, Shimon. 1987. "The Evolution of the Egyptian Nationality Laws and Their Application to the Jews in the Monarchy Period." In Shimon Shamir (ed.). *The Jews of Egypt: A Mediterranean Society in Modern Times*. Boulder, CO: Westview Press, pp. 33–67.
Shamir-Tulipman, Ayelet. 2004. "The Local Stranger: Embodiment of Hybridity within Modern Hebrew Literature—Reading of Three Novels" (in Hebrew). PhD thesis, University of Haifa.
Shammās (Shammas), Anton (Anṭūn). 1974. *Hard Cover* (in Hebrew). Tel Aviv: Sifriyat Poalim.
——. 1974a. *Asīr Yaqẓatī wa-Nawmī*. Jerusalem: al-Sharq.
——. 1974b. *In Two Voices* (in Hebrew). Haifa: Bet HaGefen.
——. 1976. "Arabic Literature in Israel after 1967" (in Hebrew). *Skirot* 2. Tel Aviv: Machon Shiloah, Tel Aviv University Press.
——. 1979. *No Man's Land* (in Hebrew). Tel Aviv: Ha-Kibbutz Ha-Me'uḥad.
——. 1982–1983. "The Return to My Home, the Return to Lebanon" (in Hebrew). *Ḥadarim* 3, pp. 19–22.
——. 1984. *Ṣayd al-Ghazāla*. Tel Aviv: Dār al-Mashriq.

——. 1985. "The Meeting Which Took Place; the Meeting Which Will not Take Place" (in Hebrew). *Moznaim*, September, pp. 30–2.
——. 1985a. "On Right and Left in Translation" (in Hebrew). *Iton 77*, May–June, pp. 18–19.
——. 1986. "My Fight against the Windmills of the Intellectuals" (in Hebrew). *Moznaim*, September, pp. 26–7.
——. 1986a. "The Guilt of the Babushka" (in Hebrew). *Politika* 5–6 (February–March), pp. 44–5.
——. 1987. *Arabesques* (in Hebrew). Tel Aviv: Am Oved.
——. 1988. *Arabesques*, trans. Vivian Eden. London: Viking.
——. 1989. "Your Worst Nightmare." *Jewish Frontier*, July–August, p. 10.
——. 1990. "He's Got the Roles Mixed Up: Observations on the Figure of the Arab in the Israeli Cinema in the Wake of *Avanti Popolo*" (in Hebrew). In Rafi Bukaee. *Avanti Popolo* (in Hebrew). Jerusalem: Kinneret, 1990, pp. 7–17.
——. 1993. "The Departure: The Most Bitter Year" (in Hebrew). *Haaretz*, September 15, p. B3.
——. 1994. "Arab Male, Hebrew Female; The Lure of Metaphors." In Fatma Müge Göçek and Shiva Balaghi (eds.). *Reconstructing Gender in the Middle East*. New York: Columbia University Press, pp. 167–73.
——. 2003. ""The Drowned Library." In Isabelle de Courtivron (ed.). *Lives in Translation: Bilingual Writers on Identity and Creativity*. New York: Palgrave Macmillan, pp. 111–28.
Shammās, Maurice (Mūrīs). 1979. *al-Shaykh Shabtāy wa-Ḥikāyāt min Ḥārat al-Yahūd*. Shfaram: Dār al-Mashriq.
Shannon, Jonathan. 2007. "Performing al-Andalus, Remembering al-Andalus: Mediterranean Soundings from Mashriq to Maghrib." *Journal of American Folklore* 120.477, pp. 308–44.
Shapira, Anita. 2009. "The Jewish-People Deniers." *Journal of Israeli History* 28.1, pp. 63–72.
Sharīf, Nihād. 1981. *Alladhī Taḥaddā al-I'ṣār*. Cairo: al-Hay'a al-Miṣriyya al-'Āmma li-l-Kitāb.
Sha'shū'a, Salīm. 1959. *Fī 'Ālam al-Nūr*. Nazareth: Maṭba'at al-Ḥakīm.
——. 1976. *Ughniyyāt li-Bilādī*. Jerusalem: Majallat al-Sharq.
Shā'ul, Anwar. 1930. *al-Ḥaṣād al-Awwal*. Baghdad: Maṭba'at al-Jam'iyya al-Khayriyya.
——. 1955. *Fī Ziḥām al-Madīna*. Baghdad: Sharikat al-Tijāra wa-l-Ṭibā'a al-Maḥdūda.
——. 1980. *Qiṣṣat Ḥayātī fī Wādī al-Rāfidayn*. Jerusalem: Rābiṭat al-Jāmi'iyyīn al-Yahūd al-Nāziḥīn min al-'Irāq.
——. 1983. *Wa-Bazagha Fajr Jadīd*. Jerusalem: Rābiṭat al-Jāmi'iyyīn al-Yahūd al-Nāziḥīn min al-'Irāq.
Shaw, George Bernard. 1962. *Pygmalion*. London: Longman.
Sheehi, Stephen. 2004. *Foundations of Modern Arab Identity*. Gainesville: University Press of Florida.
Shehadeh, Hasseb. 1997. "The Hebrew of the Arabs in Israel (in the Light of Two Matriculation Examinations, 1970, 1972)." In M'hammed Sabour and Knut S. Vikør (eds.). *Ethnic Encounter and Culture Change: Papers from the 3rd Nordic Conference on Middle Eastern Studies, Joensuu 1995*. Bergen, Norway: Nordic Society for Middle Eastern Studies, pp. 49–71.
Shenberg, Galia. 1998. "Diglossia and Bilingualism: Storytelling by Druze Women" (in Hebrew). *'Iyyun ve-Mehkar be-Hachsharat Morim* (Gordon College, Haifa) 21, pp. 21–9.
Shenhav (Shenhav-Shahrabani), Yehouda. 1999. "The Jews of Iraq, Zionist Ideology and the Property of the Palestinian Refugees of 1948: An Anatomy of National Accounting." *International Journal of Middle East Studies* 31.4, pp. 605–30.
——. 2002. "Ethnicity and National Memory: The World Organization of Jews from

Arab Countries (WOJAC) in the Context of the Palestinian National Struggle." *British Journal of Middle Eastern Studies* 29.1, pp. 27–56.
——. 2002a. "The Phenomenology of Colonialism and the Politics of 'Difference': European Zionist Emissaries and Arab-Jews in Colonial Abadan." *Social Identities* 8.4, pp. 521–44.
——. 2003. *The Arab Jews: Nationalism, Religion and Ethnicity* (in Hebrew). Tel Aviv: Am Oved.
Shenhav (Shenhav-Shahrabani), Yehouda and Mendel, Yonatan. 2019. "From the Neoclassical to the Binational Model of Translation." *Journal of Levantine Studies* 9.2, pp. 5–21.
Sherara, Yosef (= Yoram Kaniuk). 1984. *A Good Arab* (in Hebrew). Tel Aviv: Kinneret.
Shiblak, Abbas. 1986. *The Lure of Zion: The Case of the Iraqi Jews*. London: Saqi.
——. 2005. *Iraqi Jews: A History of Mass Exodus*. London: Saqi.
Shiḥāda, Rāḍī. 1985. "al-Masraḥ al-Filasṭīnī Bayna al-Karr wa-l-Farr." *al-Karmil* 16, pp. 245–53.
——. 1989. "*Masraḥ al-Ḥakawātī al-Filasṭīnī*." *al-Karmil* 31, pp. 172–91.
——. 1997. *Hawājis Masraḥiyya*. Acre: Manshūrāt al-Aswār.
Shiloah, Amnon. 1992. *Jewish Musical Traditions*. Detroit, MI: Wayne State University Press.
——. 2002. "The Activity of Jewish Musicians in Classical Algerian Music and Related Areas" (in Hebrew). *Pe'amim: Studies in Oriental Jewry* 91, pp. 51–64.
——. 2011. "Encounters between Jewish and Muslim Musicians throughout the Ages." In Michael M. Laskier and Yaacov Lev (eds.). *The Convergence of Judaism and Islam: Religious, Scientific, and Cultural Dimensions*. Gainesville: University Press of Florida, pp. 272–83.
Shimoni, Baruch. 2007. "Ethnic Demonstration and Cultural Representation: From Multiculturalism to Cultural Hybridization, the Case of Mizrahi-Sabras in Israel." *HAGAR: Studies in Culture, Polity and Identities* 7.2, pp. 13–34.
Shimony, Batya. 2013. "Shaping Israeli-Arab Identity in Hebrew Words: The Case of Sayed Kashua." *Israel Studies* 18.1, pp. 146–69.
Shinar, Dov. 1987. *Palestinian Voices: Communication and Nation-Building in the West Bank*. Boulder, CO: Lynne Rienner.
Shklovsky (Shklovskij), Victor (Viktor). 1966. *Theorie der Prosa*. Frankfurt am Main: Fischer.
Shohat, Ella. 1989. *Israeli Cinema: East/West and the Politics of Representation*. Austin: University of Texas Press.
——. 1992. "Antinomies of Exile: Said and the Frontiers of National Narrations." In Michael Sprinker (ed.). *Edward Said: A Critical Reader*. Oxford: Blackwell, pp. 121–43.
——. 1997. "Columbus, Palestine and Arab-Jewish: Toward a Relational Approach to Community Identity." In Keith Ansell-Pearson et al. (eds.). *Cultural Readings of Imperialism: Edward Said and the Gravity of History*. London: Lawrence & Wishart, pp. 88–105.
——. 1997a. "Sephardim in Israel: Zionism from the Standpoint of Its Jewish Victims." In Anne McClintock et al. (eds.). *Dangerous Liaisons: Gender, Nation, and Postcolonial Perspectives*. Minneapolis: University of Minnesota Press, pp. 39–68.
——. (ed.). 1998. *Talking Visions: Multicultural Feminism in a Transnational Age*. New York and Cambridge, MA: New Museum of Contemporary Art and MIT Press.
——. 1999. "The Invention of the Mizrahim." *Journal of Palestine Studies* 29.1, pp. 5–20.
——. 2003. "Reflections of an Arab Jew." In Loolwa Khazzoom (ed.). *The Flying Camel*. New York: Seal Press, pp. 115–21.
Shohet, Nir. 1982. *The Story of an Exile: A Short History of the Jews of Iraq*, trans. A. Zilkha. Tel Aviv: Association for the Promotion of Research, Literature and Art.
Siksik (Sikseck), Ayman. 2010. *To Jaffa* (in Hebrew). Tel Aviv: Miskal.

——. 2014. *al-ʿAwda ilā Yāfā*, trans. Muḥammad Ibrāhīm al-Ghabbān. Cairo: Cairo University.
——. 2016. *Tishrīn* (*Blood Ties*) (in Hebrew). Tel Aviv: Ahuzat Bayit.
Silber, Marcos. Forthcoming. "Reassessing the Acculturation Paradigm: Popular and Mass Culture in Interwar Poland." (I thank Prof. Silber for providing me with the text of the article before its publication.)
Silberstein, Laurence J. 1991. *New Perspectives on Israeli History: The Early Years of the State*. New York: New York University Press.
——. 1999. *The Postzionism Debates: Knowledge and Power in Israeli Culture*. New York: Routledge.
Silverfarb, Daniel. 1986. *Britain's Informal Empire in the Middle East: A Case Study of Iraq, 1929–1941*. New York: Oxford University Press.
Silverman, Netanel Haim. 2019. "Rereading Identity Cards: The Early Anticolonial Poetics of Mahmoud Darwish and Their Hebrew Afterlives." PhD thesis, University of Toronto.
Simon, Reeva S. 1986. *Iraq between the Two World Wars: The Creation and Implementation of a Nationalist Ideology*. New York: Columbia University Press.
——. 1997. "The Imposition of Nationalism on a Non-Nation State: The Case of Iraq during the Interwar Period, 1921–1941." In James Jankowski and Israel Gershoni (eds.). *Rethinking Nationalism in the Arab Middle East*. New York: Columbia University Press, pp. 87–104.
Sivan, Emmanuel. 1988. *Arab Political Myths* (in Hebrew). Tel Aviv: Am Oved.
Slyomovics, Susan. 1987. *The Merchant of Art: An Egyptian Hilali Oral Epic Poet in Performance*. Berkeley: University of California Press.
——. 1994. "Performing *A Thousand and One Nights* in Egypt." *Oral Tradition* 9.2, pp. 390–419.
——. 1998. *The Object of Memory: Arab and Jew Narrate the Palestinian Village*. Philadelphia: University of Pennsylvania Press.
——. 2013. "Who and What Is Native to Israel? On Marcel Janco's Settler Art and Jacqueline Shohet Kahanoff's "Levantinism." *Settler Colonial Studies* 4.1, pp. 27–47.
Smilansky, Saul. 2007. *10 Moral Paradoxes*. Oxford: Blackwell.
Smith, Anthony D. 1991. *National Identity*. Harmondsworth: Penguin.
Smith, Wilfred Cantwell. 1963. *Islam in Modern History*. New York: Mentor.
Smooha, Sammy. 1978. *Israel: Pluralism and Conflict*. Berkeley: University of California Press.
——. 1984. *The Orientation and Politicization of the Arab Minority in Israel*. Haifa: Jewish-Arab Center.
Snir, Reuven. 1988. "Cultural Changes as Reflected in Literature: The Beginning of the Arabic Short Story by Jewish Authors in Iraq" (in Hebrew). *Peʿamim: Studies in Oriental Jewry* 36, pp. 108–29.
——. 1988a. "The Books: Blessing or Curse: A Study of 'The Books' by Mīshīl Ḥaddād" (in Hebrew). *Journal of the Teachers of Arabic Language* 4, pp. 9–16.
——. 1989. "The Arab–Israeli Conflict as Reflected in the Writing of Najīb Maḥfūẓ." *Abr-Nahrain* 27, pp. 120–53.
——. 1990. "'A Wound Out of His Wounds': Palestinian Arabic Literature in Israel" (in Hebrew). *Alpayim* 2, pp. 244–68.
——. 1991. "'We Were Like Those Who Dream': Iraqi-Jewish Writers in Israel in the 1950s." *Prooftexts* 11, pp. 153–73.
——. 1991a. "Figliastri pieni d'amore: Scrittori arabi in lingua ebraica." *La Rassegna Mensile di Israel* 57.1/2 (June/August), pp. 245–53.
——. 1991b. "Achilles's Heel or Narcissus' Reflection?" (in Hebrew). *Alpayim* 4, pp. 202–5.
——. 1992. "Step-Sons and Lovers" (in Hebrew). *Moznaim*, May, pp. 6–9.

——. 1992a. "'al-Zayt fī al-Miṣbāḥ Lan Yajiffa'—Jadaliyyat al-Burj al-'Ājī'/al-Manāra fī Mir'āt al-Shi'r al-Multazim." *al-Karmil: Studies in Arabic Language and Literature* 13, pp. 7–54.
——. 1993. "The Poetic Creative Process according to Ṣalāḥ 'Abd al-Ṣabūr." In Ami Elad-Bouskila (ed.). *Writer, Culture, Text: Studies in Modern Arabic Literature.* Fredericton, NB: York Press, pp. 74–88.
——. 1993a. "Original and Translation on the Contact Line" (Hebrew). In Sasson Somekh (ed.). *Translation as a Challenge: Papers on Translation of Arabic Literature into Hebrew* (in Hebrew). Tel Aviv: Tel Aviv University Press, pp. 21–39.
——. 1993b. "Al-Adīb Muharrijan: Mulāḥaẓāt Ḥawla Dawr al-Adīb al-Filasṭīnī fī al-Ḥalba al-Thaqāfiyya al-Isrā'īliyya." *Mawāqif* (Haifa and Nazereth), March/April, pp. 52–61.
——. 1993c. "al-Tanāfur al-Ma'rifī fī Thaqāfat al-Aghlabiyya Izā' Thaqāfat al-Aqalliyya fī Isrā'īl." *Filasṭīn al-Thawra,* May 16, pp. 28–9.
——. 1993d. "The Beginnings of Political Palestinian Theater: *Qaraqāsh* by Samīḥ al-Qāsim" (in Hebrew). *HaMizrah HeHadash* 35, pp. 129–47.
——. 1993e. "Baghdad My Beloved City" (Hebrew). *Haaretz,* April 23, 1993, p. B9.
——. 1994a. "The 'World Upsidedown' in Modern Arabic Literature: New Literary Renditions of an Antique Religious Topos." *Edebiyât* 5.1, pp. 51–75.
——. 1994b. "'Under the Patronage of Muḥammad': Islamic Motifs in the Poetry of Jewish Writers from Iraq" (in Hebrew). In Tamar Alexander et al. (eds.). *History and Creativity in the Sephardi and Oriental Jewish Communities* (in Hebrew). Jerusalem: Misgav Yerushalayim, pp. 161–93.
——. 1994c. "Arabic Literature in the 20th Century: An Historical Dynamic Functional Model" (Hebrew). *HaMizrah HeHadash* 36, pp. 49–80.
——. 1994d. "A Study of *Elegy for al-Ḥallāj* by Adūnīs." *Journal of Arabic Literature* 25.2, pp. 245–56.
——. 1995. "'Hebrew as the Language of Grace': Arab-Palestinian Writers in Hebrew." *Prooftexts* 15, pp. 163–83.
——. 1995a. "Palestinian Theatre: Historical Development and Contemporary Distinctive Identity." *Contemporary Theatre Review* 3.2, pp. 29–73.
——. 1995b. "The Image of the Jew in Modern Arabic Culture" (in Hebrew). *Moznaim,* January, pp. 32–4.
——. 1995c. "Bawākīr al-Masraḥ al-Siyāsī al-Filasṭīnī: Samīḥ al-Qāsim wa-Masraḥiyyat Qaraqāsh." In Ṭāriq Rajab (ed.). *Mutāba'āt Naqdiyya fī Adab Samīḥ al-Qāsim.* Haifa: al-Wādī li-l-Ṭibā'a wa-l-Nashr, pp. 63–103.
——. 1996. "Palestinian Theatre as a Junction of Cultures: The Case of Samīḥ al-Qāsim's *Qaraqāsh.*" *Journal of Theatre and Drama* 2, pp. 101–20.
——. 1996a. "Maḥmūd Darwīsh: Birds without Wings" (in Hebrew). *Helicon: Anthological Journal of Contemporary Poetry* 18, pp. 47–61.
——. 1997. "'And I Hallucinate in No-Man's Land': Arab-Palestinian Writers in Hebrew" (Hebrew). *Hebrew Linguistics* 41/42, pp. 141–53.
——. 1997a. "Zionism as Reflected in Arabic and Hebrew *Belles Lettres* of Iraqi Jewry" (in Hebrew). *Pe'amim: Studies in Oriental Jewry* 73, pp. 128–46.
——. 1998. "Synchronic and Diachronic Dynamics in Modern Arabic Literature." In Shimon Ballas and Reuven Snir (eds.). *Studies in Canonical and Popular Arabic Literature.* Toronto: York Press, pp. 87–121.
——. 1998a. "Intersecting Circles between Hebrew and Arabic Literature" (in Hebrew). In Yosef Tobi (ed.). *Contacts between Arabic Literature and Jewish Literature in the Middle Ages and Modern Times,* vol. I (in Hebrew). Tel Aviv: Afikim, pp. 177–89.
——. 1998b. "The Palestinian al-Ḥakawati Theater: A Brief History." *Arab Studies Journal* 6.2/7.1, pp. 57–71.
——. 1999. "Virginia Woolf in Arabic Literature: Translations, Influence, and Reception." *Virginia Woolf Miscellany* 54, pp. 6–7.

——. 2000. "'Al-Andalus Arising from Damascus': Al-Andalus in Modern Arabic Poetry." *Hispanic Issues* 21, pp. 263–93.
——. 2000a. "The Emergence of Science Fiction in Arabic Literature." *Der Islam* 77.2, pp. 263–85.
——. 2000b. "Women in the Arabic *Belle-Lettres* of Iraqi Jewry in the 20th Century" (in Hebrew), *Pe'amim: Studies in Oriental Jewry* 82, pp. 119–49.
——. 2001. *Modern Arabic Literature: A Functional Dynamic Historical Model*. Toronto: York Press.
——. 2001a. "'Postcards in the Morning': Palestinians Writing in Hebrew." *Hebrew Studies* 42, pp. 197–224.
——. 2002. *Rak'atān fī al-'Ishq: Dirāsa fī Shi'r 'Abd al-Wahhāb al-Bayyātī*. Beirut: Dār al-Sāqī.
——. 2002a. "'My Heart Beats with Love of the Arabs': Iraqi Jews Writing in Arabic in the Twentieth Century." *Journal of Modern Jewish Studies* 1.2, pp. 182–203.
——. 2002b. "Science Fiction in Arabic Literature: Translation, Adaptation, Original Writing and Canonization." *Arabic Language & Literature* (Seoul) 2, pp. 209–29.
——. 2004. "'Forget Baghdad!': The Clash of Literary Narratives among Iraqi Jews in Israel." *Orientalia Suecana* 53, pp. 143–63.
——. 2004–2005. "'Will Homer Be Born After Us?': Intertextuality and Myth in Maḥmūd Darwīsh's Poetry in the 1980s." *al-Karmil: Studies in Arabic Language and Literature* 25/26, pp. 17–85.
——. 2005. "Arabic Literature by Iraqi Jews in the Twentieth Century: The Case of Ishaq Bār-Moshe (1927–2003)." *Middle Eastern Studies* 41.1, pp. 7–29.
——. 2005a. *Arabness, Jewishness, Zionism: A Clash of Identities in the Literature of Iraqi Jews* (in Hebrew). Jerusalem: Ben-Zvi Institute for the Study of Jewish Communities in the East.
——. 2005b. "'When the time stopped': Ishaq Bār-Moshe as Arab-Jewish Writer in Israel." *Jewish Social Studies* 11.2, pp. 102–35.
——. 2005c. *Palestinian Theatre*. Wiesbaden: Reichert Verlag.
——. 2005d. "The Emergence of Palestinian Professional Theatre after 1967: al-Balālīn's Self-Referential Play *al-'Atma* (*The Darkness*)." *Theatre Survey* 46.1, pp. 5–29.
——. 2006. *Religion, Mysticism and Modern Arabic Literature*. Wiesbaden: Harrassowitz Verlag.
——. 2006a. "Arabic in the Service of Regeneration of Jews: The Participation of Jews in Arabic Press and Journalism in the 19th and 20th Centuries." *Acta Orientalia* (Budapest) 59, pp. 283–323.
——. 2006b. "'Arabs of the Mosaic Faith': Chronicle of a Cultural Extinction Foretold." *Die Welt des Islams* 46.1, pp. 43–60.
——. 2006c. "'Till Spring Comes': Arabic and Hebrew Literary Debates among Iraqi-Jews in Israel (1950–2000)." *Shofar: An Interdisciplinary Journal of Jewish Studies* 24.2, pp. 92–123.
——. 2006d. "My Childhood Blossomed on the Waters of the Tigris": The Arabic Literature of Iraqi Jews in the 20th Century." *Bulletin of the Royal Institute for Inter-Faith Studies* 8.1/8.2, pp. 29–68.
——. 2008. "'Other Barbarians Will Come': Intertextuality, Meta-Poetry, and Meta-Myth in Maḥmūd Darwīsh's Poetry." In Hala Khamis Nassar and Najat Rahman (eds.). *Mahmoud Darwish, Exile's Poet: Critical Essays*. Northampton, MA: Interlink Books, pp. 123–66.
——. 2009. "The Arab Jews: Language, Poetry, and Singularity." *Art and Thought* 9, pp. 40–47.
——. 2010–2011. "Baghdad, Yesterday: On History, Identity, and Poetry" (in Hebrew). *Pe'amim: Studies in Oriental Jewry* 125–7, pp. 97–156.

——. 2012. "Who Needs Arab-Jewish Identity? Fragmented Consciousness, 'Inessential Solidarity', and the 'Coming Community' (Part 1)." *Journal of Modern Jewish Studies* 11.2, pp. 169–89.
——. 2013. "Double Exclusion and the Search for Inessential Solidarities: The Experience of Iraqi Jews as Heralding a New Concept of Identity and Belonging." In David Tal (ed.). *Israeli Identity between Orient and Occident*. London: Routledge, pp. 140–60.
——. 2015. *Mahmud Darwish: Fifty Years of Poetry* (in Hebrew). Tel Aviv: Keshev.
——. 2015a. "Who Needs Arab-Jewish Identity? Fragmented Consciousness, 'Inessential Solidarity', and the 'Coming Community' (Part 2)." *Journal of Modern Jewish Studies* 14.2, pp. 299–314.
——. 2015b. *Who Needs Arab-Jewish Identity? Interpellation, Exclusion, and Inessential Solidarities*. Leiden: Brill.
——. 2017. *Modern Arabic Literature: A Theoretical Framework*. Edinburgh: Edinburgh University Press.
——. 2019. "World Literature, Republics of Letters, and the Arabic Literary System: The 'Modernists' in the Defendants' Bench—A Review Article." *Mamlūk Studies Review* 22, pp. 137–92.
——. 2019a. *Arab-Jewish Literature: The Birth and Demise of the Arabic Short Story*. Leiden: Brill.
——. 2019b. "Arab-Jewish Identity: For a Long Time, There Has Been No Such Thing" (in Hebrew). *Haaretz*, April 10, 2019.
——. 2019–2020. "A Handful of Lentils"—Maryam Al-Mullā as a Feminist Iraqi-Jewish Activist." *al-Karmil: Studies in Arabic Language and Literature* 40/41, pp. 133–61.
——. 2020. "'Washing Away the Shame': A Forgotten Arab-Jewish Author as a Pioneer against Honor Killing." *Shofar: An Interdisciplinary Journal of Jewish Studies* 38.1, pp. 109–45.
——. 2020a. "Who Needs Arab-Jewish Identity? On Politics of Identity, Social Capital, and Academic Ethics" (in Hebrew). *Jama'a: Interdisciplinary Journal of Middle East Studies* 25, pp. 317–52.
——. 2020b. "A Piece of Merchandise': An Arab-Jewish Author Struggling for Women's Rights." *Journal of Oriental and African Studies* (Athens) 29, pp. 159–81.
——. 2021. "'If I Forget Thee, O Baghdad': The Demise of Arab-Jewish Identity and Culture." *Asian and African Studies* 30.1, pp. 173–88.
——. 2021a. "An Unspoken Agreement: The Demise of Arab-Jewish Culture and Identity." *Mediterranean Review* 14.1, pp. 123–54.
——. 2021b. "'My Arabic is Mute': The Demise of Arabic Literature by Iraqi Jews and Their Shift to Writing in Hebrew." *Quest. Issues in Contemporary Jewish History* 19, pp. 162–214.
——. 2021c. "'What Has Been Written Upon the Forehead, the Eye Must See': An Arab-Jewish Author between Baghdad and an Israeli Transit Camp." *Miscelánea de Estudios Árabes y Hebraicos* 70, pp. 169–90.
——. Forthcoming. "'My Iraq Was Lost Forever': Naïm Kattan and the Demise of Arab-Jewish Culture."
Sobernheim, M. 1978. "Ḳarāḳūsh." *The Encyclopaedia of Islam*, 2nd edn. VI, pp. 613–14.
Soman, Neha et al. 2021. "The Duality of Arab Israeli Identity and the Politics of Survival in Sayed Kashua's *Let It Be Morning*." *Rupkatha Journal on Interdisciplinary Studies in Humanities* 13.3, pp. 1–10.
Somekh, Sasson. 1987. "The Participation of Egyptian Jews in Modern Arabic Culture." In Shimon Shamir (ed.). *The Jews of Egypt: A Mediterranean Society in Modern Times*. Boulder, CO: Westview Press, pp. 130–40.
——. 1989. "Lost Voices: Jewish Authors in Modern Arabic Literature." In Mark R. Cohen and Abraham L. Udovitch (eds.). *Jews among Arabs: Contacts and Boundaries*. Princeton, NJ: Darwin Press, pp. 9–14 (= Wirth-Nesher 1994, pp. 188–98).

——. 1991. *Genre and Language in Modern Arabic Literature*. Wiesbaden: Harrassowitz Verlag.
——. 1995. "Baghdad Jewish Journalists, 1946–1948" (in Hebrew). *Kesher* 17, pp. 108–13.
——. 2007. *Baghdad Yesterday: The Making of an Arab Jew*. Jerusalem: Ibis Editions.
Soons, C. A. 1959. "Cide Hamete Benengeli: His Significance for 'Don Quijote.'" *Modern Language Review* 54.3, pp. 351–7.
Sophocles. 2007. *Sophocles: Oedipus the King*, ed. Ian Johnston. Arlington, VA: Richer Resources.
Sorek, Tamir. 2001. "Arab Football (Soccer) in Israel" (in Hebrew). PhD thesis, Hebrew University of Jerusalem.
——. 2003. "Palestinian Nationalism Has Left the Field: A Shortened History of Arab Soccer in Israel." *International Journal of Middle East Studies* 35.3, pp. 417–37.
——. 2006. *Playing with Identities: Arab Soccer in a Jewish State* (in Hebrew). Jerusalem: Magnes Press.
——. 2007. *Arab Soccer in a Jewish State: The Integrative Enclave*. Cambridge: Cambridge University Press.
——. 2015. *Palestinian Commemoration in Israel: Calendars, Monuments, and Martyrs*. Stanford, CA: Stanford University Press.
——. 2020. *The Optimist: A Social Biography of Tawfiq Zayyad*. Stanford, CA: Stanford University Press.
Stahl, Abraham. 1978. *Israel's Communities: Literary Chapters, Ways of Life, and History* (in Hebrew). Tel Aviv: Am Oved.
Starr, Deborah A. 2008. *Remembering Cosmopolitan Egypt: Culture, Society and Empire*. London: Routledge.
——. 2017. "Chalom and 'Abdu Get Married: Jewishness and Egyptianness in the Films of Togo Mizrahi." *Jewish Quarterly Review* 107.2, pp. 209–30.
——. 2020. *Togo Mizrahi and the Making of Egyptian Cinema*. Oakland, CA: University of California Press.
Steinschneider, Moritz. 1902. *Die Arabische Literatur der Juden*. Frankfurt am Main: J. Kauffmann.
Stern, Samuel Miklos. 1963. "Arabic Poems by Spanish-Hebrew Poets." In Moshe Lazar (ed.). *Romanica et occidentalia etudes dédiées à la mémoire de Hiram Peri*. Jerusalem: Magnes Press, pp. 254–63.
Stetkevych, Jaroslav. 1969. "Arabism and Arabic Literature: Self-View of a Profession." *Journal of Near Eastern Studies* 28.3, pp. 145–56.
——. 1973. "The Confluence of Arabic and Hebrew Literature." *Journal of Near Eastern Studies* 32.1/2, pp. 216–22.
Stewart, Devin J. 1997. "Cide Hamete Benengeli, Narrator of *Don Quijote*." *Medieval Encounters* 3.2, pp. 111–27.
Stillman, Norman A. 1979. *The Jews of Arab Lands*. Philadelphia, PA: Jewish Publication Society of America.
——. 1991. *The Jews of Arab Lands in Modern Times*. Philadelphia, PA: Jewish Publication Society of America.
——. 1991a. "Myth, Countermyth, and Distortion." *Tikkun* 6, pp. 60–4.
——. 1996. "Middle Eastern and North African Jewries Confront Modernity: Orientation, Disorientation, Reorientation." In Harvey E. Goldberg (ed.). *Sephardi and Middle Eastern Jewries: History and Culture in the Modern Era*. Bloomington: Indiana University Press, pp. 59–72.
——. 2011. "Judaism and Islam: Fourteen Hundred Years of Intertwined Destiny? An Overview." In Michael M. Laskier and Yaacov Lev (eds.). *The Convergence of Judaism and Islam: Religious, Scientific, and Cultural Dimensions*. Gainesville: University Press of Florida, pp. 10–20.

Stroud, Scott R. 2007. "Orientational Meliorism in Dewey and Dōgen." *Transactions of the Charles S. Peirce Society: A Quarterly Journal in American Philosophy* 43.1, pp. 185–215.
Stroumsa, Sarah. 1995. "On Jewish Intellectuals Who Converted in the Early Middle Ages." In Daniel Frank (ed.). *The Jews of Medieval Islam: Community, Society, and Identity*. Leiden: Brill, pp. 179–97.
al-Subkī, Tāj al-Dīn. 1992. *Ṭabaqāt al-Shāfi'iyya al-Kubrā*, ed. 'Abd al-Fattāḥ al-Ḥilū and Maḥmūd Muḥammad al-Ṭanājī. Cairo: Dār Iḥyā' al-Kutub al-'Arabiyya.
al-Suhrawardī, Shihāb al-Dīn. 1993. *Maqāmāt al-Ṣūfiyya*, ed. Emile Maalouf. Beirut: Dar el-Machreq Sarl Éditeurs.
Sulaiman, Khalid A. 1984. *Palestine and Modern Arab Poetry*. London: Zed Books.
Sulaymān, Muḥammad. 1988. *al-Ṣiḥafa al-Filasṭinyya wa-Qawānīn al-Intidāb al-Bariṭānī*. Nicosia: Bīsān Press.
Sulaymān, Ramzī. 2005."From Hegemony to Partnership" (in Hebrew). www.mahsom.com, June 30, 2005, available at: https://www.adalah.org/uploads/oldfiles/newsletter/heb/jun05/comi1.pdf, last accessed November 7, 2021.
Suleiman, Camelia. 2017. *The Politics of Arabic in Israel: A Sociolinguistic Analysis*. Edinburgh: Edinburgh University Press.
Suleiman, Yasir and Muhawi, Ibrahim (eds.). 2006. *Literature and Nation in the Middle East*. Edinburgh: Edinburgh University Press.
Sulivan, Jean. 1994. "Minor Writers/Authentic Words." *Religion & Literature* 26.3, pp. 59–79.
Sūsa, Aḥmad Nissīm. 1936. *Fī Ṭarīqī ilā al-Islām*. Cairo: al-Maṭba'a al-Salafiyya.
——.1986. *Ḥayātī fī Niṣf Qarn*. Baghdad: Dār al-Shu'ūn al-Thaqāfiyya al-'Āmma.
Suyoufie, Fadia. 2015. "Maḥmūd Darwīsh's *Athar al-farāshah*: The Poetics of Proximity." *Journal of Arabic Literature* 46, pp. 93–124.
al-Suyūṭī, Jalāl al-Dīn. [n.d.]. *al-Muzhir fī 'Ulūm al-Lugha wa-Anwā'ihā*. Cairo: Dār Iḥyā' al-Kutub al-'Arabiyya.
——. [n.d.1]. *Nuzhat al-Julasā' fī Ash'ār al-Nisā'*. Cairo: Maktabat al-Qur'ān.
Swift, Todd (ed.). 2003. *100 Poets against the War*. Cambridge: Salt Publishing.
Szyska, Christian. 2001. "Geographies of the Self: Text and Space in Anton Shammas's *Arabesques*." In Roxane Haag-Higuchi and Christian Szyska (eds.). *Narrated Space in the Literature of the Islamic World*. Wiesbaden: Harrassowitz Verlag, pp. 217–32.
Ṭāhā (Taha), Ibrāhīm. 1990. *al-Bu'd al-Ākhar*. Nazareth: Rābiṭat al-Kuttāb al-Filasṭīniyyīn.
——. 1997. "Duality and Acceptance: The Image of the Outsider in the Literary Work of Shimon Ballas." *Hebrew Studies* 38, pp. 63–87.
——. 2000. "The Palestinians in Israel: Towards a Minority Literature." *Arabic and Middle Eastern Literatures* 3.2, pp. 219–34.
——. 2021. "Intertextuality in Samīḥ al-Qāsim's Poetry: A Philosophy of Blending." In Meir Hatina and Yona Sheffer (eds.). *Cultural Pearls from the East: In Memory of Shmuel Moreh, 1932–2017*. Leiden: Brill, pp. 91–105.
Tal, David. 2017. "Jacqueline Kahanoff and the Demise of the Levantine." *Mediterranean Historical Review* 32, pp. 237–54.
——. 2017a. "Between Politics and Politics of Identity: The Case of the Arab Jews." *Journal of Levantine Studies* 7.1, pp. 57–77.
al-Ṭālib, 'Umar Muḥammad. 1987. *Malāmiḥ al-Masraḥiyya al-'Arabiyya al-Islāmiyya*. Beirut: Dār al-Āfāq al-Jadīda.
Talmon, Rafael. 2000. "Arabic as a Minority Language in Israel." In Jonathan Owens (ed.) *Arabic as a Minority Language*. Berlin: Mouton de Gruyter, pp. 199–220.
Talmud Babli, Sotah (Jerusalem, 1981) (photostat of the 1884 edition of Vilnius).
Tannenbaum, Michal. 2014. "'With a Tongue Forked in Two': Translingual Arab Writers in Israel." *International Journal of Bilingualism* 18.2, pp. 99–117.
Ṭarrāzī, Philip de. 1913 [vols I–II]; 1914 [vol. III]; 1933 [vol. IV]). *Ta'rīkh al-Ṣiḥāfa al-'Arabiyya*. Beirut: al-Maṭba'a al-Adabiyya.

Tart, Charles T. (ed.). 1969. *Altered States of Consciousness*. New York: Wiley.
Tarzi, Nazli. 2022. "Virtual Museum Retraces the Lost Art of Arab Puppetry." *The New Arab*, January 20, 2022, available at: https://english.alaraby.co.uk/features/virtual-museum-retraces-lost-art-arab-puppetry, last accessed January 27, 2022.
Tauber, Eliezer. 1995. *The Formation of Modern Syria and Iraq*. Ilford: Frank Cass.
Taufar, Barbara. 2001. *Der Uhrmacher*. Munich: Langen Muller.
Taylor, John Russell. 1984. *The Penguin Dictionary of the Theatre*. Harmondsworth: Penguin.
Tchernichovski, Saul. 1950. *Poems* (in Hebrew). Jerusalem: Schocken.
ten Bos, René. 2005. "Giorgio Agamben and the Community without Identity." *Sociological Review* 53.1, pp. 16–29.
The Talmud of Babylonia, XVII, Tractate Sotah. 1984, trans. Jacob Neusner. Chico, CA: Scholars Press.
Thompson, Thomas Levi. 2017. "Speaking Laterally: Transnational Poetics and the Rise of Modern Arabic and Persian Poetry in Iraq and Iran." PhD thesis, University of California, Los Angeles.
Tibawi, Abd al-Latif. 1974. *Arabic and Islamic Themes: Historical, Educational and Literary Studies*. London: Luzac.
Tibi, Bassam. 1990 [1981]. *Arab Nationalism: A Critical Enquiry*. Houndmills: Macmillan.
Tobi, Yosef. 1995. "The Reaction of Rav Sa'adia Gaon to Arabic Poetry and Poetics." *Hebrew Studies* 36, pp. 35–53.
——. 1996. "The Flowering of Judeo-Arabic Literature in North Africa, 1850–1950." In Harvey E. Goldberg (ed.). *Sephardi and Middle Eastern Jewries: History and Culture in the Modern Era*. Bloomington: Indiana University Press, pp. 213–25.
——. 2000. "Sa'adia Gaon, *Poet-Paytan*: The Connecting Link between the Ancient Piyyut and Hebrew Arabicised Poetry in Spain." In Tudor Parfitt (ed.). *Israel and Ishmael: Studies in Muslim–Jewish Relations*. Richmond: Curzon, pp. 59–77.
——. 2002. "Translations of Sa'adia Gaon's Liturgical Works into Arabic." In Yitzhak Avishur and Z. Yehuda Avishur (eds.). *Studies in the History and Culture of the Jews in Babylonia* (in Hebrew). Or-Yehuda: BJHC, pp. 203–21.
——. 2004. *Proximity and Distance: Medieval Hebrew and Arabic Poetry*. Leiden: Brill.
——. 2017. "Jewish Connections and Connotations in the Poetry of Imru' al-Qays (ca. 497–545 CE)." In Nader Masarwah et al. (eds.). *In the Inkwell of Words: Studies in Arab Literature and Culture—In Honour of Professor Albert Arazi*. Mauritius: Noor Publishing, vol. II, pp. 194–390.
Tobi, Yosef and Tobi, Zivia. 1998. "Mythicization of a Popular Singer: Oral and Written Traditions about Hbiba Msika (Tunis, 1903–1930)" (in Hebrew). *Jerusalem Studies in Jewish Folklore* 19/20, pp. 187–210.
Tottoli, Roberto. 1999. "Origins and Use of the Term *Isrā'īliyyāt* in Muslim Literature." *Arabica* 46, pp. 193–210.
——. 2002. *Biblical Prophets in the Qur'ān and Muslim Literature*. Richmond: Curzon.
——. 2021. "New Material on the Use and Meaning of the Term *Isrā'īliyyāt*." *Jerusalem Studies in Arabic and Islam* 50, pp. 1–42.
Toury, Gideon. 1995. *Descriptive Translation Studies and Beyond*. Amsterdam: John Benjamins.
Trimingham, J. Spencer. 1971. *The Sufi Orders in Islam*. Oxford: Clarendon.
Tsoffar, Ruth. 2006. "Forget Baghdad: Roundtrip to the Promised Land." *Anthropological Quarterly* 79.1, pp. 133–43.
Tsur, Yaron. 2003. *The Evolution of a Culture: The Jews of Tunisia and Other Islamic Countries* (in Hebrew). Jerusalem: Zalman Shazar Center for Jewish History.
Ṭūqān, Fadwā. 1985. *Riḥla Ṣa'ba Riḥla Jabaliyya*. Acre: Dār al-Aswār.
al-Ṭūsī, Abū Naṣr al-Sarrāj. 1960. *al-Luma'*. ed. 'Abd al-Ḥalīm Maḥmūd and Ṭāhā 'Abd al-Bāqī Surūr. Cairo: Dār al-Kutub al-Ḥadītha.

Tzelgov, Eran. 2009. "A Personal Conversation with Elias Khoury" (in Hebrew). *Daka: Journal for Poetry and Criticism* 5.
al-Udhari, Abdullah (ed. and trans.). 1984. *Mahmud Darwish, Samih al-Qasim, Adonis.* London: Saqi.
Urian, Dan. 1996. "Perspectives on Palestinian Drama and Theatre: A Symposium." In Linda Ben-Zvi (ed.). *Theater in Israel.* Ann Arbor: University of Michigan Press, pp. 323–45.
——. 2001. "Mizrahi and Ashkenazi in the Israeli Theatre." *Arabic and Middle Eastern Literatures* 4.4, pp. 19–36.
——. 2004. *The Ethnic Problem in Israeli Theatre* (in Hebrew). Tel Aviv: Open University.
'Uthmān, I'tidāl. 1988. *Iḍā'at al-Naṣṣ.* Beirut: Dār al-Ḥadātha.
Van Leeuwen, Richard. 1999. "The Poet and His Mission: Text and Space in the Prose Works of Maḥmūd Darwīsh." In Stephan Guth et al. (eds.). *Conscious Voices: Concepts of Writing in the Middle East.* Beirut: Orient-Institut der DMG, pp. 265–6.
Varghese, Gabriel. 2020. *Palestinian Theatre in the West Bank: Our Human Faces.* New York: Palgrave Macmillan.
von Grunebaum, Gustave E. 1962. *Modern Islam: The Search for Cultural Identity.* Berkeley: University of California Press.
Wādī, Ṭāhā. 2001. *al-Qiṣṣa Dīwān al-'Arab: Qaḍāyā wa-Namādhij.* Cairo: al-Sharika al-Miṣriyya al-'Ālamiyya li-l-Nahsr—Longman.
Wagner, Mark S. 2009. *Like Joseph in Beauty: Yemeni Vernacular Poetry and Arab-Jewish Symbiosis.* Leiden: Brill.
Wallin, Johanna (ed.). 2017. *Rehearsing Freedom: The Story of a Theatre in Palestine.* New Delhi: LeftWord.
Walters, Keith. 2021. "Introduction: The Arabic Language and Identity." In Reem Bassiouney and Keith Walters (eds.). *The Routledge Handbook of Arabic and Identity.* New York: Routledge, pp. 3–10.
Wannūs, Sa'd Allāh. 1989. *al-Fīl Yā Malik al-Zamān wa-Mughāmarat Ra's al-Mamlūk Jābir.* Beirut: Dār al-Ādāb.
Wasserstein, David J. 1991. "The Language Situation in al-Andalus" In Alan Jones and Richard Hitchcock (eds.). *Studies on the Muwaššaḥ and the Kharja.* Reading: Ithaca Press, pp. 1–15.
——. 1993. "Samuel Ibn Naghrīla Ha-Nagid and Islamic Historiography in al-Andalus." *Al-Qanṭara* 14, pp. 109–25.
Wensinck, A. J. and Mensing, J. P. (eds.). 1936–1969. *Concordance et Indices de la Tradition Musulmane.* Leiden: Brill.
White, Hayden V. 1978. *Tropics of Discourse: Essays in Cultural Criticism.* Baltimore, MD: Johns Hopkins University Press.
——. 1987. *The Content of the Form: Narrative Discourse and Historical Representation.* Baltimore, MD: Johns Hopkins University Press.
Wickstrom, Maurya. 2012. *Performance in the Blockades of Neoliberalism: Thinking the Political Anew.* New York: Palgrave Macmillan.
Wiet, Gaston. 1966. *Introduction à la littérature arabe.* Paris: Maisonneuve et Larose.
Williams, Patrick. 2014. "Postcolonialism and Orientalism." In Geoffrey Nash et al. (eds.). *Postcolonialism and Islam: Theory, Literature, Culture, Society, and Film.* London: Routledge, pp. 48–61.
Wilson, Arnold T. 1936. *Loyalties Mesopotamia, 1914–1917: A Personal and Historical Record.* London: Oxford University Press.
Wilson, Edmund. 1941. *The Wound and the Bow: Seven Studies in Literature.* Cambridge, MA: Houghton Mifflin.
Wimsatt, W. K. and Beardsley, Monroe 1946. "The Intentional Fallacy." *Sewanee Review* 54.3, pp. 468–88.

Wirth-Nesher, Hana (ed.). 1994. *What is Jewish Literature?* Philadelphia: Jewish Publication Society of America.

Wisse, Ruth R. 2000. *The Modern Jewish Canon: A Journey through Language and Culture*. New York: Free Press.

Wistrich, Robert S. 1987. "The Modernization of Viennese Jewry: The Impact of German Culture in a Multi-Ethnic State." In Jacob Katz (ed.). *Toward Modernity: The European Jewish Model*. New Brunswick, NJ: Transaction, pp. 43–70.

Yāghī, 'Abd al-Raḥmān. 1981. *Ḥayāt al-Adab al-Filasṭīnī al-Ḥadīth: Min Awwal al-Nahḍa ḥattā Awwal al-Nakba*. Beirut: Dār al-Āfāq al-Jadīda.

Yaḥyā, Rāfi'. 2003. "Qaṣīdat al-Aṭfāl al-Jadīda." *Mawāqif* (Haifa) 36/37, pp. 148–64.

Yannakakis, Ilios. 1997. "The Death of Cosmopolitanism." In Robert Ilbert and Ilios Yannakakis (with Jacques Hassoun) (eds.). *Alexandria 1860–1960: The Brief Life of a Cosmopolitan Community*, trans. Colin Clement. Alexandria: Harpocrates Publishing, pp. 190–94.

Yāqūt. 1991. *Mu'jam al-Udabā'*. Beirut: Dār al-Kutub al-'Ilmiyya.

Yardeni, Galya (ed.). 1967. *The Basket of Grapes: Israeli Stories from the First Aliya Period* (in Hebrew). Jerusalem: Bialik Institute.

Yazbak, Mahmoud. 1998. *Haifa in the Late Ottoman Period, 1864–1914: A Muslim Town in Transition*. Leiden: Brill.

Yehoshua, Abraham B. 1988. "In Search of the Sephardi Lost Time, Somewhat" (in Hebrew). In Ya'qūb Yehoshua (ed.). *Nostalgic Jerusalem* (in Hebrew). Jerusalem: Keter, pp. 8–11.

——. 1989. *The Wall and the Mountain* (in Hebrew). Tel Aviv: Zmora-Bitan.

——. 2001. *The Liberating Bride* (in Hebrew). Tel-Aviv: Ha-Kibbutz ha-Me'uḥad.

——. 2003. *Diokan 2: Two Interviews and Notes by Yotam Reuveny* (in Hebrew). Tel Aviv: Nimrod.

——. 2004. *The Liberated Bride*, trans. Hillel Halkin. Orlando, FL: Harvest/Harcourt.

——. 2011. *Spanish Charity* (in Hebrew). Tel Aviv: Ha-Kibbutz ha-Me'uḥad.

Yehoshua, Ya'qūb (Yaacob). 1974. *Ta'rīkh al-Ṣiḥāfa al-'Arabiyya fī Filasṭīn fī al-'Ahd al-'Uthmānī (1908–1918)*. Jerusalem: Dār al-Ma'ārif.

——. 1979. "A Very Remote Draft" (in Arabic). *al-Sharq*, July–September, pp. 67–77.

Yehuda, Zvi. 1980. *From Babylon to Jerusalem* (in Hebrew). Tel Aviv: Iraqi Jews' Traditional Cultural Center.

——. 1996. "Iraqi Jewry and Cultural Change in the Educational Activity of the Alliance Israélite Universelle." In Harvey E. Goldberg (ed.). *Sephardi and Middle Eastern Jewries: History and Culture in the Modern Era*. Bloomington: Indiana University Press, pp. 134–45.

——. 2017. *The New Babylonian Diaspora The Rise and Fall of the Jewish Community in Iraq, 16th–20th Centuries C.E.* Leiden: Brill.

Yinnon, Abraham. 1981. "Tawfiq Zayyād: We Are the Majority Here" (in Hebrew). In Aharon Layish (ed.). *The Arabs in Israel: Continuity and Change* (in Hebrew). Jerusalem: Magnes Press, pp. 213–40.

Youssef, Mary. 2018. *Minorities in the Contemporary Egyptian Novel*. Edinburgh: Edinburgh University Press.

Yudkin, Leon I. 1982. *Jewish Writing and Identity in the Twentieth Century*. London: Croom Helm.

——. 1992. *Beyond Sequence: Current Israeli Fiction and Its Context*. Northwood: Symposium Press.

Zafrani, H. 1980. *Littératures dialectales et populaires juives en Occident Musulman: l'écrit et l'oral*. Paris: Éditions Geuthner.

Zajda, Joseph. 2009. "Nation-Building, Identity and Citizenship Education: Introduction." In Joseph Zajda et al. (eds.). *Nation-Building, Identity and Citizenship Education*. Dordrecht: Springer, pp. 1–11.

Zaydān, Jurjī. 1913. *Ta'rīkh Adab al-Lugha al-'Arabīyya*. Cairo: Maṭba'at al-Fajjāla.
al-Zayyāt, Aḥmad Ḥasan. 1960. *Ta'rīkh al-Adab al-'Arabī*. Cairo: Maktabat Nahḍat Miṣr.
Zeidel, Ronen. 2009. "A Question of Language and Audience: On the Possibility of 'Iraqi Novels' in Hebrew." *Hebrew Studies* 50, pp. 229–43.
——. 2013. "Writing about the 'Other': Israel in Recent Iraqi Novels." *Arabica* 60, pp. 778–94.
——. 2018. "On the Last Jews in Iraq and Iraqi National Identity: A Look at Two Recent Iraqi Novels." *Journal of Modern Jewish Studies* 17.2, pp. 207–21.
Zenner, W. P. 1988. "Aleppo and the Kibbutz in the Fiction of Amnon Shamosh." *Shofar: An Interdisciplinary Journal of Jewish Studies* 6.3, pp. 25–35.
Zimhoni, Dafna. 1988. "The Beginnings of Modernization among the Jews of Iraq in the Nineteenth Century until 1914" (in Hebrew). *Pe'amim: Studies in Oriental Jewry* 36, pp. 7–34.
al-Ziriklī, Khayr al-Dīn. 1984. *al-A'lām*. Beirut: Dār al-'Ilm li-l-Malāyīn.
Zohar, Zvi. 2007. "Non-Ashkenazic Jewry as the Ground of Contemporary Israeli Multiculturalism." *Revista de Historia Actual* 5, pp. 137–48.
——. 2013. *Rabbinic Creativity in the Modern Middle East*. London: Bloomsbury.
Zubaida, Sami. 2002. "Entertainers in Baghdad: 1900–50." In Eugene Rogan (ed.). *Outside In: On the Margins of the Modern Middle East*. London: I. B. Tauris, pp. 219–22.
Zuhur, Sherifa (ed.). 2001. *Colors of Enchantment: Theater, Dance, Music, and the Visual Arts of the Middle East*. Cairo: American University in Cairo Press.
Zurayk, Constantine K. 1956. *The Meaning of the Disaster*. Beirut: Khayat.

Index

Note: The definite article *al-* is not taken into consideration in the alphabetical order. It appears in this form throughout the entire book before solar and lunar letters. The following terms and their derivatives do not appear in the Index as independent terms or appear only partly: Arab, Arabic, Arabized, Baghdad, culture, Egypt, identity, Iraq, Islam, Israel, Jew, Jewish, Muslim, *Nakba*, Palestine, short story, text, theater, West, Zionism.

'Abbās, Hiyām, 64
Abbās, Iḥsān, 95n
al-'Abbūshī, Burhān al-Dīn, 43
al-'Abbūshī, Sāmiḥ, 57
'Abd al-Nāṣir, Jamāl (Gamal Abdel Nasser), 124
'Abd al-Ṣabūr, Ṣalāḥ, 78, 80, 295
'Abd al-Wahhāb, Muḥammad, 279
Abel, 111, 115, 129
al-Ablaq, 193, 234
Abraham, 169, 182, 224n
Absurd, absurdity, 18, 62, 79, 85, 294
Abū Ghūsh, Usāma, 147n
Abū Jābir, Rīmā, 290n
Abū Sālim (Abu Salem), François, 55–6, 59, 64–6, 70–1
Abū Shanab, Hānī, 57
Abū Shbaḥot, 205
Abū Warda, Yūsuf, 147n
Abyaḍ, Georges, 41
Achebe, Chinua, 93
Aciman, André, 212, 353
Acre (Akko, 'Akkā), 99, 100, 255n
'Adas, Shafīq, 305
Aden, 103
Adīb al-Qāṣṣ, 251, 270; *see also* Ballas, Shimon
Adon (Adūn), Rā'ida, 174
Adorno, Theodor, 141
Adūnīs ('Alī Aḥmad Sa'īd), 94n, 120, 308
Agamben, Giorgio, 1, 18, 346
Aghāsī (Aggasi), Iliyāhū (Eliyahu), 244n
Agnon, Shmuel Yosef, 271
Aḥada 'Ashara Kawkaban (poetry collection), 100
Aharon, Ezra, 230
Aharon, Zakkay Binyamin (Binyāmīn Hārūn), 241
Ahava Bein ha-Dekalīm (book for youth), 266
Ahavat Sha'ūl (novel), 280
Ahavat Tzion (novel), 209n
Ahl al-Dhimma, 195
Aḥmad, 'Abd al-Ilāh, 238
Aḥmad, Zakariyyā, 79
Aḥrār wa-'Abīd (collection of short stories), 223n
'Ā'ilat al-Masraḥ (theatrical troupe), 31, 55, 57, 74
Akher, 272; *see also* Other; ben Avuya, Elisha
Alcalay, Ammiel, 272n, 318n
Aleppo, 223n, 373
Alexandria, 14, 24, 37, 210, 212
  Alexandrian cosmopolitanism, 15

Alf Layla wa-Layla, 39, 63, 140, 205, 273; *see also A Thousand and One Nights*
Algeria, Algerian, 203, 204, 231n, 253n
ʿAlī, Muḥammad, 37
Ali, Tariq, 366n
alienation, 20–1, 82, 92, 161, 166, 274, 287, 294, 300
Ali, Agha Shahid Ali, 168–9
ʿAlī, Fāḍil, 147n
ʿAlī, Muḥammad Kurd, 100n
ʿAliyya, 236n
ʿAliyyat ha-Noʿar, 277, 281
Allāh wa-l-Zahra wa-Qiṣaṣ Ukhrā (collection of short stories), 303
Allen, Woody, 62
Alliance Israélite Universelle (AIU), 211, 214, 215, 219n, 221, 252, 270
Aloni, Nissim, 294n
Aloni, Shulamit, 69
Althusser, Louis Pierre, 2–6, 191, 331
American, 13, 21, 23–4, 60, 62, 125, 126, 127, 130, 168, 208n, 234, 235, 251, 262, 263, 272, 274n, 288, 325, 348, 353, 366n
Amichai, Yehuda, 143, 150, 166, 168, 169, 171–2, 183
Amīn, Aḥmad, 225
Amir, Aharon, 154
ʿAmīr, Elī, 251, 277–82, 313
ʿāmmiyya, 57, 304; *see also* dialect; vernacular
Amor, Meir, 328
Anā min al-Yahūd (short story), 284–90
anarchy, anarchist, 11, 125, 295
al-Anbāʾ (newspaper), 55, 293
Andalus, Andalusian, 97–101, 106, 115, 158n, 198–203, 224, 317, 365–6; *see also* Spain
Anna Karenina (novel), 267
Anthills of the Savannah (novel), 366
Antichrist, 88–90
Antigone (play), 84, 88
anti-Jewish, 224n, 272
anti-Semitism, 232
anti-Zionism, 43, 232, 250, 346
Antonius, George, 222n
apocalypticism, 88–90
Apparatus, 2–4, 8
Appiah, Kwame Anthony, 13–14, 17n
ʿaql, 141
ʿAql, Saʿīd, 153
al-ʿAqqād, ʿAbbās Maḥmūd, 209–10, 225
Arab Book Fund, 46, 244
Arabeskot (novel), 151, 153n, 154, 164–5, 166, 167, 170, 176n, 178
Arabian Peninsula, 194
Arabization, 196, 202, 203, 205n, 208n, 218
Arabness, viii, 176, 223, 225, 239, 243, 323, 330, 342, 345, 346, 350n
Arab Revolutionary Committee, 123, 340
Aramaic, neo-Aramaic, 196, 197, 204
ʿArāyidī, Naʿīm, 25, 32–3, 147, 150, 153–64, 173–6, 183, 313
Aristotle, Aristotlian, 295
Armillus, 88
Arna's Children (film), 70n
al-Asadī, Bahāʾ al-Dīn ibn ʿAbd Allāh, 79; *see also* Qarāqūsh
Ashʿab mi-Baghdad (book for youth), 273
Ashrāṭ al-Sāʿa (The Signs of the Day of Judgment), 89
ʿAshrāwī, Ḥanān Mīkhāʾīl, 53
Ashrāwī, Imīl, 57
Ashkenazi, Ashkenazim, 176, 177n, 190, 236, 251, 262, 266–9, 274–5, 277, 278, 280, 286, 309, 320, 327, 329–30, 338, 345n
Asia, Asian, 11, 23, 50, 77, 124, 127
assimilation, 82, 150n, 182n, 213n, 215, 222, 230, 330
Association for Civil Rights in Israel (ACRI), 268
Association of Arabic Language Poets, 244
Assyrian, 218, 221
Aswār al-Quds wa-Qiṣaṣ Ukhrā (collection of short stories), 302
atheist, 19
Athens, 101, 102, 107, 128n
A Thousand and One Nights, 39, 48, 205, 267, 273, 279; *see also Alf Layla wa-Layla*
al-ʿAtma (play), 57, 70
attachment, 9, 188, 203, 212, 261, 334
indissoluble attachment, 340–2
Aufklärung, 216; *see also Haskala*; Enlightenment; *Nahḍa*; renaissance
Auschwitz, 23, 141

Austria, Austrian, 208n, 216, 217, 221, 294, 335
author, 272, 280–2, 296–7, 302–5, 357–8, 362–6, 368, 375
 death of the author, 362–6, 375
 implied author, 4n, 272, 280, 282, 296, 297, 302, 305, 328, 357, 358, 362, 368
autobiography, autobiographical, 71, 151, 182, 190, 208n, 210, 213n, 240n, 243, 273, 278, 279, 280, 282, 285, 293, 295, 296, 303, 305; *see also* biography, biographical
Avanti Popolo, 93, 143–5
Avi-Shlomo (Avishai), Mordechai, 306n
ʻAwn, Īmān, 59
al-Ayyām (novel), 303
Ayyām al-ʻIrāq (novel), 303n, 306–7
Ayyūb (Job), 129
Ayyūb, Dhū al-Nūn, 238
al-ʻAzabī, Muḥammad, 306n
al-Azdī, Abū al-Muṭahhar, 203–4
ʻAzza Ḥafīdat Nafratītī (autobiography), 210
ʻAzzām, Ṣāliḥ, 147n
ʻAzzī, Asad, 147n

al-Bāb (play), 50
Babel, Babylon, Babylonian, 196, 204, 205, 214, 231, 234, 304, 313, 322–4
 Babylonian Academy at Sūra, 197
 Babylonian Exile, 213, 323
 Babylonian Talmud, 218n
 The Babylonian Jewry Heritage Center (BJHC), 231n, 242
 Tower of Babel, 168
Baʻḍ al-Nās (collection of short stories), 223n
Baghdad
 As a "Jewish" city, 218
 Ashʻab mi-Baghdad, 273
 Baghdad Law College, 292, 378n
 Forget Baghdad (documentary film), 175n, 309, 323, 344n
al-Baḥrī, Jamīl, 43
Bakhtin, Mikhail, 362
Bakrī, Muḥammad, 147n
al-Balālīn (theatre troupe), 57
Balbūl, Yaʻqūb, 224, 241, 292
Balfour, Arthur James, 218n
Balfour Declaration, 43, 151, 218, 224, 338, 341
Ballas, Shimon, 175–6, 208n, 220n, 241, 251, 262, 269–77, 314, 323, 324, 349, 360, 361
Banū Isrāʼīl, 209n, 239
Barabash, Uri, 64
barbarians, barbarism, barbaric, 96, 117–30, 136, 141
Bār-Moshe, Isḥāq (Isaac), 26, 190–1, 219–20, 241, 292–312, 358
Barnes, Djuna, 5
Barthes, Roland, 362–5, 375
Bashkin, Orit, 315–17
Basra,196, 305
Baṣrī, Mīr, 226, 228, 233, 234, 238, 240, 292, 310n, 357
al-Baṣṣūn, Nīrān, 358n, 367
al-Baṣṣūn, Salīm, 292, 367
Bataille, Georges, 351–2
Bauman, Zygmunt, 6–12, 18, 332–5
al-Bayādir (magazine), 54
Baydas, Khalīl, 370n
Baydas, Riāḍ, 156n
Bayna al-Nahrayn, 226
Bayt fī Baghdad (novel), 305, 307
al-Bayyātī, ʻAbd al-Wahhāb, 80
Beardsley, Monroe, 363
Beck, Ulrich, 16–17
Beckett, Samuel, 64
Bedouin, 194, 218n
Begin, Menahem, 210
Be-Gūf Rishon (novel), 274
Behar, Almog, 284–90, 321, 361–2
Behar, Moshe, 319–20
Beirut, 24, 37, 55, 103, 104, 114, 134, 137, 204, 207n, 217, 232n
belonging, belongingness, viii, 2, 3, 4, 8, 18, 19, 26, 32, 147, 177n, 180, 191, 192, 268, 326, 327, 333–8, 334, 344, 345, 347, 351, 356, 372
ben Avuya, Elisha, 272
Benengeli, Cide Hamete, 365
Ben Hanania, Yehoshua, 228n; *see also* Yehoshua, Yaʻacob
Benite, Zvi Ben-Dor, 318–20
Benjamin, Walter, 141

Bennett, Andrew, 354, 364, 375
Ben Zvi, Yitzḥak, 246
Berber, 98, 366n
Berdugo, Sami, 329
Berlin, 11, 81
Beyond the Walls (film), 64
Bhabha, Homi K., 174
Bialik, Haim Nachman, 253n, 360
Bible, biblical, 100, 110, 129, 169, 197, 200, 208, 209, 271; *see also* Torah
Biesecker, Barbara, 338
Bilā-Līn (theatre troupe), 57
Bildungsroman, 279
bilingual, bilingualism, 25, 32, 143–84, 204
Bin'Amāra, Muḥammad, 134n
binary, 16, 191, 236, 337, 342, 343
biography, biographical, 147n, 237–8, 356–8, 361, 365; *see also* autobiography, autobiographical
al-Bīra, 49
Bismi al-Ab wa-l-Umm wa-l-Ibn (play), 61
Blau, Joshua, 200
Blindness (novel), 287
Bombay, 339
Book of Psalms, 322
Bosnia, 11, 22
bourgeois, bourgeoisie, 2, 18–19, 69, 86, 87, 92, 251
  bourgeois ideology, 2
  classlessness of the bourgeoisie, 18
  petty bourgeoisie, 18–19
Brazilian, 11
Bread Givers (novel), 288
Brecht, Bertolt, 25, 31, 49, 58–60, 68, 81–2, 85–91
Breton, André, 301
Britain, British, 1, 23, 24, 43, 250, 305, 306, 366n
  British High Commissioner, 224
  British mandate, 38, 53, 211, 218
brotherhood, 48, 130, 190, 241, 249, 253, 256, 257, 260, 283
  Arab-Jewish brotherhood, 48, 189, 244, 247, 249, 283
Buddhists, 19, 21n
Bukaee, Rafi, 143n, 144, 145
Būluṣ, Sarkūn, 368n
Burg, Avraham, 280n
Burke, Kenneth, 337–8
al-Bustānī, Buṭrus, 217
Butterfly Effect, 94, 373–5
"By the Rivers of Babylon," 322–4

Cain, 111, 129
Cairo, 41, 123, 149, 197, 205, 209–13, 230, 237, 280, 293, 299, 311, 340
  Cairene Trilogy, 266, 303
  Cairo Genizah, 197
Caliphate, 124, 196
canon, canonical, 25, 33, 42, 96, 153, 156, 172, 173, 175, 179, 188, 191, 205, 206, 207, 213, 214, 237, 238, 243, 267–9, 275, 306, 308, 309, 312–14, 347, 365
captivity, 322
Carné, Marcel, 64
carpe diem, 279
Carr, Edward Hallett, 346
Carthage, 313n
catharsis, 295
Cather, Willa, 288
Cavafy, Constantine P., 120–30
Censorship, 45, 47, 53–4, 58, 67–8, 78, 80, 91, 231n, 253, 276, 314, 370n
Chaim (Ḥaim), Chacham Yoseif, 217
Chalghi, 205
Cheikho (Shaykhū), Louis, 206–7
Cherem, 217
Chetrit, Sami Shalom, 243, 325–7, 330, 346
Chicano, 11
Choueiri, Youssef M., 350n
Christ, Christianity, Christian, 11, 19, 24, 25, 32, 37, 42, 88–90, 98, 115, 143, 147, 150, 153, 154, 155, 156, 172, 183, 186, 188, 195, 198, 200, 203, 207, 214, 217, 218, 219, 220, 221, 223, 232, 235, 237, 239, 244n, 263, 265, 268, 270, 275, 280, 291, 292n, 305, 307n, 310n, 311, 313, 314n, 320, 328, 338, 339, 340, 341, 350, 352, 366n, 368, 369
Church (Catholic), 366n
cinema, films, movies, 4, 16, 41, 58, 60, 62, 64, 70, 79n, 143–4, 146, 147, 155n, 175n, 178n, 210, 211, 227n, 265, 270, 278, 284n, 309, 323, 344, 350, 361n
Cixous, Hélène, 351

classical, 32, 41n, 59, 138, 179, 200, 203, 225, 231, 239, 256, 273
classical Arabic language, 207, 230
classical Arabic poetry, 107, 108, 109
classical bias, 204
neoclassical poetics, 32, 96, 108
clown, 174, 263, 264, 268
Coetzee, John Maxwell, 121–9
cognitive dissonance, 25, 33, 93, 148–9, 173, 267, 269, 271, 285, 312–13
colonialist, colonialism, 64n, 70n, 93, 174, 179, 188, 224, 236n, 274, 274, 275n, 319, 349, 368
Communist, Communism, 26, 47–8, 54, 70, 144n, 173, 190, 232, 239, 244, 250–5, 259, 260, 264, 265, 268, 274, 279, 283–4, 346
Communist Manifesto, 255
Communist Party (Iraq), 270
Communist Party (Israel), 45, 47, 244–5, 270
Conrad, Joseph, 93
conversion, convert, converted, 154n, 201–2, 207–8, 211, 237, 272, 366n
convivencia, 353
Copenhagen, 235, 285
Cordova, 97, 98, 142
cosmopolitan, cosmopolitanism, 14–17, 23–4, 212n, 227, 270, 273, 275, 335, 360
coup d'état, 239, 305
cowboy, 62, 262–3
Crime and Punishment (novel), 5
Crusoe, Robinson, 7–8
culture (definition)
Curiel, Henri, 274
curriculum, 219, 220, 232, 281

al-Dabābīs (play), 57
Dabka, 40, 65
al-Dahāna, 270
Dā'irat al-Khawf al-Ḍabābiyya (play), 57–8
al-Dajjāl, 88
Dalālat al-Ḥā'irīn, 197–8
Dal'ūnā, 40n
Damascus, 39n, 50, 340
Daniel, Ezra Ben Menaḥem, 251
Daninos, Abraham, 203
Dante, 167
Daqqāqāt, 205
al-Darb (journal), 47n
Dār al-Idhā'a al-Isrā'īliyya, 210, 293
al-Darīnī, Labība, 49
Darwīsh, Maḥmud, xii, 4n, 25, 28, 32, 51, 77, 94, 96–142, 169, 256, 352, 372–5
Darwīsh, Salmān Ya'qūb, 220, 234
Darwīsh, Shalom, 223n, 231, 241, 250n, 292, 340, 359–60
Dā'ūd, Sihām, 147n
Davis, Diane, 1, 22, 337n, 351n
Ḍaw, Salīm, 93, 145, 147n
Dayan, Moshe, 89, 282
DDT spray, 176n, 265
Debord, Guy, 19–20
de Cervantes, Miguel, 365
deconstruction, 6
Deleuze, Gilles, 274
democracy, democratic, 11, 23, 24, 153, 154, 155, 157n, 174, 181, 243, 269n
Derrida, Jacques, 178, 281, 365
Der Uhrmacher (novel), 217n
de Ṭarrāzī, Philip, 206, 338
deterritorialization, reterritorialization, 152, 274
deus ex machine, 83, 299
Dewey, John, 21
dialect, 46, 145, 197, 203, 205, 206, 219, 230n, 304, 324, 346; *see also* *'āmmiyya*; vernacular
diaspora, 24, 113, 181n, 235, 360
dichotomy, dichotomizing, dichotomous
Dijla, 233, 235, 367; *see also* Tigris
Dijla (newspaper), 223
dina de-malkhuta dina, 218n
al-dīnu li-llāhi wa-l-waṭan li-l-jamī', 217–18, 350, 369
discrimination, 95, 304
Don Quixote (novel), 365–6
Dostoyevsky, Fyodor, 5
Drory, Rina, 200–1
Druze, 25, 32, 147, 154n, 155, 156, 159, 172, 183, 263, 313
al-Dubb al-Quṭbī wa-Qiṣaṣ Ukhrā (collection of short stories), 300
Dutch, 24, 164n, 266

dwarfing (of the father figure), 251, 279n
dybbuk, 286, 288

Eckhart, Meister, 297n
'Edot Mizrāḥ, 236n, 237n, 343–4
El-Ariss, Tarek, 317
elegy, 195, 228–9, 280n
Elias, Arieh, 49
Eliraz, Israel, 177
elite, elitist, elitism, 15–16, 29, 45, 47, 69, 70, 92, 197, 214, 215, 218, 221, 230, 268, 314n, 339, 340, 347, 350
elusive, elusiveness, 9, 229, 334, 364, 375
emancipation, 226, 236
Encyclpaedia Palastina, 46–7
Engels, Friedrich, 255
enjambment, 256, 258
Enlightenment, 216–17, 221n, 229, 318; *see also Aufklärung*; *Haskala*; *Nahḍa*; renaissance
escapism, 232, 239, 295
establishment (cultural, literary), 26, 45–50, 74, 90, 92, 127n, 129, 161, 173, 189–91, 242, 244–5, 249–53, 266–8, 271, 280, 283–4, 308, 313, 327
estrangement, 161, 274, 286, 287
ethnic, ethnical, ethnicity, 6, 21, 23, 30–1, 36, 171, 176, 177n, 183, 187, 191, 196, 219, 221, 226, 236, 265, 275, 280, 294, 308, 323,332, 341, 345, 347
  ethnic cleansing, 319, 342
  ethnic identity, 7, 177n, 187, 190, 293
Euphrates, 213, 234, 235, 252, 323
exclusion, exclusionist, exclusionary, 25–6, 56n, 82, 191, 217, 237–8, 330, 336–46
exile, 71, 97, 102, 158n, 163, 169, 181, 204, 245, 274, 283, 287, 311–12
  Babylonian Exile, 196, 213, 322–3, 366n, 371
  exiled writers, 171
  Negation of Exile, 309
Existentialism, existential, existentialist, 70, 170, 190, 279, 293–9, 327, 357

Fāḍil, 'Abd al-Ḥaqq, 238
al-Fajr, (newspaper), 252
Fallah, Dalia, 177
Falsafat al-Thawra (book), 124
Fanon, Frantz, 179, 202
al-Frāfīr (theater troupe), 58
Faraḥ, Najwā Qa'wār, 48
Faraj, Murad (Morad Farag), 208–9
al-faraj ba'da al-shidda, 83
Fargeon, Maurice, 212
Farḥāt, Muḥammad 'Alī, 94n
Farhūd, 232, 239, 306–7
Fatā Isrā'īl (pseudonym), 228–9
Fatimid, 197
Fawzī, Ḥusayn, 273
Fayṣal (King of Iraq), 186, 223, 231, 233, 237, 339, 369
Fedayeen, 302
Feiner, Shmuel, 229
feminist, feminism, 5, 6, 17, 187, 205–6, 274, 332, 335, 337
fetishization, 21
Fī 'Ālam al-Nūr (poetry collection), 245
al-firdaws al-mafqūd (The Lost Paradise), 98, 100, 106, 115, 137
Firqat al-Masraḥ al-Filasṭīnī (theater troupe), 57
Firqat al-Mukhtabar al-Masraḥī al-Sūrī (theatre troupe), 39
First World War, 29, 30, 36, 38, 41n, 123, 217, 226, 235, 340
Fish, Stanley, 96
Flaubert, Gustave, 267
fluid, fluidity, 6, 9, 11n, 14–15, 276, 327, 334, 347, 351
flying saucers, 299
Forget Baghdad (documentary film), 175n, 309, 323, 344n
Foucault, Michel, 355, 363–4, 375
fragmentation (of identities, dynasties), 16, 98, 341, 344
France, French, 2, 15, 24, 37, 41, 42, 55, 56, 60, 64, 66, 70, 127, 144, 156n, 164, 172, 179, 183, 208, 209, 212, 213, 215, 225, 227, 242, 266, 270, 274, 309, 319, 331, 336, 340, 348, 362, 373
fuṣḥā, 199, 225, 226, 304, 314, 317n, 348
Frayn, Michael, 7–8
Freemason, 293
free verse, 108, 110, 245, 258

Gaonim, 204
Gaspar, Francine, 55
Gaspar, Lorand, 55
Gavras, Costa, 64
gay, 3, 11, 13, 23, 331
Gaza Strip, ix, 25, 32, 42, 44, 50, 53, 66, 74, 91, 96, 180n, 282, 352, 372; *see also* Occupied Territories
Gelblum, Arye, 343
gender, 5, 13, 23, 178n, 346n
Genizah, 197
German, Germany, viii, 5, 11, 16, 31, 66, 81, 82, 193, 225, 226, 266, 297, 306, 309, 336, 340, 348
  German Jews, 215, 216, 221, 222, 236, 292
Ge'ūt ha-Naḥal (novel), 262n
al-Ghad (journal), 47n
Ghanāyim, Muḥammad Ḥamza, 147n
Gharāyiba, Ibrāhīm, 313n
al-Ghazālī, Naẓim, 237
ghost, ghosts, 262, 295, 317, 364, 375
Ghunayma, Yūsuf Rizq Allāh, 221
Gibb, H. A. R., 124
Gibraltar, 98
Gilboa, Amir, 261–2
Gilroy, Paul, 1, 350
Ginosar, Yossi, 269
global, globalization, 9, 12, 14, 17, 312, 335, 344–9
  global capitalism, 19
  global diaspora, 360
Globish, 15
Goitein, Shelomo Dov, 193
Golden Age, 124, 158n, 341
Gordon, Judah Leib, 230
Gormezano-Goren, Yitzhak, 212
Granada, 98, 100, 199
Greek, 5, 11, 64, 65, 80, 83, 120, 128n, 138n, 189, 193–4, 196, 266, 272, 323
Greenblatt, Stephen, 355–6
Guattari, Félix, 274
gypsy, 11

Ḥabībī, Emīl, 39n, 36n, 41, 42, 48, 62, 164n, 283
Ha-Cohen, Mordechai, 215n
Ḥaddād, 'Ezra, 224
Ḥaddād, Mīshīl, 48, 125n
Ḥaddād, Suhayl, 145, 147n
Haifa, 38, 39, 43, 47, 49, 51, 52, 69, 92, 135, 150, 159, 166, 178n, 183, 262, 263, 265, 293
  Haifa Municipal Theater, 148n, 155n, 265n, 266
hailing, 2–5, 191–2, 331, 337–43; *see also* interpellation
Ḥājj-Dibsī, Khawla, 147n
Ha-Kalla ha-Meshaḥreret (novel), 327–8
ḥakawātī, 39, 59–60, 278
al-Ḥakawātī (theatrical troupe), 25, 31, 59–67, 69, 73, 74
al-Ḥakīm, Tawfīq, 225
Ha-Kol mi-Ba'ad la-'Anaf (poetry collection), 261–2
ḥāl (a mystical "state"), 297
Ḥalabī, Rafīq, 147n
Ha-Levanon (newspaper), 215
Hall, Stuart, 1, 6, 21, 187, 332
Ha-Ma'abara (novel), 262, 270–2
Ha-Maggid (newspaper), 215, 217
Ḥamdān, Mas'ūd, 147n
Ha-Merkaz le-Shilūv Moreshet Yahudūt Sepharad ve-ha-Mizraḥ, 267
Hanley, Will, 15–16
Hanna K. (film), 64
Ha-'Olam (newspaper), 216
Ḥaqīqat al-Amr (weekly), 45
al-Ḥaqq 'alā al-Ḥaqq (play), 57
Harari, Yuval Noah, 325, 334–6
Ḥārat al-Yahūd (the Jewish Quarter in Cairo), 210–11
al-Ḥarīrī, Abū Muḥammad al-Qāsim ibn 'Alī, 200
al-Ḥarīrī, Rafīq, 115
Hašek, Jaroslav, 87
al-Ḥashara (play), 58
Hashemite, 44, 52, 326n
ḥashw, 108
al-Ḥāṣid (journal), 228–9
Haskala, 209n, 216, 229–30, 318; *see also Aufklärung*; Enlightenment; *Nahḍa*; renaissance
Ḥasūt (novel), 251
Ḥatsotsra ba-Wadī (novel), 265
Ḥattā Yajī' al-Rabī' (poetry collection), 190, 253n, 283

Ḥawādith al-Zamān, 226
Ḥawādith Kiskish Bek, 79n
Ḥāwī, Khalīl, 137–8
Haykal, Muḥammad Ḥussayn, 225
Ha-Yoresh (novel), 274
Ha-Zphira (newspaper), 215
Heart of Darkness (novel), 93
Ḥeder Na'ūl (novel), 274
hegemony, hegemonic, 3, 146, 179, 269, 309, 312–13, 343, 345n
Helen (of Troy), 128
Hellenistic, 189, 196
Herbert D. Katz Center for Advanced Judaic Studies, 315–17
heresy, heretic, 88, 272, 281
hero, heroine, heroic, anti-hero, 11n, 18n, 39n, 47, 48, 50, 61, 75, 87, 90, 170, 178, 232, 242n, 243n, 260, 263, 266, 272, 273, 274, 280, 294, 295, 296, 299, 326, 335, 366; *see also* protagonist
Herzl, Theodor, 127
Hesse, Hermann, 178
heteroglossia, 360–2
High Commissioner for Iraq, 224
Ḥikāyat al-'Ayn wa-l-Sinn (play), 64
Hikmet, Nazim, 57
al-Hilāl (journal), 225
al-Ḥilla, 272
Hindus, 19
Ḥinna ceremony, 205
Hirschberg, H. Z., 215
Ḥisqīl (Yeḥeskel), Sāsūn (Sassoon), 216
Histadrut (General Federation of Labor), 45–6, 52, 55, 62, 244, 248
historicization, 8, 188
Hitbaharūt (novel), 273
Hitler, Adolf, 80
Hobsbawm, E. J., 19–20, 29
Ḥofen shel 'Arafel (novel), 251
Holocaust, 126, 242n, 262, 264, 280
Homer, 116, 117, 126, 136–7
Ḥoref Aḥaron (novel), 274
Hourani, Albert, 225
Hugi, Jacky, 322
Hugo, Victor, 41
Huis Clos (play), 263
Ḥukm Qarāqūsh (operetta), 79
Ḥula Valley, 279
Hulagu, 123–5, 129
ḥumaynī, 203
Ḥūraysh (Ḥoresh), Yūsuf, 230
Ḥūrī, Mūsā, 323
Ḥusayn, Rāshid, 147n
Ḥusayn, Ṣaddām, 126, 272, 307
Ḥusayn, Ṭāhā, 41, 270, 303
al-Ḥusaynī, Jamāl, 369
al-Ḥusaynī, Isḥāq Mūsā, 41
Ḥuṣīn, Shlomo Bekhor, 215
Ḥusnī, Da'ūd, 210
al-Ḥuṣrī, Sāṭi', 222, 237, 339
Hussein, Taha, 225; *see also* Ḥusayn, Ṭāhā
hybrid, hybridic, hybridity, hybridization, 24, 25, 188, 198, 227, 238, 244, 285, 286, 287, 306, 312, 336, 346n, 347, 348, 369
hyperbole, hyperbolic, 89

Iberia, 98, 366
ibn 'Ādiyā', al-Samaw'al, 193, 194, 207, 223, 228, 232, 233, 234, 291, 310
  awfa min al-Samaw'al, 194
  Ibn al-Samaw'al, 228
  al-Samaw'al School, 232n
ibn 'Arabī, Muḥyī al-Dīn, xvi
Ibn al-Athīr, 225
ibn al-balad, 206, 210
ibn 'Ezra, Moshe, 199
Ibn Gabirol, 199
Ibn Kammūna al-Isrā'īlī, 198
Ibn Khaldūn, 225
ibn Killis, Ya'qūb, 197
ibn Mas'ūda, Shālūm (Shalom) Dāwūd, 209–10
ibn Maymūn, Mūsā, 197; *see also* Maimonides
ibn Naghrīla, Ismā'īl, 199; *see also* Shmuel ha-Nagid
Ibn al-Rūmī, 225
ibn Sahl al-Ishbīlī al-Isrā'īlī, Ibrāhīm, 201–2
Ibn Taymiyya, 198
ibn Tibbon, Yehuda, 198–9
ibn Yūsuf, Sa'īd al-Fayyūmī, 197; *see also* Gaon, Sa'adia
Ibrāhīm, George, 49
Ibrāhīm, Ḥāfiz, 211
Ibsen, Henrik, 326

identity, 9–11, 24–6, 30, 36–8, 154–5, 169–70, 187–91, 221, 236–8, 242–4, 314–24, 325–51; *see also* subjects, subjectivity
Arab identity, 30, 37, 221, 236, 242, 342
Arab-Jewish identity, 1, 24, 26, 188, 191, 238, 244n, 285, 314–24, 326n, 328, 336, 344, 347, 349–50, 355, 358, 362, 368
cultural identity, 6, 21, 154, 155, 178, 187, 227, 332, 345n, 347
communal identity, 228, 327, 356
essential identity, 344
ethnic identity, 7, 177n, 187
fluid identity, 11
identity crises, 9, 169–70
identity politics, 285, 320, 324, 346, 355
inessential solidarities, 1, 26, 191, 325–51
Israeli identity, 154, 167, 369
Israeli-Jewish identity, 345
Jewish identity, 244n, 276, 342
Jewish-Zionist identity, 188, 238, 336
Mizrahi identity, 346, 349n
national identity, 30, 36, 37, 38, 53, 75, 135n, 180n, 190, 244n, 293, 336
postmodern identity, 10
primordialist/non-primordialist, 187
Idrīs, Muḥammad Jalā', 311n
Idrīs, Yūsuf, 4n
Ighbāriyya, Ayman Kāmil, 147n, 174
Iliad, 223
iltizām, 24,78
al-'Imārī, Murād 'Abd Allāh, 292
in medias res, 275
Institut du Monde Arabe, 318–20
intentional fallacy, 363
interference (cultural), 35, 195, 205
interpellation, 2–5, 191, 268, 288, 331, 336–44; *see also* hailing
Intifāḍa, 25, 32, 63, 66, 70, 96, 268, 352
invented tradition, 278
Iqbāl, Muḥammad, 297
Iran, Iranian, 114, 250, 323; *see also* Persia, Persian
Iran-Iraq War, 272
al-Īrānī, Mu'ayyad Ibrāhīm, 43
Isḥāq, Salīm, 226
Ishtayya (Shatayye), Muḥammad, 67
Israel (Ceresi, Shīrīzī), Marcel (Marsīl)
Isrā'īlī (=Jewish), 198, 201, 209n, 239
Banū Isrā'īl, 209n, 239
al-Isrā'īlī (an Arabized Jew who converted to Islam), 198, 201
Isrā'īliyyāt, 239
Istanbul, 24, 340
Italy, Italian, 1,11, 12, 20, 24, 37, 66, 144, 164n, 212, 288, 309, 335, 336
al-Ittiḥād (newspaper), 47, 54, 245, 251

al-Jadīd (jouranl), 47, 54, 245, 252, 256
Jāhiliyya, 233; *see also* pre-Islamic
Jalīlī, Yā 'Alī (play), 62
Jamaican, 1, 187
Jamāl al-Dīn, Jabbār, 307n
Jamāl al-Dīn, Samīr, 309n
Jameson, Fredric, 281
al-Janābī, 'Abd al-Qādir, 301
Japan, Japanese, 11, 66, 67n, 309, 348
Jarīdat al-Masraḥ, 57
al-Jarīma al-Ghāmiḍa (novel), 270
al-Jarrāḥ, Nūrī, 121n, 176n
al-Jawzī, Jamīl, 42–3
al-Jawzī, Naṣrī, 40–3
Jenīn, 69–70, 265
Jesuit, 55, 206
Jesus, 48, 88, 116, 224n
Jewish Agency, 277, 280n
Jewish literature, 153, 203n, 359–60
Joseph, 100, 106–16, 129
Joyce, James, 140, 172, 364–5
Jubrān (Gibran), Jubrān Khalīl, 270
Jubrān, Wisām, 310n
Judeo-Arabic, 196–8, 204–6, 324
Judt, Tony, 17n, 23
Julius Caesar (play), 89

Kafka, Franz, 288, 294
Kafr Qāsim Massacre, 253–6
Kahanoff, Jacqueline, 212–13
Kaḥīla, Najīb, 241
Kanafānī, Ghassān, 50
Kandinsky, Wassily Wassilyevich, 273
Kant, Immanuel, 216–17
al-Kanz (play), 57

Karagöz, 40
Karaite, Karaites, 200, 208–9, 210, 211
Karkabī, Ḥabīb Ibrāhīm, 46
al-Kashkūl (theatrical troupe), 57
Kashua, Sayed (Sayyid Qashshū'a), 147n, 148, 155n
Kassabova, Kapka, 12
al-Kātib, Sālim (Shalom Katab), 241
Kattan, Naïm (Na'īm Qaṭṭān), 240, 353
al-Kaylānī, Rashīd 'Ālī, 239
Kedourie, Elie, 218, 240, 307, 339n
Kellner, Douglas, 9–10, 12
Kenan, Amos, 63
Kennedy, Ann, 5
Kennedy, Robert F., 18n, 335n
Khalīl, 'Āmir, 59, 67
Khalālyila, Ibrāhīm, 59
Khalīfa, Mārsīl (Marcel Khlife), 113–15
Khamīs, Ṣalība, 70
kharja, 199
khayāl al-ẓill, 40
Khayr, Nazīh, 147n
al-Khayyām, 'Umar (Omar Khayyam), 226n
Khazar, 351n
Khedhourie (Khaḍḍūrī), Sassoon, 234–5
Khedhourie (Khaḍḍūrī), Shā'ul Nājī, 234–5
Khūrī, Ilyās (Elias Khoury), 313n, 372
Khūrī, Makram, 147n
Khūrī, Salīm, 48–9
al-Khurūj min al-'Irāq: Dhikrayāt 1945–1950 (memoir), 304
Khuṭba fī Ādāb al-'Arab, 217
kibbutz, kibbutzim, 170, 177, 277–82
King Lear (play), 364–5
Kitāb al-Aghānī, 225
Kitāb al-Muḥāḍara wa-l-Mudhākara, 199
Knesset, 173, 269n, 280n
Kol ha-'Am (newspaper), 270
Koran, xvi, 169; *see also* Qur'ān
Korsgaard, Christine, 21–2
Koskas, Marco, 353
Kovner, Abba, 262
Kūfiyya (*kaffiyeh*), 133n
Kūhīn (Cohen) brothers (Zakī and Salīm), 204
Kurd, Kurdish, Kurdistan, 205n, 218, 345n, 361n
al-Kurd, Muṣṭafā, 57
Kuttāb, Da'ūd, 59
al-Kuwaytī, Dāwūd, 230
al-Kuwaytī, Ṣāliḥ, 230

Lammā Injanenā (play), 58
Landau, J. M., 43
Landshut, Siegfried, 224
last Mohicans, 26, 190, 291–324
Laṭīf, Māzin, 320–1
Latin, 11, 348
Lazari-Moyal, Esther (Istīr Azharī-Mūyāl), 205–6
League of Nations, 224, 250
Lebanon, Lebanese, 7, 29, 38, 56, 115, 137, 147n, 153, 176n, 187, 205, 206, 220n, 222, 225, 313, 350, 352, 372
  Lebanon 1982 war, 25, 32, 96, 100, 106, 265, 352
  Lebanese Civil War, 53, 113
Leda, 128n
leisure, 10, 12–13
Lemarachand, Joseph (Jean Sulivan), 162n
Levant, Levantine, Levantinism, 3, 15n, 212–13, 331, 343
Libya, 104
Lifton, Robert Jay, 5–6
lingua franca, 15, 154, 196n, 198
Lithuania, 216
liturgical, 197, 199–200, 204, 214, 231, 261n
Lo bi-Mkoma (novel), 274
London, 66, 216, 240n, 359
  London Matriculation Examination, 219
London, Jack, 270
Lorca, Federico Gracía, 169
Lubeck, Jackie, 59, 64
Luqa' ibn Luqa (play), 39n

ma'abara, ma'abarot (immigrant camp), 262, 270, 277–8
Maalouf, Amin (Amīn Ma'lūf), 7, 22n, 187
al-Ma'arrī, Abū al-'Alā', 115, 225
machismo, 11
Madame Bovary (novel), 267
al-Madina, 234n

al-Madrasa al-Ḥadītha, 209–10
Mafriyaḥ ha-Yonīm (novel), 278–80
Maḥāmīd, Muḥammad, 59
Maḥberot Iti'el, 200
Mahdī, 88
Maḥfūẓ, Najīb, 266, 280, 303
Maḥjūb, Maḥjūb (play), 35, 61–2
Maimonides (Mūsā ibn Maymūn), 197–8
mainstream, 15, 146n, 200, 273, 280, 292, 330
mainstream Arabic literature, 226, 292
mainstream Israeli society, 264–9
majlis, 197
majnūn, 45, 49, 169, 229, 361
Makmal, Yūsuf, 227
al-Makr, 52
Maktūb (translation project), 348–9
Mālikī, Sa'd Ya'qūb, 212
Manchester, 292, 311, 319, 336
al-Manfalūṭī, Luṭfī, 225
Mani, Sulayman Menahem, 261
Manṣūr (the Caliph), 214n
Manṣūr, 'Aṭāllāh, 147n, 169, 173n
Mappu, Avraham, 209n
maqām (in music), 230
maqāma, 11n, 200, 204
al-Maqrīzī, 197
Marcos (Rafael Sebastián GuillénVicente), 11–12
marginalization, marginalized, 8, 11, 32, 94n, 96, 187, 236, 237n, 238, 264, 267, 276, 308, 333
Marinetti, Filippo Tommaso, 20
market, 17–19, 249
market triumphalism, 17, 335
Marmorstein, Emile, 214
Marquez, Gabriel Garcia, 112
Marx, Karl, 255
Marxist, Marxism, 2, 78, 86, 331, 341n
Maṣālḥa, Salmān, 106, 108, 147, 149, 164
Māsarjawayh, 196
Maṣārwa, Ṭāriq, 49
Ma'sāt al-Ḥallāj (verse drama), 78
al-Mashriq (journal), 207n
al-Mashriqī, Aḥmad, 210; *see also* Mizrāḥī, Tūgū (Togo)
mask, masks, 79–80, 83, 154n, 325; *see also qinā'*
Maskil, Maskilim, *maskilic*, 229–30
al-Masraḥ al-Jāmi'ī (theatre troupe), 58
masrḥ al-maqhā, 57
al-Maṭba'ī, Ḥamīd, 237–8
matruz, 204
Mā Warā' al-Ḥayāt wa-Qiṣaṣ Ukhrā (collection of short stories), 303
Mawāsī, Fārūq, 147n
mawlid, mawālid, 39
Mayan, 11
al-Māzinī, Ibrāhīm 'Abd al-Qādir, 225
McDonald, 269
McKibben, Bill, 18
Megged, Aharon, 278
melting pot, 154, 155, 236, 345n
Melucci, Alberto, 12–13, 335
Memmi, Albert, 183–4, 353
memoirs, 16, 41, 151, 190, 220, 272, 278, 293, 303n, 304, 308, 324
memory, memories, memorialization, 4, 13, 63, 123, 135, 146, 160, 161n, 163, 169, 210, 242n, 252, 255n, 260n, 270–1, 301, 304, 307, 309, 319, 352, 360, 361n, 369
collective memory, 135n, 146n, 253n, 352
Mer-Khamīs, Arna, 70
Mer-Khamīs, Juliano, 70
Mesopotamia, 29, 196–7, 218, 226, 320, 323, 339
Messiah, Messianic, 204, 231, 281, 340
meta-culture, ix
meta-fiction, 26, 285, 295, 300, 352, 353, 356–9, 361, 365, 366
meta-myth, ix, 32, 97
metaphor, 11, 59, 94n, 163, 295n, 297, 374
metaphysics, metaphysical, 6, 187, 297, 299, 300, 305n, 332
meta-poetic, meta-poetry, 32, 97, 106, 110, 116, 120, 121, 136, 141
meter, xii, 108, 110, 117, 171, 199, 256, 258; *see also* prosody
Michael, Sami (Sāmī Mīkhā'īl), 175, 214n, 220n, 235, 262–9, 313, 323, 324, 344, 349
Middle Ages, medieval, 35, 83, 89, 123, 124, 189, 193, 196, 197, 198n, 199, 204, 208n, 209, 224, 246, 273, 292n, 294, 297, 298, 366n

migration, emigration, immigration, immigrant, émigré, 236, viii, ix, 13, 15, 17, 26, 45, 97, 102, 158, 188, 189, 192, 210, 211, 227, 240, 241–3, 250–2, 261–6, 269–70, 277–83, 302, 310–11, 324, 325, 329n, 335, 337, 341–7, 358–60
  mass immigration, 229n, 235n, 241, 303–4, 307
Mīkhā'īl (Michael), Murād, 220, 241, 292
Mīkhā'īl, Nādiyā, 57
Miller, Carolyn, 338
Miller, Judith, 347–8
Ministry of Absorption (Israel), 277
Ministry of Agriculture (Israel), 265
Ministry of Culture (Israel), 69
Ministry of Culture (Palestine), 67
Ministry of Education (Israel), 52, 150, 232n, 267, 277
Ministry of Religious Affairs (Israel), 359
minority, minorities, 11, 23, 32, 44, 49, 52, 135, 144, 146–7, 154–5, 172–5, 178, 182, 190, 214, 226, 239, 242, 244–5, 250–6, 266, 283–4, 313, 321, 352, 360, 366n
Miron, Dan, 171
al-Miṣbāḥ (journal), 228–9
Mishmar Ha-'Emek, 277
Mishnah, 271
Miṣr fī Qalbī (memoir), 308–9
Mista'revim (*Musta'ribūn*), 236n
Mizrahi, Mizrahim, Mizrahiness, 3, 127n, 134n, 176, 210, 236–7, 243, 262, 267–9, 274n, 275, 311, 313, 317n, 320, 323, 327, 329, 331, 343–50
  Mizrahi identity, 346, 349n
  Mizrahi radical intellectuals, 347–50
Mizrāḥī, Tūgū (Togo), 210; *see also* al-Mashriqī, Aḥmad
Mnouchkine, Ariane, 60
modernity, modernism, modernization, 1, 9–10, 15–16, 29, 33, 37, 51, 60–1, 65, 69, 92, 95, 150, 161–2, 194, 214–15, 226, 230–1, 236, 245, 256, 258, 294, 308, 364
  modern (definition), 9n
  postmodern, postmodernism, postmodernity, 6, 9–12, 17, 56, 187, 332, 335, 372
  premodern, 9, 35
Mohawk, 11
Molière, 37, 207
  monolithic, 72, 324, 343
monolithic category, 191, 337
monopoly, monopolization, 20, 209
Moor, Moorish, 365, 366n
Moreh, Shmuel, 223, 241, 243, 292, 314, 321, 324, 349, 358
Mosad, 321
Moses, Mosaic, 25, 189, 193–240, 291, 310
Moshe, Salmān, 230
mother tongue, 25, 32, 146, 148n, 149, 163, 222n, 261, 291, 362
Mount Carmel, 159
Moyal, Shimon (Shim'ūn Mūyāl), 205–6
Msika (Messika), Ḥabība (Ḥbiba), 204n
al-Mu'allim, Idwār, 59
muḍāri, 118
Mudhakkirāt Dajāja (novel), 41
Mudhakkirāt Khādima (novel), 270–1
Mughāmarat Ra's al-Mamlūk Jābir (play), 39n
Muḥammad (the Prophet), 39, 202, 224, 297
al-Mujtama' (magazine), 45
Mūl ha-Ḥoma (collection of short stories), 273–4
al-Mullā, Maryam, 292, 358, 367
multiplicity, multiple (identities, subjectivities, meanings), 8–10, 16, 24, 28, 68, 95, 174, 188, 308, 311, 330–1, 333, 341, 348, 362, 370–2
Mulūk al-Ṭawā'if, 98
al-Muqtaṭaf (journal), 225
Murād, Laylā, 208n, 211
Murād, Salīma, 208n, 230, 237, 279
Muṣāra'a Ḥurra (play), 57
Mūṣayrī (Mosseri), Albert, 212
Mūṣayrī (Mosseri), Mazal-Mathilde, 212
mushrikūn, 198
music, musician, musical, 57, 59, 64, 65, 79, 82, 107, 113, 167, 173, 179n, 203, 204n, 210, 230–1, 273, 279, 299, 328
  First Congress of Arabic Music, 230, 311
  Jewish-Arab Musical Youth Orchestra, 310
Musil, Robert, 335
al-Mutanabbī, Abū al-Ṭayyib, 225
muwashshaḥ, 199

My Antonia (novel), 288
mysticism, mystic, mystical, 140–1, 193–4, 200, 294, 297–300, 305n, 348; *see also* Sufism
myth, mythical, mythological, 29, 32, 60, 71, 85, 97, 106, 110, 111, 115, 117, 119, 123, 126–9, 136, 213n, 273, 281, 341, 363
  meta-myth, ix, 32, 97, 116, 121
  "neo-lachrymose" countermyth, 341

Na'ar Ha-Ofanayim (novel), 282
Nahḍa 42, 207, 317–18; *see also* *Aufklärung*; *Haskala*; Enlightenment; renaissance
al-Nāhiḍ (theatrical troupe), 52
Naḥūm (Nahum) Effendi, Rabbi Chaim, 209
Nakba, viii, ix, 24–6, 31–2, 71, 73, 93–142, 146, 188, 352–4
  "Jewish Nakba," 353
Nakhla, 'Āmir (Amer), 173
name, names, 42, 120, 133, 139, 165, 216, 267, 342, 347, 365
  nickname, 273, 275
  pen name, 177, 251, 270
Naqqāra-Ḥaddād, Salwā, 147n
al-Naqqāsh, Marūn, 37
al-Naqqāsh, Salīm, 37
Naqqāsh, Samīr, 175, 220n, 241, 267n, 284, 288, 292, 307, 311, 315, 332, 360, 361, 362
narrative, narration, narrator, 4, 5, 26, 61, 63, 71, 82, 95, 113, 121–4, 136, 140, 154, 155n, 164, 167–70, 208n, 262–3, 274–5, 279, 285–8, 297, 299–300, 303, 305–9, 313, 324, 356–62, 366, 368
  narrativization of the self, 8, 188, 331–6
  Zionist (master) narrative, 237, 274, 277–8, 282
al-Nashāshībī, Rāghib, 224
Nashrat Aḥwāl al-Jaww (play), 57
nation, national, nationalist, nationalism, nationality, ix, 6, 15–17, 23, 25, 29, 36, 43, 48, 50–1, 124, 155, 176, 178n, 180, 187, 188–90, 194, 203, 211, 218, 221–2, 235, 237–9, 242n, 243, 245, 248, 251–4, 260, 262, 269, 274, 279, 283, 286, 312, 313, 317, 325, 330, 332, 334, 336, 339, 340, 342, 344, 351–2, 356, 368
  bi-national, 368
  Egyptian nationalism, 207, 211
  Iraqi nationalism, 219, 222, 225
  Jewish nationalism, 152, 154, 173, 179, 229, 232, 309
  national songs and anthems, 61–2, 113
  National Arab Movement, 231, 232
  national identity, 21, 30, 36–8, 53, 75, 135n, 180n, 190, 244n, 276, 293, 336
  national language, 29, 200
  national Palestinian theater, 58–9, 67, 74
  Palestinian nationalism, viii, 24–5, 29–31, 37–8, 52n, 53–5, 58–9, 68–9, 73–4, 92, 155
  transnational Jewish networks, 53, 326n
nation-state, 16, 17, 29–30, 36, 218, 230n, 233, 338
Navon, Yitzhak, 294n
Nazi, Nazism, 22, 80, 232, 250, 305
Near East, 189, 196
Nebot, Didier, 353
Nebuchadnezzar II, 323
neo-Arab-Jewish, 346, 348
neo-Aramaic, 205n
neo-lachrymose, 341
neo-Ṣūfī, viii
Nevo, Eshkol, 63n
New Year, 200
New York, 24
  as a Jewish city, 218
Nietzsche, Friedrich, 281
Nigerian, 93, 366
Ninth of Av, 200; *see also* Tish'a Be-'Av
Nobel Prize, 266, 268, 271
North Africa, North African, 156n, 172, 194, 204, 206, 215n, 327, 331
nostalgia, 5, 15, 16, 20, 98, 165, 283, 309, 314n, 350
novel, novels, novelist, 4, 5, 7, 41, 50, 63n, 77, 87, 93, 94–5, 112, 121–3, 129, 147n, 148, 149, 151, 155n, 156, 164, 170, 173n, 175, 176n, 178, 182, 183, 190, 208n, 209n, 213, 217n, 225, 240n, 251, 262, 265–7, 270–4, 278–82, 287, 288, 293, 300, 303–6, 312, 315n, 321, 324, 327–9, 350, 353, 361n, 365–7; *see also riwāya*
novella, 273–7, 288

Nye, Naomi Shihab, 126–7
Nzūla wa-Khayṭ al-Shayṭān: Riwāya 'Irāqiyya (novel), 315n

'Obadyā, Ibrāhīm, 231n, 233, 241, 292
Obermeyer, Jacob, 217
obscurity/clarity (literary), 95n, 308n
Occupied Territories, 24, 44, 50, 52–4, 57–9, 64, 66n, 67, 69, 74–5, 213, 242, 268; *see also* Gaza Strip; West Bank
October Revolution, 225n, 260n
Oedipus the King (play), 83
Old Testament, 304
'oleh ḥadash, 277
Oneness, 376
Oppenheimer, Yochai, 280–1
Oren, Yosef, 280n
Orient, Orientalism, Oriental, Orientalist, Orientalization, 3, 45, 123, 124, 127n, 146, 164, 176, 190, 213, 215, 225, 226, 236, 244, 251, 265, 267–8, 278, 280, 281, 297, 309, 311n, 313, 317, 319, 331, 343, 359, 369
Orientalism (book), 126, 129
Other, otherness, 135n, 173, 272, 276–7, 268, 312, 345; *see also* Akher
Otot Stav (collection of novellas), 273
Ottoman, 15, 38, 215, 216, 226, 370
  Ottoman Empire, 15, 225
oud, 230
outsider, 136, 172, 272, 274, 294
Oz, Amos, 294n

Paḥonīm ve-Ḥalomot (book for youth), 266
Pamuk, Orhan, 4n
pan-Arabism, pan-Arab, 69, 92, 232, 239, 320
Paris, 55, 56, 128, 176n, 213, 240n, 270, 273, 274, 318, 320
Paris (from troy), 128n
Parks, Tim, 19
Passover, 200
patriot, patriotic, patriotism, 186, 189–90, 219, 222, 223, 229, 233–4, 242–7, 250–1, 310, 317, 339, 369
Pedaya, Haviva, 311n, 317n
Peer Gynt: A Dramatic Poem (play), 326
Pentecost, 200
performativity, performative, 6, 187, 332, 360–2, 365
Persia, Persian, 114, 169, 195, 205n, 226n, 339, 348; *see also* Iran, Iranian
persona, 97–8, 105, 110, 112–13, 115–16, 119, 136–7, 325; *see also* speaker
philological, 208, 316
Piamenta, Moshe, 306n
pilgrim, pilgrimage (as a metaphor for modern life), 11
Piscator, Erwin, 31, 81–2
Plato, 14, 295n
player (as a metaphor for postmodern life), 11
pluralistic, plurality, pluralism, 25, 173, 177n, 189, 193, 203, 265, 267, 338, 350
Poland, Polish, 6, 11, 66, 278, 292, 306, 309, 312, 327, 332
Polytheists, 198
"positive" culture, literature, 45–50, 74, 244, 284
post-Cartesian, 6, 187, 332
postmodern, postmodernism, postmodernity, 6, 9–12, 17, 56, 187, 332, 335, 372
preference, preferences (literary, aesthetic), 33, 69, 92, 150, 153, 156, 164, 166, 173, 190, 192, 201, 233, 261, 264, 269, 272, 291, 293, 302, 337, 345
pre-Islamic, 24, 189, 195–6, 207, 211, 228, 232, 310, 314, 368; *see also* Jāhiliyya
primitive, primitivism, 46, 342–3
primordial, primordialist, non-primordialist, 7, 9, 187, 366n
prison, imprisonment (political), 62, 66, 78, 122, 234, 254–5, 260
  "prison-house of language," 281
  the body in the soul, 235
professionalization (in theatre), 50–67, 91
prose poem, 110, 301
prosody, 108n, 171; *see also* meter
protagonist, 7, 66, 170, 208, 270, 272, 273, 274, 278–80, 282, 288, 294, 297–9, 328, 364, 366–7; *see also* hero
protest, 47, 56, 59, 66, 115, 125, 152, 155n, 161, 174, 224n, 233, 235, 245, 251, 252, 253, 256, 265, 266, 269, 320

Proteus, 5
  protean (self), 5–6
  proteanism, 6
pseudonym, 54, 162, 176, 177, 228, 356
psychoanalysis, 6, 17, 187, 332, 335, 364, 375
Puzo, Mario, 288

al-Qabānjī (al-Qebbantchi), Muḥammad, 231
al-Qabbānī, Abū Khalīl Aḥmad, 38
Qabbānī, Nizār, 75, 105
qadar, 198
Qadhdhāfī, Mu'ammar, 104
qalb, 141
Qamar, Victor, 51
Qambar 'Ali quarter (in Baghdad), 376
al-Qānūn al-Asāsī al-'Irāqī, 339–40
Qaraqāsh (verse drama), 25, 31, 51, 55, 73–93
Qarāqūsh, 40n, 78–80, 85
qaṣīda, xii, 95, 106–9, 169, 199
Qāsim, 'Abd al-Karim, 233
al-Qāsim, Samīḥ, 25, 31, 51, 55, 73–93, 141
Qasmūna, 202
Qa'wār, Jamāl, 48
Qaws Quzaḥ (magazine), 293
al-Qayrawānī, Ibn Rashīq, 94
al-Qays, Imru', 195
qinā', 79–80; *see also* mask
al-Qiṣṣa Dīwān al-'Arab, 95
Qiṭ'at Ḥayāt (play), 57
Quebec, 376
Qur'ān, Qur'anic, 26, 100, 111, 114, 153, 189, 310; *see also* Koran
  knowledge among Jews, 195–8

Ra'anana, 285
Rabin, Yitzḥak, 69, 161, 272
race, racial, 6, 16, 22, 104, 187, 221, 222n, 224, 276, 332, 340
radio, 42, 50, 62, 77, 114, 244, 286
Rāḥīl Shaḥmūn School, 292
al-Rā'ī, 'Alī, 74, 90, 95
Ramadan, 39, 40
Ramallah, 31, 49, 55, 57, 58, 69, 74, 77, 92
Raqṣat al-Maṭar wa-Qiṣaṣ Ukhrā (collection of short stories), 300
Rasā'il Ikhwān al-Safā (encyclopedic work), 225
al-Rashīd, Hārūn (the Caliph), 42
Ratosh, Yonathan, 155
rebab, 39
Regev, Miri, 69
Rejwan, Nissim (Nissīm Rajwān), 213, 218, 221, 225
renaissance, 37, 98, 205; *see also* *Aufklärung*; *Haskala*; Enlightenment; *Nahḍa*; renaissance
repressive state apparatuses (RSAS), 3
resistance, 25, 31, 50, 59, 64n, 67–9, 72, 73–93, 331
revolution, revolutionary, revolutionized, 19, 38, 50, 68, 69, 84, 86, 88, 91, 92, 105–6, 120, 124, 130, 217, 225–6, 254, 255, 281, 288, 303n, 370
  Arab Revolutionary Committee, 123, 340
  Iranian revolutionary songs, 114n
  October Revolution, 255n, 260n
  Young Turk Revolution, 225
rhetoric, rhetorical, 1, 3, 59, 60, 89, 95, 105, 106, 111, 117–19, 121, 198n, 199, 246, 331, 337–42
rhyme, xii, 108–10, 117, 118, 171, 199, 256, 258
al-Rīḥānī, Najīb, 79
al-Risāla (journal), 225
al-Riwāya (journal), 225
riwāya, 37, 95, 300, 315n; *see also* novel
  al-riwāya dīwān al-'arab al-jadīd, 95
  al-riwāya mir'āt al-sha'b, 95
  Riwāyat al-Bakhīl (play), 37
Robinson Crusoe (novel), 7–8
Roman, Romanic, 189, 193, 366
  Roman Empire, 120, 125
romances, 225
Romania, 327
Romanticism, romantic, 16, 124, 208, 263, 328
Rooke, Tetz, 374–7
Rotberg, Roi, 282
Rothschild, Lord, 218
Roumani, Judith, 353
Royal School of Medicine (Baghdad), 376n
Royle, Nicholas, 354–5, 364, 375

Rubā'iyyāt, 226n
al-Rubā'iyya al-'Irāqiyya, 306
Rūmānū (Romano), Jāk, 210–11
al-Ruṣāfī, Ma'rūf, 224, 228
Russia, Russian, 31, 172, 213, 273, 278, 309, 348

Sa'adia Gaon, 197
Sabra, 243, 278, 280, 285, 330, 345n
Sab' Sanābil Hazīla (poetry collection), 376
Sadan, Dov, 360
al-Sādāt, Anwar, 62, 210
al-Sa'dūn, 'Abd al-Muḥsin, 229
al-Ṣafadī, Muḥyī al-Dīn al-Ḥajj 'Īsā, 43
Said, Edward W., 126, 267n, 317, 347–8, 370
al-Sa'īd, Nūrī, 304
Ṣāliḥ, Anṭwān, 52
Samīr Mārid, 251; *see also* Michael, Sami
al-Sammāk, Mahdī, 219n
Samra, Dāwud, 237
Samuel, Herbert, 224
Sanbar, Elias, 127
San Cristobal, 11
Sandel, Michael J. 18n, 336
San Francisco, 11
Ṣanū',Ya'qūb (James Sanua), 38, 207–8, 274
Saramago, José, 287
Sāra al-Qurayẓiyya, 195
Ṣarrāf, Aḥmad Ḥāmid, 226n
Sartre, Jean-Paul, 78, 263–4
Sassoon, David Solomon, 237n
Savary, Jérôme, 60
al-Sawāfirī, Kāmil, 38
al-Sayyāb, Badr Shākir, 195n
al-Sayyid, Maḥmūd Aḥmad, 238
Scheherazade, 140
Scheindlin, Raymond P., 202
Schimmel, Annemarie, 297
schizophrenic, schizophrenia, 192, 287, 294
Scholem, Gershom, 348
Second World War, 119, 250
secular, secularist, secularization, 9, 35, 126, 197, 199, 214–15, 217–19, 221–2, 225–7, 230, 235–6, 268, 270, 314n, 339–40, 350, 369
Sefarad, 203
self
  many-sided self, 216–17
  narrativization of the self, 5, 188, 331–6
  performative self, 5, 187, 332
  protean self, 5–6
  self-consciousness, 22, 366
  self-control, 13
  self-denial, 286
  self-justification, 264
  self-referential, 274re
  self-reflexive, 9
  self-sustaining subject, 6, 332
Semah, David, 190, 218n, 241, 252, 253–60, 283, 292, 314, 324
Sephardi, Sephardim, Sephardic, 3, 236n, 261, 267, 275, 280, 317, 327, 328, 331, 343–4, 346n, 349n, 353
  Sephardic Federation in the United States, 277
Seville, 98
sexual, sexuality, 5, 22, 115, 122, 128, 129, 264, 266, 279, 280, 298, 299n
Shabak (General Security Services), 269
shā'ir, 39n
  shā'ir al-rabāba, 39
Shakespeare, William, 89, 145
Shammās, Anṭūn (Anton), 25, 32–3, 135, 147, 149, 156, 162–84, 313, 353
Shammās, Maurice (Abū Farīd), 210
Shammāsh School, 214, 219, 220, 252
Shamosh, Amnon, 243
al-Shams (*al-Chams*) (newspaper), 212
Shamshūn wa-Dalīla (play), 40
Shapira, Ronen, 310n
Sharḥ, 197
Sharīf, Nihād, 298–9
al-Sharqāwī, 'Abd al-Raḥmān, 80
Sha'shū'a, Salīm Murād (Shelomo Shashoua), 241
shaṭaḥāt, 141
Shā'ul, Anwar, 193, 227–30, 233–5, 237–40, 243, 251n, 272, 291, 292, 310, 340, 357
Shavīm ve-Shavīm Yoter (novel), 265
Shavit, Ari, 127n

Shaw, George Bernard, 178
Shawqī, Aḥmad, 45, 49, 208n
al-Shaykh Shabtāy wa-Ḥikāyāt min Ḥārat al-Yahūd (collection of short stories), 210
Ṣebaḥiyī, 205
Shedīm ba-Martef (play), 266
Shedīm Ḥumīm (book for youth), 266
Shem, Semitic, 152, 186, 209, 211, 223, 285, 339, 369
Shenhav (Shaharabani), Yehuda, 243–4, 346–9
al-Shibbath, Salīm, 230
Shiblak, Abbas (ʻAbbās Shiblāq), 222
Shiḥāda, Rāḍī, 59, 64
Shiḥaybar brothers (Anṭwān and Ilyās), 204
Shiite, Shias, 198, 199n, 218
Shīna, Salmān, 228
Shimoni, Baruch, 345n
al-shiʻr dīwān al-ʻArab, 43, 94, 136
shiʻr ḥurr, 108; *see also* free verse; *shiʻr al-tafʻīla*
shiʻr al-tafʻīla, 108n; *see also shiʻr ḥurr*
Shklovsky (Shklovskij), Viktor, 96
Shlonsky Prize, 261–2
Shmuel ha-Nagid, 199, 202; *see also* ibn Naghrīla, Ismāʻīl
Shohat, Ella, 176, 269, 309, 317, 318, 323, 328, 331n, 346, 347
Shoḥet, Nīr, 241
Ṣidqī, Bakr, 305
Siksik, Ayman, 147n, 149
al-Sindbād (Sinbad), 273
singularity, 2, 5, 18–19, 326, 329, 344–6
Smilansky, Saul, 13
Solo (novel), 274
Somekh, Sasson, 241, 252, 258, 284, 303n, 314, 324, 350
song, singer, 4, 16, 39, 57, 64, 82, 85, 97, 106, 113, 138, 144, 160, 166, 174, 200, 203–5, 210–11, 230–1, 237, 244, 248, 256, 279, 280, 322
Sorbonne, 270
South Africa, 11
Spain, Spanish, 11, 16, 98, 164n, 169, 193, 198, 200, 236n, 328, 353, 366; *see also* Andalus
speaker, 4, 12, 111, 267, 275, 323, 325, 337, 370; *see also* persona
Stahl, Abraham, 278
Stern, Samuel Miklos, 200
Stetkevych, Jaroslav, 318, 348
Stillman, Norman A., 214, 316
storytellers, 39, 56, 57, 59–60, 270, 278; *see also ḥakawātī*
straw-man arguments, 315–16
stream-of-consciousness, 275, 294
stroller (as a metaphor for postmodern life), 11
strophe, strophic, 40, 109, 199, 203
structural, structuralism, poststructuralism, 1, 17, 64, 335
subjects, subjectivity, viii, 2, 4–6, 9, 16, 187–8, 191–2, 327, 330–2, 334, 336–7, 341–7, 361, 365; *see also* identity
  self-sustaining subject, 16
  social subjects, 9, 188, 334
  subject position, 3–4, 9–10, 188, 330–1, 334
subversive, subversion, 145–6, 331
Sūfa Bein ha-Dekalīm (book for youth), 266
Sufism, Ṣūfī, viii, 141, 193, 200, 226, 297–8, 300, 305; *see also* mysticism
Sulaymān, Ramzī, 174
Sulivan, Jean, 162
ṣundūq al-dunyā/ṣundūq al-ʻajab, 39, 58
Sunnī, Sunnis, 218
Sūq ʻUqāẓ, 55
surrealist, surrealistic, surreal, 65, 183, 263, 285, 300, 301
Sūsa, Aḥmad Nissīm (Ahmed Sousa), 207n, 237, 272
suture, 8, 334
al-Suwaydī, Tawfīq, 220–1
symbiosis, symbiotic, 26, 188–9, 193–5, 199, 218, 221–3, 229, 264, 291–2, 305, 352–3, 368
symbol, symbolic, symbolism, viii, 8, 30, 31, 37, 42, 46, 47, 59, 60, 61, 65, 90, 92, 122, 151, 158, 161, 180, 236n, 243, 249, 263, 265, 273, 277, 288, 299, 334, 365
synagogue, 217

Syria, Syrian, 29, 37–8, 40, 43, 75, 105, 121, 124, 147n, 155, 157, 165, 176, 196, 198, 205, 206, 207, 220, 225, 243, 265, 308, 323
Sznaider, Natan, 16–17

taf'īla, 108
al-ṭāghūt, 83, 88
Taḥkemonī, 200
Talmud, Talmudic, 196, 218n, 247, 272
Tamārī, Salīm, 127n
Tanqīḥ al-Abḥāth li-l-Milal al-Thalāth, 198
al-Ṭanṭāwī, 'Alī, 220
Tanzimat refroms, 214
taqiyya, 147n
Ṭarābsha, 'Adnān, 59
Tarnegol Kapparot (novel), 251, 278, 281–2
taskīn, 118
taswīf, 118–19
Taufar, Barbara, 217n
al-Ṭā'ūn (play), 57
Tayma', 234n
Tchernichovski, Saul (Shaul), 253
Tel-Aviv Mizraḥ (novel), 271n
ten Bos, René, 19
Te'omīm (play), 266
al-Thaqāfa (journal), 225
Thawrat al-Zanj (play), 39n
Théâtre du Soleil, 60
theatrical presentation of the self, 56, 372
The Caucasian Chalk Circle (play), 58, 81–2, 86, 87, 88
The Fortunate Pilgrim (novel), 288
The Good Soldier Švejk (play), 87
The Iron Heel (novel), 270
The Merchant of Venice (play), 143–5
The Museum of Innocence (novel), 4n
Tigris, 123, 213, 234, 235, 252, 279, 323, 367
Tish'a Be-'Av, 323; *see also* Ninth of Av
Toledo, 98
Tolstoy, Leo, 267
Tom ha-Bikkūr (novel), 274
Torah, xvi, 247, 272; *see also* Bible
tourist (as a metaphor for postmodern life), 11–12
tradition, traditional, 3, 5, 9, 13, 15, 19, 23, 30, 32–6, 39, 44, 47, 55, 58–69, 75, 82–3, 88–96, 106–8, 114n, 127, 133n, 138n, 147n, 172, 178–9, 188-9, 195–209, 215, 222n, 229–44, 266, 277–8, 292–7, 302–3, 311n, 324, 346n, 352, 357, 363, 370–5
transnationalism, 17, 53, 326n
travellers, 139, 216, 217
"trailed travelers," 26, 366–7
tribe, tribes, 9, 32, 97, 103, 162, 194, 195, 223, 325, 334, 336
trilogy, 266, 271, 272n, 280, 303–4, 306–8
Tripoli (Lebanon), 103
Tripoli (Lybia), 215n
Tsdaka, Rina, 281
Tūmā, 'Āyida, 265n
Tunis, Tunisia, Tunisian, 55, 66, 183, 204n, 212, 213, 222, 313n, 353
Ṭūqān, Fadwā, 77
Ṭūqān, Ibrāhīm, 40
Turkey, Turks, Turkish, 11, 40n, 57, 123, 205n, 225, 226, 323, 339
Ṭuwayq, Na'īm Ṣāliḥ, 227

Ughniyyāt li-Bilādī (poetry collection), 248
Ulysses (novel), 364–5
Umm Kulthūm, 210, 244, 282
UNESCO, 310n
United States, 23, 62, 66, 67n, 104, 126, 166, 167. 206, 213, 267n, 272, 277
un-Jew, 152–4, 274
al-'Uṣba (magazine), 239–40, 250
'Uṣbat Mukāfaḥat al-Ṣahyūniyya, 239–40, 250
utopia, utopian, 48, 154, 155, 165, 256, 260, 273, 283, 321

vagabond (as a metaphor for postmodern life), 11
Ve-Hu Akher (novel), 208n, 272
Verfremdungseffekt (V-Effect), 82
vernacular, 30, 36, 57, 197, 199, 226; *see also 'āmmiyya*; dialect
Victoria (novel), 266–7
Vienna, 216
Vilna, 216
Visigoths, 98

Wādī, Ṭāhā, 95
Waiting for Godot (play), 64
Wajdī, Anwar, 211
Wannūs, Sa'd Allāh, 39n
waqt (mystical time), 297, 305n
ibn al-waqt, 297
Warā' al-Sūr wa-Qiṣaṣ Ukhrā (collection of short stories), 293, 299, 310
Ward Aqall (poetry collection), 25, 32, 96–7, 106–10, 116, 136–7
al-Warsha al-Fanniyya (theatre troupe), 58
Watad, Muḥammad, 147n
Weizmann, Chaim, 224n
West, Western
Western civilization, 6, 98
Western colonialism, 236n
Western culture, 93, 179n, 214
Western literature, 5, 227, 312, 365
Westernization, Westernized, 146, 218, 219n, 230n, 231, 236n
Western values, 278
West Bank, ix, 25, 31, 32, 37, 44, 49, 50, 53–5, 64–7, 72, 74, 91, 96, 180n, 265, 352; *see also* Occupied Territories
Wickstrom, Maurya, 71
Wilson, Arnold Talbot, 338–9
Wilson, Edmund, 295n
Wimsatt, William Kurtz, 363
al-Wirdānī, Ibrāhīm, 305–6
Wolfensohn, Isrā'īl (Israel) (Abū Dhu'ayb), 211
Wolman, Dan, 278
Woolf, Virginia, 294
world upside down, 86, 89–90

Yalde Ḥuts (novel), 272
Yannakakis, Ilios, 14–15
Yasmīn (novel), 280–1
al-Yawm (newspaper), 45
Yawm al-Arḍ (The Day of the Land), 53
Yawmān fī Ḥazīrān (novel), 306–7
Yehoshua, A. B., 154, 167, 327–8
Yehoshua, Ya'acob, 327
Yehuda, Avraham Shalom, 224
Yehuda, Zvi, 215
Yehuda al-Ḥarīzī, 200
Yemeni, Yemenite, 203, 286
Yezierska, Anzia, 288
Yiddish, 315
Yishuv, 280
Yizrael Valley, 278
Young Turks, 225, 226
Yūnus al-A'raj (dramatized poem), 57

Zach, Natan, 171
al-Zahāwī, Jamīl Ṣidqī, 228
zajal, 4n, 40
al-zaman al-jamīl, 314n, 350
Zamīr, Shlomo, 241
Zapatista, 11
Zaydān, Jurjī, 225
Zaydān, Maḥmūd, 147n
Zayyād, Tawfīq, 77, 253n, 255
al-Zayyāt, Muḥammad Ḥasan, 225
Zeh ha-Devarim (novel), 329
Zeus, 128n
Ziffer, Benny, 349n
Zilkha, Nuriel, 241
Zion, Zionist, Zionism, 135, 145, 147n, 150, 152, 178, 188, 191, 204n, 206, 209, 211, 218, 222, 224–5, 227–9, 231–2, 235–6, 238–40, 242–3, 250–1, 267–8, 270, 272, 274n, 277–82, 291, 304–5, 307–11, 313, 318–21, 322, 324, 327, 331, 334, 336–51, 359, 368–9
Zionist discourse, 127
Zionist (master) narrative, 237, 274, 277–8, 282
Zirid, 199
Zoroastrian, 195
zuhd, zuhhād, 298, 300
al-Zuhūr (newspaper), 226
Zurayk, Constantine, 124–5

EU representative:
Easy Access System Europe
Mustamäe tee 50, 10621 Tallinn, Estonia
Gpsr.requests@easproject.com

www.ingramcontent.com/pod-product-compliance
Lightning Source LLC
Chambersburg PA
CBHW061703300426
44115CB00014B/2537
* 9 7 8 1 3 9 9 5 0 3 2 2 8 *